Companion to
American Children's
Picture Books

Companion to American Children's Picture Books

Connie Ann Kirk

Greenwood Press
Westport, Connecticut • London

Library of Congress Cataloging-in-Publication Data

Kirk, Connie Ann.
   Companion to American children's picture books / Connie Ann Kirk.
      p. cm.
   Includes bibliographical references and index.
   ISBN 0–313–32287–2 (alk. paper)
   1. Picture books for children—United States—Bibliography.   2. Children's literature, American—
Bio-bibliography—Dictionaries.   3. Children—Books and reading—United States—Dictionaries.   4.
Children's literature, American—History and criticism.   I. Title.
   Z1033.P52K57 2005
   011.62—dc22   2005003395

British Library Cataloguing in Publication Data is available.

Library of Congress Catalog Card Number: 2005003395
ISBN: 0–313–32287–2

First published in 2005

Greenwood Press, 88 Post Road West, Westport, CT 06881
An imprint of Greenwood Publishing Group, Inc.
www.greenwood.com

Printed in the United States of America

⊗™

The paper used in this book complies with the
Permanent Paper Standard issued by the National
Information Standards Organization (Z39.48–1984).

10 9 8 7 6 5 4 3 2 1

To Mum, who first read to me,
and to my sons, Ben and John,
who also first read to me

Contents

Alphabetical List of Entries

Preface

I originally proposed this project when I went to look for a book like this one for my work in both writing and studying American picture books for children and did not find one in the library or in the bookstore. Researching and compiling information for over 400 entries has been a challenging task, but reading and thinking about so many examples and aspects of the picture book art form have been a true pleasure.

Thanks go to the writers, artists, editors, art directors and designers, publishers, librarians, and educators I have known over several years who have made me aware of the pleasures and topical issues relating to American children's picture books. Much of this reference is the result of reading thousands of picture books and researching subjects related to them over many years, but the work also benefited from the shared knowledge of the community of children's literature professionals who communicate through a variety of means, including academic and professional conferences, journals, newsletters, Web sites, Internet forums, reference books, biographies, books of criticism, and many other sources.

I thank Greenwood editor George Butler for accepting my proposal for this project and for his patience as I worked it through to completion. Thanks to poet and author Liz Rosenberg for providing early encouragement of my serious interest in picture books as an art form while I was in graduate school. I am also grateful to publisher and editor Philip Lee, cofounder of Lee and Low Books, for calling to accept my own first picture book manuscript for publication the very day after my first child went off to college. It seems for me, as perhaps for many others, that childhood and parenting remain irrevocably linked through the treasury of this special literary form.

Invaluable assistance for this project came from my receiving the Ezra Jack Keats/de Grummond Collection Children's Literature Research Fellowship in 2004. The fellowship allowed me to conduct research at the comprehensive de Grummond Children's Literature Collection at the University of Southern Mississippi in Hattiesburg. Thanks to all the authors, artists, and their estates who have donated manuscripts, papers, and artwork to the collection for use by scholars. Special thanks for the fellowship experience go to Dr. Deborah Pope, Executive Director of the Ezra Jack Keats Foundation; GinaMarie Pugliese, curator of the de Grummond Children's Literature Collection; and the helpful staff at the reading room of the McCain Library and Archives.

Other libraries, museums, organizations, and services that helped provide picture books, book lists, secondary material, referrals, references, recommendations, or other information for the *Companion* include the American Library Association, headquartered in Chicago; the Child_Lit Listserv moderated and archived at the Archibald S. Alexander Library, Rutgers University, New Brunswick, New Jersey; the Children's Literature Association, headquartered in Battle Creek, Michigan; the Eric Carle Museum of Picture Book Art in Amherst, Massachusetts; the Library of Congress, Washington, DC; the New York Public Library; North Hall Library at Mansfield University, Mansfield, Pennsylvania; the Rosenbach Library and Museum in Philadelphia; and the Southeast Steuben County Library System of upstate New York.

I especially wish to thank John Kirk, research assistant extraordinaire, for his valuable aid in helping locate and transport hundreds of picture books to and from library shelves for this project. As anyone who works with a number of these books at one time knows, they pile up quickly, and tote bags full of them tend to grow heavy even more quickly than that. Thanks go to my family for their continuing endurance, love, and support. Many of the books presented here are part of our family library and represent some of our family's most cherished memories.

Lastly, I thank the reader for picking up this volume to browse through or to use as a resource. It is my hope that this reference will promote the appreciation of, and conversation about, the genre in new and intriguing ways. It is intended to be an informative and convenient tool for those who create, read, and/or study American children's picture books and most of all, for those who share them with a child.

ABOUT THE *COMPANION*

The *Companion* contains more than 400 entries on authors, artists, works, and general topics related to the creation, study, and enjoyment of American picture books for children. With thousands of picture books for children published in the United States each year to choose from, the author of a guide such as this one needs to be selective as well as purposeful in her selections. Anyone who has young children or who has visited the children's section of his or her local public library knows how quickly picture books pile up and spill over in a young child's world. From all of these possibilities, how does one choose which ones to highlight as the best quality or most important or most popular or interesting representatives of the form?

SELECTION CRITERIA FOR THE *COMPANION*

Picture book title entries for the *Companion* come from a variety of sources and are intended to give a good cross-section of critically acclaimed and popular books as well as picture books of historical and scholarly interest. The first choice made to narrow the field was to limit works entries to fiction, poetry, biographies, and some concept books, such as alphabets. There are many fine nonfiction and informational picture books for children. These books, however, outnumber storybooks and are often written in series with the direct purpose of educating the reader, somewhat as supplementary textbook material. There are exceptions, but for the purpose of the *Companion*, most informational books have been omitted.

Since the most prominent and visible picture books in American culture are usually the ones that have won awards for illustration and/or text, selection from the remaining possibilities began in those areas. All American Library Association (ALA) Randolph Caldecott Medalists and Honor Books from 1938 through press time are included in the *Companion*, as are all Charlotte Zolotow Award books for text. All John Newbery Award and Honor books that happen to be picture books (most are not) are included, as are the few children's picture books that have won the National Book Award. In addition, picture book winners of the Coretta Scott King Book Award and Pura Belpré Awards are here. Honorees from these awards were omitted due to space constraints, but all are listed in the appendixes. Still other picture book works entries come from those recognized and/or recommended by the Asian American and Native American Indian communities, titles that were solicited through research and interviews with members of those groups.

Remaining picture books have been selected from the following categories and sources, depending on ease of availability as well as the balance in subject matter, diversity, popularity, effect on the form of picture books, or other considerations that they provide the *Companion*: the New York Public Library's (NYPL) 100 Picture Books Everyone Should Know; the *New York Times* Best Books for Children as listed in *The New York Times Parent's Guide to the Best Books for Children* by Eden Ross Lipson (Children's Book editor of the *New York Times*); lists from *The Essential Guide to Children's Books*, edited by Anita Silvey (editor of *Horn Book Magazine*) as well as Silvey's *100 Best Books for Children*, and other listings. Books listed by all of the various sources above represent a good sampling of critically acclaimed as well as popular and classic American picture books.

Entries for a few other picture book titles are included for their historical and scholarly value to the genre before, or contemporary with, the onset of the awards commended by the American Library Association beginning in 1938 and other children's book award entities. These entries are identified with the distinction "Of historical/scholarly interest." A couple of picture books are selected as recommendations from my own twenty years' experience as an author, scholar, college professor, former school librarian, and parent. These are designated as "Author's choice."

The eleven authors and artists selected among the thousands of possibilities for individual entries were chosen primarily for the quality and quantity of the distinctions they have received from American children's literature professional organizations and/or their influence on the field of American children's picture books, in particular—in other words, the members of this small group are among the top of the established and preeminent authors and artists in the field. This selection includes the seven artists to date who have won more than one Caldecott Medal and the four additional authors or artists who work primarily in picture books and have won the Laura Ingalls Wilder Medal for their body of work in children's literature.

Entries on general topics such as distinctions, organizations, museums, collections, and other related topics were chosen with the book's usefulness to educators, librarians, other children's literature professionals, and scholars of children's literature in mind. Though several of the organizations, for example, are not concerned exclusively with picture books, their connections to that genre in particular are highlighted within their entries. General topics of children's literature that are concerned primarily with areas outside of picture books are not included. As an aid for entries that include information about the artistic media used in creating the book, several media entries with quick, single-sentence descriptors are included throughout the *Companion*. Further information about artistic media may be found from the sources given in the bibliography.

No book like this one on a subject this large can be definitive. It is my hope that important omissions, as well as any questionable inclusions, are limited and that this resource will provide a good introduction and convenient reference for the children's picture book genre throughout its American history as well as its existence in the United States in the early years of the twenty-first century. The author is open to suggestions for improvement from readers made through the publisher for use in subsequent editions.

HOW TO USE THE *COMPANION*

The *Companion* was organized in a way to be useful to its audience of general readers, librarians, professors, teachers, students, scholars, editors, authors, artists, and others who have an interest in American children's picture books. It is alphabetical by picture book title, authors'/artists' last names, and general topics of interest. Each works entry contains the author's and artist's names; publisher and year of publication; summary of the story (including names of major characters); media used in the illustrations, if known; any known anecdotes about the book's genesis, production, or reception, or stories of interest about the author/artist; distinctions; birthdays of authors/artists when they are known; and Library of Congress subject headings related to that book. Some works entries also contain, where appropriate, cross-listings within the *Companion* as well as a listing of recommended further reading. Author/artist entries include a brief biographical treatment and survey of that person's career as it relates to American picture books for children. Entries on general topics contain brief information about organizations, artistic media, or other relevant subjects.

Probably the easiest way to use the *Companion* is to thumb through alphabetically by authors' and artists' last names, book title, or general topic. One may also begin with the index, which will show whether or not an entry exists under the heading one is trying to locate. The appendixes contain several useful lists for quick information that does not require the reading of a full entry. These include all Caldecott Medal and Honoree Books listed chronologically by award, alphabetically by artist, alphabetically by author, and alphabetically by title. Readers will also find listings of Coretta Scott King Book Awards and Honorees; Pura Belpré Award and Honorees; Charlotte Zolotow Awards for Best Picture Book Text; selected review journals/periodicals; and Reading Rainbow Books. Birthdays of authors/artists of books that have entries in the *Companion* are listed both alphabetically and chronologically, when available. Listings of titles covered in the *Companion* grouped by subject areas are followed by a full bibliography divided into categories.

Introduction

WHAT IS A PICTURE BOOK?

One cannot begin a discussion of picture books without first defining exactly what one means. The phrase "picture book" can be applied to a variety of objects—a coffee-table book of photography by Ansel Adams; a family photo album; a visual biography of a nineteenth-century poet with reproductions of archival photos, documents, manuscripts, and objects. In children's literature, a picture book is best described first by distinguishing it from an illustrated book, since both contain several pictures and both occupy the largest share of shelf space in the children's and young adult section of libraries and bookstores.

An illustrated book may be a novel such as *The Adventures of Tom Sawyer* by Mark Twain. The novel has some pictures on a few pages scattered throughout the book. The pictures may take up an entire page or part of a page. They may be decorative, such as borders or motifs at the beginnings of new chapters. The function of the pictures is to illustrate, illuminate, or interpret the text. By contrast, in a picture book like *Make Way for Ducklings*, written and illustrated by Robert McCloskey, the artwork appears on every page, often dominating the space. Sometimes the artwork even expands across two pages facing one another and interplaying with one another, a feature of picture books that is called the *spread*. In a picture book, the illustrations take on an equal role with the text in the telling of the story. It may be possible to discern the story from the pictures alone, but usually the text and illustrations must work in conjunction for the story to be told and fully appreciated. The symbiotic nature of the written and visual forms in picture books is so close that there are even some critics who wish to demonstrate it by spelling the form as *picturebook*, with no separation at all between the pictures and the book.

Picture books have much in common with two other art forms—poetry and film. Like poetry, picture book text is minimal (most picture books are thirty-two pages long, 1,000–1,200 words or less total, and with only a few lines of text per page). Each word is vital and carefully chosen. There is frequent use of poetic devices in picture book texts—such as alliteration, assonance, repetition, and imagery. Also like poetry, most picture book texts do not rhyme, though they are stereotyped as always doing so. The aural quality of the words, however, makes both poetry and picture books appealing when read aloud. There is a rhythm to picture book prose and poems that is important to the overall effect. Similar to line breaks or stanzas in poetry, the line breaks and the turn of a page in a picture book play an important role in pacing its rhythm. It is no accident that occasionally picture book texts are actually poems, rhyming or not, that spread across several pages and are illustrated.

Akin to film, or perhaps even drama, as an art form, picture books rely on the eye's visually taking in images as well as the writing (dialogue and narrative) one hears (or reads) to fill in the blanks that make the story a story. Also like film, the product of the book itself is a collaboration, and authors and artists of picture books often play one medium of storytelling off the other in the same work. For example, the text may say one thing is happening, and the pictures show something quite different going on. In film, the audience hears the words of dialogue being said by the actors, but the camera reveals the actors' gestures and facial expressions as the words are being said, or it may show an action occurring outside the window that neither character is aware is happening. In this way, text and visual art combine to tell the full story or operate ironically to tell a more complex story that the attentive reader/listener/viewer will appreciate.

Young readers or read-to's enjoy looking at the pictures in picture books, and this process helps them learn to digest material from a book without actually reading the text. Some educators believe that children first learn to "read" pictures by moving their eyes left to right, top to bottom through a picture book; others disagree and see children looking all over any given picture book page in random order. After they do begin reading text, often children are aided by the pictures to discern the meanings of new words. The rhythm of the poetic prose in a picture book often helps a child in remembering or reciting the text. This is another reason that the text in picture books is so important and difficult to write; it must stand up to repeated rereadings aloud to wiggling young people and more than likely by tired adults who are spending quality time with these same energetic young ones. As any parent knows, "repeated readings" is an understatement when a child latches on to a favorite story. Words, voice inflection, and other aspects of the performance of reading a picture book aloud are important to young children; they sense when the rhythm of a book is broken by an adult wanting to skip or rush through one of their favorite books.

With the distinction between a picture book and an illustrated book made, it is useful to note the variations of children's picture books that exist. There are picture books with no text at all (though these are rare) and those that are known as concept books, some with very little text. Concept books usually do not tell a story but instead introduce an idea such as the alphabet or counting numbers. Picture storybooks are the most common and are likely what most people envision when they think of picture books for children. These books contain enough text that they tell a complete story with a beginning, middle, and ending. Just as in full-length books for adults, picture books for children may be nonfiction or fiction. Fiction picture books may include historical fiction, realistic fiction, fantasy, mystery, folklore, fairy tales, and so forth. Nonfiction picture books include biographies, history, informational books such as books about science or geography, nursery rhymes, and poetry.

Typically, a picture book for children is oversized compared to a book for adults. This is designed purposely not only to accommodate the child's physical ease with larger print but also to accommodate the artwork. Some books are designed almost as toys with fold-out pages, holes, sound, or other devices or tactile features inside their covers. Some are intentionally designed very small to fit in a child's hand or are cut into particular shapes that correspond in some way with the subjects of the books.

Perhaps Barbara Bader, in her classic book, *American Picturebooks from Noah's Ark to The Beast Within*, defines the genre of the picture book best:

> A picturebook is text, illustrations, total design; an item of manufacture and a commercial product; a social, cultural, historical document; and, foremost, an experience for a child. As an artform it hinges on the interdependence of pictures and words, on the simultaneous display of two facing pages, and on the drama of the turning of the page. On its own terms its possibilities are limitless. (1)

A BRIEF HISTORY OF THE AMERICAN PICTURE BOOK FOR CHILDREN

The world's first picture book for children is traditionally agreed on by scholars to be *Orbis Sensualium Pictus*, translated as *A World of Things Obvious to the Senses Drawn in Pictures* or *The Visible World*. The book was written by Johan Amos Comenius and originally published in Nuremberg, Germany, in 1654. It remained in print well into the nineteenth century. An early edition available in America included a 1777 edition printed for S. Leacroft in London. The volume has the distinction of being the first textbook for children to incorporate visual aids as part of the instruction. Pages included pictures of objects or subjects with lists of Latin and English words (or other languages) that correspond to them. Older children used the book to learn Latin; younger children paged through the book as a picture book for entertainment or for help in learning to read.

In his preface, Comenius explains his justification for the use of pictures in his texbook:

> For it is apparent, that Children (even from their Infancy almost) are delighted with Pictures, and willingly please their eyes with these sights: And it will be very well worth the Pains to have once brought it to pass, that scare-crows may be taken away out of Wisdoms Gardens. (iii)

Between 1682 and 1820 there were more than 800 books published in the United States for children. These were primarily religious tracts, catechisms,

Bibles, and other spirituality-related works. The first American book for children has been conventionally agreed on by scholars to be one published in the colonies—John Cotton's catechism, *Spiritual Milk for Boston Babes in New England: Drawn Out of the Breasts of Both Testaments for Their Souls' Nourishment*. The book was published between 1641 and 1645. Many American books from the eighteenth century were reprints of books from England or other countries in Europe. Factors such as increased nationalism after the War of 1812, the growth of literacy, advancements in book printing, schools, and the development of a social class capable of purchasing books in the United States increased demand for a uniquely American literature by the mid-nineteenth century. Authors and poets such as Nathaniel Hawthorne, Ralph Waldo Emerson, Walt Whitman, Edgar Allan Poe, Herman Melville, Catherine Maria Sedgwick, Lydia Child, Harriet Beecher Stowe, Louisa May Alcott, Frances Hodgson Burnett, Mark Twain, Susan Warner, and others dominated the books and periodicals created for both adults and young people. However, none of their works would be what we would call picture books for younger children today.

While novels such as *Little Women* and *The Adventures of Tom Sawyer* were illustrated, picture books in the form readers would recognize today as those in which the text and illustration collaborate to tell a story remained reprints of English and European authors for some time in the United States. The three best-known British illustrators, Randolph Caldecott, Kate Greenaway, and Walter Crane, were all famous in America as well through reprints of the expensive gift picture books of the day.

After World War I, many illustrators immigrated to America, bringing with them techniques and philosophies that had been cultivated in European picture books. The timing of this influx with the growth in children's library services and increased interest on the part of publishing houses in creating more books for the growing children's market combined to launch the true beginning of children's picture books in America. In 1919, Macmillan established an editorship for oversight of its new children's book division and asked Louise Seaman (later Bechtel) to occupy the new position. Much of the early history of American picture books (as well as American children's books of all kinds) coincides with new editorships from this same time—Ernestine Evans at Coward-McCann, for example, and May Massee at Doubleday and later at Viking. Women's professional experience as teachers and librarians ironically placed them in powerful business positions at key moments early on in the development of the American children's book industry.

At first, picture books were still not something that was solicited by these new American editors. The British gift books of Crane, Caldecott, and Greenaway were still popular in the United States, and to these were added the more recent imports of Beatrix Potter and Leslie Brooke. Book printing was still in its infancy in America and could not compare with the quality achieved in Europe. In 1923, however, poster artist C. B. Falls created a woodblock alphabet book for his daughter, *ABC Book* (Doubleday, 1923), which May Massee included on her first book list. Though it owed much to the better-illustrated *The Square Book of Animals* (Heinemann, 1899) by British author Arthur Waugh and illustrator William Nicholson, Falls' alphabet book was regarded as a victory in American printing. Even after the success of this book, picture books remained unsolicited, partly due to the wide success of the illustrated novel at that time. Original American picture books appeared only as special occasions arose for artists who wished to produce them.

Only when Ernestine Evans formed the opinion that the best artists in America should be solicited for illustrating children's books did the trend begin to change. She had heard of a one-woman show at the Weyhe Gallery in New York by artist Wanda Gág. Gág was the daughter of German immigrants who were both artists. When she approached her, Evans found Gág willing to do a book. She created *Millions of Cats*, and Evans immediately accepted it for publication. With the book's publication and popular success in 1928, most scholars designate this book and that year as the beginning of the modern era of American children's picture books. One of the book's distinguishing features was the use of the double-page spread where text and pictures continued from one page across to the other. The twentieth century would become a time when more picture books were published than ever before as well as a time when the possibilities of the genre became explored in ever-increasing dimensions.

Other literary events of the early twentieth century that seemed to have cemented the validity of children's books among American book buyers were the establishment by publishers of Children's Book Week in 1919; the American Library Association's (ALA) new award for children's books (novels, information books, and picture books), which it called the John Newbery Medal in 1922; and the ALA's subsequent establishment of the Caldecott Medal for picture book illustration in 1938. Meanwhile, the new editors of children's divisions within publishing houses made landmark decisions on what to publish and encouraged the work of authors and artists who went on to create what have become American classics of the genre. May Massee, for example, published such books as *The Story of Ferdinand* (1936), written by Munro Leaf and illustrated by Robert Lawson; *Madeline* (1939), written and illustrated by Ludwig Bemelmans; and *Make Way for Ducklings* (1941), written and illustrated by Robert McCloskey.

Following the pioneer editors, the next generation at midcentury who had learned from them continued to be influential forces in publishing. Perhaps most notable among this second generation is the legendary Ursula Nordstrom. Nordstrom nurtured into being such now-classic American picture books as *Harold and the Purple Crayon* by Crockett Johnson (1954) and Maurice Sendak's *Where the Wild Things Are* (1963), in addition to novels for children such as E. B. White's beloved *Charlotte's Web*. Other editors of this generation included Margaret K. McElderry at Harcourt, Brace and later at Atheneum and Simon and Schuster. Walter Lorraine of Houghton Mifflin was also beginning his career.

As printing technology advanced, the possibilities for picture book illustration also increased. Artists could employ color through the 3-color and 4-color processes. For the 3-color process, for example, the artist would paint the black portions of the picture first on a *keyplate*. Then the artist would preseparate the other colors, painting the primary colors of red, yellow, and blue on separate *overlays*. The overlays would allow some colors to blend when they were stacked together. For example, the blue and yellow portions of the overlays that were in the same area of the picture would appear green when the overlays were stacked on top of one another. Other overlays provided outlines, shading, or bold color. Artists needed patience and skill to produce overlays in a way that achieved the correct color enhancements they wanted in the completed picture.

American picture books published during World War II reflected these simple black-and-white and basic color designs. Many of them, such as *An American ABC* (Macmillan, 1941) and *The Rooster Crows: A Book of American Rhymes and Jingles* (Macmillan, 1945), both written and illustrated by Maud and Miska Petersham, had patriotic themes. Others, such as Virginia Burton's *The Little House* (Houghton Mifflin, 1942), expressed authors' social concerns such as that book's warning about the negative aspects of urban expansion.

As with other art forms, picture books reflect what is going on in the society at the time. Books such as Marcia Brown's 1950s *Cinderella* (Scribner, 1954) and *Puss in Boots* (Scribner, 1952) retold favorite European fairy tales for the relatively docile postwar baby boom generation. By the time their younger siblings were enjoying picture books, the turbulence of the 1960s and the civil rights movement was making its effect on writers and illustrators. Sendak's *Where the Wild Things Are* (Harper, 1963) seemed to predict the troubles that would plague the nation over the next few years at the same time that it began to explore the emotional truth and rage that had built up in young people over the false pretenses created in the homogenized era of the 1950s. Keats's *The Snowy Day* (Viking, 1962) and Steptoe's *Stevie* (Harper, 1969) bookmarked the decade with representations of African American children that had not been seen in mainstream picture books before that time.

The 1960s opened the door to the 1970s, when a new trend in children's literature, coined *multiculturalism*, emphasized telling stories of minority children from their point of view. In particular, this decade looked to the motherlands of minority ancestors and others for retellings of folktales. Verna Aardema's *Why Mosquitoes Buzz in People's Ears: A West African Folktale* (Dial, 1975), illustrated by Diane and Leo Dillon, exemplifies this group, as do *The Golem: A Jewish Legend* by Beverly Brodsky McDermott (Lippincott, 1976), Gerald McDermott's *Anansi the Spider: A Tale from the Ashanti* (Holt, 1972), and Tomie dePaola's Italian *Strega Nona* (Prentice-Hall, 1975).

By the mid-1980s, a revolution in printing technology brought on a golden age of picture book illustration. High-speed presses, computers and more sophisticated and affordable software, and electronic scanners allowed for crystal-clear reproduction of artwork of all kinds, and this brought a new generation of innovative artists and designers to the field of children's picture books. The artwork of Paul O. Zelinsky's elaborate and colorful *Rumpelstiltskin* (Dutton, 1986) and Nancy Willard's book *A Visit to William Blake's Inn: Poems for Innocent and Experienced Travelers*, illustrated by Alice and Martin Provensen (Harcourt, 1981), were both possible to reproduce in lush, full color.

Themes and techniques continued to evolve from the 1990s into the early years of the twenty-first century in American children's picture books. More books written from the authentic perspectives of Latina, Native American, African American, Asian American, and other minority and female perspectives appear each year, though the number is still lower than many librarians, educators, and other concerned readers and book buyers would like to see. Just before the turn of the millennium, the first picture book illustrated completely by 3-D computer graphic design, *Nova's Ark*, by David Kirk (Scholastic, 1999), ushered in what some see as a new tool of art and others fear as too much of an intrusion of technology into picture book creation. The difference between books as toys and toys as books blurred as never before as technology made the distinction between the two at times almost indecipherable. Baby board book versions of classic picture books began to appear more frequently, opening up the picture book to even younger audiences.

Thousands of picture books for children are created by American publishers each year, yet very few of them remain in print for long. Rightly or wrongly, publishers judge longevity through sales. It is up to fans of the picture book form to support their favorites from the genre to help keep them in print. They can do this through purchase, reading, sharing, and otherwise promoting their favorite picture books and by sharing them with a child who will want to see their own favorite storybooks stay in print for the next generation.

PARTS OF A PICTURE BOOK

The parts of a picture book include the cover (also called the binding); the dust jacket; front matter and back matter; and the interior pages. All parts of a quality picture book are designed carefully to make the best presentation of the artwork and text possible.

Covers and Dust Jackets

Most picture books are first issued in *hardcover* or *clothbound* form; the terms mean the same thing and are interchangeable. Covers are manufactured of thick, sturdy cardboard and are covered with either cloth or glossy paper. *Endpapers*, usually heavy stock white paper, but sometimes color coordinated to match the illustrations or even illustrated themselves, are glued to the inside of the front and back covers to cover the cardboard on the inside and seal the edges of the cloth or paper that cover the outside. *Spines* of hardcover picture books, the place where the pages are held together, may be either glued or sewn. Typically in hardcover books they are sewn. Covers may also be issued in *trade bindings* or *library bindings*. The type of binding refers to the thickness of the covers and the strength of the bindings at the spine of the book. Trade binding is the form that is traditionally sold in bookstores to consumers. Library-bound books typically have thicker covers, tighter bindings, and possibly even thicker pages to facilitate repeated use by many hands and are sold to school and public libraries by companies specializing in that market. After a hardcover edition has been released and sold for a while, publishers may decide to issue a *paperback* edition of the book. If the paperback is issued first, without a hardcover edition at all, that edition is called an *original paperback*. If the paperback is issued at the same time as the hardcover edition, that circumstance is called a *simultaneous publication*.

The function of a *dust jacket* is as its name suggests—to protect the cover from dust and markings. Dust jackets are made of paper; the portions folded inside the front and back covers are called the *front flap* and *back flap*. The dust jacket also serves as a marketing tool for publishers. Brief summaries, biographical information, and short review blurbs about the book or previous books by the author and or artist normally appear on the dust jacket. Often, the artwork on a picture book dust jacket is the same as the cover proper, but sometimes it is different. Occasionally publishers print a map or poster on the inside of the dust jacket as a special feature for children, but since most readers keep books in their jackets, this is not a frequent practice.

Front Matter and Back Matter

The pages at the beginning and at the ending of the book are called *front matter* and *back matter*. In picture books, these pages may or may not be illustrated. Front matter is made up of the *half-title page*, *ad card*, *title page*, *title page verso*, the *copyright page*, and the *dedication page*. Rarely appearing in picture books, but not unheard of, are additional pages in the front matter including *acknowledgments*; *preface*; *foreword*; *table of contents*; and possibly another *half-title page* or a *part-title page*. *Back matter* may be made up of any, all, or none of the following: *epilogue*; *afterword* and/or *author* and/or *illustrator's note*; *appendix*; *glossary*; *source notes*; *bibliography*; *index*; and biographical information such as *About the Author* and/or *About the Illustrator*.

Half-Title Page

If it is used, on this first page in the book appears simply the title with nothing else. The half-title page is not always used and is an old-fashioned practice from the days when this page served as the cover of books, which were normally unbound. On the *verso*, or reverse side, of this page may appear a listing of the author's and/or artist's other works. This listing is called the *ad card*. If the verso contains an illustration, this is called a *frontispiece* and often combines with the *title page* to form a double-page illustration *spread*.

Title Page

Each book has a *title page*, which contains important information. The *recto*, or front of the title page, contains the full title and subtitle of the book; names of the author, illustrator, translator, adaptor or reteller; possibly an editorial imprint; and the publishing company. The page may also include the year the book was published and edition information.

Copyright Page

The *title page verso* or *copyright page* on the back of the title page contains a good deal of important information about the book, usually in small print. This includes the original year of publication shown as the copyright date with the copyright symbol ©. There may be one date or several dates, indicating different editions published in different years. Sometimes "First Edition" will be noted if that is the case, or "First American Edition" for a book originally published outside the United States, or perhaps "First Paperback Edition" for that instance. If the book is adapted from another printed source, such as an eighteenth-century folktale, sometimes this source is listed in the fine print of the copyright page. Information about a book's first edition outside the United States (if it is not American in origin) normally appears here as well.

There is a difference between the terms *printing* and *edition*. An edition is a version of a book copied many times over from one set of plates. A printing is a set number of copies made at one time. For example, a first edition may have an initial printing of 10,000 copies, but if it sells quickly and well, a subsequent print run of 50,000 copies may be made. In both cases, the pages are the same, so the edition is the same. Publishers signify printings by a series of numbers at the bottom of the copyright page. The way to determine which printing of a book a reader is looking at is to find the lowest number is the series. Publishers may number printings in descending order on the page—10 9 8 7 6 5 4 3 2 1—or they may scramble the numbers in a code by a pattern of even numbers going forward and odd numbers going backward—2 4 6 8 10 9 7 5 3 1. Both nomenclatures above denote a first printing of that edition. In subsequent printings, the lowest number, wherever it appears in the series, is the number of the printing. For example, both 6 8 10 9 7 and 10 9 8 7 6 indicate the edition is in its sixth printing.

Library of Congress Cataloging-in-Publication data, or CIP for short, is often included on the copyright page. This may appear almost as a miniature library catalog card, containing information such as the book's title, author and illustrator, publisher and date of publication; Dewey and Library of Congress (LOC) classification numbers; a two-line summary of the book; and subject headings under which the book is categorized at the Library of Congress. In addition, the ISBN, or *International Standard Book Number*, may appear here, but it almost always appears as a bar code on the back cover and dust jacket of the book to aid in the book-selling and ordering process. Separate editions of a book (not printings), for example, the hardcover and paperback, will have different ISBNs. The independent numbering system helps track the exact edition of any book for which someone may be looking.

Additional information that may be found on the copyright page includes *photo credits*; notes on the *media* used in the artwork; *typography* style names and sources; and possibly the *book designer's* name. With the increase in kinds and varieties of artwork used in picture books because of the more recent flexibility provided by advances in printing technology, noting the artist's media, especially, used for the book is becoming a more frequent practice.

Dedication and Other Front Matter Pages

Most picture books have dual dedications—one from the author usually followed by his or her initials and one by the illustrator acknowledged in the same way. An *acknowledgment page* may offer more detailed words of gratitude for particular help on researching a subject for a book or some other assistance or inspiration. A *preface* may describe the genesis of the book, information about its creation, or what it means to the author; it may also include acknowledgments. Sometimes this or other information may occur under other headings such as the *author's note* or *a note to parents*. If a *foreword* is included, it is usually introductory remarks made by someone other than the creators of the book, usually a recognized name or authority in the subject of the book.

Nonfiction picture books in particular and even some fictional picture books that are broken up into shorter stories may have a *table of contents* listing chapter titles and page numbers. Following a table of contents, if there is one, may appear another half-title page (with just the title of the book again) or a *part-title page*, which may give the title of the first part, or chapter, of the book. For example a nonfiction picture book about deserts as an ecosystem may have a part-title page "Chapter One: The Land."

Back Matter

A picture book's *back matter* may include an *epilogue*, which is a description of what happens after the main action of the story has ended or additional information about the subject. An *afterword* is normally the author's comments on the book, its creation, or its effect on him or her after it is completed. In picture books, this is often labeled "Author's Note." An *appendix* offers lists, table, graphs, or other useful information; a *glossary* lists terms used in the book and their definitions. Sometimes picture books offer a glossary of words from other languages, such as Spanish, used in the text, or a table of Zuni words and their English translations. *Source notes* detail where information came from within chapters in longer books. These will likely not be referenced in picture books by page number, though they may be; these notes, if they appear at all in a picture book, will usually be listed more generally. A *bibliography* in the endpapers of a picture book will be a listing either of sources used in composing the book or of sources recommended for further reading or both. Here, the source material is listed alphabetically by author's last name and may also be categorized into kinds of media such as books, periodicals, electronic media (CD-ROMs, DVDs, video and audio recordings, and so forth), and Internet Web sites. Sometimes nonfiction picture books use an *index*, which alphabetically lists subtopics and their page numbers in the book to help get children used to using this research tool. A *biographical note* at the end of a picture book may have the title "About the Author" or "About the Illustrator" and sometimes gives educational information, where the author/artist lives, perhaps other books by him or her, and occasionally a brief anecdote about the book's inspiration or creation.

Interior Pages

In a fiction picture book, the story will occur, of course, on the interior pages. Elements of these pages concern the text of the story, the illustrations, any decorations, and the design of the page.

Text

Picture book text may rhyme, or it may be unrhymed poetry or prose. The text may be long or short on each page and overall, and it may use simple words that a very young child can understand, or it may use more mature language more appropriate to a third or fourth grader or older. Many of the award-winning picture books highlighted in the *Companion* could not be easily read independently by beginning readers, which is why Random House and its most famous author, Dr. Seuss, initiated the Beginning Reader series in 1957 with *The Cat in the Hat* and other books. While many readers consider a book such as *The Cat in the Hat* to be a picture book because it contains pictures on every page that add to the telling of the story, the beginning reader is technically not the same genre of children's literature as a picture book. One distinction is that the language is purposely written to help children learn to read, so its intent is more educational than literary per se, for that reason.

The design of the text on the page of a picture book and where it appears are the work of the *book designer*, who chooses the typeface style, size, and *value* or lightness or darkness of the print. The editor usually organizes the text across the pages, deciding where to divide text, but this is often done in conjunction with the illustrator and/or book designer or art director.

Illustrations

The artwork that helps tell the story is called the illustrations, though the term often lumps storytelling art and decorative art together. In addition, the term illustration suggests that the art simply accompanies the text of a picture book, when it actually plays a much more important role in this genre by telling at least one-half of the overall story children will experience. Illustrations may fill up a page to its edges, a term called *bleed*, or they may be situated somewhere on a page with or without borders, or they may expand across two pages open opposite one another in a larger drawing that plays one page off another in a *spread*. Normally, a spread may not accommodate the *gutter*, or the area where the pages come together, though sometimes *borders* of white space or decoration are incorporated there as part of the design.

Decorative artwork might entail art along the borders of the page, a sidebar, illustrated letters, and so forth. Decorative art may enhance the story's presentation but it does not normally move the story forward as the illustrations do.

Design

Important elements such as the *layout* of the page, the location and positioning of text and illustration; the *typography* of the print; and any borders are typically the work of the *book designer*, who may be the illustrator or a graphics artist at the publishing company or book production company.

The entire package, all parts of a picture book working together, creates an image and tells a story. When all of the elements of a picture book work hand in hand successfully, that picture book has benefited from a collaboration of many people who share a common vision. The result is not only a meaningful or entertaining story well told through words and pictures but also a book that is aesthetically pleasing as a physical object.

HOW PICTURE BOOKS WORK

As typically the first books that young children are exposed to, picture books play an important role in acquainting children with how to handle a book as well as what to expect from written and drawn stories and concepts. Some educators believe that picture books also develop skills in children that are precursors to reading, skills such as focusing one's attention on print and pictures, looking at the linearity of stories from left to right and top to bottom, and gradually associating the words on a page to a picture and a sound. The writing, illustrating, and designing of a picture book take many of these factors into account.

Picture book text is generally quite brief. The story must have a beginning, middle, and an end and accomplish its narrative arc in approximately 1,000 words or less (though this number varies). Because it is difficult to illustrate a story throughout the pages of a picture book using only one setting (though Margaret Wise Brown and Clement Hurd's classic *Goodnight Moon* actually does just that, keeping the reader in the ever-darkening "great green room" the entire time), most picture books change settings frequently throughout the story so that different pictures and scenes are possible and these keep the story moving forward (setting does actually change in *Goodnight Moon* as the room darkens and small shifts in the clock, locations of animals, and so forth occur at each turn of the page). The importance of movement through pictures makes plot motifs such as the journey a frequent device in the writing of picture books. Examples of books that show journeys with a variety of settings, both real and imaginary, include *Millions of Cats* by Wanda Gág, *Make Way for Ducklings* by Robert McCloskey, *Where the Wild Things Are* by Maurice Sendak, *Kitten's First Full Moon* by Kevin Henkes, and many others.

Authors use various techniques to capture and keep a reader's or read-to's attention in a short, picture book story. Some of these strategies include structure, rhythm, rhyme, repetition, questions and answers, alliteration, pacing, and others. Though the author of a picture book story may or may not divide up his or her own text while working on the manuscript, in a traditional thirty-two-page picture book, there are normally fourteen to fifteen segments, or sections of text divided across the pages. Each of these may be a few words to a few sentences long. Within that structure, the author must present a main character, create a problem for that character, attempt one or two solutions to the problem, reach a turning point in the plot in regard to the problem, then provide an ending. Authors have found various ways to do this, but the plot in a picture book story is really not so different from that of any other work of fiction—it simply must be accomplished all the more quickly with fewer numbers of words and in language young children can understand. Sometimes picture book authors make "dummies," or small booklets, where they lay out their text in order to simulate a picture book without the pictures in order to get a sense of the overall pacing and rhythm of the story. This helps them conceptualize and rework what Barbara Bader calls "the drama of the turning of the page" to its best effect.

Within this structure, picture book authors focus on techniques of making language engaging and ear-catching, since most picture books are read aloud to individuals or groups of children. This involves devices one finds in poetry—techniques such as alliteration, assonance, rhyme, repetition, rhythm, and perhaps line breaks. Other useful techniques in terms of language involve the use of imagery, dialogue, and questions and answers, among many others. The best picture books, like any story, keep moving and cause the reader to care about the characters and what happens to them. Whether they are humorous or dramatic, picture book stories must have an ending that is satisfying to the reader or listener—it is not fair to a reader to have a "trick" ending that cannot be substantiated by what happened before in the story. Though many picture book stories use the dream as a device to explain a journey of some kind into a fantasy world, fantasy alone need not depend on a logical explanation of this kind.

The story is self-contained, yet it is told in a way that allows an illustrator room to expand and color in the story through his or her interpretation of the text. Accomplishing this balancing act that works on all levels within thirty-two pages is more difficult than it seems to most readers. However, most readers and listeners identify with a picture book story that is well written. Each word and its placement are so integral to the story that children, as parents and other caregivers know, will correct a reader who leaves something out or who disrupts the rhythm of the text in some way.

Illustrations for a picture book are created using a variety of tools central to art. Rather than techniques of language, illustrators use visual elements in telling their part of the story, techniques such as line, shape, texture, color, and value. The illustrator knows that the top half of the page is the more fantastic and spiritual realm of the visual space. Images occupying this area often carry a feeling of freedom and happiness or rebellion against gravity, in all of its forms. The lower half of the page represents "groundedness," as in stability. It can also be used effectively to suggest sadness or limitations. The middle of the page occupies the viewer's center of attention. The sides and corners of the page are the peripheries of the viewer's typical view of the action on the page. An image in the corner will appear to be "cornered" to the viewer, emotionally. Background to the artist's drawing is another important consideration. White is considered to be "safer" and to simulate daylight to the eye; a black background suggests darkness, night, and danger.

Lines drawn or painted on the open space of the page are either straight or curved and may be either thin or thick. A horizontal line draws the eye across the page onto the next page, if the picture is a double-page spread. A horizontal line suggests movement in an orderly fashion, such as a casual walk. It also conveys stability and calmness. Vertical lines stop action and put the eye's attention in a more limited space, as though the action is somehow caught in time. Vertical lines suggest energy. Oblique or slanted lines create motion, tension or excitement, such as a ball rolling down a steep hill. Artists also place lines in their composition to point to, or otherwise bring attention to, other details in the picture.

Shapes are either curved or angular. Typically, curved shapes are used to depict nature—for example, human beings, animals, the sun and moon. Angular shapes, such as rectangles, normally represent objects that are made by humans such as books, robots, houses, and buildings. Pointed shapes carry a more ominous or dangerous emotional feeling to them to the viewer than do rounded shapes. When an artist wishes to give "humanlike" traits to an inanimate object, one way that may be achieved visually is to soften the shape of the object to make it more curved than angular. In *The Little House* (Houghton Mifflin, 1943), Virginia Burton curves the sides and top of the house so that it seems more alive.

Texture refers to tactile quality of the surface of a shape. Artists can portray a hard and smooth surface, a soft surface, and a rough, scratchy, or bumpy surface. This is achieved through the artist's choice of media as well as his or her drawing. For example, charcoal and pastels normally have a softer appearance than pen and ink or woodblocks. The surface on which the art is created may also contribute to the overall sense of texture. It may be textured to begin with, such as a painting on tree bark, or it may work with the media on it to give the appearance of a new texture.

Color is another interesting aspect of picture book illustration to consider, and color work contains its own vocabulary. *Hue*, for example, refers to distinct colors, such as red or yellow. *Value* is the lightness or darkness of the color. *Achromatic* colors range from black to white, with shades of gray in between. *Monochromatic* are shades or values within one color, from a pale blue to a dark blue. *Chroma* refers to the level of brightness or dullness of the color. The *primary colors*, as many kindergartners can recite, are red, yellow, and blue; *secondary colors* are made from combinations of primary colors, such as orange (red and yellow), green (blue and yellow), and purple (blue and red).

Colors on the same page may either be *complementary* or *analogous*. If a picture is painted in analogous colors, it means the primary and secondary colors are related by hue, such as red and orange or blue and green. If they are complementary, the colors have no hue in common, such as red and green or yellow and purple. Colors described as warm are often shades of the sun, such as yellow, orange, or red. Colors described as cool are frequently shades of the earth and water, such as green and blue. Artists use color to send different messages about their subjects in the story. For example, color may be used to help set the mood of the book, whether it is serious or funny, set back in time or in the present day, or if the emotions of the characters are happy or sad.

Another artistic technique used to set the mood of the book is *value*. Value refers to how dark or light the color appears. The artist mixes a color with black to darken the value or white to lighten it. In black-and-white artwork, value helps give dimension and perspective to the page. Color that has no value variation is called *flat*.

Another important consideration to the artist as he or she goes about telling the visual version of the story in a picture book is the *composition* of the pictures. Composition refers to the plan or design of the elements of the picture on the page, and artists give this aspect of their work a great deal of thought. Design principles they consider in composing the picture include dominance, balance, contrast, gradation, alternation, variation, harmony, and unity.

Dominance can show importance in four chief ways: (1) creating a quantity of features in the picture in the same way—for example, making more of the elements warm by using warm colors for more of them; (2) making something larger—a large object near a small one makes the larger one appear dominant and stronger; (3) using brightness—a brighter image appears dominant to a dull one because it catches the eye's attention first; and (4) using contrast—a light-colored object against a dark background will stand out as more dominant, and vice versa.

In a picture book, as in all visual art, balance of composition may be *symmetrical* (formal) or *asymmetrical* (informal). This may be achieved through the number of shapes, the size of them, or their respective colors. *Contrast*, such as an angular shape placed next to a round one, gives a sense of disruption or vitality—its immediate impact is to get us to look at both more closely. *Gradation* in an element of composition represents change in time, distance, or motion. Patterns may be established by *alteration*, for example, using one thin line and one dark line in the border decoration of a picture book page. *Variation* changes line, texture, shape, value, and color, adding complexity to the overall picture. One visual technique that slows down the pace of a story is *harmony*, in which the basic picture is the same, but with only a slight change in it from the last picture, such as the small changes in the great green room in *Goodnight Moon*. Unity of composition can be achieved through repeating, or echoing, one element of the picture within the picture. For example, the eye picks up objects of different shapes but the same color as having unity with one another.

Other aspects of the artwork for a picture book include *media* and *style*. Media involve choices such as drawing, painting, printmaking, collage, or photography, and it also entails choices among these basic media. For example, in drawing, the artist may choose to use pen and ink, pencil or graphite, pastels, or scratchboard. Paint choices include gouache, poster paint, tempera, watercolor, oil paint, and acrylics. In printmaking artists may choose what medium other than paper they are going to use, substances such as stone, cardboard, metal, wood, or linoleum. Collage may incorporate fabric or paper or even three-dimensional objects glued to a background. Photography is a frequent medium for nonfiction books and concept books, and artists must decide whether it will be used in combination with another medium or stand alone.

Some readers over time are able to identify picture book artists' work from the cover or from a few pages or even a single new image rendered by them without even knowing their names. That is because artists often develop their own *style*. Style also refers to the way art is made by several artists who over time have come to depict life or fantasy in a certain way. For example, a *realistic* style attempts to portray life as it looks to the human eye. An *abstract* style bends perspective and proportion, taking the figures and images out of the realm of reality. *Surrealistic* art blends realism with some element of the fantastic, such as frogs flying on lily pads over suburban neighborhood houses in David Wiesner's *Tuesday*. Maurice Sendak used an *impressionistic* style in *Mr. Rabbit and the Lovely Present* (Harper, 1962) by Charlotte Zolotow. This style emphasizes broken or refracted light. *Expressionism* is a common artistic style used in picture books. It is a style that uses elements of abstract art to convey the artist's emotion about the subject. A picture book example is *A Chair for My Mother* (Greenwillow, 1982) by Vera Williams. Barbara Cooney's *Ox-Cart Man* by David Hall is an example of *naïve* art, which is depicted as one-dimensional, flat without depth, giving an innocent and primitive feel to the images. *Folk art* is also flat and usually involves intricate patterns and simplified shapes, and color is a key element. *Cartoon art* emphasizes line for the effect of exaggeration and absurdity. Often cartoon art is chosen by picture book artists who are illustrating a humorous story. Alternatively, it can be used to provide a lighter emotional cushion between the reader and a more serious subject.

The text and pictures work in tandem to tell the story or to explain a concept. While a reader reads the text aloud, the eyes of the listener travel over the pictures, sometimes in top-to-bottom and left-to-right order, sometimes randomly around one page or both pages open in a double-page spread. Information is taken in both aurally and visually at the same time. The plan of the pages has been carefully laid out so that the pictures on the right-hand side of the spread are not a story spoiler for what is happening on the left, but they may create anticipation about what is going to happen next. The listener learns to look forward to the next part of the story. The turn of the page brings a pause full of suspense or anticipation in some books; it can be a moment of high drama. Depending on the story, the best authors are aware of this element of the form and use it purposefully to good effect.

Sometimes the illustrations depict the text almost word for word, but in better picture books, the illustrations add knowledge to the text for the reader/viewer. From the pictures, one can glean the mood of the book, information about a character such as what he or she looks like, expression, gestures, choice of clothing, and so forth. Action can also be portrayed in more detail through the pictures—What do the characters look like in different situations in the story? When they sit in a tree? Walk a city street? Setting is amplified through illustration as well. The time, place, circumstances, culture, and elements of a fantasy world may all be portrayed in details that the text may suggest or to which it only alludes. Sometimes text and pictures work purposefully against one another to create an ironic effect. A child loves to catch the humor of a story that is saying one thing, while the pictures are telling a completely different story.

If one doubts the necessary collaboration of a picture book, all one needs to do is read the text of one separate from the pictures or see the pictures of another separate from the text. While some texts stand on their own as poetry or poetic prose that tells a story, and some collections of pictures give the basic idea of the story and what happens, each is diminished in effect by the absence of the other. The experience is similar to listening to a movie without being able to see it, or vice versa.

When one considers the choices an author and artist each must make to create a picture book, one's appreciation goes up for choices that have been made in such a way as to be most effective as text or art. That admiration only increases when these choices work collaboratively well together to match picture with story in a way that makes a unified, aesthetically pleasing, and meaningful book.

EVALUATING A PICTURE BOOK

In evaluating a picture book critically as a work of art, the book reviewer considers all of the elements of text, illustration, and book design and makes a judgment as to how these all work together successfully or unsuccessfully to present a coherent whole for the kind of book the team is producing. Knowing how picture books are made, the details that make up each of their components as well as seeing and reading thousands of picture books, is what makes book reviewers and their assessments so helpful to potential buyers. Reviewers often have knowledge of child development and the classroom or library environment as well, in addition to what else is on the marketplace that might be similar to the book in question. Their evaluations are based on professional experience and knowledge of the field.

An educator may evaluate a picture book first simply by the subject matter she or he is looking to read about in the classroom, then by whether the language seems appropriate to the students and their ages and interest in class. Some teachers may be less familiar with professional reviews but may instead depend on suggestions given in teaching journals and magazines or from the school or public librarian. It is not unusual for an elementary teacher to choose favorite picture books about different subjects in the curriculum and use those workable books over and over again, year after year.

Librarians have seen hundreds of picture books and have shared them with hundreds of children in story hours and through both patron and professional recommendations. They often know what picture books are the most popular with children and which ones read best aloud. Librarians are usually quite familiar with the published reviews of certain books, and they have their own opinions based on their own voluminous reading. Perhaps it is no accident that a committee of librarians each year chooses the children's picture books that will be honored with the Caldecott Medal. Some observers, however, comment that since the Caldecott award is based on art, artists should be involved on the award committee. The award was founded and continues to be sponsored by the Association of Library Service to Children division of the American Library Association.

Evaluating a picture book on its own basis against a standard of quality involves examining the text, pictures, and design. Is the language appropriate for the targeted age audience? Does it tell a story with a beginning, middle, and end? Are the language and story engaging? Is it believable, or is it fantasy that allows the reader to believe it for the duration of the story? Is the narrator reliable so that the reader trusts enough in the narrator to be carried away by the story? Does the story create empathy for its characters? Does the reader care what happens to the characters? Does the story keep moving, or does it weigh down in the middle? Does the story work on more than one level? If so, what are the levels and themes? Is the language condescending to its young readers or respectful? Does the ending seem manipulated or organically grown from the rest of the story? Is there an aftereffect to this book as in a desire to reread it right away or a lingering thought that one takes away?

Pictures in a picture book should hold their weight in showing more details about the story and not simply illustrate what is already written. Does one learn, for example, more about the physical attributes of the characters or setting from the visual details in the pictures? Do the pictures help answer questions in the reader's mind such as, What was it like? How do each of the elements of composition, use of space, choice of media, style, and so forth contribute to the overall book? Is the art itself, separate from the book, striking? Does the art make a unique contribution to the story? Is there a feeling that the text and pictures were "born" together, that they are equal parts of a whole?

Book design should combine the text and illustrations in a style and manner that enhance the story being told. Does the design reflect the mood of the story? Are elements clear, and is necessary information easy to find? Is the book cleverly designed? Are the size and shape of the book appropriate for its illustrations, intent, and audience? Is the text clear and easy to read against the colors of the background on the page?

Critiquing a picture book for reading aloud to a group of children may have a few additional elements of consideration. Does the text read well aloud, for example or does the text become clumsy on the tongue in spots? Is it simple enough that children can follow along while listening in a setting that may have distractions? Are there textual techniques in the prose such as repetition that may aid in listening? Pictorially, are the illustrations large enough that children will be able to see them from some distance farther away than a parent's lap? Is there an aspect of the story that allows for questions, observations, comments, or other active participation from a young audience? Often, it takes reading several books on a similar topic to know which of them is more "readable" aloud to a group than others. Librarians and teachers also sometimes consider the length of time it takes to read a certain picture book chosen for a class period. This can vary book to book more than one may at first realize.

A feature educators sometimes use to give variety to reading-aloud time is to play audio versions of picture books read by professional actors with music and sound effects in the background. Just like millions of radio program fans from generations before them, many children enjoy making up the pictures in their own minds from a good story well told through an oral performance. Learning to read well aloud with good expression is a lesson that can be learned from listening to professional performances of readings (separate from oral storytelling) as well.

Evaluating a picture book for an individual child as a parent, relative, or other caregiver can sometimes be a tricky task. One recommendation is for loved ones to share a book they like themselves with their child. Their enthusiasm will not only help the child appreciate the book alongside their adult loved one but also be an opportunity to share values in books and subject matter, writing, and art together. Children are quick to let their adults know if a book is too advanced in concept or language for them. Subject matter may be a natural choice for the selection of a picture book. If one's child is zealous over trains, for example, it is a wonderful experience to share books of various kinds on a similar subject. This teaches the child about different approaches that are available in books.

Of course, the best evaluator of a picture book that is intended for a child is the child himself or herself. It is easy to find the personal award winners in a child's room. They are the ones she looks at again and again, and they are the titles after which they are read, the child immediately says, "Read it again!"

FURTHER READING

Allen, Marjorie N. *100 Years of Children's Books in America, Decade by Decade*. New York: Facts on File, 1996.

Bader, Barbara. *American Picturebooks: From Noah's Ark to The Beast Within*. New York: Macmillan, 1976.

Bang, Molly. *Picture This: How Pictures Work*. New York: SeaStar Books, 2000.

Bang, Molly. Foreword by Rudolf Arnheim. *Picture This: Perception and Composition*. Boston: Little, Brown, 1991.

Burlingham, Cynthia. "Picturing Childhood: The Evolution of the Illustrated Children's Picture Book." University of California at Los Angeles, http://www.library.ucla.edu/libraries/special/childhood/pictur.htm, accessed on September 15, 2004.

Comenius, Johan Amos. Trans. Charles Hoole. *Orbis Sensualism Pictus*. London: John Sprint, 1705.

Horning, Kathleen T. *From Cover to Cover: Evaluating and Reviewing Children's Books*. New York: HarperCollins, 1997.

Kirk, Connie Ann, ed. "Picture Books with Texts and Picture Inconsistencies." Kay E. Vandegrift's Children's Literature Web site, http://www.scils.rutgers.edu/~kvander/ChildrenLit/PictureInconsistencies.htm, accessed on April 19, 2004.

Nikolajeva, Maria, and Carole Scott. *How Picturebooks Work*. New York: Garland, 2001.

Nodelman, Perry. *Words about Pictures: The Narrative Art of Children's Picture Books.*
Athens, GA and London: University of Georgia Press, 1988.

Silvey, Anita, ed. *Children's Books and Their Creators.* Boston: Houghton Mifflin,
1995.

Vandergrift, Kay E. "Notes for the Analysis of a Picture Book." Rutgers University, New Brunswick, NJ, http://www.scils.rutgers.edu/~kvander/Syllabus/
pictureanalysis.html, accessed on April 19, 2004.

A

ABC Book (Doubleday, 1923). Written and illustrated by C. B. Falls.

SUMMARY: This alphabet concerns itself exclusively with animals, real and imagined. For example, M is for mouse, and C is for cat, but U is for unicorn.

MEDIA: Woodblocks and 4-color printing.

ANECDOTE: Falls, predominantly a poster designer, created the book for his three-year-old daughter, who liked big books with lots of pictures. When it appeared on editor May Massee's Doubleday book list in 1923, the world awakened to the possibility of children's picture books originating from the United States. Falls was regarded as "the finest color printer in America." Though his book owes much to the British picture book *The Square Book of Animals* by Arthur Waugh and illustrated by William Nicholson (Heinemann, 1899) and is not viewed to be as technically refined as that book in its depiction of swans' necks and horses, for example, the fine quality of its overall design and printing brought it attention and favor from both children and adults. In a country that had been used to importing its picture books from Europe because of its own lack of printing expertise, the success of Falls' book brought the children's picture book genre home to Americans and opened a new era in book publishing in the United States.

DISTINCTION: Of historical/scholarly interest.

BIRTHDAY: Not available.

SUBJECT: Alphabets.

The ABC Bunny (Coward McCann, 1933). Written and illustrated by Wanda Gág; hand-lettered by Howard Gág.

SUMMARY: A rabbit hops through the alphabet in a whimsical, rhyming series of adventures as it makes its way home. A musical score of "ABC Song" by Flavia Gág, the artist's sister, begins the book, and the rest of the pages illustrate the lyrics. Some letters are predictable, A for apple, for example; but others, like V for view and M for mealtime, are less so. Illustrations are black and white; large capital letters on each page appear in red. The hand-lettering is done by the artist's brother, Howard Gág. Readers of Gág's classic, *Millions of Cats*, may enjoy this earlier book by the same author and artist.

MEDIA: Lithographs and hand-lettering.

ANECDOTE: Wanda Gág wrote this book for her small nephew, Gary, in 1933.

DISTINCTION: 1934 Newbery Honor Book.

BIRTHDAY: Wanda Gág: March 11, 1893.

SUBJECTS: Alphabets; Rabbits—Fiction.

See Also: Gág, Wanda; Millions of Cats; Nothing at All; Snow White and the Seven Dwarfs.

Abraham Lincoln (Doubleday, 1939). Written and illustrated by Ingri and Edgar Parin d'Aulaire.

SUMMARY: This is a story of Abraham Lincoln's life from his birth to Thomas and Sally Lincoln in the log cabin in Kentucky in 1809 through his days on the farm and the prairie to his presidency in Washington, D.C., and the Civil War. Favorite anecdotes about Lincoln borrowing books to educate himself and stuffing papers into his top hat are included with other depictions of life in the nineteenth century. The book was praised in the *New York Times* of its day for the "high standard" it set in biographies for children under ten years of age.

MEDIA: Lithographic pencil on stone.

ANECDOTE: While traveling and camping across America for several weeks doing research for this book, the d'Aulaires drove a car that cost them only twenty-five dollars. They nicknamed the car "Maybe," because they were never sure each time they got in it whether or not it would start. Edgar Parin d'Aulaire's maternal grandfather from Texas enlisted in Lincoln's army at the age of sixteen, even though he came from a plantation in the Southwest.

DISTINCTION: 1940 Caldecott Medal.

BIRTHDAYS: Edgar d'Aulaire: September 30, 1898; Ingri d'Aulaire: December 27, 1904.

SUBJECTS: Lincoln, Abraham (1809–1865); Presidents—United States—Biography.

Acetate. Artist's medium. Clear plastic film, normally overlaying other media.

Africa Dream (HarperCollins, 1977). Written by Eloise Greenfield; illustrated by Carole Byard.

SUMMARY: A young child dreams one night of going to long-ago Africa. She goes shopping at the marketplace for perfume and jewelry. She reads strange words in books and understands what they mean; she rides a donkey and sees her grandparents' faces with faces like those of her parents. She dances the hello dance to her uncles' drums and sings the hello song. She walks all over Africa until her grandmother, who looks like her mother, holds her, and she goes back to sleep.

MEDIA: Possibly charcoal.

ANECDOTE: Carole Byard went to Africa for the first time on a grant from the Ford Foundation. She made another trip to Nigeria as a delegate to an international black arts conference.

DISTINCTION: 1978 Coretta Scott King Award for Illustration.

BIRTHDAYS: Carole Byard: July 22, 1941; Eloise Greenfield: May 17, 1929.

SUBJECT: Africa—Fiction.

See Also: Cornrows; Nathaniel Talking; Working Cotton.

The Ageless Story, with Its Antiphons (Dodd, Mead, 1939). Written and illustrated by Lauren Ford.

SUMMARY: The book opens with a letter from the author and illustrator to her goddaughter, Nina, in which she explains why she created the book. She teaches her goddaughter about the Benedictines and their chants and the recovery of their music. The book is not intended to teach the chants and how to sing them, but instead it is to help readers find the music more familiar. The book then moves into what it calls the "Ageless Story" of Christ's boyhood as told in the Gospel of Luke. The rest of the book depicts antiphons in Latin and Gregorian music on the left-hand side of page spreads with illustrations and English translations of the antiphons on the right-hand side. Biblical figures appear in clothing and surroundings that suggest New

England, not the Middle East. Initial capitals of the antiphons are illuminated in the style of the Renaissance monks. Both sides of the spreads are framed in a repeating pattern of flowers with a family listening to, and singing, the antiphons along the bottom. Shiny gold accents further illuminate the pages.

MEDIA: Painting, possibly with gold leaf accents.

ANECDOTE: Lauren Ford informs her goddaughter, Nina, in the opening letter that the New England setting for the scenery and clothing in the book is local and familiar rather than true to the Middle East because she wants her goddaughter to recognize God in her own surroundings, to know that God is everywhere. The book was created as a gift to her goddaughter from "Auntie Lauren" of Bethlehem, Connecticut.

DISTINCTION: 1940 Caldecott Honor Book.

BIRTHDAY: Not available.

SUBJECTS: Bible stories; Music.

Airbrush. Artist's medium. A device that sprays paint or ink in a fine mist.

ALA. *See* American Library Association (ALA).

ALA Notable Children's Books. Distinction. Each year a committee from the American Library Association's (ALA) subdivision, the Association for Library Service to Children (ALSC), evaluates and chooses books published by American publishers for children the previous year that they believe to be noteworthy or worth pointing out for having exemplary qualities. Criteria for judging books that are notable include exemplary text, illustration, design, format, use of language, and belief in the interest and expected acceptance by children. After reading thousands of books each year, the committee makes its decision on what books it will place on the notable list at the midwinter ALA meeting each January. The list is an aid to children and librarians in selecting books to read. The notable children's book sticker is a black and gold seal with the word "Notable" in large type across the center. Lists are published on the ALA Web site and in various publications accessible to librarians.

See Also: American Library Association (ALA).

Alexander and the Terrible, Horrible, No Good, Very Bad Day (Atheneum, 1972). Written by Judith Viorst; illustrated by Ray Cruz.

SUMMARY: Alexander goes to bed with gum in his mouth and wakes up with gum in his hair. This is the first of several problems to occur that day, a bad day that makes Alexander want to escape by moving to Australia. Difficulties range from getting no toy prize in his cereal box, to not getting a window seat in Mrs. Gibson's carpool, to dropping from Paul's best friend to his third best friend behind Philip Parker and Albert Mayo. His mother does not put a dessert in his lunch, and Dr. Fields tells him at their family dentist appointment after school that he has a cavity and has to come back to have it filled. Alexander fights with his brothers, Nick and Anthony, and gets into trouble with his mother because of it. At the shoestore, Nick and Anthony get the colors of sneakers they want, but Alexander's choice is all sold out. At his father's office, where they go to pick him up, Alexander has several accidents with the copier and the telephone. There are lima beans that he hates for dinner and kissing on television that he hates to watch. His bath is too hot, and he is made to wear his pajamas with trains on them that he doesn't like to bed. Even in bed, Alexander has problems when his Mickey Mouse light burns out and the cat decides to sleep with Anthony instead of him. His mother tells him that everyone has days like this, even people in Australia.

MEDIA: Pen and ink.

ANECDOTE: Critics complain that the book is one long whining session and that Alexander wants to run away from his problems in his desire to go to Australia. Fans enjoy the exaggeration of problems that make Alexander's bad day even worse than their own and the honest reaction of wanting to move away when difficulties pile up.

DISTINCTIONS: *New York Times* Best Book for Children; NYPL 100 Picture Books Everyone Should Know; *100 Best Books for Children.*

BIRTHDAY: Judith Viorst: February 2, 1931.

SUBJECT: Humorous stories.

Alexander and the Wind-Up Mouse (Pantheon, 1969). Written and illustrated by Leo Lionni.

SUMMARY: All Alexander the mouse wants are a few crumbs, but when he appears out of his hole to get them, someone screams and a broom swings after him. One day no one is home, and Alexander hears a noise in Annie's room. It is another mouse, much like himself except this one has a large key on its back and two little wheels. His name is Willy the wind-up mouse, and he is Annie's favorite toy. He is cuddled and able to sleep in her bed between her doll and her teddy bear. Alexander is glad to make a friend; he asks Willy to go to the kitchen with him to find a few crumbs, but Willy can move only when someone winds his key. He doesn't mind this limitation of his freedom, though, because he is so loved. Soon, Alexander loves Willy, too. The two friends tell each other stories and tales of their adventures. When Alexander is back in his hole at night, however, he thinks of how much Willy is loved and wishes he could be a wind-up mouse and be loved that way, too.

One day, Willy tells Alexander that he heard that there is a magic lizard in the garden. The magic lizard can turn one animal into another. Alexander goes to see him. The magic lizard tells Alexander to bring him a purple pebble when the moon is round. Try as he might, Alexander cannot find one that color. The next time he goes to visit Willy, he finds him in a box with old toys. Annie has had a birthday party where the children brought lots of new toys, and Willy is to be thrown away. Beside the box lies a purple pebble. Alexander takes the pebble to the magic lizard; there is a full moon. Instead of asking to be turned into a wind-up mouse, Alexander asks if Willy could be changed into a real mouse, like him. There is a flash of blinding light, and the purple pebble disappears.

Alexander runs back to the house to find the box of old toys empty. He worries that he is too late. When he goes back to his hole, he hears a squeak and discovers Willy there. The magic lizard has changed him. The two friends are so happy they run out into the garden and dance until morning.

MEDIA: Collage.

ANECDOTE: Lionni did not begin to create picture books for children until he started making them for his grandchildren. He went on to become one of children's favorite picture book authors and artists.

DISTINCTION: 1970 Caldecott Honor Book.

SUBJECT: Mice—Fiction.

BIRTHDAY: Leo Lionni: May 5, 1910.

See Also: Frederick; *Inch by Inch*; *Swimmy*.

All Around the Town (J. B. Lippincott, 1948). Written by Phyllis McGinley; illustrated by Helen Stone.

SUMMARY: This is a rhyming alphabet book with sights from the city. Each letter names an object, then the verse below it describes the object and its function in city life. For example, A is for aeroplane; B is for bus; I is for ice on the ice-skating rink at Rockefeller Center in New York. The illustrations are dated to the city life of the late 1940s.

MEDIA: Undetermined.

ANECDOTE: Phyllis McGinley's daughters were each paid fifty cents by Ludwig Bemelmans for their idea to include a dog in his new book, *Madeline's Rescue*.

DISTINCTION: 1949 Caldecott Honor Book.

BIRTHDAY: Phyllis McGinley: March 21, 1905.

SUBJECTS: City and town life—Poetry; Children's poetry—American; Alphabet rhymes; Alphabet.

All Falling Down (Harper, 1951). Written by Gene Zion; illustrated by Margaret Bloy (Graham).

SUMMARY: As fall draws near, this rhyming story shows the different kinds of things that fall—leaves, apples, sand castles, flower petals, nuts. Then the season changes, and the snow falls; ice-skaters fall. In spring, the rain falls, and shadows fall as the days grow longer. Finally, night falls, and so does Grandma's ball of yarn when she knits, and Daddy's head when he nods off to sleep. Jimmy's blocks fall from the house he has built, and he goes off to bed. In the morning, Daddy doesn't fall but lifts Jimmy out of his crib and gives him a light toss. As Jimmy falls, Daddy catches him, and a new day is beginning.

MEDIA: Undetermined.

ANECDOTE: The idea for the book came from a sketch Margaret Bloy Graham drew of her children collecting apples in an orchard. She and her husband, Gene Zion, collaborated on this book.

DISTINCTION: 1952 Caldecott Honor Book.

BIRTHDAY: Gene Zion: October 5, 1913.

SUBJECT: Seasons—Fiction.

All in the Morning Early (Holt, Rinehart, and Winston, 1963). Written by Leclaire Alger (pseud. Sorche Nic Leodhas); illustrated by Evaline Ness.

SUMMARY: In this rhyming story, early one morning Sandy from Perthshire is sent on an errand by his mother to the mill with a sack of corn. On his way, he meets a huntsman with a horn, two ewes, three gypsies, four farmers, five wee lads, six hares, seven geese, eight burnybees, nine larks, and ten bonny lassies with ribbons gay. All of these add to the group, until they form a long parade on the way to the mill. When he reaches the mill, Sandy tells them that this is as far as he is going, and the rest go on their way.

MEDIA: Undetermined.

ANECDOTE: Librarian Leodhas informs her readers that the story has been in her Scottish family for three generations, at least 150 years, but that she modified some of the words for an American child audience.

DISTINCTION: 1964 Caldecott Honor Book.

BIRTHDAY: Evaline Ness: April 24, 1911.

SUBJECTS: Counting; Country life—Fiction; Scotland—Fiction.

Alphabatics (Aladdin, 1992; Bradbury, 1986). Compiled and illustrated by Suse MacDonald.

SUMMARY: In this alphabet book, letters roll and tumble until they situate at an angle or are blown up out of the frame of the picture in a way that suggests a figure that the illustrator then draws and completes. The figure begins with that letter. For example, an upside-down A becomes an ark; the oval inside the small letter b blows up to become a balloon; the curve of a C becomes the smile of a clown; Zs multiply until they become the stripes on a zebra.

MEDIA: Cells, vinyl acrylic, gouache.

ANECDOTE: Suse MacDonald showed her artist's portfolio to forty-seven publishers and art directors before *Alphabatics* was accepted for publication.

DISTINCTION: 1987 Caldecott Honor Book.

BIRTHDAY: Suse MacDonald: March 3, 1940.

SUBJECTS: Alphabet; English language—Alphabet.

Alphabet City (Viking, 1995). Compiled and illustrated by Stephen T. Johnson.

SUMMARY: This is a wordless alphabet book showing capital letters in objects around a typical city. Johnson found the sights in actual urban settings but then painted them for the book in realistic details that appear strikingly like photographs. For example, the A is the end of a yellow sawhorse at a construction site; E is a traffic light painted from the side; G is a curlicue in iron at the top of an old-fashioned lamppost; T is the open space between buildings with a crosswalk between them. Viewers enjoy finding the letters, which are not always immediately apparent at first glance, thus training the eye to look closely at intricacies in the urban landscape.

MEDIA: Paintings created with pastels, watercolors, gouache, and charcoal on hot pressed watercolor paper.

ANECDOTE: The artist set criteria for himself in accepting the alphabet letters he found in the city—they all had to be capital letters, readily visible in all seasons of the year, and located outside or in indoor public places where anyone could see them. Inspiration for the idea came from his noticing the A in the sawhorse and an S in a decorative keystone.

DISTINCTION: 1996 Caldecott Honor Book.

BIRTHDAY: Stephen T. Johnston: May 29, 1964.

SUBJECTS: Alphabet; City and town life.

ALSC. *See* Association for Library Service to Children.

Always Room for One More (Holt, Rinehart, and Winston, 1965). Written by Leclaire Alger (pseud. Sorche Nic Leodhas); illustrated by Nonny Hogrogian.

SUMMARY: This rhyming book is set in Scotland. Lachie MacLachlan and his wife and ten children (*bairns*) must share their extra food and provisions, since there is a storm outside. They hail passersby to come on into the house. A tinker comes in, then a tailor, sailor, *gallowglass* (soldier), fishing lass, a merry wife, four peat-cutters, Piping Rury the Ranter, a shepherd boy, and his shepherd dog. The people take up the whole house, but Lachie says there is always room for one more. There are music and dancing. Unfortunately, the house eventually falls down, dumping all of the people outside. For a while, they feel sad, until Lachie gets impatient with the gloom and tells them all they can build a new house, which they do. They build a house twice as tall and twice as wide that fits them all, and they say that there will always be room for one more. The book concludes with the music and lyrics for the Scottish song that inspired the book and an explanation of the story's origins as well as of the Scottish words used in the story.

MEDIA: Black pen with colored pastels and wash; 3-color preseparated art.

ANECDOTE: Nonny Hogrogian listened to Scottish music while writing this book. Sorche Nic Leodhas told Nonny that her first attempt at drawing a Scotsman came out with the bone structure of a Romanian.

DISTINCTION: 1966 Caldecott Medal.

BIRTHDAYS: Nonny Hogrogian: May 7, 1932; Sorche Nic Leodhas: January 8, 1898.

SUBJECTS: Folk songs, Scots—Scotland—Texts; Folk songs, Scots.

See Also: Hogrogian, Nonny.

The Amazing Bone (Farrar, Straus and Giroux, 1976). Written and illustrated by William Steig.

SUMMARY: Pearl the pig dawdles on her way home one beautiful day and considers the different kinds of work that adults do that she

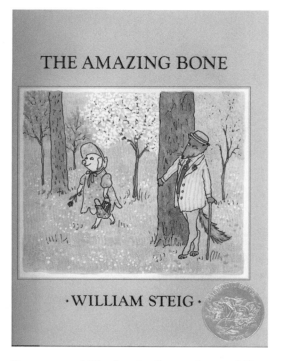

Front cover of *The Amazing Bone*, written and illustrated by William Steig. The book earned Steig a 1977 Caldecott Honor Award the same year he won a Newbery Honor Award for *Abel's Island*. (Reprinted by permission of Farrar, Straus and Giroux, LLC: *The Amazing Bone* by William Steig. Copyright © 1976 by William Steig. www.fsgkidsbooks. com.)

might do herself. She watches the street sweepers; she watches the bakers on Parsnip Lane. On Cobble Road, she watches the men at Maltby's barn pitch horseshoes. She sits down in a forest later on and admires the spring flowers. Her pretty dress makes her feel like a flower herself. She comments aloud that she loves everything. A voice answers that it loves everything, too. Pearl learns that the voice is coming from a bone that is lying by a rock near her. The bone can speak in any language and make any sound. Pearl is astonished and delighted. The bone cannot explain itself or its abilities other than to say that it dropped out of a witch's basket and never wanted to return because the witch was always complaining.

Pearl puts the bone in her purse to take home. She leaves the purse open so that she and the bone can converse. On the way, she and bone fend off robbers, but then they meet a sly fox who is too smart to be outwitted by the noises the bone makes. He takes them both back to his house to prepare Pearl for his meal. It's nothing personal he says. When Pearl and bone are about to meet their fate, the bone begins saying magic words that cause the fox to shrink until he is the size of a mouse. Pearl is saved. She takes the bone back to her parents, who first think the voices are Pearl's imagination until they get used to the idea that the bone can talk and make sounds. The bone becomes a family friend and lives with them, sleeping with Pearl each night and keeping her company.

MEDIA: Possibly watercolor.

ANECDOTE: This book won the 1977 Randolph Caldecott Honor Award the same year Steig's *Abel's Island* won a John Newbery Honor Award.

DISTINCTION: 1977 Caldecott Honor Book.

BIRTHDAY: William Steig: November 14, 1907.

SUBJECT: Pigs—Fiction.

See Also: Doctor De Soto; Sylvester and the Magic Pebble.

An American ABC (Macmillan, 1941). Written and illustrated by Maud and Miska Petersham.

SUMMARY: Published the year the United States entered World War II, this picture book presents the alphabet with a patriotic theme. A is for America, B is for the Liberty Bell, and so on. Similar to several picture books of this period, the text for each page is longer than it is for many later American picture books, often taking up an entire page for each letter. Readers and listeners are educated on themes of Americana through the alphabet: Christopher Columbus, Daniel

Boone, Emigrants, Freedom, George Washington, the Hudson River, Independence, Jamestown, the Knickerbocker family, Abraham Lincoln, the *Mayflower*, the National Anthem, Old Glory, the Pledge of Allegiance (the words "under God" are not yet included in this 1941 version), Quakers, Redskins (dating this book for contemporary discussion of Native American Indians), South America, Thanksgiving, United States (with only forty-eight states at this time), Valley Forge, the White House, Xmas (Christmas, the Christian holiday again somewhat dating this book for contemporary discussion of the country and religion), Yankee Doodle, and Z for "Zeal, an American trait."

MEDIA: Pencil and preseparated watercolor.

ANECDOTE: This book was published in 1941; Maud Petersham's son later served in World War II, and she tried to control her worry by collecting and singing songs and rhymes. The Petershams used to joke that each of their books required both of them to complete because Maud was right-handed and Miska was left-handed. Miska's name at birth was Petrezselyem Mihaly. He changed it later because no one could pronounce it. As a young man, Miska once gave the last few coins he owned to aid survivors of the *Titanic*.

DISTINCTION: 1942 Caldecott Honor Book.

BIRTHDAYS: Maud Petersham: August 5, 1889; Miska Petersham: September 20, 1888.

SUBJECTS: Alphabet; United States—History.

See Also: The Rooster Crows: A Book of American Rhymes and Jingles.

American Library Association (ALA). Organization. Founded in Philadelphia in 1876, ALA is the largest and oldest professional organization of librarians in the world. With more than 64,000 members, the organization has influence in the picture book world in many ways, not least of which is its buying

Each year since 1938, the American Library Association has awarded the Caldecott Medal to the American artist of the most distinguished American children's picture book published the previous year. Named after the British artist Randolph J. Caldecott, the Caldecott Medal was designed in 1937 by René Paul Chambellan. (Courtesy American Library Association.)

power for public, school, and university library collections that are prime and steady purchasers of children's books. Another means of influence is through its annual awards and book lists, which give attention to dozens of picture books out of the thousands that are published each year. These awards include the Randolph Caldecott Medal and Honor Books, Pura Belpré Awards, and Notable Book Lists. ALA is also in association with the Coretta Scott King Foundation that awards the Coretta Scott King Awards each year.

The ALA's mission is to promote public access to information as well as the highest-quality library and information services and promote the profession of librarianship. It creates its own publications as well as lobbies for freedom of information access in political circles and holds both annual and midwinter conferences. ALA is an organization that outside groups turn to for book lists on themes, since it can enlist its members in committees to provide a thorough and comprehensive listing. Eleven divisions of the umbrella organization include the Association of Library Service to Children (ALSC), which is the branch most involved with picture books for children.

Further Reading: http://www.ala.org

See Also: Association for Library Service to Children (ALSC); Caldecott Medal, Randolph; Coretta Scott King Book Awards; Pura Belpré Award.

America's Ethan Allen (Houghton Mifflin, 1949). Written by Stewart Holbrook; illustrated by Lynd Ward.

SUMMARY: This book is much longer than most picture books—ninety-six pages—with a great deal more text on each page than one traditionally sees today. Readers may be surprised to find it as a Caldecott Honor Book, since it is obviously intended for older readers. It is a dramatized biography of the American Revolutionary War hero Ethan Allen. Born in 1737 in the wilds of Connecticut, Allen goes on to lead the Green Mountain Boys against the Yorkers and then against the British. His most famous battle was at Fort Ticonderoga. Though he and his men were successful in capturing the fort from British control, he was later sent to Britain as a prisoner of war. His size and roughness impressed the British. Instead of keeping him, they sent him to Cork, Ireland, where he was met with appreciation, since the Irish did not like the British either and had heard of Allen's Fort Ticonderoga success. From there, he was boarded on a ship to Cape Fear, North Carolina, with British soldiers and was incarcerated still later in a cell in New York City. Finally, his release was traded for the release on the American side of a British colonel.

Colonel Allen met with George Washington at Valley Forge and went on to do much more for the Green Mountains area he loved so well, which would become the state of Vermont. He returned to Bennington to a hero's welcome but died on February 12, 1789, just two years before Vermont declared statehood.

MEDIA: Full-color gouache paintings.

ANECDOTE: Ward illustrated six Newbery Honor books and two Newbery Medal books.

DISTINCTION: 1950 Caldecott Honor Book.

BIRTHDAY: Lynd Ward: June 26, 1905.

SUBJECTS: Allen, Ethan, 1738–1789; Revolutionaries—United States—Biography; Soldiers—United States—Biography; United States—History—Revolution, 1775–1783; Vermont—History—Revolution, 1775–1783; United States—History—Revolution, 1775–1783—Biography.

Anansi the Spider: A Tale from the Ashanti (Holt, Rinehart, and Winston, 1972). Adapted and illustrated by Gerald McDermott.

SUMMARY: In a prologue, the author explains the function of folklore, mythology, and legends in culture in general and in the Ashanti people's traditions in particular. The Ashanti live in Ghana of West Africa. They are artisans and weavers and weave symbols of their culture and past into their work. The Anansi is a spider, a trickster, that is one of these symbols. The author says that the following story is one of the tricksters' adventures that have been passed down in Ashanti culture. Anansi has six sons; their names are See Trouble, Road Builder, River Drinker, Game Skinner, Stone Thrower, and Cushion. Anansi wanders off and gets himself into trouble. His six good sons come to his rescue. See Trouble sees that his father needs help. Road Builder takes the sons to his aid. River Drinker takes up the water to catch the fish that had swallowed Anansi. Game Skinner cuts him out of the fish. Stone Thrower casts a stone at a falcon that picks up Anansi. Cushion softens Anansi's return to earth. The family of spiders is happy, and they return home. They see a globe of light in the woods. Anansi wants to reward the son who rescued him with the globe of light, but he cannot decide which son should receive the reward. He calls on Nyame, the God of All Things, to help him decide. Seeing the family begin to argue over who deserves the reward, Nyame takes the globe of light up to the sky where they all can see it and keeps it there, where it remains as the sun lighting the world, even now.

MEDIA: Preseparated 4-color artwork outlined in ink.

ANECDOTE: McDermott's film version of the story won a Blue Ribbon for children's films at the American Film Festival in 1970. McDermott's career in picture books came from his film work, not the other way around.

DISTINCTION: 1973 Caldecott Honor Book.

BIRTHDAY: Gerald McDermott: January 31, 1941.

SUBJECTS: Ashanti (African people)—Folklore; Anansi (Legendary character); Folklore—Africa.

Anatole (Whittlesey House, 1956). Written by Eve Titus; illustrated by Paul Galdone.

SUMMARY: Anatole is a French mouse who lived in a village near Paris. His wife's name is Doucette, and his children are Paul and Paulette, Claude and Claudette, and Georges and Georgette. In the small mouse village at night, the husbands ride in pairs on bicycles around town looking for food to feed their families. Gaston is usually Anatole's partner. One night, as they try to secure a crumb from a kitchen, Anatole overhears a woman say how disgraceful mice are to France. He tells Gaston that they must leave. Gaston has a different attitude; he says that people are people and mice are mice, but Anatole does not like being looked down upon by people. He has his honor to uphold. He decides that for all the food the humans supply him and his family, he should do something back.

One night, he types many little signs and takes them on his bicycle to the Duval Cheese Factory. There he goes to the tasting room and tries all the cheeses, sticking a sign with his opinion, good, not good, and so on, into the cheese. The next morning, no one knows who left the signs and did all the cheese tasting, but when M'sieu Duval arrives and did some tasting of his own, he agrees with the reviews. The cheese makers make changes to improve the not-good cheeses, and business begins to do very well. Business does so well that Henri Duval leaves a typed letter for Anatole, offering him a job as Vice President in charge of cheese tasting. He can have all the cheese he wants every evening and French bread that will be left for him as well, and someday maybe M'sieu Duval and he will meet. Anatole's wife and family are proud of his new job as a cheese taster business-mouse, and he invites Gaston to be his partner.

MEDIA: Possibly pen and ink with gray wash over graphite with paper collage.

ANECDOTE: The book began as a bed-time story that Eve Titus told her son Ricky about the business where his father worked.

DISTINCTION: 1957 Caldecott Honor Book.

BIRTHDAY: Eve Titus: July 16, 1922.

SUBJECTS: Mice—Fiction; Cheese—Fiction.

See Also: Anatole and the Cat.

Anatole and the Cat (Whittlesey House, 1957). Written by Eve Titus; illustrated by Paul Galdone.

SUMMARY: In a sequel to *Anatole*, now the mouse is respected in all of France as the expert cheese taster at the Duval Cheese Factory. One night as Anatole and his partner Gaston work at the factory tasting cheeses, they hear a cat upstairs. They are afraid and make many mistakes in the signs they write for the cheeses, but as long as the cat does not come downstairs, they can keep doing their work. On their way out that night, however, they see the cat on the stairs; they pedal home on their bicycles as quickly as they can.

The workers show the crazy signs to M'sieu Duval the next day. Since he trusts Anatole, he tells them to do what the signs say. Gaston does not return to work with Anatole that night; he is too afraid. Anatole types a letter to leave for M'sieu Duval, telling him that he does not like cats, and he cannot return to work for him if the cat is still allowed to come to the factory at night. M'sieu Duval writes back his apologies that his family pet had gotten into the factory, and that he will do his best to keep it from happening again. However, Anatole believes that if the cat escaped once from home, it could do it again. His solution is to tie a bell around the cat's neck to serve as a warning. He goes to a hardware store and buys a cat trap, setting it with catnip that evening.

Charlemagne the cat is caught in the trap that night. Anatole goes in the cage and ties the bells on the cat bravely while it was sleeping. He also leaves a typed memo saying why the cat was belled and that M'sieu Duval needs to watch him more carefully. M'sieu Duval types Anatole a note as well that thanks him for the idea and tells him that a new cheese has been named after him. One of the mixed-up notes said to add cucumber seeds to one cheese, and it turned out to be a favorite with customers.

MEDIA: Possibly pen and ink with gray wash over graphite with paper collage.

ANECDOTE: French is occasionally used throughout the book; for example, the heading of the interoffice memo reads: "Fromagerie Duval."

DISTINCTION: 1958 Caldecott Honor Book.

BIRTHDAY: Eve Titus: July 16, 1922.

SUBJECTS: Mice—Fiction; Cats—Fiction.

See Also: Anatole.

And to Think I Saw It on Mulberry Street
(Vanguard, 1937). Written and illustrated by Dr. Seuss (Theodor S. Geisel).

SUMMARY: Marco's father wants him to quit telling tales about what he saw on Mulberry Street on his way home from school. Still, Marco can't help his imagination as he sees a man with a horse and cart on Mulberry Street expand into many more complicated and fanciful visions. The horse becomes a zebra, reindeer, elephant, and an elephant with two giraffes. The wagon becomes a chariot, sleigh, then a brass band. Embellishments include a trailer with an observer, a Rajah driving atop the elephant, a police escort on motorcycles, a grandstand with the mayor and other officials waving, an airplane dropping confetti, a Chinese man, Magician, and a man with a ten-foot beard. Marco returns home and is tempted to tell his father what he *really* saw on Mulberry Street but abides by his father's wishes and tells him that he saw just a horse and wagon.

ANECDOTE: This book is the first of forty-four books for children written by "Dr. Seuss." It was turned down by twenty-eight publishers before it was accepted. The author wrote down the refrain and several beginning draft lines in a bar aboard the *M.S. Kungshold.* The rhythm of the refrain, "And this is a story that no one can beat / when I say that I saw it on Mulberry Street," was the rhythm of the motors aboard the ship. The rhythm galloped annoyingly through the author's mind for a week after he left the ship. The book is filled with images from Geisel's hometown of Springfield, Massachusetts. Springfield images include the name of the street itself, the appearance of the mayor (taken after Mayor Fordis Parker), and the red motorcycles the police ride, which suggest red Springfield Indian motorcycles.

MEDIA: Undetermined.

DISTINCTION: Of historical/scholarly interest.

BIRTHDAY: Dr. Seuss: March 2, 1904.

SUBJECTS: Imagination—Fiction; Stories in rhyme.

See Also: Bartholomew and the Oobleck; Geisel, Theodor (Ted) Seuss; *If I Ran the Zoo*; *McElligott's Pool*.

Andy and the Lion (Viking, 1938). Written and illustrated by James Daugherty.

SUMMARY: In a three-part picture book, Andy checks out a book about lions from the library, and his adventures begin. In part one, he reads the book all during dinner and all evening. His grandfather tells him about shooting lions using both barrels, and Andy dreams that night about hunting lions. He is still thinking about lions as he gets ready for school the next day. In part two, Andy is on his way to school when he sees a lion's tail behind a rock. He chases the lion, and the lion chases him all around the rock until they get tired. Lion shows Andy that he has a thorn in his paw. Andy removes the thorn with pliers he always carries in his pocket, and they become friends. Andy goes on to school, and the lion goes on his way. In part three, a circus has come to town, and the biggest lion escapes into the crowd. Just as the crowd is about to capture the lion, Andy stands before him and tells the crowd that the lion is his friend. The book ends with Andy leading the lion down the street in a parade, then taking his book back to the library.

MEDIA: Charcoal.

ANECDOTE: The story is a retelling of the fable Androcles and the Lion. During World War I, James Daugherty painted camouflage colors on ships.

DISTINCTION: 1939 Caldecott Honor Book.

BIRTHDAY: James Daugherty: June 1, 1889.

SUBJECT: Fables.

The Angry Moon (Little, Brown, 1970). Story retold by William Sleator; illustrated by Blair Lent.

SUMMARY: Lupan and Lapowinsa are friends out one summer night walking. Lapowinsa laughs at how funny the moon looks with all the marks on its face, but Lupan tells her not to laugh at the moon. Suddenly, a rainbow appears and takes Lapowinsa away, leaving Lupan alone. Lupan takes his bow and arrow and tries to strike the moon or a star; he thinks the moon has taken his friend. Each arrow does not come back, but he keeps shooting them until soon a chain of arrows hangs down from the sky. Lupan touches it; the arrows become a ladder. For some reason, he puts branches in his hair and climbs up the ladder. He keeps climbing through darkness and heavy rain.

In the morning, the sun is very bright, and Lupan feels that the branches on his head have grown and bear blue and red berries. He eats the berries and drops the empty branches down to the ground. He falls asleep, and soon he hears a voice saying that it is taking him to his grandmother. A little boy takes him to an old woman. She explains to Lupan that she saw how brave he was and she helped him come to the sky world. The moon has captured his friend. He must eat and become strong; after that, he must take four things to the moon's house to rescue Lapowinska—a pinecone, a fish eye, a rose, and a piece of stone. He can hear Lapowinska's cries. When he gets to the moon's house, he sees that she is in a smoke hole and is burning.

Quickly, he drops the pinecone in the hole, and she escapes. When the pinecone has burned all the way and stopped crying in place of Lapowinska, the moon becomes angry at being tricked and rolls after the two friends. Lupan throws the fish eye behind him, and water appears with a boat to take the two friends away. On the shore, the moon almost catches up with them. Lupan throws the rose, and thickets grow to stop the moon yet again. Lastly, Lupan throws the stone, and a mountain grows to hold back the moon. The moon cannot roll over it; it simply rolls up and down one side again and again.

The two friends find the grandmother and

thank her for her help. She tells them the ladder is still there, and they can return to earth whenever they like. When they go down the ladder, they are covered with a fine mist that glistens on them, and the ladder turns back into arrows. Back on earth, the two friends live a long and happy life, telling their story of the angry moon and the sky world that gets passed down many generations.

MEDIA: Pen-and-ink drawings with acrylic glazes; full-color paintings.

ANECDOTE: The legend that inspired this story was recorded by Dr. John R. Swanton in the Bureau of American Ethnology, Bulletin 39, *Tlingit Myths and Texts*, Government Printing Office, Washington, D.C., in 1909. Though the illustrations are based on Tlingit designs, they are not necessarily authentic renderings.

DISTINCTION: 1971 Caldecott Honor Book.

BIRTHDAY: Blair Lent: January 22, 1930.

SUBJECTS: Tlingit Indians—Folklore; Indians of North America—Folklore.

Animals of the Bible, a Picture Book
(Frederick A. Stokes, 1937). Selected by Helen Dean Fish; illustrated by Dorothy P. Lathrop.

SUMMARY: The first book to win a Caldecott Medal, this work retells Bible stories that include animals. Stories from the Old Testament include "The Story of the Creation of the Animals"; "The Serpent and Eve"; "The Story of the Animals Saved in the Ark"; "The Dove Who Served Noah"; "Abraham's Ram"; "Isaac's Camels at Rebekah's Well"; "The Scapegoat"; "Balaam's Ass"; "David Saves His Sheep from a Lion and a Bear"; "The Ravens Who Fed Elijah"; "God Talks to Job about the Animals"; "Behemoth"; "Leviathan"; "The Thirsting Heart"; "The Mighty Eagle"; "God's Care of the Animals"; "Daniel's Lions"; "The Story of Jonah and the Great Fish"; and "Some Other Animals of the Old Testament." Stories from the New Testament include "Animals Around the Christmas Manger"; "The Flocks of the Christmas Shepherds"; "The Prodigal Son's Swine"; "The Foxes Have Holes"; "The Family Dogs"; "The Netful of Fishes"; "The Good Samaritan's Own Beast"; "The Sheep of the Good Shepherd"; "The Palm Sunday Colt"; "As a Hen Gathereth Her Chickens"; "Peter's Cock"; and "The Peaceable Kingdom." Underneath most stories are the book, chapter, and verse from the King James Bible from which the story is adapted.

ANECDOTE: This book was the first ever to win the Caldecott Medal for excellence in illustration of picture books for children. In her acceptance speech, Lathrop looked out at the audience and said she wished they were animals with furry faces, because then she would better know what to say to them. While she worked on the pictures for the book, she had trouble with her animal models because they kept falling asleep.

Throughout American publishing history, Helen Dean Fish was only the third editor to work full-time on children's books. As a child, she loved the stories in the Bible about animals the best. She enjoyed one about Samson's foxes that had burning brands tied to their tails, but she did not include it in the book for fear children would tie a burning brand to the tail of an animal. Fish selected the text for the Caldecott Honor Book of the same year, *Four and Twenty Blackbirds*.

MEDIA: Black-and-white lithographs.

DISTINCTION: 1938 Caldecott Medal.

BIRTHDAYS: Helen Dean Fish: February 7, 1889; Dorothy Lathrop: April 16, 1891.

SUBJECT: Bible—Natural history.

See Also: Four and Twenty Blackbirds: Nursery Rhymes of Yesterday Recalled for Children of Today.

Ape in a Cape: An Alphabet of Odd Animals
(Harcourt, 1952). Written and illustrated by Fritz Eichenberg.

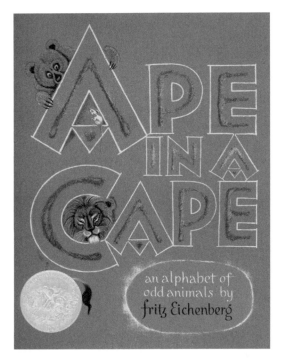

Cover of *Ape in a Cape: An Alphabet of Odd Animals*, written and illustrated by Fritz Eichenberg. Eichenberg escaped to New York from Nazi Germany, beginning a successful art career that spanned much of the twentieth century. (Copyright © 1952 by Fritz Eichenberg. Copyright © by Harcourt, Inc. All rights reserved.)

SUMMARY: This is a rhyming alphabet book with animals in unusual moods, settings, costumes, or with objects. For example, B is for a bear in despair; C is a carp with a harp; J is a bluejay in May; and P is a pig in a wig. X is for Rex, which is a king lion.

MEDIA: Woodcuts; acetate separations.

ANECDOTE: Eichenberg escaped Nazi Germany and moved to New York to begin a prolific artistic career that spanned a large portion of the twentieth century. He later became a Quaker. His art was recently celebrated in a traveling exhibition, "Witness to the 20th Century: An Artistic Biography of Fritz Eichenberg."

DISTINCTION: 1953 Caldecott Honor Book.

BIRTHDAY: Fritz Eichenberg: October 24, 1901.

SUBJECTS: Alphabet; Animals—Pictorial works.

April's Kittens (Harper, 1940). Written and illustrated by Clare Turlay Newberry.

SUMMARY: April lives in New York City with her parents, Margaret and Charles, and a black cat named Sheba. Their apartment is so small that April still sleeps in a crib to save space, even though she is six years old. Charles says they live in a "one-cat apartment" and warns Sheba not to have babies; there is simply not room. Despite the warning, Sheba has three kittens, one black and two tiger-striped. April adores them, but Charles keeps warning that the kittens cannot stay. He tells Margaret to find homes for them before their daughter becomes attached. Soon, the family talks about naming them, and April's father names them Charcoal, Butch, and Brenda. The kittens learn to drink milk from a dish. The family discusses keeping Brenda and giving Sheba and the other two away. April likes Brenda best, but she does not say so because she does not want to hurt the other kittens' feelings. Perhaps Aunt Helen in the country will take Sheba, April's mother suggests. Soon, Mrs. Dalton arrives with Geoffrey, and they choose Butch to take home. Miss Elwell comes the next day, and she adopts Charcoal. April is relieved each time that she still has Brenda. However, now she must choose between Sheba and Brenda, since they still live in a one-cat apartment. April tosses and turns in bed that night with her decision. Her mother notices April's feet touching the bottom of the crib. Though she is small for her age, at six, she has now completely outgrown the crib. Margaret shows this to Charles, and he agrees that it is time to move to a bigger apartment. When April asks, he tells her that it can be a two-cat apartment, and they can keep both Sheba and the kitten, Brenda. April joyfully makes up a cat song about purring, then purrs herself back to sleep.

MEDIA: Ink, charcoal, and watercolor.

ANECDOTE: The first picture Newberry drew was of a cat when she was two years old. Cats play an important part in each of her four Caldecott Honor books.

DISTINCTION: 1941 Caldecott Honor Book.

BIRTHDAY: Clare Newberry: April 10, 1903.

SUBJECTS: Cats—Fiction; Apartment houses—Fiction.

See Also: Barkis.

Arrow to the Sun: A Pueblo Indian Tale

(Viking, 1974). Written and illustrated by Gerald McDermott.

SUMMARY: The book retells a story of the Pueblo Indians. The sun sends life to a maiden living in a pueblo, and that life becomes a boy. The Boy is not accepted by the other children because he has no father. They ask him where his father is, and this makes the Boy and his mother sad. The Boy sets out to search for him. He asks the Corn Planter, the Pot Maker, and the Arrow Maker where his father is, but no one knows. The Arrow Maker turns the Boy into a special arrow and shoots him to the sun. The Boy asks the mighty Lord if he is his son, and the Lord replies that he might be or he might not. He must prove himself through tests. He must pass through the Kiva of Lions, the Kiva of Serpents, the Kiva of Bees, and the Kiva of Lightning. The Boy passes through all of these successfully. When he passes out of the Kiva of Lightning, he is changed to have the sun's power. The Father sends him back to earth as an arrow to bring his spirit to the earth. When he returns to the pueblo, the people celebrate with the Dance of Life.

MEDIA: Gouache and ink; black line pre-separated; art reproduced using the 4-color process.

ANECDOTE: When he was a child, McDermott performed in a radio program of myths and legends.

DISTINCTION: 1975 Caldecott Honor Book.

BIRTHDAY: Gerald McDermott: January 31, 1941.

SUBJECT: Pueblo Indians—Folklore.

See Also: McDermott, Gerald.

Ashanti to Zulu: African Traditions (Dial, 1976). Written by Margaret Mugrove; illustrated by Leo and Diane Dillon.

SUMMARY: This is an alphabet book that teaches the language and customs of twenty-six different African peoples who live on the continent. For each letter, the name of an African group is given with its pronunciation, then a description of a custom of that group. Paragraphs are presented on each page underneath the Dillons' award-winning artwork. The peoples include Ashanti, Baule, Chagga, Dogon, Ewe, Fanti, Ga, Hausa, Ikoma, Jie, Kung, Lozi, Masai, Ndaka, Ouadai, Pondo, Quimbande, Rendille, Sotho, Tuareg, Uge, Vai, Wagenia, Xhosa, Yoruba, and the Zulu. A map of the continent appears at the back of the book that shows where concentrations of the twenty-six peoples live.

ANECDOTE: Musgrove took care in making her text authentic by living and researching in Ghana, where she worked as an English teacher, as well as studying African language and traditions at the University of Massachusetts and Yale. The Dillons tried to depict a man, woman, and child as well as a dwelling, artifact, and local animal in each painting. They spent three months researching the illustrations but had all of them painted within one month.

MEDIA: Pastels, watercolors, and acrylics; frames in watercolor and black ink.

DISTINCTION: 1977 Caldecott Medal.

BIRTHDAYS: Diane Dillon: March 13, 1933; Leo Dillon: March 2, 1933; Margaret Musgrove: November 19, 1943.

SUBJECTS: Ethnology—Africa; Alphabet; Africa—Social life and customs.

See Also: Dillion, Diane, and Leo; *Why Mosquitoes Buzz in People's Ears.*

Association for Library Service to Children (ALSC). Organization. A major division of the professional organization American Library Association (ALA), ALSC is involved in promoting the profession of children's librarianship and the relationship among children's books, citizen literacy, libraries, and patrons. It was officially formed as a division of the ALA on June 24, 1941, though its name underwent several incarnations before that time. The ALSC was formed from several smaller groups such as the Children's Library Association; the American Association of School Librarians; and the Young People's Reading Round Table.

Among its many functions as an advocate for children's literature and children's literature professionals, ALSC is the branch of ALA that awards the best-known annual prizes for children's books in the United States. Committees for each award form from the organization's 3,700 members, and each committee deliberates choices for a year. The awards are normally announced at the ALA midwinter meeting each January. The awards include the John Newbery Medal for most distinguished contribution to American literature for children; the Randolph Caldecott Medal for excellence in illustration of the most distinguished children's picture book published the previous year; the Laura Ingalls Wilder Medal for a substantial and lasting contribution to literature for children over a number of years and publications; the Pura Belpré Award to the Latino/Latina writer and illustrator whose work best affirms and celebrates Latino culture in a book for children; and the Robert F. Sibert Informational Book Medal for most distinguished informational book.

Other awards granted by the ALSC include the Andrew Carnegie Medal for best video production for children; the Mildred L. Batchelder Award for outstanding translation; and the Mary Hill Arbuthnot Honor Lecture Award for a citizen of any country who has served as a librarian, writer, illustrator, critic, historian, or teacher of children's literature and made a lasting contribution to children's literature. In addition, the ALSC works in cooperation with the Coretta Scott King Foundation to publicize and promote the winners and honor books each year of the Coretta Scott King Book Award for distinguished African American authors and artists of books for children. The organization also publishes annual lists of Notable Children's Books.

Within its ranks, ALSC promotes children's librarianship in both public and school libraries through publications, conferences, Internet discussion lists, scholarships, products, partnerships, events, and other methods.

Contact Information: ALSC, ALA, 50 Huron Street, Chicago, IL 60611-2795; (800) 545-2433, ext. 2163; Fax: (312) 944-7671; E-mail: alsc@ala.org.

Further Reading: http://www.ala.org/ALSC.

B

Baboushka and the Three Kings (Houghton Mifflin, 1960). Written by Ruth Robbins, illustrated by Nicolas Sidjakov.

SUMMARY: Three kings lose their way in a snowstorm while following the star to where the child known to them as the Babe was born. They stop at Baboushka's hut to see if she will show them the way. Instead, she asks them to come in and spend the night, warming by her cozy fire; they will find their way better in the morning. The three men, however, are in a hurry and tell her that if she cannot come with them, they must continue on in their sleigh. In the morning, Baboushka decides their journey must be important, and this must not be an ordinary baby they are looking for; she decides to follow them. She packs a few chosen gifts and sets off. She goes from village to village asking after the newborn child, but no one has seen him. On her way, she pauses to enjoy the children she sees playing in the new snowfall with their dogs, but she does not stop for long.

Her journey is commemorated each year after Christmas when children receive small, but special, gifts in memory of Baboushka setting out anew to find the Christ Child. Music by Mary Clement Sanks and lyrics by Edith M. Thomas to the song "Baboushka" are provided at the back of the book.

MEDIA: Tempera and felt-tip pen in four colors.

ANECDOTE: Nicolas Sidjakov's Russian background and his four-year-old son gave him inspiration for his artwork for this book.

DISTINCTION: 1961 Caldecott Medal.

BIRTHDAY: Nicolas Sidjakov: December 16, 1924.

SUBJECTS: Folklore—Russia; Christmas—Fiction.

Baldwin Library of Historical Children's Literature. Collection. This collection, begun in librarian Ruth Baldwin's forty-year career, comprises more than 90,000 volumes of British and American children's literature published from the early 1700s to the 1990s. One of its highlights is the inclusion of 800 children's works from early America that is the second largest such collection in the country. Other features of interest to picture book enthusiasts include books printed in both Britain and the United States; nineteenth-century alphabet books; Little Golden Books; editor Louise Seaman Betchel's papers including correspondence with Berta and Elmer Hader and Maud and Miska Petersham; and other materials.

Contact: Baldwin Library of Historical Children's Literature, University of Florida, George A. Smathers Libraries, Department of Special Collections, P.O. Box 117007, Gainesville, FL 32611-7007; (352) 392-9075; Web site: http://web.uflib.ufl.edu/spec/bald win/baldwin.html; email: ritsmit@mail.uflib. ufl.edu.

Bambino the Clown (Viking, 1947). Written and illustrated by Georges Schreiber.

SUMMARY: A small man from Italy comes to America. He is called Bambino because he is so small; bambino is the Italian word for child. Bambino lives on Main Street across from the General Store where he can see the river and the church steeple. He loves it there, since the church bells seem to ring out his name. He loves children, and he loves to laugh; he is a clown who always has lots of people around him. Bambino has a pet sea lion named Flapper. One day, Bambino meets Peter, a boy who is sad because the wind has blown away his hat. Peter wants to learn to be a clown, so Bambino takes him home to cheer him up and teach him. Peter sees Bambino's huge collection of costumes, makeup, and props. He plays with Flapper, who lives in his own pool in Bambino's backyard. Bambino gives Peter a free ticket to one of his shows.

At the show, Peter sees Bambino transform into a clown. The clown tries to play a double-bass and a bass-tuba, but funny things keep preventing him from doing so. Flapper joins the act, balancing balls and other objects on his nose. Bambino falls from a tower of tables and chairs and picks himself up again. After the show, Peter and his friends wait outside for Bambino, who talks to them about how clowns make other people happy, even if they themselves have lost their hats. The town church bells ring their "Bam-bim, Bam-bim," and everyone is happy again.

MEDIA: Possibly watercolor.

ANECDOTE: Schreiber's career started by his painting portraits of world celebrities.

Among others, he painted Albert Einstein, Gertrude Stein, Sinclair Lewis, H. G. Wells, Thomas Mann, and Paul Von Hindenberg. *Bambino the Clown* was his first book for children. He wrote and illustrated a sequel in 1959, *Bambino Goes Home*.

DISTINCTION: 1948 Caldecott Honor Book.

BIRTHDAY: Georges Schreiber: April 25, 1904.

SUBJECTS: Clowns—Fiction; Sea lions—Fiction; Seals (Animals)—Fiction.

Barkis (Harper, 1938). Written and illustrated by Clare Turlay Newberry.

SUMMARY: James receives a cocker spaniel puppy named Barkis from his Uncle Jimmy for his ninth birthday. His older sister, Nell Jean, has a kitten named Edward. Both children are jealous of the other's pets. Nell Jean wants to share the cat and dog, saying they each belong to both of them, but James does not. Nell Jean has not shared Edward with him previously, so why should he share his birthday dog with her? One day, Barkis pushes open the screen door and gets outside. He steps down the stairs and rolls around in the grass. Nell Jean, who has been reading, sees Barkis go outside, but she does not stop him. She thinks that James should take care of it, but she does not tell him about Barkis either. Soon, kindness wins out, and she looks outside the window for Barkis but cannot find him. When she goes outside to look, she finds puppy Barkis has just fallen into the icy creek. She rescues him and brings him home.

Their mother warms Barkis so that he does not become ill. After a close call, Barkis comes back around and is fine by dinner. James thanks his sister by offering to share Barkis and Edward. Ridden with guilt, Nell Jean confesses her previous neglect of Barkis, but James generously maintains his offer that both siblings call each pet half their own. Nell Jean is moved by her brother's generosity and understands how he would like to call Barkis mostly his own. She suggests that they each call their own pet mostly theirs but also partly their siblings'. Like the siblings, Barkis and Edward, who were previously leery of one another (Edward gave Barkis a scratch on the nose when he first arrived), begin to get along better as well.

MEDIA: Charcoal pencil and watercolor wash.

ANECDOTE: Newberry wanted to be a portrait painter but had more success painting cats, her lifelong love.

DISTINCTION: 1939 Caldecott Honor Book.

BIRTHDAY: Clare Newberry: April 10, 1903.

SUBJECTS: Dogs—Fiction; Brothers and sisters—Fiction.

See Also: April's Kittens

Bartholomew and the Oobleck (Random House, 1949). Written and illustrated by Theodor Seuss Geisel (pseud. Dr. Seuss).

SUMMARY: King Derwin of the Kingdom of Didd is angry with the four things of rain, fog, snow, and sunshine that come down to the earth from his sky. Bartholomew Cubbins is the King's page who saves the day. The King asks his magicians to make something new to fall from the sky, and they come up with *oobleck*. Green drops fall from the sky the next morning, and the King is overjoyed. He asks the bell ringer to call for a holiday. However, everything is getting covered with a green, molasses-like substance, the oobleck. Bartholomew goes to the trumpeter to have him blow a warning, but his trumpet is gummed up with oobleck. He goes to the Captain of the Guards, but he eats some oobleck, and his mouth glues shut. It is no use. Oobleck is everywhere, gumming up the works. The Royal Laundress is stuck to her clothesline; the Royal Fiddlers are stuck to their fiddles; and the King's crown is stuck to his head and his seat to his throne. The King tells Bartholomew to have the magicians stop making oobleck fall from the sky, but their cave

on Mountain Neeka-tave is covered with the stuff.

Cubbins has the idea that no one but the King can stop the mess. He tells him that he must say he is sorry in simple words; no fancy magical words will do. The King is indignant, but soon the weight and stickiness of the oobleck make him apologize. As soon as he does, the oobleck stops falling from the sky. The oobleck melts away from everywhere it has fallen. The kingdom celebrates when Bartholomew Cubbins takes the King by the sleeve and leads him to the bell tower, where the King himself rings the bell calling for a holiday. The King now knows that the four things that fall from the sky—fog, rain, sunshine, and snow—are good enough.

MEDIA: Pencil, crayon, and watercolor.

ANECDOTE: The story has often been read as a statement against air pollution.

DISTINCTION: 1950 Caldecott Honor Book.

BIRTHDAY: Dr. Seuss: March 4, 1904.

SUBJECT: Fantasy.

See Also: And to Think I Saw It on Mulberry Street; Geisel, Theodor (Ted) Seuss; *If I Ran the Zoo*; *McElligott's Pool*.

Baseball Saved Us (Lee and Low, 1993). Written by Ken Mochizuki; illustrated by Dom Lee.

SUMMARY: In Camp, Dad builds a baseball field after his son Teddy talks back to him disrespectfully. Teddy has never talked that way to his father before, so Dad knows it is time to create the field to help cut the tension in Camp. The Camp is an internment camp in the desert where Japanese Americans were held under suspicion during World War II. The narrator of the story is a small Japanese American boy who likes to play baseball but has always been the last boy picked at school because he is small and does not play well.

During the course of the story, Teddy plays much more ball on the field his father has built, and the game helps raise the spirits of many of the internees. After the war, Teddy faces discrimination back at school, when the other children will not sit with him in the cafeteria because of his ancestry. When he plays ball, however, they see he has improved from his days playing at the Camp and they start calling him Shorty as an affectionate nickname. Just as his anger at the steady glare of the security guard at Camp helped him make a hit in a game there, Teddy's response to racial slurs at the ballpark back home pushes him to hit another home run. An author's note at the beginning of the book briefly explains the internment camps that actually existed in the United States from 1942 to 1945.

MEDIA: Scratched encaustic beeswax on paper and oil paint.

DISTINCTION: Asian American-commended book.

BIRTHDAYS: Dom Lee: May 4, 1959; Ken Mochizuki: May 18, 1954.

SUBJECTS: Japanese Americans—Evacuation and relocation, 1942–1945—Fiction; World War, 1939–1945—United States—Fiction; Baseball—Fiction; Prejudices—Fiction.

Batik. Artist's medium. A process where paint is applied to a wax-resistant surface in wax and the wax is taken away to leave the paint on the surface desired.

Bear Party (Viking, 1951). Written and illustrated by William Pène du Bois.

SUMMARY: The bears at Koala Park in Australia usually play all day, but one day they become angry with one another. They get angrier and angrier. They become so angry that they stop looking at one another; and instead look straight ahead and growl. There is one old and wise bear who lives at the top of the eucalyptus tree. He thinks the behavior of the other bears is terrible. He decides to hold a costume ball where the bears will not recognize each other. The bears choose their own costumes—there are an Indian Bear, a Sleeping Bear, a Spanish Bear, French Bear, Angel Bear, Clown Bear, a Nurse, a Bullfighter, a Chinese Bear, a Hunting Bear, a Dancing Bear, a Knight, a Turkish Bear, and a Napoleon Bear. The bears do all kinds of dances, including rhumbas, sambas, bunny hugs, turkey trots, and difficult dances they make up themselves.

When the party is over, the wise old bear tells them to take off their costumes and throw them in a pile on the ground. They hang their masks on the tree. Since the bears all look alike, and they had been unfriendly for so long, they can no longer tell each other apart. They begin to quarrel all over again. The wise old bear solves the problem by having each bear put its costume back on. They have another party. When they see how much fun they have, they decide to keep one part of their costume to wear as a souvenir after the party is over. When they do this, they can tell each other apart once more, and they are no longer angry. Soon, the souvenirs are no longer needed to tell each other apart, and the wise old bear at the top of the eucalyptus tree is pleased with their behavior. He has determined that they need more parties at Koala Park.

MEDIA: Undetermined.

ANECDOTE: While the story uses the term "bears" throughout, the illustrations depict Australian koalas, which are not bears but marsupials. Du Bois won the Newbery Medal in 1948 for *The Twenty-One Balloons*.

DISTINCTION: 1952 Caldecott Honor Book.

BIRTHDAY: William Pène du Bois: May 9, 1916.

SUBJECTS: Animals—Fiction; Bears—Fiction; Koalas—Fiction; Behavior—Fiction.

Beautiful Blackbird (Atheneum, 2003). Written and illustrated by Ashley Bryan.

SUMMARY: In Africa, there are birds of only solid colors—red, yellow, purple, orange, blue, pink, and black. All the birds vote that the most beautiful bird in the land is the blackbird. The other birds do a Beak and Wing Dance and a Show Claws Slide to celebrate how beautiful Blackbird is. Ringdove asks Blackbird if he can paint a ring of black around his neck to give him some of Blackbird's beauty. Blackbird tells Ringdove that what makes a bird beautiful is what is on the inside. Nevertheless, after the Sun-Up Dance the next morning, he makes a mixture of black in his medicine gourd and paints a ring with his feather brush for Ringdove. The other birds see this ornamentation and want black markings, too, and that is how the birds received black markings—strips, rings, dots, tips, and other designs—on their feathers.

MEDIA: Paper collage.

ANECDOTE: The scissors shown in the endpapers of the book are the same scissors Bryan's mother used for her embroidery and sewing and that Bryan then used to cut paper for the collages in the book. The story is adapted from a tale of the Ila-speaking peoples of Zambia, formerly known as Northern Rhodesia.

DISTINCTION: 2004 Coretta Scott King Award for Illustration.

BIRTHDAY: Ashley Bryan: July 13, 1923.

SUBJECTS: Ila (African people)—Folklore; Folklore—Zambia.

Ben's Trumpet (Greenwillow, 1979). Written and illustrated by Rachel Isadora.

SUMMARY: Ben plays his imaginary trumpet in the night air, sitting on his stoop and listening to the jazz music from the Zig Zag Jazz Club. He goes by the club on his way home from school and listens to the musicians practice—the pianist, the saxophonist, the trombonist, and the drummer. Ben likes the trumpet best of all. He plays his own imaginary trumpet all the time, for his family, and out on the stoop. One day someone walks by and tells him he likes his horn. It is the trumpet player from the Zig Zag Jazz Club. When Ben plays his trumpet in front of his schoolmates, they laugh and make fun of him, saying that he has no trumpet. Ben walks slowly home and does not play his trumpet that night while he listens to the music from the club. When the trumpet player goes by again, he asks Ben where his horn is; when Ben says he does not have one, they go to the club. There, the trumpet player lets Ben hold a real trumpet and begins teaching him how to play.

MEDIA: Pen and ink.

ANECDOTE: Rachel Isadora likes to write, draw, and dance. She was a professional ballerina at eleven years of age and studied at the School of American Ballet (affiliated with the New York City Ballet) on a Ford Foundation Scholarship. She later danced with the Boston Ballet. A foot injury caused her to change careers. She says her favorite art form of all is music.

DISTINCTION: 1980 Caldecott Honor Book.

BIRTHDAY: Not available.

SUBJECT: Musicians—Fiction.

See Also: Duke Ellington: The Piano Prince and the Orchestra.

Between Earth & Sky: Legends of Native American Sacred Places (Harcourt, 1996). Written by Joseph Bruchac; illustrated by Thomas Locker.

SUMMARY: Delaware Indian Little Turtle asks his Uncle Old Bear about sacred places. Before the powwow where peoples from all across the continent will come together, Uncle Old Bear teaches his nephew about places that are sacred to ten groups of them: Wampanoag (East), Gay Head on Martha's Vineyard, Massachusetts; Seneca (North), Niagara Falls, New York and Canada; Navajo (West), El Capitan, Kayenta, Arizona; Cherokee (South), Great Smoky

Front cover of *Between Earth & Sky: Legends of Native American Sacred Places*, written by Joseph Bruchac (Abenaki) and illustrated by Thomas Locker. The book features ten of the many landscapes of the North American continent that are especially important to Native Americans. (Copyright © 1996 by Joseph Bruchac. Copyright © by Harcourt, Inc. All rights reserved.)

Mountains, North Carolina and Tennessee; Papago (West), Painted Desert, Arizona; Hopewell (Center), Great Serpent Mound, near Hillsboro, Ohio; Cheyenne (Above), Rocky Mountains from Alaska to New Mexico; Hopi (Below), Grand Canyon, Arizona; Walapai (Balance Lost), Mesa Verde, Colorado; and Abeneki (Balance Held), Lake Champlain, New York, Vermont, Canada. Little Turtle discovers that every place is sacred as long as one carries the teachings in one's heart.

A map showing locations of Native American lands of these ten groups and many others on the continent also labels the sacred places featured in the book. A key gives a listing of the tribe, symbol, and location of the sacred places. Finally, a glossary at the end of the book provides pronunciations of several of the Native American Indian words used throughout the book.

MEDIA: Oil on canvas.

ANECDOTE: The seven directions of the Native American Indian are East (birth), North (youth), South (adulthood), West (time of being an elder), Above (Sky), Below (Earth), and the place Within (one's spirit). According to teachings, each person needs all of the seven directions in order to be balanced.

DISTINCTION: Native American Indian-commended book.

BIRTHDAY: Joseph Bruchac: October 16, 1942.

SUBJECTS: Folklore—North America; Indians of North America—Folklore.

See Also: Thirteen Moons on a Turtle's Back.

The Big Snow (Macmillan, 1948). Written and illustrated by Berta and Elmer Hader.

SUMMARY: Mrs. Cottontail and the littlest rabbit spot the Canada geese flying south overhead. Mrs. Cottontail tells her child that it is time for them to prepare for the winter. They must eat to grow a thicker coat to keep them warm. The fat little groundhog sees the geese and goes to bed for the winter. When Mrs. Chipmunk spots them, she retires, her mouth full of seeds. Various birds and animals discuss whether or not they are going south, depending on their natural habits. Most of those featured will stay—the red cardinals, the red and gray squirrels, the deer, and the wood mouse. Hibernating animals head toward their dwellings such as raccoons to their logs. Soon, the first snow arrives, and the animals such as the deer, skunks, and mice leave their tracks in the snow from dancing. The owls see a rainbow around the moon that means more snow is on its way. They hoot their warning to the animals, and soon the heavy snow begins. The rooftops are covered, and the fields are deep in snow. The animals have difficulty finding food, and they are hungry. A little old man comes out of the stone house and shovels a path. Soon, a little old woman comes out and spreads seeds, nuts, and bread crumbs out for the birds and animals. The blue jays are the first to spot it; they cry, "Food, food, food," and all the animals come running to the walk in front of the stone house to eat the food the little old woman has spread out for them. When the groundhog emerges from his hutch on February 2, he sees that the heavy snow is still there and that there will be six more weeks of winter. He is right. That winter is long, cold, and snowy, but the little old man and woman keep helping the animals by feeding them until spring arrives. Black-and-white drawings are interspersed with color paintings.

MEDIA: Watercolor.

ANECDOTE: Inspiration for the book came from a heavy snowfall during the winter of 1947. The Haders themselves were the models for the little old man and woman, since they fed the animals that year.

DISTINCTION: 1949 Caldecott Medal.

BIRTHDAYS: Elmer Hader: September 7, 1889; Berta Hader: February 6, 1891.

SUBJECTS: Animals—Fiction; Winter—Fiction.

The Biggest Bear (Houghton Mifflin, 1952). Written and illustrated by Lynd Ward.

SUMMARY: Young Johnny Orchard lives near an apple orchard out in the country. Whenever Johnny walks by other people's barns, he is envious of the bearskins that hang on the outside of them. There is no skin outside the Orchards' barn. One day Johnny goes to the woods to shoot a bear. Instead, he brings home a bear cub. The bear cub eats maple sugar. All throughout the year, the bear eats food at the farm. It eats the mash for the chickens; it eats the apples in the orchard; it eats Mr. McCarroll's cornfield and the McLeans' maple sap. The bear grows bigger and bigger. After about a year, Mr. McLean, Mr. Pennell, and Mrs. McCarroll come to see Johnny's father. Something must be done about Johnny's pet bear. Mr. Orchard sits Johnny down and explains to him that the bear must go.

Johnny takes him out to the woods and leaves him there, but he comes back. He takes him out farther, but he comes back again. He takes him beyond Watson's hill and leaves him eating blueberries, but he finds his way back to Johnny again. Johnny rows him out to Gull's Island, but the bear comes back again, hardly even wet. Johnny's father talks to Johnny and tells him there is only one thing left to do. Johnny takes his gun and the bear and heads back out to the woods.

When they get there, the bear starts sniffing something and runs fast in the direction of the scent. Johnny crawls in after him into a small log house. They are trapped. When the trappers come, it turns out all for the good—they are trying to find a bear to take to the zoo, and this bear is even bigger than they had hoped to find. Johnny may visit him

The Biggest Bear, written and illustrated by Lynd Ward, won the 1953 Caldecott Medal. (Copyright © 1952 by Lynn Ward. Copyright © Houghton Mifflin Company. All rights reserved.)

whenever he wants, and when he does, he brings maple sugar with him.

MEDIA: Opaque watercolor.

ANECDOTE: In a gesture that would be questioned today, the staff of Houghton Mifflin presented Lynd Ward with a copy of this book bound in bearskin. When he was a boy, Ward was an avid hunter of squirrels, rabbits, and birds. He did encounter a bear once but realized that his .22 would only wound it.

DISTINCTION: 1953 Caldecott Medal.

BIRTHDAY: Lynd Ward: June 26, 1905.

SUBJECT: Bears—Fiction.

Bill Peet: An Autobiography (Houghton Mifflin, 1989). Written and illustrated by Bill Peet.

SUMMARY: This book is a 190-page autobiography of the artist Bill Peet. Each page contains extensive text and at least one drawing, sometimes more. Peet was born in Grand-view, Indiana, on January 29, 1915. His father deserted his family after he served stateside in World War I, so Peet never really knew him. His grandmother bought them a house on the edge of the city, and Bill loved going up into the attic and drawing pictures all through his boyhood. He says the first books he illustrated for children were the textbooks in which he drew in the margins that later became best-sellers at used book sales. The autobiography chronicles memorable events of the artist's childhood at relatives' farms, attending school, entering art competitions, and so forth, then moves primarily into an account of his professional artistic career. It also gives a brief discussion of his adult family—how he met his wife, Margaret, and incidents with his son, Bill Jr.

Over half of the volume describes his years working for Walt Disney Studios. Peet joined Disney in 1937 and stayed there for twenty-seven years working on such Disney classic films as *Snow White and the Seven Dwarfs*; *Pinocchio*; *Fantasia*; *Dumbo*; *Peter Pan*; *Song of the South*; *Cinderella*; *Alice in Wonderland*; *Sleeping Beauty*; *101 Dalmatians*; *The Sword in the Stone*; and *Jungle Book*. He also worked on Disney propaganda films during World War II including *Education for Death* and *Victory through Air Power*. His jobs at Disney included beginning as an "in-betweener," an artist who draws hundreds of drawings to move a character from one place to another; to a sketch man; then story man; to writing the screenplays for *101 Dalmatians*; *Sword in the Stone*; and *Jungle Book*. In 1964, Peet separated from Disney Studios over a dispute about an actor's accent for the voice of the leopard character in *Jungle Book*.

All the while he worked for Disney, Peet had a love-hate relationship with the man who gave the studio its name. Peet had always wanted to branch out on his own and become involved either in fine art, selling his original work in galleries, or as an author and artist of children's books. When he left Disney, he was well on his way in his children's books career. Disney died a little over a year after Peet left the studio, and the artist relates how the larger-than-life figure influenced him and his work for some time afterward. Bill Peet went on to publish over thirty books for children and explains in detail at the close of his autobiography how the most autobiographical of his books is *Chester the Worldly Pig*.

MEDIA: Pencil.

ANECDOTE: Bill Peet died on May 11, 2002, at the age of eighty-seven. He and his wife, Margaret, the "woman in the front row of art class" to whom he dedicates this book, were married for sixty-four years. He wrote that his infant son, Bill, influenced how he conceived and drew the pictures of the endearing baby Dumbo in the Disney film. Some of the turbulence in Peet's relationship with Walt Disney resulted from his not receiving credits in the films he worked on. Some Disney films do credit him, though credits appear with various names such as Bill Peed; William Peed; and Bill Bartlett Peet.

DISTINCTION: 1990 Caldecott Honor Book.

BIRTHDAY: Bill Peet: January 29, 1915.

SUBJECT: Peet, Bill—Autobiography; Authors, American—twentieth century—Biography; Children's stories—Authorship; Illustrators—United States—Biography; Animators—United States—Biography; Walt Disney Productions; Peet, Bill; Authors—American; Illustrators.

Binder. Artist's medium. The ingredient in paint that holds the pigment and the liquid media together.

Black and White (Houghton Mifflin, 1990). Written and illustrated by David Macaulay.

SUMMARY: Four stories occur simultaneously throughout the book; the pages are quartered with a story happening continuously in each quarter from page spread to page spread. In the top left corner of each spread is "Seeing Things," a story of a boy riding a train that gets delayed. In the bottom left quadrant there is "Problem Parents," a story about a boy and his parents who come home behaving strangely. At the top right is "A Waiting Game," a train depot where gathering crowds await a late train's arrival. In the lower right quarter of the spread is the story "Udder Chaos," where cows leave their fields and become impossible to find. In a virtuoso manipulation of narrative and time, Macaulay intersects and weaves apart and together the four stories until at the end of the book, the reader sees that they have all been told through the imagination of a boy playing at home with a train set accompanied by his black-and-white dog.

MEDIA: Various, including: "Seeing Things," watercolor; "Problem Parents," ink line and wash; "A Waiting Game," watercolor and gouache; and "Udder Confusion," gouache paint.

ANECDOTE: David Macaulay took seven years to complete this book, and the artistic media for each story is different. When making his acceptance speech for the 1991 Caldecott Medal, Macaulay divided his talk into four separate minispeeches.

DISTINCTION: 1991 Caldecott Medal.

BIRTHDAY: David Macaulay: December 2, 1946.

SUBJECT: Literary Recreations.

See Also: Castle; Cathedral.

Blueberries for Sal (Viking, 1948). Written and illustrated by Robert McCloskey.

SUMMARY: Little Sal goes with her mother to Blueberry Hill to pick blueberries. As they go up the hill, Little Sal puts some berries into her small bucket, but then she eats as many as she picks. Soon, she eats the berries in her bucket as well and eats those she finds on bushes behind her mother. Sal puts one berry in her mother's larger bucket, but then takes it back out with a few others to eat. Mother tells her to pick her own. Little Sal goes down the slope and sits down among berries because she is tired. She goes right on eating the berries around her.

On the other side of Blueberry Hill a mother bear and her cub are eating blueberries, too. They are fattening up for the long winter. Little Bear gets tired of following and sits down among blueberry bushes and eats the berries right there. Back on the other side of the hill, Little Sal runs out of berries near her and runs to catch up with her mother. She hears a noise behind a rock and thinks that is her mother. Instead, it is a mother crow and her children. She hears another noise she thinks must be her mother, but instead it is Little Bear's mother. Little Sal follows along behind her.

Little Bear runs out of berries and goes to find his mother. He hears a noise he thinks might be her, but instead it is a mother partridge and her children. Little Bear hears another noise and finds Little Sal's mother picking berries. Little Bear follows her. Things are all mixed up on the hill. Both mothers are surprised when they find Little Sal and Little Bear are following the wrong mothers. They go hunting for their little ones. Little Sal's mother finds her when she hears the sound of berries hitting the bottom of her little bucket, still mostly empty. Little Bear's mother hears her baby's munching and swallowing. Reunited, both mothers and young ones go back down their respective sides of the hill. The bears have eaten enough berries to keep them full all winter, and Little Sal and her mother have picked enough blueberries to can and keep for their winter.

MEDIA: Possibly lithographs.

ANECDOTE: Robert McCloskey was the first artist to receive two Caldecott Medals. Little Sal and her mother are based on McCloskey own wife and daughter.

DISTINCTION: 1949 Caldecott Honor Book.

BIRTHDAY: Robert McCloskey: September 15, 1914.

SUBJECTS: Mother–child—Fiction; Bluberries—Fiction; Bears—Fiction.

See Also: Journey Cake, Ho!; *Make Way for Ducklings*; McCloskey, Robert; *One Morning in Maine*; *Time of Wonder*.

Boats on the River (Viking, 1946). Written by Marjorie Flack; illustrated by Jay Hyde Barnum.

SUMMARY: This rhythmic story describes the Hudson River of the 1940s coming down from the mountains and opening into the sea at New York Harbor and highlights the different kinds of boats that sailed on it at that time. Boats depicted include the ferryboat, paddle-wheel riverboat, ocean liner, tugboat, motorboat, sailboat, rowboat, freight boat, submarine, and an American warship. Since the story is set in the time of World War II, sailors are depicted on leave from the warship and visiting people's houses, stores, and the zoo in New York City. Boats do not visit the city this way, the book instructs young children; they stay in the river. In fog, the boats all look gray and let the sailboat pass, since it has no motor. At night, the boats light up with a red light on the left, a green light on the right, and a white light on top.

MEDIA: Undetermined.

ANECDOTE: The book was first published in 1946 but was reissued in 1991.

DISTINCTION: 1947 Caldecott Honor Book.

BIRTHDAY: Marjorie Flack: October 23, 1897.

SUBJECT: Boats—Fiction.

Book Design. As with any book, picture books for children go through a design process to determine what the physical book itself will look like. Since picture books by their composition contain a strong visual element, book design is particularly relevant to their overall effect on the reader or listener. Sometimes the illustrator of a picture book is also the book's designer, or the designer may be a separate graphics artist within the publishing company or a book production company. In considering the design for a picture book, the designer must take into account the intended audience and use, the ways in which the story and artwork work together, and ways in which the book's design may enhance the overall effect of the story's presentation. Areas within the book designer's purview include the size and shape of the book, the cover design, and page design.

The size and shape of a picture book normally indicate how it is intended to be shared with children. For example, a small size may indicate that the book has a story about a small subject such as baby bunnies, or there is a desire on the part of the book's creators for an intimate relationship between the story and a young child so the book is made small enough to be held in his or her small hands. On the other hand, small books are difficult to share with a group or even on a lap with a parent. The larger, oversized format (usually larger in height and/or width than a conventional hardcover book for adults) is more typical for picture books. This makes the book easier for children to enjoy in a group as part of library story hours or on the laps of their adult caregivers at bedtime. The larger format also allows more room for a fuller display of artwork that is so necessary to the picture book experience. A picture book may be longer horizontally (called landscape) or vertically (called portrait). The decision of which sides are the longer ones must coincide with, and enhance, the artwork and story. The overall feel of the book is also taken into consideration—for example, a book with many exterior scenes of a character walking on a journey may be better suited to the landscape design, which would suggest the journey taking place across long pages, left to right. A

book about trees, which have a vertical orientation, may be designed in the portrait format.

The covers, both front and back, of a picture book set the tone for the story; they give basic information such as title, author, illustrator, and publisher; and they entice a reader or book buyer to open the book. The book cover may have a different illustration or set of illustrations than a book jacket. The jacket usually includes "flaps," the portion of the jacket that folds inward a short ways on the front and back covers. Book flaps normally contain a short summary of the story on the front flap and brief biographical information about the author and artist and perhaps short review comments about the book or other titles by the same creators on the back flap. A "wraparound" illustration is one in which the covers or book jacket form one expanded picture when opened. Other kinds of covers include illustrations that are separate from front to back and may duplicate an illustration from inside the book or be a different picture added to the book. Typically, the back cover contains a smaller vignette or scene than the front.

Page design is another important factor for the book designer to consider and includes elements such as layout, borders, and typography. These must be decided not only for the story pages themselves but also for the pages at the beginning and ending of a book, commonly called front matter and back matter. Front matter includes the half-title page, title page, dedication, and copyright. Back matter may include pages such as an author's note with more information about the subject or about the author and artist sections with short biographies. These pages may be distinct from the story pages with no illustrations, or they may have decorative hints of the illustration to come or be elaborately illustrated.

Layout for the story pages involves choosing where the artwork will be placed on a spread (two pages open opposite to one another in a picture book) and where the text will be located in relation to the artwork. Designers must consider if the pictures will be set at the bottom of the page with the print above, for example, or if they will be in borders with the print underneath. Which visual element goes where may suggest where a reader's eyes will go first when turning the page, and this plays a role in choices over placement similar to headlines in a newspaper. Normally, editors work with the illustrators beforehand in deciding how to break up the text over the usual thirty-two pages of a picture book; however, designers collaborate on this as well.

Borders affect how the illustrations are presented and make a statement about the story. For example, if the illustrations are all within boxes or decorated frames, this sends a different signal to the eye aesthetically than illustrations that are borderless and take up the entire page, even appearing to run off the page or "bleed." Gutters (the space where the pages come together at the spine) need to be thought of when planning how the artwork will be displayed across a spread. If adequate care is not taken, some of the artwork will disappear where the pages come together, but to break up the artwork deliberately at this position by putting borders of space or decoration there is to create a different overall effect in the spread when the book lies open. Borders and layout are another clear concern for pages that are to contain sidebar information.

Typography elements include font design, size, color, and boldness. There are many designs of typography, and the book designer decides which one best suits the story, artwork, and readability for children and those who will read to them. Sometimes letters become part of the artwork itself, such as the first letter of a sentence being illustrated as in the centuries-old illuminated manscripts of monks.

Though the book design is an important aspect of the overall picture book presentation, it is perhaps the least known and appreciated part of the collaborative efforts among author, artist, editor, designer, and art director. Often the dust jacket or book designer is credited only in small print on the cover, such as at the bottom of the back flap. With more attention paid to the increasing variety of book designs made possible by computer technology, perhaps picture book designers and art directors will become better known in the future for their valuable contributions to the process.

Book of Nursery and Mother Goose Rhymes (Doubleday, 1954). Written and illustrated by Marguerite De Angeli.

SUMMARY: The book is a collection of 376 nursery rhymes with more than 260 illustrations. Most of the pictures are black-and-white, though there are a handful that are in color. There is a foreword by the illustrator describing the genesis of the book. An index of first lines closes the book. Samples of rhymes include "A carrion crow sat on an oak," "Flour of England, fruit of Spain," "Little Johnny Morgan," "Sing a song of sixpence," "Yankee Doodle came to town," and "One misty, moisty, morning."

MEDIA: Sharp Wolf pencils and watercolor.

ANECDOTE: This book is one of three Caldecott Honor books to have a Mother Goose/nursery rhyme collection theme. De Angeli utilized her children when they were small as well as her grandchildren as models for the young people in the illustrations. Later she was surprised to recognize her own brothers and sisters and even her parents gathered around the table in the illustration for "God bless the Master of This House." De Angeli lived to be nearly one hundred years old.

DISTINCTION: 1955 Caldecott Honor Book.

BIRTHDAY: Marguerite De Angeli: March 14, 1889.

SUBJECT: Nursery rhymes.

The Boy of the Three-Year Nap (Houghton Mifflin, 1988). Written by Diane Snyder; illustrated by Allen Say.

SUMMARY: A poor widow and her son live on the banks of the Nagara River where the cormorants fish for food. The widow sews kimonos all day for the rich women in town. She works nonstop. Her son, Taro, however, is healthy but lazy. All he wants to do is eat and sleep. Whenever she asks him to do anything such as fix the leaking roof or otherwise help repair their house, Taro says he will do it after his nap. People say that if no one wakes him, Taro could sleep for three years straight. He becomes known as the "Boy of the Three-Year Nap."

One day a wealthy merchant builds a mansion next door. Taro looks at the mansion, the carp in the pond, and the merchant's fat rice sacks between his naps. He tells his mother to sew him a black kimono and a priest's hat. He has come up with a plan to help them in their poverty. When the garments are done, Taro puts them on and adds makeup that makes him look like a samurai warrier. He tells his mother not to mention this to anyone. The merchant takes his walk and scorns the widow for being so soft with her son. He should not be sleeping at dusk. Then he goes to the shrine of the ujigami, who is the village's patron god. There he sees a goblin in black robes. The ujigami tells the surprised and frightened merchant that he is the god and that it has been decreed that the merchant's daughter marry Taro next door. The merchant protests but agrees when the fierce ujigami threatens to turn his daughter into a clay pot.

The merchant visits the widow the next day and tells her that his daughter must marry her son. After asking what the mysterious ujigami looks like, the widow sees what her son has

The Boy of the Three-Year Nap, retold by Diane Snyder, illustrated by Allen Say, is one of many examples of retold folktales among American children's picture books. It was a Caldecott Honor book in 1989. (Copyright © 1988 by Diane Snyder; illustrations by Allen Say. Copyright © Houghton Mifflin Company. All rights reserved.)

been up to; she tells the merchant that his daughter could not live in a house like hers that is so much in need of repairs. The merchant agrees and fixes the widow's house. When he asks again for the marriage, the widow says that they have only one room in the house, and the merchant's daughter will still not be happy. The merchant adds rooms onto it as well. He asks the widow if he has her consent now for the marriage. Her last objection is that Taro does not have a job. Saying they will ruin him, the merchant gives Taro a job managing his storehouse.

Taro tells his mother that the job was not part of his plan, but the widow replies that she has a plan of her own. The couple marries in a grand celebration and lives happily. Taro counts his father-in-law's rice sacks and is no longer the laziest man in town.

MEDIA: Brush-line, pen and ink, and watercolor.

ANECDOTE: Say nearly gave up art to take up photography right before the publication of this book. This story was so familiar to Say as a Japanese American that he nearly turned down the opportunity to illustrate it because he thought it lacked interest. Diane Snyder wanted to retell an entire collection of Japanese folktales, but this story grew into a book by itself.

DISTINCTION: 1989 Caldecott Honor Book.

BIRTHDAY: Allen Say: August 28, 1937.

SUBJECTS: Laziness—Folklore; Folklore—Japan.

See Also: Grandfather's Journey.

The Bremen-Town Musicians (Doubleday, 1980). Retold and illustrated by Ilse Plume.

SUMMARY: A donkey is getting too old to work for his master, and he knows his master is thinking of doing away with him so that he will not have to feed him anymore. Since the donkey has a fine bray, he thinks he might go to Bremen, where he could join in with the street musicians there and make music. He heads off for town. On his way, he meets an old dog that can no longer hunt. His master intends to shoot him. The donkey invites him to Bremen with him to add his bark to the music they will make. In likewise manner, the animals meet an old cat and rooster on their way. They join in the trek to Bremen, each hoping to make music of their own particular kind.

The small band of animals decides to sleep in the woods when they spy a lit cottage. They go there and climb on top of one another to look in the window. There they see a band of robbers. The animals fall through the window, scaring the robbers away. Inside, the animals find food and then curl up each in their own way of finding comfort for the night. When one robber returns to the house to see if they had not been scared away too soon, he confronts each of the animals in turn in the dark. He returns to his band telling them that a witch now occupies the house, and they can never return. The animals de-

cide the house is a cozy place to live, and they stay there and make their music rather than going on to Bremen.

MEDIA: Possibly colored pencil and graphite.

ANECDOTE: The book is a retelling of a Grimm's fairy tale.

DISTINCTION: 1981 Caldecott Honor Book.

BIRTHDAY: Wilhelm Karl Grimm (German): February 24, 1786.

SUBJECTS: Fairy tales; Folklore—Germany.

Brown, Marcia (1918–   ). Artist, author. Marcia Brown has the unique distinction of being the only "triple-crowned" Caldecott Medalist so far awarded in history. Born on July 13, 1918, in Rochester, New York, Brown was the daughter of a minister and once dreamed of becoming a medical doctor. Medical school was too costly, so she opted to attend the New York State College for Teachers at what is now Albany University (SUNY). There she majored in very different classes than medicine or the sciences—English and drama. She also studied painting at college and at the Woodstock School. After college, Brown taught for three years at Cornwall High School in the lower Hudson Valley but left for New York City in 1943 to pursue yet another dream—of writing and illustrating books for children. In order to fund this ambition, she became an assistant librarian at the rare book collection for the New York Public Library. She also studied at the New School for Social Research, Art Students' League at Columbia University.

Brown's first book was *The Little Carousel* (1946). The story is based on an actual carousel she watched be delivered to the Italian neighborhood of Greenwich Village. She watched its delivery from her apartment window on Sullivan Street. When she had a dummy of the book prepared, she ventured to the publishing offices at Scribner. She had once heard editor Alice Dagleish give a speech, and she admired the other books the company had published. She was so nervous when she arrived, however, that when she was told Ms. Dagleish was too busy to see her, she burst into tears. She went outside, thinking she would take her book to editor May Massee around the corner at Viking. When she got there, there was an elevator strike going on, and Ms. Massee's office was on a high floor. Rather than climb so many stairs, Brown decided to go back and wait for Dagleish to be free to see her. Alice Dagleish took the book, and Brown has published her many books with Scribner ever since.

Though Brown has lived most of her life in New York City, she has traveled extensively and incorporated much of what she has learned in her travels in her books. She has visited such places as Mexico, Europe, the Middle East, the former Soviet Union, the Virgin Islands, and China. She once taught a puppetry class at University College in Jamaica. Through her travels as well, she began adopting a variety of artistic techniques in her work. She has used paper cuts, gouache, photography, pen and ink, watercolors, and wood and linoleum blocks.

Brown is best known for her enthusiastic experimentation with a variety of artistic techniques as well as the spare text and strong images in her books. Her more than thirty children's books have been translated into languages such as German, Japanese, Spanish, Afrikaans, and Xhosa-Bantu. In a career that has spanned over thirty-nine years, Brown earned three Caldecott Medals (*Cinderella, or the Little Glass Slipper*, 1955; *Once a Mouse*, 1962; and *Shadow*, 1983) and two Caldecott Honors (*Puss in Boots*, 1953; and *The Steadfast Tin Soldier*, 1954).

For *Shadow* (1982), one of her last books, Brown's arthritic hands forced her to abandon the woodblock technique she wanted to use and instead adopt a method of cut-paper. She returned to the work later after illness and blotted woodblock images on transluscent paper in a way that suggested a landscape that had been scarred by its history. Her intricate work on this project earned her a third Caldecott Medal.

Marcia Brown retired from actively creating children's books in the mid-1990s, but she continues to create her art. She claims to have never known an artist who ever fully retired. The artist was awarded the Laura Ingalls Wilder Medal by the American Library Association in 1992 for her lifetime of achievement in children's literature.

Further Reading: Brown, Marcia. "Organized Wonders: Laura Ingalls Wilder Acceptance Speech." *The Horn Book Magazine* 68, no. 4 (July 1, 1992): 429.

See Also: Cinderella, or The Little Glass Slipper; *Once a Mouse*; *Puss in Boots*; *Shadow*; *Stone Soup*.

Brown, Margaret Wise (1910–1952). Author. One of the most prolific and influential American authors of picture books for children was born on May 23, 1910, in Greenpoint in Brooklyn, New York. The middle child of middle-class parents, Robert Bruce and Maude Margaret, Brown was brought up in a comfortable lifestyle in Whitestone, Long Island. She was closer to her father's family than her mother's. Brown's paternal grandfather, B. Gratz Brown, had served as a leader in the Civil War and had also been senator and governor of Missouri.

Brown loved nature and often entertained her siblings, pets, and other children from the neighborhood with stories she would make up or lyrics she would change to familiar tunes like "Dixie." She often played on the beaches and in the woods by herself. She and her sister attended boarding school in Switzerland in 1923 while her parents were in India, and the future author found the experience both disruptive and challenging. She

Author Margaret Wise Brown (*right*) and companions. In her brief forty-two years, Brown wrote and published more than 100 books for children. The author of the classic *Goodnight Moon*, illustrated by Clement Hurd, Brown's poetic prose continues to influence authors of picture books for the very young. (Photo by Morgan Collection/Getty Images.)

later attended Dana Hall, where she learned more self-reliance and confidence. At Dana Hall, Margaret earned the nickname of "Tim" from the color of her hair appearing to be the same shade of light brown as timothy hay. Both she and her sister did well there academically.

Brown wanted to attend college, but at first her father was against it. Her mother, however, allowed her to attend Hollins College near Roanoke, Virginia, where she graduated in 1932. When she entered graduate school at the Bank Street College of Education in New York, Brown gravitated to the teachings of Lucy Sprague Mitchell, who taught a "here-and-now" approach to children and literature. Previously, children's books were predominantly fantasy, but Mitchell believed that children responded well to books about their everyday lives. Her exposure to Mitchell and her own observations and good ear for children and the way they talked and told each other stories ignited Brown's future career.

Her first book was *When the Wind Blew*, published by Harper in 1937. She became editor of William R. Scott Publishing Company, and in 1938, four of her books were published. The *Noisy Book* series, which encouraged children to listen and echo everyday sounds they heard all around them, quickly became popular, and Brown's career as a children's book author was well engaged. Soon, her books were selling so well that she was able to purchase a retreat from the city, a house with no electricity, telephone, or bathroom, on an island off the coast of Maine that she called "The Only House." She had another small house in the midst of skyscrapers in New York that she called "Cobble Court."

Brown's lifestyle included inviting artists to The Only House when they were working on books together. Her group of friends called themselves "The Bird Brain Club." One book that came out of her beloved retreat was *The Little Island*, published under the pseudonym Golden MacDonald and illustrated by

Leonard Weisgard. The book won the Caldecott Medal in 1947. Another title, *A Child's Good Night Book*, illustrated by Jean Charlot, won a 1944 Caldecott Honor. In 1952, while on a book tour in France, Brown became ill with appendicitis and required immediate hospitalization in Nice. Near the end of her recovery, she was up dancing around at the thought of soon leaving the hospital. She kicked her leg up can-can style and was struck with an embolism that shot from her leg to her brain and killed her instantly. She was forty-two.

Brown's influence on American children's picture books over her short life can hardly be overstated. She published more than one hundred picture books, employing her quiet, everyday themes, poetic prose, and keen awareness for the sensibilities of very young children. Many of her books were the first books that generations of American children encounter on the laps of their mothers and fathers at bedtime. Her best-known bedtime book, *Goodnight Moon*, was published in 1947 and has sold millions of copies worldwide. Brown's other influences include furthering the artistic careers of prominent illustrators such as Garth Williams and Clement Hurd and convincing author Gertrude Stein to write the children's fantasy *The World Is Round*, now considered a classic. She was also instrumental in moving book production toward the evolution of the board book format for very young children. Since her books were written with very small children in mind, many readers do not fully appreciate Brown's gifts as a fine poet.

Books by Margaret Wise Brown include *When the Wind Blew*, illustrated by Rosalie Slocum (1937); *Noisy Book*, illustrated by Leonard Weisgard (1939); *The Runaway Bunny*, illustrated by Clement Hurd (1942); *A Child's Goodnight Book*, illustrated by Jean Charlot (1943); *Little Lost Lamb*, illustrated by Leonard Weisgard (1945); *The Little Fur Family*, illustrated by Garth Williams (1946);

The Little Island, illustrated by Leonard Weisgard (1946); *Goodnight Moon*, illustrated by Clement Hurd (1947); *The Important Book*, illustrated by Leonard Weisgard (1949); *My World*, illustrated by Clement Hurd (1949); *Little Fur Tree*, illustrated by Barbara Cooney (1953); and *Wheel on the Chimney*, illustrated by Tibor Gergely (1954).

Further Reading: Blos, Joan W. *The Days Before Now: An Autobiographical Note by Margaret Wise Brown*. New York: Simon and Schuster, 1994; Marcus, Leonard. *Margaret Wise Brown: Awakened by the Moon*. Boston: Beacon Press, 1992.

See Also: A Child's Good Night Book; Goodnight Moon; The Little Island; Little Lost Lamb.

Brown Bear, Brown Bear, What Do You See?

Brown Bear, Brown Bear, What Do You See? (Holt, Rinehart, and Winston, 1967). Written by Bill Martin Jr.; illustrated by Eric Carle.

SUMMARY: Using rhythm, rhyme, color, alliteration, and animals, this book teaches about color, animals, and language. The animals are brown bear, red bird, yellow duck, blue horse, green frog, purple cat, white dog, black sheep, goldfish, and . . . a teacher.

MEDIA: Collage.

ANECDOTE: Bill Martin Jr. had a Ph.D. in early childhood education. The artwork was redone for a reissue of this book in celebration of its twenty-fifth anniversary in 1992. The book has sold over 2 million copies and was the first picture book that Eric Carle illustrated.

DISTINCTIONS: *New York Times* Best Book for Children; NYPL 100 Picture Books Everyone should know.

BIRTHDAYS: Eric Carle: June 25, 1929; Bill Martin Jr.: March 20, 1916.

SUBJECTS: Color—Fiction; Animals—Fiction; Stories in rhyme.

See Also: Carle, Eric; Eric Carle Museum of Picture Book Art; *The Very Hungry Caterpillar.*

C

Caldecott, Randolph J. (1846–1886). Artist. Caldecott is the British artist for whom the prestigious Caldecott Medal for a distinguished illustrator of American picture books for children is named. He was born on March 22, 1846, in Chester, England. Caldecott was a good student who began drawing animals at the age of six. When he was fifteen, he moved to Whitchurch to work in a bank. He lived in the countryside two miles from town. While he lived there, he enjoyed hunting and fishing and going to cattle fairs. His tall, handsome figure with light brown hair and vibrant blue-gray eyes was often seen at these activities carrying his sketchbook.

In 1872, Caldecott moved to London to pursue a career in art. He began supplying artwork to publications such as the *London Graphic* and *London Society*. Readers enjoyed his humorous sketches of hunting, animals, and other scenes. He also studied at the British Museum and the zoological garden. The editor of the *London Society*, Henry Blackburn, became a friend and mentor to Caldecott. Caldecott illustrated Blackburn's book *The Harz Mountains* in 1872. Blackburn took Caldecott's sketches with him to America, and soon American periodicals such as *Harper's Magazine* and the *New York Daily Graphic* began featuring his work. In Caldecott's time, his pen-and-ink drawings were photographed onto a wooden block; these images were then engraved by careful engravers. Reproductions of Caldecott's work benefited from the fine work of engravers such as J. D. Cooper and Edmund Evans.

In the summers of the early 1870s, Caldecott lived at a cottage owned by Blackburn at Farnham Royal. There he created the art for such works as Washington Irving's *Old Christmas* (1876) and *Bracebridge Hall* (1877). With the publication of these two books, Caldecott's reputation as an illustrator was established. Caldecott moved to Northern Italy and the Riviera because of his chronic difficulties with health. There he continued sending illustrations to the *Graphic* and worked on artwork for books such as Alice Carr's *North Italian Folk* (1878).

By 1879, Caldecott was back in England, living in "Wybournes," a little house near Sevenoaks. During this time and with the encouragement of Edmund Evans, the artist began work on the sixteen picture books for which he is most known today. He also illustrated the work of others such as Juliana H. Ewing's *Daddy Darwin's Dovecote* (1884), *Jackanapes*, and *Lob Lie-by-the-Fire*. On March 18, 1880, he married Marian H. Brind in the Church of St. Martins-of-Tours in Chelsford,

Kent. Randolph's brother Alfred, who had become a priest, aided in the ceremony.

In late 1885, the Caldecotts sailed to America aboard the steamship the *Aurania*. They made their way by train down the East Coast to Florida, again with hopes that the warmer climate there would aid Randolph's frail health. They did not stay in New York because it was so cold; however, they planned on visiting it longer on their return trip. On their way south, they visited Philadelphia, Washington, D.C., and Charleston, South Carolina. Randolph drew sketches in each city. The Caldecotts did not like the spider webs of telephone wires they saw or the hustle and bustle of the cities. The blatant commercialism of billboards and other advertisements bothered them. Randolph poked fun at these by sketching one drawing with hunters using the billboards as jumps for their horses. They did like the cleanliness of the Philadelphia and Washington streets and the red houses with white doors and gray shutters. Caldecott intended to send the *London Graphic* artwork of scenes from America. Unfortunately, by the time he reached South Carolina, he was very ill, and the sketches he made there would be his last. That winter, the weather the couple experienced living at the Magnolia Hotel was particularly harsh for the Florida climate. Caldecott died from heart disease on February 13, 1886, in St. Augustine. He was thirty-nine.

Caldecott's art is best known for its fluidity of motion. Now regarded as his most characteristic work, *The Three Jovial Huntsmen* features scenes of hunters in full flight on their horses with dogs running alongside. Caldecott was also known for his satire. Much of his work contains humorous, though not malicious, commentary on nineteenth-century society and customs. In addition to his pen-and-ink illustrations, Caldecott worked in clay and oils. His work was exhibited at the Royal Academy in London.

Caldecott is buried at the Evergreen Cemetery in St. Augustine, Florida. His grave is maintained by the Randolph Caldecott Society of America. In London, a memorial in the form of a tablet was installed in the crypt at St. Paul's Cathedral. The tablet depicts a peaceful Breton child holding a picture of the artist. The artist died at the height of both his life and career. In 1938, Frederic D. Melcher of the American Library Association established the Randolph Caldecott Medal to reward distinguished artwork in American children's picture books in his honor. In the United States, the Caldecott name is linked with the Caldecott Medal awarded to children's picture books each year, which features a scene from *The Diverting History of John Gilpin* on the front.

The sixteen *Picture Books* Caldecott produced were published in pairs with printings of 10,000 each by Routledge publishers. Caldecott was paid a penny for each copy. As each installment in the series became more popular, printings grew to more than 100,000. In London and America, they were published by Frederick Warne & Company. Caldecott and Evans insisted the series be called *Picture Books* rather than "toy books" as some previously illustrated books for children had been termed because the pictures interpret rather than decorate the story. It is possible to "read" the story by looking at the pictures alone. Because of the new arrangement Caldecott worked out with Evans to receive no flat fee for his work but instead a penny for each copy sold or nothing if no copies sold, Caldecott's work for this series is thought to be the first time an illustrator was paid royalties for his artwork appearing in books.

The sixteen *Picture Books* in the series are *The House That Jack Built* and *The Diverting History of John Gilpin* (1878); *Elegy on a Mad Dog* and *The Babes in the Wood* (1879); *Sing a Song for Sixpence* and *The Three Jovial Huntsmen* (1880); *The Farmer's Boy* and *Queen of Hearts* (1881); *The Milkmaid* and *Hey Diddle*

Diddle and Baby Bunting (1882); *A Frog He Would A-Wooing Go* and *The Fox Jumps over the Parson's Gate* (1883); *Come Lasses and Lads* and *Ride a Cock Horse and a Farmer Went Trotting* (1884); and *The Great Panjandrum* and *Mrs. Mary Blaize* (1885).

Caldecott's illustrations in other books include *The Harz Mountains: A Tour in the Toy Country* by Henry Blackburn; *Old Christmas: Selections from the Sketch Book* by Washington Irving; *Bracebridge Hall: Selections from the Sketch Book* by Washington Irving; *North Italian Folk: Sketches of Town and Country Life* by Alice (Mrs. Comyns) Carr; *Breton Folk: An Artistic Journey in Brittany* by Henry Blackburn; *What the Blackbird Said* by Mrs. Frederick Locker; *A Sketchbook of R. Caldecott's: Original Sketches for the Four Seasons*, engraved and reproduced by Edmund Evans; *Some of Aesop's Fables with Modern Instances* from new translations by Alfred Caldecott (the artist's brother); frontispiece for *Jackanapes* by Juliana H. Ewing; *Daddy Darwin's Dovecote* by Juliana H. Ewing; *The Owls of Olynn Belfry* by A.Y.D.; *Jack and the Beanstalk* by Hallam Tennyson; *Lob-Lie-by-the-Fire* by Juliana H. Ewing; and *Randolph Caldecott's Sketches* with an introduction by Henry Blackburn.

In 1887, publisher George Routledge printed 1000 copies of a collectible book called *The Complete Collection of Randolph Caldecott's Pictures and Songs*. The books were autographed by engraver Edmund Evans and quickly sold out. The rare editions are still prized by collectors today.

Further Reading: Lewis, Marguerite. *Randolph Caldecott: The Children's Illustrator*. New York: Hagerstown, MD: Alleyside Press, 1992; Billington, Elizabeth T., ed., *The Randolph Caldecott Treasury*, with an appreciation by Maurice Sendak. New York: F. Warne, 1978; Blackburn, Henry. *Randolph Caldecott: A Personal Memoir of His Early Art Career*. [London: Low et al., 1886]. Detroit: Singing Tree Press, 1969; Engen, Rodney K. *Randolph Caldecott: Lord of the Nursery*. London: Oresko Books, 1976.

See Also: Caldecott Medal; Caldecott Society of America.

Caldecott Medal. Every year since 1938, the American Library Association (ALA) has awarded the Randolph Caldecott Medal to the American artist of the most distinguished American children's picture book published the previous year. The recognition was originated by Frederick G. Melcher of the ALA, who thought that picture books should have an award similar to the John Newbery Award given to children's books (primarily novels). The ALA adopted the prize and agreed to name it after the British artist Randolph J. Caldecott. At first, nominations for the two categories were kept separate. In 1977, the ALA decided that books could be nominated for both or either award. Criteria for selection, among others, include that the artist must be American or a resident of the United States, that the artwork be original and not dependent on any other source for its enjoyment, and that the work must be a picture book, meaning that the pictures must be integrally involved in the telling of the story, not merely functioning as decoration for the text. The picture book must also have a clear intent of being created for a child audience. The committee that decides on the winner may consider other elements of the book such as its text and design as they coordinate with the pictures, but it should not reward books based on lessons the book teaches or popularity of the book or the artist.

The medal itself was designed in 1937 by René Paul Chambellan. The medal is made of bronze and is embossed with the winner's name and the year on the back. It is presented to the winner in a velvet covered box. On the front of the medal appears a scene from pages 12 and 13 of Randolph J. Caldecott's picture book *The Diverting Story of John*

RANDOLPH CALDECOTT,
Born 1846 ; Died 1886.

Randolph J. Caldecott (1846–1886)—the successful British illustrator for whom the Caldecott Medal is named. Caldecott is buried in St. Augustine, Florida. (Hulton Archive/Getty Images.)

Gilpin. The scene shows John Gilpin flying away astride a runaway horse, accompanied by geese, dogs, and onlookers in swift movement and commotion. The scene of animals and motion is characteristic of Caldecott's nineteenth-century art. The reverse side depicts Caldecott's illustration from *Sing a Song of Sixpence*, showing a butler stepping high, presenting the pie of four and twenty blackbirds before the king. Under the illustration is space for the name of the recipient and the date.

Around the illustration on the front of the medal are the words, "The Caldecott Medal." In addition to the artist's name and the year on the back of the medal appears another Caldecott illustration and the inscription: "For the Most Distinguished American Picture Book for Children . . . Awarded Annually by the Children's and School Librarian's Sections of the ALA."

Each year, one medalist is chosen as the winner, and other honor books, formerly called "runners-up," may also be named. Metallic seals (gold for winners and silver for honor books) representing the medals are affixed to the front covers of medalists and honor books in bookstores and in libraries and become a notable and salable feature for children's picture books among the public. While the award is given to the illustrator of the picture book, both the book's author and illustrator benefit from the increased attention and promise of longevity that the award bestows.

See Also: Caldecott, Randolph J.; Caldecott Medalists (Multiple); Caldecott Society of America.

Caldecott Medalists (Multiple). Each year since 1938, there has been only one Randolph Caldecott Medal awarded for outstanding illustration in a children's picture book, with several others artists receiving Honors designations. To date, only seven artists have earned more than one Caldecott Medal during their careers: Marcia Brown with the most at three (1955, *Cinderella, or The Glass Slipper*; 1962, *Once a Mouse*; and 1983, *Shadow*); Barbara Cooney with two (1959, *Chanticleer and the Fox*; 1980, *Ox-Cart Man*); husband-and-wife collaborators Leo and Diane Dillon, who are the only artists to win Caldecott Medals two years in a row (1976, *Why Mosquitoes Buzz in People's Ears*; 1977, *Ashanti to Zulu: African Traditions*); Nonny Hogrogrian with two (1966, *Always Room for One More*; 1972, *One Fine Day*); Chris Van Allsburg (1982, *Jumanji*; 1986, *Polar Express*); and David Wiesner with two (2000, *Tuesday*; 2002, *The Three Pigs*). Other artists have earned multiple honor book recognitions or combinations of one medal and one or more honor book awards. See Appendix B for listings of these multiple honorees.

See Also: Appendix B; Caldecott, Randolph J.; Caldecott Medal, Caldecott Society of America.

Caldecott Society of America. Organization. This is the American branch of the parent organization, the Randolph Caldecott Society of the United Kingdom. The American group is headquartered in St. Augustine, Florida, where Randolph Caldecott is buried at Evergreen Cemetery. The society regards one of its missions as maintaining the gravesite and celebrating Caldecott's life by keeping flowers on his grave. Another function is the donation of the annual ALA-awarded Caldecott Medal and Honor picture books to the Randolph Caldecott Room at the St. Johns County Main Public Library in St. Augustine. Interest in study of the British illustrator is also encouraged, and the American and British branches cooperate and support one another's efforts at honoring Caldecott's legacy of art.

See Also: Caldecott, Randolph J.; Caldecott Medal.

Caps for Sale: A Tale of a Peddler, Some Monkeys and Their Monkey Business (Scott, 1940). Written and illustrated by Esphyr Slobodkina.

SUMMARY: A cap peddler sells his wares through the village by walking up and down the streets wearing identical caps one after the other on top of his head. He wears his own checked cap, topped by a stack of gray caps under a bunch of brown caps under a bunch of blue caps topped off by a stack of red caps. He calls out that the caps are fifty cents each. One morning, no one is interested in buying caps, and the peddler does not have money to buy lunch. He decides to go for a walk in the country instead. While there, he gets tired and sits down carefully under a tree, leaning back against the trunk slowly so as not to disturb the stack of caps on his head.

When he awakens, the peddler discovers that the checked cap is the only one still on his head. He looks around, but cannot see the other caps anywhere. Finally, he looks up and sees many monkeys in the tree each wearing a cap. He speaks to them, shakes his finger at them, shakes both fists at them, stomps one foot and then two feet at them to try to get them to give him back the caps, to no avail. The monkeys simply chatter, shake a finger, shake both fists, and stomp their feet right back at him. Finally, the peddler gives up in anger and disgust and throws his cap to the ground and begins to leave. At that, all the monkeys throw their caps down to the ground as well. The peddler picks them back up one by one and restacks them all on his head and goes about selling caps once again.

MEDIA: Cut-out collage and watercolor.

ANECDOTE: Slobodkina lived in a small town in Siberia where peddlers went through the village carrying and selling their wares. Her inspiration for the drawings was nineteenth-century painter Henri Rousseau—from him she adopted the mustache on the peddler and the mischievous looks on the monkeys' faces. A sequel is *Circus Caps for Sale.*

DISTINCTIONS: *New York Times* Best Book for Children; NYPL 100 Picture Books Everyone Should Know; *100 Best Books for Children.*

BIRTHDAY: Esphyr Slobodkina: September 22, 1908.

SUBJECTS: Peddlers and peddling—Fiction; Hats—Fiction; Monkeys—Fiction.

Carle, Eric (1929–   ). Artist. In almost any contemporary library or bookstore in the United States, Eric Carle's colorful picture books are in plentiful supply and prominent display. The popular artist was born on June 25, 1929, in Syracuse, New York, to German immigrants Erich Carle and Johanna Oeschläger Carle. Carle began kindergarten in the United States, where his interest in art was encouraged. At the age of six, however, after a visit from his Grandmother Carle to the United States, Carle and his family moved back to Germany. Carle disliked his new school. Life in Germany during the war was complicated and difficult. Carle's father was drafted into Hitler's army, and young Eric was taken from his bed, sometimes two or three times a night for several months, to bomb shelters to be protected from Allied bombing. Eventually, he was sent away with other children to live with foster families in the country in an attempt to avoid this danger. After the war, Carle's father was imprisoned in a prisoner-of-war camp.

The boy used to dream of building a bridge across the ocean from Germany to the United States so that he could return to the life of his idyllic younger childhood that he remembered so fondly. He and his father used to take walks in the woods where his father taught him to appreciate nature. He would turn over rocks and point out to Eric the small insects and other creatures that lived underneath them. Another key figure in Carle's creative development was his Uncle August. August liked to tell stories, and he and Eric had a game where Eric would ask for a story and August would tell him he needed to wind up his thinking machine first. Eric would make an imaginary winding motion beside his Uncle August's temple until the kindly man told him to stop because at that moment he had thought of a story.

When the war was over, and he was a teenager, Carle attended art school at the prestigious *Akademie der bildenden Kunste* in Stuttgart. He was enrolled two years younger than normal beginners at the school, and this led him to be a bit overconfident. As a consequence, Professor Schneidler demoted him from his status as an art student to that of a typesetter's apprentice at the school. Carle learned his lesson and picked up all the knowledge he could about typography before finally being allowed to resume his status as an art student. At age twenty-two, he took his accomplished portfolio and forty dollars and finally reached his dream of returning to the United States.

Carle moved to New York in May 1952, where first he stayed with his uncle, then moved to an apartment near Broadway and 57th Street. He met and was mentored by the artist Leo Lionni, who was then working for *Fortune Magazine*. Eventually, Carle landed a job as a graphic designer in the promotion department of the *New York Times*. After that, he worked as the art director in an advertising agency for several years. Ironically, Eric Carle was drafted by the U.S. Army and was asked to serve in Germany as the mail clerk for his unit. He was allowed to go back to his old home each night and sleep in the bed he had had in his youth.

One weekend back in Germany he ran into an old colleague, and through him he met the colleague's sister, Dorothea Wohlenberg. A relationship developed, and the couple was married one month before Carle's discharge. Dorothea returned to New York with Eric and lived in Queens, where their daughter, Cirsten, was born. Later they moved to Irvington-on-Hudson, where their son, Rolf, was born. The couple had a sad separation four years later, and Eric threw himself into his work and spending time with his children for the next ten years.

One day, the well-respected author and educator Bill Martin Jr. asked Eric to illustrate one of his picture books for children. This became *Brown Bear, Brown Bear, What Do You See?*, which is now often regarded as a classic of the picture book form for young children. Carle's best-known book, *The Very Hungry Caterpillar*, came about when he was fooling around with a paper punch. He punched a hole through several layers of paper, and this made him think of a bookworm. He suggested the idea of Willy the green worm to his editor, Ann Beneduce, who liked it but was not as sure about a bookworm as the main character. She suggested a caterpillar. Eric liked this idea, and the book was born.

To create the book, Eric implemented what would become his trademark medium—the tissue paper collage. At first, he used commercially colored tissue paper, but later on he began painting his own mixtures of color and patterns over an acrylic base on white tissue paper and storing them by color families in large, flat cabinet drawers. In his present work, when he chooses a figure or design, he goes to these drawers and pulls out possible sheets of colored paper that he might use. Then he cuts the collage shapes he needs from each paper, gluing them on the design with polymer wallpaper paste.

The Very Hungry Caterpillar takes a bit of poetic license with scientific fact. Caterpillars actually emerge from the chrysalis, not the cocoon as the one does in the story. Carle admits that cocoon was simply a better word to use in the text. Since it was originally published in 1969, the book has been translated into thirty languages and has sold over 20 million copies worldwide. The artist reissued the book in 1989 with all new, slightly more vibrant and textured artwork, the originals done with materials that will stand up better archivally to the trials of time.

In 1971, Carle met a teacher of special children, Barbara Morrison. When she came to dinner, she brought Eric a single-stemmed anthurium wrapped in translucent white paper. The match seemed destined; they married in 1973 and moved to western Massachusetts. Several years later, the Carles decided to spend winters in the village of Northampton, where they could be closer to town activities and interact with the community. They return to their Berkshire home in the summers. In 1995, the Carles established a foundation that would begin work on their dream of establishing the first full-scale museum of picture book art in the United States.

The Eric Carle Museum of Picture Book Art opened to the public in Amherst, Massachusetts, in November 2002.

Eric Carle has earned several distinctions for his contributions to children's literature. Probably the most notable is the 2003 Laura Ingalls Wilder Medal, which is awarded by the American Library Association to an author or artist whose books, over many years, have made a lasting and significant contribution to children's literature. One of the artist's chief concerns for children is the moment of separation when very young children head off to school leaving their families for the first time. He is also a keen observer who appreciates nature. The insects and bugs from his walks with his father in the woods show up frequently in his work. Book design through "paper engineering" is perhaps one of the features for which he is most known—several of his books have die-cut holes, chirping sounds, twinkly lights, or other toylike features that surprise and delight young children.

Carle's many books include *Brown Bear, Brown Bear, What Do You See?* by Bill Martin Jr. (1967); *1, 2, 3, to the Zoo* (1968); *The Very Hungry Caterpillar* (1969); *Pancakes, Pancakes!* (1970); *The Tiny Seed* (1970); *Do You Want to Be My Friend?* (1971); *The Mixed-Up Chameleon* (1975); *The Very Busy Spider* (1984); *The Mountain That Loved a Bird* (1985); *Papa Please Get the Moon for Me* (1986); *A House for Hermit Crab* (1987); *The Lamb and the Butterfly* (1988); *The Very Quiet Cricket* (1990); *Polar Bear, Polar Bear, What Do You Hear?* by Bill Martin Jr. (1991); *Draw Me a Star* (1992); *The Very Lonely Firefly* (1995); *From Head to Toe* (1997); *Flora and Tiger: 19 Short Stories from My Life* (1997); *Hello, Red Fox* (1998); *Dream Snow* (2000); *Slowly, Slowly, Slowly, Said the Sloth* (2002); *Panda Bear, Panda Bear, What Do You See?* by Bill Martin Jr. (2003); and *Mister Seahorse* (2004).

Further Reading: Carle, Eric. *The Art of Eric Carle.* New York: Philomel, 1996; Klingberg, Delores R. "Profile: Eric Carle." *Language*

Arts 54 (April 1977): 445–452; Video: *Eric Carle: Picture Writer* (Putnam, 1993); Web site: http://www.eric-carle.com/.

See Also: Brown Bear, Brown Bear, What Do You See?; Eric Carle Museum of Picture Book Art; *The Very Hungry Caterpillar*.

The Carrot Seed (Harper, 1945). Written by Ruth Krauss; illustrated by Crockett Johnson.

SUMMARY: A young boy plants a carrot seed and weeds and waters it every day. His mother tells him she is afraid nothing will come up; his father is afraid nothing will come up; his older brother knows nothing will come up. The boy still keeps weeding and watering. At first nothing does come up; then nothing comes up again. Finally, one day a carrot does come up as the boy knew it would—and a big orange carrot it is, too, so big he must carry it away in a wheelbarrow.

MEDIA: Possibly ink.

ANECDOTE: This book was Crockett Johnson's picture book debut. The muted browns and yellows of the illustration make the bright orange of the carrot at the end of the book even more distinctive. Maurice Sendak called the work a "perfect picture book" and "the granddaddy of all picture books in America." Chris Van Allsburg included the book among his choices for a Western canon of children's literature. Johnson and Krauss were married.

DISTINCTIONS: *New York Times* Best Books for Children; NYPL 100 Picture Books Everyone Should Know; *100 Best Books for Children*.

BIRTHDAYS: Ruth Krauss: July 25, 1901; Crockett Johnson: October 20, 1906.

SUBJECTS: Gardening—Fiction.

See Also: Harold and the Purple Crayon.

Casey at the Bat: A Ballad of the Republic Sung the Year 1888 (Handprint Books, 2000). Written by Ernest Lawrence Thayer; illustrated by Christopher Bing.

SUMMARY: The popular narrative verse about Casey of the Mudville nine is illustrated line by line on pages looking like a nineteenth-century scrapbook. Yellow newspaper clippings, postcards, old money, tickets, medals, and other memorabilia lie atop line drawings done in the style of nineteenth-century newspaper illustrations depicting the scene as the game unfolds. Close examination of the myriad of clippings yields surprises of twenty-first-century writing depicted as though it were a clipping from a nineteenth-century newspaper, including commentary on the poem, the game, and so forth.

MEDIA: Pen-and-ink scratchboard engravings for the main illustrations; newspaper and scrapbook background done with mirrored photocopies on acetate, 100 percent cotton-rag watercolor paper soaked in warm acetone baths and watercolors.

ANECDOTE: "Casey at the Bat" was first published in the *San Francisco Examiner* on June 3, 1888. Though the Library of Congress gives him a citation as though he were a real person ("Brian Kavanagh Casey, 1859–1946"), Casey was a fictional character only. The error speaks to how embedded this character is in the American psyche. Christopher Bing is a Boston Red Sox fan.

DISTINCTION: 2001 Caldecott Honor Book.

BIRTHDAY: Ernest Lawrence Thayer: August 14, 1863.

SUBJECTS: Casey, Brian Kavanagh (1859–1946)—Poetry; Baseball players—Poetry; Baseball—Poetry.

Castle (Houghton Mifflin, 1977). Written and illustrated by David Macaulay.

SUMMARY: The book traces the story of the construction of a fictional castle—that of Lord of Aberwyvern of Wales, the former Kevin le Strange, and his wife, Lady Catherine. In the twenty-eight years between 1277 and 1305, several castles were actually built to aid King Edward I of England in conquering

Wales. They were built by the king but also by wealthy lords in the region; Lord Kevin is modeled after one of these noblemen. Master James of Babbington is modeled after one of the many master engineers who designed such fortifications. The book includes diagrams of the interior of the castle, tools, and other relevant aspects of castle building. The drawings aid readers in visualizing the process from the first temporary houses for the builders and soldiers built on the limestone bluff chosen for the site to the dungeons, trusses, turrets, and moat, to the whitewashing of the walls and towers of the castle with lime to create an imposing appearance. Weapons for defense of the fort are also presented that might ward off an attack by the imaginary Prince Daffyd of Gynedd. A glossary of relevant architectural terms appears at the back of the book.

MEDIA: Pen and ink.

ANECDOTE: Macauley completed his first drawing at the age of eight; it was of a fire engine. He had an interest in castles from his early years in England before his family moved to the United States when he was eleven. He has a bachelor's degree in architecture.

DISTINCTION: 1978 Caldecott Honor Book.

BIRTHDAY: David Macaulay: December 2, 1946.

SUBJECTS: Castles—Fiction; Fortification—Fiction.

See Also: Black and White; Cathedral: The Story of Its Construction.

The Cat in the Hat. *See* Geisel, Theodor (Ted) Seuss.

Cathedral: The Story of Its Construction
(Houghton Mifflin, 1973). Written and illustrated by David Macaulay.

SUMMARY: The book traces the story of the building of Chutreaux, an imaginary

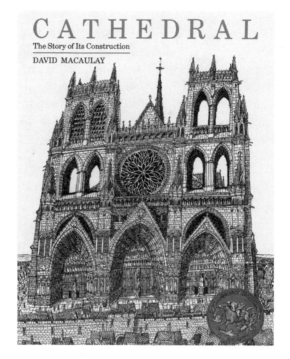

Front cover of *Cathedral: The Story of Its Construction,* written and illustrated by David Macaulay. This 1974 Caldecott Honor book addresses one of several nonfiction topics Macaulay has helped explain visually through his use of detailed pen-and-ink drawings. (Copyright © 1973 by David Macaulay. Copyright © by Houghton Mifflin Company. All rights reserved.)

Gothic cathedral built somewhere in twelfth- through fourteenth-century France. Flemish architect William of Planz is hired to design the church. Master craftspeople are hired to do the building. Lumber and stone must be found, cut, and brought to the cathedral site. Each stone quarried is marked three times— once with a marking of where it will go in the cathedral, once to show what quarry it comes from so the quarry will be paid, and once to show which quarryman cut the stone so that he will be paid. Tools of the various necessary trades are also depicted and discussed. Foundations, crypts, flying buttresses, gargoyles, rose windows, as well as all other parts of a cathedral are described in detail with discussion of how they fit into the overall plan. As work on the cathedral goes on over many years, master builders who die must be replaced. Robert of Cormont replaces William of Planz, and Etienne of Gaston replaces him when Robert falls accidentally from a scaffold and dies. The cathedral in the book, representative of the real thing, takes eighty-six years to complete. A glossary of relevant architectural terms appears at the back of the book.

MEDIA: Pen and ink.

ANECDOTE: *Cathedral* was David Macaulay's first book. Macauley has a bachelor's degree in architecture. Born in England, he attended the Rhode Island School of Design before settling in the United States. The author admits that the book suggests that work on cathedrals proceeded nonstop, when that was not the case. Interruptions in work invariably occurred from many factors.

DISTINCTION: 1974 Caldecott Honor Book.

BIRTHDAY: David Macaulay: December 2, 1946.

SUBJECTS: Cathedrals; Architecture, Gothic.

See Also: Black and White; Castle.

A Chair for My Mother (Greenwillow, 1982). Written and illustrated by Vera B. Williams.

SUMMARY: Rosa's mother works at the Blue Tile Diner. Rosa works alongside her sometimes, helping clean off the salt and pepper shakers, filling the ketchup bottles, and cutting up onions. Josephine at the diner tells her she does a good job and gives her a few coins. Both Rosa's money and her mother's tips go in the jar they keep at home. The jar is a savings bank for a new chair for Rosa's mother. There was a fire in their house not so long ago, and they lost everything. Grandma, Aunt Ida, and Uncle Sandy all help out. The neighbors help, too. Soon, Rosa and her mother have an apartment furnished with some of the things they need, but not all. There are no couch and no soft chair for Rosa's mother and Grandma to sit in. They

are saving coins until the large jar is full, when they will go buy a soft chair with big roses on it for mama.

Finally, the jar is full and can fit no more coins. Rosa and her mother and grandmother go shopping and find the chair they have been hoping to buy. They have enough money. Aunt Ida and Uncle Sandy bring it home in their truck, since they know Rosa and her mother do not want to wait until it can be delivered. Now, Rosa's mother has a comfortable place to put up her feet after a long day of working as a waitress, and Rosa has a place to snuggle with her on her lap.

MEDIA: Watercolor.

ANECDOTE: This book is the first of a trio of books about Rosa and her mother and grandmother. The other two are *Something Special for Me* (1983) and *Music, Music for Everyone* (1984).

DISTINCTION: 1983 Caldecott Honor Book.

BIRTHDAY: Vera B. Williams: January 28, 1927.

SUBJECTS: Family life—Fiction; Saving and investment—Fiction; Chairs—Fiction.

Chanticleer and the Fox (Crowell, 1958). Adapted from Geoffrey Chaucer's *Canterbury Tales* and illustrated by Barbara Cooney.

SUMMARY: A widow lives peacefully minding her dairy farm and raising her two daughters. She has three pigs, three cows, and a sheep named Molly. She has a colorful rooster whose crow is finer and louder than any other rooster's in the land. His name is Chanticleer. The rooster has seven hens as wives. Demoiselle Partlet, the one with the prettiest throat, is his favorite.

One night, Chanticleer has a dream that a doglike beast, with fur between yellow and red and with tail and ears tipped in black, has tried to kill him. Demoiselle Partlet admonishes Chanticleer, assuring him that he is brave and should not be frightened by mere dreams. With that, Chanticleer flies down to the ground and preens and prunes while the hens gather around him. Soon a fox comes by and compliments him on his singing. The fox tells him he has not heard any rooster sing so well since he knew Chanticleer's father. He also knew his mother, who had visited him. He asks the rooster to sing again to see if he sings as well as his father. When he does so, Chanticleer closes his eyes and beats his wings; he steps up on his toes and crows. At that, the fox grabs him about the neck and runs off with him toward the woods.

At hearing the hens' shrieks, the widow, her daughters, the hogs, and the cows all run after them. Chanticleer tells the fox that he should simply turn around to them all and say that he is going to eat the rooster whether they follow him or not. The fox answers that that is exactly what he is going to do, but when he says this, Chanticleer flies free up into a tree. Both the rooster and the fox exchange morals that they have learned from the episode. Rooster has learned not to be tricked by flattery, and fox has learned not to talk when he shouldn't.

MEDIA: Preseparated art; black and white on scratchboard; colors on Dinobase.

ANECDOTE: The story is adapted from "The Nun's Priest's Tale" of Geoffrey Chaucer's *Canterbury Tales*, which the author read once while she was ill. Cooney used her own live chickens and plants from her garden as models for the illustrations. The Christmas after she completed the book, she discovered that she was making gingerbread forms out of the characters to hang on her tree as ornaments.

DISTINCTION: 1959 Caldecott Medal.

BIRTHDAY: Barbara Cooney: August 6, 1917.

SUBJECTS: Fables; Animals—Fiction.

See Also: Cooney, Barbara; *Island Boy*; *Miss Rumphius*.

Charcoal. Artist's medium. Pencils or unwrapped pieces of carbon.

Charlotte Zolotow Book Award. Distinction. In honor of longtime Harper editor Charlotte Zolotow, a medal and $1,000 cash are awarded each year by the Cooperative Children's Book Center (CCBC). The CCBC is the children's literature library of the School of Education, the University of Wisconsin-Madison. The prize is given annually to the author of the best picture book text published in the United States the previous year. The award is intended to draw similar attention and recognition for picture books that are exceptionally well written in the same way that the Randolph Caldecott Medal recognizes art.

The award was initiated in 1998 to honor the career of Charlotte Zolotow, who worked as an editor at Harper for thirty-eight years and also wrote over seventy picture books. Zolotow attended the University of Wisconsin from 1933 to 1936 on a writing scholarship. The Zolotow medal is bronze; a metallic seal depiction of it is affixed to the cover of each year's winner. It was designed by Harriet Barton, who designed the logo for Zolotow's book imprint at Harper. The medal has a tulip (adapted from the crocus of the Charlotte Zolotow imprint) with the initials "CZ" on either side of it and also the words "Charlotte Zolotow Award/CCBC." In addition to the award, there are up to three Honor Books and up to ten titles the CCBC calls "Highly Commended." All of these distinctions are intended to bring attention to American picture books for children with quality writing.

Selection is made by the CCBC award committee, and winners are announced each January. An award ceremony in the spring honors Charlotte Zolotow's career by bestowing the awards on that year's winners and also features a free and public lecture by an invited children's literature professional. The lecture is a separate distinction from the award. The Charlotte Zolotow lectures to date have been given by Karla Kuskin (1998); Katherine Paterson (1999); Jean Craighead

George (2000); Robert Lipsyte (2001); Kevin Henkes (2002); Naomi Shahib Nye (2003); and Linda Sue Park (2004).

See Also: Clever Beatrice; Farfellina and Marcel; Lucky Song; The Night Worker; Snow; What James Likes Best; When Sophie Gets Angry—Really, Really Angry.

Chato and the Party Animals (Putnam, 2000). Written by Gary Soto; illustrated by Susan Guevara.

SUMMARY: Cool cat Chato's friend, Novio Boy, is an orphan from the pound who has never had a birthday party; he doesn't even know when his birthday is. When he attends Chorizo's party at the mice house in the *barrio*, he becomes sad as he always does at birthday parties. Chato, being a party animal, decides to throw Novio Boy a party. He enlists the help of his friends. Sharkie, the D. J., will play tunes. Chato cooks many dishes and also purchases a *piñata*. He fills water balloons. Finally, the guests arrive including twins Mas and Menos, Sharkie, Flirty, Samba, Pelon, and Peloncito. Chorizo arrives with the family of mice on his back. When they all ask where Novio Boy is, Chato realizes that he has not invited him. They all go looking for the birthday cat. He is not in the sycamore tree and not on Senora Ramirez's garage roof. They begin to think he has been kidnapped, and they go back to Chato's very sad. Suddenly, Novio Boy appears with two friends. He has been dumpster hopping. When he learns that the party is for him, he has the best birthday of his life. Chato tells him that he must have been born on the first day of summer because he likes to play so much. Novio Boy tells his friends they are *mi familia*. There is a glossary of Spanish words used in the story and their English translations in the front of the book.

MEDIA: Undetermined.

ANECDOTE: This book is the sequel to *Chato's Kitchen*.

DISTINCTION: 2001 Pura Belpré Award for Illustration.

BIRTHDAYS: Susan Guevara: January 27, 1956; Gary Soto: April 12, 1952.

SUBJECTS: Cats—Fiction; Parties—Fiction; Birthdays—Fiction; Los Angeles (Calif.)—Fiction.

See Also: Chato's Kitchen.

Chato's Kitchen (Putnam, 1995). Written by Gary Soto; illustrated by Susan Guevara.

SUMMARY: Chato, a cool cat from East L.A., invites a family of mice (*ratoncitos*) who are new to the *barrio* (neighborhood) to dinner. He also invites his cool friend, Novio Boy. In English and Spanish, the foods Chato prepares for the meal and the new home Mami and Papi mouse settle flavor the story with vocabulary from both languages. When the mice invite Chorizo, or Sausage, with them to the meal, Chato agrees, thinking now he will have a tasty meal of six mice instead of five. When the mice arrive, the cats discover that Chorizo is a dachshund, and they end up eating the tasty treats they have made in Chato's kitchen rather than the mice they had hoped to have. Treats from Chato's kitchen include *arroz* (rice); *carne asada* (grilled steak); *chiles rellenos* (stuffed chili peppers); *enchiladas*; *fajitas*; *flan*; *frijoles* (beans); *guacamole*; *salsa*; *tamarindo* (drink made from tamarind fruit); and *tortillas*. The mice prepare and bring with them cheese *quesadillas*. A glossary of Spanish words with their English translations, including Chato's menu, appears at the front of the book.

MEDIA: Undetermined.

ANECDOTE: Gary Soto is also a poet who teaches at the University of California at Berkeley.

DISTINCTION: 1996 Pura Belpré Award for Illustration.

BIRTHDAYS: Susan Guevara: January 27, 1956; Gary Soto: April 12, 1952.

SUBJECTS: Cats—Fiction; Mice—Fiction; Mexican Americans—Fiction; Los Angeles (Calif.)—Fiction.

See Also: Chato and the Party Animals.

Chicka Chicka Boom Boom (Simon and Schuster, 1989). Written by Bill Martin Jr. and John Archambault; illustrated by Lois Ehlert.

SUMMARY: In a rhyming alphabet, the letters go up a coconut tree in groupings that dare the next group of letters to join them. When the tree becomes top-heavy, the letters all fall down and are picked up and mended with Band-Aids by their capital letter "parents" and other adult caretakers. After nightfall, little letter A slowly climbs back up the coconut tree in another determined effort that implies the antics are ready to begin all over again.

MEDIA: Cut-paper collage.

ANECDOTE: The bold bright letters and bouncing rhyming text are particularly popular and successful with young children learning the alphabet and how to read. Already educating and entertaining a second generation, the book is becoming a late-twentieth-century classic alphabet.

DISTINCTIONS: *New York Times Best Book* for Children; NYPL 100 Picture Books Everyone Should Know; *100 Best Books for Children.*

BIRTHDAYS: Bill Martin Jr.: March 20, 1916; Lois Ehlert: November 9, 1934.

SUBJECTS: Alphabet; Stories in rhyme.

Children's Book Council (CBC). Organization. The CBC is a collective of American trade children's book publishers and packagers that promotes reading and the enjoyment of children's and young adult books. It is also the official sponsor of both Young People's Poetry Week and Children's Book Week. Many American picture book artists' work have been featured in the CBC's well-known Children's Book Week posters produced annually since 1919, many of which have become collector's items. A chronological review of the posters offers a historical glance through American styles, interests, and sensibilities through the twentieth and early twenty-first centuries. The CBC publishes book lists, promotional products to encourage literacy, and other materials used by libraries and schools as well as information useful to authors and artists of children's books.

Contact: The Children's Book Council, 12 W. 37th Street, 2nd floor, New York, NY 10018-7480. (212) 966-1990. Web site: http://www.cbcbooks.org; email: info@cbcbooks.org.

Further Reading: Marcus, Leonard S. *75 Years of Children's Book Week Posters: Celebrating Great Illustrators of American Children's Books.* New York: Knopf, 1994.

Children's Literature Association (ChLA). Organization. ChLA is a professional organization made up of children's literature experts such as professors, teachers, librarians, authors, artists, and others who are primarily interested in the study and literary analysis of children's and young adult literature. The association takes the picture book genre seriously as a literary art form that stands alongside any adult form of fiction, nonfiction, or poetry as being worthy of critical analysis and scholarly inquiry. ChLA sponsors an annual academic conference where picture books for children, along with middle grade and young adult books, are featured prominently in papers, plenaries, and panel discussions. Literary criticism of picture books, as well as reviews of secondary books about the genre, appear in the organization's publications, *Children's Literature Association Quarterly* and *Children's Literature.*

Contact: Children's Literature Association, P.O. Box 138, Battle Creek, MI 49016-0138; (269) 965-8180.

A Child's Calendar (Holiday House, 1999). Written by John Updike; illustrated by Trina Schart Hyman.

SUMMARY: Updike has written a poem for each month of the year, using the collective first person "we" as children as the speaker for each. Titles for each poem are the month's names. Most poems are written in short quatrains with a rhyme scheme of *abcb*, though there is also frequent use of slant rhyme. Each poem describes children's lives in that time and season of the year.

MEDIA: Pen and ink; watercolor.

ANECDOTE: John Updike is a prolific and internationally renowned American author known for his novels, short stories, essays and literary criticism, including the popular *Rabbit* series about Harry "Rabbit" Angstrom. His work frequently appears in *The New Yorker*.

DISTINCTION: 2000 Caldecott Honor Book.

BIRTHDAYS: Trina Schart Hyman: April 8, 1939; John Updike: March 18, 1932.

SUBJECTS: Months—Poetry; American poetry; Children's poetry, American.

A Child's Good Night Book (Scott, 1943). Written by Margaret Wise Brown; illustrated by Jean Charlot.

SUMMARY: In this bedtime story book, everything is getting sleepy and going to bed. The sun goes to the other side of the world, and it gets dark. Birds sleep; fish sleep with their eyes open; sheep stop leaping and baaing and go to sleep. Wild things such as lions and monkeys and mice go to sleep. Sailboats and engines go to sleep. Baby kangaroos stop jumping, and cats stop purring. Bunnies close their eyes. Children stop whistling; they say their prayers and get under the covers. The book ends with a short prayer that God will look over all the sleeping things.

MEDIA: Color lithographs.

ANECDOTE: Brown was an editor at W. R. Scott publishers.

DISTINCTION: 1944 Caldecott Honor Book.

BIRTHDAY: Margaret Wise Brown: May 23, 1910.

SUBJECT: Bedtime—Fiction.

See Also: Brown, Margaret Wise; *Goodnight Moon; The Little Island; Little Lost Lamb.*

The Christmas Anna Angel (Viking, 1944). Written by Ruth Sawyer; illustrated by Kate Seredy.

SUMMARY: Text is extensive in this picture book. Anna and Miklos take a sleigh ride with their father, Matyas Rado, to the bakery on St. Nicholas Eve, the saint's feast day (not Christmas Eve). Their horses' names are Istvan and Janos. In the village, they buy what they can afford after three years of war. There are no Christmas cakes this year at the bakery, only bread. The children are disappointed to have no Christmas cakes. Back home, Mari Rado, the children's mother, urges them to eat their dinner, but the children are excited for the arrival of St. Nicholas. When St. Nicholas arrives with his decorated robes and tall staff, the children are frightened at first. He asks whether they have been good, and what present each would like for Christmas. Anna says she would like a white muff with a hot potato in it to warm her hands. Miklos wants a knife, boots, and a present for his puppy, Ferko. St. Nicholas looks to their parents, and both nod.

The children decorate the tree with new ornaments they make. Then St. Lucy's Day (feast day) arrives, and the children play with the hens. The army had come and counted all the wheat on the farm. They were not allowed to sell it to make flour for such frivolities as Christmas cakes. However, there is a hint that Mari has managed to hide some away. Anna thinks of angels in the sky having wheat and being able to make Christmas cakes for their tree. She prays to her special Anna Angel that that will happen. On Christmas Eve night, Anna Angel appears and makes Christmas cakes in shapes Anna's family loves for the tree. Mari's is a manger; Matyas's is the shepherd; Miklos loves the Three Kings; and Anna's is shaped like a clock with the hands set at midnight.

On Christmas morning, the family rejoices in the miracle of the Christmas cakes. The soldiers did not find all the white flour; the family finds hope for peace.

MEDIA: Undetermined.

ANECDOTE: The Hungarian born Kate Seredy visited the United States in 1922 and lived there the rest of her life.

DISTINCTION: 1945 Caldecott Honor Book.

BIRTHDAYS: Ruth Sawyer: August 5, 1880; Kate Seredy: November 10, 1899.

SUBJECT: Christmas—Fiction.

See Also: Journey Cake, Ho!

Cinderella, or The Little Glass Slipper
(Scribner, 1954). Translated from Charles Perrault; illustrated by Marcia Brown.

SUMMARY: The familiar fairy tale of Cinderella is retold in relatively extensive text.

MEDIA: Gouache, crayon, watercolor, and ink.

ANECDOTE: The fairy tales normally attributed to Frenchman Charles Perrault may have been actually written by his father, Pierre Perrault, who may have given the credit to his son.

DISTINCTION: 1955 Caldecott Medal.

BIRTHDAYS: Marcia Brown: July 13, 1918; Charles Perrault (French): January 12, 1628.

SUBJECTS: Fairy tales; Folklore—France.

See Also: Brown, Marcia; *Dick Whittington and His Cat*; *Henry Fisherman*; *Puss in Boots*; *Shadow*; *Skipper John's Cook*; *Stone Soup*.

Clever Beatrice: An Upper Peninsula Conte
(Atheneum, 2001). Written by Margaret Willey; illustrated by Heather Solomon.

SUMMARY: Beatrice lives with her mother in the upper peninsula of Michigan. She likes riddles, and she is very clever and smart. Her mother tells her they are almost out of porridge. Beatrice says that she will go out and get them some money. Her mother tells her there are only two ways to get money there in the woods. One is to cut down trees with the lumberjacks, but that is no job for such a small girl. The other is to find the giant on the other side of the woods who likes to gamble on his strength. That does not seem suitable for such a small girl either. Beatrices asks if the giant is smart and is told that rich giants don't need to be smart.

After watching the lumberjacks down a large tree, Beatrice finds the giant and challenges him to a bet on strength. She tells him that she can strike a blow harder than his. They agree to hit the giant's front door. After the giant hits his door, Beatrice points to the large tree just felled by the lumberjacks down the mountain and leads him to believe she knocked it down to provide him with a new door after she would knock that one down. The giant believes her and pays her the ten gold coins of their bet rather than allow her to hit the door.

Challenges and cleverness continue through two more bets—fetching water and throwing a large iron bar. The giant is not happy to keep paying Beatrice off, but neither is he smart enough to realize that she is bluffing her way through the bets. With the water, she ties a rope around the entire well and threatens to pull it over to the giant's house; with the iron bars, she asks whether the giant knows anyone in each direction, north, south, east, and west, so that she can call to them to duck their heads and not be hurt when she hurls the bar their way. The giant stops her each time rather than allow her to take away his water well or hurt any of his relatives. Beatrice runs home with a silver bag full of the giant's gold coins.

MEDIA: Watercolor, collage, acrylic, and oils.

ANECDOTE: The story is an adaptation of a Canadian *conte*, a form of folklore similar to an American tall tale. French Canadians brought the form to the upper peninsula of northern Michigan, where they were attracted by the lumber trade.

DISTINCTION: 2002 Charlotte Zolotow Award.

BIRTHDAY: Margaret Willey: November 5, 1950.

SUBJECTS: Folklore—Michigan; Tall tales.

Click, Clack, Moo: Cows That Type
(Simon and Schuster, 2000). Written by Doreen Cronin; illustrated by Betsy Lewin.

SUMMARY: Farmer Brown has an unusual problem—his cows like to type. They type all day. They leave messages for him that their barn is cold and that the cows need electric blankets. The chickens are cold, too, and they also want electric blankets. When the blankets do not appear, the cows type a note that they will not give milk, and the chickens will not give eggs. Farmer Brown gets his own typewriter out and types a response—blankets will not be coming, and he demands that the cows and chickens produce milk and eggs. He sends his note through Duck, who is neutral in the dispute. The cows have a meeting that night in the barn. All the other animals listen in, but they do not understand the cows' "moo" language. The cows type a note with their typewriter offering the typewriter in exchange for the blankets with instructions about how and where the exchange is to take place. The note is returned to Farmer Brown by the arbiter, Duck. Farmer agrees and

leaves the blankets at the appointed place and time and waits for Duck to bring him the typewriter. Instead, Duck and his fellow ducks type Farmer Brown a note requesting a diving board for the pond.

The book, though humorous and light-hearted, contains elements that may remind older readers of George Orwell's novel, *Animal Farm*.

MEDIA: Watercolor.

DISTINCTION: 2001 Caldecott Honor Book.

BIRTHDAY: Betsy Lewin: May 12, 1937.

SUBJECTS: Cows—Fiction; Domestic Animals—Fiction; Typewriters—Fiction.

Cock-a-Doodle Doo: The Story of a Little Red Rooster
(Macmillan, 1939). Written and illustrated by Berta and Elmer Hader.

SUMMARY: A mother duck and her ducklings are surprised when a little red chick hatches out of an egg as part of her family. The farmer is surprised, too, but he thinks the little red chick will make out all right with the ducks. When the ducks float into the pond, the little red chick steps in and right back out again. He does not like getting wet. When the ducks say, "Quack-quack," the chick says, "Peep-peep." The chick begins to get very lonely, since he is so unlike the ducks. One day from the other side of a hill, the little chick hears a call to come home; he understands it. He tries to fly over but cannot. He starts to walk there, even though the ducks warn him to come back and not go into the woods where there are wild animals. First, he encounters a crow. Then he sees an owl. The little chick stays very quiet so as not to be noticed. He sees a mouse scurry away from the owl. The chick sees a skunk, raccoon, three gray squirrels, a fox, chipmunk, rabbit, and dogs. All the while he is following the cock-a-doodle-doo call to come home from the farm on the other side of the hill.

When he reaches the farm, he is not home yet. He has adventures with a turkey, geese, and a hawk before he finally arrives in the barn where there is a family of little yellow chicks much more like himself. As time passes, the little red chick grows to be a rooster that wakes the farm every morning.

MEDIA: Watercolor.

ANECDOTE: The Haders were married in 1919. They collaborated on over one hundred books.

DISTINCTION: 1940 Caldecott Honor Book.

BIRTHDAYS: Berta Hader: February 6, 1891; Elmer Hader: September 7, 1889.

SUBJECT: Animals—Legends and stories of.

See Also: The Big Snow; *The Mighty Hunter*; *White Snow, Bright Snow*.

Collage. Artist's medium. A collection of materials or objects laid out in a design chosen by the artist; also torn paper laid out in a design or picture.

Color Preseparation. Artist's medium. In this process, the artist paints the colors for a finished drawing by drawing the objects that are to be the same color all on one transparent surface separate from the others. For example, green grass and leaves would be on one sheet; blue flowers and sky on another. When all the drawings are overlaid on top of one another, the completed picture emerges with all colors together where they should be. Printing processes do this mechanically, but if the artist does it before printing, it is called preseparation.

Color Zoo (HarperCollins, 1989). Written and illustrated by Lois Ehlert.

SUMMARY: Solid color-blocking and geometric cut-outs are cleverly configured to create images of animals on the right-hand side of page spreads and plain shapes on the other. Shapes depicted are star, circle, square, triangle, rectangle, heart, oval, diamond, octagon, and hexagon. Animals are tiger, mouse, fox, ox, monkey, deer, lion, goat, and snake. Colors are blue purple, red purple, pink, red, orange, yellow orange, yellow, yellow green, green, dark green, blue green, blue, dark blue, brown, gray, and black. Keys to all three concepts are included in the back of the book.

MEDIA: Paper collage and die-cut forms.

ANECDOTE: Ehlert rigged up her first drawing board by propping up a bread board against a can on a card table.

DISTINCTION: 1990 Caldecott Honor Book.

BIRTHDAY: Lois Ehlert: November 9, 1934.

SUBJECTS: Color—Study and teaching (Elementary); Visual perception—Study and teaching (Elementary); Color; Shape.

Coming on Home Soon (Penguin, 2004). Written by Jacqueline Woodson, illustrated by E. B. (Earl Bradley) Lewis.

SUMMARY: Mama loves Ada Ruth more than rain and snow, and Ada Ruth loves her that much, too. One day, Mama tells Ada Ruth that she is going to Chicago to work during the war to make some money for the family, but she will be coming on home soon. Ada Ruth waits behind with Grandma, and the long wait to hear anything from Mama is very hard. Ada Ruth keeps writing letters to Mama, who is washing trains in the city. One day, a small black kitten appears and the little girl feeds it some milk, though Grandma warns her not to get attached. Finally, a letter arrives from Mama with money in the envelope and the promise that she will be coming on home soon. Grandma and Ada Ruth reread the letter many times, and it seems the kitten has found favor with Grandma after all and will be staying. The last page is wordless, an illustration of Mama walking toward the house through the snow, coming on home.

MEDIA: Watercolor on Arches paper.

ANECDOTE: There is no author's note, but Mama's explanation to Ada Ruth, as well as the illustrations throughout the book, makes the point clear that black women, as well as white, were hired in the city during World War II to do jobs that men who were away at war used to do. Lewis dedicates the book to men and women in current wars, a long way from home.

DISTINCTION: 2005 Caldecott Honor Book.

BIRTHDAY: E. B. Lewis: December 16, 1956.

SUBJECTS: Separation (Psychology)—Fiction; Mother and child—Fiction; Grandmothers—Fiction; African Americans—Fiction; World War, 1939–1945—United States—Fiction.

Conté Pencil. Artist's medium. Square-shaped drawing chalk that comes in colors of sepia, black, white, and sanquine.

The Contest: An Armenian Folktale (Greenwillow, 1976). Retold and illustrated by Nonny Hogrogian.

SUMMARY: Two robbers live near the village of Erzingah. One, Hmayag, does his robbing by day and spends his evenings with his betrothed, Ehleezah. The other, Hrahad, does his by night and sees his betrothed, Ehleezah, by day. Ehleezah is seeing both men, but they don't know that fact or each other. In order to find more riches for Ehleezah, both robbers decide to go rob in the next province. Ehleezah packs *bokhjahs* (bags of food) for both of their journeys. When both robbers stop under a pomegranate tree, they meet one another, and both open their *bokhjahs*. Each contains cheese, olives, dried meat, one tomato, three scallions, and four apricots. After discussing other things they have in common, the robbers discover that they are both engaged to the same woman. They begin to quarrel.

They decide to have a contest to decide which man is the cleverer robber and will marry Ehleezah. Hmayag steals jewels from a man who is taking his wife's gems to be re-paired. When he arrives at the jeweler's, both he and the jeweler see the stones. The man returns home, but on the way Hmayag again switches the jewels for the stones. His wife is upset that they have not been repaired. This goes back and forth a few times until finally Hmayag keeps the jewels.

Hrahad finds a hammer and spikes and nails them into the Ishkhan's palace wall. Once inside, he and Hmayag roast the fattest hen from the Ishkhan's henhouse. Hrahad sneaks past the guard into the Ishkan's chamber and whispers to him in his sleep. He explains the plight of the two robbers and asks him to decide which one should marry Ehleezah. The Ishkhan, thinking he is dreaming, says both robbers have been clever, then rolls over to dream another dream. The robbers decide that Ehleezah doesn't deserve either one of them. They decide to stay in the province. Meanwhile, Ehleezah of Erzingah has found yet another man to spend time with in their absence.

MEDIA: Colored pencils and crayons for color; pencil drawings for black and white.

ANECDOTE: Nonny Hogrogian is a double Caldecott Medal winner. She studied woodcut with Antonio Frasconi at the New School for Social Research in New York City.

DISTINCTION: 1977 Caldecott Honor Book.

BIRTHDAY: Nonny Hogrogian: May 7, 1932.

SUBJECT: Folklore—Armenia.

See Also: Hogrogian, Nonny.

Cooney, Barbara (1917–2000). Author and artist. Cooney and a twin brother were born in Room #1127 of the Hotel Bossert in Brooklyn, New York, on August 6, 1917. Her immigrant grandfather, who arrived in the country with thirty cents in his pocket, had built the hotel, which was one of the largest in Brooklyn Heights. Cooney's family lived there for two weeks before moving to Long Island, where she would grow up. Barbara

Author and artist Barbara Cooney (1917–2000) worked in a variety of different media, but she is perhaps best known for her picture books featuring watercolors of Maine and New England, where she lived much of her life. (AP/Wide World Photos.)

was the daughter of a stockbroker father and an artist mother. Her German immigrant great-grandfather was also a professional artist who painted "Cigar Store Indian" figures and oil landscapes. Though Barbara showed an early interest in art, her mother did not give her lessons beyond how to clean her brushes. She did, however, allow her to play with her art materials. Having both access to materials and a lack of instruction, which encouraged self-exploration, were two aspects of her growing up that Cooney later attributed to helping her become an artist.

Cooney spent summers on the coast of Maine all through her childhood, and it was from this experience that her famous love for New England and the coastline of Maine began. She enjoyed playing in fields and woods with other children and always felt she needed to be able to go outdoors and preferably live near the sea. She later found city life to be too confining. Cooney studied studio art and art history at Smith College and graduated in 1938. When she began looking for art work, she was told that she needed to fa-

miliarize herself more with the limitations of black and white that were needed for printing, so she studied lithography at the Art Students' League in New York City. *Ake and His World*, her first illustrated book for children written by the Swedish poet Bertil Malmberg, was published in 1940. A year later the first book she illustrated and also wrote, *King of Wreck Island*, was published.

During World War II, Cooney entered the Women's Army Corps but left when she married her first husband, Guy Murchie, and became pregnant with their first child. Murchie was an author and war correspondent. They had two children, Gretel and Barnaby. The couple divorced five years into the marriage. In 1949, Barbara married a country doctor, Charles Talbot Porter. They had two more children, Charles Talbot Jr. and Phoebe. Cooney said her children had barely opened their eyes before she had drawn them in a sketch pad she took with her to the hospital. The couple raised all four children in Pepperell, Massachusetts. Cooney later moved to a house that included a studio designed by one of her sons along the Damariscotta River in Maine, close to her beloved sea.

Cooney's art media for picture books changed over the years, in part due to innovations in printing technology. She began with scratchboard and pen and ink but later moved on to pen and ink with wash, casin, collage, watercolor, and acrylics. Her over one hundred illustrated books for children include *Little Fur Tree* by Margaret Wise Brown (1954); *Owl and the Pussy-Cat* by Edward Lear (1969); *Squawk to the Moon, Little Goose* by Edna Mitchell Preston (1974); *Lexington and Concord, 1775: What Really Happened* by Jean Colby (1975); *Emma* by Wendy Kesselman (1980); *Roxaboxen* by Alice McLerran (1991); *Emily* by Michael Bedard (1992); *Letting Swift River Go* by Jane Yolen (1992); and many others. Her fine etchings for *Chanticleer and the Fox* (1958), a retelling of Chaucer's tale, won her a Caldecott Medal in 1959.

Cooney picked up a second Caldecott Medal in 1980 for illustrating Donald Hall's *Ox-Cart Man*. Enhancing the New England theme of the book, she used wood as the basis for her painting. While she was at work on the book, she was building a house by the shore near South Bristol, Maine. She met Leon, a carpenter working on the house, who had a red beard that she particularly liked, and she wanted to draw it in the book. After researching social customs, she found that beards were popular in the New Hampshire setting of the story from around 1803 to 1847. She further narrowed the timeline to 1832 by researching when turnstiles were still in existence as well as when there was a brick market in Portsmouth. For the scene where the ox-cart man kisses his ox, Cooney used another carpenter named Markie as a model and asked him to kiss a lamp. Markie was so pleased to be part of the project that he built a mahogany box for Cooney's illustrations when they were finished and ready to be shipped. On the outside of the box, Cooney painted an ox before she mailed it off to her publisher.

The works that Cooney herself admitted were the most autobiographical are a trilogy of picture books made up of *Miss Rumphius* (1982), *Island Boy* (1988), and *Hattie and the Wild Wave*s (1990). The first inspiration for *Miss Rumphius* came from a woman named Hilda whom Cooney had met. Hilda was born on July 5, 1898, and had planted lupine seeds much as Johnny Appleseed had done with apple seeds. The autobiographical elements in the book include Cooney's belongings such as an embroidered shawl, armchair, and a picture of her grandson, as well as locations in New England where she had lived, and a conservatory similar to the one at her alma mater, Smith College. The theme of making the world better by making it more beautiful is perhaps the most autobiographical element of all in the book, since this is the goal of many artists, including Cooney. *Miss Rumphius* won the National Book Award in 1983.

Island Boy expresses a life Cooney said she would have liked to have had—living on an island off the coast of Maine. It is inspired by a late-nineteenth-century man living in Maine whom Cooney heard of and then researched. She employed her love of nature all throughout the book and especially her admiration for where the sky and sea meet at the horizon and the way the sun and moonlight dance on the water. She called the book her "hymn to Maine." *Hattie and the Wild Waves* not only echoes her own growing up as a future artist but it is also the story of Cooney's mother growing up in Brooklyn. Of all of the books Cooney wrote and/or illustrated, she called this trilogy her "heart."

Barbara Cooney died on March 10, 2000, not quite making it to the hundred years of age she hoped to reach. In 1989, the Maine Library Association developed the Lupine Award, named after the lupines in *Miss*

Rumphius. The award is given each year in recognition of children's books written or illustrated by residents of the state or which have subjects about, or are set in, the state of Maine. The governor of Maine recognized Cooney's contributions in 1997, calling her "a State Treasure."

DISTINCTIONS: 1959 Caldecott Medal; 1980 Caldecott Medal; 1983 National Book Award.

Further Reading: Cooney, Barbara. "Caldecott Medal Acceptance." *Horn Book* (August 1989): 378–82.

See Also: Caldecott Medalists (Multiple); *Chanticleer and the Fox*; *Emily*; *Miss Rumphius*; *Ox-Cart Man*; Printing Technology.

Cooperative Children's Book Center (CCBC). Library. The CCBC is the children's literature library of the School of Education, the University of Wisconsin-Madison. It is the entity that awards the annual Charlotte Zolotow Award for best American children's picture book text and also publishes *CCBC Choices*, a bibliography of children's books considered noteworthy by the CCBC that were published the previous year. The library maintains a moderated Internet discussion list for those interested in children's literature: ccbc-net.

Contact: CCBC, 4290 Helen C. White Hall, 600 North Park Street, Madison, WI 53706; (608) 263-3720.

Corduroy (Viking, 1968). Written and illustrated by Don Freeman.

SUMMARY: Corduroy is a toy bear that lives in the toy department of a store. He wears green corduroy overalls, but he has a problem—one of the buttons on his shoulder straps is missing. Because of the missing button, Corduroy has been passed over by children who would have otherwise liked to take him home. A little girl named Lisa sees him and wants to take him, but her mother says she has already spent too much money that day and besides, the bear does not look new because of his missing button. The little girl goes away sad.

Corduroy did not realize he was missing a button, so he decides that evening while the store is closed, he will see if he can find it. By accident, he steps onto an escalator that takes him to the furniture department upstairs. Corduroy has always wanted to live in a place with such nice furniture. He sees a button on a mattress and tries to pull it off, thinking it must be his lost button. When he pulls on the tied button, he falls against a floor lamp, which attracts the attention of the night watchman. When the watchman investigates, all he sees are the tops of Corduroy's fuzzy brown ears above a sheet on the biggest bed in the furniture department. He takes Corduroy back to the toy department downstairs.

The next morning as Corduroy is waking up, he sees the very same girl in front of him who was there the day before. Lisa tells him that she went home and counted the money in her piggy bank, and she has enough money to buy him. When she buys him, the clerk asks if she'd like a box, but instead the girl takes Corduroy right out of the store and runs up four flights of stairs to her family's apartment and straight to her room. There, she sews on a new button for her new brown bear. Corduroy sees the nice little girl's bed and the smaller bed his size in Lisa's room. He appreciates her taking care of his button and decides she must be a friend.

MEDIA: Possibly ink and watercolor.

ANECDOTE: Don Freeman's artwork is part of the collections of the Smithsonian National Portrait Gallery, the British Museum, and other museums. *Corduroy* was one of the first mainstream American picture books for children to feature an African American child.

DISTINCTIONS: *New York Times* Best Book for Children; NYPL 100 Picture Books Everyone Should Know.

BIRTHDAY: Don Freeman: August 11, 1908.

SUBJECTS: Toys—Fiction; Fantasy.

Coretta Scott King Book Awards. Sometimes great things start out in small ways, and such was the case with the origin of the Coretta Scott King (CSK) Book Awards. Two school librarians, Glyndon Greer and Mabel McKissick, were attending the 1969 American Library Association conference in Atlantic City, New Jersey. Both arrived by chance at the booth of a publisher, John Carroll. Both were interested in receiving a poster of Dr. Martin Luther King Jr. that the publisher was handing out. Dr. King had been shot just the year before, and social unrest was still high across the United States. The little group got talking about how it was a shame that African American authors and illustrators received no recognition for their work in children's literature through the various award programs. John Carroll suggested to the two librarians that they pursue such an award. The award grew out of that initial conversation when the librarians went home and went to work. They were able to enlist the help of four others: Harriet Brown of New York; Beatrice James, president of the New Jersey Library Association; Roger McDonough, New Jersey State librarian; and Ella Gaines Yates, assistant director of the Montclair Public Library.

The award is given to honor the life of Dr. Martin Luther King Jr., and his wife, Coretta Scott King's, continued work for peace and justice. Outstanding children's books written or illustrated by African American authors and artists published in the previous year that continue Dr. King's work toward peace, justice, and understanding are eligible for consideration. The first award was given in 1970 by the New Jersey Library Association at its annual gala. Lillie Paterson was the first author recipient, for her biography of the civil rights leader, *Martin Luther King, Jr., Man of Peace* (Garrard, 1969), illustrated by Victor Mays. Two years later, the CSK group held a breakfast as part of the annual ALA conference, but it was still not officially affiliated with the organization.

The CSK group awarded its first award to illustrators in 1974, to George Ford for his artwork in the biography *Ray Charles* (Crowell, 1973), written by Sharon Bell Mathis. Mathis won the author award that same year. Also that year, the seal was designed that would be affixed to award-winning books in the future. It was designed by internationally known Atlanta artist Lev Mills. The basic design is a circle with a pyramid positioned in front of it. An African American child reads a book in the center of the pyramid. Around the top arc of the circle are arrayed the words, "Peace," "NonViolent Social Change," and "Brotherhood." The words, "Coretta Scott King Award," appear at the bottom of the circle. Lines fanning out from the book meet five main religious symbols; this symbolizes nonsectariansim. The circle represents continuity of movement from one idea to another. The pyramid represents Atlanta University, where the award was centered at the time the seal was designed, as well as representing strength. At the peak of the pyramid is a dove carrying an olive branch, which represents the peace that Dr. Martin Luther King Jr. taught. Two rays connect the dove with the words "Peace" and "Brotherhood" on the circle. The colors for winners and honor books seals have changed since the original design. Previously, the winner seal was bronze, and the honor book seal was pewter. Though these seals are still appropriate, the more recent colorations are bronze and black for winners and pewter and black for honor books.

In 1979, Mrs. King attended and spoke at the tenth-anniversary celebration of the CSK Award Breakfast at the ALA convention in

Dallas, Texas. In 1980, the group became affiliated with the Social Responsibilities Round Table of the ALA. In 1982, the CSK awards became officially affiliated with the American Library Association and have remained part of it ever since. In 1995, a new category was added to the awards—the New Talent Award recognizes the promising work of African American authors and artists who have fewer than three book publications.

The award does not distinguish between novels and picture books in its categories; however, artists of picture books frequently win the CSK Award for Illustration.

Further Reading: Smith, Henrietta, ed. *The Coretta Scott King Awards Book, from Vision to Reality*, Chicago: American Library Association, 1994; Smith, Henrietta, ed. *The Coretta Scott King Awards Book*, 1970–1999, Chicago: American Library Association, 1999.

See Also: Appendix F.

Cornrows (Coward, 1979). Written by Camille Yarbrough; illustrated by Carole Byard.

SUMMARY: Shirley Ann (nickname, Sister) and her little brother Mike (nickname, Brother) like to play outside until it is dark. Sister has nicknamed Brother as MeToo because everything she does, he wants to do, too. After dark when the children must come in, their Mama and Great-Grammaw like to tell stories. Some of the stories are about life in Alabama. One evening, Great-Grammaw fixes Mama's hair in cornrows. Sister explains these braids are called that because they look like the rows of corn that the old folks planted down south. Sister wants cornrows, too. So does, of course, MeToo.

As she braids, Great-Grammaw sings and tells the story of braids in Africa and other symbols of the inner spirit that manifested in fancy carved royal stools, sculptured ware, and ritual masquerade. The symbols were de-signed to give praise, and they helped people stay strong. People all over Africa from Senegal to Somali and from Egypt to Swaziland wore braids. People could tell a lot about others from the design woven into their braids—whether they were royalty, married, what gods they worshiped and what tribe or clan they were from and so forth. People wearing cornrows were put in chains and brought to America as slaves.

Now, as Great-Grammaw sings, she tells the children that they can name their cornrows after anything they want to give praise to a school, a teacher, poem, fish, proverb, star—anything at all. They can name them after important African Americans—such as Malcolm, Dr. King, Du Bois, Rosa Parks, Harriet Tubman, and others. Sister decides to name hers after Langston Hughes because she just learned one of his poems. MeToo names his after his hero, Batman. Sister thinks he is such a baby. Through the cornrows the children not only learn some of the history of their ancestors but also the history of their people in America.

MEDIA: Possibly charcoal.

ANECDOTE: In addition to her writing, Camille Yarbrough is an accomplished actress, composer, and singer. Carole Byard's artwork has appeared in both solo and group exhibitions.

DISTINCTION: 1980 Coretta Scott King Award for Illustration.

BIRTHDAY: Carole Byard: July 22, 1941.

SUBJECTS: African Americans—Fiction; Hair—Fiction.

See Also: Africa Dream.

The Creation (Holiday, 1994). Poem by James Weldon Johnson; illustrated by James E. Ransome.

SUMMARY: Paintings of a country preacher sitting underneath a tree and preaching to children sitting around him are interspersed with images from nature. The text is a poetic sermon adapted from the book of Genesis. After each thing created—light, sun, moon, and stars, the earth, land and water, animals, and man—God proclaims, in the accent of the southern preacher, "That's good!"

MEDIA: Possibly oil paintings.

ANECDOTE: Ransome's grandmother, who raised him, asked him to read to her from the Bible. The illustrations he saw of people in flowing robes, landscapes, and intricate architecture inspired him to try his hand at drawing. James Weldon Johnson's poetic sermons are collected in *God's Trombones: Seven Negro Sermons in Verse*.

DISTINCTION: 1995 Coretta Scott King Award for Illustration.

BIRTHDAY: James E. Ransome: September 25, 1961.

SUBJECTS: Creation—poetry; Children's poetry—American; American poetry—Afro-American authors; Bible stories—O.T.; Johnson, James Weldon, 1871–1934; Creation.

Crow Boy (Viking, 1955). Written and illustrated by Taro Yashima.

SUMMARY: Chibi, which means "tiny boy," is found underneath the schoolhouse on the first day of school in a Japanese village. No one in the village knows who he is. He does not talk or play with the others. He is given a desk and chair off by himself. Chibi is able to amuse himself by staring at the ceiling, a patch on a classmate's clothing, or the window. Each day he comes to school with the same lunch, a rice ball rolled in a leaf. Sometimes he wears strange clothing that does not look like the other children's clothes. Five years go by this way.

In sixth grade, a new teacher, Mr. Isobe, takes the children outside the school and into the fields. There, he and the class discover all of the things about nature that Chibi knows. Mr. Isobe hangs up Chibi's drawings and talks with him when no one else is around. At the talent show that year, the students are amazed when Chibi gets on the stage, and it is announced that for his talent, he is going to imitate crows. He mimicks crow calls in the morning, father crow calls, happy crow calls, and more. People in the audience begin to recognize where Chibi may have come from. At the end of his performance, he imitates crows in an old tree, making an even more distinctive sound.

The audience knows that Chibi comes a long way from home on the other side of the mountain for school each morning. Mr. Isobe explains that Chibi learned the crow calls from walking that long distance each day for six years. The others are ashamed at how they treated Chibi. They no longer called him Chibi but Crow Boy, and at graduation, Crow Boy is the only student to earn a perfect attendance award. As an adult in the village, Crow Boy seems to like his new name and his job selling charcoal that his family has made. Everyone is now friendly to him, and he makes the happy crow sound as he rounds the hills back to his family each evening with small purchases he makes in the village for them.

MEDIA: Pencil and brush separations.

ANECDOTE: Yashima was born in Japan and was given the name Jun Atsuchsi Iwamatsu. He spoke out against the Japanese government in the pre–World War II era and spent time in and out of jail in Japan because of it. He and his wife immigrated to the United States in 1939. His first children's book was *The Village Tree* (1953), which was published at a time of post-war elevated interest in Japan in the United States.

DISTINCTION: 1956 Caldecott Honor Book.

BIRTHDAY: Taro Yashima: September 21, 1908.

SUBJECT: Folklore—Japan.

Curious George (Houghton Mifflin, 1941). Written and illustrated by H. (Hans). A. (Augusto) Rey.

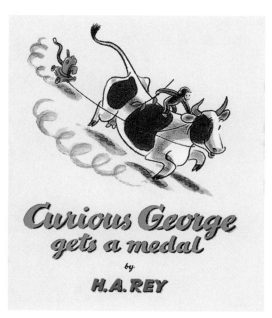

Cover of *Curious George Gets a Medal*, written and illustrated by H. A. Rey. *Curious George*, and its sequels, are still popular with children sixty years after its first publication. However, the stories featuring a monkey captured in the wild and brought to live in the city have lost favor among some contemporary wildlife enthusiasts. (Copyright © 1941 by H. A. Rey. Copyright © by Houghton Mifflin Company. All rights reserved.)

SUMMARY: George is a monkey that lives in Africa. His curiosity gets the best of him at times. When he sees a man with a yellow hat, George becomes curious about the hat and tries to put it on his head. He ends up being caught by the man. The man with the yellow hat takes him back with him to the city, where he says he will take him to live in the zoo. On the boat, George sees some seagulls and tries to fly as they do. He falls overboard. The sailors rescue him. In the city, George tries to use the telephone as the man does. He ends up calling the fire department and is taken to prison. George escapes. Then he sees a man selling balloons, and he wants one, too. He winds up with the whole bunch. Holding on, George rides into the sky with the balloons, looking down at, and enjoying, the city below. He lands on top of a traffic light. All the people in the cars are so surprised to see him that commotion in the intersection ensues. The man with the big yellow hat is there and rescues George. He pays the balloon man for all of the balloons. They get in a car and arrive at the zoo, where George gives balloons to all the other animals and seems happy.

MEDIA: Undetermined.

ANECDOTE: There are several sequels to *Curious George*, including *Curious George Takes a Job* (1947); *Curious George Rides a Bike* (1952); *Curious George Gets a Medal* (1957); *Curious George Learns the Alphabet* (1963); and *Curious George Goes to the Hospital* (1966). The *Curious George* books are translated into at least a dozen languages, including Japanese, Afrikaans, and Hebrew.

DISTINCTIONS: *New York Times* Best Book for Children; NYPL 100 Picture Books Everyone Should Know; *100 Best Books for Children*.

BIRTHDAY: H. A. Rey: September 16, 1898.

SUBJECT: Monkeys—Fiction.

D

Dash and Dart (Viking, 1942). Written and illustrated by Mary and Conrad Buff.

SUMMARY: Twin fawns, Dash, a male, and Dart, a female, lay in the forest ferns and the meadow grasses and learn to eat, stand, leap, and with the help of their mother, Doe, they grow through the seasons of the year. They have an adventure with bear cubs and play games with squirrels over who will get the acorns that fall from the tree. Mini "chapters" of lyrical prose include "Two Fawns," "Twin Sister," "Mother Doe," "Dash Stands Up," "Learning Things," "Sounds," "Bears," "September," "Hunger," "Dash and Dart Grow Up," "Who Gets the Acorn?," "Winter," and "Spring." By spring, Dash is worried that he has not yet grown any antlers but later discovers them by looking at himself in the water. He knows one day he will be King of the Forest.

MEDIA: Possibly lithographs.

ANECDOTE: Conrad did the pictures and Mary did most of the writing on the couple's many books for children. Known for simplicity in their portrayals of nature, they were runners-up three times for the *Newbery Award*—for *Big Tree* (1946) a story about "Wa Wo Na," a sequoia tree; *The Apple and the Arrow* (1951), a story about William Tell; and *Magic Maize* (1953).

DISTINCTION: 1943 Caldecott Honor Book.

BIRTHDAYS: Conrad Buff: January 15, 1886; Mary Marsh Buff: April 10, 1890.

SUBJECT: Deer—Fiction.

The Day We Saw the Sun Come Up (Scribner, 1961). Written by Alice E. Goudey; illustrated by Adrienne Adams.

SUMMARY: A boy and his sister Sue get up early one morning and watch the sun come up. They are fascinated with it all day, watching its path across the sky and the changes in their shadows and the shadow of their cat, Christopher. They discover that sunlight cannot travel through them and it cannot travel through clouds. At the end of the day, their mother explains the earth's rotation relative to the sun, and the children experiment with an apple, two pins to represent them, and a flashlight to represent the sun.

MEDIA: Graphite and gray wash with white gouache separations.

ANECDOTE: The book contains an author's note at the front that instructs children about the sun as a star.

DISTINCTION: 1962 Caldecott Honor Book.

BIRTHDAY: Adrienne Adams: February 8, 1906.

SUBJECT: Sun—Fiction.

See Also: Houses from the Sea.

de Grummond Children's Literature Collection. Located at the McCain Library and Archives of the University of Southern Mississippi, the de Grummond Collection is made up of research materials concerning British and American children's literature. There are original manuscripts and artwork for over 1,200 authors and artists; over 80,000 books dating from 1530 to the present; and more than 250 periodical titles. The collection is used for research in children's literature but also in other fields such as history and American studies.

Lena Young de Grummond taught children's literature at the School for Library Science at the university during the 1960s. While she was there, she believed that her students would benefit from seeing artifacts of the creative process in the making of children's books in the form of original manuscripts and artwork rather than restrict their exposure to textbooks and the finished product. De Grummond began writing to children's book authors and artists to see whether they would be willing to send her samples of their raw materials. The first to respond were Bertha and Elmer Hader, who sent her dummy books and other materials for their book *Ding, Dong, Bell* (1957). De Grummond kept writing letters, and soon she had obtained work from Lois Lenski, Elizabeth Coatsworth, and Roger Duvoisin. Decades later in the early twenty-first century the collection ranks as one of the most prestigious and valuable in children's literature in the world with over 4,000 cubic feet of original material housed in over 5,500 containers.

Highlights for those interested in picture books include the major repository of the work of Ezra Jack Keats; an extensive collection of British illustrator Kate Greenaway's original artwork; artwork by Randolph Caldecott; two Caldecott Medals (Slobodkin's 1943 and Keats's 1963); an early printed edition of Aesop's fables; and eighteenth-century editions of *Orbis Pictus*.

Contact: de Grummond Children's Literature Collection, Box 5148, Hattiesburg, MS 39406; (601) 266-4349; Web site: http://www.lib.usm.edu/~degrum/.

The Desert Is Theirs (Scribner, 1975). Written by Byrd Baylor; illustrated by Peter Parnall.

SUMMARY: The desert seems such a dry, plain place, but the poetic text of this book shows its multidimensions and its appeal for animals, plants, and the Desert People, the Papago Indians. The book tells the creation story of the Papago, where Earthmaker patted dirt into mud in his hands, and a greasewood bush grew there. Coyote helped spread seeds, and Spider People sewed the earth and sky together with no hills in between. Elder Brother instructed the people how to live on the desert and how to ask for rain.

The Desert People share the land with the desert plants such as the saguaro cactus, mesquite, yucca, grass, corn, and squash, and they enjoy the cactus blooms and berries. Wildlife sharing the land include the coyote, buzzard, gopher, badger, hawk, snake, fox, horned toad, spider, ant, deer, and pack rats. The people, plants, and wildlife all share in the desert and enjoy its quiet mysteries and the gift of a rare rainfall.

MEDIA: Possibly pen and ink.

ANECDOTE: Byrd Baylor spent much time outside in her childhood. Once, she was allowed to study under a mesquite tree during school. She is the author of four Caldecott Honor books.

DISTINCTION: 1976 Caldecott Honor Book.

BIRTHDAYS: Byrd Baylor: March 28, 1924; Peter Parnall: May 23, 1936.

SUBJECTS: Desert Ecology; Deserts; Ecology.

See Also: Hawk, I'm Your Brother; *The Way to Start a Day*; *When Clay Sings*.

Dick Whittington and His Cat (Scribner, 1950). Written and illustrated by Marcia Brown.

SUMMARY: Dick Whittington is an orphan boy living in England. He is too young to work, so he travels about the countryside in pretty ragged condition. One day a wagoner asks him to hop aboard, and he takes him to London. Dick has heard that the streets of London are paved in gold; he wants to get some for himself. When he gets there, all he sees are muddy roads. He is even more lonely and destitute in London than he was in the country. A kind man hires him to help with his hay for a few days, but soon the boy is on the streets and hungry again. He collapses at the property of a rich merchant named Mr. Fitzwarren. The kind merchant has the grumpy cook feed him and give him a job in the kitchen. Unfortunately, he sleeps in the garret with the mice and rats. One day, a man gives Dick a penny for shining his shoes. Dick tries to buy a cat with the penny, but the girl gives him one instead. Miss Puss eats scraps Dick brings her from the kitchen and takes care of the mice problem in the garret, so Dick can sleep.

One day, Mr. Fitzwarren asks all his servants to give him something to offer in trade on the ship he has ready to sail. Dick owns nothing but Miss Puss. Miss Alice feels sorry for Dick and gives him money to buy another cat, but he still misses Puss. Finally the cook mistreats him so poorly that Dick runs away on All-Hallows Day. Sitting and listening to the Bells of Bow, Dick seems to hear them call him the lord mayor of London. Dick goes back to the cook, thinking he should take his beatings if it is his job to one day become the mayor.

In the meantime, the ship has landed off the Barbary coast, and trade has begun with the Moors. The king's court is filled with good food of every kind, but it is also filled with rats and mice. The captain remembers Puss and trades her to the king for many riches. He is glad to have a means to get rid of the vermin in his palace. Not only did Miss Puss take care of that, but she was warm and soft in the queen's lap and allowed herself to be petted. The king was so pleased that he purchased the entire ship's cargo and paid ten times the value of the cargo for the cat alone. When the ship returns, Dick receives the money and can afford to clean himself up, buy a house, and good clothes. He becomes a gentleman and marries Miss Alice. The mayor of London attends the wedding, and Dick gets a job as sheriff. Later, he has three terms as mayor of London, where he meets King Henry V and his queen, and they become mutual admirers.

MEDIA: Cut linoleum.

ANECDOTE: This folktale is well known in England.

DISTINCTION: 1951 Caldecott Honor Book.

BIRTHDAY: Marcia Brown: July 13, 1918.

SUBJECTS: Whittington, Richard, d. 1423—Legends; Folklore—Great Britain.

See Also: Cinderella, or The Little Glass Slipper; *Henry Fisherman*; *Puss in Boots*; *Shadow*; *Skipper John's Cook*; *Stone Soup*.

Did You Hear Wind Sing Your Name? An Oneida Song of Spring (Walker, 1995). Written by Sandra De Coteau Orie; illustrated by Christopher Canyon.

SUMMARY: Through a series of fourteen questions, the text asks readers if they have observed with all their senses a full day of the small natural details of spring. Details include such things as the tracks of a turtle, the sweet smell of a cedar tree, the taste of the rain, the blue of the sky reflected in violets, and the song of one's name in the wind.

MEDIA: Undetermined.

ANECDOTE: The Oneida live on lands in

what is now called the states of New York and Wisconsin. Sandra De Coteau Orie is an Oneida author. The illustrations of beads in the opening pages pay tribute to Oneida beadwork, a frequent means of self-expression.

DISTINCTION: Native American Indian-commended.

BIRTHDAY: Not available.

SUBJECTS: Spring—Fiction; Nature—Fiction; Oneida Indians—Fiction; Indians of North America—Fiction.

Dillon, Diane and Leo (1933– ; 1933–). Authors/Artists. As a husband-and-wife artistic duo, the Dillons are the only artists to date to win two consecutive Caldecott Medals. They have also won two Coretta Scott King Awards for Illustration, among many other honors. Their lives have seemed to intertwine almost from the beginning, long before their names began appearing together on the covers of children's books and in entries in references about children's literature. Their childhoods were quite different, but it was art that brought them together.

Leo Dillon was born on March 2, 1933, in Brooklyn, New York. His father owned a trucking company, and Leo and his sister grew up in Brooklyn. Leo was a loner who liked to draw as a means of dealing with his emotions, including his frustration over racial discrimination. Though he was talented in art and worked for, and was mentored by, poet and painter Ralph Volman of the Marcus Garvey political movement, it was expected that he would go into either law or medicine. However, Leo's life did not go that way. He joined the marines and served in the Korean War. After his service, he worked at his father's business for a time, then enrolled in the Parsons School of Design. Working quietly on his artwork at a table in a studio there, he began to notice the artwork of a fellow classmate, Diane Sorber.

Diane Sorber, it turned out, was born eleven days after Leo on March 13, 1933, but on the other side of the United States, in Glendale, California. Her father was a teacher, and she grew up with her brother living in thirteen different places, locations such as Van Nuys, North Hollywood, and Morristown, New Jersey. Her artwork became one of the only consistencies in her life. Even though her father was an educator, and he gave her some tips on techniques like shadowing from his knowledge of drafting, Diane's career aspirations were not taken seriously because her family believed she would grow up to become a housewife. She admired the work of modern artists such as fashion illustrator Dorothy Hood. She had to work to attend college classes at Los Angeles College in California and one semester at Skidmore College before she arrived at Parsons.

The two art students thought very highly of each other's art, even to the point of competing with one another. By graduation their mutual admiration had turned to a personal relationship as well. After a brief breakup, they came back together and married in 1957 and embarked on a career together as commercial artists. They marketed themselves under the name Studio 2, which made them sound like they were representatives of a larger company of artists. The two in their company name, however, was quite literally just Leo and Diane. At first, they worked independently, and the competition they endured in art school continued. At one art show where both of their work was exhibited, they suffered through several hours of wondering who would sell more art by the end of the night. As it turned out, both of their exhibitions totally sold out. It was then that they realized they might succeed best as a team working on individual pieces of art together.

Their first picture book for children was *The Ring and the Prairie: A Shawnee Legend* written by John Bierhorst (Dial, 1970). In 1976, they won their first Caldecott Medal for illustrating Verna Aardema's *Why Mosqui-*

toes Buzz in People's Ears (Dial, 1975). For that book, they used vellum cut-outs, frisket masks, and watercolors applied by airbrush. In an unprecedented feat, they won the Caldecott Medal again the next year for Margaret Musgrove's *Ashanti to Zulu: African Traditions*, where they used pastels, watercolors, and acrylics. The Dillons work as true collaborators on their art. They say that even they can no longer tell when they look at a finished piece of art where the work of one of them leaves off and the other begins. It is almost as though a third artist emerges from the application of both of their talents.

After a five-year hiatus, the Dillons returned to children's books when they illustrated Mildred Pitts Walter's *Brother to the Wind* (Lothrop, 1985). The couple has one son, Lee, who is also an artist. Lee has collaborated with his parents. For Leotyne Price's retelling of *Aïda* (1990), for example, Lee worked on the frame borders for which he was inspired by the art of sixteenth-century Dutch artist Hieronymus Bosch. Other works from the couple in both picture books and other books for young people include *The People Could Fly* by Virginia Hamilton (1985); *The Girl Who Spun Gold* by Virginia Hamilton (Blue Sky, 2000); *The Sorcerer's Apprentice* by Nancy Willard (Blue Sky, 1993); and *To Every Thing There Is a Season: Verses from Ecclesiastes* (Scholastic, 1998).

The couple is known for the diversity of their artwork. They have worked in watercolor, pastel, acrylic, and frisket as well as other media such as crewel, plastic, and leading made of liquid steel. While the media and style may change from book to book according to the subject matter, the Dillons' work is regarded in all cases as being of stellar quality. Some projects have required extensive research about the locations that are being represented such as Nigeria in Africa; other illustrations contain whimsical elements.

In addition to illustrating children's books, the Dillons have created art for album cov-ers, advertisements, movie posters, paperback book covers, and magazines. They have been remodeling a brownstone in Brooklyn for over forty years. Leo and Diane and their son Lee all have studios there. Though they must pass the art being worked on back and forth, Leo and Diane now work on different floors because they can listen to their own favorite music without bothering each other. Their work continues its high quality and symbiotic nature, much to the benefit of children and those who share books with them.

DISTINCTIONS: 1976 Caldecott Medal; 1977 Caldecott Medal; Coretta Scott King Award for Illustration, 1991 and 1996.

Further Reading: Dillon, Leo, and Diane Dillon. "The Art of Illustrating Picture Books." *Washington Post Book World* (February 18, 1988): 4.

See Also: Ashanti to Zulu: African Traditions; *Why Mosquitoes Buzz in People's Ears*.

Dinobase. Artist's medium. Out of date, this was a method of sandblasting acetate to make it rough like lithographic stone.

The Dinosaurs of Waterhouse Hawkins
(Scholastic, 2001). Written by Barbara Kerley; illustrated by Brian Selznick.

SUMMARY: The book chronicles the true tale of a modelmaker, Benjamin Waterhouse Hawkins, who, in 1853, unveiled his models of dinosaurs in London. His models become part of the Queen Victoria and Prince Albert's new art and science museum, the Crystal Palace. Hawkins worked with scientist Richard Owen to fill in the blanks left by dinosaur fossils to re-create full-size models. The process from research to drawing to a small clay model, a life-size clay model, iron skeleton, mold, and finally the full-size completed model is described.

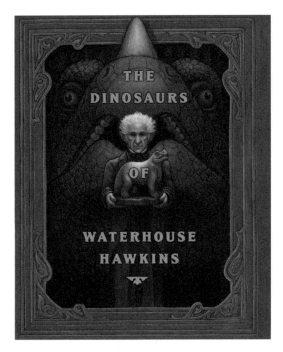

Front cover of *The Dinosaurs of Waterhouse Hawkins*, written by Barbara Kerley, illustrated by Brian Selznick. This story of the British dinosaur model maker is illustrated in acrylics; Zelnick received a Caldecott Honor in 2002. (Illustration by Brian Selznick from *The Dinosaurs of Waterhouse Hawkins* by Barbara Kerley. Published by Scholastic Press/Scholastic Inc. Jacket illustration copyright © 2001 by Brian Selznick. Reprinted by permission.)

Waterhouse had the approval of the queen, but he planned a special event to host the leading scientists of the day to review his work. He held their dinner in the iguanodon model. The leading paleontologists of the day attended and were delighted with what they saw. Hawkins was invited to America to build dinosaur models there. He built a Hadrosaurus for the Academy of Natural Sciences in Philadelphia and gave lectures around the country about dinosaurs. He was supposed to build a structure similar to the Crystal Palace at Central Park, but the project was stopped by William "Boss" Tweed, a corrupt politician who controlled much of the city. Tweed thought the project was a waste of money. While Hawkings continued

his work, vandals broke into his workshop and smashed his models. They even buried some of the chunks in the park. Hawkins accused Tweed of masterminding the misdeeds, but he was asked to forget about his project and move on.

Hawkins took his work to Princeton Univesrity and the Smithsonian Institution in Washington, D.C. Despite Tweed's setback that cost Hawkins two years of his life and work, he still provided these institutions with models and paintings of American dinosaurs. He was the first modelmaker to do this. At seventy-one, he went home to England and lived at Fossil Villa, his home near the Crystal Palace. There, his dinosaur models remain in the park. Somewhere under Central Park are remains of other Hawkins models.

MEDIA: Acrylics.

ANECDOTE: The artist had access to Hawkins' original drawings for his research on this book. On the last day of studying the dinosaur models at Crystal Palace Park in London, Selznick was bitten by a goose. He drew the goose into the book on the second to the last page.

DISTINCTION: 2002 Caldecott Honor Book.

BIRTHDAY: Not available.

SUBJECTS: Hawkins, B. Waterhouse (Benjamin Waterhouse), 1807–1889; Dinosaurs—Models—History—Nineteenth Century; Modelmakers—Great Britain—Biography; Modelmakers; Dinosaurs.

Distinctions. American children's picture books regularly receive awards and other distinctions from nonprofit organizations representing librarians, educators, and other children's literature professionals; from review journals and other periodicals and organizations; and from states and other municipalities to recognize works of merit in both writing and art in the picture book form. These distinctions are one way to help differentiate quality picture books from the thousands that are published each year in the United States. Distinctions are a coveted treasure in the world of picture book publishing—they help draw attention to a book, spur its sales to libraries, schools, and the general public, lengthen print life, and most importantly bring readers to titles who may have not otherwise heard of them among a sea of other possibilities.

The most widely recognized and influential distinction for American children's picture books today is the Randolph Caldecott Medal, awarded annually since 1938 by the American Library Association (ALSC division) for distinguished illustration in a picture book published the previous year. In addition to the one Medalist each year, a few Honor Books may be also designated. Before the onset of the Caldecott Medals, the John Newbery Medal was occasionally awarded to picture books. Most Newbery Medalists and Honor Books, however, are novels. Other distinctions for artwork in American children's picture books include the Coretta Scott King Awards. These prizes, given annually by the Coretta Scott King Foundation in cooperation with the ALA and the Social Responsibilities Round Table since 1970, are awarded for several categories, but in the picture book area they are awarded to an outstanding picture book illustrated by an African American in the previous year. There can be honor books awarded in this category as well. The Pura Belpré Award honors the same achievement by a Latino/a American artist every two years. The ALA also generates its annual lists of Notable Books, which include several picture book titles.

Besides the American Library Association, several American universities have also joined the ranks of those bestowing awards on children's books, including the picture book genre. The only award given specifically for outstanding text in any American picture book published the previous year, for example, is the Charlotte Zolotow Book Award

given by the Cooperative Children's Book Center (CCBC) of the University of Wisconsin-Madison School of Education. The CCBC also publishes an annual annotated bibliography, *Choices*, which contains dozens of children's and young adult books published the previous year that are recommended by the CCBC staff. The Lee Bennett Hopkins Poetry award occasionally recognizes picture books in its dedication to honoring the best books of poetry written for children in the review period. It is administered by the Pennsylvania Center for the Book at Penn State University. Picture books for children have also received the prestigious National Book Award (also American Book Award).

Review journals and other periodicals are also influential through the awards they bestow or through the notable lists they generate about American children's picture books. The *Horn Book Magazine* and the *Horn Book Guide* are arguably among the most prestigious of these review journals and join with their sister publication the *Boston Globe* to bestow the *Boston Globe-Horn Book Award*. Likewise, the *New York Times* picks its best picture books of the previous year to complement its weekly best-seller lists. Starred reviews in the widely subscribed and authoritative *School Library Journal* almost always initiate a heightened interest in a picture book by librarians who serve that important reading audience.

To honor authors and artists in their state, many schools and other organizations grant state or regional awards to picture books for children. These are often, but not always, limited to authors and artists from that geographical area. Some of these state and regional distinctions include Texas Bluebonnet Awards; South Carolina Children's Book Awards; the Dorothy Canfield Book Award (Vermont); Knickerbocker Award for Juvenile Literature (New York); Massachusetts Children's Book Award; William Allen White Book

Award (Kansas); Young Hoosier Book Award (Indiana); Rebecca Caudill Young Readers' Book Award (Illinois); and the Georgia Children's Book Award, among many others.

In a time when the sea of information has grown exponentially, getting any one book noticed can be sometimes difficult. As the number of distinctions rises into the dozens for American picture books for children, readers may wonder which distinctions to follow as the best guidelines for purchasing or recommending books for young people. Often books fall on more than one list, and that is a good sign of a quality book viewed from differing perspectives. However, other books slip unnoticed beneath the radar of even devoted, widely read committees looking for the best, so it is still up to the individual reader in the end to read well and widely and make his or her own choices for the family, classroom, or library. The best distinction any picture book can receive is being a favorite that is read (or read to) over and over by an individual child or one that is shared as an old favorite by a parent or grandparent with a special young person in the family.

See Also: Caldecott Medal; Charlotte Zolotow Book Award; Coretta Scott King Book Awards; Pura Belpré Award.

Doctor De Soto (Farrar, Straus and Giroux, 1982). Written and illustrated by William Steig.

SUMMARY: Doctor De Soto is a popular mouse dentist with animals of all sizes. He stands on a ladder for larger animals; for very large animals, he has a special room where he is hoisted up on a pulley pulled by his assistant, his wife. He wears galoshes to keep his feet dry in patients' mouths, and his drill is so tiny, his patients don't feel a thing. Naturally, Doctor De Soto will not treat cats or other animals that are harmful to mice like him. It says this on his sign.

One day a fox in great pain comes to see

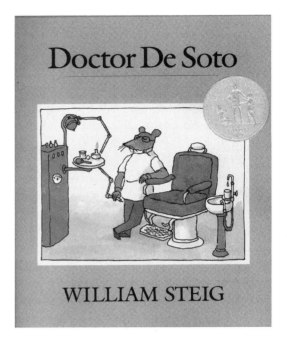

Front cover of *Doctor De Soto*, written and illustrated by William Steig. The story about a mouse dentist has the distinction of earning a Caldecott Honor award for Steig in 1983 as well as the National Book Award the same year. (Reprinted by permission of Farrar, Straus and Giroux, LLC: *Doctor de Soto* by William Steig. Copyright © 1982 by William Steig. www.fsgkidsbooks.com.)

Doctor De Soto. The Doctor tells him he does not see animals that are dangerous to mice; didn't the fox see the sign? When he sees how much pain the fox is in, however, he lets him in. Doctor De Soto bravely goes into the fox's mouth to pull the bad tooth. The fox is so preoccupied with his toothache that he barely notices how tasty the dentist mouse is in his mouth. However, the De Sotos worry all night about the fox returning the next day for the conclusion of his treatment. When he does arrive, the fox has clearly decided to eat the mice when they are done treating his teeth. Instead, Doctor De Soto applies an adhesive coating to the teeth that makes the fox's mouth stay glued shut for a few days. The De Sotos are saved from harm, and the fox must go on his way with better teeth but no mice for dinner. Pleased with this outcome, the De Sotos decide to take the rest of the day off.

MEDIA: Possibly ink, watercolor, and colored pencil.

ANECDOTE: William Steig was a well-known cartoonist for *The New Yorker* before he began a second career later in life in children's books.

DISTINCTIONS: 1983 Newbery Honor Book; 1983 National Book Award.

BIRTHDAY: William Steig: November 14, 1907.

SUBJECTS: Animals—Fiction; Dentists—Fiction; Mice—Fiction.

See Also: The Amazing Bone.

Don't Let the Pigeon Drive the Bus!

(Hyperion, 2003). Written and illustrated by Mo Willems.

SUMMARY: A bus driver parks his bus and asks the reader to keep an eye on things. In particular, he says to remember not to let the pigeon drive the bus. The crafty pigeon appears and tries every possible way to fool the reader into allowing him to drive—from outright asking, to begging and pleading, to rationalizing, to saying that his cousin Herb drives a bus almost every day. Self-pity and trying to fool the reader by playing a game of driving a bus are other tactics. The pigeon offers monetary bribes, promises to be the reader's best friend, coaxes that the reader's mom would let him drive, screams, and tries several other methods. Finally, the bus driver reappears and thanks the reader for not letting the pigeon drive the bus. As the bus drives off, the pigeon sees a truck and sets new sights on driving that.

MEDIA: Dark Stabillo pencil (8046), colored and composited in Photoshop.

ANECDOTE: Mo Willems has won six Emmys. There are several sequels to the book with the popular pigeon character, including *The Pigeon Finds a Hot Dog!*, *The Pigeon Loves Things That Go!*, and *The Pigeon Has Feelings Too!*.

DISTINCTION: 2004 Caldecott Honor.

BIRTHDAY: Not determined.

SUBJECTS: Pigeons—Fiction; Bus Drivers—Fiction.

See Also: Knuffle Bunny.

Dr. Seuss. *See* Geisel, Theodor (Ted) Seuss.

Drummer Hoff

(Prentice-Hall, 1967). Adapted by Barbara Emberley; illustrated by Ed Emberley.

SUMMARY: This rhyming text shows how a canon is loaded and fired. Characters include Drummer Hoff (who "fires it off"), Private Parriage, Corporal Farrell, Captain Bammer, Sergeant Chowder, Major Scott, and General Border. Each character plays a role in providing the carriage, barrel, rammer, powder, shot, and finally the order to fire the canon, which occurs at the end of the book—*kaboom!*

MEDIA: Woodcuts and ink.

ANECDOTE: Ed Emberley used just three colors—red, yellow, and blue—to illustrate this book. Any other color that appears is the result of a blend of these. The artist frequently uses a parade motif in his books such as the people here involved in firing the canon, or the animals in *One Wide River to Cross*. This technique is no doubt inspired from his two years' experience in an army parade unit on Governor's Island. He thought few people would be interested in *Drummer Hoff* and was surprised when the book became so popular.

DISTINCTION: 1968 Caldecott Medal.

BIRTHDAYS: Barbara Emberley: December 12, 1932; Ed Emberley: October 19, 1931.

SUBJECT: Folk songs.

See Also: One Wide River to Cross.

Duffy and the Devil: A Cornish Tale

(Farrar, Straus and Giroux, 1973). Retold by Harve Zemach; illustrated by Margot Zemach.

SUMMARY: Squire Lovel of Trove is not married, and Old Jone, his housekeeper, is losing her sharpness so she can no longer sew or knit. He goes out to Buryan Churchtown in search of aid for Jone. There he finds an unwanted, lazy girl getting kicked out of her house; her name is Duffy. He hires Duffy to do the fine work and brings her back to his house. Duffy claims that she can work only when she is alone and no one is watching, but secretly in the attic she does not know the first thing about the spinning wheel. She makes a deal with the devil. The devil will spin and knit stockings for Squire Lovel. He will do all of Duffy's work for her for three years. At the end of that time, the devil will take her away unless Duffy can tell him his name.

Duffy lives the easy life, and the devil's work is so fine that Squire Lovel marries her. Soon, the three years are almost up. Duffy worries and confesses to Jone about the deal with the devil. Jone turns out to be a witch who offers to help. She arranges for Lovel to fall down a so-called fuggy-hole to observe a witches' meeting and hear the devil's name when he comes to visit the meeting. Lovel tells Duffy the name when he describes his strange adventure to his wife. When she next confronts the devil, she says his name, and he disappears. Unfortunately, so does every article of clothing that he ever spun or knit, and Lovel ends up naked. Duffy proclaims that she will never knit again, and she never does.

MEDIA: Pen and ink drawings with watercolor.

ANECDOTE: Harve Zemach met his wife and collaborator, Margot, when he was studying at the University of Vienna on a Fulbright Scholarship. Harve's real name is Harvey Fishchtrom, but he changes it on books he does with his wife.

DISTINCTION: 1974 Caldecott Medal.

BIRTHDAYS: Harve Zemach: December 5, 1933; Margot Zemach: November 30, 1931.

SUBJECTS: Folklore—England; Folklore—Cornwall (England: County).

Duke Ellington: The Piano Prince and the Orchestra (Hyperion, 1998). Written by Andrea Davis Pinkney; illustrated by Brian Pinkney.

SUMMARY: Edward Kennedy Ellington was born in Washington, D.C., on April 29, 1899. He told his friends to call him Duke. His parents, Daisy and J. E. Ellington, signed him up for piano lessons when he was young, but he preferred baseball to the music he was learning to play. He gave up the piano. Many years later, Duke heard a new kind of music called ragtime. This caused him to pick up playing the piano again. By the time he was nineteen, he was playing professionally in cabarets and clubs. He was a fine dresser and a favorite with the ladies. Soon he left Washington, D.C., with his band, the Washingtonians, and went to New York City. There they played in Harlem clubs such as Barron's Exclusive, the Plantation, Ciro's, and the Kentucky Club. People liked their music, and they became popular. When they were asked to play at the Cotton Club, Duke's career took an even brighter turn. He and his band changed their name to Duke Ellington and His Orchestra; there were twelve of them now, and when they played, they were often heard over the radio.

People who could never go to the Cotton Club listened to Duke's music such as *Creole Love Call* and *Mood Indigo* on the radio. Often, Duke told his band to jam, playing anything they pleased in the middle of a song. Sonny Greer played drums; Joe "Tricky Sam" Nanton, played trombone; Otto "Toby" Hardwick jammed on his saxophone; and James "Bubber" Miley played trumpet. People at the Cotton Club liked to dance to the music, too. Some of their dances were called the black bottom, the fish-tail, and the Suzy-Q. They bought Duke's records as well.

Duke hired songwriter and musician Billy

Strayhorn in 1939. Together, they wrote songs such as *Take the "A" Train*, which became a big hit in 1941. As a tribute to his people, Duke composed *Black, Brown, and Beige*. The suite of songs debuted at New York's prestigious Carnegie Hall on January 23, 1943, and Duke was heralded as a serious composer of a new style of music. Ellington died on May 24, 1974, but his swing jazz music lives on.

MEDIA: Scratchboard renderings with gouache, luma dyes, and oil paint.

ANECDOTE: Brian Pinkney was inspired for this book by his love of jazz and playing the drums. He had also heard that Duke Ellington's music was a lot like painting.

DISTINCTIONS: 1999 Caldecott Honor Book; 1999 Coretta Scott King Honor Book for Illustration.

BIRTHDAYS: Andrea Davis Pinkney: September 25, 1963; Brian Pinkney: August 28, 1961.

SUBJECTS: Ellington, Duke, 1899–1974; Jazz musicians—United States—Biography; Musicians; African Americans—Biography.

Dye. Artist's medium. Liquid color ingredient that is absorbed by a surface and changes the color of that surface. Dye becomes part of the surface, not a medium applied on top of it.

E

The Egg Tree (Scribner, 1950). Written and illustrated by Katherine Milhous.

SUMMARY: Carl and Katy wake up Easter morning looking for the eggs the Easter Bunny was to leave. They see the Bunny and wake up their cousins—Susy, Luke, Johnny, and Appolonia. Grandmom smiles; it is time for the Easter Egg Hunt. Katy and Carl have less luck finding eggs than their cousins. Katy finally goes to the attic, where she finds a box-ful of beautiful eggs, more beautiful than the other Easter eggs. She takes them downstairs. Grandmom smiles; she has forgotten about those eggs. Carl wins the prize for finding the most eggs; Katy wins for finding the prettiest. As the children have treats, Grandmom tells them that she painted the beautiful eggs in that very kitchen when she was a young girl and put them away to keep forever. She now lets each of the children choose one for their very own. Carl chooses an egg with a horse on it; Katy chooses one with a bird sitting on a branch. They hang the eggs on an Easter Egg tree. The children ask their grandmother if she will teach them how to paint eggs. She does, and they decorate an even larger Easter Egg tree, one with hundreds of eggs on it that is so large that people come from all around to see it.

MEDIA: Tempera.

ANECDOTE: Inspiration for the book came from the Historical Society of Reading, Pennsylvania, which one year decorated a tree with 1,400 eggs and put it on exhibition. The year *The Egg Tree* was published, the author made fifteen egg trees that she sent to various libraries and bookstores. The author's mother sold her wedding ring to get enough money to send her daughter to art school.

DISTINCTION: 1951 Caldecott Medal.

BIRTHDAY: Katherine Milhous: November 27, 1894.

SUBJECTS: Easter eggs—Fiction; Easter—Fiction; Pennsylvania Dutch—Fiction.

Ella Sarah Gets Dressed (Harcourt, 2003). Written and illustrated by Margaret Chodos-Irvine.

SUMMARY: Ella Sarah gets up one morning and knows just what she wants to put on for the day—pants that are pink polka-dot, a dress with orange and green flowers on it, socks that are purple-and-blue-striped, yellow shoes, and a red hat. Her mother says this outfit is too dressy and suggests something else; her father says it is too fancy, and he suggests other clothes, too; her sister says it is too silly and recommends a hand-me-down outfit that she has outgrown. However, Ella Sarah puts on all the clothes she chooses any-

Ella Sarah Gets Dressed, written and illustrated by Margaret Chodos-Irvine, is illustrated with a variety of printmaking techniques on Reeves paper. It is a 2004 Caldecott Honor book. (Copyright © 2003 by Margaret Chodos-Irvine. Copyright © by Harcourt, Inc. All rights reserved.)

way. She thinks it looks nice. Then the doorbell rings, and she answers it. Standing there are her friends who are also obviously playing dress-up, and they think she looks just right, too.

MEDIA: Variety of printmaking techniques on Rives paper.

ANECDOTE: The book is dedicated to the creator's own Ella Sarah.

DISTINCTION: 2004 Caldecott Honor Book.

BIRTHDAY: Not available.

SUBJECTS: Clothing and dress—Fiction; Individuality—Fiction.

ellington was not a street (Simon and Schuster, 2004). Written by Ntozake Shange; illustrated by Kadir Nelson.

SUMMARY: The book is an autobiographical poem celebrating "men who changed the world" who visited Shange's upper middle-class home when she was a child. The visitors included: Paul Robeson, W.E.B. (William Edward Burghardt) Du Bois, Ray Barretto, Earlington Carl "Sonny Til" Tilghman, John Birks "Dizzy" Gillespie, Dr. Kwame Nkrumah, Edward Kennedy "Duke" Ellington, Virgil "Honey Bear" Atkins, and the vocal group the Clovers. As each of the visitors comes into the home, he is greeted by the warmth of Shange's father and the community that has gathered there before him. The men discuss politics, music, civil rights, and other subjects. They are from the city and the country and from Africa, and they eat together, play music and sing, and enjoy each other's company and the company of their wives. As the men gather, a little girl listens, falls asleep, and grows up among them.

The poem is a tribute to these men and the community they formed as well as to Shange's father and the stability, nobility, and memory of Shange's childhood home and upbringing. The book closes with biographical sketches of each of the men, as well as the poem reprinted all on one page. The poem itself is titled "Moon Indigo," after an Ellington song, and is reprinted from Shange's collection *A Daughter's Geography*.

MEDIA: Oils.

ANECDOTE: Shange changed her name from her birthname of Paulette Williams in 1971. Ntozake Shange (pronounced en-to-zaki shong-gay) means "she who comes with her own things" and "she who walks like a lion" in the Zulu language of Xhosa. She is a poet, novelist, and playwright well known for her work *for colored girls who have considered suicide/when the rainbow is enuf*. Nelson's work includes art for both film and television. He was conceptual artist for the Steven Spielberg film *Amistad*, as well as for the Oscar-nominated animated feature *Spirit: Stallion of the Cimarron*.

DISTINCTION: 2005 Coretta Scott King Award for Illustration.

BIRTHDAY: Ntozake Shange: October 18, 1948.

SUBJECTS: Afro-American civil rights workers—Poetry; Afro-American artists—Poetry; Afro-American girls—Poetry; Children's poetry, American; Afro-Americans—Poetry; American poetry.

Emily (Doubleday, 1992). Written by Michael Bedard; illustrated by Barbara Cooney.

SUMMARY: A family moves in across the street from the poet Emily Dickinson when a note slips through the mail slot in the door. The note is accompanied by pressed bluebells and is an invitation for Mother to come play piano for the reclusive woman known about town as "the Myth." It is winter, and she says that the playing would help remind her of spring. The little girl narrator overhears Mother and Father talking about the woman, and she asks to go with Mother when she plays. Father explains that the woman writes poetry, and he tries to explain what the mystery of poetry is to his little daughter. The girl decides to take with her some lily bulbs that they have brought with them to plant at the new house. She is a bit afraid to visit the mysterious woman but thinks that perhaps the woman may be a bit fearful herself.

As Mother plays in the Dickinson Homestead parlor to Emily listening somewhere out of sight, the little girl manages to sneak away to see Emily sitting at the top of the stairs. There, she gives her the lily bulbs. Pleased at the sight of her and at her gift, Emily writes her a poetic note to take home. With Father, the little girl plants the lily bulbs that are left and welcomes in the spring. She learns that nature, poetry, and people are all sometimes mysterious, but that is not necessarily a bad thing.

MEDIA: Oil paintings.

ANECDOTE: The Dickinson Homestead in Amherst, Massachusetts, long existing with its red brick exterior, was repainted the ochre color depicted in this book in the summer of 2004. The color is truer to the time when the poet lived there.

DISTINCTION: Author's choice.

BIRTHDAY: Barbara Cooney: August 6, 1917.

SUBJECTS: Emily Dickinson (1830–1886)—Fiction; Neighborliness.

See Also: Chanticleer and the Fox; *Miss Rumphius*; *Ox-Cart Man*.

The Emperor and the Kite (World, 1967). Written by Jane Yolen; illustrated by Ed Young.

SUMMARY: Djeow Seow means "the smallest one," and that is the name of the tiny princess in China who is the focus of this story. Her four older brothers and four older sisters are given all the attention, and they help their father rule the land. Djeow Seow never gets any attention and has no one to play with. She plays with her kite of paper and sticks, flying it every day. A monk sees her flying the kite and offers a prayer. Djeow Seow thanks him.

One day, a group of evil men come and kidnap her father, the emperor. They wall him up in a tower and then say that he is dead. The four older brothers and sisters are not there; they mourn and cannot bring themselves to do anything about it. Djeow Seow, so small and unnoticed in the corner, sees the men take her father and knows what is up.

She builds a small hut out of twigs. Every day she fills a basket with food and sails her kite to the top of the tower where her father can get it. She keeps him alive. One day the monk passes by and says a different prayer about the kite that gives the princess an idea. She makes a rope and sends it up to her father. When he flies out of the tower, his robes look like a kite. He returns to his empire and restores his rule and never again ignores his tiniest daughter. His other children return and are surprised to see the tiniest princess exalted. All she wanted was love. She rules well beside the emperor on a tiny throne and

The Eric Carle Museum of Picture Book Art, Amherst, Massachusetts. Founded by picture book creator Eric Carle and his wife Barbara, the museum opened in 2002 and is the first full-scale museum in the United States devoted to domestic and international picture book art. The museum features rotating exhibits of prominent picture book artists and hosts special events throughout the year that celebrate the art young children often first encounter. (The Eric Carle Museum of Picture Book Art, Amherst, Massachusetts, photograph by Paul Shoul.)

takes over the reign of his empire when he dies, reigning with loyalty and gentleness.

MEDIA: Paper cuts.

ANECDOTE: Jane Yolen has written more than two hundred books for children. *Newsweek* magazine has called her "America's Hans Christian Andersen."

DISTINCTION: 1968 Caldecott Honor Book.

BIRTHDAYS: Jane Yolen: February 11, 1939; Ed Young: November 28, 1931.

SUBJECTS: Folklore—China; Fathers and daughters—Folklore; Kites—Folklore.

See Also: Lon Po Po: A Red-Riding Hood Story from China; Owl Moon; Seven Blind Mice.

Engraving. Artist's medium. Cutting into a surface to make words or a design or picture.

Eric Carle Museum of Picture Book Art. Opened in November 2002, the Eric Carle Museum of Picture Book Art is the first museum in the United States to be dedicated solely to the presentation and appreciation of children's picture book art. It is located in Amherst, Massachusetts, near an apple orchard and adjacent to the Hampshire College campus. The museum features galleries of rotating exhibits of original artwork by both American and international picture book artists. One of the missions of the facility is to celebrate the art that viewers first encounter as children. By connecting and reconnecting museumgoers to the art they experienced in childhood, the museum creators hope to promote visual literacy in art of all kinds. Children learn to "read" pictures by developing skills in art appreciation and interpretation. The museum is accessible to young children and encourages their engagement with the art they recognize from books that have been read to them at home, in libraries, and in school.

In addition to exhibits, the museum hosts visiting artists, special performances, films, educational workshops, and other events for educators, students, and the public. In addition to two large galleries, the museum contains a picture book library, art studio, and theater. A research area, containing secondary material for use by scholars of the picture book art form, is under development.

Contact: 125 West Bay Road, Amherst, MA 01002. (413) 658-1100. Web-site: http://www. picturebookart.org.

See Also: Brown Bear, Brown Bear, What Do You See?; Carle, Eric; *The Very Hungry Caterpillar.*

F

F Pencil. Artist's medium. A graphite pencil of medium hardness.

Fables (Harper, 1980). Written and illustrated by Arnold Lobel.

SUMMARY: The book is a collection of twenty fables, each one page long with a spoken moral at the end. The fables are "The Crocodile in the Bedroom"; "The Ducks and the Fox"; "King Lion and the Beetle"; "The Lobster and the Crab"; "The Hen and the Apple Tree"; "The Baboon's Umbrella"; "The Frogs at the Rainbow's End"; "The Bear and the Crow"; "The Cat and His Visions"; "The Ostrich in Love"; "The Camel Dances"; "The Poor Old Dog"; "Madame Rhinoceros and Her Dress"; "The Bad Kangaroo"; "The Pig at the Candy Store"; "The Elephant and His Son"; "The Pelican and the Crane"; "The Young Rooster"; "The Hippopotamus at Dinner"; and "The Mouse at the Seashore." Morals to the tales include such advice as there is such a thing as too much order; changes in routine can be good; and small risks can add to life's excitement.

MEDIA: Gouache and pencil.

ANECDOTE: Arnold Lobel's editor, Charlotte Zolotow, suggested he illustrate some of Aesop's fables, but Lobel didn't like the violence presented in them. When an accident resulted in a broken ankle, forcing him to sit still for long periods, Lobel decided to write his own fables and wrote about one a day. They are the twenty new fables that make up this book.

DISTINCTION: 1981 Caldecott Medal.

BIRTHDAY: Arnold Lobel: May 22, 1933.

SUBJECTS: Fables—American; Children's stories, American; Animals—Fiction; Fables.

See Also: On Market Street.

The Faithful Friend (Simon and Schuster, 1995). Written by Robert D. San Souci; illustrated by Brian Pinkney.

SUMMARY: Monsieur Duforce, a sugar plantation owner on the island of Martinique in the Caribbean, lost his wife in childbirth. He hires a widow from the village of Le Vauclin to teach his son, Clement, and care for him. She is to bring her own new son, Hippolyte, to the plantation house with her and raise the boys together. When the boys grow to be handsome and intelligent young men, Clement shows Hippolyte a picture of Pauline, the niece of Monsieur Zabocat, who lives in Macouba. He tells him that he wants Hippolyte to come with him to ask her uncle for her hand in marriage the next day. Hippolyte warns his friend Clement that one cannot tell much about a person from just a picture and that possibly Pauline has a sharp tongue, but he cannot change his mind, and they set off. Hippolyte has also heard that Pauline's uncle may be a wizard.

On their way through lush tropical lands, they come upon a dead poor man. Hippolyte tells Clement that they must give the man a proper burial, so they do so. Finally, they reach the plantation and meet Pauline. She is even more beautiful than the picture and is also very pleasant. Monsieur Zabocat invites the young men to dinner, though he really wants Hippolyte to sit with the servants. When Clement proposes to Pauline, and she accepts, her uncle is furious. He wants to take her to France and choose a match for her there. Pauline refuses to go and says that while she is grateful for her uncle's help all these years, she must follow her heart. The uncle banishes all three young people, and they leave.

On their way back to Le Vauclin, they become sleepy and lie down in the forest. Hippolyte is unable to sleep, however, and keeps watch. Three women, who are actually zombies sent on a mission by Pauline's uncle, plot to destroy the couple by poisoned water in a brook. Hippolyte hears their plot and protects them from drinking water, though he does not tell them what he has seen. The three zombies plot again using a mango, and again that plot fails because of Hippolyte's watchfulness over the couple. The zombies plot that a serpent will bite the couple on their wedding night, and the person who tells them any of their plots will turn to stone. Clement's father is pleased with the coming marriage and invites people from all around. Hippolyte sneaks into the bridal chamber and waits. When the couple comes in, a *fer de lance* appears, the deadliest snake on the island. Hippolyte cuts it in half, and the pieces disappear.

Monsieur Zabocat accuses Hippolyte of being jealous of Clement. At first, Clement and the others do not believe it, but when Hippolyte does not defend himself, they become angry, and Clement orders him out of the house. Hippolyte begins to tell of the zombies and their plots. As he tells each plot, more of his body turns to stone. Finally, he is all stone when he explains about the serpent in the wedding chamber. Clement feels terrible about Hippolyte's sacrifice. He says he will do anything to bring his friend back to life.

An old man steps forward from the guests and tells him that if he is willing to trade places, he may bring his friend back to life. Clement agrees, and the old man turns Hippolyte back to life. However, instead of reaching for Clement to turn to stone, the old man turns Monsieur Zabocat to stone. He tells the party that he was the poor man the young men gave the Christian burial to on their way to Pauline's. Because Clement was willing to give up his life for his friend, he is able to break the curse and return it to its source. Both friends continue to live in happiness, now with Clement married to Pauline.

MEDIA: Scratchboard and oil.

ANECDOTE: The tale is adapted from a story recorded in Elsie Clews Parsons' *Folk-Lore of the Antilles, French and English*, published in 1943 by the American Folk-Lore Society.

DISTINCTION: 1996 Caldecott Honor Book.

BIRTHDAYS: Robert D. San Souci: October 10, 1946; Brian Pinkney: August 28, 1961.

SUBJECTS: Folklore—Caribbean Area; Folklore—Martinique.

See Also: The Talking Eggs.

Farfallina & Marcel (HarperCollins, 2002). Written and illustrated by Holly Keller.

SUMMARY: Farfallina is a caterpillar who eats a portion of a leaf that is providing shade for a gosling underneath it. In this way, Farfallina meets Marcel. The two become friends. They like to play hide-and-seek. Farfallina hides close to the ground because she knows Marcel cannot climb. Marcel hides close by, because he knows Farfallina moves very slowly. The caterpillar likes Marcel's eyes and soft feathers. Marcel likes Farfallina's colors and nice smile.

One day, Farfallina tells Marcel that she is feeling a bit strangely, and she must go up to the top of a tree. Marcel decides to wait for her. When Farfallina does not come back, Marcel keeps returning to the tree each day until he finally gives up. He sees himself in the reflection in the pond and sees that he has changed into a mature goose. He misses his friend. Farfallina one day becomes a butterfly. She has no idea how long she was up in the tree. When she flies down to find Marcel, she cannot find him. She sees a goose on the pond but does not recognize her friend. The two meet all over again and begin a new friendship until the butterfly tells the goose her name. The two friends are reunited and become lifelong friends. When autumn comes, they decide to go south together.

MEDIA: Watercolor.

ANECDOTE: Farfallina means butterfly in Italian. The story was inspired by a song about a farfallina Keller's friend learned in Italy.

DISTINCTION: 2002 Charlotte Zolotow Book Award.

BIRTHDAY: Not available.

SUBJECTS: Friendship—Fiction; Growth—Fiction; Caterpillars—Fiction; Geese—Fiction.

Feather Mountain (Houghton Mifflin, 1951). Written and illustrated by Elizabeth Olds.

SUMMARY: Long ago, birds had no feathers. It didn't matter how big or little they were, they still had little pink bodies without any feathers at all. The other animals laugh at the naked birds, but mostly the birds ignore them and keep on singing. Soon an owl talks them into finding some kind of covering. As the news spreads, the birds become self-conscious of their naked bodies and forget to sing. They want coverings that will help them seek food in the woods, fly, and swim. They turn to the old owl for advice. The owl tells them they should appeal to the Great Spirit for help.

The Great Spirit tells the birds that their coverings have been waiting on Feather Mountain all along for them to come pick up. The turkey buzzard agrees to go get them. The buzzard flies a long way to Feather Mountain, where he eventually finds trees of feathers. The feathers are beautiful and of every shape and kind. Turkey buzzard first decides on plumes for himself and takes the most beautiful. When he realizes that he cannot fly with feathery long plumes, he puts some back and takes more plain-colored feathers for his body. He flies back as many feathers as he can carry.

When the other birds see the beautiful feathers, they begin to quarrel about which bird gets which feathers. The turkey buzzard sets out to distribute and affix the feathers in an orderly fashion, each according to the birds' habitat and way of life. They use glue, pins, and pots of paint to give each bird just the right colors, including dying their beaks and feet. One page spread in the book shows many different kinds of birds and their names. The birds are satisfied now that they are warm and comfortable. Their young are born with feathers and coloring just like their parents. When the birds fly off together, they remind the turkey buzzard of the many colors of Feather Mountain.

MEDIA: Preseparated art and watercolor wash (4-color).

ANECDOTE: Dozens of different kinds of birds and their plumage are featured in the book.

DISTINCTION: 1952 Caldecott Honor Book.

BIRTHDAY: Not available.
SUBJECT: Birds—Fiction.

Finders Keepers (Harcourt, 1951). Written by William Lipkind (pseud. Will); illustrated by Nicolas Mordvinoff (pseud. Nicolas).

SUMMARY: Two dogs dig in the yard and find a bone. The dog with white on its tail is named Winkle. The dog with a spot on its head is Nap. Both dogs claim the bone. Nap says he saw it first; Winkle says he touched it first. They ask a passing farmer, Mr. Haymaker, whose bone it should be. The farmer asks the dogs to help him get his wagon out of a rut. After they do so, the farmer gives them some hay and says that nobody cares about a bone. This procedure continues through Mr. Tuftichin, the goat who cares more about horns and Mr. Hairtrimmer, who cares more about giving haircuts. Mr. Longshanks is a fancy dog who offers to take care of the bone while they decide. When he goes to make off with it, Nap grabs one end of the dog and Winkle the other until they loosen the bone from Mr. Longshanks' mouth. They decide to each nibble on the opposite end of the bone, and that solves the problem.

MEDIA: Acetate color separations for line reproduction.

ANECDOTE: Nicolas Mordvinoff did not like the initial proofs for *Finders Keepers* and started the illustrations all over again. Before he was awakened to be told he had won the Caldecott Medal, Mordvinoff was dreaming of being in a boxing ring with a prize-fighter. William Lipkind attended Columbia Law School. His education in negotiating settlements may have contributed to the plot of this story.

DISTINCTION: 1952 Caldecott Medal.

BIRTHDAYS: William Lipkind: December 17, 1904; Nicolas Mordvinoff: September 27, 1911.

SUBJECT: Dogs—Fiction.

See Also: The Two Reds.

Fish for Supper (Dial, 1976). Written and illustrated by M. B. (Marilyn Brooke) Goffstein.

SUMMARY: Grandmother gets up at 5 o'clock every morning and rows out on the lake to go fishing all day. She brings hooks, lines, bobbers, and sinkers. She brings fruit for lunch. Her catch includes perch, crappies, sunfish, and occasionally a big northern pike. In the evening, she cleans the fish, cooks it in butter, and bakes fresh rolls. Then she sits down to eat her supper slowly in order to watch out for fish bones. She does the dishes and goes to bed to prepare for another early morning of going fishing.

MEDIA: Ink drawings.

ANECDOTE: M. B. Goffstein's first book for children was *The Gats* (1966). Rather than do many sketches as she plans her books, Goffstein says that she does her thinking out ahead of time, then starts to draw.

DISTINCTION: 1977 Caldecott Honor Book.

BIRTHDAY: M. B. Goffstein: December 20, 1940.

SUBJECTS: Fishing—Fiction; Grandmothers—Fiction.

Fish in the Air (Viking, 1948). Written and illustrated by Kurt Wiese.

SUMMARY: There is a little boy named Fish who receives fish shoes for his birthday from his mother. His father buys him a fish-shaped lantern at the Lantern Festival. When it comes time to fly kites, Little Fish asks his father, Big Fish, to buy him the biggest kite shaped like a fish. They go to town and the street where kites are made, and father buys Little Fish the kite he wishes for. After they pass through the South Gate to the open fields where kites are flown, a big wind called a Tai Fung scoops up the kite and Little Fish up with it.

Up in the air go the fish kite and Little Fish. Little Fish lands first on the straw hat of a man who is carrying fish, then on the nose of a grouchy man writing letters. Next, the boy and his kite sail to the nose of one of the dragons guarding the South Gate. People in the fields look up and wonder at the two fishes they see in the air. At the river, a fisherman, Old Man Lo, has his net in the water. He is fishing the same way his father and all his ancestors did, by dropping a net and taking a nap while waiting for fish. He does not see Little Fish, who drops into the river after a Fish Hawk snatches the fish kite and rips it to shreds with its beak.

Little Fish comes up in Old Man Lo's net. Just as he is surprised, Big Fish, the boy's father, offers the fisherman a silver dollar if he will haul in this fish for him. He does, and Little Fish is saved; Big Fish has his son returned; and Old Man Lo has his money. After this excitement, Little Fish tells his father that now he wants the smallest fish kite there is.

MEDIA: Ink and watercolor.

ANECDOTE: Wiese was born and educated in Germany but spent six years in China; five in Australia; and four in Brazil before moving to the United States.

DISTINCTION: 1949 Caldecott Honor Book.

BIRTHDAY: Kurt Wiese: April 27, 1887.

SUBJECTS: Kites—Fiction; China—Fiction.

Five Little Monkeys (Houghton Mifflin, 1952). Written and illustrated by Juliet Kepes.

SUMMARY: Buzzo, Binki, Bulu, Bibi, and Bali are five mischievous monkeys that try to avoid Tiger the Terrible. When Lion is sleeping, they drop coconuts on his head. Elephant, Wart Hog, Water Buffalo, Zebra, Gnu, Peccary the wild pig, Hartebeest, Crocodile, Leopard, Quagga, Eland, Mouse Deer, and Nilghai all suffer under the boistrousness of the five little monkeys. They hatch a plan to stop them. They put bananas in a pit and lure the monkeys into it. Of all the animals, Peccary is the only one to feel sorry for them as a hunter approaches the pit. After they assure everyone they will mend their ways, Lion is convinced to lower a tree into the pit so the monkeys can escape.

For a while the monkeys behave themselves and are even nice to the other animals. However, they really turn the corner when they defend Piccary from Tiger the Terrible, who is about to eat him. All five monkeys grab hold of Terrible and hang him from a tree. Swinging him, they make him feel sick until he promises to leave them all alone and even announce to them when hunters are coming from the plain. Piccary, again sympathetic to another suffering animal, convinces the others to let Terrible go. The animals all cheer the five monkeys for the best good deed of all.

MEDIA: Preseparated ink and watercolor wash (4-color).

ANECDOTE: Kepes lived in Cambridge, Massachusetts, for fifty-three years. She carved five bronze birds in various stages of flight that were then embedded in a brick wall beside the Clarendon Avenue Park in that city. They are still visible. *Five Little Monkeys* was innovative in the early 1950s for its use of color on some pages (when color separation was still sometimes a tiresome procedure), quick brushwork that animated the monkeys, and overall book design.

DISTINCTION: 1953 Caldecott Honor Book.

BIRTHDAY: 1919.

SUBJECT: Monkeys—Fiction.

Fly High, Fly Low (Viking, 1957). Written and illustrated by Don Freeman.

SUMMARY: In San Francisco, a pigeon lives inside the letter B of the sign "Bay Hotel" at the top of a tall building. Pigeons nearby think this one must be fussy to want to live where he does, but a white dove thinks he must have a good reason. Each day, the white dove and the pigeon from the letter B fly together, hoping Mr. Hi Lee will come by and feed them some special crumbs in Union Square. Hi Lee names the birds Sid and Midge. Sid and Midge fly in and out of the Golden Gate Bridge and other famous San Francisco landmarks and soon begin making a nest in Sid's letter B. Midge lays two eggs. One day while Sid is away, the letter B shakes, and Midge thinks it is an earthquake, but instead some workmen are taking down the sign. They spot Midge's nest in the B and say they will not throw it away, but they take it away anyway and Midge, her nest, and the eggs with it.

When Sid returns, he begins searching for the missing B and his family. Fog rolls in, making the search even more difficult. Sid hides in front of a green traffic light, making traffic bottle up with confused drivers; he hides underneath the bell of a cable-car in the rain, then jumps when the bell rings and startles him. He starts to blame people for his problems, when he remembers the nice people in the park. He decides to go to Union Square, but he has to walk, since he is too weak to fly. Mr. Hi Lee picks him up and puts him in his warm pocket. He says he will take him to a bakery for something to eat. At the bakery, they are putting up a new letter B in the sign, and there Sid finds his family. The little eggs hatch, and the family is happy. The old pigeon neighbors come to visit and have to admit that Sid knew what he was doing by building his home in the letter B.

MEDIA: Colored pencil accented by outlines in ink.

ANECDOTE: Don Freeman was born in San Diego.

DISTINCTION: 1958 Caldecott Honor Book.

BIRTHDAY: Don Freeman: August 11, 1908.

SUBJECT: Birds—Fiction.

See Also: Corduroy.

The Fool of the World and the Flying Ship: A Russian Tale (Farrar, Straus and Giroux 1968). Retold by Arthur Ransome and illustrated by Uri Shulevitz.

SUMMARY: An old peasant and his wife have three sons. Two of the sons are clever, but one son is the Fool of the World. The Czar announces that he will give his daughter, the Princess, in marriage to anyone who builds him a flying ship that can sail through the sky like a ship on water. The two clever sons set off to achieve this task. They are sent off with the best clothes and food their parents can provide. When the Fool wants to go, he is discouraged until he pleads so long that his mother finally gives in. She gives him dry black crusts and water rather than the white rolls and corn brandy she gave his brothers.

On his way, the Fool meets an ancient man and generously agrees to share his food with him, though he warns him that the food is not fit for guests. When he opens his bag, he finds that God has turned his rations into white rolls, meats, and the best corn brandy. The ancient man tells him that God takes care of the simple folk. After they eat, the ancient tells the Fool where to go in the forest and what to do. When the Fool does these things, a flying ship appears. The Fool sails away. On his journey, he meets several other simple people, or *moujiks*, peasants, whom he invites aboard the ship—Listener; Swift-goer, who hops about on one leg; Far-shooter, a man with a gun searching for birds too far away to shoot; Eater; Drinker; a man with a stack of sticks he said could turn into soldiers; and a man with straw. With this fully loaded flying ship, the group reaches the Czar's palace.

The Czar does not want his daughter to marry a peasant, so he gives the Fool several tests to pass. The first is to bring him magic water before he completes his meal. Listener, Swift-goer, and Far-shooter all help the Fool accomplish this task. Another is that all the people on the ship should eat twelve roasted oxen and enough bread that could be baked

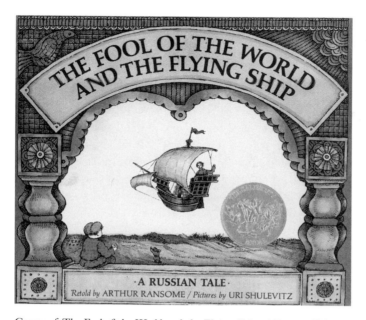

Cover of *The Fool of the World and the Flying Ship: A Russian Tale*, retold by Arthur Ransome, illustrated by Uri Shulevitz. During the Cold War, Shulevitz received the Caldecott Medal in 1969 for his work on this book. (Reprinted by permission of Farrar, Straus and Giroux, LLC: *The Fool of the World and the Flying Ship: A Russian Tale* retold by Arthur Ransome, pictures by Uri Shulevitz. Copyright © 1968, renewed 1996 by Uri Shulevitz. www.fsgkidsbooks.com.)

in forty ovens. Eater helps with this task. Then they are to drink forty barrels of wine with forty bucketfuls in every barrel. Drinker does this. Then the Czar wants the Fool to bathe in red-hot water to prepare for the wedding. The *moujik* with the straw puts straw in the water to make it cool.

Finally, the Czar tells the Fool that he must be able to defend the Princess. He must raise an army of soldiers. The Fool agrees to this last task but tells the Czar that if he is put off again, he will take the Princess by force with war on the Czar's country. The peasant with sticks helps him do this. The Czar is so afraid of the Fool's army that he offers him fine clothes and jewels and begs him to marry his daughter.

When the Fool is dressed in fine clothes, he is handsome to the Princess, who falls in love with him, and he with her. The Czar and Czaritza like him, too, and God has taken care of the simple people.

MEDIA: Pen and brush with black and colored inks.

ANECDOTE: The story was originally published in 1916 in Arthur Ransome's *Old Peter's Russian Tales*. Uri Shulevitz lived in Warsaw, Poland, as a very young child during World War II. Two of his memories from those years were a bomb killing about a third of the people waiting with him in a bread line and another bomb demolishing the stairs to his apartment.

DISTINCTION: 1969 Caldecott Medal.

BIRTHDAYS: Arthur Ransome: January 18, 1884; Uri Shulevitz: February 27, 1935.

SUBJECT: Folklore—Russia.

The Forest Pool (Longman, 1938). Written and illustrated by Laura Adams Armer.

SUMMARY: Somewhere in Mexico, Diego is sleepy and dreaming. He dreams of hummingbirds. Ruby-throat is about to tell him how many hummingbird feathers it took years ago to make a royal cloak for King Montezuma. His pet parrot, Polly, keeps repeating a refrain, saying that she has been here before; she has been here before. This wakes up Diego, who sees his friend, Popo, approaching.

Popo has found an iguana in the woods and wants to catch him for the boys' zoo. Diego picks a large orange from his mother's tree. On his way, he tells his mother about his dream, and she tells him that many years ago their people lived in Tzin-tzun-tzan, the city of the hummingbirds. They were keepers of the royal birds. She has had the same dream of them; all of their family has.

Diego and Popo go to catch the iguana. They find him in a tree above a pool. When Polly joined Diego's family, she had been given to them by a fisherman who had found her with a note attached to her claws. He could not read the note, so he gave Polly to Diego's father. The note said that the pearls were in the pool. Popo tells Diego that the iguana is very wise and old. Iguanas were on the earth before human beings. Popo says that the iguana knows the answers to all their questions; it just cannot talk. He thinks Polly and the iguana will like each other in the zoo.

The iguana takes the orange but then jumps down from the tree into the pool. Diego is disappointed and later asks his father to catch the iguana for him. He has caught many iguanas before. Father is making a silver bracelet for Mother when Diego finds him. He says that he is busy, but he does take time to catch the iguana. When he returns, the boys play with the iguana for awhile, but soon it slips off into the woods again. They are disappointed once more before Mother explains to Diego that the iguana must live in the woods where it will be happy, just as they are happy at their house. When Father emerges with the silver bracelet for Mother, he also has a string of pearls for her that he found at the tree where the iguana was. Polly had made a scratch in the tree where they were found, announcing that he had been there before.

MEDIA: Undetermined.

ANECDOTE: The Aztecs really did adorn Montezuma's ceremonial cloaks with the tiny, irridescent feathers of the hummingbird. No one alive now knows how many feathers it took to decorate the cloak—except perhaps wise, old iguana, who has never told.

DISTINCTION: 1939 Caldecott Honor Book.

BIRTHDAY: Laura Adams Armer: January 12, 1874.

SUBJECTS: Hummingbirds—Fiction; Iguanas—Fiction; Mexico—Fiction; Parrots—Fiction.

Four and Twenty Blackbirds: Nursery Rhymes of Yesterday Recalled for Children of Today (Lippincott, 1937). Collected by Helen Dean Fish; illustrated by Robert Lawson.

SUMMARY: The editor collects twenty-four lesser known and anthologized nursery rhymes. They include "Little Dame Crump," "Merry Green Fields of England," "The Old Gray Goose," "The Robber Kitten," "The Ragman," "Joe Dobson," "Poor Lady Dumpling," "Old Mother Tabbyskins," "The Hungry Fox," "Frog Went A-Courting," "The Keys of Heaven," "Dame Trot and Her Comical Cat," "The Old Crow," "Come Hither Little Puppy Dog," "Old Crummles," "Jim Finley's Pig," "We Are All Nodding," "The Tragic Tale of Hooty the Owl," "The Two Foxes," "The Little Red Hen," "Mr. Bourne and His Wife," "The Bumble-Bug," "Cluck, Cluck," and "Rufflecumtuffle."

In the back of the book is the music for the following: "Little Dame Crump," "Merry Green Fields of England," "The Old Gray

Goose," "Joe Dobson," "Old Mother Tab-byskins," "The Hungry Fox," "Frog Went A-Courting," "The Keys of Heaven," "The Old Crow," "Old Crummles," "We Are All Nod-ding," "Mr. Bourne and His Wife," and "Cluck, Cluck."

MEDIA: Drawings in pen and tempera.

ANECDOTE: Helen Dean Fish was inspired to collect these nursery rhymes in memory of her mother, who first shared many of them with her as a child. She also wished to rescue the rhymes from becoming lost, since they were less familiar.

DISTINCTION: 1938 Caldecott Honor Book.

BIRTHDAY: Robert Lawson: October 4, 1892.

SUBJECT: Nursery rhymes.

See Also: Animals of the Bible: A Picture Book.

4-Color Process. Printing process or artist's medium. Four colors: black, cyan, magenta, and yellow, are printed on four separate plates. When printed together, the colors on the plates combine to create the full picture. New colors using combinations of any of these four also emerge.

Fox Went Out on a Chilly Night: An Old Song (Doubleday, 1961). Written and illustrated by Peter Spier.

SUMMARY: The book illustrates the lyrics to the song, and the music and lyrics appear in the back. The fox goes to a farm one night and takes some geese off with him to the town. Mother Giggle-Gaggle, the farmer's wife, wakes up farmer John and tells him the fox has run off with their gray goose. John runs to town with his gun and blows his horn. Soon, the fox arrives at his warm den where there are his wife and ten little foxes. They cook the goose and cut it up, and the little ones chew on its bones.

MEDIA: Pen and ink and watercolor on blue boards.

ANECDOTE: Peter Spier's father owned a complete set of Caldecott picture books. As a child, Peter scribbled with a red crayon on every page of the books and received a spanking as a result. When Spier won the Caldecott Medal in 1978 for *Noah's Ark*, his father presented him with the scribbled set.

DISTINCTION: 1962 Caldecott Honor Book.

BIRTHDAY: Peter Spier: June 6, 1927.

SUBJECTS: Animals—Fiction; Songs.

See Also: Noah's Ark.

Frederick (Random House, 1967). Written and illustrated by Leo Lionni.

SUMMARY: In the mouse world, Frederick is the only one who does not appear to be doing anything. All through the spring, summer, and fall, the other mice are busy collecting food for winter by the wall where they live, but Frederick sits perfectly still, daydreaming and taking in the sunsets and other natural wonders around him. When winter comes, he tells stories and poems to the other mice who are hibernating for the season. It is then that the other mice realize and appreciate that Frederick had been hard at work all along, noticing and remembering details from the world and composing stories and poems with which to entertain them all through the long, dark winter.

MEDIA: Collage with mixed media.

ANECDOTE: Italian artist Leo Lionni was a graphics artist whose work appeared in such venues as *Fortune* Magazine. He began his collage career in picture books by telling his grandchildren stories on a long train ride, tearing pieces of paper from magazines.

DISTINCTION: 1968 Caldecott Honor Book.

BIRTHDAY: Leo Lionni: May 5, 1910.

SUBJECTS: Imagination—Fiction; Mice—Fiction; Poetry—Fiction; Poets—Fiction; Seasons—Fiction; Storytelling—Fiction; Winter—Fiction; Work—Fiction.

Free Fall (Lothrop, 1988). Written and illustrated by David Wiesner.

SUMMARY: This is a wordless picture book. A boy falls asleep in bed reading a book. A page tears out of the book and enters the boy's dreams, and he is transported to a castle in the Middle Ages. The boy, as well as knights, kings, queens, and other characters from the book, move in and out of the book and in and out of past and present time, seemingly following the missing page. Everyone is falling, and each building or other structure deconstructs into pages that fall and keep the boy falling afterward. The boy falls past a dragon, a chess board, a glass with spilled juice, a croissant, a bowl of cereal, spoon, and salt shaker. A falling leaf becomes a swan, and the boy glides on its back. The swans and leaves rush forth on water filled with cereal flakes and fish that splashes up to the boy's bed and returns him safely under the covers.

When he awakes, both the boy and the viewer see a goldfish bowl on the boy's nightstand with pigeons outside his window, and in his room a toy dragon, salt shaker, spoon, chess pieces, books, and plate with a croissant.

MEDIA: Watercolor.

ANECDOTE: Flying is a frequent motif in Wiesner's books.

DISTINCTION: 1989 Caldecott Honor Book.

BIRTHDAY: David Wiesner: February 5, 1956.

SUBJECTS: Dreams—Fiction; Stories without words.

Freight Train (Greenwillow, 1978). Written and illustrated by Donald Crews.

SUMMARY: A train with large colored cars runs across a track. Readers see the train from the back and move forward through the pages to the engine. There are a red caboose, an orange tank car, yellow hopper car, green cattle car, blue gondola car, purple box car, black tender, and black steam engine. The tender has the date 1978 on the side of it, and the engine the capital letters N&A. It is a freight train. The train moves through tunnels, by cities, across trestles, through darkness and daylight until it is gone.

MEDIA: Preseparated art; airbrush with transparent dyes.

ANECDOTE: Donald Crews' recollections of traveling to Florida from New Jersey to stay with his grandparents each summer vacation inspired this book.

DISTINCTION: 1979 Caldecott Honor Book.

BIRTHDAY: Donald Crews: August 30, 1938.

SUBJECTS: Color; Railroads—Trains.

Frisket Mask. Artist's medium. During airbrushing or painting, this thin paper covers areas where paint is not desired.

Frog and Toad Are Friends (Harper, 1970). Written and illustrated by Arnold Lobel.

SUMMARY: This is an I-Can-Read book consisting of five stories: "Spring," "The Story," "A Lost Button," "A Swim," and "The Letter." In "Spring," Frog convinces Toad to get up out of bed, since it is spring. He has to tear the pages off the calendar from November until May for Toad to believe him. He has been hibernating all winter. In "The Story," Toad is not feeling well (he is looking green), and takes to his bed. He asks Frog to tell him a story. Frog tries very hard to think of a story to tell Toad. He walks on the porch; he stands on his head; he pours glasses of water over his head; and finally he bangs his head against the wall, all in an effort to think up a story to tell Toad. None of these work, but now Frog is feeling worse than Toad, and Toad is well, so they switch places. Frog asks for a story if Toad knows one, and Toad recounts Frog's activities in trying to think up a story for him. By the time he comes to the end of the story, Frog has fallen asleep.

In "A Lost Button," Toad loses a button off of his jacket while he and Frog are out walking. Frog helps him look for it. They find all kinds of buttons—square, black, one with two holes, small buttons, thin buttons. Toad puts them all in his pocket, but they have still not found the one that matches the one he lost. Finally, Frog and Toad go home, and Toad finds the four-holed, thick, white, round button he lost on the floor inside his house. He knows that he has caused Frog a lot of work for nothing. To repay him, Toad sews all of the buttons they collected onto his jacket and gives the jacket to Frog. Frog really enjoys the jacket and jumps with happiness. None of the buttons come off because Toad had sewn them on very well.

The story "A Swim" attracts several animals to Frog and Toad's exploits. The two friends decide it is a great day for swimming. They head down to the river. Frog is ready to jump in as is, but Toad tells him that he wears a bathing suit. Toad does not want to be seen in his suit because he says he looks very funny in it. Frog allows Toad to get in the water and does not look. Soon, however, a turtle crawls by the riverbank, and Toad asks Frog to tell him to go away because he does not want the turtle to see him in his bathing suit. The turtle stays out of curiosity. This continues with a group of lizards, a snake, two dragonflies, and a field mouse. They all stay because they want to see the funny sight of Toad in his bathing suit; they have not seen something funny in quite some time. Toad does not get out of the river until he is very cold and freezing. When he finally does, all the animals, including Frog, laugh. Toad does, in fact, look very funny in his suit! When Frog tells him this, Toad says he knows and that is why he said so. He takes his clothes and goes home.

The concluding story, "The Letter," shows the strong friendship between Frog and Toad. Frog sees Toad sitting on his porch and asks him why he looks so sad. Toad says it is his sad time of day, the time of day when the mail comes, except that he never gets any mail. Frog sat down with him and waited for a while. Then Frog tells Toad that he must go; he has something to do. Frog goes home and writes Toad a letter. He finds a snail and asks the snail to deliver the letter. Then he goes back to Toad's house and tells him that he should wait for the mail again. Toad has gone to bed to take a nap. He will not get up to check for mail because he says he never gets any. When he sees Frog looking out his window for so long looking for mail, he does get up. Frog admits that he knows Toad will get mail because he has sent him a letter. Toad asks him what the letter says, and Frog tells him that the letter says he is glad Toad is his best friend and signs it as his best friend, Frog. Toad agrees that this makes a very nice letter, and they sit down on the porch happily to wait for it. It takes snail four days to deliver the letter; when it finally arrives, Toad is still happy to receive it.

MEDIA: Pencil drawings in three colors.

ANECDOTE: Sequels to this book include *Frog and Toad Together* (1972); *Frog and Toad All Year* (1976); and *Days with Frog and Toad* (1979). Arnold Lobel grew up in Schenectady, New York, where he lived with his grandparents. Though he is probably best known for the Frog and Toad books, he wrote and illustrated twenty-eight books and illustrated over seventy for other authors. He was married to Anita (Kempler) Lobel, who is another children's book author and illustrator. They collaborated on *On Market Street*, which was a 1982 Caldecott Honor Book. Arnold wrote the text for that book, and Anita did the artwork.

DISTINCTION: 1971 Caldecott Honor Book.

BIRTHDAY: Arnold Lobel: May 22, 1933.

SUBJECTS: Frogs—Fiction; Toads—Fiction.

See Also: On Market Street.

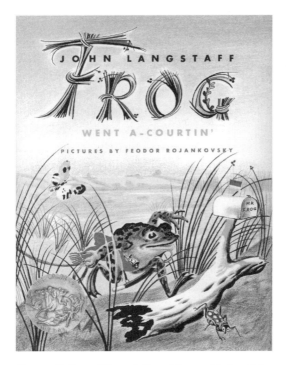

Cover of Frog Went A-Courtin', retold by John Langstaff, illustrated by Feodor Rojankovsky. Randolph J. Caldecott also illustrated this Scottish folk song in the nineteenth century. (Copyright © 1955 by Feodor Rojankovsky. Copyright © by Harcourt, Inc. All rights reserved.)

Frog Went A-Courtin' (Harcourt, 1955). Retold by John Langstaff; illustrated by Feodor Rojankovsky.

SUMMARY: In rhyming couplets, the text describes Frog's proposal and marriage to Miss Mouse. Wearing boots, sword, and pistol, Frog rides his horse to her house and makes his proposal. Miss Mouse says they must obtain permission from her Uncle Rat. Uncle Rat gives his approval, and the wedding is on. Miss Rat from Pumpkin Town makes the dress; a moth lays out the tablecloth; and Mister Coon brings a spoon. A bumblebee plays a banjo; a flea dances a jig; a goose plays fiddle; and two ants dance. A fly eats all the wedding pie, and a chick eats so much he gets sick. With all this celebrating going on, the party does not see the cat who puts a stop to all that. Frog and Mouse go to France to begin their happy life together. Music is written at the end of the book.

MEDIA: Brush, ink, and crayon on acetate separations.

ANECDOTE: The story was brought to America from Scotland, and here it was transformed by many oral tellings of adults to children and children to adults. The music is from a version Langstaff heard children sing in the Appalachians. This story is one of two Caldecott-honored books that were also illustrated by Randolph Caldecott years earlier. The other is *Three Jovial Huntsmen*. Rojankovsky sent his editor, Margaret McElderry, several letters dotted with illustrations of frogs. Bob Dylan recorded "Froggie Went A-Courtin'" on his album *Good As I Been to You*, in 1992.

DISTINCTION: 1956 Caldecott Medal.

BIRTHDAYS: John Langstaff: December 24, 1920; Feodor Rojankovsky: December 24, 1891.

SUBJECT: Folk Songs—United States.

The Funny Little Woman (Dutton, 1972). Retold by Arlene Mosel; illustrated by Blair Lent.

SUMMARY: In Old Japan, there was an old woman who liked to laugh and make dumplings out of rice. One day, a dumpling rolls off the table and into a crack in the floor. The funny little woman reaches in the hole for it, but the earth gives way, and she falls down to an underground road where she meets statues of the gods. She asks Jizo Sama if he has seen her dumpling. He tells her he has but that she should not follow it, because it has gone too close to the wicked *oni* (monsters). The other statues warn her the same way. The little woman simply laughs and says that she is not afraid of the *oni*.

Soon, an *oni* comes by, and the little woman hides behind Jizo Sama. The *oni* smells her humanness. Just when the *oni* might leave, it hears the little woman laugh. The *oni* takes the little woman home with him, where he makes her cook for all the other *oni*. She must put just one grain of rice in the kettle and stir with a magic paddle the *oni* gives her; the kettle soon fills with rice. She thinks about how many rice dumplings she could make with such a paddle.

After some time, the little woman misses her house. She puts the magic paddle in her belt and gets into a boat and starts rowing across the river. At first the *oni* do not see her, but when they do, they do not swim, so they lie down and drink up all the water from the river, leaving the little woman stuck in the mud. When the *oni* see her stuck there, they laugh the laugh of the funny little woman and all the water spills back out of their mouths, floating the boat up once again. The woman rows to safety at her old house, where she uses the magic paddle to make lots of rice dumplings, enough to sell and make her one of richest women in Japan.

MEDIA: Pen-and-ink drawings with full-color acrylic glazes; full-color paintings.

ANECDOTE: The story is based on *The Old Woman and Her Dumpling* by Lafcadio Hearn (1850–1904). Lent used the increased income from the book after it won the Caldecott Medal to move out of the city to the country. Both of Mosel's daughters became librarians.

DISTINCTION: 1973 Caldecott Medal.

BIRTHDAYS: Arlene Mosel: August 27, 1921; Blair Lent: January 22, 1930.

SUBJECT: Folklore.

G

Gág, Wanda (1893–1946). Author and artist. Wanda Hazel Gág (pronounced "gog") was born in New Ulm, Minnesota, on March 11, 1893, the eldest of seven children. Her father, Anton, was an artist and photographer, and her mother, Lissi, was a homemaker whose health was poor after the birth of her last child. Both were German immigrants from Bohemia in Eastern Europe. They expressed both their heritage and their interests in the unique home they built on 226 North Washington Street in New Ulm in 1894. The home contained skylights, open turrets, and an artist's studio in the attic that were especially unusual features for the time.

When Gág was fifteen, her father became seriously ill with tuberculosis. On his deathbed, he whispered to his eldest child, *"Was der Papa nicht thun konnet', muss die Wanda halt fertig machen."*—"What your Papa could not do, Wanda will have to finish." Gág took this deathbed request seriously and worked to help support her family through selling her art in the form of postcards and placecards and illustrations for the *Journal Junior* supplement to the *Minnesota Journal*. Her work also appeared in *Youth's Companion* and in a section of the *Women's Home Companion* called "Aunt Janet's Pages." All of this work was completed while Gág was still in high school.

After graduation, Gág taught in a one-room schoolhouse in New Ulm for a year, then left to attend art schools in St. Paul and Minneapolis. She received a scholarship to attend art school in New York City and went there but returned in February 1918, when her mother died. After settling her younger siblings' living arrangements with other families in New Ulm, she returned to New York to study and market her art. For a while, she had a job painting designs on lampshades when times for selling her artwork were slow.

She managed to eke out a living through various clients and projects, but the artist never stopped experimenting with techniques and subjects. One project involved boxes that she designed to be folded, piled one on top of the other, and read in continuation. These "story boxes" included titles such as "The House That Jack Built" and "Four Little Happy Workers on the Farm." Unfortunately, Gág poured all of her savings into this project to try to make it marketable, but it never took off. Another innovative project was "Cross-Word Puzzle Fairy Stories" that she created in 1925 and that appeared in several publications. While working at this stage of her career, Gág boarded with a family that had two children. She often entertained the children by telling stories; then she would try

Portrait of young artist Wanda Gág, 1917. Years later, Gág's *Millions of Cats* broke new ground in American picture books and is considered a classic of the form. (© Minnesota Historical Society/Corbis.)

to market the stories for publication. None of these was successful. This included an early version of *Millions of Cats*, which was typed up for her around 1923 by her sister, Dele. All the while, she continued to display her sketches, watercolors, and lithographs in galleries throughout the East, including the New York Public Library in 1923 and the Weyhe Gallery in New York City in 1926, 1930, and 1940.

It was during the Weyhe Gallery exhibition in 1926 that editor Ernestine Evans of the new children's books department at Coward-McCann saw Gág's work and asked whether she might be interested in creating a children's book. Gág mentioned *Millions of Cats* and presented the manuscript and unfinished art to Evans within the month. Evans liked the book and asked Gág to revise the story and finish the illustrations for publication.

In 1927, Gág moved to Tumble Timbers near Glen Gardner, New Jersey, and began to focus more intensely on children's books. Leaving the city for the countryside more like she knew growing up was an important step for her work. She met Earle Marshall Humphreys, who would become a steady companion. Another friend, Jack Grass, brought Gág two kittens from a nearby farm to serve as models for completing *Millions of Cats*. She experimented with the book, once trying red lettering and cats that were chocolate brown and other matters of composition. Humphreys offered some suggestions on the text.

Finally, Gág decided on black and white as the basic colors for the book. One innovation that stuck was her decision to move the cats and text across pages that were open opposite one another. This is one of the first and certainly most influential uses of the double-page spread in picture books for children, and Gág is traditionally given credit for this advance in the development of the genre. Her brother, Howard, hand-lettered the text, and this attribute completed the folklike design of a book that told a folklore-like story of an old man and woman who wanted a cat for companionship. Its refrain, "Hundreds of cats, thousands of cats, millions, and billions and trillions of cats" went on to become one of the most familiar and recognizable lines in American children's literature. The lyrical story is equally told by unforgettable black-and-white images that Gág aptly described as "small, sturdy peasant drawings."

Millions of Cats was published in 1928 to rave reviews that Gág kept in a scrapbook. It went on to be given the Newbery Honor Book Award in 1929. This success opened the door to other books like *The Funny Thing* (Coward-McCann, 1929) and *Snippy and Snappy* (Coward-McCann, 1931). *The ABC Bunny* (Coward-McCann, 1933) won a 1934 Newbery Honor Book Award. It featured one of the first instances in an alphabet book of a continuing story running from one letter to the next. Her

Snow White and the Seven Dwarfs, which she created to challenge Disney's homogenization of the story in his 1938 film, won a Caldecott Honor Book Award in 1939. *Nothing at All*, which was about an invisible dog and which was her last original picture book, won the same award in 1942. She also illustrated *Gone Is Gone* (Coward-McCann, 1935), a retelling of a Grimm's fairy tale, and published other illustrated Grimm's tales in *Tales from Grimm* (Coward-McCann, 1936) and *More Tales from Grimm* (Coward-McCann, 1947).

In 1931, Gág moved to her permanent home—a farm she called All Creation, which was located near Milford, New Jersey, in the Musconetcong Mountain area. Several of her siblings lived there on and off over the years, proving that she went on to fulfill the promise she made to her father on his deathbed. Some say Gág and Humphreys married in 1930. Documents such as diaries available to scholars only since 1993 and housed at the University of Pennsylvania Special Collections suggest that they were together but not married until 1943. The documents also suggest that Gág lived a life that was filled with more risk, independent spirit, and adventure than scholars previously realized.

In 1945, Gág set about to work on her second collection of Grimm's fairy tales, when a visit to her doctor gave her family bad news. Earle Humphreys reportedly kept the prognosis from her that she had lung cancer and was expected to live only three months. They went to Florida, where it was thought the warm climate might ease her discomfort and where she worked on drawings for the book from her bed. Defeating the odds, she went on to live seventeen more months and nearly completed the book. Gág died on June 27, 1946. From the detailed notes she left to her editor and minus a few unfinished drawings, the book was published in 1947 very close to the way she had intended.

Wanda Gág's awards include the Lewis Carroll Shelf Award given posthumously for *Millions of Cats* and the Kerlan Award for her body of work, given in 1977. The house in New Ulm, Minnesota, was placed on the National Register of Historic Places and is now open to the public during limited hours, for special events, and by appointment. The residents of the town celebrate Gág's birth each March.

DISTINCTIONS: 1929 and 1934 Newbery Honor Book, 1939 and 1942; Caldecott Honor Books; 1977 Kerlan Award.

See Also: The ABC Bunny; Millions of Cats; Nothing at All; Snow White and the Seven Dwarfs.

The Garden of Abdul Gasazi (Houghton Mifflin, 1979). Written and illustrated by Chris Van Allsburg.

SUMMARY: Alan Mitz is given the job of dog-sitting Fritz for Miss Hester when she goes to visit her cousin Eunice. Fritz had once bitten Eunice, so he had to stay home. Alan tries to do a good job with the troublesome Fritz. Fritz likes to chew everything in sight, and he wears Alan right out, until Alan takes a nap on the couch. He has put his hat (the thing Fritz most likes to chew) under his shirt to try to protect it.

Alan is awakened by a bite on the nose from Fritz. Fritz wants to go for his afternoon walk. While they are out, they see a gate to a garden with a warning that no dogs are allowed. Fritz breaks free of his leash and bolts up the path anyway. Alan chases behind Fritz through the topiary garden. Losing Fritz, Alan comes upon the big house of Gasazi, the magician. He believes the dog has been captured there and fearfully approaches the door. Before Alan can ring the bell, Gasazi the Great opens the door. Inside, Alan politely asks for Fritz, and Gasazi says he may have him. They go back outside. A group of ducks comes by, and Gasazi tells Alan that one of the ducks is Fritz. He says he changes dogs he finds in his garden to ducks. When Alan

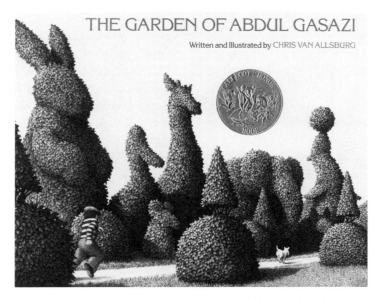

Cover of *The Garden of Abdul Gasazi*, written and illustrated by Chris Van Allsburg. Van Allsburg's picture book debut was rendered in carbon pencil on Strathmore paper and garnered him a 1980 Caldecott Honor. (Copyright © 1979 by Chris Van Allsburg. Copyright © by Houghton Mifflin Company. All rights reserved.)

begs him to change Fritz back, Gasazi tells him that only time can do that, and it might take just a day, or it might take years. Alan takes the duck in his arms, but suddenly the duck grabs his hat and flies off with it, disappearing into the clouds.

Back at Miss Hester's, Alan tells her the whole story. Miss Hester tries to hide a smile and tells Alan that Fritz was in the front yard when she got back. She says that no one can turn dogs into ducks and that Gasazi must have tricked him. Alan feels foolish and promises never to allow himself to be tricked like that again. He heads for home. After he leaves, Fritz turns up on the porch with Alan's hat which he may have, or may not have, flown away with before.

MEDIA: Carbon pencil on Strathmore paper.

ANECDOTE: This book was Chris Van Allsburg's first picture book. The artwork was critically acclaimed, but some reviewers at the time objected to the ominous quality of Mr. Gasazi's topiary for young children.

DISTINCTION: 1980 Caldecott Honor Book.

BIRTHDAY: Chris Van Allsburg: June 18, 1949.

SUBJECTS: Magicians—Fiction; Dogs—Fiction.

See Also: Jumanji; The Polar Express.

The Gardener (Farrar, 1997). Written by Sarah Stewart; illustrated by David Small.

SUMMARY: Through a series of twelve letters, Lydia Grace Finch tells Mama, Papa, and Grandma how life is in the city where she goes to live with Uncle Jim for a while, "until things get better." Lydia lives with her uncle and helps him with his bakery from August 1935 until her father gets a job in July 1936, and she can go back home. It is the depression, and times are hard. Lydia hopes to make Uncle Jim smile. She brings seeds with her and ends up planting window boxes and an entire rooftop garden to surprise him. The letters detail her progress through the

Front cover of *The Gardener*, written by Sarah Stewart, illustrated by David Small. Small's 1998 Caldecott Honor book is one example of many collaborations between husband and wife teams in the picture book world. (Reprinted by permission of Farrar, Straus and Giroux, LLC: *The Gardener* by Sarah Stewart, pictures by David Small. Pictures copyright © 1997 by David Small. www.fsgkidsbooks.com.)

seasons until the garden is in full bloom in June. Lydia makes friends with Emma, who agrees to teach her more about baking if Lydia will teach her the Latin words for different flowers. Like her namesake, her grandmother, Lydia takes her gardening with her wherever she goes and says gardeners "never retire."

MEDIA: Watercolor, ink pen line, and crayon.

ANECDOTE: Sarah Stewart and David Small are married and have collaborated on other picture books as well, including *The Library*. Small received an M.F.A. from Yale University and taught art at the college level for many years before working full-time as an artist.

DISTINCTION: 1998 Caldecott Honor Book.

BIRTHDAYS: Sarah Stewart: August 27, 1938; David Small: February 12, 1945.

SUBJECTS: Gardening—Fiction; Uncles—Fiction; Letters—Fiction.

Geisel, Theodor (Ted) Seuss (pseud., Dr. Seuss) (1904–1991). Author and artist. The man who came to be known to millions of children around the world as "Dr. Seuss" was born Theodor Seuss Geisel in Springfield, Massachusetts, on March 2, 1904. His father, Theodor Robert Seuss, worked in a brewery for many years, but when Prohibition closed down the plant, he became the curator of parks in the New England town. The park facilities included a small zoo. Geisel faced difficulties in school with the other children over his German heritage during World War I, but his childhood overall was apparently a pleasant one. He often went fishing with his father and spent a good deal of time watching and playing with the animals such as the baby lions and the antelope at the zoo in Springfield where his father worked. Asked whether his childhood influenced his work, however, Geisel responded that he did not think so; in fact, he remarked in his characteristic, provocative style used in interviews, "I think I skipped my childhood." He never had a formal art class but one in high school which he quit after thinking the style being taught did not match his own. All the while, he continued to "doodle" his own sketches and drawings and read widely.

Geisel graduated from Central High School and attended Dartmouth with the intention of eventually going on to Oxford and acquiring a Ph.D. in English literature. At Dartmouth, he became interested in cartooning and stayed long hours at the offices of the college humor publication, *Jack-o-Lantern*, at times when he should have perhaps been studying. His grades reflected this other emphasis he placed on his time. When his father

American author and illustrator Dr. Seuss (Theodor Seuss Geisel, 1904–1991) sitting at his drafting table in his home office in La Jolla, California, with a copy of his newly published book, *The Cat in the Hat*. The photo was taken April 25, 1957, well before the artist sported the famous snowy white hair and beard of his later years. (Hulton Archive/Getty Images.)

asked about his future plans, he told him that he intended to go to Oxford on a Campbell scholarship. When the scholarship did not materialize, the family found other means to send him to Oxford, since the young scholar's father had already announced his son had won the Campbell scholarship in the local newspaper.

While in England, Geisel met Helen Palmer. At the same time, he became disillusioned with teaching literature and longed to tour around Europe instead. His tutor at Oxford counseled him to abandon his earlier plan and withdraw from Oxford. Not long afterward, Geisel and Palmer married, and the couple soon returned to the United States. Geisel began working in New York City as a freelance illustrator, earning low pay for small jobs here or there. Finally, Geisel had a break from hard times when he was asked to write and illustrate advertising for a bug spray. His

ad, "Quick Henry, the Flit!," was very successful, and he earned $12,000 for it in the midst of the depression. Although he continued to be successful in advertising and cartooning, his work appearing in such publications as *Vanity Fair*, *The Saturday Evening Post*, and *Judge*, Geisel soon found that his heart was not in that line of work. Perhaps it had not drifted as far away from teaching as he had originally thought. He began planning to write a children's book.

Taking an ocean liner to Paris for a vacation, he noticed the rhythm of the ship's motors. The rhythm kept beating in his brain over and over, until he put words to the rhythm in his head, "And to think that I saw it on Mulberry Street." Mulberry Street was a street from his hometown, Springfield. As he said the words to the rhythm over and over in his mind, a story developed that he continued to work on after he got home. The manuscript and artwork for the book were rejected at least twenty-seven times before Geisel ran into a friend from Dartmouth who agreed to publish it. The book was an immediate success.

Geisel's whacky characters and rhyming texts appeared first in magazines in the beginning, then later in books. This was true of *The 500 Hats of Bartholomew Cubbins* (Vanguard, 1938), for example, *Bartholomew and the Oobleck* (Random House, 1949), *Horton Hears a Who!* (Random House, 1954), and *Horton Hatches the Egg* (Random House, 1940). During World War II, Geisel was commissioned as a captain in the U.S. Army in the information and education division. He was sent to Hollywood, California, where he produced films for the military, including *Your Job in Germany* and *Design for Death. Your Job in Germany* was released to the public in 1945 by Warner Bros. as a feature film retitled *Hitler Lives*. It was awarded the Academy Award for best short subject documentary in 1946. *Design for Death* also won an Academy Award a short time later—for best documentary feature. In 1950, Geisel would go on to win yet a third Academy Award, this time for the animated cartoon *Gerald McBoing Boing.* His television work was also recognized decades later with a Peabody Award in 1971 for his popular television specials *How the Grinch Stole Christmas* and *Horton Hears a Who!*

A lesser-known fact about Geisel's career is that before, during, and after the war, he produced political cartoons and embedded political satire and his own worldview within his several of books. The character Yertle of *Yertle the Turtle and Other Stories* (Random House, 1958), for example, is patterned after Hitler, and the story is a parody of totalitarian government. A theme of the equal value and worth of all people rings throughout his work; for example, the star that makes the Sneetches different in *The Sneetches and Other Stories* turns from a flaw to a gift in that story and may be suggestive of the Jewish Star of David. The value of all people "no matter how small" in *Horton Hears a Who!* refers to the Japanese after World War II and their efforts to develop democracy. The Grinch in *How the Grinch Stole Christmas* is a personification of commercialism of a religious holiday. *The Lorax* became Geisel's parable about the need to save the environment; *The Butter Battle Book* was about nuclear disarmament. A later book, *Marvin K. Mooney, Will You Please Go Now!* (Random House, 1972), disguises Richard Nixon as a child. Geisel must have taken some satisfaction in the coincidence that the day after the book was published, Nixon resigned from the presidency.

Geisel also incorporated autobiographical elements into his books. *If I Ran the Zoo*, for example, is a tribute to his father and the Springfield zoo that he ran. *And to Think I Saw It on Mulberry Street* refers to the same street in his hometown of Springfield. He dedicated *If I Ran the Circus* to his father, "Big Ted of Springfield, the finest man I'll ever know." *McElligott's Pool* calls back to his fishing days with his father.

In the 1950s, Geisel was approached to create a book that would help launch Random House's new program of Beginning Books. A 1954 article by John Hersey in *Life* magazine helped bring national attention to a concern about literacy, and educators and publishers were charged with the challenge of coming up with better and more interesting ways of teaching American children how to read than continuing to use the bland *Dick and Jane* types of readers. Geisel's task was to come up with a book written only in words of one syllable from a limited, designated list that would better engage children's interest. He thought the task would be easy enough to do in a couple of days; however, the challenge proved to stump the author/artist for over two years. Finally searching the word list over and over again, he fixed on the rhyme between the single-syllabled words "cat" and "hat," and the classic beginning reader, *The Cat in the Hat*, was born. The story of a cat's decidedly subversive visit to a children's home while their mother is away is composed of only 223 total words. The book was published by Random House in 1957 as both a textbook for classrooms and as a trade book for commercial sales. The book was immediately successful. Geisel went on to become president of the publisher's Beginning Book division, and his wife Helen became its editor in chief.

Writing under the pseudonym of "Dr. Seuss," apparently awarding himself the Ph.D. that he had not pursued at Oxford, Geisel went on to write seventeen limited vocabulary books for the Beginning Books series, and it is these books for which he is best known. The famous *Green Eggs and Ham* that many twenty-first-century American parents and grandparents can still recite by heart contains just fifty words. Pseudonyms other than Dr. Seuss that the author used during the years include Theo LeSieg, which is Geisel, spelled backwards, and one borrowing his second wife's maiden name, Stone, as the author, Rosetta Stone, of *Because a Little Bug Went Ka-Choo!*

Helen Palmer Geisel died on October 23, 1967, and the author remarried within a year to Audrey Stone Diamond on August 5, 1968. He had had no children from his first marriage but increased his family with two stepdaughters, Lea and Lark, on marrying Audrey. He and Audrey established a home at the top of Mount Soledad in LaJolla, California—a house they called "the Tower." Its remote location was made even more private by the fact that it could be reached only by one narrow, winding road. By now, "Dr. Seuss" was a national celebrity but managed to maintain his privacy at the Tower. The license plate on his car read, "GRINCH," and the author and artist collected cats in the form of figurines, prints, and other cat-themed objects. The couple did have one real cat for several years, named appropriately, "Thing 1."

Theodor Geisel died on September 24, 1991, at the age of eighty-seven, from an illness that had lasted several months. Geisel did not want a funeral or memorial stone, so instead his legacy has been passed down through the monetary donations his survivors have made to memorials of different kinds in his honor. There is the Dr. Seuss National Memorial, for example, at Springfield, Massachusetts, and the bulk of his papers are held at the Dr. Seuss Collection of the Mandeville Special Collections Library in the Geisel Library at the University of California at San Diego. Interestingly, years before, the papers for *The Lorax* wound up at the Lyndon Baines Johnson Presidential Library after a mixup over a Democratic dinner conversation the author had with Liz Carpenter, the president's former press secretary. She had discussed with him Lady Bird Johnson's environmental work.

Dr. Seuss is best known for his beginning reader series of books that are sometimes confused by readers as picture books. Two of his actual picture books for children won Caldecott Honor Book Awards—one in 1948 for *McElligott's Pool* and the other in 1950 for *Bartholomew and the Oobleck*. His forty-six books for children were enormously popular among all age groups, as evidenced by two publications—*The Butter Battle Book* (1984) and *Oh, the Places You'll Go* (1990), which broke records for how many weeks they remained on the adult edition of the *New York Times* best-seller list. His books have sold more than 200 million copies in twenty languages as well as Braille since 1937. In the 1980s, Geisel's popularity was bolstered by additional critical recognition. In 1980, he was awarded the Laura Ingalls Wilder Award for his body of work and contribution to children's literature, and in 1984 he was awarded the Pulitzer Prize.

DISTINCTIONS: 1984 Pulitzer Prize; 1980 Laura Ingalls Wilder Award; 1971 Peabody Award for the animated cartoons, *How the Grinch Stole Christmas* and *Horton Hears a Who*; 1951 Academy Award for *Gerald McBoing-Boing*; 1950 Caldecott Honor for *Bartholomew and the Oobleck*; 1948 Caldecott Honor for *McElligott's Pool*; 1947 Academy Award for *Design for Death*; 1946 Academy Award for *Hitler Lives*.

Further Reading: Geisel, Audrey. *The Secret Art of Dr. Seuss.* New York: Random House, 1995; Geisel, Theodor. *Dr. Seuss Goes to War: The World War II Editorial Cartoons of Theodor Seuss Geisel.* New York: New Press, 2001; Krulak, Victor H., et al. *Theodor Seuss Geisel: Reminiscences and Tributes.* Hanover, NH: Dartmouth, 1966, 1996; Lathem, Connery Edward, *Who's Who & What's What in the Books of Dr. Seuss.* Hanover, NH: Dartmouth College, 2000; Morgan, Judith, and Neil Morgan. *Dr. Seuss and Mr. Geisel: A Biography.* New York: Random House, 1995; Nel, Philip. *Dr. Seuss: An American Icon.* New York: Continuum, 2004.

See Also: And to Think I Saw It on Mulberry Street; *Bartholomew and the Oobleck*; *McElligott's Pool.*

George and Martha (Houghton Mifflin, 1972). Written and illustrated by James Marshall.

SUMMARY: The book is made up of "five stories about two great friends," who are two hippos. The stories are "Split Pea Soup"; "The Flying Machine"; "The Tub"; "The Mirror"; and "The Tooth." In "Split Pea Soup," Martha likes to make the soup, but George hates to eat it. After hiding some soup in his loafers to avoid hurting her feelings after eating ten bowls of soup in one day, George is told by Martha that he should have told her he does not like the soup. She only likes to make it, not eat it. She offers to make them chocolate chip cookies instead. In "The

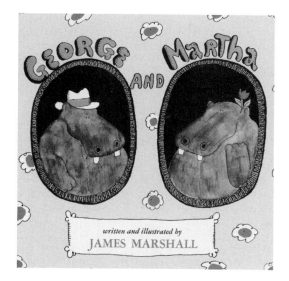

George and Martha, written and illustrated by James Marshall, contains five interrelated stories. (Copyright © 1972 by James Marshall. Copyright © by Houghton Mifflin Company. All rights reserved.)

Flying Machine," George sits in the basket of a hot-air balloon and tells Martha that he wants to be the first of his species to fly. Martha asks him why he is not yet flying, since he is in the machine, and he replies that he does not know. Martha suggests that perhaps the basket is too heavy, and George gets out to make the basket lighter. When the balloon takes off without him, Martha says that she would rather have George on the ground with her anyway.

In "The Tub," George likes to peek in windows and once peeks in while Martha is taking her bath. When the tub ends up outside the window upside down on George's head, he understands that Martha needs her privacy and that he should never do that again. The story, "The Mirror," is about Martha's preference for looking at herself in the mirror. She thinks it's fun and even wakes up in the night to look at herself in a mirror. George gets tired of her doing this and draws a funny picture of her and pastes it to the mirror. When Martha is dismayed, George explains that that is what happens when one looks at herself or himself too much in the mirror.

Martha stops doing it. In the last story, "The Tooth," George falls while roller-skating to Martha's house and breaks his right front tooth. He feels terrible about it, but Martha tries to help him feel better. The next day, he goes to the dentist, Buck McTooth, "D. D.," who gives him a gold tooth as a replacement. Martha tells him he looks handsome with the new tooth. Friends help friends feel better, and they also tell them the truth.

MEDIA: Possibly pen and ink and water-color.

ANECDOTE: There are several sequels to this book. They include *George and Martha Rise and Shine*; *George and Martha Encore*; *George and Martha Back in Town*; *George and Martha Round and Round*; *George and Martha One Fine Day*; and *George and Martha Tons of Fun*. Marshall once said that after creating the first George and Martha book for children, he had found the work he knew he wanted to do all his life.

DISTINCTION: *New York Times* Best Book for Children; NYPL 100 Picture Books Everyone Should Know.

BIRTHDAY: James Marshall: October 10, 1942.

SUBJECT: Friendship—Fiction.

See Also: *Goldilocks and the Three Bears*.

Gillespie and the Guards (Viking, 1956).

Written by Benjamin Elkin; illustrated by James Daugherty.

SUMMARY: The king invites three brothers to join the Royal Guards because of their gifted eyesight. He tells his kingdom that anyone who can fool the new guards will win a medal set with diamonds. People arrive in disguise, including a boy from Keokuk disguised as a dog; a man from Switzerland dressed as a clock; and a lady from Winnipeg in a peppermint candy dress. The guards see through all the disguises, and this makes them famous. Now that they are famous, they are not sure how they should behave. After talk-

ing it over, they decide they should act serious and proud.

A boy named Gillespie comes to play with the prince each day and becomes friends with the guards. Now that they are acting haughty, Gillespie decides he will try to fool them to make them smile again and not be so serious. One day he goes home with a wagon full of leaves. This makes one guard smile a little, since he sees nothing hidden beneath the leaves. He writes it down in the Royal Guard Book. The next day, Gillespie does the same thing with a pile of sand. The next day he does the same thing with stones. More days he fills the wagon with piles of grass, weeds, tin cans, and bottles. The guards never see anything hidden beneath the piles, but each day they mark what Gillespie is taking out with him in the wagon in the Royal Guard Book.

One day, Gillespie asks to see the king and reports that he has succeeded in fooling the guards. The king holds up the book and says that he knows everything Gillespie has taken from him. Gillespie invites him to his home to see what he has taken that the guards did not catch. The king is so intrigued that he summons his royal carriage, and an entire royal parade goes to Gillespie's home. There, Gillespie opens a garage full of little red wagons taken from the palace storeroom of toys. The king presents Gillespie with the medal with diamonds, and the three brothers go back to being not so serious. Gillespie becomes famous, too, from wearing his medal around town.

MEDIA: Possibly charcoal and ink.

ANECDOTE: Daugherty illustrated more than forty books by other authors and was influenced by Walt Whitman's poetry in his instilling of American vitality into his characters.

DISTINCTION: 1957 Caldecott Honor Book.

BIRTHDAYS: Benjamin Elkin: August 10, 1911; James Daugherty: June 1, 1889.

SUBJECTS: Contests; Guards—Fiction; Wagons—Fiction.

See Also: Andy and the Lion.

The Girl Who Loved Wild Horses (Dutton, 1978). Written and illustrated by Paul Goble.

SUMMARY: There is a girl in the village who loves horses and tends to them for the tribe. One day there is a fierce storm that chases the horses out of the village. The girl goes with them, riding a horse courageously, clinging to its mane. When the storm clears, they find themselves lost in hills the girl does not recognize. A spotted stallion appears and welcomes them to the land of the wild horses. There, the girl is very happy. Meanwhile, the villagers go out looking for the girl and the horses. When they find her, the spotted stallion tries to keep her and a spotted colt away from them. Finally, the girl falls from her horse when it stumbles, and the villagers take her home.

At home, the girl is sick and unhappy. She says the wild horses are her relatives. Since her family in the village loves her, they allow her to go back to the wild horses to live. They give her the best horse in the village. The spotted stallion comes down from the hills with the wild horses, and the villagers paint the wild horses' bodies and put eagle feathers in their manes and tails. Everyone is happy, and each year the girl gives the village a new colt. One year she is not seen; then she is never seen again. Years later, hunters see a beautiful mare with the spotted stallion and believe it is the girl. They are pleased to know that they have relatives among the Horse People.

MEDIA: Full-color pen and ink and watercolor.

ANECDOTE: Paul Goble's interest in Native American culture began with the stories his mother read to him by Grey Owl and Ernest Thompson Seton. This story is a combination of many legends. Goble has been adopted into both the Yakima and Sioux tribes.

DISTINCTION: 1979 Caldecott Medal.

BIRTHDAY: Paul Goble: September 27, 1933.

SUBJECTS: Fairy tales; Indians of North America—Fiction; Horses—Fiction.

Giving Thanks: A Native American Good Morning Message (Lee and Low, 1995). Written by Chief Jake Swamp; illustrated by Erwin Printup Jr.

SUMMARY: The book is adapted from the Thanksgiving Address of the *Haudenosaunee*, or Iroquois, the Six Nations. The Six Nations are the Mohawk, Oneida, Cayuga, Onondaga, Seneca, and Tuscarora. Thanks are given to Mother Earth, the blue water, the cool green grass, sweet fruits and berries, herbs for medicine, the animals and trees, the birds and their songs, the Four Winds, and Grandfather Thunder Beings (storms). Thanks are also given to Elder Brother Sun, Grandmother Moon, the stars, Spirit Protectors, and most of all thanks go to the Great Spirit. At the end of the book, the Thanksgiving Address is given in a basic form in the *kaniakehaka* (Mohawk) language.

MEDIA: Acrylic on canvas.

ANECDOTE: Chief Jake Swamp (Tekaronianeken) was born on the Akwesasne Mohawk Reservation in upstate New York. He has given the Thanksgiving Address around the world as well as at the United Nations.

DISTINCTION: Native American Indian-commended.

BIRTHDAY: Not available.

SUBJECTS: Mohawk Indians; Speeches, addresses, etc., Mohawk; Human ecology; Nature—Religious aspects.

The Glorious Flight: Across the Channel with Louis Blériot, July 25, 1909 (Viking, 1983). Written and illustrated by Alice and Martin Provensen.

SUMMARY: Riding in his car with his family, Mama (Alice) Blériot and children Alceste, Charmaine, Suzette, Jeannot, and Gabrielle, Louis Blériot sees an airship fly overhead. The sight inspires him to build airplanes, and he begins trying out constructions and taking on injuries, one after another until finally his *Blériot VII* flies successfully. When he sees a prize is being offered to the first person to fly across the English Channel, Papa Blériot takes the risk because that's the kind of man he is.

On July 25, 1909, he flies his *Blériot XI* out over the Channel for thirty-seven minutes. Lost in the fog, he worries that he won't make it until he sees the White Cliffs of Dover underneath him. Blériot is the first person to cross the English Channel in a machine heavier than air, forever afterward linking sky, water, and land.

MEDIA: Acrylic and pen and ink.

ANECDOTE: The story is based on the true event of Blériot's crossing. The plane's design was later adopted for French and Italian military use in World War I and could fly up to 45 miles per hour. One replica of many made of the *Blériot XI* can be seen at the National Museum of the United States Air Force in Dayton, Ohio.

DISTINCTION: 1984 Caldecott Medal.

BIRTHDAYS: Alice Provensen: August 14, 1918; Martin Provensen: July 10, 1916.

SUBJECTS: Blériot, Louis (1872–1936); Air pilots; Airplanes—Design and construction.

Goggles! (Macmillan, 1969). Written and illustrated by Ezra Jack Keats.

SUMMARY: In an urban lot, Peter finds a pair of motorcycle goggles. He calls through the pipe to tell his friend Archie about them. Archie appreciates how great they are. They decide to go to Archie's house and sit on the steps. On their way, a gang of older boys sees the goggles and tells Peter to give them to them. Peter's dog,

Willie, growls at them, and Peter tells Archie to hold him. With the goggles in his pocket, Peter puts up his fist. Archie can't believe Peter is standing up to the gang and gasps. When Peter turns to check on Archie, he gets socked to the ground, and the goggles land out in the open. For a second, everyone stares at them. Then, Willie picks them up and disappears in a hole in the fence. Archie and Peter agree to go to their hideout in different directions to throw off the gang. It works, and soon Willie has joined them.

The big boys are close to the hideout, but they don't see Peter, Archie, or Willie. Peter throws them off by pretending to call to Willie to meet him in the parking lot. The big boys run off in that direction, and the friends escape to Archie's front steps after all. They agree that from there with the goggles, "things look real fine."

MEDIA: Oil paint and collage.

ANECDOTE: Keats was born in Brooklyn, the child of Polish immigrants.

DISTINCTION: 1970 Caldecott Honor Book.

BIRTHDAY: Ezra Jack Keats: March 11, 1916.

SUBJECTS: Bullies—Fiction; City and town life—Fiction; African Americans—Fiction.

See Also: Keats Foundation; *Snowy Day.*

Goin' Someplace Special (Atheneum, 2001). Written by Patricia McKissack; illustrated by Jerry Pinkney.

SUMMARY: 'Tricia Ann wants to go to the place she calls "Someplace Special." Her grandmother, Mama Frances, finally agrees to let her go out in the city by herself but not before she reminds her to hold her head up and remember that she belongs to somebody. Along her way, 'Tricia Ann must ride in the back of the bus. She cannot sit on a park bench by the Peace Fountain her grandfather helped build because it is marked "For Whites Only." When she gets accidentally swept into the Southland Hotel's grand lobby at the arrival of a celebrity and is kicked out, she runs to the Mission Church garden and starts to cry. Maybe it is not worth the trouble of facing so much discrimination after all to get to Someplace Special.

While she is there, she is comforted by Blooming Mary, a woman who tends the garden for no particular reason. Mary tells 'Tricia Ann to listen for her grandmother, and she will be right there with her. 'Tricia Ann listens and hears Mama Frances' words of encouragement and determination. Blooming Mary gives her a bright orange zinnia, and 'Tricia Ann is on her way once again. When she passes by the Grand Music Palace, a small boy named Hickey introduces himself and tells her he is six years old today. He asks her if she is coming in to the theater, but suddenly his big sister tugs on his arm and tells him that colored people have to sit up in the Buzzard's Roost. 'Tricia Ann tells Hickey that she is not coming in; she is going somewhere else that is more special; Hickey says that he would like to go.

Finally, at the corner, 'Tricia Ann sees the big building she's been searching for. When she sees it, she loses all her feelings of embarrassment, hurt, and anger. It is the Public Library, where a sign reads "All are Welcome."

MEDIA: Pencil and watercolor on paper.

ANECDOTE: The story is an autobiographical account of McKissack's youth in Nashville, Tennessee, in the 1950s. In the author's note, McKissack explains that during the 1950s Jim Crow laws kept blacks and whites segregated in Nashville, but the library board quietly voted to open all of their buildings to everyone. Since she felt welcome in the library, she checked out more books and learned her grandmother's value of reading and its relationship to freedom.

DISTINCTION: 2002 Coretta Scott King Award for Illustration.

BIRTHDAYS: Patricia McKissack: August 9, 1944; Jerry Pinkney: December 22, 1939.

SUBJECTS: Segregation—Fiction; African Americans—Fiction; Nashville (Tenn.)—Fiction.

The Golden Kite Award. Distinction. Originated in 1973, the Golden Kite Award is presented annually by the Society of Children's Book Writers and Illustrators to members of the society who have written and illustrated the most outstanding children's books the previous year. It is the only children's book award given by peers in the profession. In most recent years, categories have included fiction, nonfiction, picture book text, and picture book illustration. Honor books are also recognized in each category. The author of the picture book that won the illustration award and the illustrator of the picture book text award each receive a certificate. The Golden Kite is a statuette of a child flying a kite. Picture books were added as a separate category starting in 1982 for illustration and in 1996 for text.

Picture book text winners include: Amy Timberlake for *The Dirty Cowboy*, illustrated by Adam Rex (Farrar, Straus and Giroux, 2003); Sarah Wilson for *George Hooglesberry: Grade School Alien*, illustrated by Chad Cameron (Tricycle, 2002); J. Patrick Lewis for *The Shoe Tree of Chagrin*, illustrated by Chris Sheban (Creative, 2001); Jane Kurtz for *River Friendly, River Wild*, illustrated by Neil Brennan (Simon, 2000); Deborah Hopkinson for *A Band of Angels*, illustrated by Raul Colon (Atheneum, 1999); Christine O' Connell George for *Old Elm Speaks: Tree Poems*, illustrated by Kate Kiesler (Clarion, 1998); Marguerite W. Davol for *The Paper Dragon*, illustrated by Robert Sabuda (Atheneum, 1997); Diane Stanley for *Saving Sweetness*, illustrated by G. Brian Karas (Putnam, 1996).

Winners of the picture book illustration award in the 2000s and 1990s include Loren Long for *I Dream of Trains*, written by Angela Johnson (Simon, 2003); Marla Frazee for *Mrs. Biddlebox*, written by Linda Smith (Harper, 2002); Beth Krommes for *The Lamp, the Ice, and the Boat Called Fish*, written by Jacqueline Briggs Martin (Houghton Mifflin, 2001); David Shannon for *The Rain Came Down* (Blue Sky, 2000); Amy Walrod for *The Little Red Hen (Makes a Pizza)* (Dutton, 1999); Uri Shulevitz for *Snow* (Fararr, Straus and Giroux, 1998); Robert Sabuda for *The Paper Dragon* (Atheneum, 1997); Holly Berry for *Market Day* (Harper, 1996); Dennis Nolan and Lauren Mills for *Fairy Wings* (Little, Brown, 1995); Keith Baker for *Big Fat Hen* (Harcourt, 1994); Kevin Hawkes for *By the Light of the Halloween Moon* (Lothrop, 1993); Patricia Polacco for *Chicken Sunday* (Philomel, 1992); Barbara Lavallee for *Mama, Do You Love Me?* (Chronicle, 1991); and Jerry Pinkney for *Home Place* (Macmillan, 1990).

During the 1980s, picture book illustration winners were Richard Jesse Watson for *Tom Thumb* (Harcourt, 1989); Susan Jeffers for *Forest of Dreams* (Dial, 1988); Arnold Lobel for *The Devil & Mother Crump* (Harper, 1987); Suse MacDonald for *Alpabatics* (Bradbury, 1986); Judith St. George for *The Mount Rushmore Story* (Putnam, 1985); Don Wood for *Little Red Riding Hood* (Harcourt, 1984); Trina Schart Hyman for *Little Red Riding Hood* (Holiday, 1983); and Tomie dePaola for *Giorgo's Village* (Putnam, 1982).

Goldilocks and the Three Bears (Dial, 1988). Retold and illustrated by James Marshall.

SUMMARY: This Goldilocks is a naughty girl who does exactly as she pleases. When her mother asks her to go buy muffins in the next village but not go through the woods because of the bears she has heard that live there, Goldilocks promptly disobeys. The three bears are in their house having breakfast. Papa Bear says the porridge is "scalding"; and Baby Bear drops to the floor and says he's dying. Fed up with both of them, Mama Bear tells them that is quite enough. Papa Bear suggests that they all go for a ride on their rusty old bicycle while the porridge cools.

Goldilocks strides right into the house without even knocking. She tries the biggest bowl of porridge, the medium, and the smallest. She finds them to be too hot and cold and just right, as in the traditional story. The same thing happens with the chairs and the beds. The end of the story goes pretty much as the traditional tale as well, with Baby Bear discovering Goldilocks in his bed, and Papa Bear's waking the girl up. At seeing the three bears around her, Goldilocks jumps out the window. When Baby Bear asks who she was, Mama Bear replies she doesn't know but hopes they never see her again, and they don't.

MEDIA: Pen and ink and watercolor.

ANECDOTE: Marshall died at just over fifty years old. Once he made up the existence of a cousin, "Edward Marshall," whom he claimed lived in a crematorium with his eighteen children. He did this in order to publish an easy-to-read book, *The Cut-Ups*, outside of an exclusive agreement he had with his publisher.

DISTINCTION: 1989 Caldecott Honor Book.

BIRTHDAY: James Marshall: October 10, 1942.

SUBJECTS: Folklore; Bears—Folklore; Three bears.

See Also: George and Martha.

Golem (Clarion, 1996). Retold and illustrated by David Wisniewski.

SUMMARY: The book retells a Jewish legend from a time of racial and religious discord in Prague. According to the legend, in

1580, riots were occurring all over Prague from a "Blood Lie" that stated that the Jews were mixing the blood of Christian children with the flour and water of their unleavened Passover bread. The "Blood Lie" caused much violence and persecution against the Jews. From a message he received in the night, Rabbi Loew creates Golem, a giant man, out of clay to protect the Jews. On his forehead, he writes in Hebrew, *emet*, "truth." The Golem, whom the rabbi calls Joseph, is simple-minded. He enjoys simple pleasures such as the sunrise. He does as he is asked and protects the Jews, bringing their persecutors to jail without harming them. Soon, however, the riots grow worse, and with them Golem's size and strength grow larger and stronger. When the people come to the gates of the ghetto to do the Jews harm, Golem has grown to an immense size and kills and wounds many of them.

The rabbi is summoned by the emperor to Prague Castle and asked to destroy Golem; in exchange, the Jews will live in peace. The rabbi agrees. Golem has performed his duty and will return to the earth from which he came. However, Golem does not want to return to clay. He asks his father, the rabbi, if he may stay alive because he enjoys life so much. He says he will disobey and not turn to clay. The rabbi erases the "e" from *emet* on Golem's forehead, leaving the Hebrew word, *met*, or "death," and Golem disintegrates. Legend has it that he will rise again should the Jewish people ever really need him to ward off their enemies. In Hebrew, Golem means "shapeless mass."

MEDIA: Color-aid, coral, and bark cut papers.

ANECDOTE: The author/artist copied figures from comic books as a child. He attended the Ringling Brothers and Barnum & Bailey Circus Clown College and performed for two years. To cut papers used in this book, Wisniewski used between 800 and 1,000 blades in his knife.

DISTINCTION: 1997 Caldecott Medal.

BIRTHDAY: David Wisniewski: March 21, 1953.

SUBJECTS: Judah Loew ben Bezalel, ca. 1525–1609—Legends; Golem; Legends—Jewish; Jews—Czech; Republic—Folklore; Folklore—Czech Republic.

The Golem: A Jewish Legend (Lippincott, 1976). Retold and illustrated by Beverly Brodsky McDermott.

SUMMARY: Learned Rabbi Yehuda Lev ben Bezalel lives behind thick walls in the Prague ghetto. One night his wife, Rivka, has a dream that people have accused the Jews of baking matzos with the blood of Christian children. She predicts an angry mob will attack the ghetto. The Rabbi believes her and says he will make a man out of clay to protect them. He summons his pupils, Isaac and Jacob, to help. In the attic of the synagogue, under a pile of old prayer books, the Rabbi takes out a lump of clay. He tells his pupils that he has been summoned by God to use their magic to raise up the Golem.

Rabbi Lev forms the clay, and it becomes a man in a burst of fire. The man cannot speak, the Rabbi says, because while he can give him the shape of a human being, only God can give him the gift of speech. The Golem will remain mute. The Golem becomes a familiar sight protecting the ghetto and its people at synagogue and during feast days. Passover eve, the Gentiles become jealous of the harvest of the Jews when their tables lay empty. They storm the ghetto, but the Golem grows huge and crushes them. He keeps going, destroying everything in sight.

The Rabbi tells him to stop. When the Golem opens his mouth, the name of God falls out, and the Golem begins to crumble. The Rabbi picks up the ball of clay and returns it to the synagogue, where he replaces it again underneath the old prayer books.

MEDIA: Gouache, watercolor, dye, and ink on watercolor paper.

ANECDOTE: Beverly Brodsky McDermott was married to Gerald McDermott. Her inspiration for *The Golem* came while watching a 1920s German film on the subject when she was living in the south of France. Two years of research included study of the Hebrew alphabet as well as the magical attributes given to it by the Cabbalists, Jewish mystics. As she worked on the paintings, McDermott claims the figure of the Golem in her art dissolved from a humanlike being to blotches of clay that collapsed and returned to the earth, leaving a meaningful silence behind.

DISTINCTION: 1977 Caldecott Honor Book.

BIRTHDAY: Not available.

SUBJECTS: Judah Löw ben Bezaleel, ca. 1525–1609; Golem; Jews—Folklore; Folklore.

See Also: Golem.

Good-Luck Horse (McGraw-Hill, 1943). Written by Chih-Yi Chan; illustrated by Plato Chan.

SUMMARY: Good luck and bad luck trade places throughout this story set in ancient China. A lonely boy makes a horse out of paper that he can hold in his hand. Magically, the horse becomes real and is named "Good-Luck Horse" by the magician, but good luck does not always come in the way one expects.

MEDIA: Possibly pen and ink and wash.

ANECDOTE: The story was adapted from a Chinese legend.

DISTINCTION: 1944 Caldecott Honor Book.

BIRTHDAY: Not available.

SUBJECT: Horses—Fiction.

Goodnight Moon (Harper, 1947). Written by Margaret Wise Brown; illustrated by Clement Hurd.

SUMMARY: In this classic American bedtime story, Little Bunny goes to bed in the "great green room" and says goodnight to all of the everyday things he sees—things like a comb and a brush, mittens, a telephone, and a bowl full of mush. An old lady rocking and knitting in a rocking chair in the room whispers "hush" and provides gentle comfort as the scene gradually darkens with each page; the clock advances through time; and a mouse and other movements and noises settle into sleep. The text of the book is recognized for its poetic tenderness for young children.

MEDIA: Tempera.

ANECDOTE: Brown wrote the story upon waking up one morning, as though she had dreamed it. She first called it *Goodnight Room*. She called editor Ursula Nordstrom and read it to her over the phone, and Nordstrom accepted the manuscript for publication immediately. Brown knew she wanted Clement Hurd to illustrate the book, and since she was a successful author by that time who had Nordstrom's respect, after a brief consideration of a few other illustrators while Hurd was overseas, the editor brought Hurd on board.

The setting of this picture book occurring entirely in one room posed a challenge for the illustrator, who would not have the usual variety of settings to conceptualize from the text and depict. The movement, then, instead of place to place, passes through time, the room gently darkening with each page, and other changes happening subtly, such as the movements of the moon, the clock's hands, and the mouse. At first, Hurd wanted to draw people instead of bunnies for the characters, but Brown and Nordstrom preferred rabbits and later convinced Hurd that he drew better rabbits than people. Discussion over early drawings showed the trio's concern about every aspect of the artwork—from the perceived softness of the yarn to the proximity of the mouse to the child's bed, to the amount of detail on the cow's udders in the picture on the wall.

Hurd may have borrowed a few images from other books of the day in his depiction of the great green room. In one early drawing, the "old lady" was indeed a gray-haired woman sitting in the rocking chair. The image bears a striking resemblance to the old woman in Wanda Gág's *Millions of Cats* in the scene where she and the old man sit by the lamp with a cat playing at their feet. The everyday objects on the bunny's table, particularly the brush and comb, are very similar to those photographed in Edward Steichen's *The First Picture Book* (Harcourt, Brace, 1930). When the final decision was made to make the people characters into bunnies, Hurd tipped his hat to Brown's book *The Runaway Bunny* by depicting a scene from that book in the picture on the wall behind the "old lady." In an earlier drawing with the old woman, the picture behind her was a map of the Americas. At one time as well, Hurd had depicted the child in bed as a black boy similar to a boy who had stayed with him and his wife in Connecticut over the summer of 1946 as a participant in the Fresh Air program. The picture was not considered seriously not because the portrayal of a young black boy in a picture book for children of the 1940s would be groundbreaking but because Hurd's drawing was unsatisfactory to him and the others.

Goodnight Moon was published on September 3, 1947, and was well received by reviewers. It sold a healthy 6,000 copies in its first run. It did not become a runaway best-selling classic, however, until a surge in sales began inexplicably in 1953, the year after Brown died. From that time on, it became and has remained one of the best-selling and highest regarded American picture books for children of all time. The paperback edition first appeared in 1977. Since 1979, it has been translated into several languages, including Japanese, French, Hebrew, Swedish, Spanish, and Korean. The book was first made into a successful board book for babies in 1991.

MEDIA: Tempera.

DISTINCTIONS: *New York Times* Best Book for Children; NYPL 100 Picture Books Everyone Should Know; *100 Best Books for Children.*

BIRTHDAYS: Margaret Wise Brown: May 23, 1910; Clement Hurd: January 12, 1908.

SUBJECTS: Bedtime—Fiction; Rabbits—Fiction.

Further Reading: Leonard S. Marcus, *Margaret Wise Brown: Awakened by the Moon.* Boston: Beacon Press, 1992; *Goodnight Moon, with a 50th Anniversary Retrospective* by Leonard S. Marcus. New York: HarperCollins, 1997.

See Also: A Child's Good Night Book; Brown, Margaret Wise; *The Little Island.*

Gouache (pronounced gwäsh). Artist's medium. A painting process using opaque colors.

Grandfather Twilight (Philomel, 1984). Written and illustrated by Barbara Berger.

SUMMARY: Each evening, Grandfather Twilight, who lives in the woods, closes his book, removes his glasses, and goes to a large chest that contains an endless strand of pearls. There, he removes one pearl and goes for a walk. As he walks, the pearl grows, spreading a glow of light all around. When Grandfather Twilight gets to the sea, he gives the pearl to the sky, where it becomes the moon. Then he goes home and goes to bed.

MEDIA: Acrylic.

ANECDOTE: The book is dedicated to the author's father. The chest of pearls is taken from a wooden chest that used to sit in her parents' room when she was growing up.

DISTINCTION: *New York Times* Best Book for Children.

BIRTHDAY: Barbara Helen Berger: March 1, 1945.

SUBJECTS: Twilight—Fiction; Night—Fiction; Moon—Fiction.

Grandfather's Journey (Houghton Mifflin, 1993). Written and illustrated by Allen Say.

SUMMARY: The author's grandfather is a young man when he leaves Japan for the United States. He wears Western clothes for the first time on the steamship across the wide Pacific Ocean. The ocean amazes him; it takes three weeks to cross. Once in America, he walks many days and also rides trains and riverboats. He sees the tall rock formations in the deserts and the wide fields of grain. He sees cities and tall mountains and clear rivers. On his journey, he meets men of all colors. He likes the Sierra Mountains of California the best and never thinks about going back to Japan to live.

The grandfather returns to Japan to marry his childhood sweetheart and bring her to America. They establish a home by the San Francisco Bay and soon have a baby daughter. Having a daughter and seeing her grow makes the grandfather think back to his own childhood in Japan. He thinks of his old friends and the mountains and the rivers there. He buys songbirds as pets to try to recreate the sounds he remembers, but he still feels he needs to go back. When his daughter is almost grown-up, he takes his wife and her back to Japan.

He is glad to visit with his old friends again and to see the mountains and rivers he has missed as well. He moves to the city so that his daughter from San Francisco can be more comfortable. She meets a man there and marries him. Later, the author is born. The author enjoys visiting his grandfather on weekends and hearing all about California. They plan a trip to go to America, but that is when World War II breaks out. At the end of the war, bombs fall that destroy the grandfather's home and city.

The last time the author saw his grandfather, he still wanted to see California again. He never made it. The author goes himself once he becomes a young man. There, he has a daughter of his own. Now, he misses the rivers and mountains of his childhood in Japan, and he misses old friends. So, he goes back occasionally. When he is in one country, however, he always finds himself missing the other. In this way, he believes he has come best to know his grandfather, whom he misses very much.

MEDIA: Watercolor.

ANECDOTE: Allen Say was born in Yokohama, Japan, and came to the United States when he was sixteen, to San Francisco, where he lives now. At the 1994 Caldecott award dinner, Say sat beside Lois Lowry. They discovered during dinner that they both lived in Tokyo at the same time; Lowry lived around the corner from Say's school. In his speech, Say related that he was born the first year the Caldecotts were awarded. For his illustrations, Say didn't model them after real people, except for the narrator. He was surprised to realize later that his mother as a young woman ended up looking like a girl he had been fond of in middle school.

DISTINCTION: 1994 Caldecott Medal.

BIRTHDAY: Allen Say: August 28, 1937.

SUBJECTS: Grandfathers—Fiction; Voyages and travels—Fiction; Homesickness—Fiction; Japanese Americans—Fiction; Japan—Fiction; United States—Description and Travel—Fiction.

The Graphic Alphabet (Orchard, 1996). Written and illustrated by David Peletier.

SUMMARY: Using graphic design and computers, Peletier devotes one letter and one word to each page. The letter is presented in a way to suggest pictures that the word helps viewers to interpret. For example, the letter D is a block red letter placed belly-side down so that two short "horns" of the letter poke up and the curved portion below suggest a face. The word below it is "Devil." For the letter E, the letter is thick and placed flat and at an angle so that the edges of the letter are prominent like buildings, and the word below it is "Edge." X is an X-ray of a hand with crossed fingers.

MEDIA: Computer-generated images reproduced in full color.

ANECDOTE: In the late 1990s, computers became a more frequent tool in picture book illustration.

DISTINCTION: 1997 Caldecott Honor Book.

BIRTHDAY: Not available.

SUBJECT: Alphabets.

Graphite. Artist's medium. Sticks of carbon for drawing.

Green Eggs and Ham. *See* Geisel, Theodor (Ted) Seuss.

Green Eyes (Capitol, 1953). Written and illustrated by A. Birnbaum.

SUMMARY: Green Eyes is a white cat that will be one year old soon. She was born in the spring in the country. She tells the reader the story of her life so far. She used to live in a red box and tried very hard to climb out of it. When she got out, she ran around a tree many times and got tired. She remembers the first time she saw chickens, cows, and goats that lived on a nearby farm. When she watched the farmer milk the cows, she received a bowl of warm milk. When it was summer, the cat played outside all day, hiding in the cool grass when it got hot. Some said she looked like a lion in the jungle then. In the fall, Green Eyes chased a fallen leaf in the wind. In the winter, it was too cold to play outside, so the cat enjoyed curling up in her box by the radiator.

Now that it is spring again, Green Eyes is a year old and no longer a kitten. She has a new, bigger pink box. She visualizes how she will spend the rest of the spring, then the summer, fall, and winter because she has seen them all once before.

MEDIA: Not available.

ANECDOTE: For the book's fiftieth anniversary, Golden Books published a deluxe edition; the illustrations look still fresh and contemporary. The cat's gender is not discernible from the text, but perhaps the pink box for the grown cat is a clue.

DISTINCTION: 1954 Caldecott Honor Book.

BIRTHDAY: Not available.

SUBJECTS: Cats—Fiction; Animals—Infancy—Fiction; Seasons—Fiction.

The Grey Lady and the Strawberry Snatcher (Four Winds, 1980). Conceived and illustrated by Molly Bang.

SUMMARY: This is a wordless picture book about a Grey Lady who loves strawberries and who has just purchased some and is taking them home. On her way, she is stalked by the Strawberry Snatcher, who reaches for the strawberries on the red brick sidewalks, city streets, on paths, and in the woods. Bang's illustrations move the Grey Lady in and out of the pictures, blending with the grey background in many cases, to suggest her elusiveness to the Strawberry Snatcher. Finally, when she disappears in the woods, the Strawberry Snatcher finds himself in front of blackberry bushes, which delight and satisfy him. Meanwhile, the Grey Lady has made it home to her grey family, who all enjoy the berries she has brought with her.

MEDIA: Watercolor, occasionally with white gouache undercoat on gray construction paper.

ANECDOTE: Molly Bang once illustrated medical manuals for UNICEF and Johns Hopkins Center for Medical Research.

DISTINCTION: 1981 Caldecott Honor Book.

BIRTHDAY: Molly Bang: December 29, 1943.

SUBJECTS: Strawberries—Fiction; Stories without words.

See Also: Ten, Nine, Eight; When Sophie Gets Angry—Really, Really Angry.

H

Half a Moon and One Whole Star (Macmillan, 1986). Written by Crescent Dragonwagon; illustrated by Jerry Pinkney.

SUMMARY: A rhyming text shows what goes on in the summer night while Susan sleeps. Some creatures sleep; others wake. Her parents talk on the porch; their friends, the Steinkamps, say their farewell. Johnny walks down the street with his saxophone; he will play while Susan sleeps and bakers bake. A sailor on watch alone on the prow of a ship sees the half moon and one whole star and knows that morning is not far away. As morning nears, Johnny will go to bed, and so will the nocturnal animals who have been up with him. The baker and sailor will end their nighttime work and go to bed, too. When the sun is fully up, the half moon and one whole star will slip out of sight and Susan will have another summer day to get ice cream, run, swim, and play.

MEDIA: Not available.

ANECDOTE: The book is dedicated by the author to Susan Sims Smith, presumably the Susan of the story.

DISTINCTION: 1987 Coretta Scott King Award for Illustration.

BIRTHDAYS: Crescent Dragonwagon: November 25, 1952; Jerry Pinkney: December 22, 1939.

SUBJECTS: Night—Fiction; Sleep—Fiction; Stories in rhyme.

Hansel and Gretel (Dodd, 1984). Retold by Rika Lesser; illustrated by Paul O. Zelinsky.

SUMMARY: A woodcutter cannot afford to feed his wife and children, so his wife comes up with a plan. They must build a fire and leave the children there alone. Hansel and Gretel hear their mother's plan. Gretel is fearful, but Hansel tells her he has an idea. Then he goes outside and gathers up shiny white pebbles and puts them in his pocket and goes back to bed. When their parents take them to the woods, Gretel puts the bread they give them under her apron, and Hansel often turns toward the house. He pretends to look back with longing at the house, but instead he is dropping pebbles in the path. After a fire is built, their mother tells them they are going to find more firewood, and they will be right back. When the couple does not return, Gretel begins to cry. When the moon comes up, Hansel leads Gretel down the path to the house, following the trail of white pebbles.

Instead of being happy as Husband was to see her children, the mother was very angry. She tells Husband that he must take the children deeper into the forest. This time, Hansel leaves a secret trail of bread crumbs. This time, however, the animals of the forest eat them up before the children can use them to find their way home. For three days, the children wander about the forest; on the third day, they come to a house made of bread and covered with sweets. An old woman inside hears their calls and comes out to invite them inside for food. Once the children are asleep, the old woman takes Hansel and puts him in a stall to fatten him up. She tells Gretel she is going to eat him.

Hansel doesn't fatten up, no matter how much food she takes to him. Gretel is making bread, when the old woman decides to push her into the oven. Gretel is on to her plan, however, and asks her to show her how far to put the bread in first. When the old woman gets close to the oven, Gretel pushes her in and closes the door. She and Hansel escape and run, but first they take jewels and other riches from the old woman's house. The children run home, where their mother had died, but their father rejoices at their return. With the money from the jewels and treasures, the father and his children live well and happily.

MEDIA: Oil paintings.

ANECDOTE: Zelinsky is a former student of Maurice Sendak. Rika Lesser helped Zelinsky with the writing of his 1998 Caldecott Medal Book, *Rapunzel*.

DISTINCTION: 1985 Caldecott Honor Book.

BIRTHDAYS: Rika Lesser: July 21, 1953; Paul O. Zelinsky: February 14, 1953.

SUBJECTS: Fairy tales; Folklore—Germany.

See Also: Rapunzel; Rumpelstiltskin.

Happy Birthday, Moon (Prentice-Hall, 1982). Written and illustrated by Frank Asch.

SUMMARY: Bear thinks it would be nice to give Moon a birthday present, but he doesn't know when Moon's birthday is. When he calls to the moon from atop a tree, Moon doesn't answer. Bear rows across a river, walks through the woods, and climbs a mountain, until he appears to be closer to Moon. He begins to call to Moon again. When he asks his questions now, he hears the echo of his own voice and thinks this is the moon replying to him. When the moon "responds" that its birthday is tomorrow and it wants a hat, Bear grows excited. He empties out his piggy bank, goes to the store, and chooses a hat for Moon. He puts the hat on a tree branch in his yard and waits. As the moon crosses the sky, it soon appears to be right beneath the hat, trying it on. Bear is happy that the hat fits Moon so well.

During the night the hat falls out of the tree onto Bear's doorstep. When Bear wakes up, he thinks Moon has given him a hat for his birthday, too. He puts it on, and it fits just right, but just then the wind takes off with it, and the hat is lost. Bear rows across the river, walks through the forest, and climbs the mountain again to have another chat with the moon. Moon does not speak to Bear at first. Fearing Moon might be angry with him, Bear tells him what happened, that he lost the hat he gave him. Moon replies in kind that it lost the hat he gave him. Bear says he still loves Moon, and Moon says he still loves Bear.

MEDIA: Not determined.

ANECDOTE: Asch taught as a Montessori teacher in India and New Jersey. He was influenced as a children's book author by Maurice Sendak and E. B. White.

DISTINCTION: *New York Times* Best Book for Children.

BIRTHDAY: Frank Asch: August 6, 1946.

SUBJECTS: Bears—Fiction; Birthdays—Ficton; Moon—Fiction.

The Happy Day (Harper, 1949). Written by Ruth Krauss, illustrated by Marc Simont.

SUMMARY: The bears, field mice, snails, squirrels, groundhogs and other animals are all asleep for the winter. One day, they all open their eyes and sniff. They sniff some

Front cover of *Harlem: A Poem*, written by Walter Dean Myers, illustrated by Christopher Myers. The author celebrates his hometown of Harlem in this book, while his son received both a 1998 Coretta Scott King Honor award for illustration and a Caldecott Honor award. The art of creating picture books is handed down in several authors' and artists' families, sometimes beginning with collaborations such as this one. (Illustration by Christopher Myers from *Harlem: A Poem* by Walter Dean Myers. Published by Scholastic Press/Scholastic Inc. Jacket illustration copyright © 1997 by Christopher Myers. Reprinted by permission.)

more, and they run. All the animals run to the same spot in the forest where they smell the scent. It is a happy day because there they find a single yellow flower growing up through the snow, signaling spring.

MEDIA: Charcoal.

DISTINCTION: 1950 Caldecott Honor Book.

BIRTHDAYS: Ruth Krauss: July 25, 1901; Marc Simont: November 23, 1915.

SUBJECTS: Bears—Fiction; Winter—Fiction.

Harlem: A Poem (Scholastic, 1997). Written by Walter Dean Myers; illustrated by Christopher Myers.

SUMMARY: The book is a poem about Harlem, as the title indicates, full of images of the migration there, the A train, the Apollo, the blues, Langston and Countee, the Cotton Club, 110th Street, funeral cars, open fire hydrants, basketball, front steps, music, and lots of people, some happy and some not. The author says the A train continues a journey in Harlem that began on the banks of the Niger River in Africa and that is not yet over.

MEDIA: Ink, gouache, and cut-paper collage.

ANECDOTE: Walter Dean Myers grew up in Harlem. Christopher Myers is his son.

DISTINCTIONS: 1998 Caldecott Honor Book; 1998 Coretta Scott King Honor Book for Illustration.

BIRTHDAY: Walter Dean Myers: August 12, 1937.

SUBJECTS: African Americans—Poetry; Children's Poetry—American; American Poetry; Harlem (New York, N.Y.)—Poetry.

Harold and the Purple Crayon (Harper, 1955). Written and illustrated by Crockett Johnson.

SUMMARY: Wearing his blue pajamas, bald-headed Harold thinks things over and decides to take a walk in the moonlight. Since there is no moon, he first draws one with his purple crayon, then draws a straight path for his walk. As the need arises on his journey, Harold draws a shortcut, a one-tree forest, apples, a dragon, an ocean, a boat, beach, picnic, nine pies in flavors that Harold likes best, a hungry moose, a porcupine, a hill that turns into a mountain, a hot-air balloon, grass, a house, windows, a city of buildings with many windows, a police officer, his bedroom window, his bed, and his covers. At the end of Harold's adventure, the purple crayon falls to the floor, and Harold falls asleep under the covers drawn snugly up to his chin.

MEDIA: Possibly ink.

ANECDOTE: There were several sequels to the book, including *Harold's Fairy Tale*, *Harold's Trip to the Sky*, *Harold at the North Pole*, *Harold's ABC*, *Harold's Circus*, and an early reader, *A Picture for Harold's Room*. Crockett Johnson is a pen name for David Johnson Leisk. Johnson drew the comic strip "Barnaby" starting in 1942 and running for 21 years. It was adapted into a play and a book, as well as developed for radio and television. Johnson's scant-haired appearance was not unlike Harold's or Barnaby's.

DISTINCTIONS: *New York Times* Best Book for Children; NYPL 100 Picture Books Everyone Should Know; *100 Best Books for Children*.

BIRTHDAY: Crockett Johnson: October 20, 1906.

SUBJECT: Fantasy.

See Also: The Carrot Seed.

Harry the Dirty Dog (Harper, 1956). Written by Gene Zion; illustrated by Margaret Bloy Graham.

SUMMARY: Harry is a white dog with black spots, but when he needs a bath, he runs the other way. One day, he grabs the scrubbing brush and buries it in the garden and runs away. He gets dirty on his adventures in the streets, at the railroad tracks, at a construction site, and near a pile of coal. He is so dirty that he is unrecognizable to his family when he gets home. His white fur has turned black, and his black spots appear lighter, so that his coloring appears reversed. Harry tries to do jumps and tricks for his family to convince them he is Harry, but they do not believe it is he. Finally, he finds the scrubbing brush and runs upstairs to the bathroom. The family sees that this little dog wants a bath, so they give him one, and as they do, they discover Harry. All are happy and well, and Harry takes a nap at the end of the book from all his adventures. However, he has hidden the scrubbing brush underneath his dog bed.

MEDIA: Possibly pencil, charcoal, and watercolor.

ANECDOTE: Zion and Graham were married.

DISTINCTIONS: NYPL 100 Picture Books Everyone Should Know; *100 Best Books for Children*.

BIRTHDAYS: Gene Zion: October 5, 1913; Margaret Bloy Graham: November 2, 1920.

SUBJECT: Dogs—Fiction.

See Also: All Falling Down; The Storm Book.

Have You Seen My Duckling? (Greenwillow, 1984). Written and illustrated by Nancy Tafuri.

SUMMARY: In this nearly wordless book, Mother Duck searches for her missing duckling who has wandered off chasing a butterfly. The other ducklings tell her that one of them is missing, and the search begins. As Mother Duck inquires of various other pond animals such as birds, beavers, fish, and other waterfowl whether each has seen her baby, keen observers of the book can see the little duckling hidden among the greenery and other locations on each page. Finally, Mother Duck spots the little duckling next to the turtle in the water. When the baby rejoins his family swimming in a line, the turtle follows close behind as the butterfly flies again overhead, tempting the duckling to stray once again.

MEDIA: Watercolors and pastels.

ANECDOTE: Nancy Tafuri's husband gave her the idea for this story; he suggested that she write about the mallard duck and her young that lived on their property.

DISTINCTION: 1985 Caldecott Honor Book.

SUBJECTS: Lost children—Fiction; Ducks—Fiction; Ponds—Fiction.

Hawk, I'm Your Brother (Scribner, 1976). Written by Byrd Baylor; illustrated by Peter Panall.

SUMMARY: Rudy Soto wants to fly, not like a sparrow but like a hawk, gliding high. That is his only dream where he lives at Santos Mountain. He feels like he could be a hawk's brother. One day, he steals a baby hawk from its nest, thinking perhaps he can learn the magic of flight from it and be the hawk's brother. Though he is otherwise kind to the bird, he keeps the hawk tied and caged. The hawk cries to its bird brothers in the sky who have learned to fly. The sky shines in the hawk's eyes, day after day, and Rudy learns he must climb Santos Mountain and let the hawk go. When he does, the hawk calls down to him as a brother, and Rudy lives the rest of his days hearing and answering the call of his hawk brother. The day he let him go was the day he felt himself fly free in the wind.

MEDIA: Possibly pen and ink.

ANECDOTE: Baylor writes frequently about the Southwest.

DISTINCTION: 1977 Caldecott Honor Book.

BIRTHDAYS: Byrd Baylor: March 28, 1924; Peter Parnall: May 23, 1936.

SUBJECTS: Hawks—Fiction; Flight—Fiction.

See Also: *The Desert Is Theirs*; *When Clay Sings*.

Henry Fisherman (Scribner, 1949). Written and illustrated by Marcia Brown.

SUMMARY: Henry wants to work as a fisherman at St. Thomas, Virgin Islands, like his father, Jonas. Jonas says that he is still too little to go to sea in his boat, the *Ariadne*; he is too tempting for sharks. Henry finds other things to do in St. Thomas as he waits to get old enough to go to sea. He holds the day's water on his head in a pail without spilling it, washes clothes with his sister Bianca, fetches fresh tropical fruits such as pawpaw, pineapple, and bananas for his mother; and tends to the family's three goats—Jimmy, Annie, and Eleanor—in the field. Each day, he spends much of his time at the docks, dreaming of going out on the fishing boat. One day, Henry goes out to sea with his father and dives for the fishpot. He does his job well, but he narrowly escapes a shark. His father says he is ready to be a fisherman; he dives well and swims fast enough now to escape danger.

MEDIA: Possibly collage.

ANECDOTE: The book is dedicated to the children of St. Thomas and is written in island dialect.

DISTINCTION: 1950 Caldecott Honor Book.

BIRTHDAY: Marcia Brown: July 13, 1918.

SUBJECTS: Fishing—Fiction; Virgin Islands—Fiction.

See Also: *Cinderella, or The Little Glass Slipper*; *Dick Whittington and His Cat*; *Stone Soup*.

Hershel and the Hanukkah Goblins (Holiday, 1989). Written by Eric Kimmel; illustrated by Trina Schart Hyman.

SUMMARY: On the first night of Hanukkah, Hershel of Ostropol arrives in the village hoping to see the lit candles and have plates of potato latkes, but instead the village is dark. He learns from the rabbi that there is no Hanukkah celebration because the goblins that haunt the synagogue on the hill blow out the candles and dump the latkes on the floor. They do not allow the Jewish people to practice their faith all year, but it is particularly hard for them during Hanukkah. Hershel offers to rid the synagogue of the goblins, but he learns that he must stay eight nights there and light the Hanukkah candles each night; on the eighth night, a goblin must light them; then the spell of the goblins will be broken.

Hershel fools the first goblin, who is very small. He crushes a boiled egg in his hand, and the goblin believes that he is strong enough to crush stone. The second night, Hershel lures a plump goblin to eat pickles and gets his hand stuck in the pickle jar. The third night, he makes up his own version of the dreidel game and causes the third goblin to lose all his gold and go away. Each night Hershel fools another goblin and lights another candle. Finally, the last night of Hanukkah, the King of the Goblins arrives. Hershel plays into his pride by telling him that he cannot see him unless he lights all of the candles. When the King does this, the synagogue explodes, leaving the completely lit menorah, and Hershel returns to the village, which can celebrate Hanukkah again.

An author's note explains the origin of the holiday as well as how to play the dreidel game.

MEDIA: India ink and acrylic paint.

DISTINCTION: 1990 Caldecott Honor Book.

BIRTHDAYS: Trina Schart Hyman: April 8, 1939; Eric Kimmel: October 30, 1946.

SUBJECTS: Hanukkah—Fiction; Goblins—Fiction.

See Also: A Child's Calendar.

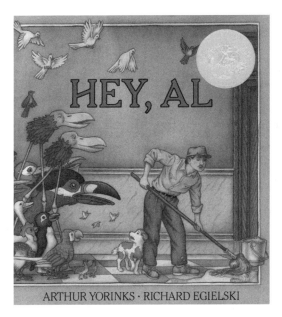

Cover of *Hey, Al*, written by Arthur Yorinks, illustrated by Richard Egielski. The collaborators were first introduced by Maurice Sendak. (Reprinted by permission of Farrar, Straus and Giroux, LLC: *Hey, Al* by Arthur Yorinks, pictures by Richard Egielski. Pictures copyright © 1986 by Richard Egielski. www.fsgkidsbooks.com.)

Hey, Al (Farrar, Straus and Giroux, 1986). Written by Arthur Yorinks; illustrated by Richard Egielski.

SUMMARY: Al and his dog, Eddie, live together on the West Side. Al is a janitor and a quiet man. They struggle to make a go of it in a tiny apartment. Eddie really wants a house with a backyard where he can run around. While he's shaving one day, Al sees a large bird poke its head through the bathroom window. The bird invites him and Eddie to his place. The next day, the bird comes for them and flies them to a beautiful island in the sky. The island is a tropical paradise full of colorful birds of all sorts. Al and Eddie decide they love it. Pretty soon, though, they discover that they are turning into birds with beaks and feathers. Al says he would rather mop floors than become a bird. Eddie and Al fly away, but Eddie falls into the sea. Al arrives home and is sad, but Eddie arrives soon afterwards; he is a good swimmer. Al begins to paint and fix up their apartment, knowing that he has traded paradise in the sky for heaven on earth with Eddie.

MEDIA: Watercolor.

ANECDOTE: Yorinks used money from the sale of this book to buy rural property in Nova Scotia, where there are lots of birds. As a child, he was afraid of birds due to his aunt allowing one to fly loose in her house and also to the Alfred Hitchcock movie, *The Birds*. Maurice Sendak arranged a meeting between Yorinks and Egielski because he thought their work complemented each other. They saw each other for the first time in an elevator.

DISTINCTION: 1987 Caldecott Medal.

BIRTHDAYS: Arthur Yorinks: August 21, 1953; Richard Egielski: July 16, 1952.

SUBJECTS: Birds—Fiction; Dogs—Fiction.

Hide and Seek Fog (Lothrop, 1965). Written by Alvin Tresselt; illustrated by Roger Duvoisin.

SUMMARY: A lobsterman is the first to see the fog rolling in. He drops one more lobster pot and makes his way back to shore. Families vacationing call in their children from the beach and move inside their cottages. A thick fog passes over the coastline and settles in the town for three days. It is the worst fog in twenty years. While it is foggy, the lobsterman repairs lobster pots, and the fathers, discouraged that the fog is ruining their vacations, take the mothers to town to do some shopping. The mothers help children make scrapbooks by the fire. The children are the only ones who enjoy the fog. They play hide-and-seek in it among the rocks. Finally, the thick fog breaks on the third afternoon, and the day is sunny and clear again, the sun sparkling off the ocean. The lobsterman checks out his boat to ready it for the next day's sail; sailors prepare their boats for a race around the islands; and the families are back out on the beach having a clambake with their children.

MEDIA: Full-color gouache.

ANECDOTE: The book is set in a seaside village on Cape Cod. Alvin Tresselt was the editor of *Humpty Dumpty Magazine* from 1952 to 1965.

DISTINCTION: 1966 Caldecott Honor Book.

BIRTHDAY: Alvin Tresselt: September 30, 1916.

SUBJECTS: Fog—Fiction; Weather—Fiction.

See Also: White Snow, Bright Snow.

Hildilid's Night (Macmillan, 1971). Written by Cheli Durán Ryan; illustrated by Arnold Lobel.

SUMMARY: An old woman named Hildilid lives in the hills near Hexham. She hates the night and all of its creatures such as bats, owls, moles, voles, and moths, and she also dislikes the stars, shadows, sleep, and moonlight. One night she tells her old wolfhound that she wonders why no one has thought to sweep the night away. She takes twigs and makes a broom and commences sweeping. It doesn't work.

Next, Hildilid sews a sack to fill it with the night, but that doesn't work either. Her other attempts include trying to boil the night in a cauldron, tying it up in vines, shearing it, feeding it to the wolfhound, tucking it into her bed, dipping it in the well, burning it with a candle, singing it lullabies, pouring it milk, shaking her fist at it, smoking it in the chimney, stamping on it, spanking it, and digging a grave for it. She even spits at the night, but the night doesn't notice. Hildilid decides not to notice the night and turns her back on it. Just then, the sun comes up, but now Hildilid is so tired from struggling against the night that she goes to bed and sleeps all day. She wants to be fresh for the next night when she plans to turn her back on the night and disregard it as the night disregards her.

MEDIA: Possibly pen and ink.

ANECDOTE: It has been said that the book is used to help calm children who are afraid of the dark.

DISTINCTION: 1972 Caldecott Honor Book.

BIRTHDAY: Arnold Lobel: May 22, 1933.

SUBJECT: Night—Fiction.

See Also: Fables; Frog and Toad Are Friends; On Market Street.

Hogrogian, Nonny (1932–). Author and artist. One of only seven double Caldecott award-winning artists, Hogrogian was born in the Bronx on May 7, 1932, to Rachel Ansoorian and Henry Mugerditch Hogrogian. Her parents were of Armenian descent, and both were interested in art. Hogrogian's mother was a painter, and her father spent time copying the works of masters such as Monet, Homer, and Renoir, on weekends. Hogrogian played with her father's paints from about the age of three. By the time she reached high school, she had a burning desire to become an artist and applied for admission into the selective School of Music and Art in New York. As part of the application process, she was asked to make a contour drawing. Though the concept was new to the young artist, she worked on a drawing that showed she was getting the idea of what it was the administrators were looking for. Had she had a second chance at the drawing, Hogrogian has said, she may have been admitted. As it was, her admission was declined, and her ambition to study art seriously and her confidence in her work took a hard hit.

Instead of counting on a school to educate her in art, then, Hogrogian set out to teach herself. She began with the contour drawing that had been her downfall at the school and went on to teach herself lettering. She also picked up techniques along the way as best she could from people she met. One artist who made and sold cards taught her to dry-brush while she colored in the cards for a nickel each; her aunt taught her how to paint. She also picked up how to do etching, lithography, and woodcutting. At Hunter College in New York, Hogrogian was finally able to study more formally and majored in art. There, she studied such techniques as fabric design, illustration, and stage set design. Her formal education continued with lessons from Antonio Grasconi at the New School of Social Research and at the Haystack Mountain School of Crafts in Maine. After she accomplished this training, Hogrogian acquired a job at a book publisher as a book designer and art buyer.

Hogrogian's creative desires continued to challenge her. While she enjoyed designing books for others and illustrating some books on her own, she found the work less and less satisfying because she was consistently working with other people's ideas and art. She began to consider quitting her job to seek a master's degree in order to pay more attention to the development of her own artistic themes and styles. Just as she was completing the paperwork for the application, Hogrogian discovered that she had been awarded the 1966 Caldecott Medal for *Always Room for One More*, written by Sorche Nic Leodhas (the pseudonym of Alger LeClaire). It seems that applications to art schools portended radical changes in Hogrogian's future more than once in her life.

Winning the award allowed her to spend more time on her own art and ideas. At the same time, it increased her national exposure and instilled in Hogrogian a sense of responsibility to live up to the reputation she now held in the field. When she had illustrated Sorche Nic Leodhas' *Gaelic Ghosts* (Holt, 1963), he had told her that the figures had more of a Romanian look than a Scottish one, and Hogrogian took this criticism seriously. When she worked on *Always Room for One More*, she did her homework in a vigorous bout of research that included studying photographs of Scottish people, listening to Scottish music, looking at slides of Scottish cottages, and analyzing Scottish clothing from books in the library to determine what Lachie and his cohorts might wear.

One person who admired Hogrogian's new reputation and artistic style was writer and poet David Kherdian, who first saw one of Hogrogian's books in a bookstore in Santa Fe, New Mexico. Kherdian contacted Hogrogian about creating the cover for his new book of poems. They enjoyed sharing each other's Armenian heritage, and Hogrogian agreed to do the work. After some time of corresponding, they met in New York when Kherdian arrived there to attend a reception in his honor as the new editor of *Ararat* magazine in 1971. On March 17, 1971, the two were married. They embarked on a mutual life of writing and art by moving to an old farmhouse in New Hampshire. There, Kherdian worked for the state's Poet-in-the-Schools program and on his poetry. Hogrogian created her art, taking freelance projects of up to four books a year. The couple had animals and a garden and kept in touch with family and friends for companionship.

Working solely in the arts is difficult on almost anyone's finances, and the couple worked hard to keep things going. Hogrogian was about to turn to the doors of a school one more time to make a change in her life—this time as a teacher. She thought a steady, reliable income was what the couple needed. She and her husband sat huddled together near the fire in their New Hampshire farmhouse discussing the situation one January evening when the electricity had gone out during a storm. Lazily drinking brandy and launching into a series of possibilities in her thinking, Hogrogian lightheartedly posed the suggestion to her husband that maybe she would win another Caldecott Medal. David told her how silly and unlikely this was, but Hogrogian protested. She was drawing book after book, at a steady rate, after all. The couple playfully speculated in this way until the lights came back on, then both went back to their work for another hour or so. Just as she was finishing her work for the day, Hogrogian received the phone call from Anne Izard that she had, indeed, won a second Caldecott Medal, this one for *One Fine Day*, which she both wrote and illustrated. The second medal allowed Hogrogian to slow down her output and spend time working to her satisfaction on fewer, more choice projects.

The couple moved to another farmhouse in Oregon and pursued their mutual and independent creative projects. In 1977, Hogrogian won a Caldecott Honor Book Award for *The Contest*. Hogrogian illustrated several of her husband's books, including his *The Road from Home: The Story of an Armenian Girl* (Knopf, 1979), which was about David's mother and her actual experience of seeing the death and destruction portrayed in the novel. The book won a 1980 Newbery Honor Book Award. By the 1990s, the couple returned to New York state and settled in Spencertown.

Hogrogian is most appreciated for her versatility as an artist and her ability to set the proper mood in a picture book so that the artwork matches the story being told. For example, she abandoned her favored woodcutting for *Always Room for One More* when the heather suggested to her that the artwork needed a lighter touch. Instead, she used pen-and-ink line and crosshatch with gray wash and lavender and green pastels. In *One Fine Day*, she turned to oils full of rich and warm color. Not only her artwork but also her writing have been acknowledged as lively and engaging for children.

Hogrogian's publications began to taper off in the 1990s, but not before she had written and created artwork for several memorable picture books for children.

DISTINCTIONS: 1966, 1972 Caldecott Medals (one of only seven existing double medalists); 1977 Caldecott Honor Book.

Further Reading: Hogrogian, Nonny. "Caldecott Award Acceptance." *Horn Book Magazine* (August 1966): 419–421; Hogrogian, Nonny. "Caldecott Award Acceptance: How the Caldecott Changed My Life—Twice." *Horn Book Magazine* (August 1972): 352–355.

See Also: Always Room for One More; *The Contest*; *One Fine Day*.

Hondo & Fabian (Henry Holt, 2002). Written and illustrated by Peter McCarty.

SUMMARY: Fabian is a cat, and Hondo is a dog. Their favorite places are the windowsill (Fabian) and the floor (Hondo). Hondo goes on an adventure in the car. He meets his dog friend Fred at the beach. Meanwhile, Fabian plays with the baby girl at home. While Hondo and Fred dive in the waves, Fabian has fun with the toilet paper.

Hondo would like to eat the fish the man has caught in the ocean; Fabian would like to eat the turkey sandwich he sees on the table. Finally, Hondo comes home, and he and Fabian eat their dinner side by side from their bowls. Plump and satisfied, they go back to their favorite places (floor and window) and go to sleep, and the baby goes to sleep, too.

MEDIA: Pencil on watercolor paper.

DISTINCTION: 2003 Caldecott Honor Book.

BIRTHDAY: Not available.

SUBJECTS: Dogs—Fiction; Cats—Fiction; Pets—Fiction.

Hosie's Alphabet (Viking, 1972). Written by Hosea, Tobias, and Lisa Baskin; illustrated by Leonard Baskin.

SUMMARY: Many of the words for this book are unusually long and complex for an alphabet book, and some of the drawings may be a bit scary for very young children, making this picture book perhaps more appropriate for older children. For example, P is for "primordial protozoa," and L is for "the omnivorous swarming locust," while demons, vultures, dragons, and gargoyles make up some of the other images. For the right child or group of children, the book challenges the ears with wordplay and the eyes with edgy artwork.

MEDIA: Watercolor.

ANECDOTE: This book started as a project in the Baskin family when Leonard's three-year-old son, Hosea, asked him to draw an alphabet. Hosea, his brother, Tobias, and their mother, Lisa, wrote the words, and Leonard drew the pictures.

DISTINCTION: 1973 Caldecott Honor Book.

BIRTHDAY: Leonard Baskin: August 15, 1922.

SUBJECT: Alphabet.

A House Is a House for Me (Viking, 1978). Written by Mary Ann Hoberman; illustrated by Betty Fraser.

SUMMARY: In rhyming verse, this book describes houses and dwellings of various animals and moves to more abstract concepts such as houses for reflections and hums. Houses and dwelling objects or other words of inclusion or enclosure used in the book include hill, hive, hole, web, nest, rug, coop, sty, fold, barn, kennel, hutch, shed, castle, puddles, lakes, sea, shell, igloo, teepee, pueblo, wigwam, garage, hangar, dock, terminal, husk, pod, nutshell, glove, stocking, shoe, boot, box, teapot, cup, carton, bed, barrel, bottle, pot, sandwich, cookie jar, bread box, coat, hat, a mirror for reflections, a throat for a hum, pockets, pens, peaches for pits, trash cans, garbage for germs, envelopes, earmuffs, eggshells, bathrobes, baskets, bins, ragbags, rubbers, roasters, tablecloths, toasters, tins, a book for a story, a rose for a smell, heads for a secret; a garden is home for a garden; a stall is home to a donkey, and earth is home for it all. The illustrations show other possibilities for house and home, such as a baseball mit for a baseball, a kangaroo pouch for its baby, and a pincushion for pins.

MEDIA: Not available.

ANECDOTE: Hoberman is a poet whose work has appeared in *Harper's* and the *Southern Poetry Review*. Some of the illustrations depict well-known children's stories such as *Alice's Adventures in Wonderland* and *The Story of Ferdinand*.

DISTINCTION: 1983 National Book Award.

BIRTHDAY: Mary Ann Hoberman: August 12, 1930.

SUBJECTS: Dwellings—Fiction; Stories in rhyme.

The House That Jack Built—La Maison Que Jacques a Batie: A Picture Book in Two Languages (Harcourt, 1958). Written and illustrated by Antonio Frasconi.

SUMMARY: The popular building nursery rhyme is given in English, then French, line by line. Vocabulary includes house, malt, rat, cat, dog, cow, maiden, man, priest, and cock.

The book ends with questions about the rhyme in English with responses in French.

MEDIA: Woodcuts.

ANECDOTE: Frasconi immigrated to the United States from South America and had difficulty learning English. When he began creating picture books, he wrote many bilingual books to help his son, Pablo, understand that there are many languages to use to say something. His work pre-dates the late-twentieth-century and early twenty-first-century focus on bilingual books for children.

BIRTHDAY: Antonio Frasconi: 1919.

DISTINCTION: 1959 Caldecott Honor Book.

SUBJECTS: Children's poetry—English; Children's poetry—French; French language—Readers; Nursery rhymes; Nursery rhymes—English; Nursery rhymes—French.

Houses from the Sea (Scribner, 1959).

Written by Alice E. Goudey; illustrated by Adrienne Adams.

SUMMARY: A boy and his sister go to the beach and pick up its natural treasures. The book describes these shells and other things. Shells discussed include moon shells, jingle shells, cockleshells, cowrie shells, keyhole limpets, periwinkle, wedge shells, wentle-traps, scallops, top shells, slipper shells, turret shells, clamshells (also known as quahogs), and welk shells. Other creatures and elements from the sea mentioned are the sandpiper, Hippa crabs, butterflies, seaweed, seagull, and hermit crabs. At the end of the book is a spread with all the different kinds of shells labeled with their names and an author's note about how shells are made.

MEDIA: Possibly watercolor.

ANECDOTE: Goudey spent summers in Maine. Adams once said that the most exciting time of being a book illustrator was not when the book arrived complete but the moment of beginning a new book with the hope of making it better than the one before.

DISTINCTION: 1960 Caldecott Honor Book.

BIRTHDAY: Adrienne Adams: February 8, 1906.

SUBJECT: Shells.

See Also: The Day We Saw the Sun Come Up.

Hush! A Thai Lullaby (Orchard, 1996).

Written by Minfong Ho; illustrated by Holly Meade.

SUMMARY: A mother is trying to keep things quiet for her sleeping baby, but creatures from the wild keep endangering the quiet. A mosquito is weeping, a lizard is peeping, a cat is creeping. Animals and their sounds get increasingly larger—a monkey is swinging, a buffalo is sweeping, and finally an elephant is shrieking. The mother runs and tells each of them to hush, that her baby is sleeping. By the time night falls and the moon is out, the mother herself is asleep at the windowsill, exhausted from hushing all of the animals. Of course, by then her baby is wide awake.

MEDIA: Cut-paper collage with ink.

ANECDOTE: The author grew up in Thailand, falling asleep to the various soft sounds of the countryside. Later, as a mother, she made up the rhyming words of this lullabye to sing her own baby to sleep when they were in northern Thailand.

DISTINCTION: 1997 Caldecott Honor Book.

BIRTHDAYS: Minfong Ho: January 7, 1951; Holly Meade: September 14, 1956.

SUBJECTS: Lullabies—American; American poetry; Thailand—Poetry.

I

I Read Signs (Greenwillow, 1983). Conceived and photographed by Tana Hoban.

SUMMARY: This is a concept book about signs. The reader sees "environmental print" in the form of photographs of thirty everyday road signs. Often a child is able to read the signs with the additional aids of the size, color, and shape of the sign and relating the signs in the book to signs she or he sees in the world and how the signs change people's behavior. For example, the STOP sign is octagonal, red with white letters, and people do what the sign says when they read it.

MEDIA: Photography.

ANECDOTE: Tana Hoban likes to encourage children to look at everyday objects all around them in new ways. She was born in Philadelphia of Russian immigrant parents and has lived in Holland, England, and France. She has created more than two dozen children's books. Her photographs are also part of the collection of the Museum of Modern Art. Though not related to this picture book, the first word American poet Sylvia Plath read as a child in the 1930s, according to her mother, was the word "POTS," which she read by reversing the letters on a STOP sign. The book has helped children recognize and read these familiar words in their environment.

DISTINCTION: Author's choice.
BIRTHDAY: Not available.
SUBJECTS: Traffic signs and signals; Street signs; Signs and signboards.

i see the rhythm (Children's, 1998). Written by Toyomi Igus; illustrated by Michele Wood.

SUMMARY: The book traces African American history from its roots in Africa through the 1990s using the motif of music. Each double-page spread contains art, poetic text, a description of a musical style, and a timeline of historical events related to African American history and culture. Kinds of music addressed include African tribal music; slave songs; blues; ragtime; jazz; swing; female jazz singers; bebop; cool jazz; Gospel; rhythm and blues and soul; rock and roll; funk; rap and hiphop.

MEDIA: Possibly oil on canvas.

ANECDOTE: Wood places a little girl character, Missy (her nickname when she was small), into every scene of the book. She is not always easy to find, and this makes a scavenger hunt possible to find her in each picture. The author and artist collaborated to tell Wood's personal story in a picture book that won the American Book Award in 1997. That book is titled *Going Back Home: An Artist Returns to the South.*

DISTINCTION: 1999 Coretta Scott King Award for Illustration.

BIRTHDAY: Not available.

SUBJECTS: African Americans—Music—History and criticism.

If All the Seas Were One Sea (Macmillan, 1972). Written and illustrated by Janina Domanska.

SUMMARY: A rhyming text explains how great it would be if all the seas, trees, axes, and men were one sea, tree, ax, and man. The man would cut the tree with his ax; it would fall into the great sea and make a large splash.

MEDIA: Etchings on zinc plates with brush-and-ink overlays.

ANECDOTE: Janina Domanska was born in Poland and was a prisoner in a concentration camp during World War II. She studied art in Poland and Italy.

DISTINCTION: 1972 Caldecott Honor Book.

BIRTHDAY: Janina Domanska: 1912.

SUBJECTS: Children's poetry; Nursery rhymes.

If I Ran the Zoo (Random House, 1950). Written and illustrated by Theodor Seuss Geisel (pseud. Dr. Seuss).

SUMMARY: Young Gerald McGrew tells what new things he'd like to see in a zoo. He'd open the cages and let all the old-fashioned animals out, then put new animals in. His new animals include a ten-footed lion; hens that roost on each others' topknots; an Elephant-Cat; a Bustard; a Flustard; and more. Young Gerald McGrew would rig up his Skeegle-Mobile and go looking around the world for different and new kinds of beasts such as Joats, Lunks, a Mulligatawny, an Iota, Thwerll, Chuggs, Mazurka, Gusset, a Gherkin, Gasket, Gooch, a Natch, Obsk, a Russian Palooski, an It-Kutch, a Preep, a Proo, a Nerkle, Nerd, and Seersucker. Others include Bippo-no-Bungus and a Fizza-

ma-Wizza-ma-Dill. He would have the best zoo in the world for all the fantastic and new creatures he had to show; that's what he'd do.

MEDIA: Pencil, ink, and watercolor.

ANECDOTE: Theodor Geisel's father ran a zoo in Springfield, Massachusetts.

DISTINCTION: 1951 Caldecott Honor Book.

BIRTHDAY: Dr. Seuss: March 2, 1904.

SUBJECTS: Fantasy; Stories in rhyme.

See Also: Bartholomew and the Oobleck; Geisel, Theodor (Ted) Seuss; *McElligott's Pool*.

If You Give a Mouse a Cookie (Harper, 1985). Written by Laura Jaffe Numeroff; illustrated by Felicia Bond.

SUMMARY: Like a persistent child, if the mouse takes a cookie from a boy he is not satisfied. He will want milk, and that will make him want a straw and then a napkin. He'll want a mirror to be sure he doesn't have a milk mustache, but then when he sees himself, he will want a pair of nail scissors to give his hair a trim. Then he'll need a broom to sweep up the hair from his trim off the floor. He'll probably get carried away washing all the floors in the house and then want a nap because he's so tired. For this, he'll need a box for a bed that the boy will have to make, and some covers and a pillow. Then, of course, he will want a story.

As the boy reads him the story, he'll ask to see the pictures, then he'll want to draw a picture of his own. Next, he'll ask for paper and crayons. He'll want to sign his name with a pen and then he'll need Scotch tape to tape his drawing to the refrigerator. After all that, he'll be thirsty again from looking at the refrigerator, and he'll ask for a glass of milk. . . . and another cookie!

MEDIA: Possibly pen and ink, watercolor, and colored pencils.

ANECDOTE: Numeroff dedicated the book to her parents.

DISTINCTION: *New York Times* Best Book for Children; NYPL 100 Picture Books Everyone Should Know.

BIRTHDAYS: Felicia Bond: July 18, 1954; Laura Jaffe Numeroff: July 14, 1953.

SUBJECT: Mice—Fiction.

In Daddy's Arms I Am Tall: African Americans Celebrating Fathers (Lee, 1997). Selected and illustrated by Javaka Steptoe.

SUMMARY: The book is an anthology containing an Ashanti proverb and 12 poems to and about fathers. Poems and poets include "in daddy's arms," by Folami Abiade; "Artist to Artist," by Davida Adedjouma; "Promises," by David A. Anderson; "Lightning Jumpshot," by Michael Burgess; "Tickle Tickle," by Dakari Hru; "Her Daddy's Hands," by Angela Johnson; "My Granddaddy Is My Daddy Too," by Dinah Johnson; "The Things in Black Men's Closets," by E. Ethelbert Miller; "Black Father Man," by Lenard D. Moore; "My Father's Eyes," by Sonia Sanchez; "Seeds," by Javaka Steptoe; and "The Farmer," by Carole Boston Weatherford.

MEDIA: Mixed media of collage and paintings, including torn and cut paper with pastel, appliqué, and found objects.

ANECDOTE: Steptoe is the son of illustrator John Steptoe, whom he occasionally helped as a child by modeling for his illustrations. This book was Javaka's stellar debut. He says he uses found objects and scraps of materials in his collages to represent the history of his people, who made art out of the scraps of life in order to survive 400 years of hardship and oppression.

DISTINCTION: 1998 Coretta Scott King Award for Illustration.

BIRTHDAY: Javaka Steptoe: April 19, 1971.

SUBJECTS: Children's poetry, American—African American authors; Fathers—United States—Poetry; African American fathers—Poetry; Men—United States—Po-etry; African American men—Poetry; Fathers—Poetry; African Americans—Poetry; American poetry—Collections.

In My Mother's House (Viking, 1941). Written by Ann Nolan Clark; illustrated by Velino Herrera.

SUMMARY: The book contains twenty-nine poems about the land, animals, vegetation, customs, and culture of the Tewa people. The poems include "Home," "The Pueblo," "The People," "The Council," "Fields," "Arroyos," "Pasture," "Land," "Lakes," "Rivers," "Ditches," "Irrigation," "The Windmill," "The Spring," "The Pipeline," "Cows," "Sheep," "Goats," "Horses," "Trees," "Juniper," "Wild Plants," "Indian Tea," "Yucca," "Chamiso," "Guaco," "Wild Animals," "Birds," and "Mountains." Most of the artwork is made up of black-and-white line drawings; however, a few are rendered in vibrant color.

MEDIA: Possibly pen and ink and pastel.

ANECDOTE: Clark is regarded as one of the first authors for young people to write of Native Americans and their cultures with accuracy and respect. During Clark's days as a student at New Mexico Highlands University, she taught Tewa Indians at the Tesuque Pueblo in Santa Fe. Her first publication was a poem that appeared in a local newspaper and celebrated New Mexico's becoming the 47th state of the United States in 1912.

DISTINCTION: 1942 Caldecott Honor Book.

BIRTHDAY: Ann Nolan Clark: December 25, 1896.

SUBJECTS: Tewa Indians—Poetry; Indians of North America—Poetry; Children's Poetry, American; American Poetry.

In the Forest (Viking, 1944). Written and illustrated by Marie Hall Ets.

SUMMARY: A boy gets a new horn and hat and goes for a walk in the forest. While he is there, he meets up with animals along the way that stop what they're doing and follow behind him in his walk until there is a long parade, led by the boy. They reach a clearing where there is a table, and there they have a party with food the animals brought with them and food they found there. They play games such as drop-the handkerchief, London-bridge-is-falling-down, and hide-and-seek. The boy was "It" for hide-and-seek, and all the animals hid except the rabbit, which stood still. Just as the boy is about to go looking for the animals in the game, his father comes looking for him to take him home. When the boy says that the animals are hiding, Dad says that maybe they will wait to play another day, because now it is late. The animals in the parade and party are lion, who needed to comb his hair; two elephant babies, who had been taking a bath; two big brown bears, who had been counting their peanuts and eating their jam; a set of kangaroo parents, who were teaching their baby how to hop (the baby comes along in the mother's pouch); a gray stork; two monkeys; and the rabbit.

MEDIA: Paper batik.

ANECDOTE: Marie Ets enjoyed walking in the woods and forests of her native state, Wisconsin.

DISTINCTION: 1945 Caldecott Honor Book.

BIRTHDAY: Marie Hall Ets: December 16, 1893.

SUBJECT: Animals—Fiction.

See Also: Just Me; *Mister Penny's Race Horse*; *Mr. T. W. Anthony Woo*; *Nine Days to Christmas*; *Play with Me*.

In the Night Kitchen (Harper, 1970). Written and illustrated by Maurice Sendak.

SUMMARY: Mickey hears thumps in the night and wakes to shout down for it to be quiet. When he does, he falls out of his bed and out of his clothes and out of the building into the mixing bowl in the night kitchen of bakers who all look like Oliver Hardy from the movies. The bakers mix and stir and get ready to put the cake batter in the Mickey Oven, when Mickey pops out of the batter and into the bread dough where he fashions an airplane and takes off with a cup to bring back milk needed for the cake. Flying his plane over the Milky Way and diving it into a huge milk bottle, Mickey sinks to the bottom with his cup and then swims to the top where he pours milk down into the batter below. The three Oliver Hardy bakers are happy and finish making their Mickey cake. Mickey slides down a slide into his bed where he's back home, safe and dry. The story ends by explaining that this is why we now have cake each morning.

MEDIA: Line drawings and wash.

ANECDOTE: Sendak admitted that the montage of images in the book is a tribute to New York City, where he grew up (in Brooklyn) as well as to Busby Berkeley musicals, Walt Disney, Mickey Mouse, and 1930s movies that he enjoyed such as *King Kong*. Mickey's nudity (and anatomical correctness), representative of humanity's primal nature in the story, has inhibited some teachers and librarians from using it at story time. Sendak has said that he is aware of some adults drawing a diaper on the pages to cover Mickey's frontal nudity.

Autobiographical details in the book abound and include that the book is dedicated to Sadie and Philip, who were Sendak's parents; the clock on top of the radio in Mickey's room bears the name "Jennie," the name of Sendak's beloved Sealyham terrier. "Q. E. Gateshead" on the building behind Mickey as he falls back into his room is the name of the hospital where Sendak was treated for his heart attack while in Europe in 1967. At the bottom of the second page where the three bakers appear is a sack of flour on its side—in small print at the bottom of the sack are the words "Killingworth, Connecticut." This is the town where Jennie was born. The sack of flour held upside down by one of the bakers on that same page contains Jennie's name as well as the names of her breeders; the date

1953 on that same bag of flour represents the year that Sendak started longing for a dog and made arrangements with the breeders to receive the runt of the litter. In the scene where Mickey flies over the Milky Way, a tiny lightpost sign over the elevated train says "Jennie Street"; on the page where Mickey is tinkering with the plane's propeller, there are words on a building behind him that read, "Patented June 10th, 1928," which is Sendak's birthday.

On the page with four sections that show Mickey kneading, punching, pounding, and pulling dough, the buildings behind him have the words, "Philip's Best Tomatoes," "Eugene's," and "Sadie's Best," another tribute to Sendak's parents, and Eugene is a good friend who took Jennie to be relieved of her suffering when she was dying from cancer. When Mickey falls into the bowl of batter, there is a building behind him shaped like a bottle of Tabasco and labeled, "Kneitel's Fandango"; this is a reference to Kenny Kneitel, the Kenny of Sendak's book *Kenny's Window*, who was a serious collector of Mickey Mouse paraphernalia from the 1930s. "Woody's Salt" on the opposite page refers to Wood Gelman, editor of Nostalgia Press. The "Schickel" building on the spread where Mickey flies over the tall milk bottle is a reference to Richard Schickel. Schickel wrote the biography, *The Disney Version: The Life, Times, Art, and Commerce of Walt Disney* (Simon, 1968). The book triggered Sendak's memory and inspiration for using Mickey Mouse, a character created the year he was born, as a metaphor in his work. In *In the Night Kitchen*, the oven and its label, "Mickey Oven," are done in the characteristic Disney style from the Mickey Mouse cartoons.

DISTINCTION: 1971 Caldecott Honor Book.

BIRTHDAY: Maurice Sendak: June 10, 1928.

SUBJECT: Fantasy.

See Also: Sendak, Maurice; *Where the Wild Things Are.*

In the Small, Small Pond (Henry Holt, 1993). Written and illustrated by Denise Fleming.

SUMMARY: Pond creatures such as tadpoles, frogs, raccoons, geese, dragonflies, turtles, herons, minnows, beavers, and swallows do the things they do in a pond as the seasons pass. They make noises, dip, snap, doze, and wriggle. Large alliterative and rhyming words describe the pictures of the pond creatures doing what they do best in the water. By winter, the pond sleeps under its layer of ice.

MEDIA: Colored cotton pulp poured through hand-cut stencils.

ANECDOTE: A previous illustrator of licensed characters such as the Care Bears, Fleming enrolled in a paper-making class, which resulted in her signature illustration technique.

DISTINCTION: 1994 Caldecott Honor Book.

BIRTHDAY: Denise Fleming: January 31, 1950.

SUBJECTS: Pond animals—Fiction; Stories in rhyme.

In the Time of the Drums (Hyperion, 1999). Written by Kim L. Siegelson; illustrated by Brian Pinkney.

SUMMARY: Mentu is a boy born on an island near Teakettle Creek. He is being raised by his grandmother, Twi, who was born in Africa and has never forgotten the ways of her homeland. Twi can play a drum she made in the African way and teaches Mentu how to do so as well. She tells him that one day he will have to be strong and that knowing the African stories and ways she teaches him will help him. One day a ship bearing African people in chains arrives at the island. They are Ibdo people from Benin. Twi plays her drum to communicate with them down below deck. The people in chains below deck look up in hope that after all this time perhaps they have been taken back to their homeland. They beat the bottom of the ship with their feet in reply.

However, the Ibdo people have been brought to the island to be sold as slaves. Twi tells Mentu some last messages to remember and then tells him she must leave him. Mentu, still very young, does not understand and wants to go wherever Twi is going, but she tells him he cannot. She tells him to remember the things she has taught him. Twi has seemed all along to have magical powers and secrets. Both the white people and black people on the island have been afraid of her. Now, her secret powers become known.

The Ibdo people will not leave the dock and touch foot on the land they know will result in their enslavement. Despite their efforts, the Spanish captain and crew cannot make them move onto the land. Soon, Twi begins to run toward the dock. All of her years drop behind her as she runs, and she is now young and strong. She calls to them and tells them to come, that she will take them home through the water. She takes the people by the hand, and together they walk toward Teakettle Creek and down into the water. As the water rises over their shoulders and up their necks, the chains binding them disappear, and the people sing that the water can take them home. They keep walking until each one of them has disappeared underneath the water.

Mentu grows up to be strong and good. He teaches the African ways taught to him by his grandmother Twi to his children and their children. He teaches them to play the drums with a rhythm that echoes what is deep in their hearts. People today still know how to play these drums because they held onto that which would keep them strong.

MEDIA: Scratchboard.

ANECDOTE: The tale is an adaptation of a story that has been passed down through generations of African Americans living near the Sea Islands off Georgia and South Carolina. It is often told as a ghost story. There are several accounts that the event of the Ibdo people's choice of physical death and spiritual freedom over slavery occurred at Dunbar Creek on St. Simons Island. Kim Siegelson sat down beside the creek where the Ibdo people were said to enter the water, and she listened. She says this story is what she heard and that she added the element of the people returning home by walking back across the Middle Passage under water. The African drums drawn in the book are from Brian Pinkney's private collection. He is a drummer, so he found the project particularly meaningful.

DISTINCTION: 2000 Coretta Scott King Award for Illustration.

BIRTHDAY: Brian Pinkney: August 28, 1961.

SUBJECTS: Slave insurrections—United States—Fiction; Slave insurrections—Fiction; African Americans—Fiction; Igbo (African people)—Fiction; Grandmothers—Fiction.

Inch by Inch (Ooblensky, 1960). Written and illustrated by Leo Lionni.

SUMMARY: One day a robin was about to eat an inchworm, when the inchworm defended himself by saying that he is useful because he can measure things. Robin asks him to measure his tail, which the inchworm does and finds to be five inches long. Robin takes the inchworm to other birds who can use something measured. Inchworm measures the flamingo's neck, the toucan's beak, the heron's leg, the pheasant's tail, and the entire length of a hummingbird. When the nightingale encounters the inchworm, it wants its song measured. Inchworm tries to explain that it only measures things, not songs, but the nightingale insists that if the inchworm did not measure his song, it would eat him up. Inchworm has an idea; he tells the bird to sing, and inchworm begins to measure, inch by inch, the distance between himself and the nightingale as the inchworm escapes to safety.

MEDIA: Rice paper collage and crayon.

ANECDOTE: Leo Lionni began his career writing and illustrating children's picture books when he was a grandfather entertaining his grandchildren.

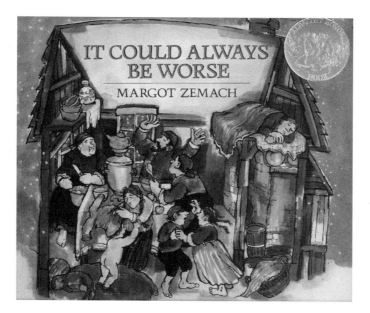

Cover of *It Could Always Be Worse*, retold and illustrated by Margot Zemach, which was a 1978 Caldecott Honor book. (Reprinted by permission of Farrar, Straus and Giroux, LLC: *It Could Always Be Worse* by Margot Zemach. Copyright © 1976 by Margot Zemach. www.fsg kidsbooks.com.)

DISTINCTION: 1961 Caldecott Honor Book.

BIRTHDAY: Leo Lionni: May 5, 1910.

SUBJECT: Insects—Fiction.

See Also: Frederick.

India Ink. Artist's medium. A permanent black ink that is made of lampblack and glue binder.

It Could Always Be Worse (Farrar, Straus and Giroux 1976). Retold and illustrated by Margot Zemach.

SUMMARY: A man, his wife and six children, and the man's mother all live together in a small hut. They are poor; it is crowded, and it is noisy. The man goes to the rabbi for advice on what to do to improve the sitation. Rabbi asks the man if he has any chickens, roosters, or geese. The man does. Rabbi tells him to let all of the birds into his hut to live.

After a while, the man can't stand it any longer, and he goes back to the rabbi again for help; he says things couldn't be worse. The rabbi asks if he has a goat. The cycle repeats with the goat and then a cow until finally there are so many animals and so much commotion in the house that the man goes back one last time to the rabbi. Finally, the rabbi tells him to let out all the animals from his little hut. When he does so, the man now enjoys the room and quiet with his family.

MEDIA: Possibly watercolor.

ANECDOTE: Margot Zemach often did her artwork with two cats close by—one in her lap and one lapping up the paint water.

DISTINCTION: 1978 Caldecott Honor Book.

BIRTHDAY: Margot Zemach: November 30, 1931.

SUBJECTS: Jews—Folklore; Folklore.

See Also: Duffy and the Devil.

J

Jambo Means Hello: Swahili Alphabet Book (Dial, 1974). Written by Muriel Feelings; illustrated by Tom Feelings.

SUMMARY: Swahili is spoken in the African nations of Zaire, the Congo, Kenya, Somalia, Tanzania, Zambia, Malwi, Mozambique, and the Malagasy Republic. This book is an introduction to the Swahili language. Each letter introduces a new Swahili word with its pronunciation and English translation. Further information about the word (e.g., *arusi*, wedding) educates readers on cultural details. For example, readers are told that an *arusi*, wedding, is celebrated by an entire village, not just the couple's families. Examples of words and their translations include *baba*, father; *chakula*, food; *jambo*, hello; *mama*, mother; and *karibou*, welcome. Letters Q and X are not included, presumably because they are not part of the Swahili alphabet or there are no corresponding words that begin with those letters or sounds in Swahili.

MEDIA: Black ink, white tempera, and linseed oil on textured board with tissue paper; bookprinting done by photographing the original artwork in double-dot and printing it in two different colored inks—black and ochre.

ANECDOTE: High humidity gave Tom Feelings problems with the tissue paper he used in creating the artwork for this book. Muriel Feelings once worked through the United Nations as an art teacher in Uganda.

DISTINCTION: 1975 Caldecott Honor Book.

BIRTHDAY: Muriel Feelings: July 31, 1938.

SUBJECTS: Alphabet; Swahili language—Alphabet; Swahili language—Dictionaries; Africa, Eastern—Social life and customs; Africa, East—Social life and customs.

John Henry (Dial, 1994). Retold by Julius Lester; illustrated by Jerry Pinkney.

SUMMARY: This is a retelling of the traditional tall tale of John Henry as the strong man who competed with a steam driller cutting a hole through a mountain for the railroad. In Lester's version, Henry sets up the contest, not the steam driller's owner. Henry dies from a burst heart after winning the cutting competition and is said to be buried under the White House lawn.

MEDIA: Pencil, colored pencil, and watercolor.

ANECDOTE: Lester uses versions of the story from various written sources, such as the novel *John Henry* (1931), by Roark Bradford, in his retelling. He also uses his experience as a folksinger to incorporate elements of the story as it is told in folk songs. He said that he was inspired to write the text to the story that Jerry Pinkney was illustrating after considering that the legendary John Henry, whether an actual man or an invention, reminded him of Dr. Martin Luther King Jr. Both figures work hard at their respective efforts until their hearts break. Both men, he said, died in tragic ways, but should be remembered most by the examples of their lives.

DISTINCTION: 1995 Caldecott Honor Book.

BIRTHDAYS: Julius Lester: January 27, 1939; Jerry Pinkney: December 22, 1939.

SUBJECTS: John Henry (Legendary character)—Legends; African Americans—Folklore; Folklore—United States.

See Also: Mirandy and Brother Wind.

Joseph Had a Little Overcoat (Viking, 1999). Retold and illustrated by Simms Taback.

SUMMARY: Joseph's overcoat gets worn, and he cuts it down to make a jacket. When that gets worn, he cuts it down to make a vest. Die-cuts in the pages of the book show the garment as it was before and then cut down to the new garment. Through this process, Joseph makes from his overcoat a jacket, vest, scarf, necktie, handkerchief, and finally a button. One day, Joseph loses the button. Now he has nothing. He decides to write a book about his overcoat, which shows that you can always make something out of nothing. The music and lyrics to the Yiddish folk song, "I Had a Little Overcoat," appear in the back of the book.

MEDIA: Watercolor, gouache, pencil, ink, and collage; die-cut pages.

ANECDOTE: Friends of Tabeck noticed that Joseph looked remarkably like him.

DISTINCTION: 2000 Caldecott Medal.

BIRTHDAY: Simms Tabeck: February 13, 1932.

SUBJECTS: Toy and movable books; Folklore—Europe, Eastern; Jews—Folklore; Coats—Folklore.

See Also: There Was an Old Lady Who Swallowed a Fly.

Journey Cake, Ho! (Viking, 1953). Written by Ruth Sawyer; illustrated by Robert McCloskey.

SUMMARY: On the other side of Tip-Top Mountain live Merry, the old woman, Grumble, an old man, and a boy named Johnny. They each have lots of work to do, and everything they need is close by them on the mountain top. Raucus, a crow, watches for any trouble. After a very long time, some trouble begins. A fox takes off with the hens one night; another night a wolf takes away the sheep. Raucus caws the alarm, but it is too late each time. One day a pig wanders away from the farm, and a cow falls in a creek and breaks its leg.

In the morning, Merry and Grumble send Johnny off to find a new family to care for him and avoid all the trouble. They give him a Journey Cake for his travels, a large round cake. Johnny heads out, but soon his Journey Cake falls out of his sack and starts rolling. Johnny runs after the Journey Cake, calling hi and ho. As it rolls by various animals, the animals began running after it, too, joining in the fun of the race to catch the Journey Cake and eat it for themselves. Soon, they travel down and up until they find they are all at the place they started. The Journey Cake has led them all back home.

MEDIA: Undetermined.

ANECDOTE: Robert McCloskey was Ruth Sawyer's son-in-law.

DISTINCTION: 1954 Caldecott Honor Book.

BIRTHDAYS: Ruth Sawyer: August 5, 1880; Robert McCloskey: September 15, 1914.

SUBJECT: Folklore—United States.

See Also: *Blueberries for Sal*; *Make Way for Ducklings*; McCloskey, Robert; *One Morning in Maine*; *Time of Wonder*.

Juanita (Scribner, 1948). Written and illustrated by Leo Politi.

SUMMARY: Antonio and Maria Gonzalez name their shop, or *puesto*, on Olvera Street after their daughter, Juanita. While they work, they raise Juanita there. On her fourth birthday, Antonia plays her "Las Mañanitas," or the Mexican birthday song. The music and lyrics are in the book. Juanita has a party. Near Easter time, the Old Mission Church is decorated with flowers in preparation for "The Blessing of the Animals." Juanita washes her dove and puts a green ribbon around its neck for the blessing. Señora Carmela brings a burro; Ramon and his wife, Salina, are there. They organize the activities, which include a parade of the animals. Señor Francisco walks at the end of the parade with his old dog, Blanco. This is Blanco's twelfth blessing. Ramon walks up and down beside the parade to be sure all is well; he has a macaw on his shoulder. Antonia plays the dove song, "La Paloma," when the parade passes the shop. The music for this song, too, is in the book. At the door of the church, the priest blesses each animal with holy water. The people meet at the Old Plaza to visit with one another, happy after they and their animals have all received their blessing.

At the end of the day, Maria hangs Juanita's Easter dress up in preparation for the next day and rocks Juanita and sings her a lullabye, "Duérmete niña" (music and lyrics also in the book). The old Mission bells chime during the night, signaling all is well.

MEDIA: Possibly tempera.

ANECDOTE: Politi was born in California but returned to Italy with his immigrant parents for several years, where he studied art. When he came back to the United States, he settled on Olvera Street in a Mexican neighborhood in Los Angeles. The street be- came the setting of several of his picture books.

DISTINCTION: 1949 Caldecott Honor Book.

BIRTHDAY: Leo Politi: November 21, 1908.

SUBJECT: Mexican Americans—Fiction.

See Also: *Pedro, the Angel of Olvera Street*; *Song of the Swallows*.

The Judge: An Untrue Tale (Farrar, Straus and Giroux, 1969). Written by Harve Zemach; illustrated by Margot Zemach.

SUMMARY: Five prisoners are individually brought before the Judge. Each of them warns of something horrible approaching, and with each prisoner's story, the thing approaching gets more and more described. The Judge does not believe any of their stories and puts them all in prison. Finally, the door is opened by a monster that eats the Judge, and all the prisoners are freed.

MEDIA: Watercolor, pen and ink.

ANECDOTE: Harve's birth name was Fischstrom; he took his wife's last name as her husband and collaborator.

DISTINCTION: 1970 Caldecott Honor Book.

BIRTHDAYS: Harve Zemach: December 5, 1933; Margo Zemach: November 30, 1931.

SUBJECT: Stories in rhyme.

See Also: *It Could Always Be Worse*.

Jumanji (Houghton Mifflin, 1981). Written and illustrated by Chris Van Allsburg.

SUMMARY: Peter and Judy's parents have gone to the opera one cold day in November. They will be bringing home guests, so they caution the children not to mess up the house while they are gone. The children immediately remove everything from their toy boxes and make a mess. Then they go outside. They are bored. At the base of a tree, Peter finds a board game called Jumanji. The children take

Cover of *The Judge: An Untrue Tale*, written by Harve Zemach, illustrated by
Margot Zemach. As illustrator, Margot Zemach received the Caldecott
Honor in 1970 for this book on which she collaborated with her husband.
(Reprinted by permission of Farrar, Straus and Giroux, LLC: *The Judge: An
Untrue Tale* by Harve Zemach, pictures by Margot Zemach. Pictures copyright © 1969 by Margot Zemach. www.fsgkidsbooks.com.)

Front cover of *Jumanji*, written and illustrated by Chris Van Allsburg.
In 1982, the book earned the artist his first Caldecott Medal and was
later made into a film. (Copyright © 1981 by Chris Van Allsburg.
Copyright © by Houghton Mifflin Company. All rights reserved.)

it home; Judy reads the instructions; and they begin to play. One warning to the game is that once begun, the game cannot be finished until one player reaches the Golden City.

As they begin to take their turns around the board, animals suddenly appear in the house. These include a lion and monkeys. A monsoon season begins on one space Judy lands on when she must lose a turn, and rain arrives in the house. Other strange things that arrive according to the words on the board include a lost guide; a rhinoceros stampede; a python; sleeping sickness; and a volcano eruption. Finally, Judy reaches the end and says, "Jumanji," making all the strange appearances go away.

Mother and Father wake the children when they get home. They set out a puzzle for the children to work on. Mrs. Budwing and her sons, Walter and Daniel, are among the guests. As Peter and Judy go to work on the puzzle their parents want to occupy them, they spot Daniel and Walter outside running through the trees with a game box under one arm.

MEDIA: Conté pencil with conté dust.

ANECDOTE: Van Allsburg often gets his ideas from asking "What if" questions. He asked himself what if two children were bored and invented a board game. *Jumanji* was the result.

DISTINCTION: 1982 Caldecott Medal.

BIRTHDAY: Chris Van Allsburg: June 18, 1949.

SUBJECTS: Games—Fiction; Play—Fiction.

See Also: The Garden of Abdul Gasazi; *The Polar Express*; Van Allsburg, Chris.

Just a Minute: A Trickster Tale and Counting Book (Chronicle, 2003). Written and illustrated by Yuyi Morales.

SUMMARY: Grandma Beetle wakes at dawn to a knock on the door. There, she sees Señor Calavera, a skeleton who tips his hat to her. He tells her it is time for her to come

For his *Just a Minute: A Trickster Tale and Counting Book*, Latin American author and illustrator Yuyi Morales received the 2004 Pura Belpré Award for Illustration. (From *Just A Minute: A Trickster Tale and Counting Book* by Yuyi Morales. © 2003 by Yuyi Morales. Granted with permission from Chronicle Books, LLC.)

with him. Grandma Beetle cannot leave her house yet, however, because she has too much to do. She tells Calavera to wait just a minute; she has various chores to complete. As she adds up the minutes, Calavera counts them in Spanish. Her chores include sweeping one house; boiling two pots of tea; making three pounds of corn into tortillas; four fruits to slice; five cheeses that need melting; six pots of food to cook; seven *piñatas* that require filling with candy; eight food platters to arrange on the table; nine grandchildren who arrive for a party; and ten guests (including Calavera) to sit at the table. It is Grandma Beetle's birthday. When she blows out all the candles in a big cloud of smoke, Calavera makes a discreet exit. He leaves a note behind that Grandma Beetle reads after the party. It says that the party was a scream, and she can count on his coming again next year.

MEDIA: Acrylic and mixed media on paper.

ANECDOTE: Morales was born in Mexico but now lives in the United States. She used to be a puppet maker and host of a Spanish-language radio show for children.

DISTINCTION: 2004 Pura Belpré Illustrator Award.

BIRTHDAY: Not available.

SUBJECTS: Folklore—Mexico; Counting.

Just Me (Viking, 1965). Written and illustrated by Marie Hall Ets.

SUMMARY: A little boy is playing alone at the farm. He sees a bird sitting on a post by the barn and that his cat, Biddy, is after it. He warns the bird, and the bird flies away. When Biddy goes off seeking other prey, the boy crawls down on the ground like the cat. This begins a series of adventures where the boy encounters different animals around the farm and fields and attempts to act just like them. He sees a rooster, a pig, a rabbit, a snake, a cow, their goose named Gongky, their horse, Flora, a squirrel, Spunky the goat, a frog, and a turtle. Finally, he sees his father tying up the boat, and he wants a ride, so he runs just like himself to catch him, and they sail out in the pond.

MEDIA: Paper batik.

ANECDOTE: Ets was one of the few American artists working on picture books for children in the 1930s and 1940s and helped set a standard of excellence in art for American children's books.

DISTINCTION: 1966 Caldecott Honor Book.

BIRTHDAY: December 16, 1895.

SUBJECT: Animals—Fiction.

See Also: In the Forest; *Mister Penny's Race Horse*; *Mr. T. W. Anthony Woo*; *Nine Days to Christmas*; *Play with Me*.

K

Keats Foundation. Organization. Named after picture book author and artist Ezra Jack Keats (1916–1983), the Keats Foundation is a not-for-profit corporation that was founded in 1964. At Keats's death in 1983, there were no heirs, so his will directed that royalties from his books go to the foundation for the purpose of benefiting humanity. Since that time, Keats's friend, Dr. Martin Pope, professor emeritus of chemistry from New York University, and his wife, Dr. Lillie Pope, as well as Dr. Deborah Pope and a board of directors, have worked to see Keats's wishes be fulfilled through the philanthropic work of the foundation. The foundation has become well known in the field of children's literature for its benefits to children, children's literature and libraries and collections, and its encouragement and aid to the creators of children's literature and the scholars who study it.

Projects funded by the Keats Foundation include but are not limited to the New York Public Library's Ezra Jack Keats New Writer's and New Illustrator's Award for Children's Books; the Annual Ezra Jack Keats Lectureship and Children's Book Festival at the University of Southern Mississippi; the Keats/de Grummond Research Fellowship at the de Grummond Children's Literature Research Library at the University of Southern Mississippi; minigrants to public schools and public libraries; and the Ezra Jack Keats Scholarship for Children's Book Research at the Kerlan Collection at the University of Minnesota (awarded to authors and artists), among other ongoing projects.

Keats was born Jacob Ezra Katz on March 11, 1916, in Brooklyn, the son of Polish immigrants Benjamin Katz and Augusta Podgainy Katz. His parents met after they immigrated to the United States from Warsaw, Poland, and their marriage was an arranged one after the Polish custom. Keats's father worked in Pete's Coffee Shop, and making ends meet was difficult for the family. Ezra was the third child, and the family lived in a duplex at 438 Vermont Street. Often, Ezra had to do the family's errands and returned with complaints from debtors that caused tension in the household and discord between his parents. Ezra sought refuge from the family's depression-era troubles by going to the library and also through his art. At the Arlington Branch of the Brooklyn Public Library, Keats and a childhood friend, Martin Pope, enjoyed looking at books together. Ezra sought out art books while Pope gravitated to the books about science.

Keats had an early interest in art that was encouraged by his mother but frowned on by his father, who worried that a starving artist would literally not make enough money to feed himself. The day before his son's high school graduation, Benjamin Katz died. Ezra found clippings in his father's wallet about his art awards, and he knew then that his father had been proud of his talent all along.

Although he was awarded three scholarships to art school, Ezra was needed at home to help support his family. He worked by day and attended art classes as he could in the evening. The Works Progress Administration (WPA) hired him in 1937 as a muralist. Three years later, he took on work as a comic-book illustrator, and by 1942 he was illustrating the backgrounds for Captain Marvel comic strips. During World War II, he joined the U.S. Air Corps and designed camouflaged patterns. After his honorable discharge two years later, he suffered from ill health and depression. When the war was over, he officially changed his name from Jacob Ezra Katz to Ezra Jack Keats, presumably to escape the anti-Semitic prejudice of the time.

From 1954 onward, Keats illustrated fifty-five books for children. His first illustrated book was *Jubilant for Sure* by Elizabeth Hubbard Lansing (1954). He wrote his first book in 1960, *My Dog Is Lost!* (Crowell, 1960; Viking, 1999). Through many years of illustrating picture books for children, New York native Keats noticed that none of the characters were ever black children. In 1962, he broke that mold quite consciously, making his character, Peter of *The Snowy Day*, a black child. The story has a universal theme of Peter and his companions enjoying playing in the snow. It won Keats the 1963 Caldecott Medal. Because of this picture book and the several others that feature Peter that appeared later such as *Whistle for Willie* (Viking, 1964); *Peter's Chair* (Harper, 1967); *A Letter to Amy* (Harper, 1968); *Goggles!* (Macmillan, 1969); *Hi, Cat!* (Macmillan, 1970); and *Pet Show!* (Macmillan, 1972); Keats has often been credited, however imperfectly, with opening the

door for the multicultural movement in American children's picture books. *Goggles!* won a 1970 Caldecott Honor Book Award.

The author and artist was well known around the world in his lifetime. In Japan, for example, his book *Skates!* (Watts, 1973), which is about two dogs' adventures on roller skates, caused such a sensation that children all over Tokyo began roller-skating. Parents petitioned the city to build a roller-skating rink, and when the rink was opened, a plaque bearing Keats's name was part of it, placed there in honor of the artist's influence.

Keats never married or had children of his own, and he lived in his apartment at 444 East 82nd Street in New York City for many years. He died on May 6, 1983, of a heart attack. The Keats Foundation is a living legacy of an important American children's picture book artist, a legacy that continues to breathe life into American children's picture books in both their creation and their appreciation by children.

See Also: Goggles!; *The Snowy Day*.

Kerlan Collection. Archival collection. One of the largest and most comprehensive collections of children's literature materials in the world, the Kerlan Collection is housed at the Elmer L. Andersen Library at the University of Minnesota in Minneapolis. The collection includes more than 90,000 children's books, chiefly by twentieth-century American authors; original manuscripts and artwork related to more than 10,000 titles; more than 300 periodical titles; and more than 1,200 reference titles.

The collection is named for alumnus Irvin Kerlan, M.D. (1912–1963), chief of medical research for the Food and Drug Adminstration of the United States in Washington, D.C. Kerlan was a private collector of children's literature during the 1940s. In 1949, he donated his collection to the university and kept adding to it until his death in 1963. At that time, the collection comprised more than

9,000 books, manuscripts, and illustrations. At the collection's fiftieth anniversary in 1999, the work of more than 1,800 authors and artists of children's books was represented. These include American picture book authors and artists such as Wanda Gág, Jane Yolen, Berta and Elmer Hader, Clement Hurd, Emily Arnold McCully, Mifong Ho, Barbara Cooney, Taro Yashima, Margaret Wise Brown, and hundreds of others.

In addition to its holdings and services to the research and scholarly community, the Kerlan Collection sponsors lectures, programs, special exhibits, and awards. Each year, the collection grants the Ezra Jack Keats/Kerlan Memorial Fellowship to promising authors and artists who wish to study their craft using Kerlan's materials. A Kerlan-Grant-in-Aid fellowship aids scholars who wish to travel to the library to study the collection as part of their research in children's literature. The organization also bestows an annual Kerlan Award to children's literature professionals including authors, artists, editors, publishers, and educators who have contributed to children's literature in a significant way and have also made a unique contribution to the Kerlan Collection. Past picture book-related winners of the Kerlan Award include Roger Duvoisin, Tomie dePaola, Margaret Wise Brown, Barbara Cooney, Eve Bunting, and Jane Yolen.

Contact: The Children's Literature Research Collections, Kerlan Collection, 113 Elmer L. Andersen Library, 222 21st Avenue South, Minneapolis, MN 55455; (612) 624-4576; Web site: http://special.lib.umn.edu/clrc/kerlan.html; email: clrc@tc.umn.edu.

King Bidgood's in the Bathtub (Harcourt, 1985). Written by Audrey Wood; illustrated by Don Wood.

SUMMARY: King Bidgood is in the bathtub, and he won't come out. The Page asks several people from the kingdom what they should do, and each one in turn tries to get

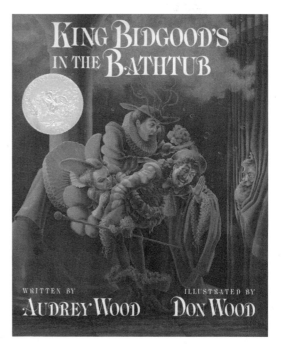

King Bidgood's in the Bathtub, written by Audrey Wood, illustrated by Don Wood, earned the husband of the pair a 1986 Caldecott Honor. (Copyright © 1985 by Don Wood. Copyright © by Harcourt, Inc. All rights reserved.)

him out. However, each activity they present to the king ends up being done in the tub with him. The knight does battle; the Queen has lunch; the Duke goes fishing; the entire Court comes in for a Masquerade Ball. Each person leaves in turn without convincing the king to get out of the water. Finally, the Page has an idea of what to do. He pulls the plug, letting the water out of the tub, and the king comes out with it.

MEDIA: Possibly oil on pressed wood.

ANECDOTE: Don Wood claims that some of the paintings for this book have a cat hair or two in them because his cat, Gizmo, would not leave him alone while he worked.

DISTINCTION: 1986 Caldecott Honor Book.

BIRTHDAY: Don Wood: May 4, 1945.

SUBJECTS: Kings, queens, rulers, etc.—Fiction; Baths—Fiction.

Kitten's First Full Moon (Greenwillow, 2004). Written and illustrated by Kevin Henkes.

SUMMARY: Kitten sees a full moon for the first time and thinks that it is a bowl of milk. She wants to taste the milk, so she tries to lick the sky, but a bug lands on her tongue instead. She jumps toward the moon but falls down the porch steps. The bowl of milk still sits in the sky. Kitten decides to chase it. She runs along the sidewalk, garden, pond, and all the way up a tree, but she does not catch it. At the top of the tree, she becomes afraid to come down until she sees the moon reflected in the pond. This bowl of milk looks even larger than the one in the sky. She is having quite a night. She races down the tree and leaps into the pond. She not only discovers that there is no milk there, but now she is wet, tired, and unhappy in addition to being hungry. Kitten finally heads back home, and there she finds a real bowl of milk waiting for her on the porch.

MEDIA: Gouache and colored pencil.

ANECDOTE: Henkes cites Clare Turlay Newberry's artwork of cats in books such as *Marshmallow* as well as Jean Charlot's work in books like *A Child's Good Night Book* by Margaret Wise Brown as inspirations for this book for very young children. The book grew out of a sentence that stood out to him from an abandoned project he had written about circles. Henkes used only black and white for the illustrations because he thought color was unnecessary to a story about the moon in the night sky, a white kitten, and a bowl of milk. His novel *Olive's Ocean* was a 2004 Newbery Honor book.

DISTINCTION: 2005 Caldecott Medal.

BIRTHDAY: Kevin Henkes: November 27, 1960.

SUBJECTS: Cats—Fiction; Animals—Infancy—Fiction; Moon—Fiction.

See Also: Charlotte Zolotow Book Award; *Lilly's Purple Plastic Purse*; *Owen*.

Knuffle Bunny: A Cautionary Tale (Hyperion, 2004). Written and illustrated by Mo Willems.

SUMMARY: Daddy and Trixie, who is still too young to speak words, go on an errand to a laundromat in Brooklyn. They go past scenes from the neighborhood. At the laundromat, Trixie helps her daddy put the clothes in the washing machine and the coins in the slot. They start up the washer and leave to go home until the wash is done. Only a block or so away, however, Trixie realizes that something is missing—her beloved Knuffle Bunny was thrown into the washer with the clothes. Since she cannot speak words, Trixie tries several ways unsuccessfully to let her daddy know that something is terribly wrong. She makes unrecognizable sounds, points, cries, and shouts. She goes limp as dead weight. As soon as they arrive home, Trixie's mommy asks where Knuffle Bunny is, and the family now recognizes the problem. They all rush back to the laundromat and look for Trixie's bunny. At first they do not find it among the clothes they pull out of the washer. Then Trixie's daddy decides to roll up his sleeves and really dive into the machine to get a better look. When he saves the day by retrieving the soggy Knuffle Bunny, Trixie calls out her bunny's name in delight and these are the first words she has ever spoken.

MEDIA: Hand-drawn ink sketches and digital photography.

ANECDOTE: Willems was a scriptwriter and animator on the children's television program *Sesame Street* for nine years and has won six Emmys. He has created independent short films and also television programs such as the Cartoon Network's *Sheep in the Big City* and Nickelodeon's *The Off-Beats*.

DISTINCTION: 2005 Caldecott Honor Book.

BIRTHDAY: Not available.

SUBJECTS: Lost and found possessions—Fiction; Toys—Fiction; Fathers and daughters—Fiction; Self-service laundries—Fiction.

See Also: Don't Let the Pigeon Drive the Bus.

L

Laura Ingalls Wilder Medal. Distinction. Awarded by the American Library Association's Association for Library Service to Children division, the award honors authors or illustrators whose books published in the United States have made a substantial and lasting impact on children's literature over a period of years. The medal is named after American novelist Laura Ingalls Wilder (1867–1957), author of the famous "Little House" series of books about growing up on the prairie of the American Midwest. The bronze medal was designed by artist Garth Williams, who illustrated the Little House books. Inaugurated in 1954 with Wilder herself as the first recipient, the honor was given every five years between 1960 and 1980. Between 1980 and 2001 the award was bestowed every three years, and since 2001 the medal has been awarded every two years.

Of the fourteen winners to date, five of the American authors and artists among them have made a significant share of their contribution to children's literature through the medium of picture books. These include Eric Carle, Marcia Brown, Theodor Seuss Geisel (Dr. Seuss), Ruth Sawyer, and Maurice Sendak. Other authors and artists who have won the medal include Clara Ingram Judson, E. B. White, Beverly Cleary, Jean Fritz, Elizabeth George Speare, Virginia Hamilton, Russell Freedman, and Milton Meltzer. Often regarded as similar to a "lifetime achievement award" among children's literature professionals, the Laura Ingalls Wilder Medal is arguably one of the most prestigious awards that can be bestowed on an author or artist of children's literature in the United States.

Leo the Late Bloomer (Harper, 1971). Written by Robert Kraus; illustrated by José Aruego.

SUMMARY: Young tiger Leo cannot read or write or talk or draw or eat neatly. His father becomes concerned about his development, but his mother tells his father to be patient, that Leo is simply a late bloomer. She tells him that a watched late bloomer does not bloom. Leo's father tries not to watch throughout the rest of the summer and on through the winter. Finally, in the spring Leo reads, writes, draws, eats neatly, and says not one word, but an entire sentence.

MEDIA: Possibly wash.

ANECDOTE: Aruego was born in the Philippines. Kraus formed his own publishing company in 1965, Windmill Books, in order to write the text for picture books for which he could invite his favorite artist friends from *The New Yorker* to illustrate.

DISTINCTION: *100 Best Books for Children.*

BIRTHDAYS: Robert Kraus: June 21, 1925; José Aruego: August 9, 1932.

SUBJECT: Tigers—Fiction.

Lilly's Purple Plastic Purse (Greenwillow, 1996). Written and illustrated by Kevin Henkes.

SUMMARY: Lilly loves everything about school—the desks, pencils, the food at lunchtime, and especially her teacher, Mr. Slinger. Mr. Slinger is smart and wears artsy shirts with a different tie every day. He provides crunchy, tasty snacks. He provides a Lightbulb Lab where the students can express their ideas by drawing and writing when their work is done. Lilly and her friends, Chester, Wilson, and Victor, all want to become teachers one day. At home, Lilly plays school where she is the teacher and her little brother Julius is the pupil.

One day, Lilly wants to show Mr. Slinger and the class the new purple plastic purse that Grammy and she got while shopping over the weekend. The purse plays a tune when it is opened, and she also has three shiny quarters and sparkly new sunglasses. Unfortunately, Lilly is impatient to share these things with the class, even after Mr. Slinger asks her to wait several times. He has to take the things from her and put them at his desk until the end of the day. Back in the Lightbulb Lab, Lilly writes a nasty note and picture about Mr. Slinger and slips them into his bookbag before she goes home. She says she no longer wants to be a teacher when she grows up.

When Mr. Slinger gives her back her things to take home, she finds a note from him in her purse. In it, he says that today was a hard day and that tomorrow would be better, and he encloses a tasty snack. Lilly feels terrible now about the nasty note she left Mr. Slinger. She goes home and tells her parents everything that happened. Her mother writes him a note, and her father reassures her that Mr. Slinger will probably understand. Lilly writes a new note and takes everything in with her the next day. She has a talk with Mr. Slinger, who allows her to show the class all her new exciting things. Then they share Lilly's snacks with everyone, and she says she wants to be a teacher again when she grows up, at least on days when she does not want to be a scuba diver or a surgeon or a diva.

MEDIA: Watercolor paints and black pen.

ANECDOTE: The character of Lilly is in two previous Henke picture books—*Chester's Way* and *Julius, the Baby of the World*. Henkes saw a little girl in an airport with a purple plastic purse, and that gave him the idea of what to give Lilly for her own story.

DISTINCTIONS: *New York Times* Best Book for Children; NYPL 100 Picture Books Everyone Should Know; *100 Best Books for Children*.

BIRTHDAY: Kevin Henkes: November 27, 1960.

SUBJECTS: School—Fiction; Teachers—Fiction; Mice—Fiction.

Linoleum Cuts. Artist's medium. Cuts are made into a block of linoleum, and it is used in a relief printing process.

Lion (Viking, 1956). Written and illustrated by William Pène du Bois.

SUMMARY: In the sky, there is a Drawing Room in a place called the Animal Factory where all the animals and their names and their noises are made up by artists who look like angels. One day, Artist Foreman, who became a boss after inventing "worm" when he was young but who has not drawn in a very long time, decides to create a new animal. He names it "lion," but he does not know yet what it will look like or what sound it will make. Since he has been a boss over the other artists, it has been some time since he has drawn a new animal. He begins to draw a small, colorful creature that looks something, but not quite, like a lion we know today. He decides it will make a peeping sound. He shows it to the other artists and asks, in turn, what one word they would say to improve his animal. In turn, the other artists suggest size, feathers, color, legs, haircut, until finally there is nothing left to improve. When Artist Foreman shows the lion to his boss, Chief Designer, the designer asks if the lion roars, and Artist Foreman decides that it does. Chief Designer agrees to send it down to earth to be king of the beasts. Artist Foreman is pleased with himself and sits back in the drawing room and roars like a lion.

MEDIA: Pen and india ink; color preseparated on Dinobase with lithographic pencil.

ANECDOTE: As this book indicates, Du Bois was always interested in invention. His 1948 Newbery Medal winner, *The Twenty-One Balloons*, also attests to this interest.

DISTINCTION: 1957 Caldecott Honor Book.

BIRTHDAY: William Pène du Bois: May 9, 1916.

SUBJECTS: Animals—Fiction; Lions—Fiction; Fantasy.

Lithograph. Artist's medium. A design is painted on stone or a printing plate that is treated in a way so as to print only the desired design and not the entire surface.

Little Bear's Visit (Harper, 1961). Written by Else Holmelund Minarik; illustrated by Maurice Sendak.

SUMMARY: This "I Can Read Book" is made up of four stories: "Grandmother and Grandfather Bear," "Mother Bear's Robin," "Goblin Story," and "Not Tired." In the first story, Little Bear comes to visit his grandparents. He enjoys Grandmother's cooking and playing with Grandfather. He tells Grandfather that Father told him not to get him too tired. After they play a while, he asks Grandfather to tell him a story, but Grandfather falls asleep. Instead Little Bear and Grandmother go to the summer house, where she tells him the next story in the book. In "Mother Bear's Robin," Grandmother tells

Little Bear about a robin that Mother found and cared for when she was little and the robin was just a chick. She loved the robin and cared for it well inside the house, but one day the robin was sad and wanted to go outside and be free to fly. Mother took it outside and let it go. The robin returns every year, and its children do also. Grandmother points to a robin beside them, and tells Little Bear that this is one of that robin's children's children.

In "Goblin Story," Grandfather has awakened from his nap, and Little Bear asks him for a story. Grandfather tells of a little goblin that is frightened out of its shoes when he hears a thump inside a cave he passes by. As the goblin keeps walking, there is a noise of something following him, stepping right along behind him. The goblin jumps into a hole in a tree out of fear but then he sees that the thing making the noise was just his shoes that had followed him after he jumped out of them. Little Bear laughs at the story, saying that he is glad this will not happen to him because he does not wear shoes. He likes it that way. In the last story, Little Bear is sleepy, waiting for Mother and Father Bear to come take him home. He hears them come in and start talking with Grandmother and Grandfather, but he is both awake and asleep. When he hears Father say that they will go fishing, he asks him if they really will do that, and Mother sees that he has heard what they have been saying all along. He tells Grandfather that they had fun, and they do not get tired. Grandfather agrees that grandfathers and little cubs have fun and do not get tired, but sure enough Little Bear is asleep on Father's shoulder as they go out the door to go home.

MEDIA: Pen and ink with wash separations.

ANECDOTE: A prequel to this book, *Little Bear*, launched the I Can Read Book series. Ursula Nordstrom, Minarik's editor at Harper and Row, liked the concept of providing books with simple texts for new readers. Minarik wrote the books not only for her first graders, whom she taught for many years, but also for her daughter, who was an early reader.

DISTINCTION: 1962 Caldecott Honor Book.

BIRTHDAYS: Else Holmelund Minarik: September 13, 1920; Maurice Sendak: June 10, 1928.

SUBJECT: Bears—Fiction.

See Also: Sendak, Maurice; *Where the Wild Things Are.*

The Little Engine That Could (Platt, 1930). Written by "Watty Piper"; illustrated by Lois Lenski.

SUMMARY: A small train engine works at a station where it performs short and light tasks like moving cars from one switch track to another. One day, a load needs to be carried over a hill, but the larger engines cannot or will not do it for one reason or another. Finally, the request falls on the Little Engine, which responds, "I think I can; I think I can." As she climbs the mountain, the Little Engine keeps saying her mantra until she makes the peak and starts the easy run down the other side, saying, "I thought I could; I thought I could."

MEDIA: Undetermined.

ANECDOTE: Watty Piper is not an individual, but the pen name for the publishing company Platt & Munk. In 1954, Platt & Munk published a slightly different text with new color illustrations by George and Doris Hauman. Another edition appeared in 1976, illustrated by Ruth Sanderson. Platt & Munk claims trademarks for the title and the familiar line from the story and made much of its annual profits from the wide sales of this one popular story alone.

The 1930 edition gives credit to Mabel C. Bragg for the story, called the *Pony Engine* and copyrighted in 1910 by George H. Doran and Company. Bragg, a health educator in Boston,

never claimed to have originated the story. In fact, this origin is not likely to be the authentic one. Finding the origin of the story with its famous lines of encouragement has yielded several possibilities but nothing conclusive.

When copyright was challenged beginning in 1949 by Mrs. Elizabeth M. Chmiel claiming that her cousin, Frances M. Ford, had written the story in 1910 under the pseudonym "Uncle Nat," the publishers issued a $1,000 reward for documented proof of the story's origin. As a result of that search, another possible origin came forth, a 1906 story called "Thinking One Can" that appeared in *Wellspring for Young People*, a Sunday school publication, and that was later reprinted in a Daughters of the American Revolution (DAR) publication. There have been other printings of similar versions of the story as well, dating from 1906 to 1916, including in the *Kindergarten Review* and *The Riverside Second Reader*. The mystery of the story's origin is almost as large as the popularity of its famous lines and message. Ironically, Putnam now owns both Platt & Munk and Grosset and Dunlap, the house that challenged the copyright.

Feminist readers have sometimes cried foul in that the story usually portrays the larger, stronger engines as male and the Little Engine with the more menial tasks to do as female.

DISTINCTIONS: Of historical/scholarly interest; *New York Times* Best Book for Children.

BIRTHDAY: Lois Lenski: October 14, 1893.

SUBJECTS: Trains—Fiction; Transportation—Fiction.

The Little House (Houghton Mifflin, 1942). Written and illustrated by Virginia Lee Burton.

SUMMARY: Little House is happy and strongly built, living in the countryside. The man who built her planned that she should

Cover of *The Little House*, written and illustrated by Virginia Lee Burton. Burton received the 1943 Caldecott Medal for this book, published during World War II, that depicts what some read as a commentary on urbanization. (Copyright © 1942 by Virginia Lee Burton. Copyright © by Houghton Mifflin Company. All rights reserved.)

never be sold and that his great-great grandchildren and their great-great grandchildren would live there happily. As she enjoys the sunshine and the starlight at night, Little House can see the lights of the city way off in the distance and occasionally wonders what it would be like to live there. Little House stays where she is through all four seasons: spring, summer, fall, and winter, watching children grow and play. She stays there for many, many years watching horses and carriages come down the road, then surveyors, then construction equipment, and cars and trucks. Gradually, she watches as construction begins and more houses are built around her. Soon, there are many houses and many more roads. Soon after that tall buildings spring up around Little House until no one wants to live in her anymore. She sits and watches as the streets become dirty and crowded around her and a trolley line is built right in front of her.

Now, she is finding out what it is like to live in the city. She can no longer tell which season is which, and she misses the flowers

and other aspects of nature in the countryside. One spring morning, the great-great granddaughter of the man who built the house comes to see Little House. The woman recalls that Little House looks like the house her grandmother lived in as a young girl except that it used to be on a hill that overlooked daisies and apple trees. They ask the Movers if the house can be moved. Since Little House was so well built, the Movers said she could, and soon she is moved to the countryside where there are daisies and apple trees. Once again, there is also a family living inside her who take care of her. Little House is happy and never wonders about what living in the city would be like again.

MEDIA: Watercolor.

ANECDOTE: Burton's father was the first dean of the Massachusetts Institute of Technology; her mother was a poet and painter who called herself Jeanne D'Orge. Burton first wanted to become a dancer but changed career plans when she studied art with George Demetrios, a well-known sculptor whom she later married.

DISTINCTION: 1943 Caldecott Medal.

BIRTHDAY: Virginia Lee Burton: August 30, 1909.

SUBJECTS: Dwellings—Fiction; City and town life—Fiction.

See Also: Song of Robin Hood.

The Little Island (Doubleday, 1946). Written by Margaret Wise Brown (pseud. Golden MacDonald); illustrated by Leonard Weisgard.

SUMMARY: There is a little Island out in the sea. Mists cover it, and spiders sail cobwebs on it in the morning. In the spring, tiny flowers sprout there. Soon, lobsters make their way to the Island and hide under rocks where they shed their old shells and put on new ones. Seals bring their young to spread out on the rocks, birds nest their young, strawberries turn red, and it is summer. Fish jump out of the water near the Island, and boats sail to it.

One boat brings a kitten who thinks the Island is very small and tells it so. The Island replies that the kitten is small, too. The kitten says that it is part of the bigger world around the Island, and the Island is by itself. The Island tells the kitten a secret that the kitten has to believe on faith—the land is connected all underneath the water. The kitten likes secrets, so he believes. The kitten sails away in his boat. Night and a storm come to the Island; autumn and winter come, too. The Island is by itself, but it is also part of the larger world around it.

MEDIA: Gouache.

ANECDOTE: Weisgard used Vinalhaven, an island off the coast of Maine, as the inspiration for the island in the book. When Weisgard won the Caldecott Medal, Margaret Wise Brown gave him a pocketwatch as a gift. In return, Weisgard gave Brown a box of gold Caldecott Medal seals. She used them on the dummies of her works in progress for inspiration.

DISTINCTION: 1947 Caldecott Medal.

BIRTHDAY: Margaret Wise Brown: May 23, 1910.

SUBJECTS: Islands—Fiction; Seasons—Fiction.

See Also: Brown, Margaret Wise; *Goodnight Moon*; *Little Lost Lamb*.

Little Lost Lamb (Doubleday, 1945). Written by Margaret Wise Brown (pseud. Golden MacDonald); illustrated by Leonard Weisgard.

SUMMARY: A little black sheep is born in every flock. The shepherd watches over them all. The little black sheep is always roaming off by himself. One day, the lamb gets away without the shepherd seeing him. His mother bah-s for him; the shepherd looks for him, but the little lamb is lost. He is having a good time by himself. The shepherd wants to find him, but he also has to get the other sheep all down to the valley before dark. Finally, he leads them down. In the valley, the sheep will be safe from mountain lions and other dangers.

That night, the shepherd cannot stop thinking about the little lost sheep, and he cannot sleep. In the night, he and his dog climb the mountain to the high valley. They hear a mountain lion and scare it away just in time to find the lamb. The shepherd returns the lamb to the flock and sings his soothing song into the night.

MEDIA: Undetermined.

DISTINCTION: 1946 Caldecott Honor Book.

BIRTHDAY: Margaret Wise Brown: May 23, 1910.

SUBJECTS: Lambs—Fiction; Sheep—Fiction; Shepherds—Fiction.

See Also: Brown, Margaret Wise; *A Child's Good Night Book*; *Goodnight Moon*; *The Little Island*.

The Little Machinery (Doubleday, 1926). Written and illustrated by Mary Liddell.

SUMMARY: The Machinery lives near the railroad tracks in the woods and works all the time. The animals admire its industriousness. It "improves" on nature by helping birds build their nests; bears hibernate in beds rather than in natural habitats; and eagles get their talons sharpened by machine. Soon its domination over nature is total, but by the end it seems the animals have exploited it rather than the other way around.

MEDIA: Possibly pencil and pen and ink.

ANECDOTE: The book has been called the "first picture book for modern children." Having no human characters and not in print for long, the book is a curious paradox of fairy tale and the mechanization of America in the 1920s.

DISTINCTION: Of historical/scholarly interest.

BIRTHDAY: Not available.

SUBJECT: Machinery—Fiction.

See Also: Nova's Ark.

Little Red Riding Hood (Holiday, 1983). Retold and illustrated by Trina Schart Hyman.

SUMMARY: Elisabeth is Little Red Riding Hood in this retelling of the classic story. Everyone calls her by that name since she so often wears the red hood her grandmother made her. This wolf ends up eating both the grandmother and Riding Hood, who are saved from his stomach by a huntsman who happens to hear the wolf snoring in the cottage. The illustrations do not show it, but the text tells that the huntsman cuts open the wolf's stomach to retrieve the grandmother and Riding Hood, then skins the wolf. One of the last drawings shows the huntsman going off in the woods, the wolf skin slung over his shoulder. Little Red Riding Hood has learned her lesson about not wandering off in the woods, even though she has obeyed her mother's request to say please and thank you and good morning when on an errand.

MEDIA: Ink and acrylic.

ANECDOTE: Hyman was particularly known for her illustrations of folklore and myths. For this classic tale, she had to go against her preference for not putting clothing on animals because she did not believe in anthropomorphism.

DISTINCTION: 1984 Caldecott Honor Book.

BIRTHDAY: Trina Schart Hyman: April 8, 1939.

SUBJECTS: Fairy tales; Folklore—Germany; Little Red Riding Hood. English; Rotkäppchen.

See Also: Saint George and the Dragon.

Lon Po Po: A Red-Riding Hood Story from China (Philomel, 1989). Retold and illustrated by Ed Young.

SUMMARY: A woman lives alone in the country with her three daughters—Shang, Tao, and Paotze. She goes to visit her mother and tells the children not to let anyone in. A wolf sees her leave and goes to the cottage disguised as their grandmother, their Po Po. Tao and Paotze believe the wolf and let it in. The wolf climbs into bed with the children, and Shang feels the wolf's tail and claws. Shang lights the candle and sees the wolf's face before it blows the candle out. She is the oldest child but also the cleverest, so instead of running, she suggests that the wolf must be hungry.

The children climb a ginko tree to get nuts, supposedly for their grandmother, but instead of bringing them back to the wolf, they stay up in the tree. They offer to haul up the wolf in a basket so that it can get some nuts, for they tell the wolf that the nuts are magic and must be eaten only by those who pick them. Each time they try, they let go of the rope, and the wolf falls to the ground. On the last try, the fall bumps the wolf's head and breaks its heart, and it dies. The children climb down and go back to bed. The next day, the children tell their mother the story when she returns from their grandmother's.

MEDIA: Watercolor and pastels.

ANECDOTE: Ed Young did not always appear to be a winner. Once when he was young, he brought home a bad report card, and his mother said she didn't know what was going to become of him. On his first visit to the Harper and Row offices, a guard led him to the freight elevator because he thought he was a delivery person. His interest in art as a career began after winning a badge design contest at the University of Illinois, where he was studying architecture. The dedication page contains a blended picture of a wolf and an old woman combined and thanks all the wolves of the world who have given their name to represent the darkness in human beings.

DISTINCTION: 1990 Caldecott Medal.

BIRTHDAY: Ed Young: November 28, 1931.

SUBJECT: Folklore—China.

See Also: The Emperor and the Kite; Seven Blind Mice.

Lucky Song (Greenwillow, 1997). Written and illustrated by Vera B. Williams.

SUMMARY: Evie is lucky because she gets what she wants all day long. She wants to wear something new, so she puts on a hat she finds on a rack. She wants something new to play with, so her grandfather makes her a kite. The door opens when she wants to go out; her legs and the wind cooperate when she wants to climb a hill and fly her kite. When she wants someone else to see her kite, her mother looks. Grandma fixes her supper when she wants to go home and eat. Her sister provides a blanket and her father a song when she wants these things. Evie is a lucky girl with a lucky song.

MEDIA: Watercolor paints.

ANECDOTE: Williams was born in California and obtained a degree in graphic art at Black Mountain College in North Carolina. She is well known for strong female characters and the diversity of characters depicted in her books.

DISTINCTION: 1998 Charlotte Zolotow Award.

BIRTHDAY: Vera B. Williams: January 28, 1927.

SUBJECTS: Day—Fiction; Kites—Fiction; Singing—Fiction.

See Also: A Chair for My Mother; "More More More," Said the Baby.

M

Madeline (Simon and Schuster, 1939). Written and illustrated by Ludwig Bemelmans.

SUMMARY: In this classic rhyming picture book, Madeline is the smallest of twelve girls who live in a boarding school in Paris, an old house covered with vines. Little Madeline is not afraid of mice or tigers. One night, the schoolmistress, Miss Clavel, wakes up and realizes that something is not right—Madeline is crying. Dr. Cohn is called and diagnoses appendicitis, and Madeline goes to the hospital to have her appendix removed. While she is there, the other girls miss her and come to visit her in her room. There are many gifts in the room, including a dollhouse from Papa. Madeline shows off her scar to the others. The girls are so impressed that during the following night, they all wake up Miss Clavel with their own crying. They all want their appendixes out, too. Miss Clavel tells them to be grateful they are well and to go back to sleep.

MEDIA: Possibly brush, pen, and watercolor.

ANECDOTE: Madeline is named after the author's wife, Madeline Freund, but is said to have more of the characteristics of his own feistiness. The book illustrates several actual scenes from around Paris including the Eiffel Tower (cover and another scene), the Opera (scene with lady feeding the horse), the Place Vendome (scene with police chasing a thief), the Hotel des Invalides (scene with wounded soldier), Notre Dame (rainy day), the Gardens at the Luxembourg (sunny day), the Church of the Sacre Coeur (behind the little girls skating), and the Tuileries Gardens facing the Louvre (in the scene where a man is feeding birds). There is a well-known inconsistency in this book on the page where the girls are at the table after visiting Madeline, but Madeline is still in the hospital. There are twelve girls at the table where there should only be eleven. Madeline's appendix removal was inspired by a girl across the hall from Bemelmans when he was in the hospital after a car accident; she had had her appendix removed. The book is also inspired partly from Bemelmans' memories of his mother's stories about living in a convent as a child in Bavaria.

DISTINCTION: 1940 Caldecott Honor Book.

BIRTHDAY: Ludwig Bemelmans: April 27, 1898.

SUBJECTS: Sick—Fiction; Stories in rhyme; France—Fiction.

See Also: Madeline's Rescue.

Madeline's Rescue (Viking, 1953). Written and illustrated by Ludwig Bemelmans.

SUMMARY: Madeline joins her class walking in two straight lines as they visit the zoo, where she is not afraid of the tiger. On the way home, however, Madeline walks along the railing of a bridge and falls into the river. She is rescued by a dog. The girls take the dog home, where she proves to be clever and helpful. They name her Genevieve. At the first of May, however, the trustees make their annual inspection of the school and determine that no dogs should be allowed. Lord Cucuface puts Genevieve out the door. Madeline vows to Genevieve that she will have vengeance and find her.

Miss Clavel and the twelve girls look for Genevieve all about Paris, but they do not find her. During the night, Miss Clavel turns on her light and finds Miss Genevieve outside under a streetlight. The girls begin fighting over who will sleep with Genevieve when she is restored to the school. Miss Clavel must turn on her light again and resolve the problem by saying that if the girls continue to argue over her, the dog will have to go. For the third time that night, something is not quite right, and Miss Clavel turns on her light. She discovers that Genevieve has given birth to enough puppies that each girl may have a dog of her own.

MEDIA: Brush, pen, and watercolor.

ANECDOTE: Madeline's fearlessness and attitude toward the world make her a favorite children's book character among feminists. Bemelmans paid Phyllis McGinley's daughters fifty cents each for their suggestion that he include a dog in the next Madeline book. Another inspiration came from Bemelmans seeing a group of girls and their teacher watching a dog retrieve an artificial leg from the Seine.

DISTINCTION: 1954 Caldecott Medal.

BIRTHDAY: Ludwig Bemelmans: April 27, 1898.

SUBJECTS: Dogs—Fiction; Stories in rhyme; Paris (France)—Fiction; France—Fiction.

See Also: Madeline.

Magic Windows (Children's, 1999). Written and illustrated by Carmen Lomas Garza; as told to Harriet Rohmer; edited by David Schecter; translated by Francisco X. Alarcón.

SUMMARY: This bilingual book contains fourteen pieces of artwork as well as comments on each piece that also address concepts and customs related to Mexican Americans, cut-paper art, and/or Garza's own life and work. Each explanation is in English, then in Spanish. Titles for the pieces are "Nopal Cactus" (*"Nopalitos"*); "Offering for Antonio Lomas" (*"Ofrenda para Antonio Lomas"*); "Dance for the Day of the Dead" (*"Baile en el Día de Los Muertos"*); "Paper Flowers" (*"Flores de Papel"*); "Little Tortillas for Mother" (*"Tortillas para Mamá"*); "Horned Toads" (*"Camaleones"*); "Hummingbirds" (*"Colibríes"*); "Fish" (*"Peces"*); "Deer" (*"Venado"*); "Turkey" (*"Guajolote"*); "Eagle with Rattlesnake" (*"Aguila con Víbroa de Cascabel"*); "Dance and Painting" (*"Baile y Pintura"*); "Flowery Words" (*"Palabras en Flor"*); and "Making Papel Picado" (*"Haciendo Papel Picado"*).

MEDIA: Cut-paper (*papel picado*).

ANECDOTE: Garza explains in the introduction that she learned cut-paper art from her grandmother and that she decided to become an artist at the age of thirteen. The art form has a long history in Mexico, beginning with bark paper banners thousands of years ago. The cut-outs are typically hung from the ceiling or on a wall so that they appear to be "magic windows." Garza also paints and has had exhibitions at major museums, such as the Smithsonian Institution.

DISTINCTION: 2000 Pura Belpré Award for Illustration.

BIRTHDAY: Not available.

SUBJECTS: Carmen Lomas Garza—Family; Mexican Amerians—Social life and customs; Mexican American Families; Paper work; Spanish language materials—Bilingual; Handicraft; Mexico—Social life and customs.

Make Way for Ducklings (Viking, 1941). Written and illustrated by Robert McCloskey.

The sculpture of Mrs. Mallard and her ducklings at Boston Public Garden celebrates families as well as Robert McCloskey's 1941 classic, *Make Way for Ducklings*. The book made the park familiar to children all over the world, illustrating the global reach of picture book literature. (Photo copyright © 1995 by Ken Kirk. Courtesy Ken Kirk.)

SUMMARY: In this classic picture book, Mr. and Mrs. Mallard are ducks looking for a suitable home where they can raise a family. After searching various sites, they settle on an island in the Charles River in Boston, where Mrs. Mallard lays eggs and hatches eight ducklings. Mr. Mallard leaves his family on a trip to see the rest of the river. Mrs. Mallard must cross a busy city street to meet him at the appointed place and time of his return. After a fearful attempt, she and her ducklings are aided by Officer Michael, who stops traffic so that the little troupe may cross. The family decides to make their home in the safer area of the park, where they can follow the swan boats.

MEDIA: Lithographic crayon on stone.

ANECDOTE: McCloskey sketched ducks he kept in his bathtub in a New York City apartment for weeks in preparation for his award-winning illustrations. A life-sized, bronze statue of Mrs. Mallard and her brood sculpted by Nancy Schon was installed in Boston's Public Garden in 1987.

DISTINCTION: 1942 Caldecott Medal.

BIRTHDAY: Robert McCloskey: September 15, 1914.

SUBJECTS: Ducks—Fiction; Boston (Mass.)—Fiction.

See Also: Blueberries for Sal; McCloskey, Robert; *One Morning in Maine*; *Time of Wonder*.

The Man Who Walked between the Towers (Roaring Brook, 2003). Written and illustrated by Mordicai Gerstein.

SUMMARY: On the morning of August 7, 1974, before the two towers of the World Trade Center in New York City were completely built, French aerialist Philippe Petit performed a tightrope act between them for nearly an hour. This is the story of that performance. The day before, Petit and his friend dressed as construction workers in order to get his supplies up to the roof of the south tower. There they wait until everyone has gone home, and it is dark. Two friends on top of the north tower shoot an arrow across the space, and after some failed attempts, eventually manage to tie a seven-eighths-inch-thick cable between the towers. The task took most of the night, making it necessary that the walk take place in the morning while people were on their way to work.

Petit performed by not only walking but also running, dancing, lying down, and doing other maneuvers on the wire. By this time, he was noticed by people on the ground and the police were at the top calling at him through a blowhorn to return. Petit simply walked on the wire away from the blowhorns—he knew no one would come out to get him, nor would they untie the wire. He stayed out on the wire enjoying a sense of freedom and peace until he was satisfied with his accomplishment. Petit was taken to court, where he was ordered to perform for children in the park. When he did so, children playing with the wire almost made him fall, but he caught himself. The book concludes with a tribute to the memory of the twin towers and Petit's part in their history.

MEDIA: Ink and oil painting.

ANECDOTE: Rather than interpret this book as exploitation of the destruction of the World Trade Center two years after the terrorist attack of September 11, 2001, most readers embraced it for highlighting a more positive event in the history of the towers.

DISTINCTION: 2004 Caldecott Medal.

BIRTHDAY: Mordicai Gerstein: November 25, 1935.

SUBJECTS: Petit, Philippe, 1949– ; Tightrope walking; Aerialists—France; Aerialists; World Trade Center (New York, N.Y.).

Many Moons (Harcourt, 1943). Written by James Thurber; illustrated by Louis Slobodkin.

SUMMARY: A princess named Lenore lives in a castle near the sea. She is ten going on eleven. Lenore gets sick on raspberry tarts,

Front cover of *Many Moons*, written by James Thurber, illustrated by Louis Slobodkin. Slobodkin's 1944 Caldecott Medal for this book is housed as part of the de Grummond Children's Literature Collection at the University of Southern Mississippi—Hattiesburg. (Copyright © 1943 by James Thurber. Copyright © by Harcourt, Inc. All rights reserved.)

and the Royal Physician is worried about her and calls the King. The King promises anything Lenore desires to get her well. Princess Lenore says that she wants the moon. The King tells Lord High Chamberlain that he must get the moon to give to his daughter so that she will get well. After going down a very long list of things he had retrieved for the King (including a blue poodle), Lord High Chamberlain tells him that he cannot get him the moon, since it is so large and is made of molten copper. The King summons the Royal Wizard.

The Royal Wizard also runs down a list of things he has gotten for the King (including wolfbane and an invisibility cloak) and tells him that the moon is impossible because it is so large and made of green cheese. In like fashion and with similar results, the King summons the Royal Mathematician. Then, he summons the Court Jester, who recommends asking the princess how big she thinks the moon is, how far away, and what it may be made of. She tells him that it is made of gold, is as far away as the tree outside that holds it in its branches each night, and is the size of her thumbnail that covers it when she looks out at it. The Court Jester goes to the Royal Goldsmith and has him make a gold necklace that fits the princess' qualifications for the moon. When he gives it to her, she becomes well and goes outside again to play.

Since the princess now thinks she wears the moon around her neck, the problem now is what to do about the moon that will surely shine in her chamber window that night. The Lord High Chamberlain suggests dark glasses, but the King disregards that, saying that they will make her fall and grow ill again. The Royal Wizard suggests dark curtains, but the king says she will grow ill from those not letting in enough air. The Royal Mathematician suggests setting off fireworks every night so that she cannot see the moon, but the King says the noise will keep her awake and make her ill again from lack of sleep. The Court Jester suggests they ask the princess herself how the moon can be about her neck and also up in the sky.

When he goes to her chamber, the Court Jester sees the princess wearing her moon necklace but also looking out at the moon already visible from her window. When he asks her how the moon can be in both places, the princess explains that a new one has grown in place of the one about her neck, just as the Royal Gardener's flowers regrow where they are picked. The Court Jester thinks he sees the moon winking at him, so he returns the gesture, much relieved.

MEDIA: Pen and ink; watercolor.

ANECDOTE: James Thurber was blinded in one eye in a childhood accident while playing "William Tell" with his brothers. He was completely blind later in life. After that time, he continued to write by dictating his stories on tape recordings. Slobodkin's Caldecott Medal is part of the de Grummond Collection.

DISTINCTION: 1944 Caldecott Medal.

BIRTHDAYS: James Thurber: December 8, 1894; Louis Slobodkin: February 19, 1903.

SUBJECTS: Princesses—Fiction; Moon—Fiction.

Marshmallow (Harper, 1942). Written and illustrated by Clare Turlay Newberry.

SUMMARY: Oliver is a bachelor cat that lives in an apartment with Miss Tilly. Since he never goes outside, he does not know about the other furry animals of the world. He has not even seen mice, since Miss Tilly takes care of his every need, feeding him from her own refrigerator. One day, Miss Tilly tells Oliver that she has a surprise for him. She has brought home a small, white baby rabbit she names Marshmallow. At first, Oliver is afraid of the bunny; he has never seen another furry animal before. Then, when he sees that Marshmallow is quiet, nonthreatening, and lonely for his mother bunny, he decides to move in on the rabbit and nearly springs upon him. Miss Tilly separates the cat and rabbit just in time and decides to keep them in different rooms. She writes poems about the rabbit on her typewriter.

One day, Miss Tilly is out longer than usual. Oliver hears Marshmallow playing in the room behind the door. He is young but growing and likes to hop and flip and gnaw on things. Oliver can hear his nails scratching along the hardwood floor. Oliver is hungry. He works at the doorknob until he gets it free and goes in to watch Marshmallow. The bunny is not afraid but is so glad to see a furry animal similar to his mother that he hops over to the cat and kisses its nose and nuzzles up to its fur. Soon, Oliver has also made friends. He cleans Marshmallow with his tongue as a mother cat would her kitten. Before Miss Tilly comes home, they are fast friends and fall asleep cuddled together. Miss

Tilly can't believe her eyes, but she is glad that her pets now get along and allows them to be together from that day on. She is glad that Oliver agrees that a house is brightened when a bunny lives there.

MEDIA: Possibly charcoal.

ANECDOTE: Newberry always lived with cats in the house, so it is perhaps no surprise that they are so much a part of her work.

DISTINCTION: 1943 Caldecott Honor Book.

BIRTHDAY: Clare Turlay Newberry: April 10, 1903.

SUBJECTS: Rabbits—Fiction; Cats—Fiction; Friendship—Fiction.

See Also: April's Kittens; Barkis; T-Bone, the Baby Sitter.

Martin's Big Words: The Life of Dr. Martin Luther King, Jr. (Hyperion, 2001). Written by Doreen Rappaport; illustrated by Bryan Collier.

SUMMARY: The book relates a brief biography of the civil rights leader in simple language, using short quotations from his speeches and sermons. His death is dealt with directly and matter-of-factly. The emphasis of the book is on his preaching of a peaceful resolution to racial conflict. The book includes a listing of important dates in King's life and the movement's progress as well as additional books and Web sites for further information.

MEDIA: Watercolor; cut-paper collage.

ANECDOTE: The four candles on the last page represent the four black girls killed at the Sixteenth Street Baptist Church. Dr. King's birthday was first celebrated as a national holiday in 1986.

DISTINCTIONS: 2002 Caldecott Honor Book; 2002 Coretta Scott King Honor Book for Illustration.

BIRTHDAY: Doreen Rappaport: October 31, 1939.

SUBJECTS: King, Martin Luther, Jr., 1929–1968; King, Martin Luther, Jr., 1929–1968—Quotations; African Americans—Biography; Civil rights workers—United States—Biography; Baptists—United States—Clergy—Biography; African Americans—Civil Rights—History—twentieth Century; Civil Rights Workers; Clergy.

May I Bring a Friend? (Atheneum, 1964). Written by Beatrice Schenk de Regniers; illustrated by Beni Montresor.

SUMMARY: The King and Queen invite a small boy to the castle for tea on Sunday. The boy asks if he may bring a friend, and the royals agree, saying that any friend of a friend is a friend of theirs. So begins a series of unexpected friends brought to the castle. The boy first brings a giraffe, which sits next to him at the table and politely drinks tea with all of them. The King and Queen invite him for stew on Monday, and he asks to bring another friend, a hippopotamus, who sits beside him and eats all the food. On Tuesday, he is invited for lunch, and he brings monkeys, who are less well behaved. On Wednesday, the King and Queen invite him for breakfast. When he brings his friend, this time it is an elephant, and there is no room for it to sit with them at the table, so they sit on him. Thursday is Halloween, and he brings lions in masks. Friday is Apple Pie Day, and he brings a seal, which plays "Oh Say Can You See" on a horn and also Long Live Apple Pie. On Saturday, the King and Queen ask the boy again for tea, but he tells them his friends and he now want to invite them to tea. They all meet for tea at the zoo.

MEDIA: Pen-and-ink drawings on board in black with solid overlays and screened overlays on acetate.

ANECDOTE: Beni Montresor was knighted by the Italian government for his contribution to the arts.

DISTINCTION: 1965 Caldecott Medal.

BIRTHDAY: Beni Montresor: March 31, 1926.

SUBJECTS: Animals—Fiction; Stories in rhyme.

Mazza Museum of International Art from Picture Books. Located at the University of Findlay in Ohio, the museum's mission is to promote literacy, appreciation for the arts, and greater understanding of humanity through its collection of international picture book art. The museum claims to be the first and largest museum of original picture book art in the world.

As part of the hundredth anniversary celebration of the University of Findlay in 1982, each division at the university was given $2,000 to plan a special event. Dr. Jerry Mallett of the Education Division proposed a permanent use of the money that could be enjoyed by majors in the division as well as the entire community for years to come through the purchase of original picture book art. The money allotment for this purpose was soon exhausted, but a generous donation by alumni August and Aleda Mazza enabled the school to purchase four works of art that became the original collection. After that time, the collection grew until its 2004 level of over 2,300 pieces and continues to expand.

Artists whose works are represented in the collection include Randolph Caldecott, Peter Spier, Janet Stevens, Jan Brett, and Alice and Martin Provensen, among many others. The museum also sponsors traveling exhibits of collected artwork with themes such as dogs, animals, and the great outdoors and offers specialized tours to school groups.

Contact: Mazza Museum, University of Findlay, 1000 North Main Street, Findlay, Ohio, 45840-3695. (800) 472-9502. Web site: http://www.mazzamuseum.org. email: mazza @findlay.edu.

McCloskey, Robert (1914–2003). Artist and author. One of the biggest names in American children's picture books was born in Hamilton, Ohio, on September 15, 1914, the son of Howard Hill and Mable Wismeyer McCloskey. Like many American children growing up, McCloskey attended public school during the day and took piano lessons after school, but his love for music grew stronger than that of many children, and he went on to learn the harmonica, drums, and oboe and began to daydream about becoming a professional musician. He also developed an interest in electrical gadgets, collecting electric trains, parts of clocks, wire, and old electric motors. Once he wired up the McCloskey Christmas tree so that it would revolve and twinkle at the same time. Not unlike other notable Ohioans who liked to tinker with mechanical objects such as the Wright Brothers, McCloskey envisioned himself one day becoming an inventor. All the while, however, it was McCloskey's drawings in school that were earning him more notice than either his musical ability or his homemade electrical contraptions. Many years later, he would describe his becoming an artist of children's books as "sort of an accident."

McCloskey's school artwork and drawings for his 1932 high school yearbook earned him a scholarship to the Vesper George Art School in Boston. McCloskey accepted. On his way to art class each day, he passed through the Boston Public Gardens and noticed a family of ducks making their way to the pond. The image stuck and would be one that the artist would return to in a few years. In the meantime, he received a commission for some bas-reliefs for the municipal building of Hamilton, Ohio, and he later moved to New York City to attend the National Academy of Design. He painted for two years on Cape Cod. Despite his training, practice, and work experience, McCloskey was not successful in the early years at trying to market his artwork.

When he showed his portfolio to May Massee, the children's book editor at Viking, for example, she did not hire him but instead gave him some valuable advice. She recom-

Author-artist Robert McCloskey holds a young fan from Boston during the fiftieth anniversary celebration of his classic, *Make Way for Ducklings*, in 1991. (AP/Wide World Photos.)

mended that he shy away from his current mythological and fantasy subjects and return to the life he saw all around him, the subjects that he knew. McCloskey returned to Ohio and took up work for a while as a commercial artist. While he was there, he worked on a children's book, *Lentil*, a semiautobiographical story about a boy growing up in the Midwest and his harmonica. This time Massee liked the sepia-charcoal drawings she saw, and Viking published the book in 1940.

McCloskey made his way back east and returned to Boston, where he had a job helping Francis Scott Bradford create a mural of famous Beacon Hill figures on the Lever Brothers' Building. Again, he walked through the Boston Public Garden and noticed the ducks. This time, however, he had more time after work to stop and listen to stories about the ducks from the locals, and this kindled an idea for a story he might make into a children's book.

McCloskey returned to New York and set about studying the authentic rendering of mallard ducks in earnest. He did this in several ways, some of which have now become famous. He studied stuffed ducks at the American Museum of Natural History in New York City; sought advice from an ornithologist at Cornell University; and even purchased four ducks that he took home with him to his bathtub in his Greenwich Village apartment. There, he studied and sketched the ducks flapping in the water, waddling about the apartment, and generally being more noisy than his neighbors ever appreciated. McCloskey's novel method of research involved several weeks of following the ducks around his apartment on his hands and knees with a tissue in one hand to pick up their droppings and a sketchbook in the other to record their movements. Despite his efforts to keep them quiet, McCloskey's comical research methods eventually drove neighbors, including fellow illustrator Marc Simont, to suggest that McCloskey might return the ducks to a more natural habitat. McCloskey's intense research paid off when his classic

Make Way for Ducklings was published by Viking in 1941. The book went on to be awarded the Caldecott Medal for McCloskey's detailed sepia lithographs and is still one of the favorite American children's picture books of all time.

McCloskey's third book was *Homer Price*, another semiautobiographical story, this one told in sepia-colored charcoal about a small-town boy who enjoys gadgets. This book's text is too long to be considered a picture book, but it has another interesting anecdote attached to it that illuminates McCloskey's biography. Just as Viking was preparing to produce the book, the publisher asked McCloskey for one more illustration. World War II was on, and McCloskey had been inducted into the army and had not reread the story for a while. Hastily before leaving for the army, he drew a picture of five robbers in bed to complete the book. The book was published with this illustration; unfortunately, only four robbers existed in the story. The book was never corrected even years later for American printings, but the Japanese version took out the extra robber immediately before it was published.

During the war, McCloskey served stateside in Alabama, working on training pictures. After he returned from the army and a year abroad in Italy, he wrote and illustrated his fourth book, a sequel to *Homer Price* called *Centerburg Tales* (Viking, 1951). McCloskey met and married the daughter of storyteller and author Ruth Sawyer Durand. Robert and Peggy McCloskey had two daughters, Sally (Sal) and Jane, born in the late 1940s. From McCloskey's success, they were able to move to their own island in Penobscot Bay, Maine, near Deer Isle. Here they lived almost every summer, from May until October, and Maine became the setting of the next generation of McCloskey picture books.

The artist was inspired by his family and their life in Maine when he created *Blueberries for Sal* (Viking, 1948); *One Morning in Maine* (Viking, 1952); and *Time of Wonder* (Viking, 1957), all of which earned the artist Caldecott distinctions. The little girl and mother in *Blueberries* are depictions of Sally and Peggy in blueberry-blue lithographs. That book won a Caldecott Honor Book Award in 1949. In *One Morning*, McCloskey portrays Sally losing her first tooth, with her baby sister, Jane, as part of the story. He also included their English setter, Penny, and their black cat, Mozzarella, all done in navy blue lithographs. The village the family visits is the actual town the McCloskeys went to in order to get supplies. That book earned the artist a Caldecott Honor Book Award in 1953. *Time of Wonder* was the artist's first full-color picture book, and it took him three years to complete the watercolors that composed it. For this book, he won his second Caldecott Medal in 1958. McCloskey also illustrated one of his mother-in-law's books, *Journey Cake, Ho!*, for which he won a Caldecott Honor Book Award in 1954. The last book that he both wrote and illustrated was also set in Maine, *Burt Dow: Deep-Water Man* (Viking, 1963). McCloskey retired from creating children's books in 1970.

In addition to the five Caldecott distinctions he received for his work and many other honors, McCloskey was awarded honorary doctorates in literature from Miami University in Ohio in 1964 and Mount Holyoke College in 1967. One of the most distinct memorials to his work is the bronze sculpture that was installed in Boston Public Garden in 1987. The sculpture was created by Nancy Schon and features Mrs. Mallard and her eight ducklings walking along the thirty-five-foot walkway of old Boston cobblestone in the park. Mrs. Mallard is thirty-eight inches tall, and the ducklings range from twelve to eighteen inches. The sculpture is much beloved in Boston, and families from around the world who are familiar with McCloskey's book come to the park to enjoy the ducks. Like all public works of art, maintenance has sometimes been required for the much-loved sculpture—"Quack" once had to be recast and replaced.

The artist died on June 30, 2003, in Deer Isle, Maine. In all, he wrote and illustrated eight books and illustrated another ten for other authors. His work is remarkable and memorable for its integrity and authenticity. It is impossible to envision American children's literature without McCloskey's contributions to the unique American character represented in his picture books.

DISTINCTIONS: 1942, 1958 Caldecott Medal (one of only seven multiple medalists and second highest overall in total number of Caldecott distinctions); 1949, 1953, and 1954 Caldecott Honor Book Awards.

See Also: Blueberries for Sal; Journey Cake, Ho!; Make Way for Ducklings; One Morning in Maine; Time of Wonder.

McElligott's Pool (Random House, 1947). Written and illustrated by Theodor Seuss Geisel (pseud. Dr. Seuss).

SUMMARY: Marco sits by McElligott's pool for three hours fishing without a bite. A farmer goes by and tells him that he is a fool to fish in that pool, that there are no fish there. Marco replies that there might not be any fish, but one never knows; there might also be many fish. The pool may be very deep and connect to one of those brooks underground, where it reaches under State Highway Two-Hundred-and-Three, under Mrs. Umbroso who is hanging clothes, under the Sneeden's Hotel and out to the sea. There it might connect with water where all kinds of amazing fish live, just waiting for one of them to suggest they swim up his way. Marco imagines all this, including a pool alive with a variety of fish that have swum up from the ocean all floating next to his baited hook beneath the water. He recommends patience.

MEDIA: Pencil and watercolor.

ANECDOTE: Seuss didn't think of this book as successful, even though it won a Caldecott Honor distinction, because children didn't seem to like it as well as his other books. It lacks the dark line outlines typical of the others. Seuss dedicated the book to his father in Springfield, Massachusetts, whom he claimed was the "World's Greatest Authority on Blackfish, Fiddler Crabs and Deegel Trout."

DISTINCTION: 1948 Caldecott Honor Book.

BIRTHDAY: Theodor Geisel (Dr. Seuss): March 2, 1904.

SUBJECTS: Fishing—Fiction; Stories in rhyme.

See Also: Bartholomew and the Oobleck; Geisel, Theodor (Ted) Seuss; If I Ran the Zoo.

Mei Li (Doubleday, 1938). Written and illustrated by Thomas Handforth.

SUMMARY: It is the morning before New Year's Day, and Mei Li, a little girl with a candle-topped pigtail and her family—mother, Mrs. Wang, and brother San Yu—are making preparations for the Kitchen God's visit that evening. The Kitchen God will tell each family in China what they should do for the coming year. Uncle Wang is not working but is instead telling them all about his visit to the city. San Yu is excited to hear about it because Mrs. Wang has told him that he may go there for the New Year Fair. Mei Li is unhappy because girls are not allowed to go.

Mei Li gathers up some of her treasures—three lucky pennies and three lucky marbles, one lapis blue, one coral red, and one jade green. She bribes her way onto the sled that is taking San Yu to the city by giving him a lapis-blue marble. Igo, a small white dog, and Mei Li's thrush go with them. Mei Li gives a lucky penny to a hungry peasant girl named Lidza. Lidza is grateful and warns Mei Li to return through the Big Gate from the city before the Kitchen God comes that evening. When they arrive in the city, they see many sights such as rickshas, Mongol ponies, and women in glass coaches. It is just as exciting as Uncle Wang told them. They have lunch in the Great Square, and there Mei Li buys a firecracker. When she asks her brother to light it for her, he complains that girls have nothing to do at the New Year Fair. Just then, Mei Li asks the circus girl to lift her high and upside down, and she does. This did not impress her brother, so she goes about performing other tricks and sights. She gives him her last lucky penny to strike a tiny bell under the Bridge of Wealth, and he wins.

Soon, she goes up the hill where a fortune-teller is predicting the future with bamboo sticks. She gives the teller a coral-red marble, and she is told that she would one day rule the kingdom. Mei Li meets some other girls at the fair who help her make a crown when they hear of her fortune. She goes to a store and looks at the toys. When a gray hawk comes swooping at her out of the sky, she holds San Yu's thrush close. Soon, San Yu shows her that the hawk is his kite, and Uncle Wong comes to get them on a camel to take them back out the city gate. They have been looking for Mei Li, and now they are in danger of not getting out in time.

The camels run fast as firecrackers pop all around them, and when they get to the gate, there is Lidza holding open the doors with her feet so that Mei Li can make it out before they close. Mei Li has lost her crown in the rush. Now she comes home with no presents at all. She has given away all of her lucky pennies and marbles. The best part of going to the fair to her, however, is getting safely back home.

Mrs. Wang knows Mei Li is a princess of their hearts. They are in time for the feast. When the Kitchen God arrives, he tells them that their home is their kingdom, and to Mei Li, that she should rule all those living within it as her subjects. Mei Li sighs and agrees that this fortune will do, for now.

MEDIA: Possibly brush and lithograph pencil.

ANECDOTE: The Chinese characters on the back cover of the book are translated, "Mei Li's Chinese New Year." At the ceremony to honor the book with the Caldecott medal, Frederic Melcher, originator of the Caldecott and Newbery awards, dressed as an Asian sage, and the room was adorned with Chinese decorations.

DISTINCTION: 1939 Caldecott Medal.

BIRTHDAY: September 16, 1897.

SUBJECT: China—Fiction.

Mice Twice (Atheneum, 1980). Written and illustrated by Joseph Low.

SUMMARY: Cat was hungry and thought about what he might like to eat. He decides a mouse sounds about right, so he slyly asks Mouse to come for dinner. Mouse is smart and invites a friend to go with her—Dog. Cat decides to outsmart her the next time and sets up another dinner; this time he brings Wolf. Mouse, however, has not only brought Dog but now also Crocodile. Dinners go back and forth, including offers of Frech brie, until Lion and Wasp join the crew. Wasp stings Lion, who wrecks the house and runs out with all the other animals. Mouse thanks Wasp by offering him anything from the table that he would like.

MEDIA: Possibly watercolor and pen and ink.

ANECDOTE: Low began his career in 1933 by typesetting and printing his own work.

DISTINCTION: 1981 Caldecott Honor Book.

BIRTHDAY: Joseph Low: August 11, 1911.

SUBJECTS: Animals—Fiction; Etiquette—Fiction.

The Mighty Hunter (Macmillan, 1943). Written and illustrated by Berta and Elmer Hader.

SUMMARY: Little Brave Heart is neither big nor small, but he is brave. Though his mother wants him to go to school to become a wise leader of their people, Little Brave Heart wants to be a mighty hunter, which he thinks sounds like more fun. One morning he takes his bow and arrow and goes out to hunt. He sees a wood rat and aims, but the rat tells him that he is too small a prey for a mighty hunter and suggests the boy find the big, fat prairie dog and shoot him instead. This sequence continues through a rabbit, wildcat, antelope, and wolf until the boy reaches the buffalo. The buffalo tells him that there are not many of his kind left and that he is a friend to the Indians. He sends him through the woods, where the boy meets up with a grizzly bear. When he aims his bow, the bear asks him if he is hungry or cold and why he is hunting her. Little Brave Heart admits he is hunting simply for the fun of it. This makes the bear angry, and she chases the boy who runs until he gets all the way to the school, where his mother wanted him to be all along.

MEDIA: Watercolor.

ANECDOTE: The book is dedicated to Glacier Woman, a friend of the Haders.

DISTINCTION: 1944 Caldecott Honor Book.

BIRTHDAYS: Berta Hader: February 6, 1891; Elmer Hader: September 7, 1889.

SUBJECTS: Native Americans—Fiction; Hunting—Fiction.

See Also: The Big Snow.

Mike Mulligan and His Steam Shovel

(Houghton Mifflin, 1939). Written and illustrated by Virginia Burton.

SUMMARY: Mike Mulligan and his steam shovel, Mary Anne, dug many of the holes needed for the building of roads, skyscrapers, canals, and airfields. Then came along the gasoline shovels, electric shovels, and the Diesel motor shovels that took work away from the old steam shovels. Mike takes such good care of Mary Anne that she is as good as new, but now she has no work.

Mike reads that the small town of Popperville needs to build a new town hall. Mike takes Mary Anne, and they go to the town where they want to dig the basement of the new building. Henry B. Swap says that it would take one hundred men a week to dig the basement. Mike promises they can dig the cellar in one day, though he is not quite sure this can be done. Swap smiles in a mean way and gives the pair the job when Mike offers that they will not have to be paid if they do not make the nightfall deadline.

As work begins first thing in the morning, a little boy comes to watch, and Mike Mulligan tells him that watching is all right because he and Mary Anne work more quickly if someone is watching them. Soon, Mrs. McGillicuddy, the Town Constable, the Fire Department, and people from the nearby towns of Bangerville, Bopperville, Kipperville, and Kopperville all come to watch Mike and Mary Anne work. They dig and dig one corner after another as the sun rises and then sets overhead. By the end of the day, they have dug the square for the basement, but they have dug so fast that they have not allowed themselves a way out. Henry B. Swap suggests that the job is not entirely finished because Mike Mulligan and his steam shovel are not out of the hole. He smiles in his mean way that he will not have to pay Mike for the work.

The little boy makes a suggestion that Mary Anne becomes the furnace of the Town Hall, and Mike Mulligan becomes the janitor, so he can be paid. All agree, and the Town Hall is built above the pair. Mrs. McGillicuddy takes Mike hot apple pies where he works, and even Henry B. Swap goes down to the cellar to listen to Mike's many stories. Swap's smiles are not the mean kind anymore.

MEDIA: Crayon.

ANECDOTE: Burton's subjects reflected the interests of her young sons, Aristides and Michael. She acknowledges young Dickie Birkenbush in the book for the suggestion about what to do when Mike and Mary Anne become stuck at the bottom of the hole.

DISTINCTION: *New York Times* Best Book for Children; NYPL 100 Picture Books Everyone Should Know; *100 Best Children's Books*.

BIRTHDAY: Virginia Lee Burton: August 30, 1909.

SUBJECT: Steam shovels—Fiction.

See Also: The Little House.

Millions of Cats (Coward, 1928). Written and illustrated by Wanda Gág, hand-lettered by Howard Gág.

SUMMARY: A very old man and a very old woman live alone in a house with flowers all around it. They would be happy except there is one problem—they are very lonely. The very old woman thinks if they had a cat, they might have the company they need, so the very old man sets out to find one. He walks a long way until he comes to a hill that is covered with cats, in fact, millions and trillions of cats. He is delighted to think that now all he has to do is to choose the prettiest one and go home. However, making his selection is tougher than he first thinks. He finds a reason to take one, then two, then more. Before long, he finds that he has chosen them all.

On the way home, the millions and trillions of cats need a drink, so they stop and drink up a lake. They eat every blade of grass on a hill. When the very old man arrives home with the cats, his wife wisely says that the cats will eat them out of house and home. They can keep only one. The man suggests they allow the cats to decide who is the prettiest and who will stay. All the cats begin fighting—all of them but one thin and scruffy little one. It says that it is homely and not pretty at

all, so it didn't say anything about trying to stay. The man and woman take the little cat in and clean it and brush it until its fur shines. They feed it milk, and soon the cat grows to be plump and pretty. The man and woman are content with the cat and are happy because they are not alone anymore.

MEDIA: Black ink.

ANECDOTE: Editor Ernestine Evans sought Gág out at a one-woman art show at the Weyhe Gallery in New York City to do a children's book. Evans believed the best artists in the country should be creating picture books for children. As it turned out, Gág had always wanted to do a picture book. The book's text was hand-lettered by Gág's brother.

DISTINCTIONS: 1929 Newbery Honor Book; *New York Times* Best Book for Children.

BIRTHDAY: Wanda Gág: March 11, 1893.

SUBJECT: Cats—Fiction.

See Also: The ABC Bunny; Gág, Wanda; *Snow White and the Seven Dwarfs.*

Minty: A Story of Young Harriet Tubman (Penguin, 1996). Written by Alan Schroeder; illustrated by Jerry Pinkney.

SUMMARY: Harriet Tubman was called Minty as a child, and this is a fictionalized account of her wanting to escape in her younger years. In the story, Minty does not come when the mistress, Mrs. Brodas, calls her. Instead, she goes to the barn, where she tells the Bible story of David and Goliath to her small rag doll, Esther Lavinia Louise. When she does go to the house, she accidentally tips over a pitcher of cider on the table, the mistress burns her doll, and she is sent away from housework into the fields to be a field slave. There, she befriends Amanda, who tells the girl to have her mother, Rit, make her a bandana to keep the sweat out of her eyes in the fields.

One day, Sanders, the overseer, takes Minty to the Big Buckwater River, where the master has laid muskrat traps. Minty is to go through the water and bring in the caught game. Instead, she sets the muskrats free. When the overseer catches her, Minty is whipped and threatened with being sold downriver to the South, where she would meet with even more cruel treatment. Minty makes her wish to run away known to her family. Her father, Old Ben, teaches her about the North Star and the Drinking Gourd. She learns to swim and how to read trees.

When she sees a horse tied up outside the big house during an errand, Minty thinks this is her chance to run to freedom. Just as she almost has the rope worked free, house visitors Nathaniel and Mr. Brodas come outside and her opportunity is lost. Minty goes home crying, having lost her nerve and her chance that time, but she resolves that one day she will escape the plantation and find her freedom.

MEDIA: Pencil, colored pencils, and watercolor.

ANECDOTE: Harriet Tubman's "cradle" name was Araminta, from which comes the nickname, Minty. She was known as a "difficult" slave on the Brodas plantation on Maryland's Eastern Shore in the 1820s. After she escaped north in 1849, she aided hundreds of other slaves to freedom through the network of safe houses that came to be called the Underground Railroad. Jerry Pinkney designed the Harriet Tubman U.S. postage stamp in 1978.

DISTINCTION: 1997 Coretta Scott King Award for Illustration.

BIRTHDAY: Jerry Pinkney: December 22, 1939.

SUBJECTS: Tubman, Harriet, 1820(?)–1913—Childhood and youth; Slaves—United States—Biography; African Americans—Biography; Underground railroad; Antislavery movements—United States; Slaves.

See Also: Mirandy and Brother Wind; The Ugly Duckling.

Mirandy and Brother Wind (Knopf, 1988). Written by Patricia C. McKissack; illustrated by Jerry Pinkney.

SUMMARY: There is a cakewalk happening that night. A cakewalk is a dance competition where young people dance, are judged by their elders, and win a fancy decorated cake as a prize. Mirandy wants to dance with Brother Wind, who has blown into town on the spring air. She has heard that if she can catch Brother Wind, she can make him grant her a wish. Meanwhile, clumsy friend Ezel is expecting to be her dance partner, though they have not agreed to this officially. When Mirandy tells him she is going to dance with Brother Wind, Ezel says he is going to ask Orlinda to dance with him instead of her.

Mirandy tries various methods to capture Brother Wind. Mr. Jessup recommends pepper; Miss Pointsettia, the conjurer, recommends a spell with cider in a jug. Neither of these methods works. Mirandy keeps running into Ezel, who keeps dropping things and tripping up doing his chores. She relates her progress. Finally, she traps Brother Wind in the barn when he blows in. She shuts the door and keeps him there. At the cakewalk, Mirandy is surprised to find that Orlinda refused clumsy Ezel's invitation to be a dance partner, and she dances with him instead. Before she does, however, she asks Brother Wind to grant her wish, and they dance together like the wind and win the cake. The book also contains a recipe for a cakewalk cake and instructions on how to create a cakewalk dance event.

MEDIA: Pencil and watercolor.

ANECDOTE: Cakewalks are an African American tradition.

DISTINCTION: 1989 Caldecott Honor Book.

SUBJECTS: Dance—Fiction; Winds—Fiction; African Americans—Fiction.

See Also: Minty: A Story of Young Harriet Tubman; The Patchwork Quilt.

Mirette on the High Wire (Putnam, 1992). Written and illustrated by Emily Arnold McCully.

SUMMARY: Mirette lives with her mother at Gâteau's, a boardinghouse on English Street in Paris. There, they provide housing for performers—actors, jugglers, acrobats, and mimes. One day, the famous, but tired, tightrope walker Bellini comes to stay at Madam Gâteau's. He takes a room at the back and eats alone rather than with the others. In the back of the house, he strings a wire and occasionally Mirette sees him walking it. She asks him to teach her, but he refuses, saying that once you have a feel for the wire, you are no longer happy to be on the ground.

Mirette begins to test herself on the wire when Bellini is not around. After many falls and practice, she is able to cross. Bellini discovers her and says that her persistence may indicate that she has talent; he agrees to teach her. One evening, an agent comes to the boardinghouse and spots Bellini. He remarks on Bellini's accomplishments, including crossing Niagara Falls not just from one side to the other but also stopping and making an omelette in the middle and doing other amazing feats. Mirette wonders why he no longer performs for the public, but Bellini admits to her that he has known fear on the wire, and fear stops all performances. Bellini is sad that he has disappointed Mirette, who is still brave and loves the wire.

To face his fear and make it up to Mirette, Bellini agrees to a public performance with the agent. It is set up and ready to begin when Bellini starts out on the wire and suddenly stops. Mirette knows what the problem is. She runs to the top of the building and begins to cross the wire to meet him. Seeing her there gives Bellini back his courage, and the two complete their performance. A picture at the end of the book shows a poster suggesting that Bellini and Mirette perform together after that.

MEDIA: Watercolor.

ANECDOTE: McCully admitted that the book is a metaphor for taking risks in writing and illustrating books for children. The figure of Mirette is based on photographs of the author Colette as a child. The story first started out as a biography of the daredevil, Blondin.

DISTINCTION: 1993 Caldecott Medal.

BIRTHDAY: Emily Arnold McCully: July 1, 1939.

SUBJECT: Tightrope walking—Fiction.

Miss Nelson Is Missing! (Houghton Mifflin, 1977). Written by Harry Allard; illustrated by James Marshall.

SUMMARY: The students in classroom #207 are terribly misbehaved. In fact, they are the worst behaved students in the school. They do not do their lessons; they throw paper airplanes and spitballs; they even act up during story time. Their teacher, Miss Nelson, decides that something needs to be done. The next day, Miss Viola Swamp, wearing a black dress and long fingernails (and looking like "Maria Callas with a fake nose," according to her creator, James Marshall), arrives in the classroom. The students are taken aback by her appearance and firm manner, and they not only behave but also do more work than they have ever done before. She gives them lots of homework and does not tell them when they ask what has happened to Miss Nelson.

The class decides that this teacher is very unpleasant, and they should try to find the missing Miss Nelson and bring her back. One group goes to see Detective McSmogg, but he is no help; he deduces only that the teacher must be missing. Another group goes to Miss Nelson's house. There they find the window shades are drawn, and instead they see Miss Viola Swamp coming down the street. They run away. The students' imaginations begin to work overtime. They speculate that perhaps she was eaten by sharks or that she flew

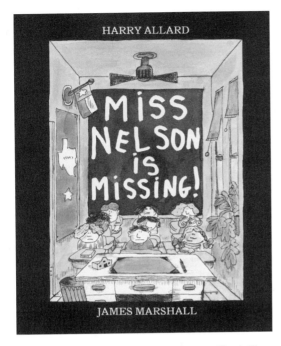

Miss Nelson Is Missing!, written by Harry Allard, illustrated by James Marshall, has been read perennially in many classrooms across the country since 1977. (Copyright © 1977 by Harry Allard; illustrations by James Marshall. Copyright © by Houghton Mifflin Company. All rights reserved.)

to Mars or that her car was taken away by angry butterflies. It seems to them that she will never return, and they miss her kindness and become discouraged.

One day, a sweet voice says good morning to the class, and suddenly Miss Nelson appears before them. The students are delighted and ask her where she has been all this time, but she says that is her little secret. She asks them why they have been all doing such good work, and they answer that the reason is their little secret. The class has learned its lesson and will behave better now for Miss Nelson. At home, Miss Nelson hangs her coat up in the closet beside the black dress she wore as Miss Swamp. Meanwhile, Detective McSmogg begins deducing a plan to search for the missing Viola Swamp.

MEDIA: Possibly pen and ink and watercolor.

ANECDOTE: Illustrator James Marshall was awakened by a telephone call at 3:00 A.M. from his collaborator, Harry Allard, who pronounced the words "Miss Nelson is missing" and then promptly hung up. Taking the bait, Marshall wondered who Miss Nelson might be and why she would be missing. Marshall spent time on a train to Chicago writing and sketching a story to answer those questions. Even though he wrote the story, Marshall honored Allard's genesis of the idea by keeping his name on the book as author. The map and state flag of Texas depicted on the cover are references to Marshall's growing up in San Antonio, Texas. However, Marshall's adult life was spent working in the Northeast.

DISTINCTIONS: *New York Times* Best Book for Children; NYPL 100 Picture Books Everyone Should Know; *100 Best Books for Children*.

BIRTHDAYS: Harry Allard: January 27, 1928; James Marshall: October 10, 1942.

SUBJECTS: Schools—Fiction; Behavior—Fiction.

Miss Rumphius (Viking, 1982). Written and illustrated by Barbara Cooney.

SUMMARY: Aging Great-Aunt Alice Rumphius met all of her goals in life as we are told by the narrator of the story, her niece. As a child, Alice lived near the sea. Her grandfather, who was an immigrant to the United States, was an artist, and she helped him with the skies in his work. When she listened to her grandfather's stories in the evenings, she said that she would travel to faraway places as he did, and she would live by the sea as he did when she got old. Her grandfather told her she must also do one more thing—she must find a way to make the world a more beautiful place. Alice wasn't sure how she would do that, but she agreed.

Alice got up, washed, ate her breakfast, went to school, did her homework, and grew up. She moved away from the sea and became a librarian whom children called Miss Rumphius. Plants inside a village conservatory during the winter kindled her desire to travel to lush islands. In her travels, she went to a tropical island, climbed tall mountains; she saw jungles and crossed deserts. When she was riding a camel once, she hurt her back, and her traveling days ended. She decided to find the place where she would live by the sea. As she got older at her pleasant cottage, she remembered her third promise to her grandfather—finding a way to make the world more beautiful.

That winter Miss Rumphius' back hurts, and she does not feel well. In the spring, a few lupines she had planted in her garden come up, and she is surprised to find more lupines over the hill when she goes to take a walk. She realizes that the birds and the wind had spread the seeds of her garden lupines there, and that gives her an idea. She purchases five bushels of lupine seeds from a catalog and takes a long walk, tossing lupine seeds wherever she goes. The people in town who see her think she is crazy. The next spring, however, thousands of lupines spring up all around, making the world a more beautiful place.

As Miss Rumphius grows very old, the townspeople call her the Lupine Lady. Sometimes little Alice's friends come in with her to listen to the Lupine Lady's stories of faraway places. Little Alice sets the same goals about going far away and coming home to live by the sea, and Miss Rumphius makes her promise to one day do something to make the world more beautiful. Little Alice agrees.

MEDIA: Acrylics and colored pencil.

ANECDOTE: Cooney called her trilogy, *Miss Rumphius*, *Island Boy*, and *Hattie and the Wild Waves*, "as close to any autobiography as I will ever get."

DISTINCTION: 1983 National Book Award.

SUBJECT: Great-aunts—Fiction.

See Also: Cooney, Barbara; *Ox-Cart Man*; Printing Technology.

Mister Penny's Race Horse (Viking, 1956). Written and illustrated by Marie Hall Ets.

SUMMARY: That autumn, Mister Penny decides to take his good crop of fruits and vegetables and his animals to show them off at the fair in Wuddle. He will not enter his horse, Limpy, at the fair because he fears that the judges would just laugh at him, though Mister Penny loves Limpy very much. He takes Mooloo, his cow; Splop, his goat; Mimkin, his lamb; Chukluk, his hen; and Doody, his rooster. Limpy pulls a cart carrying them all and feels bad that he will not be entered. He thinks the bandage on his lame leg makes him look like a racehorse, and he wants to run on the track. Mister Penny promises that if they win enough prizes at the fair, they will take a ride on the Ferris wheel.

Splop and Doody are eager to ride the Ferris wheel. They do not want to wait to win prizes to do so, so they slip out of their tents in the night. Intead, they upset the exhibits and end up getting Mister Penny and the other animals in trouble. The police the next morning ask Mister Penny and his animals to leave the fair. As Mister Penny is gathering everything up, Limpy is watching the horses race. Limpy thinks the crowd is calling to him and ends up on the track with his cart behind him and the animals in it.

Limpy runs around the track, and the people cheer to see the animals driving the cart. The director of the fair compliments Mister Penny and offers him twenty-five dollars to put on a show each day of the fair. Astonished, Mister Penny agrees but then remembers that the animals were also promised a ride on the Ferris wheel. The director is amazed and says that people will pay to watch the animals do that, and he gives them all free passes. Mister Penny is invited back the following year with his animals and is given fifty dollars instead of twenty-five dollars because of the success of showing his special animals.

MEDIA: Paper batik.

ANECDOTE: This book is a sequel to Ets' first picture book, *Mister Penny*.

DISTINCTION: 1957 Caldecott Honor Book.

BIRTHDAY: Marie Hall Ets: December 16, 1893.

SUBJECT: Horses—Fiction.

See Also: In the Forest; Just Me; Mr. T. W. Anthony Woo; Nine Days to Christmas; Play with Me.

Moja Means One: Swahili Counting Book
(Dial, 1971). Written by Muriel Feelings; illustrated by Tom Feelings.

SUMMARY: This introduction to the Swahili language is a companion to the alphabet book *Jambo Means Hello: Swahili Alphabet Book* by the same author and artist. The Swahili words for numbers one through ten are presented along with their pronunciations, English translations, and facts about the land or culture of Africa. Examples include *moja* (one); *mbili* (two); and *tatu* (three). A map of Africa at the beginning of the book shows the countries where Swahili is spoken. The introduction and author's note give background information, including the fact that *Kiswahili* is the name for the language in the language itself, spoken by about 45 million people in the eastern portion of the continent.

MEDIA: Graphite and paper collage.

ANECDOTE: Swahili is one of only about 800 African languages, but it is said to be important in learning African cultures because it serves as a unifying language among the others.

DISTINCTION: 1972 Caldecott Honor Book.

SUBJECTS: Counting; Africa, Eastern—Social life and customs; Africa, East—Social life and customs.

See Also: Jambo Means Hello: Swahili Alphabet Book.

The Moon Jumpers (Harper, 1959). Written by Janice May Udry; illustrated by Maurice Sendak.

SUMMARY: As the sun retires and goes to sleep, the moon comes up and shines all through the night. The owl and the cat are up, too, and so are two parents and four children. The children go outside and enjoy the warm summer wind, the way the moon glows on the grass. The goldfish and moonfish play together in the pond; a moth looks for moonflowers. The children climb a tree at night just to see what it is like, and they make up songs and poems. They do somersaults on the lawn and run around the house many times. It seems the later it gets, the larger the moon becomes and the more it shines. The children try to jump up and touch it, but they cannot. In their efforts, they become moon jumpers, not children. Soon father's giant shadow comes out to check his roses, and Mother calls the children inside. Since they are moon jumpers, not children, they don't want to come in, but their mother says it is time. When they do, they say good night to the moon, which is shining large in their bedroom window, and dream of the sun that will come up tomorrow.

MEDIA: Tempera.

ANECDOTE: The illustrations in the book alternate between black and white and color. Udry and Sendak were born only four days apart—Udry in Jacksonville, Illinois, and Sendak in Brooklyn, New York.

DISTINCTION: 1960 Caldecott Honor Book.

BIRTHDAYS: Maurice Sendak: June 10, 1928; Janice May Udry: June 14, 1928.

SUBJECT: Night—Fiction.

See Also: In the Night Kitchen; The Nutshell Library; Outside Over There; Sendak, Maurice; Where the Wild Things Are.

"More More More," Said the Baby: Three Love Stories (Greenwillow, 1990). Written and illustrated by Vera B. Williams.

SUMMARY: The book tells three love stories of family members for their babies—a father for his "little guy" (who is the first to call for more); a grandmother for her "pumpkin"; and a mother for her "little bird." The babies are chased after, caught up, brought close, kissed on the belly button, nibbled on the toes, and cuddled and kissed on closed, sleeping eyes in a delicious celebration of toddlerhood by their loved ones.

MEDIA: Gouache paints; lettering painted in watercolor based on Gill Sans Extra Bold Print.

ANECDOTE: Vera Williams received her inspiration for this book from her love of a new grandchild.

DISTINCTION: 1991 Caldecott Honor Book.

BIRTHDAY: Vera Williams: January 28, 1927.

SUBJECTS: Babies—Fiction; Parent and child—Fiction.

See Also: A Chair for My Mother; Lucky Song.

Mosaic. Artist's medium. Forming a picture out of tiny pieces of stone or paper or other media.

The Most Wonderful Doll in the World

(Lippincott, 1950). Written by Phyllis McGinley; illustrated by Helen Stone.

SUMMARY: A little girl named Dulcy has many dolls. However, Dulcy is never quite satisfied with the way things are. She always wants something a bit different, so though she takes care of her dolls, she keeps wishing each one of them has different hair or better clothes. One day, Mrs. Primrose gives Dulcy a new doll named Angela. She says that she once belonged to a child who lived at her house, but now she wants Dulcy to have her. Mrs. Primrose is about to leave for a trip.

On her way home, Dulcy peeks in the box at Angela and wishes she had brown hair instead of yellow. Then she sees an autumn bonfire and stops to watch. She places Angela's box a short ways away, but when she goes to get her, she cannot find her at all.

She goes home and describes Angela to her family. They agree that Angela must have been a very special doll, with clockworks and other attributes that are no longer available. Though Dulcy's father tries, he cannot find a doll just like her. One day, Dulcy's Aunt Tabby comes to visit. She is Dulcy's favorite relative. She brings her a skating doll, but Dulcy is disappointed and just tells her aunt about Angela. Her friend Margery asks about Angela, too, and Dulcy says there can be no other doll like her. Soon, all of Dulcy's friends grow tired of having their dolls and their dolls' clothes and accessories compared unfavorably to Angela's. In fact, Angela grows in Dulcy's imagination to have every outfit and item ever produced for any doll. Dulcy finds herself playing by herself, and no one is buying her any more dolls, since none of them live up to the lost Angela.

A new girl, Isabel, moves in, and Dulcy and she talk and compare their dolls. As they sit outside, Isabel begins kicking at the leaves and finds a box buried underneath them. It is Angela's box. Inside, Angela looks nothing like Dulcy remembers or has been describing to her friends. Dulcy is surprised to see the real Angela is nothing like she imagined or remembered.

Back home, Dulcy's mother has a talk with her about what is real and what is imagined and how part of growing up is knowing when to tell the difference. Dulcy decides to make up an imaginary doll that can be all of the things she wants her to be; she names her Veronica. She takes out her old dolls again and resumes playing with her old friends. When Mrs. Primrose returns from her trip and asks about Angela, Dulcy tells her the truth, but then she also tells her all the fanciful things she can about Veronica, her pretend doll. Mrs. Primrose says that Dulcy is beginning to grow up.

MEDIA: Undetermined.

ANECDOTE: McGinley won a Pulitzer Prize for *Times Three: Selected Verse from Three Decades*.

DISTINCTION: 1951 Caldecott Honor Book.

BIRTHDAY: Phyllis McGinley: March 21, 1905.

SUBJECT: Toys—Fiction.

Mother Crocodile ("Maman-Caïman"): An Uncle Amadou Tale from Senegal

(Delacorte, 1981). Written by Birago Diop; translated and adapted by Rosa Guy; illustrated by John Steptoe.

SUMMARY: Uncle Amadou tells a story that the crocodiles are the craziest of all creatures because that's what he heard from Golo, the monkey. Dia is a mother crocodile that Golo says has a good memory but is crazy. He tells this to Luke-the-Rabbit, who one day put slippers on his ears so he could run faster. He tells it to Bouki-the-Hyena whose hindquarters dip behind him because he acts like a thief or coward. He tells Thio-the-Parrot whose tongue spits out gossip from around its beak. Worst of all, though, Golo tells this about Dia to her children, the little crocodiles.

Mother Crocodile tells her children stories in order to teach them about how to get along in the world. The little crocodiles grow tired of being called away from playing to hear her stories, so they decide to believe what Golo tells them about her. One day, crows appears to warn the land and its creatures that war is approaching. The people of the East are at war with the people of the West. Dia urges her children to go with her on the trail in the river she has taught them about in order to escape. Since they now believe she is crazy, they do not go. Dia leaves to save herself.

Soon, bullets are ringing past the animals' ears. The people at war see the baby crocodiles and want their skin for purses and other things. One baby remembers the stories Dia told and leads the rest away using the trail she showed them. The moral of the story is that sometimes the old seem crazy with their stories, but the young who close their ears to them risk losing their skins.

MEDIA: Watercolor.

ANECDOTE: Diop has retold in French many of the tales he heard growing up in Senegal.

DISTINCTION: 1982 Coretta Scott King Award for Illustration.

BIRTHDAY: John Steptoe: September 14, 1950.

SUBJECTS: Folklore—Senegal; Crocodiles—Fiction.

Mother Goose

(Oxford, 1944). Selected and illustrated by Tasha Tudor.

SUMMARY: This is an anthology of seventy-seven Mother Goose nursery rhymes illustrated with both black-and-white and color drawings. A table of contents in the front of the book lists each rhyme alphabetically, though the collection is not alphabetically presented. Samples include "A swarm of bees in May"; "Hot Cross Buns!"; "Little Bo-Peep, she lost her sheep"; and "The hart he loves the high wood."

MEDIA: Possibly graphite and watercolor.

ANECDOTE: This book is one of three Mother Goose nursery rhyme books that have won the Caldecott Honor Award. At 89, Tasha Tudor lives on a farm in New England and tends to her garden using many ways of the nineteenth century. She has illustrated many beloved books for children.

DISTINCTION: 1945 Caldecott Honor Book.

BIRTHDAY: Tasha Tudor: August 28, 1915.

SUBJECT: Nursery rhymes.

See Also: Book of Nursery and Mother Goose Rhymes; Mother Goose and Nursery Rhymes; 1 Is One.

Mother Goose and Nursery Rhymes

(Atheneum, 1963). Selected and illustrated by Philip Reed.

SUMMARY: This is an anthology of sixty-six Mother Goose and nursery rhymes, each one illustrated with color wood engravings. Like many books of poetry, an index of first lines appears in the back, which honors the poetic quality of the rhymes. Examples include "As I was going to St. Ives," "Hickory, dickory, dock," "I saw a ship a-sailing," and "Rub-a-dub-dub!"

MEDIA: Wood engravings.

ANECDOTE: This book is one of three Caldecott Honor books to date to feature Mother Goose nursery rhymes.

DISTINCTION: 1964 Caldecott Honor Book.

SUBJECT: Nursery rhymes.

See Also: Book of Nursery and Mother Goose Rhymes; Mother Goose.

Mr. Rabbit and the Lovely Present

(Harper, 1962). Written by Charlotte Zolotow; illustrated by Maurice Sendak.

SUMMARY: It is the little girl's mother's birthday, and she consults with Mr. Rabbit about what to give her for a present. Mr. Rabbit asks her questions about things her mother likes. She likes red, for instance, and after suggesting several red things, the little girl settles upon apples as a good choice. She wants to give her more, however, so Mr. Rabbit asks several other questions until the little girl finds green Bartlett pears, yellow bananas, and blue grapes to give her mother. She puts them all in a basket and thanks Mr. Rabbit for his help with the lovely present.

MEDIA: Watercolor.

ANECDOTE: Zolotow is the author of more than seventy picture books but has an equally outstanding reputation as a fine editor. The Charlotte Zolotow Book Award for picture book authors is named after her.

DISTINCTION: 1963 Caldecott Honor Book.

SUBJECT: Rabbits—Fiction.

See Also: Charlotte Zolotow Book Award; Sendak, Maurice; *The Storm Book.*

Mr. T. W. Anthony Woo: The Story of a Cat and a Dog and a Mouse (Viking, 1951).

Written and illustrated by Marie Hall Ets.

SUMMARY: Michael, the cobbler of Shooshko, lives in a house with his cat named Meola; his dog, Rodigo; and a mouse friend he has made, Mr. T. W. Anthony Woo. The dog and the cat are always going at it when they see the mouse, and the cobbler's Dear Sister, Miss Dora, says there can never be any peace with them both in the house. She does not know about the cobbler's mouse friend. One day, the cobbler has to go into town to get supplies, and the cat and dog nearly destroy the house. A customer hears them and tells Miss Dora, who goes over to her brother's house to check on it. She puts both of the pets outside. She thinks a parrot like hers, Pollyandrew, makes a much more acceptable pet.

Miss Dora enjoys talking with the customers who come by and decides she will clean up the house. She throws the plate of cheese she finds with mouse tracks on it in the fire. She cooks a meal for her brother and tells him that she will be back the next day so that they may live together. The cobbler knows this is not going to work, but it takes a few incidents with the animals and Miss Dora to prove it to his sister. In the process, the cat, the dog, and the mouse all become friends, since their mutual survival depends on their getting Miss Dora to leave, which she eventually does.

MEDIA: Paper batik.

ANECDOTE: Ets attended Lawrence College, the New York School of Civics and Philanthropy, the University of Chicago, the Art Institute of Chicago, the Royal Academy of London, and Columbia University.

DISTINCTION: 1952 Caldecott Honor Book.

BIRTHDAY: Marie Hall Ets: December 16, 1893.

SUBJECT: Animals—Fiction.

Mufaro's Beautiful Daughters: An African Tale (Lothrop, 1987). Written and illustrated by John Steptoe.

SUMMARY: In Africa a long time ago lived a man named Mufaro with two beautiful daughters, Manyara and Nyasha. Manyara is jealous of Nyasha's kindness toward others. She tells her sister she will one day be queen, and Nyasha will be a servant in her household. Nyasha is sorry her sister is so unhappy, but she goes about her work growing sunflowers, yams, and vegetables. She sings as she works, and many of the villagers say this is why her crops are more beautiful than the others. A snake enters Nyasha's garden one day, and she welcomes him, saying that he may chase away creatures who would ruin her crops. Nyoka, the snake, stays.

One day, the King sends for the most beautiful girls of the village. He wants a wife. Mufara wants to send both of his worthy daughters; he does not know how Manyara treats Nyasha. Manyara tells him that her sister would be very unhappy to leave him and be Queen and that he should just send her. Mufara says that both daughters are worthy and that only the King could decide which one is better for him. That night, Manyara tries another strategy to be the one chosen—she steps out through the forest to be the first one the King would see. It is dark, and she has never been to the woods at night before, so she nearly stumbles over a small boy who appears in the path. The boy tells her he is hungry and asks for food. Manyara tells him she has brought only enough for herself and that the next day she would be his Queen; he must not bother her anymore.

Next, Manyara meets an old woman sitting on a stone who gives her advice. She tells her to be polite to a man she would meet who has his head under his arm. Manyara is mean to her also and tells her as her future Queen, she does not need advice.

The next morning, Nyasha rises and puts on her best garments. She is concerned about leaving her father, but she believes it is her duty to go, and she will accept whatever happens to her that day. When the family discovers Manyara's footprints through the woods, they determine to set out. They run across the hungry boy and the old woman. Nyasha feeds the boy and gives some sunflower seeds to the old woman in gratitude for her advice. Soon they come to a clearing where they can see the city below. Just as they are arm in arm at the city gate, Nyasha and her father see Manyara, who runs out in fear from a chamber. She tells them not to go to the King, that there is a monster there, a snake with five heads. While her father comforts Manyara, Nyasha makes her way to the chamber, where she sees Nyoka. Nyoka was the King. So were the hungry boy and the old woman. Since Nyoka knows that Nyasha is so kind and loving, he asks her to marry him, and she agrees, since she is already Nyoka's friend. Mufara thinks himself the luckiest man in the world because one of his daughters is the Queen and the other is a servant in her house.

The names in this story are African and have the following meanings: Mufaro, happy man; Nyasha, mercy; Manyara, ashamed; Nyoka, snake.

MEDIA: Crosshatched pen and ink and watercolor.

ANECDOTE: The oral folktale of Mufaro's daughters was collected from people in Zimbabwe, Africa, by G.M. Theal, who published it in his 1895 book called *Kaffir Folktales*. Designs in the illustrations are inspired from the architecture of the ruins and from the flora and fauna near where the storytellers lived.

DISTINCTION: 1988 Caldecott Honor Book.

BIRTHDAY: John Steptoe: September 14, 1950.

SUBJECTS: Fairy tales; Africa—Fiction.

See Also: The Story of Jumping Mouse.

My Friend Rabbit (Roaring Brook, 2002). Written and illustrated by Eric Rohmann.

SUMMARY: Mouse tells the story of how Rabbit is a friend who "means well" but is followed by trouble wherever he goes. When Mouse lets him play with his brand-new toy airplane, Rabbit gets it stuck in a tree with Mouse inside. Rabbit gathers many animals together, including an elephant, rhinoceros, hippopotamus, and increasingly smaller animals to reach it. The reader/viewer must tilt the book sideways to see the impressive grouping of animals stacked up to reach Mouse. The helpers are not happy when they all fall down, but Mouse flies on in the freed airplane with Rabbit hanging on the tail wing until they fly into the next tree on their path.

MEDIA: Hand-colored relief prints.

ANECDOTE: This book was published by a smaller children's publisher and brought more attention to small presses because of its award.

DISTINCTION: 2003 Caldecott Medal.

SUBJECTS: Friendship—Fiction; Rabbits—Fiction; Mice—Fiction; Animals—Fiction.

See Also: Time Flies.

My Mama Needs Me (Lothrop, 1983). Written by Mildred Pitts Walter; illustrated by Pat Cummings.

SUMMARY: Jason's mama has just come home with a new baby, and Jason decides that she needs him to help care for his sister. He refuses to go out and play; he turns down Mrs. Luby's offer of milk and cookies. He doesn't want to miss his sister crying. When she wakes up, that's when his mother says he can hold her. When she does wake up, she is hungry, and Mama feeds her at the breast. Jason cannot help. Then she falls back to sleep again. Jason cannot hold her now. Since nobody seems to need him, Jason takes Mr. Pompey, a neighbor's, offer to go feed the ducks with him. However, he feels guilty while he is away and says he must go back home because his mother needs him.

At home, Mama is calling for him. It's time to bathe the baby, and now he can help. Mama says he is a good helper when he holds the baby on a pillow in his lap. She asks him, though, why he has not gone out to play with his friends. He says that he thought she needed him. She replies that she needs a hug from him right then; and Jason realizes that he needs that, too. Then he goes out to play.

MEDIA: Pastel.

ANECDOTE: Walter visited baby clinics near where she lived in Denver, Colorado, before writing this story.

DISTINCTION: 1984 Coretta Scott King Award for Illustration.

BIRTHDAY: Pat Cummings: November 9, 1950.

SUBJECTS: Babies—Fiction; Mother and child—Fiction.

My Mother Is the Most Beautiful Woman in the World (Howell, 1945). Written by Becky Reyher; illustrated by Ruth Gannett.

SUMMARY: Marfa and Ivan go to the fields in Ukraine to harvest wheat. They work from sunup until sundown, and their children go to the fields with them. Varya is their youngest daughter, aged six. She goes also. It is hard for her to keep up with the work. She must watch out for the scythe and be sure to stack the stalks with the wheat side up. After the harvest, the family takes part in a feast to celebrate. Varya wants a fancy dress with beads, but Marfa tells her she must wait until she is older.

On another day in the wheat fields, Varya loses sight of her mother. She stumbles through the wheat until she reaches a village where several strangers stand around gossiping. She does not recognize any of them and cries out in desperation that her mother is the most beautiful woman in the world. This gives the strangers some information to go on to try to find her for the little girl.

They round up women whom the villagers

consider the most beautiful. Not one of the women, however, is Varya's mother. Finally, a plain woman with a broad face and large body comes up to the crowd, and Varya runs to her; she is her mother. The villagers say that the incident proves the old proverb that the people we love are beautiful because we love them.

MEDIA: Original gouache and watercolor reproduced by 4-match process using lithographic crayon.

ANECDOTE: The author dedicated the book to her mother, who told her the story. There is a picture frame at the end of the book that urges the child reader to put a picture of his or her mother inside, the most beautiful mother in the world.

DISTINCTION: 1946 Caldecott Honor Book.

BIRTHDAY: Ruth Stiles Gannett: August 12, 1923.

SUBJECTS: Mothers—Fiction; Folktales—Russian.

N

Nappy Hair (Knopf, 1997). Written by Carolivia Herron; illustrated by Joe Cepeda.

SUMMARY: At a backyard picnic, Uncle Mordicai tells the story, and Jimmy tapes it. He tells the story of Brenda, who has the "nappiest" hair in the world. In a cross-talk, call-and-response rhythm with the family, Uncle Mordicai uses Brenda's hair to teach the family about Africa, their family's heritage, spirituality, and personal pride. Though it might be difficult to brush each day, Brenda's hair is part of her inheritance and makes her special.

MEDIA: Not available.

ANECDOTE: This book started a controversy that made national headlines in 1998, when it was called racist and caused a third grade teacher, Ruth Ann Sherman of Brooklyn's P.S. 75, to leave her post for another teaching position in Queens after she used the book in her classroom. Parents, many of whom had not read the book and did not have students in Sherman's class, objected to images they saw on photocopied pages from the book and went to the school board to ask for Sherman's removal from the school. Eventually, the board supported Sherman, but she would have had to return to the classroom under heavy security that made her feel uncomfortable, so she elected to transfer to Queens.

The author is a respected black professor and scholar with a Ph.D. who has taught African American literature at Harvard, Mount Holyoke, and other universities and was inspired to write the book based on her own personal experience with her hair while growing up. As a child, one of her relatives was taped telling a similar story about her hair. Ironically, some blacks were uncomfortable about the subject of hair and did not like the book on that basis. Some observers commented that the strong feelings this picture book elicited speak to several issues: the state of race relations in late-twentieth-century America; subjects still regarded as taboo to discuss in public by many blacks; and the mass marketing of homogenized images of beauty in order to sell beauty and hair products. To observers of the form, the incident provides an interesting example of a children's picture book making national headlines and having a social impact.

DISTINCTION: Of historical/scholarly interest.

SUBJECTS: Afro-Americans—Fiction; Hair—Fiction.

See Also: Cornrows.

Nathaniel Talking (Black Butterfly, 1988). Written by Eloise Greenfield; illustrated by Jan Spivey Gilchrist.

SUMMARY: The book is a collection of eighteen poems spoken from the point of view of nine-year-old Nathaniel. Poems include "Nathaniel's Rap"; "Nine"; "Knowledge"; "Missing Mama"; "Mama"; "Making Friends"; "When I Misbehave"; "Education"; "I Remember"; "Grandma's Bones"; "My Daddy"; "Aunt Lavinia"; "Weights"; "Who the Best"; "A Mighty Fine Fella"; "I See My Future"; "Watching the World Go By"; and "Nathaniel's Rap (Reprise)." At the end of the book, Greenfield explains about playing "bones," in "Grandma's Bones," which is an instrument handed down from ancestors in Africa, where they really used animal bones to make the *clackety-clack* sound. She also explains the meter of the twelve-bar blues poems "My Daddy" and "Watching the World Go By" and provides readers a pattern to write a twelve-bar blues poem of their own.

MEDIA: Charcoal (interior pages).

ANECDOTE: Greenfield has won the Award for Excellence in Poetry from the National Council of Teachers of English (NCTE).

DISTINCTION: 1990 Coretta Scott King Award for Illustration.

BIRTHDAYS: Eloise Greenfield: May 17, 1929; Jan Spivey Gilchrist: February 15, 1949.

SUBJECTS: African Americans—Poetry; Children's Poetry—American; American Poetry.

National Center for Children's Illustrated Literature. NCCIL is a nonprofit organization dedicated to recognizing and promoting illustration in children's books. The idea for the center began when artist William Joyce received a phone call from the former mayor of Abilene, Texas, Dr. Gary McCaleb. The mayor had read Joyce's book, *Santa Calls*, to a group of children that day. The book's main characters live in Abilene. The mayor wanted to ask Joyce if the artwork was done by hand ("for real") or if it was computer-generated. Joyce was unsure whether the phone call was actually from the mayor, whether the call itself was "for real" or not. Their dual skepticism began a friendship and collegiality that led to the creation of the center to honor illustrators.

The center sponsors traveling exhibits of artists' work as well as hosts special exhibits in its gallery. Artists highlighted have included Mary Azarian, David Diaz, Donald Crews, Peter Sís, Betsy Lewin, David Small, Ann Jonas, Nina Crews, Ted Lewin, William Joyce, Robert Sabuda, and Ed Young. The center has an outreach and educational component dedicted to teaching children about literacy, creativity, and art. The museum opened its doors September 14, 2000.

Contact: National Center for Children's Illustrated Literature, 102 Cedar, Abilene, Texas 79601. (325) 673-4586. Web site: http://www.nccil.org. email: nccil@bitstreet.com.

The Night Worker (Farrar, Straus and Giroux, 2000). Written by Kate Banks; illustrated by Georg Hallensleben.

SUMMARY: Alex misses Papa, who always kisses him goodnight, then goes out to work while Alex and Mama sleep. Alex wants to go with him, but Papa says not tonight. Finally, one night, Alex is allowed to go with Papa to the construction site where he works as an engineer. He sees the other night workers, such as street sweepers, police officers, and delivery truck drivers. At the site, he watches the heavy machinery such as bulldozers, excavators, cement mixer, and crane and helps drive the loader that dumps dirt into a dump truck. When the workers take a break, Alex tells Papa he is tired, and they go back home, where Alex sleeps. As morning comes, he's still dreaming of one day becoming a night worker.

MEDIA: Possibly oil paintings.

Cover of *The Night Worker*, written by Kate Banks, illustrated by Georg Hallensleben. Banks received the 2001 Charlotte Zolotow Award for her text. (Reprinted by permission of Farrar, Straus and Giroux, LLC: Jacket designs from *The Night Worker* by Kate Banks, pictures by Georg Hallensleben. Pictures copyright © 2000 by Georg Hallensleben. www.fsgkidsbooks.com.)

ANECDOTE: Banks and Hallensleben also collaborated on the well-regarded *And If the Moon Could Talk*.

DISTINCTION: 2001 Charlotte Zolotow Award.

BIRTHDAY: Unavailable.

SUBJECTS: Night—Fiction; Work—Fiction; Construction workers—Fiction; Fathers and sons—Fiction.

Nine Days to Christmas: A Story of Mexico (Viking, 1959). Written by Marie Hall Ets and Aurora Labastida; illustrated by Marie Hall Ets.

SUMMARY: Ceci is old enough now to go to kindergarten, so her mother thinks she is now old enough to stay up for *posadas*, or special Christmas parties, held each night at a different house for the nine days before Christmas. They will have the first *posada* at

their house, and Ceci is excited. The next day is the last day of school until February, and Ceci begins asking people like her older brother Salvadore and their servant María when her *posada* will be. She wants to know also if she will have a *piñata*. She is disappointed when she learns that she will have to wait twenty-one days for the special days to begin. The wait is difficult.

When her mother does not take her with her to the market, Ceci speaks with her doll, Gabina. Later, at the park, she tells the ducks about the *posada* and the *piñata*. In her bath the next day, she thinks of the ducks and half-fills the tub with cold water and climbs in to be like them. Her mother is alarmed and takes her out and warms her. Finally, one day her mother invites her to go to the Mexican market with her so they can pick out her *piñata*. She takes Gabina with her. At the Christmastime market, there are so many different *piñatas* that Ceci doesn't know which one to choose. The piñatas all begin talking to her, turning this way and that from their hanging string so she can get to know them better. Each one wants her to choose it. Ceci chooses the star.

The next day preparations for the *posada* finally begin. Food is prepared, and the *piñata* is filled. That night, Ceci and her cousin Manuel lead the procession that begins every *posada*. They carry figures of Joseph and Mary on a donkey, and all the guests behind them carry candles and sing the song of the Holy Pilgrims. The procession stops at the closed door of the house, where Ceci knocks. She and the procession are told that there is no room at the inn, as is the custom, but then they are allowed in for the party to begin.

Ceci does not want anyone to break her large, golden star *piñata*. It is hung as usual, however, and the children are blindfolded and swing at it in play. Ceci hides behind a tree. When the star is broken, Ceci is upset, but a voice above her tells her to look up at the star overhead in the sky. Her special *piñata* has turned into a real star so that she and Gabina can enjoy it always.

MEDIA: Pencil on dinobase.

ANECDOTE: While Marie Hall Ets did her artwork in public in Mexico City, many people stopped and asked her questions, so she found the work difficult. All of the characters' faces were based on actual people she knew. Ets' birthday is nine days before Christmas. Her coauthor, a librarian, wanted Ets to show people in Mexico with the conveniences of modern life.

DISTINCTION: 1960 Caldecott Medal.

BIRTHDAY: Marie Hall Ets: December 16, 1895.

SUBJECTS: Christmas—Fiction; Mexico—Fiction.

See Also: In the Forest; Just Me; Mister Penny's Race Horse; Mr. T.W. Anthony Woo; Play with Me.

No, David! (Blue Sky, 1998). Written and illustrated by David Shannon.

SUMMARY: David makes all kinds of poor choices, such as playing baseball in the living room; climbing to the top shelf to get the cookie jar; tracking mud on the floor; and playing with his food. His mother says all the things most mothers have said under such circumstances, especially the word "no." Finally, David sits in the corner for "time out," but then his mother calls to him, holds him, and reassures him that yes, she loves David.

MEDIA: Acrylics and colored pencil.

ANECDOTE: Shannon made a similar book when he was a little boy that featured drawings of David doing things he was not supposed to be doing. His mother sent it to him when he grew up. The only words in the little book were "No" and "David," because those were the only words he knew how to spell at the time. He created this book as a "remake" of the one he designed as a child.

DISTINCTION: 1999 Caldecott Honor Book.

Front cover of *No, David!*, written and illustrated by David Shannon. Drawn in acrylics and colored pencil, this book is reportedly a "remake" of one Shannon made as a child and earned him a 1999 Caldecott Honor. (From *No, David!* by David Shannon. Published by the Blue Sky Press/Scholastic Inc. Jacket illustration copyright © 1998 by David Shannon. Reprinted by permission.)

BIRTHDAY: David Shannon: October 5, 1959.

SUBJECT: Behavior—Fiction.

Noah's Ark (Sea/Star, 2002). Retold and illustrated by Jerry Pinkney.

SUMMARY: The book retells the story from the Old Testament of the Bible. Noah builds an ark on the word of God and gathers animals two by two to save them from the flood that God sent to cover the earth for all the things there that displeased him. When the dove brings news of dry land, Noah praises God, and God promises never to punish the earth by flood again.

MEDIA: Pencil, colored pencil, and watercolor.

ANECDOTE: Pinkney said he was drawn to the Noah story by its epic scope and connections with nature as well as the idea it represents of human beings having responsibility and a second chance.

DISTINCTION: 2003 Caldecott Honor Book.

BIRTHDAY: Jerry Pinkney: December 22, 1939.

SUBJECTS: Noah's ark; Noah (biblical figure); Bible stories—O.T.

See Also: John Henry; Mirandy and Brother Wind; The Ugly Duckling.

Noah's Ark (Doubleday, 1977). Retold and illustrated by Peter Spier.

SUMMARY: On the first page of the book Spier translates from Dutch into English the poem "The Flood," by Jacobus Revius (1586–1658). The poem is made up of a series of short couplets that tell the Bible story of Noah's Ark. No poetic line is over three words long. The rest of the volume then retells the story from the poem with pages filled with wordless pictures.

MEDIA: F pencil on paper; watercolor and white pencil; negatives scratched.

ANECDOTE: The day Spier won the medal he was called at 4:30 in the morning to be notified. When the phone rang waking him up, he thought his parents' house was on fire. One reason Noah is shown with hardships such as swatting flies and shoveling manure in the book is because Spier thought too many Noah's Ark books for children painted too rosy a picture of a difficult experience.

DISTINCTIONS: 1978 Caldecott Medal; 1982 National Book Award.

BIRTHDAY: Peter Spier: June 6, 1927.

SUBJECTS: Noah's Ark—Pictorial works; Bible stories—O.T.; Dutch poetry.

Nothing at All (Coward, 1941). Written and illustrated by Wanda Gág.

SUMMARY: Three dogs live in doghouses in a row. Pointy lives in a kennel with a pointed roof; Curly lives in a kennel with a curved roof. The last dog is named Nothing-at-all because he is invisible. One day a little boy and girl come and take Pointy and Curly away to live with them. Nothing-at-all has a plan so that he will not be alone. On the long way to their house, he gets tired, falls asleep, and wakes up lost. On his way, he finds a hollow tree that seems like a kennel, and he stays there for shelter.

In the meantime a jackdaw bird hears him speaking to himself. Nothing-at-all tells him that now he minds how he looks and wants to look like other dogs. The bird has a magic book with a spell in it that turns nothing into something. Nothing-at-all must whirl every morning when the sun comes up for nine days. Each day, more and more of a shape of a puppy appears. On the ninth day, the little dog thanks the bird and sees the boy and girl coming down the walk with a cart carrying all three kennels, his included. He hops into the round-topped kennel and pops out when the children arrive home with the other dogs.

MEDIA: Original lithographs in color.

ANECDOTE: After Gág was diagnosed with lung cancer and given three months to live, she continued to work, even from her bed as her health worsened. She lived seventeen months longer than expected.

DISTINCTION: 1942 Caldecott Honor Book.

BIRTHDAY: Wanda Gág: March 11, 1893.

SUBJECT: Dogs—Fiction.

See Also: ABC Bunny; Gág, Wanda; Millions of Cats; Snow White and the Seven Dwarfs.

Nothing Ever Happens on My Block (Atheneum, 1966). Written and illustrated by Ellen Raskin.

SUMMARY: This book is the perfect example of text telling one story and pictures telling another. While Chester Filbert sits on the curb outside his house complaining that nothing ever happens where he lives, behind him all kinds of dramas are unfolding in the neighborhood—fires are breaking out; burglars in masks are on the run; a witch pops up in different windows; children are ringing doorbells and running away. A parachutist even lands on the sidewalk. Readers enjoy picking out all the crazy events that are going on totally unknown to Chester Filbert simply because he is not looking.

MEDIA: Color-accented pen-and-ink drawings.

ANECDOTE: After illustrating for years for other writers, this was Raskin's first picture book conceived on her own, along with her *Songs of Innocence* of the same year. She has said its moral is to stop feeling sorry for oneself and look at the world. The book is a good example of the use of irony in the picture book form.

DISTINCTION: *New York Times* Best Book for Children.

BIRTHDAY: Ellen Raskin: March 13, 1928.

SUBJECTS: Neighborhoods—Fiction; Fantasy.

Nova's Ark (Scholastic, 1999). Written and illustrated by David Kirk.

SUMMARY: Nova is playing at the workbench in his room on Roton with his dog, Sparky, beside him. He looks at an antique wooden set of animals that his father, Taspett, handed down to him before he left for his last space mission. Taspett is looking for crystal, a substance that produces energy robots need to live. At dinner with his mother, Luna, Nova receives a post disc from his father that he will be home soon; however, the disc was recorded months ago. Nova dreams of traveling through space like his father.

With his class, Nova visits the Space Center where his father works and ends up launching himself in a Glax Cruiser, shooting through space and landing on a strange, un-

known planet. He builds animals out of the parts of his spaceship, including a Sparky 2 and those like the wooden animals from his father's antique ark. He tries to communicate through space that he is alone and stranded. Eventually, a spaceship crashes on this planet with Taspett on board. Each of the animals Nova has built sacrifices a part to help Nova put his father back together. The engine of Taspett's spaceship still works, so they rebuild a way to get home. Taspett tells Nova that the planet they landed on is Zyte, which he has been looking for all along, since it is abundant with many rich crystals. When father and son arrive back on Roton, they are given a hero's welcome.

MEDIA: 3-D computer imaging.

ANECDOTE: This book is said to be the first American picture book for children to use 3-D computer imaging for all of its illustrations. Kirk began his career as a toymaker of collectible, one-of-a-kind toys and is also the author of the Miss Spider series of picture books.

DISTINCTION: Of historical/scholarly interest.

BIRTHDAY: David Kirk: 1955.

SUBJECTS: Robots—Fiction; Interplanetary voyages—Fiction; Science fiction.

Nutshell Library (Harper, 1962). Written and illustrated by Maurice Sendak.

SUMMARY: The *Nutshell Library* is a small boxed set of books, only 1½ by 2½ by 4", containing three small rhyming concept books and one cautionary tale—*Alligators All Around* is an alphabet book; *One Was Johnny* is a counting book; *Chicken Soup with Rice* is a book of months; and *Pierre* is a "Cautionary Tale in five chapters with a prologue." The rhymes in the concept books are easily memorized and aid children in learning their alphabet, numbers, and months. *Pierre* is a rhyming story about a boy who keeps saying, "I don't care" to everything and everyone around him—his mother, his father, and a lion, which decides to eat him. When the boy's parents take the lion to the doctor, Pierre falls out when the lion is tipped upside down. Finding that he is not dead, Pierre rides the lion home with his parents and decides it is better to care.

MEDIA: Possibly pen and ink and watercolor.

ANECDOTE: Each title from the set is available in larger library and paperback editions that are easier to share with a group. The title *Pierre* may have come from Sendak's love of Herman Melville, who wrote a novel with the same title, an edition of which Sendak illustrated many years later.

DISTINCTION: *New York Times* Best Book for Children.

BIRTHDAY: Maurice Sendak: June 10, 1928.

SUBJECTS: Alphabet rhymes; Counting rhymes; Months rhymes; Lions—Fiction.

See Also: Mr. Rabbit and the Lovely Present; Sendak, Maurice; *Where the Wild Things Are.*

O

Officer Buckle and Gloria (Putnam, 1995). Written and illustrated by Peggy Rathmann.

SUMMARY: When Officer Buckle comes to Napville School to give a talk about safety tips, no one ever listens. As he is leaving, the principal, Mrs. Toppel, stands on a swivel chair, even though that was Safety Tip #77 in Officer Buckle's talk. One day, Gloria, a police dog, is given to Officer Buckle to help him with his work. The next time Buckle makes a safety speech, Gloria performs each safety rule hilariously behind his back, making the audience pay enthusiastic and joyful attention. Office Buckle receives many letters of appreciation from the students, including a letter from Claire on a star-shaped piece of paper that tells him she is wearing her helmet (Safety Tip #7). The duo is requested to perform safety speeches at schools all around the area. Once, they are recorded for broadcast on television. That is when Office Buckle sees what Gloria has been doing behind his back all this time. He feels bad that the audience has not been paying attention to his rules after all, but has instead been entertained by Gloria.

The next time they are invited to give a speech, Gloria goes alone. She does not perform; instead, she stands on the stage and falls asleep; the audience falls asleep too. Mrs. Toppel stands on the swivel chair, and a large accident ensues, resulting in Claire being hit over the head with a hammer. Claire writes to Officer Buckle that she was wearing her helmet, so all is well. It is clear to everyone that Officer Buckle and Gloria are a team. This causes Buckle to add Safety Tip # 101 to his list—stay with a buddy. The front and back interior pages of the book feature stars with safety tips and Gloria's performances of them.

MEDIA: Watercolor and ink.

ANECDOTE: Gloria is based on Skipper, a dog the author once owned that got into trouble when no one was looking. Rathmann revised the manuscript for four years after it was accepted by the publisher.

DISTINCTION: 1996 Caldecott Medal.

BIRTHDAY: Peggy Rathmann: March 4, 1953.

SUBJECTS: Safety—Fiction; Police—Fiction; Dogs—Fiction; Schools—Fiction; Police Dogs—Fiction.

Olivia (Atheneum, 2000). Written and illustrated by Ian Falconer.

SUMMARY: Olivia the stylish pig lives with her parents and her little brother, Ian (who likes to copy everything she does), their dog, Perry, and cat, Edwin. Olivia is very active every day, so much so that she often wears people out; she even wears herself out. Olivia likes to try everything on before she gets dressed for the day. She likes to go sunbathing, visit museums, dance, sing songs, and paint on walls. She likes naps and going to bed at night a little less. She claims she is not sleepy and requires at least three bedtime stories. After the stories, Olivia's mother says that she loves her, even though she is so busy that she wears her out. Olivia tells her mother that she loves her anyway, too. At the museum, Olivia is inspired by Jackson Pollock's *Autumn Rhythm #30* (in the collection of the Metropolitan Museum of Art in New York) and Edgar Degas' *Ballet Rehearsal on the Set, 1874* (from the collection of the Musee d'Orsay in Paris). One of the books her mother reads to her is about the opera star Maria Callas. Especially for a pig, charming Olivia is very metropolitan.

MEDIA: Charcoal and gouache.

ANECDOTE: Ian Falconer illustrated many *New Yorker* magazine covers and dedicated this book to his children, the real Olivia and Ian. Youngest son, William, was not born in time to be a character in the book.

DISTINCTION: 2001 Caldecott Honor Book.

SUBJECTS: Pigs—Fiction; Behavior—Fiction.

On Market Street (Greenwillow, 1981). Written by Arnold Lobel; illustrated by Anita Lobel.

SUMMARY: This is an alphabet book where a boy goes shopping on Market Street. After a rhyming introduction, each letter is an item he buys, and the picture corresponds to the item transformed into the body and clothing of a person. For example, A is for apple, and the accompanying illustration shows a person with green and red apples making up the arms and legs and baskets of apples for a stomach, thighs, and feet. Apples make up the hair and hang in baskets from the fingers.

This motif of people made up of objects continues for all of the letters of the alphabet. Examples include B for books, C for clocks, and T for toys. At the end of the book, the rhyme picks back up, and the boy is shown returning home with his pile of purchases that he gives to his friend, the cat.

MEDIA: Watercolor and pen and ink.

ANECDOTE: The book was inspired by Anita Lobel's 1977 Children's Book Week poster.

DISTINCTION: 1982 Caldecott Honor Book.

BIRTHDAYS: Anita Lobel: June 3, 1934; Arnold Lobel: May 22, 1933.

SUBJECTS: Alphabet; Shopping—Fiction; Stories in rhyme.

See Also: Fables.

Once a Mouse . . . A Fable Cut in Wood (Scribner, 1961). Written and illustrated by Marcia Brown.

SUMMARY: A hermit sits thinking about big and little when a mouse comes by. The hermit sees that a crow is about to catch the mouse, and he takes the mouse out of the crow's beak. He takes the mouse back to his home and feeds him, but then a cat approaches the mouse. To save him again, the hermit quickly changes the mouse into a bigger cat. The same thing happens with a dog and then a tiger. Finally, the mouse struts about the forest with pride as a large, glorious tiger. The hermit is displeased and tells the tiger that he should be more grateful because he was once a small defenseless mouse. Instead, the tiger becomes angry and says that he will kill the hermit for saying such a thing. The hermit changes the tiger back into a mouse, and the mouse runs into the forest and is never seen again. Meanwhile, the hermit goes back to thinking about big and little.

MEDIA: Woodcuts.

ANECDOTE: The book earned Brown her second of three Caldecott medals.

DISTINCTION: 1962 Caldecott Medal.
BIRTHDAY: Marcia Brown: July 13, 1918.
SUBJECTS: Fables; Folklore—India.

See Also: Brown, Marcia; *Cinderella, or The Little Glass Slipper*; *Puss in Boots*; *Shadow*; *Stone Soup*.

One Fine Day (Macmillan, 1971). Retold and illustrated by Nonny Hogrogian.

SUMMARY: In this retelling of an Armenian folktale, a fox drinks an old woman's milk "one fine day," and she cuts off his tail, setting off a cumulative story of the fox trying to get his tail sewn back on. The old woman promises to sew the tail back if the fox gives her back her milk, but the cow wants some grass, the grass wants some water, the water wants a jug, and so on. Finally, fox comes to a good miller who gives him the grain that starts the chain of events backward again until fox has the milk for the old woman and gets his tail back so that he can return to his friends.

MEDIA: Acrylic paintings with turpentine on gesso panels.

ANECDOTE: Only hours before winning the Caldecott Medal for this book, Nonny Hogrogian had stated that it would be nice to win another Caldecott to add to the one she already had for *Always Room for One More*.

DISTINCTION: 1972 Caldecott Medal.
BIRTHDAY: Nonny Hogrogian: May 7, 1932.
SUBJECT: Foxes—Fiction.

See Also: Always Room for One More; Hogrogian, Nonny.

One Fish Two Fish Red Fish Blue Fish (Random House, 1960). Written and illustrated by Dr. Seuss (pseud. of Theodor Geisel).

SUMMARY: The theme of this beginning reader is that funny things are everywhere, as the strange, colorful characters in the book illustrate. Seuss presents imaginary creatures such as the Nook, Wump, Yink, Yop, Gack, and Zeds doing their humorous and outrageous deeds. Though there is no cohesive plot, the book is instructive about colors and counting.

MEDIA: Possibly pencil, crayon, and watercolor.

ANECDOTE: Many adults who encountered this book as children can still recite many of its rhymes.

DISTINCTION: *New York Times* Best Book for Children.
BIRTHDAY: Dr. Seuss: March 2, 1904.
SUBJECT: Stories in rhyme.

See Also: Bartholomew and the Oobleck; Geisel, Theodor (Ted) Seuss; *McElligott's Pool*.

1 Is One (Oxford, 1956). Written and illustrated by Tasha Tudor.

SUMMARY: The book counts from one to twenty using a rhyming text and illustrations from the natural world of Tasha Tudor's beloved New England countryside. Images include ducks, gourds, swallows, and apples.

MEDIA: Possibly graphite and watercolor.

ANECDOTE: Tudor said that the book not only helps teach children how to count but also expresses the pleasure in the act of counting itself.

DISTINCTION: 1957 Caldecott Honor Book.
BIRTHDAY: Tasha Tudor: August 28, 1915.
SUBJECTS: Counting; Stories in rhyme; Counting rhymes.

See Also: Mother Goose.

One Monday Morning (Scribner, 1967). Conceived and illustrated by Uri Shulevitz.

SUMMARY: On a rainy Monday, the king, queen, and prince all come to visit a little boy, but he is out. They return on Tuesday with the addition of the knight and on Wednesday with the royal guard, on Thursday with the royal cook, on Friday with the royal barber, and on Saturday with the royal jester. Each day the increasing number of visitors climbs the many stairs to the small boy's apartment, only to find that he is not home. Finally, on Sunday all the previous visitors plus a little dog come to visit him, and this time they find him home, saying that they just dropped by. The closing illustrations show the boy looking outside his apartment window on a sunny day with playing cards and other items representing the visitors to the boy's apartment.

MEDIA: Possibly pen and ink and watercolor.

ANECDOTE: The story is adapted from a French folk song.

DISTINCTION: *New York Times* Best Book for Children.

BIRTHDAY: Uri Shulevitz: February 27, 1935.

SUBJECTS: City and town life—Folklore; Kings, queens, rulers, etc.—Folklore; Folk songs—France.

See Also: Snow.

One Morning in Maine (Viking, 1952). Written and illustrated by Robert McCloskey.

SUMMARY: Sal and her little sister Jane get up and ready to go to Buck's Harbor with Daddy. When she is brushing her teeth, Sal discovers a loose tooth. She is afraid it will come out and spoil her day. Sal tells everything she sees on her way about her loose tooth—a fish hawk, a loon, and a seal. Then she tells Daddy and helps him finish digging for clams. Her mother has told her that when her tooth comes out, if she puts it under her pillow and makes a wish, it will come true.

While Sal is playing near her father, she discovers that her tooth has come out. She does not know where it is. She fishes for it in a pool of muddy water where she was, but she cannot find it. Finally, her father says that they must go back to the house or there will not be time to go to Buck's Harbor. He tells

her she is growing up and that she cannot let small things like this bother her. He encourages her to wait for another tooth to get loose to leave under her pillow. She finds a gull's feather and decides to make her wish on that, since the gull probably lost it just as she lost her tooth.

Since the motor is broken, Daddy rows all the way to Buck's Harbor village. Daddy, Sal, and Jane take the motor to Mr. Condon to fix. He pulls out a spark plug much like Sal's tooth. Then they go to Mr. Condon's brother's store. There, they see Mr. Ferd Clifford and Mr. Oscar Staples, who talk about lobsters and how the fish are biting. Sal shows the men her missing tooth. Mr. Condon offers Sal and Jane ice cream cones. On the way back, Sal carries the feather, spark plug, and ice cream. Sal remembers that she is growing up when Jane begs for another ice cream cone. She says it would ruin their dinner, which is going to be clam chowder.

MEDIA: Possibly lithographs.

ANECDOTE: Robert McCloskey and his wife moved to an island off the coast of Maine in 1946 after the birth of their daughter, Sally, the Sal of this story and *Blueberries for Sal*. Jane was Sal's real little sister.

DISTINCTION: 1953 Caldecott Honor Book.

BIRTHDAY: Robert McCloskey: September 15, 1914.

SUBJECTS: Family life—Fiction; Maine—Fiction.

See Also: Blueberries for Sal; McCloskey, Robert; *Make Way for Ducklings*; *Time of Wonder.*

One Wide River to Cross (Prentice-Hall, 1966). Adapted by Barbara Emberley; illustrated by Ed Emberley.

SUMMARY: Noah builds the ark, and the animals come. Noah's son, Japheth, plays the drum, and his son Ham plays the horn; and they come in twos. The animals come by sixes and by sevens until they come by tens and the story goes back and starts again. The ark needs to cross the Jordan, a wide river. It begins to rain, and the ark gets stuck on the mountains of Ararat. A rainbow appears in the sky to show that God promised never to flood the earth again. At the end of the book are the music and lyrics to the old folk song "One Wide River to Cross."

MEDIA: Woodcuts.

ANECDOTE: Ed Emberley used his own press to print the woodcuts for the book. Separate blocks of wood were cut for each figure or part of a design, then inked and pressed on rice paper. One page contains as many as fifty-seven different impressions.

DISTINCTION: 1967 Caldecott Honor Book.

BIRTHDAYS: Barbara Emberley: December 12, 1932; Ed Emberley: October 19, 1931.

SUBJECTS: Folk songs, English—United States—Texts; Folk songs—United States; Noah's ark—Songs and music; Animals—Songs and music.

The Origin of Life on Earth: An African Creation Myth (Sights, 1991). Retold by David A. Anderson; illustrated by Kathleen Atkins Wilson.

SUMMARY: This is a creation story of the Yoruba people of ancient West Africa. In the Yoruban religion, Olorun (pronounced oh-loe-roon) is God, and Olorun has many assistants called orishas (oh-ree-shahs). This is the story of how one orisha, Obatala (oh-bah-tah-lah), came to earth and made the first human beings. At first, all life was in the sky. Everything most people wanted they could find near the baobab tree. However, Obatala wanted to use his powers. He told Olorun about wanting to make something firm in the waters below the sky so that beings might live there and need the power of the orishas.

Obatala goes to the one who can see the future, Orunmila, who throws sixteen palm kernels into his diving tray eight times and tells him what to do.

Obatala builds a chain of gold made from the other orishas' jewelry to get down to the water. Obatala travels down the chair seven days, or the equivalent of one week. Obatala sprinkles the sand Orunmila tells him to bring, and the sand spreads and becomes firm. Obatala isn't sure what to do next. His heart beats so hard that it breaks the egg that contains all the personalities of all the orishas, and this releases Sankofa, the bird. The bird fights with the sand, spreading it around and up into dunes, putting personality into it. Finally, when he is done, Obatala falls off the chain and onto the land. He walks on the sand, spreading baobab powder from the roots of the tree, maize, and palm kernels as he goes. This makes fertile soil, and rich vegetation begins to grow.

Obatala is thirsty after walking so far, so he stops at a pool to get a drink and see himself in the reflection of the water. He is so pleased with what he sees that he takes some soil and models a figure after himself. As he works, he becomes more thirsty and drinks some palm wine. This makes his sight distorted, and he continues to make people, but some of them are deformed.

Olorun, the Sky God, sends Chameleon to see how Obatala is making out. He tells Chameleon that he has made these people, but there is no life in them. When Chameleon tells Olorun what has happened, Olorun reaches into space and grabs gases that have been swirling there. He snaps his fingers, and there is an explosion, and the ball of fire sends heat and light down to earth. To keep it from being too hot and bright, Olorun breathes on the earth, starting it rotating as it does now. As his breath crosses over the hard clay bodies of the people on Ife, the first place on earth, they soften and come to life.

MEDIA: Not available.

ANECDOTE: This book has a sequel called *The Rebellion of Humans: An African Spiritual Journey.*

DISTINCTION: 1993 Coretta Scott King Award for Illustration.

BIRTHDAY: Not available.

SUBJECTS: Creation—Folklore; Yoruba (African people)—Folklore; Folklore—Africa.

Outside Over There (Harper, 1981). Written and illustrated by Maurice Sendak.

SUMMARY: Papa goes away to sea, and Mama sits in the arbor. Two goblins watch the scene. Ida is given the responsibility of watching over her baby sister. She plays her wonder horn to rock her to sleep. While she is playing, the goblins snatch away the baby and replace her with a baby made of ice. Ida discovers it only when she hugs the baby, and the baby melts. She knows the goblins have taken her as a bride to another goblin. To rescue her sister, Ida puts on her mother's yellow raincoat, takes her horn, and backs out the window, to outside over there. Backing out is a mistake.

Ida hears her father's sailor song telling her to turn back around, and she will find the baby. She does so and finds the goblins are babies themselves, and they are in the middle of a wedding. She slows their commotion with her horn until they begin dancing. They grow tired and want to go to bed, but Ida plays all the faster, a tune the sailors dance to on the ocean. The goblin babies dance so fast they become a stream. Ida's sister is the only one who does not flow into the stream; she remains sitting in an eggshell, as calm as can be.

Ida follows the stream and carries her sister back home. She finds her mother in the arbor. She is holding a letter from Papa that asks Ida to watch over the baby and Mama for him; he will be home soon. Ida does just that.

MEDIA: Undetermined.

ANECDOTE: The artist has said that the older sister, Ida, and the baby could be his sister, Natalie, and himself. The book gave him a sense of peace when he completed it. Sendak set the story in the late eighteenth century around the time of the Brothers Grimm, their fairy tales, and Mozart's era. He places Mozart playing in a cottage on the third to the last page. Sendak considered this book the last of a trilogy exploring an "inner" theme of the darker side of children's psyches. The first two books in the trilogy are *Where the Wild Things Are* and *In the Night Kitchen.*

DISTINCTIONS: 1982 Caldecott Honor Book; 1982 National Book Award.

BIRTHDAY: Maurice Sendak: June 10, 1928.

SUBJECTS: Fantasy; Sisters—Fiction.

See Also: In the Night Kitchen; *Mr. Rabbit and the Lovely Present*; Sendak, Maurice; *Where the Wild Things Are.*

Overlay. Artist's medium. Film that is transparent or transluscent and is put over artwork. It usually contains additional details for the art that will be reproduced.

Owen (Greenwillow, 1993). Written and illustrated by Kevin Henkes.

SUMMARY: Owen is a mouse with a fuzzy yellow blanket he loves and carries with him everywhere; the blanket is called Fuzzy. Mrs. Tweezers, the nosy next-door neighbor, comments to Owen's parents that he is getting too old to carry a blanket around with him all the time. She recommends a few strategies to help break Owen away from Fuzzy. One is the Blanket Fairy. Owen stuffs Fuzzy down his pajama pants instead of under his pillow. Another is the vinegar trick. Owen takes Fuzzy outside and rolls it around in the dirt until the smell is gone. School is starting soon, and Owen cannot take Fuzzy to school. Another idea from Mrs. Tweezers is just saying no, but when his parents tell him he cannot take Fuzzy to school, then Owen starts to cry and will not stop. This gives his mother an idea. She takes Fuzzy and cuts and sews it into small handkerchiefs that Owen can carry with him to school. Everyone is happy, and Mrs. Tweezers doesn't know the difference.

MEDIA: Watercolor paints and black ink.

ANECDOTE: Henkes' favorite book as a child was a book about making books, *Is This You?*, by Ruth Krauss, illustrated by Crockett Johnson.

DISTINCTION: 1994 Caldecott Honor Book.

BIRTHDAY: Kevin Henkes: November 27, 1960.

SUBJECTS: Blankets—Fiction; Parent and child—Fiction; Mice—Fiction.

See Also: Kitten's First Full Moon; Lilly's Purple Plastic Purse.

Owl Moon (Philomel, 1987). Written by Jane Yolen; illustrated by John Schoenherr.

SUMMARY: In this poetic text, Yolen describes that late one night a child and her father go owling. The child has waited a very long time to do this, and she is up past her bedtime. They walk through the snow to the woods, where Pa makes a hooting sound. There is no reply. She is not disappointed, since her brothers have told her sometimes there is no owl. They walk on, and the child gets cold, but she doesn't say anything, because one has to be very quiet while owling.

They go deeper into the woods. It's a little scary in there, but owlers must have courage. They come to a clearing that is bright with the light of the moon on the snow. Pa hoots out again, and this time they hear an echo of an owl hooting back. A shadow flies over their heads, and the hooting sound gets closer. Finally, Pa shines his big flashlight up, and it catches a Great Horned owl just lighting on a tree branch. For what seems like a very long time, or maybe not, they look at the owl and the owl looks at them. Then the owl flies

away, and Pa and the child walk home. All one really needs to go owling is hope.

MEDIA: Pen and ink and watercolor.

ANECDOTE: While the child in the book can be interpreted to be either a boy or a girl from the illustration, she is, in fact, Yolen's daughter, Heidi, who used to go owling with her father as her brothers did before her. The book is dedicated to Yolen's husband, David Stemple.

DISTINCTION: 1988 Caldecott Medal.

BIRTHDAYS: Jane Yolen: February 11, 1939; John Schoenherr: July 5, 1935.

SUBJECTS: Owls—Fiction; Fathers and daughters—Fiction.

Ox-Cart Man (Viking, 1979). Written by Donald Hall; illustrated by Barbara Cooney.

SUMMARY: The ox-cart man fills up his cart in October with everything his family has grown or made during the rest of the year that is left over from what they need. This includes a bag of wool from the sheep they sheared in April; a shawl his wife had made from yarn she spun; and mittens his daughter had knitted. He also packs candles, linen, shingles, and birch brooms, all made by the family from materials they grew. From their garden, he loads potatoes, turnips, and cabbages, and from their orchard, apples. He brings maple sugar and a bag of goose down. He starts out for the Portsmouth Market, walking for ten days. There he sells everything, even the cart and the ox and the ox's harness.

He buys things the family will need to get them through another winter—an iron kettle, embroidery needle for his daughter, a Barlow knife for his son, and wintergreen peppermint candies. He walks all the way back home. All through the winter, they use their new tools to sew, carve, and cook more things they need and that they will take to market next year.

MEDIA: Acrylics on gesso-coated board.

ANECDOTE: Donald Hall says he heard

about this story from his cousin, who said he heard it as a young boy from an old man. The old man said he had heard it as a young boy from an old man, and so forth. While she was at work on the book, Cooney was building a house by the shore near South Bristol, Maine. She met Leon, a carpenter working on the house, who had a red beard that she particularly liked, and she wanted to draw it into the book. After researching social customs, she found that beards were popular in the New Hampshire setting of the story from around 1803 to 1847. She further narrowed the timeline to 1832 by researching when turnstiles were still in existence as well as when there was a brick market in Portsmouth. For the scene where the ox-cart man kisses his ox, Cooney used another carpenter named Markie as a model and asked him to kiss a lamp. Markie was so pleased to be part of the project that he built a mahogany box for Cooney's illustrations when they were finished and ready to be sent to the publisher. On the outside of the box, Cooney painted an ox before she mailed it off.

DISTINCTION: 1980 Caldecott Medal.

BIRTHDAYS: Donald Hall: September 20, 1928; Barbara Cooney: August 6, 1917.

SUBJECT: New England—Fiction.

See Also: Cooney, Barbara; *Emily*; *Miss Rumphius*.

P

Paddle-to-the-Sea (Houghton Mifflin, 1941). Written and illustrated by Holling C[lancy]. Holling.

SUMMARY: A boy in a cabin near Lake Nipigon makes an Indian in a canoe out of wood. He paints the toy and on the bottom carves the message that his name is "Paddle-to-the Sea" and that if anyone finds him, to please put him back in the water so that he may make it all the way to the sea. Paddle journeys from Lake Nipigon to Lake Superior, Michigan, Huron, Erie, over Niagra Falls, into Lake Ontario, and down the St. Lawrence River to somewhere off the Grand Banks of Newfoundland. On the way, Paddle has many adventures, including a time in "dry dock," when he and his canoe are repainted and a man named Bill affixes a copper plate on the bottom of the canoe. The plate urges anyone finding him to place him in water that will keep him on his way and also to scratch the name of the town where he is found on the plate. The book contains twenty-seven single-page chapters chronicling Paddle's journey to earn his name. At the end, a fisherman finds him off the Grand Banks and takes him home to his son, who marvels and dreams about what Paddle's adventures must have been. A map of Paddle's journey is located at the end of the book, and sidebars of maps with brief information along the route are included throughout.

MEDIA: Full-color oil paintings.

ANECDOTE: Holling dedicated the book to the son of a friend he paddled with in the Great Lakes.

DISTINCTION: 1942 Caldecott Honor Book.

BIRTHDAY: Holling C. Holling: August 2, 1900.

SUBJECT: Great Lakes—Fiction.

Paint. Artist's medium. Colored pigments in a smooth binder such as oil.

The Paperboy (Orchard, 1996). Written and illustrated by Dav Pilkey.

SUMMARY: The paperboy must wake up while his mother and father and sister are still sleeping. It is still dark and always cold, even in the summer. He and his dog eat breakfast out of their bowls. Then they tie the newspapers in green rubber bands and put them in a red bag for carrying. The paperboy knows how to ride his bike and carry his big red bag of papers at the same time. He knows his route by heart. His dog knows his route by heart, too, just where to sniff and where to watch for squirrels. As they continue on their route, the sun is gradually coming up. People in the neighborhood are waking up, too. By the time the paperboy has delivered his last paper, it is daylight. He goes back home, where his parents are now awake in their room, and his sister is watching Saturday morning cartoons. He and his dog go back to bed where it is still warm.

MEDIA: Acrylics and India ink.

ANECDOTE: Pilkey is also the creator of the Captain Underpants series.

DISTINCTION: 1997 Caldecott Honor Book.

BIRTHDAY: Dav Pilkey: March 4, 1966.

SUBJECTS: Newspaper carriers—Fiction; Morning—Fiction.

Pastels. Artist's medium. Pigments and gum binder pressed or rolled into sticks. Used for drawing.

Pat the Bunny (Simon and Schuster, 1940). Written and designed by Dorothy Kunhardt.

SUMMARY: A book for babies to experience different tactile and visual sensations—the fluffiness of a bunny; Daddy's scratchy face; looking in a mirror; putting a finger through Mommy's ring; and so forth.

MEDIA: Mixed media and dimensional objects affixed to pages.

ANECDOTE: This is one of the first baby activity books.

DISTINCTION: *New York Times* Best Book for Children.

BIRTHDAY: Dorothy Meserve Kurnhardt: 1901.

SUBJECT: Babies—Activities.

The Patchwork Quilt (Dial, 1985). Written by Valerie Flournoy; illustrated by Jerry Pinkney.

SUMMARY: Tanya cannot go outside because she is recovering from a cold. Instead, she watches her Grandma piece together a quilt. She promises to help her. Grandma appreciates this and says it will take about a year to make the kind of masterpiece quilt she

wants to make. The patches come from many places—Jim's favorite corduroy pants; Tanya's Halloween costume. Mama has not appreciated what Grandma is doing until Tanya explains that the quilt and Grandma are telling stories about the family; then she begins to help make the quilt, too.

After a wonderful Christmas when the house is filled with joy, Grandma becomes ill and stays upstairs in bed. Tanya is concerned and keeps working on the quilt. Her brothers Ted and Jim even cut a few squares for her, and Mama helps, too, but it is Tanya who works on it the most. Eventually, she realizes that Grandma is the only one not represented, so she quietly snips a few squares off of her old quilt to include in the family quilt. By spring, Grandma is feeling better and comes back to her chair downstairs and picks up working on the quilt, too. One day in June, she bites off the last thread, and it is done. The last square has a dedication to Tanya from Mama and Grandma that the quilt is to be hers to keep and remember.

MEDIA: Pencil, graphite, and watercolor.

ANECDOTE: Pinkney studied at the Philadelphia Museum College of Art.

DISTINCTION: 1986 Coretta Scott King Award for Illustration.

BIRTHDAY: Jerry Pinkney: December 22, 1939.

SUBJECTS: Quilting—Fiction; Grandmothers—Fiction; Family life—Fiction; African Americans—Fiction.

See Also: Mirandy and Brother Wind; The Ugly Duckling.

Pedro, the Angel of Olvera Street (Scribner, 1946). Written and illustrated by Leo Politi.

SUMMARY: On Olvera Street in Los Angeles, Pedro and his grandfather play music. Pedro sings songs, and people from all around say that he sings like an angel. Grandpa speaks to Pedro about how different things are now, that Olvera Street has been surrounded by the growing city of Los Angeles, but how the street has managed to stay the same as well. Pedro agrees that he loves Olvera Street, where many of the Mexican ways still remain.

One of these ways is the *posada*, which is a procession and festival held at Christmas. People carry candles and sing. They knock on doors, trying to find shelter for Mary and the Christ Child who will be born. Pedro, wearing small red wings, enjoys playing with the *piñata* at the festival, and it is he who manages to break it open. He takes home a music box, which he desired, and all is well at Christmas. A small angel with red wings like Pedro looks down at him and Olvera Street from the star outside his window.

MEDIA: Undetermined.

ANECDOTE: The book contains music and lyrics for "La Piñata" as well as a song about Joseph and Mary.

DISTINCTION: 1947 Caldecott Honor Book.

BIRTHDAY: Leo Politi: November 21, 1908.

SUBJECT: Mexican Americans—Fiction.

See Also: Juanita; Song of the Swallows.

Peppe the Lamplighter (Lothrop, 1993).
Written by Elisa Bartone; illustrated by Ted Lewin.

SUMMARY: In New York's Little Italy before the days of electricity, Peppe's mother is dead, his father is sick, and he needs to find work to help support his family of sisters: Giulia, Adelina, Nicolina, Angelina, Assunta, Mariuccia, Filomena, and Albina. They all live in a tenement on Mulberry Street. Peppe goes to Gennaro, the butcher, and offers to sweep, but there is no need for him. He goes to Don Salvatore, the bartender, and offers to wash glasses, but he does not need him either. He sees the candy maker, Commare Antonietta, and offers to make the torrone and string

hazel-nuts, but he is not needed there either. Neither does Fat Mary, the cigar maker, need him to count the cigars and put them in boxes.

Finally, he meets Domenico, the lamplighter, who asks him to help. Domenico must go back to Italy to get his wife and needs Peppe to light the streetlamps for him while he is gone. Peppe is delighted to have a job and runs home to tell his family. Papa, who is sick, is disappointed and angry at the job his son has found. He does not believe he has come all the way to America for his son to have the low-level job of lamplighter. Peppe does a good job lighting the lamps. He does it every night and does not miss a single lamp. As he raises the stick to the high lamp above him, the motion reminds him of lighting candles in church. He says prayers for each member of his family with each lamp, saving the last lamp as a prayer for himself that he might always be able to help light the lamps.

Still, his father's depression and shame over Peppe's job continue. It is so bad that one night, despite his sisters' repeated words of encouragement, Peppe loses heart and does not light the lamps. Instead, he stays inside and cries on his arms. That night, Assunta, his youngest sister, does not come home. Papa is worried and tells Peppe to light the lamps because the streets are dark, and Assunta cannot find her way home. That night Peppe's job is especially important. As he lights the lamps, Peppe finds Assunta sitting beneath one of them. He raises her up to light the lamp and then he brings her home. At seeing her, Papa tells Peppe to keep his job, that lighting the lamps is very important after all and that Peppe's job makes him proud.

MEDIA: Watercolor.

ANECDOTE: The story is loosely based on Bartone's grandfather living in New York's Little Italy.

BIRTHDAY: Ted Lewin: May 6, 1935.

DISTINCTION: 1994 Caldecott Honor Book.

SUBJECTS: Italian Americans—Fiction; Fathers and sons—Fiction; Brothers and sisters—Fiction; New York (N.Y.)—Fiction.

Pierre Pigeon (Houghton Mifflin, 1943). Written by Lee Kingman; illustrated by Arnold E. Bare.

SUMMARY: Seven-year-old Pierre lives in an area of Canada known as Gaspé, which is surrounded on three sides by water. Each day, Pierre helps his father unload fish at the dock. Pierre's mother also bakes bread and sells it to tourists to help the family earn more money. Pierre likes to help her as well. Pierre likes to visit a local store and look at the items on display. One object that catches his eye is a ship in a bottle that cost one dollar. Pierre knows that it is very unlikely he would ever have a whole dollar of his own to spend.

One day, Pierre is out taking care of the ox, Henri, and his cart. They see a lady who becomes frightened at Henri. She wants to paint the pasture and asks Pierre to keep Henri away while she does so. When she is finished, Pierre sees that she has painted him into the picture. She gives him a dollar for helping her with Henri. Pierre takes the money to Mr. LeClere's store to buy the ship in a bottle. He asks him how the ship got in the bottle, but Mr. LeClere does not know and asks him to tell him if he ever figures it out. Pierre buys the boat and steps carefully down the stairs of the store so that he does not trip and break it. As he arrives home, his little sister and large Newfoundland dog, Geneviève, come out to greet him. Geneviève jumps up on Pierre, and the bottle slips from his hand and breaks on the ground. The ship is still intact.

Pierre's family feels bad for his loss that night at dinner. His father mentions that he found a bottle similar to the one the boat was in and that it is in the boathouse. Pierre is grateful to have the bottle, but he has no idea how to get the ship inside of it. Then he has an idea. The masts of the boat flattened when the bottle broke. There was a fishhook on a string inside the new bottle, and the bottle was just like the one that broke. He slips the ship inside the neck of the bottle with the masts down and raises them with the fishhook. His family is glad to see the boat in a bottle, and they put it on the mantle so that Geneviève cannot get to it. When his mother tells him it is time for bed, Pierre asks to run to the store to tell Mr. LeClare how a ship grows in a bottle.

MEDIA: Preseparated gouache and ink drawings.

ANECDOTE: This was Bare's first illustrated book for children.

DISTINCTION: 1944 Caldecott Honor Book.

BIRTHDAY: Arnold Edwin Bare: June 20, 1920.

SUBJECT: Boats—Fiction.

Pigment. Artist's medium. Powders of different colors that are combined with a binder, either liquid or gum, to make paint, ink, and other media.

Play with Me (Viking, 1955). Written and illustrated by Marie Hall Ets.

SUMMARY: A little girl gets up one morning and goes to the meadow to play. She asks, in turn, a grasshopper, frog, turtle, chipmunk, blue jay, rabbit, and snake to play with her. However, when she asks them, she runs in their direction or tries to catch them, and she chases them away. She occupies herself by blowing seeds off a milkweed and watching a bug make trails in the water. When she sits by the brook, soon all the animals come back to her. Even a fawn comes out of the woods and steps nearer, since she does not make a sound. The fawn licks her cheek, and the little girl is happy now because all the animals are playing with her.

MEDIA: Graphite separations.

ANECDOTE: The idea of the animals approaching the little girl just because she is sitting still may be unrealistic, but the message of having patience with wildlife is appreciated by many readers.

DISTINCTION: 1956 Caldecott Honor Book.

BIRTHDAY: Marie Hall Ets: December 16, 1893.

SUBJECT: Animals—Fiction.

See Also: In the Forest; Just Me; Mister Penny's Race Horse; Mr. T.W. Anthony Woo; Nine Days to Christmas.

A Pocketful of Cricket (Henry Holt, 1964). Written by Rebecca Caudill; illustrated by Evaline Ness.

SUMMARY: Six-year-old Jay lives in a farmhouse with his mother and father. He is going to begin school in five days. Taking his time in the last days of summer, Jay walks about the fields and wades in the creek. As he goes, he picks up things that are interesting and puts them in his pocket. During the day, he picks up a hickory nut, a flat rock that has the fossil of a fern on one side, a gray goose feather, an Indian arrowhead that had been kicked up by a plow, white beans with red speckles on them, and a cricket.

Jay makes friends with Cricket and makes a home for him in his room. His mother gives him a tea strainer as a cage for the cricket, and each day Jay lets the cricket out to jump around and play with him. Jay feeds his pet a lettuce leaf, some banana, and a thin slice of cucumber. He gives him fresh water in a bottle cap. Every night in the dark, Cricket rubs his legs, making his cricket sound, "Chee! Chee!"

When the first day of school arrives, Jay takes out all of the other things he had in his pocket and puts Cricket in there and takes him to school. Cricket fiddles on the school bus, making his chirping sound, and the bigger boys make fun of Jay. They wonder what the teacher will do when she finds out that Jay has brought a cricket to school. In his classroom, Jay finds his seat. Cricket continues to fiddle in the dark of Jay's pocket. Pretty soon, Teacher asks who in the room has a cricket, but Jay does not reply. When she walks up and down the aisles, she discovers the cricket is in Jay's pocket, and she asks him to put him outside. Jay does not budge. She asks him again, but Jay does not move. When she asks him why he does not want to put him outside, Jay replies that he would never find him again. Teacher soon discovers that finding another cricket later also would not do because Cricket is Jay's friend.

When Teacher discovers this, she allows Jay to show Cricket to the class as show-and-tell. She gives him a drinking glass and tells him to put Cricket underneath it so the children may see him. Jay's classmates are fascinated with Cricket, and Jay enjoys showing him to them. The students ask many questions. When show-and-tell is over, the class asks Jay what he will bring in next to show. Jay thinks about the hickory nut, the gray feather, the rock with fern fossil, the Indian arrowhead, and the beans that he had taken out of his pocket and left at home. He tells them he will bring beans next time.

MEDIA: Undetermined.

ANECDOTE: The book is a popular recommendation for children just beginning school.

DISTINCTION: 1965 Caldecott Honor Book.

BIRTHDAY: Evaline Ness: April 24, 1911.

SUBJECTS: Show-and-tell presentations—Fiction; Crickets—Fiction.

The Poky Little Puppy (Simon and Schuster, 1942). Written by Janette Sebring Lowrey; illustrated by Gustaf Tenggren.

SUMMARY: Four puppies dig a hole under a fence, and when they reach the other side, they count themselves and notice that the poky little puppy is not with them. The poky little puppy is off sniffing for dessert—rice pudding. When their mother discovers the hole under the fence, the puppies are sent to bed without dessert, but the poky little puppy is late and eats up the pudding by himself. Through repetition, this action continues through chocolate custard and strawberry shortcake. The story ends with the puppies filling up the hole while their mother watches. She later rewards them, but the poky little puppy has apparently arrived late again and stolen the strawberry shortcake.

MEDIA: Not available.

ANECDOTE: As one of the twelve Little Golden Books introduced to mass audiences in the 1940s, this book has sold more than 15 million copies since 1942, making it one of the most popular children's books of all time. This fact astounds many critics who find the plot of the story illogical for children or adults. The Little Golden Books appeared in a small format and inexpensive price, which allowed them to be distributed to markets other than bookstores. They were sold in such places as grocery stores and drugstores, where they and their descendants are still marketed in the 2000s. The Little Golden Books began what many children's literature professionals regard as a "subgenre" of American children's books—one that is published for mass appeal and sales rather than literary merit. *Poky* was the first of the commercial books that have dominated picture books sales on into the early twenty-first century. Tenggren drew *Poky* after illustrating for Disney, working on such films as *Snow White* and *Pinnochio*. Prior to that, he illustrated books such as Pearl S. Buck's *The Good Earth*.

DISTINCTION: Of historical/scholarly interest. *Poky* was the first of the original twelve Little Golden Books published in 1942 by Simon and Schuster.

BIRTHDAY: Gustaf Tenggren: November 3, 1896.

SUBJECT: Dogs—Fiction.

The Polar Express (Houghton Mifflin, 1985). Written and illustrated by Chris Van Allsburg.

SUMMARY: A boy lies in bed on Christmas Eve listening for Santa's sleigh bells, a sound that a friend of his said he'd never hear. Pretty soon, a large black steam engine and cars pull up in the middle of the street outside his house. A golden light shines from the front of it, and steam rolls from the funnel, mixing with the snowflakes that are falling all around. Putting on his robe and slippers, the boy goes downstairs and out the door. The conductor tells him that this is the Polar Express, and they are on their way to the North Pole. The boy climbs aboard. In the car, he sees all kinds of children there with their pajamas on singing Christmas carols, eating candy, and drinking hot chocolate. The train makes its way through cold dark forests and around mountaintops until they see the lights of a city—the North Pole.

There in the center square are gathered thousands of elves who are there to watch Santa give the first gift of Christmas to one of the children from the train. Soon, Santa arrives with his huge sleigh and toybag. The elves and children cheer. The little boy is chosen as the child to receive the first gift, and Santa asks him what he would like for Christmas. The boy answers that he would like a bell off Santa's sleigh. Santa smiles and tells an elf to cut one. Santa gives the bell to the boy, and everyone cheers. As the clock tower strikes midnight, Santa is up and away with his sleigh. The boy puts the bell in his bathrobe pocket. Soon the children are boarding the Polar Express for the trip back home.

On his way home, the boy discovers that the bell is missing. When he looks in his pocket, he finds there is a hole in it. He becomes very sad, indeed. The other children offer to help him look for it, but just then the train heads out. The train lets him off at his front door, and the conductor cries for him to have a Merry Christmas.

THE POLAR EXPRESS

Cover of *The Polar Express*, written and illustrated by Chris Van Allsburg. In 2004, this new Christmas classic was made into a popular feature film starring Tom Hanks, bringing the appeal of picture books to an even wider audience. (Copyright © 1985 by Chris Van Allsburg. Copyright © by Houghton Mifflin Company. All rights reserved.)

On Christmas morning, the boy and his sister Sarah open their gifts. One box is wrapped in red and white striped paper. When the boy opens it, he finds a bell inside—the same bell he lost from Santa's sleigh. There is a note explaining that the bell was found on the seat in Santa's sleigh; the note is signed "Mr. C." The boy's parents say that it is too bad that the bell is broken; it does not ring for them, but the boy and Sarah both hear it ring. Over time, the boy's friends and even Sarah do not hear the bell ring anymore. The boy has grown into an old man now, but he still hears the bell ring, as do all others who still believe.

MEDIA: Full-color oil pastel on brown pastel paper.

ANECDOTE: The book is inspired by a fantasy Chris Van Allsburg once had of a train stopped outside his house and is dedicated to his sister. A popular film adaptation starring Tom Hanks as the conductor and other characters was released in 2004.

DISTINCTION: 1986 Caldecott Medal.

BIRTHDAY: Chris Van Allsburg: June 18, 1949.

SUBJECTS: Santa Claus—Fiction; Christmas—Fiction; North Pole—Fiction.

See Also: The Garden of Abdul Gasazi; *Jumanji*; Van Allsburg, Chris.

Pop Corn & Ma Goodness (Viking, 1969).

Written by Edna Mitchell Preston; illustrated by Robert Andrew Parker.

SUMMARY: Ma Goodness runs down a hill, and Pop Corn runs down the opposite hill. They run into each other, and each becomes dazed and thinks the other loves him or her. They get married, catch a horse, have a farm, and get a goat that is later killed by a bear. They have a funeral for the goat, and the bear's skin gets hung up on the outside of their house. They have children and run up and down hills with them in the winter and the spring.

MEDIA: Watercolor.

ANECDOTE: The book's nonsense rhymes and storyline may seem dated to today's readers.

DISTINCTION: 1970 Caldecott Honor Book.

BIRTHDAY: Not available.

SUBJECT: Stories in rhyme.

Prayer for a Child (Macmillan, 1944). Written by Rachel Field; illustrated by Elizabeth Orton Jones.

SUMMARY: A rhyming Christian prayer for little children is presented on the first page, then broken down in separate lines and couplets that are illustrated throughout the rest of the book. Readers follow a small girl as she gets ready for bed and "blesses" her bed and her toys, her Mother and Father, the lamplight, friends and family, and other things and people with which she is familiar. She prays for health and for all other children of different races around the world.

MEDIA: Pen and ink; watercolor.

ANECDOTE: Rachel Field wrote the prayer for her own daughter, Hannah, but died before Jones began the artwork for the book. Elizabeth Orton Jones looked hard for the toys she borrowed to draw for the book. She wanted toys that looked worn enough to be recognized as well used and loved by a child but still in good shape for the drawings. A young girl posed for the artwork of each scene.

DISTINCTION: 1945 Caldecott Medal.

BIRTHDAYS: Rachel Field: September 19, 1894; Elizabeth Orton Jones, June 25, 1910.

SUBJECTS: Bedtime prayers; Children—Prayer books and devotions—English; Prayers.

Printing Technology. The evolution of printing technology has had a great impact on American children's picture books, primarily because of its effect on the kinds and quality of artwork that could be reproduced. As printing technology advanced, the possibilities for reproducing original art in full color, in greater detail, with better quality, and at less cost have become enhanced until the early twenty-first century, when virtually any kind of image can be photographically or digitally reproduced in mass quantities for libraries and bookstores.

The earliest picture books in the American colonies, like other kinds of books, were produced on large wooden presses operated by hand. Illustrations were primarily limited to relief woodcuts that would allow ink to be picked up from the original design and pressed onto paper of various contents at a separate time from when the type for text was transferred. Chapbooks of the eighteenth century in the United States and Britain were often printed from recycled woodcuts, making them cheaper but the quality of the illustrations poor. Woodcuts had the disadvantage of requiring cruder and less detailed and intricate designs.

In addition to woodcut techniques, engravings were developed in Europe as a way of reproducing artwork for children's picture books. In this intaglio process, ink is placed on, and fills, the engraved plate and the finer lines must be pressed very hard to be picked up and copied. This made the process more expensive than woodcuts because the print for text had to be reproduced in a separate step to the illustrations. Copper was a frequent early engraved metal of choice, but its plates wore out quickly. In the 1820s, steel plates were often used instead for mass production, but pictures printed in that technique lacked the warmth and subtlety of those made with copper plates. The advantage of the engraving technique in general was that it allowed for more intricacy of design than woodcuts. Color that appeared in picture books printed from woodcuts or engraving was done either through pressing different colors at different times or for larger quantities, actual hand-coloring by groups of children, usually teenagers working around tables in assembly-line like fashion, one child coloring all the red areas, one all the blue, and so forth.

White-line wood engraving, a technique developed by Thomas Bewick in England, offered more detail than the cruder woodcuts and nearly replaced them as a technique used for children's books by the 1830s. Etching was moved forward in Europe by George Cuikshank in the 1820s and 1830s. In this intaglio process, acid burned the line into the metal plate rather than having the lines dug out through the use of tools in the steady hand of an engraver. It is important to note that most of the illustrations of these earlier periods were conceived and drawn by artists but then transferred to a printing medium such as a metal plate by an engraver, who was a separate individual with different skills. Probably the best-known artist and engraver pair was Randolph Caldecott and the master engraver Edmund Evans of England. Evans, who engraved the artwork of other well-known British illustrators such as Walter Crane, captured so much of the nuance and intricacy of Caldecott's original designs in his engravings that his fine work launched new interest in children's picture books as a respected artistic medium.

Lithography, invented by Alois Senefelder of Germany at the end of the eighteenth century, took a strong hold in illustrated books and picture books for children in various forms over the years. As the first major new way of printing developed since Gutenberg's movable type, lithography involved abandoning relief and intaglio techniques of press printing and replacing them with a chemical method that was based on the natural repulsion of oil and water. In this planographic process, grease ink or crayon drawings are worked on specially prepared limestone, which is then moistened by water. A special printer's oily ink rolls over the stone and picks up the design and then rolls over paper and prints the design on it through applying pressure. Chromolithographs developed by repeating the process with a separate color each time, taking care to align the design in the proper place for the application of the new color. Photolithography later replaced the need to draw directly on the stone plate.

By the end of the nineteenth century, photography had developed to the point that children's books could be photomechanically produced. Photography not only allowed the omission of the engraver's role of duplicating the original artwork onto a transfer medium but also enabled the direct reproduction of the artwork. After the world wars, the 4-color separation process became a popular technique. In this process, transparent overlays are used to hold portions of drawings that are rendered in only one of four colors—cyan, magenta, yellow, and black (often abbreviated as CMYK). When the overlays were stacked together, the colors blended to fool the eye that other colors were actually present as well. Artists often had to draw the overlays separately to enable the printing process.

In the 1980s, the computer was added to printing technology and advanced it to the point where virtually any visual artwork could be faithfully reproduced in children's picture books. This opened up the possibilities for picture books in a way larger than that of almost any previous method. The result has been an explosion of creativity on the part of illustrators and book designers. Artists of the third millennium depict stories through paint or pencil, photographed clay sculptures and quilts, die-cuts in paper, mixed-media collage, and many other forms—the choices seem nearly limitless.

An American artist who worked for a long time in children's picture books, Barbara Cooney, experienced the direct effect of the change in printing technology on her work.

What media she could use in her drawings in order that they reproduce in a cost-effective manner in books were directly affected by the changes in technology in the twentieth century. As an artist at first, for example, she was told she had to set her sense of color aside and work only in black and white for her work to appear in books. After college at Smith, where she employed and used a full palette of color in her original artwork, Cooney studied lithography and etching for her early work as an illustrator in New York in the late 1930s and early 1940s. She worked in wood engraving and scratchboard. Gradually, as the 4-color separation process took hold in the 1960s, she was told she could return to color but only if she were willing to work with overlays using the standard four colors of the time. As much as she loved color, Cooney disliked doing overlays. With the development of photographic 4-color reproduction, she no longer had to draw separate pieces of her artwork on different sheets.

In the late twentieth century, Cooney was elated to be able to render her art in watercolors and other media and created some of her most memorable children's picture books during the 1980s. Artists of the 2000s depict their stories in media of their choice. They have the freedom that artists of children's books before them did not have—the confidence that their work will be effectively reproduced with startling detail and quality of color and line on open pages in the laps of little children.

Pura Belpré Award. Distinction. The Pura Belpré Award, named after New York Public Library's first Latina librarian, Pura Belpré, was established by the American Library Association in 1996 to honor Latina/o writers and illustrators who best affirm and celebrate Latino culture and heritage in children's books published during the review period. Awards and honor book awards are granted for writing and illustration every two years.

The award is cosponsored by the Association for Library Service to Children division of ALA and an ALA affiliate, the National Association to Promote Library and Information Services to Latinos and the Spanish-Speaking.

Pura Belpré worked tirelessly to enhance the lives of Puerto Rican children in New York City as well as to promote awareness and appreciation for Puerto Rican folklore across the United States through preserving stories and helping them become accessible to wider audiences. The bronze medal for the award depicts Belpré reading to a Latino boy and girl.

See Also: Distinctions.

Puss in Boots (Scribner, 1952). Translated and illustrated by Marcia Brown.

SUMMARY: Brown retells Perrault's classic Puss in Boots fairy tale (for plot summary, see *Puss in Boots*, illustrated by Marcellino).

MEDIA: Possibly woodcut and watercolor.

ANECDOTE: Brown attempts to match her artwork to the subject matter of the story and often used woodcuts with fairy tales.

DISTINCTION: 1953 Caldecott Honor Book.

BIRTHDAY: Marcia Brown: July 13, 1918.

SUBJECTS: Fairy tales; Folklore—France.

See Also: Brown, Marcia; *Cinderella, or The Little Glass Slipper*; *Shadow*; *Stone Soup*.

Puss in Boots (Farrar, Straus and Giroux, 1990). Written by Charles Perrault; illustrated by Fred Marcellino.

SUMMARY: A retelling of the classic French fairy tale. A miller has three sons, and when he dies, he leaves one son his mill, the other his donkey, and the last son nothing but a cat. The young son is tempted to eat the cat and use its fur for a muff to keep warm, but then he knows he will starve. The cat hears him thinking about this plan and asks him to

Cover of *Puss in Boots*, written by Charles Perrault, illustrated by Fred Marcellino. The artist died one year after the book's publication. (Reprinted by permission of Farrar, Straus and Giroux, LLC: *Puss in Boots* a tale by Charles Perrault, pictures by Fred Marcellino. Pictures copyright © 1990 Fred Marcellino. www.fsg kidsbooks.com.)

get him a pair of boots and a sack, and he will soon prove that the man has not made out so badly after all.

Puss becomes powerful when he wears the boots. He catches rabbits easily and is so proud of his skill that he presents himself to the king. Through his trickery, he is able to acquire property from farmers and a castle from an ogre he talks into changing from a lion into a mouse that he devours. His master becomes the Marquis of Carabas. He is also able to get his master married to the king's daughter. Puss in Boots becomes a lord (hence the feathered hat, sword, and boots of his famous image) and chases mice only when he feels like it for fun.

MEDIA: Colored pencil on taupe textured illustration paper.

ANECDOTE: Marcellino died the year after the book was published.

DISTINCTION: 1991 Caldecott Honor Book.

BIRTHDAYS: Fred Marcellino: October 25, 1939; Charles Perrault: January 12, 1628.

SUBJECTS: Fairy tales; Folklore—France.

R

Rain Drop Splash (Lothrop, 1946). Written by Alvin Tresselt; illustrated by Leonard Weisgard.

SUMMARY: Rain falls on bears and frogs, down tree trunks and into.puddles, then down into a pond. The pond spills into a brook, the brook into a lake, a river; then finally the rain makes it way out into the open sea.

MEDIA: Three colors preseparated with India ink on acetate overlays.

ANECDOTE: In 1947, Weisgard was the only illustrator to have both the Caldecott and a Caldecott Honor Book in the same year. Tresselt has said that the story was initially conceived as a personified mountain stream named Hyacinth. However, the book quickly changed to a concept book about the flow of rainwater to the sea.

DISTINCTION: 1947 Caldecott Honor Book.

BIRTHDAYS: Alvin Tresselt: September 30, 1916; Leonard Weisgard: December 13, 1916.

SUBJECT: Rain—Fiction.

Rain Makes Applesauce (Holiday, 1964). Written by Julian Scheer; illustrated by Marvin Bileck.

SUMMARY: "Silly talk" nonsense text and images of intricate design stimulate the imagination.

MEDIA: Pencil and watercolors.

ANECDOTE: For some of the drawings, Bileck used puppets and dolls as models, but he tried to use his imagination for the most part, so that this could be a starting point for readers as well.

DISTINCTION: 1965 Caldecott Honor Book.

BIRTHDAY: Not available.

SUBJECT: Fantasy.

Rapunzel (Dutton, 1997). Retold and illustrated by Paul O. (Oser) Zelinsky.

SUMMARY: A couple is going to have a baby, and the woman craves the greenery, rapunzel. She claims she will die if she cannot eat all that she can of it. She eats and eats without seeming to get satisfied. A witch catches the husband going for more of her rapunzel. The witch agrees to trade the rapunzel the man's wife needs for the child. When the child is born, the trade is made.

The sorceress takes care of the girl, but when she is twelve years old, she puts her in a tower. She tells the girl to let down her hair when the witch calls, and the witch climbs up and gives her things she needs. For many years, Rapunzel lives alone in the tower having no other visitors than the sorceress.

One day a prince rides by the tower on his

white horse. He hears Rapunzel singing to the birds, and calls for her to let down her hair. When she does, Rapunzel is surprised to see the prince climb into the tower instead of the sorceress. Soon, he has won her hand, and they take part in a marriage ceremony of their own in the tower. The prince continues to visit Rapunzel by night, and the sorceress visits by day. Before long, Rapunzel is expecting a child. She does not know this is the reason that her dress is fitting tightly about the waist. The sorceress knows why and is angry and cuts Rapunzel's hair. She sends her off to the countryside to fend for herself. While there, Rapunzel gives birth to twins—a boy and a girl.

The witch fastens the long silky hair to a hook on the tower, and when the prince calls up in the evening, she lowers it down for him to climb. When he reaches the top, she pushes him off. The prince survives the long fall, but he has gone blind. He wanders about the countryside in grief for his lost Rapunzel and eyesight until one day he hears the familiar singing of his wife. When she sees him, two of her tears fall in his eyes, which clear his vision, and the prince can see his wife and children. After this, the prince takes his family back to the kingdom, where they live happily.

MEDIA: Oil reproduced in full color.

ANECDOTE: Zelinsky's idea to do a book about Rapunzel came about in part because he was constantly asked about that title incorrectly when people meant to compliment him on his other book, *Rumpelstiltskin*. One day, a wig stand appeared in the window opposite his with a blond wig placed upon it, and that was a sign to him that he should complete the book. Rather than portray the witch as ugly and the tower as unpleasant, Zelinsky paints a decorative, opulent tower and an overprotective stepmother figure who does not want to let her stepdaughter mature into adulthood. The artwork shows influence from the French and Italian Renaissance, which the artist researched partly through books and also by visiting the Metropolitan Museum of Art in New York. For a party, Zelinsky once built a Rapunzel tower out of cheese; it was bigger than the table. One year, he bought rapunzel seeds, and his wife planted them on their deck; they bloomed the first year, even though most do not bloom until the second year. Perhaps Zelinsky has even more reason than most to be a romantic since his birthday is on Valentine's Day.

DISTINCTION: 1998 Caldecott Medal.

BIRTHDAY: Paul O. Zelinsky: February 14, 1953.

SUBJECTS: Fairy tales; Folklore.

See Also: Rumpelstiltskin.

Raven: A Trickster Tale from the Pacific Northwest (Harcourt, 1993). Written and illustrated by Gerald McDermott.

SUMMARY: Raven, the trickster, arrives on the dark earth, where everything is without light. He searches for light and sees only a glimmer of it far away over the water. He flies there and finds the house of Sky Chief. His daughter kneels at the water to take a drink. Raven turns himself into a pine needle, and the girl drinks the pine needle with the water. She later gives birth to Raven as a boy child. The grandson delights Sky Chief and the elders. All while he crawls on the floor entertaining them, he is really searching for where the light is hidden in the house.

Raven sees a box in the corner of a room and makes as babies do when they want something. His mother places the bright, colorful box in front of him and opens it. Inside there are another box and another. Finally, she gets to a ball of light. Sky Chief says his grandson may have it. The ball of light is the sun. As Raven plays with the ball, he transforms back into a bird and flies off with the ball of light. He flies away and throws the ball into the sky, where it can light the earth below. This is why the people are thankful to Raven and feed him.

Front cover of *Raven: A Trickster Tale from the Pacific Northwest*, written and illustrated by Gerald McDermott. The author-artist of this 1994 Caldecott Honor book also wrote and illustrated *Anansi the Spider* and *Arrow to the Sun*. (Copyright © 1993 by Gerald McDermott. Copyright © by Harcourt, Inc. All rights reserved.)

MEDIA: Gouache, colored pencil, and pastel on heavyweight, cold-press watercolor paper.

ANECDOTE: In the back of the book is an activity for children to make a totem pole.

DISTINCTION: 1994 Caldecott Honor Book.

BIRTHDAY: Gerald McDermott: January 31, 1941.

SUBJECTS: Indians of North America— Northwest, Pacific—Folklore.

See Also: *Anansi the Spider: A Tale from the Ashanti*; *Arrow to the Sun*.

Reading Rainbow. Reading-based television program. Executive-produced and hosted by actor Levar Burton, this television program geared for young children debuted on public broadcasting stations (PBS) across the United States in June 1983. The thirty-minute show uses a mixture of live action and animation to highlight children's picture books, early readers, and early chapter books with the educa-tional purpose of encouraging reading and the enjoyment of books. In each episode, one story is read to viewers all the way through, often by a movie or television actor or other celebrity. Burton frequently visits locations pertinent to the story. A group of other books are reviewed by children. Nearly 150 episodes were taped more than fourteen seasons before funding difficulties temporarily suspended production of new shows in 2002.

In an age when children and the adults who care for them may watch up to several hours of television per day, the program Reading Rainbow has had a direct influence on picture book sales. The selection of a picture book's inclusion on the program is made by a committee of professional education consultants, and most librarians and educators agree that they are quality books, worthy of young people's time. Picture books featured on the program gain notoriety among thousands of books published per year and are often sold with the *Reading Rainbow* symbol added to the cover.

Examples of picture books featured over the years include *Ox-Cart Man*, narrated by Lorne Greene and expanded by Levar Burton's visit to Sturbridge Village in Massachusetts, demonstrating aspects of colonial life; *Mufaro's Beautiful Daughters*, narrated by Phylicia Rashad; and *Zin! Zin! Zin! A Violin*, narrated by Gregory Hines with a performance by the dance group Stomp. Despite the suspension of new programming, the show still airs daily on many PBS stations across the country where it is viewed by millions of young children.

See Also: Appendix H.

The Red Book (Houghton Mifflin, 2004). Written and illustrated by Barbara Lehman.

SUMMARY: In this wordless picture book, a young girl living in the city finds a red book in a snow bank and takes it to school. During class, she takes the book out of her bag and begins looking at the maps that are inside. She imagines being far away on a beach, where a boy sees the red book in the sand. He looks at the book and sees the city scape where the girl lives, and suddenly it is as though the boy and the girl are looking through windowpanes of the classroom and panels in the book right at one another. After school, the girl buys a bunch of balloons on the street corner. She floats up out of the wintry city but drops the book on the sidewalk right before she begins to cross the ocean. The boy, who is still looking at the red book on the beach, no longer sees the girl floating with balloons on its pages and fears what may have happened to her. Soon she has crossed the sea with her balloons and lands on the beach beside him and also back into his book. Meanwhile, the red book the girl dropped on the sidewalk by the ocean is picked up by a boy on a bicycle who looks back at us out of another panel, suggesting that the journey is about to begin all over again.

MEDIA: Watercolor, gouache, and ink.

ANECDOTE: Lehman's interest in maps and adventures in faraway places inspired this book.

BIRTHDAY: Not available.

DISTINCTION: 2005 Caldecott Honor Book.

SUBJECTS: Books—Fiction; Color—Fiction.

The Relatives Came (Bradbury, 1985). Written by Cynthia Rylant; illustrated by Stephen Gammell.

SUMMARY: The relatives pack up crackers and soda pop in the old station wagon at 4:00 in the morning and leave their home in Virginia, where the grapes are almost purple, to go visit their relations in West Virginia. There are lots of hugging and laughing, then a meal, and finally the relatives break into smaller groups and talk quietly. The relatives sleep wherever they can find and aren't fussy. They stay for weeks, helping around the garden and the house. Finally, they pack up the station wagon again at 4:00 in the morning and go back to Virginia, where the grapes are purple and ready to be picked. The house seems too big when they are gone, and everyone looks forward to next summer.

MEDIA: Graphite and colored pencil.

ANECDOTE: Cynthia Rylant often writes autobiographically, as she does in this book. She and Dav Pilkey are a couple.

DISTINCTION: 1986 Caldecott Honor Book.

BIRTHDAYS: Cynthia Rylant: June 6, 1954; Stephen Gammell: February 10, 1943.

SUBJECT: Family life—Fiction.

See Also: Song and Dance Man; When I Was Young in the Mountains.

Roger and the Fox (Doubleday, 1947). Written by Lavinia R. Davis; illustrated by Hildegard Woodward.

SUMMARY: Roger is six and is walking home from school one crisp fall afternoon.

He hears some cracking in the leaves and waits to see what is causing it; he sees a chipmunk. He has learned to be patient waiting to see wild animals from the hired hand at his family's farm, a man named Seth. When he gets home, Roger rushes to tell Seth, who he believed knew everything, about the chipmunk he had seen. Seth tells him that he had seen a fox that morning down by Still River. Roger had once seen a skunk with his older brother Dick, but he'd never seen as wild an animal as a fox. He looks for a long time that day but does not see it, and it gets cold and dark. Two weeks later, he goes to the river again looking for the fox, this time with his terrier, Scamper. Scamper makes too much noise, not like Seth's hound dog, Ranger, who the boy believes would have known better.

Roger keeps looking for the fox hole near the fallen-down tree. After several attempts, he has still not seen it and now winter is approaching. Duck hunters who see him in the woods try to convince him that there is no fox there, though Roger thought he caught a glimpse of one once. Seth said it was not easy for a city boy like Roger to stay quiet long enough to see a wild fox. This made Roger more determined than ever. For his seventh birthday, he receives a Daniel Boone hat and skis. Dad helps him learn to use the skis, and soon enough he forgets about finding the fox. Once, he surprises his mother by coming up to the door on his skis and ringing the bell. She tells him that she did not hear him coming, and this gives him an idea.

Roger gets up very early the next morning, puts on his coonskin hat and skis and heads toward the river. There, he finally sees not only one fox, but two. He can hardly ski back to Seth fast enough to tell him that he topped him after all—he has seen twice as many foxes as Seth.

MEDIA: Possibly ink.

ANECDOTE: The book has become hard to find.

DISTINCTION: 1948 Caldecott Honor Book.

BIRTHDAY: Not available.

SUBJECT: Foxes—Fiction.

The Rooster Crows: A Book of American Rhymes and Jingles (Macmillan, 1945). Written and illustrated by Maud and Miska Petersham.

SUMMARY: The book contains rhymes and jingles; finger games; rope skipping rhymes; counting-out rhymes; games; and the words to the song, "Yankee Doodle." Many of the pieces mention American locations such as New York, Chicago, Boston, and Mississippi.

MEDIA: Lithograph pencil with color separations on acetate.

ANECDOTE: In the background of the illustration for "Bye, baby bunting," the woman is in the wrong position to milk the cow. She is on the cow's left side and too close to the front. She should be on the right side and back from the front. Maud Petersham sang jingles to herself as a way of easing her worries while her son was serving in World War II. When she didn't know all the words, she began looking them up. Soon she had enough gathered together to make a book.

DISTINCTION: 1946 Caldecott Medal.

BIRTHDAYS: Maud Petersham: August 5, 1889; Miska Petersham: September 20, 1888.

SUBJECTS: Nursery rhymes—American; Children's poetry, American; American poetry; Nursery rhymes.

See Also: An American ABC.

Rosenbach Museum and Library. Located in Philadelphia, the museum was originally the 1860s town house home of brothers Dr. A.M.S. and Philip Rosenbach. The doctor was a noted dealer and collector of rare books and manuscripts, and his brother specialized in fine and decorative arts. Both brothers died in the early 1950s, and in 1954 the Rosenbach Museum and Library was formed to keep the brothers' core and most important collections intact. In 2004, the library celebrated its fiftieth anniversary.

Though its collection boasts some of the early John Tenniel illustrations for *Through the Looking Glass* and *Alice's Adventures in Wonderland* as well as the largest surviving portion of the original manuscript of Charles Dickens' *Pickwick Papers*, perhaps most notable for American picture book afficionados is the museum's Maurice Sendak collection. The holdings include more than 10,000 manuscripts and drawings by the author/artist, and something from this grouping is always on display at the museum. In 2003, the museum hosted a fortieth-anniversary exhibit of Sendak's *Where the Wild Things Are* with a gallery featuring all of the original artwork from the book.

Other items of interest to those working in children's literature include more than 600 letters of Lewis Carroll, his most rare photographs and other materials; original drawings and books by William Blake; and the manuscript and typescript of Dylan Thomas' *Under Milk Wood*. Additional literary highlights include the handwritten manuscript of Jame Joyce's *Ulysses* and a scale-model reconstruction of the living room of Marianne Moore's Greenwich Village apartment, along with several of the poet's papers and manuscripts.

Contact: The Rosenbach Museum and Library, 2008–2010 De Lancey Place, Philadelphia, PA 19103; (215) 732-1600; Web site: http://www.rosenbach.org; email: info@rosenbach.org.

Rosie's Walk (Macmillan, 1967). Written and illustrated by Pat Hutchins.

SUMMARY: Rosie the hen takes a walk around the farm and is followed unknowingly by a fox. As Rosie walks nonchalantly on her way, the fox, which is trying to catch her, gets stopped by a rake, a pond, a haystack, a sack of flour, a wagon, and a giant swarm of bees. The hen arrives home in time for supper, untouched.

MEDIA: Possibly pen and ink and paint.

ANECDOTE: Pat Hutchins is British, but she wrote *Rosie's Walk* during an extended stay in New York, and it was first published by a New York publisher. The book is often used as a good example of how text can tell one story and illustration another in a picture book.

DISTINCTION: *New York Times* Best Book for Children.

BIRTHDAY: Pat Hutchins: June 18, 1942 (British).

SUBJECT: Chickens—Fiction.

Rumpelstiltskin (Dutton, 1986). Retold and illustrated by Paul O. Zelinsky.

SUMMARY: A miller with a beautiful daughter tells the king that his daughter can spin straw into gold. The king summons the girl and locks her in a room with the command that she spin straw into gold. Since the girl does not know how to do any such thing, she begins to cry. A tiny man appears and spins straw to gold in exchange for the girl's necklace. When the king sees all the gold, he makes her spin some more, and this time she gives the little man her ring. The king puts her into an even larger room and asks that she spin some more. This time, she has nothing left to give the little man who does the spinning, so he asks her to give him her firstborn child.

The king marries the miller's daughter, and after a year passes, she gives birth to a baby boy. She has forgotten all about the little man until he arrives one day to take the child. She cries so hard that the man takes pity on her and offers to let her keep the child if she can find out his name in three days. On the first day, she mentions every name she knows, but none of them is his name. On the second day, she collects every unusual name in the countryside, but none of these is his name either. Finally, she sends her servant to try to find the little man. She does and overhears him chanting his name over the fire. When he last visits the queen, she tells him his name, and he leaves her and her family safe and never returns.

MEDIA: Oil paintings.

ANECDOTE: Zelinsky asked a stranger he saw in a Chinese restaurant to pose for the miller's daughter. *Duffy and the Devil* and *Tom Tit Tot* are versions of this same story.

DISTINCTION: 1987 Caldecott Honor Book.

BIRTHDAY: Paul O. Zelinsky: February 14, 1953.

SUBJECTS: Fairy tales; Folklore—Germany.

See Also: Rapunzel.

S

Saint George and the Dragon (Little, Brown, 1984). Retold by Margaret Hodges and illustrated by Trina Schart Hyman.

SUMMARY: This book retells the section of Edmund Spenser's *Faerie Queen* about the Red Cross Knight, George, who, after a long battle, slays the dragon that has been terrorizing Princess Uma's homeland. He marries Princess Uma but honors his pledge to the Fairy Queen to serve as her knight for six years. After his many adventures in her service, he earns his title of Saint George of Merry England.

MEDIA: India ink and acrylic.

ANECDOTE: When Hyman couldn't bring herself to depict the scene of George actually killing the dragon, Hodges suggested that she move on to show the scene right after the dragon died. The scene on the back book jacket is of Hodges and her husband coming to visit Hyman.

DISTINCTION: 1985 Caldecott Medal.

BIRTHDAY: Trina Schart Hyman: April 8, 1939.

SUBJECTS: George, Saint, d. 303; George, Saint, d. 303—Legends; Folklore—England; Knights and knighthood—Folklore; Dragons—Folklore.

See Also: A Child's Calendar; Hershel and the Hanukkah Goblins.

Sam, Bangs & Moonshine (Henry Holt, 1966). Written and illustrated by Evaline Ness.

SUMMARY: Sam lives near the harbor and tells more lies and stories than even the nearby sailors. Sam says her cat at home is a lion and that her deceased mother is a mermaid. While her father works, her friend Thomas stops by. He visits every day at the same time and believes everything Sam says. He wants to the see the baby kangaroo Sam says she has, but she is always sending him on wild goose chases to find it. Sam's father tells her that she needs to remember the difference between what is real and what is imaginary, or what he calls moonshine.

One day, Sam sends Thomas out searching for the baby kangaroo again, this time on Blue Rock. There is a storm, and Thomas and Bangs are in trouble. After several tense hours, Sam's father goes to rescue Thomas. Bangs is lost at first but returns. Sam's father tells her that Thomas almost died from her moonshine and that there is good moonshine and bad moonshine. Seeing how badly she feels, he brings her a gerbil he found on a banana boat. Sam and Bangs take the gerbil to Thomas, who is home ill from the storm. When he asks her what its name is, she says Moonshine.

MEDIA: 3-color preseparated art using Japanese pen and wash; printer's ink; roller; string.

ANECDOTE: The inspiration for Sam was a picture of a ragged girl in Ness's portfolio; Bangs came from her cat that sat on her pictures while she worked and ate her erasers. The idea for Moonshine came from Ness's tendency to tell lies when she was a child.

DISTINCTION: 1967 Caldecott Medal.

BIRTHDAY: Evaline Ness: April 24, 1911.

SUBJECT: Imagination—Fiction.

Sawyer, Ruth (1880–1970). Author and artist. The third winner of the Laura Ingalls Wilder Medal, Ruth Sawyer was born August 5, 1880, in Boston. As a child growing up in New York, Sawyer was told stories by her Irish nurse, Johanna, and became enthralled with storytelling and folklore. She went on to study both formally in Boston and at Columbia University in New York. One of Sawyer's most important achievements was that she initiated the first storytelling program for children at the New York Public Library.

Sawyer traveled to Spain and to Ireland, where she was given an assignment by the *New York Sun* to write a series of articles on Irish folklore. There she saw how the Irish "seanchies," or storytellers, performed their craft, and she came away thinking that she had nothing near the skill of these artists or Johanna whom she knew as a child. Nevertheless, she went on to write a guide to the art form called *The Way of the Storyteller* (1942, 1962), in which she does not prescribe a particular method but rather encourages a "questing" approach in which each performer seeks his or her own best way of weaving a tale.

Sawyer authored more than 200 stories, poems, articles, and periodicals in the field of children's literature. Her picture book *The Christmas Anna Angel* (1944), illustrated by Kate Seredy, won a 1945 Caldecott Honor Book Award and was one of several books Sawyer wrote on the theme of Christmas. Others include *Joy to the World: Christmas Legends* (1966), illustrated by Trina Schart Hyman; *Long Christmas* (1941), illustrated by Valenti Angelo; and *Maggie Rose, Her Birthday Christmas* (1952), illustrated by Maurice Sendak. Another picture book, *Journey Cake, Ho!* (1953), illustrated by her son-in-law, Robert McCloskey, won a Caldecott Honor Book Award in 1954.

Though two illustrators of her picture books were honored with Caldecott Honor Book Awards, Sawyer may perhaps be best known today as the 1937 Newbery Award winner for her novel *Roller Skates*. The novel is an autobiographical account of a year Sawyer spent with two aunts in upstate New York.

In her acceptance speech for the Laura Ingalls Wilder Medal in 1965, Sawyer compared her experience as an author to Wilder's in that both of them wrote books out of childhoods they believed to be of importance. The author died five years after receiving the award.

DISTINCTIONS: Laura Ingalls Wilder Medal, 1965. Author of 1945 and 1954 Caldecott Honor Books *Christmas Anna Angel*, illustrated by Kate Seredy, and *Journey Cake, Ho!*, illustrated by Robert McCloskey; 1937 Newbery Award for *Roller Skates*.

See Also: Christmas Anna Angel; Journey Cake, Ho!

Scratchboard. Artist's medium. A white board is covered with India ink, and designs are scratched into it.

Seashore Story (Viking, 1967). Written and illustrated by Taro Yashima.

SUMMARY: Children from a ballet school camp out on the shore of a deserted coastline. There, they discuss the story of Urashima, the fisherman, and the turtle. Urashima saved the life of a hurt turtle that had come to the shore to lay its eggs. As a reward, the turtle offers to take Urashima below the ocean to a beautiful place. Urashima rode on the turtle's back, and they traveled under the water for a long time. There they found a grand palace and maidens in kimonos. Urashima enjoyed the beautiful place so much and for so long, that many years went by. Urashima grew pale.

One day, he remembered the sun and the earth and wanted to return to the shore. The people of the sea gave him a lacquered box as a gift. When he returned to the shore, however, nothing was the same as when he'd left. The buildings were different, and the faces of all the people were faces he did not know. He climbed the mountain that was the only thing that looked the same and opened the box. A stream of smoke came spilling out, making his hair white. He was an old man.

The ballet class talks about the story at the beach. They ask questions and are told by their teacher that the lesson of the story is that one must not be gone from home too long and forget those one loves.

MEDIA: Watercolor and pastel.

ANECDOTE: This is a retelling of a well-known Japanese fairy tale.

DISTINCTION: 1968 Caldecott Honor Book.

BIRTHDAY: Taro Yashima: September 21, 1908.

SUBJECT: Japan—Fiction.

See Also: Crow Boy; Umbrella.

Sector 7 (Clarion, 1999). Written and illustrated by David Wiesner.

SUMMARY: This is a wordless book about a boy on a school field trip to the Empire State Building. When they reach the observation deck and cannot see anything because of heavy cloud cover, the boy is transported to Sector 7, a cloud factory and "dispatch center," where clouds are designed, made, and shot out in tubes to parts of the sky. The boy draws designs of fish at Sector 7, and then his cloud friend returns him to his class. In the sky overhead, they later see the boy's intricate fish and sea creature designs in the clouds.

MEDIA: Watercolor.

ANECDOTE: To research the book, Wiesner visited the Empire State Building on a day with zero visibility when he was the only person there.

DISTINCTION: 2000 Caldecott Honor Book.

BIRTHDAY: David Wiesner: February 5, 1956.

SUBJECTS: Empire State Building (New York, N.Y.)—Fiction; Clouds—Fiction; Stories without words.

See Also: Free Fall; The Three Pigs; Tuesday; Wiesner, David.

Sendak, Maurice (Bernard) (1928–). Artist and author. As the artist with the single most Caldecott distinctions (eight) of any other picture book illustrator as well as arguably with the most influence on the picture book form and notoriety around the world, Maurice Sendak's genius is one of the most significant artistic forces in American children's picture books of the twentieth century. His awards include the 1964 Caldecott Medal for *Where the Wild Things Are* (Harper, 1963); and seven Caldecott Honor Book Awards: 1954 for *A Very Special House* by Ruth Krauss (Harper, 1953); 1959 for *What Do You Say, Dear? A Book of Manners for All Occasions* by Sesyle Joslin (Scott, 1958); 1960 for *The Moon Jumpers* by Janice May Udry (Harper, 1959); 1962 for *Little Bear's Visit* by Else Homelund Minarik (Harper, 1961); 1963 for *Mr. Rabbit and the Lovely Present* by Charlotte Zolotow (Harper, 1962); 1971 for *In the Night Kitchen* (Harper, 1970); and 1982 for *Outside Over There* with calligraphy by Jeanyee Wong (Harper, 1981). The artist has also been awarded the Laura Ingalls Wilder Award for his significant and lasting contribution to children's literature as well as the Hans Chris-

Author/illustrator Maurice Sendak standing by a life-size scene from his classic picture book, *Where the Wild Things Are*, at an exhibit at the Children's Museum of Manhattan honoring fifty years of his work. Sendak is a master of the picture book form and is arguably the most well-known and respected picture book artist inside and outside the world of children's literature. (Time Life Pictures/Getty Images.)

tian Andersen Illustrator Medal in 1970 and the National Medal of Arts in 1996 from President Clinton at the White House, among many other awards and honors. Sendak's work is characterized by a fearless journey of discovery toward the child sensibilities in all of us, no matter how unexpected, frightening, or challenging he may find that place may be when he reaches it. Sendak's work opened up an avenue of truth about children and their real feelings that was new in picture books and was innovative in his approach to the portrayal of children as well. Sendak recognized that children are young *people* with conflicting emotions of fear and anger, whimsy and joy; they are more complex and have more going on in their emo-

tional lives than the popular image of childhood sometimes suggests.

The man who would take on nearly iconic status in American children's literature was born on June 10, 1928, in Brooklyn, New York. That this was also the same year that animator Walt Disney's character Mickey Mouse was created would not be lost on the artist some years later. He grew up the youngest of three, with his older sister, Natalie, and brother, Jack, under the care of his Polish immigrant parents, Philip and Sadie Sendak. Philip Sendak often told his children stories, and Maurice knew before he ever entered school that he wanted to grow up to become an author and an artist. Jack liked to write, and Natalie helped the boys turn their efforts into beautiful booklets that they then sold to friends on the street. When she grew older, Sendak's sister often took her younger brothers to places in the city such as Radio City Music Hall or the Roxy in Manhattan.

The sights and the sounds of the city made a big impression on the future artist. He was also influenced by comic books and Walt Disney and other films of the depression era, such as *King Kong* and Laurel and Hardy. Sendak paid homage to New York City and these other elements through incorporating several of their images in his book *In the Night Kitchen* (Harper, 1970). The young Sendak sought refuge in the fantasy world of books, art, and film when economic times were hard for his family. His father was a dressmaker and part owner of Lucky Stitching. Business was not particularly good during the depression. Since he did not own many books, one of the boy's favorite books was Mark Twain's *The Prince and the Pauper*, illustrated by Robert Lawson, which was given to him by his sister. Although he is not positive that he read the novel cover to cover, the physical presence of a book of his own—its pictures, touch, and smell—made a big impression on him.

Sendak was a sickly child. He contracted measles, double pneumonia, and scarlet fever all before the age of five. This made his parents, perhaps understandably as immigrants surviving the depression, overprotective, and young Sendak was not allowed to go outside to play with other children for weeks at a time. Instead, he stayed inside drawing pictures and making up stories. Frequently, he sat looking out his window, often at a girl across the street named Rosie. Rosie was a feisty little girl whom Sendak admired and characterized in several of his books later on, such as *The Sign on Rosie's Door* (Harper, 1960) and *Really Rosie: Starring the Nutshell Kids* (Harper, 1975). The lack of exercise from so much sedentary time in childhood caused him to gain weight, and this became an issue he has had to struggle with all of his life.

Because of his parents' overprotectiveness and his illnesses, Sendak does not remember his childhood as a particularly happy one. He remembers relatives coming over on Sundays for dinner, pinching his cheeks and otherwise fussing and bending over him, smiling at him with bad breath and yellow teeth. In the comparative absence of childhood friends, these adult visitors who came to visit as company seemed larger than life to him as the youngest child in the family. In fact, at times, their presence seemed almost monstrous. The adults appeared to have control over the situation whenever they met on these occasions, leaving little Maurice with no escape from their fawning attentions. Sendak's memories of them became one of the later inspirations for his monster characters, the "Wild Things."

Much of his adolescence was marked by World War II and its effects on his family. Several of his relatives remaining in Poland and throughout Europe died in the Holocaust, including his paternal grandfather. Word of his grandfather's death reached the family on the occasion of Maurice's bar mitzvah. His sister's fiancé was killed in action, and his brother Jack was stationed in the Pacific.

Sendak graduated from Lafayette High School a year after the war ended, in 1946. He had received attention for his art in school, working on the school newspaper and yearbook and the literary magazine. He even illustrated a book by his high school physics teacher and his colleague, Maxwell Leigh Eidnoff and Hyman Ruchlis, called *Atomics for the Millions* (Whittlesey, 1947). In exchange for the illustrations, it is said, Sendak received a passing grade and a small amount of money. Formal schooling was not his calling, however, so rather than attend art school he immediately took a job at a window-design firm instead. By 1948, he was promoted at the company, but he did not enjoy his new responsibilities. When his brother returned from the war, they designed toys for a time, making six wooden mechanical toys that they tried to market. The toys never took off, since they were too expensive to make in large quantities. When the toy store, F.A.O. Schwartz, turned down the Sendak brothers' toys, however, they did offer Maurice a job working on their window displays. It was at the toy store that the artist had a real chance to study the children's books of the day in some depth. In the evenings, he also worked on his artistic techniques at the Art Student's League.

While still with the toy store, Sendak met the influential editor Ursula Nordstrom in 1950. After seeing his artwork, Nordstrom offered him opportunities to illustrate children's books. His first book was *The Wonderful Farm* (Harper, 1951), written by Marcel Ayme. His second book, *A Hole Is to Dig* (Harper, 1952) by Ruth Krauss brought more attention, and Sendak was able to quit his job at Schwartz, move to Greenwich Village, and work at his new career as a freelance illustrator full-time.

Sendak has called the decade of the 1950s into the early 1960s his apprenticeship years as an artist. He befriended Ruth Krauss and her husband, David Johnson Leisk, otherwise known as Crockett Johnson of *Harold and the Purple Crayon* fame, and spent many weekends at their home. There they discussed art, music, picture books, and techniques. Frequently, David had to play referee for the heated discussions into which Sendak and Krauss worked themselves. The experience was a healthy one for Sendak's development as an artist. His other influences included several European illustrators such as British artists Randolph Caldecott and George Cruikshank, French artist Maurice Boutet de Monvel, and the German Wilhelm Busch. During this period, Sendak continued to illustrate picture books written by other authors. During his self-named "apprenticeship," Sendak's work captured several Caldecott Honor Book Awards.

Sendak's breakthrough came with the writing and illustrating of the 1963 publication, *Where the Wild Things Are*. It was the first of what the artist later would call a trilogy depicting children's inner lives. Parents and educators did not universally accept the book at first. In fact, Max's temper and behavior were first viewed as too subversive of authority—a rather poor message to send to children, it was thought, and the monsters depicted in the fantasy sequence were thought to be too frightening to share with children, especially at bedtime. Some children were scared by the book, the complexities of which broke the mold of bland children's books they had been used to that featured stock, well-behaved children and soft, furry animals rather than a rude boy and monsters with long claws and sharp teeth. Other children loved the book, however, and over time, the book's honest depiction of a child's frustrations and his use of fantasy to deal with his emotions and calm down became appreciated as a breakthrough in American children's picture books as well as in children's literature in general.

The artist went on to have an illustrious career in children's book illustration that has lasted more than fifty years and has resulted in more than one hundred different editions of books and projects, some written by him, others by other authors. Notable career titles from the prolific artist include *Kenny's Window* (Harper, 1956); *The Sign on Rosie's Door* (Harper, 1960); *The Nutshell Library* (Harper, 1962); *Zlateh the Goat and Other Stories* by Isaac Bashevis Singer (Harper, 1966); *In the Night Kitchen* (Harper, 1970); *Outside Over There* (Harper, 1981); *Nutcracker*, written by E.T.A. Hoffman (Crown, 1984); and, *Swine Lake* written by James Marshall (Harper, 1999).

Over the years, Sendak's interests expanded beyond picture books for children into music and theater. He has created set designs for theatrical and operatic versions of his books and with fellow illustrator Arthur Yorinks established the children's theater and touring company *Night Kitchen Theater*. He has also worked with Hollywood to produce films. His passions include Mozart, opera, and Herman Melville, and these interests frequently mix and blend with his art. It was a particular thrill for him, for example, to illustrate an edition of Melville's novel, *Pierre*.

In 1972, he bought an eighteenth-century farmhouse in Ridgefield, Connecticut, which houses his studio and is only about an hour-and-a-half train commute to Manhattan. Sendak never married or had children of his own. His adult family life is perhaps most frequently characterized by a love for animals, dogs in particular, that he has had as pets. The strong affection he had for his Sealyham terrier, Jennie, for example, is well known. He brought Jennie home with him in 1954 and had her as a beloved friend for fourteen years. Sealyham terriers are described by breeders as "the most beautiful union between cheerfulness and courage" and are known as couch potatoes with little desire for extended exercise. They shed little to none of their white, coarse fur and are good watchdogs. As a result of these traits, they make good dogs for apartment living. Jennie appears in several of Sendak's books, including *Higglety Pigglety Pop!* (Harper, 1967), that he created as a tribute to her the year after her death from cancer. In the book, Jennie is depicted near her bowl marked, "Jennie." Behind her on the wall is a picture of the Mona Lisa, which was the original name given her by her breeders. Jennie first appeared in *Mrs. Piggle Wiggle's Farm* (Lippincott, 1954), written by Betty MacDonald, and makes cameo appearances in other Sendak books as well. Max chases her down the stairs in his wolf costume in *Where the Wild Things Are*.

Sendak's art has influenced other artists and drawn attention from outside the children's picture book world, bringing an important recognition to the form. Sendak, however, does not consider himself to be a "children's" book creator. His says that he writes and illustrates books that he likes and that they are not targeted to any particular age group. Indeed, some adults believe that many of his books are more appropriate for older audi-ences. Sendak admits to being able to recall what it was like to be a child and that he is never far from reliving the emotions that he felt so many years ago. He also speaks about the openness of children and their appreciation for the truth. In his advocacy work in his golden years for causes that work to fight against issues such as childhood AIDS, war, and hunger, Maurice Sendak continues to speak on behalf of children who encounter myriad wild things.

DISTINCTIONS: 1964 Caldecott Medal; 1954, 1959, 1960, 1962, 1963, 1971, and 1982 Caldecott Honor Books (one of only seven multiple gold medalists; the single most Caldecott awards of any children's picture book artist).

Further Reading: Cech, John. *Angels and Wild Things: The Archetypal Poetics of Maurice Sendak*. University Park: University of Pennsylvania Press, 1995; Devereaux, Elizabeth. "In the Studio with Maurice Sendak." *Publisher's Weekly* 240, no. 44 (November 1, 1993): 28+; Kushner, Tony. *The Art of Maurice Sendak, 1980 to Present*. New York: Harry N. Abrams, 2003; Lane, Selma G. *The Art of Maurice Sendak*. New York: Harry N. Abrams, 1988; Sendak, Maurice. "Visitors from My Boyhood," in William Zinsser, ed., *Worlds of Childhood: The Art and Craft of Writing for Children*. Boston: Houghton Mifflin, 1990, pp. 47–69; Shaddock, Jennifer, *"Where the Wild Things Are*: Sendak's Journey into the Heart of Darkness," *Children's Literature Association Quarterly* 22, no. 4 (Winter 1997–1998): 155–159.

See Also: In the Night Kitchen; *Little Bear's Visit*; *The Moon Jumpers*; *Mr. Rabbit and the Lovely Present*; *Outside Over There*; *A Very Special House*; *What Do You Say, Dear?*; *Where the Wild Things Are*.

Seuss, Dr. *See* Geisel, Theodor (Ted) Seuss.

See Also: Bartholemew and the Oobleck; *If I Ran the Zoo*; *McElligott's Pool*.

Seven Blind Mice (Philomel, 1992). Written and illustrated by Ed Young.

SUMMARY: Seven blind mice are surprised when something strange comes by their pond. The Red Mouse investigates on Monday and finds it is a pillar. On Tuesday, the Green Mouse returns and says it is a snake. Yellow Mouse finds a spear; Purple Mouse a cliff; Orange Mouse says it is a fan that moves; Blue Mouse claims that it is nothing but a rope. With all the other mice arguing, White Mouse heads out on Sunday to see what is at the pond. She walks all over the something, from top to bottom and end to end. She goes back and tells the mice that what is there is an elephant. They all go and walk all around the elephant and see that it is so. The moral is given at the end of the story: that examining part of something provides interesting stories, but wisdom comes when viewing the whole.

MEDIA: Paper collage.

ANECDOTE: Young used to sit at the New York Central Park Zoo and sketch animals during his lunch hour.

BIRTHDAY: Ed Young: November 28, 1931.

DISTINCTION: 1993 Caldecott Honor Book.

SUBJECTS: Fables; Elephants—Folklore; Folklore—India; Stories in Rhyme.

See Also: The Emperor and the Kite; Lon Po Po: A Red-Riding Hood Story from China.

Seven Simeons: A Russian Tale (Viking, 1937). Retold and illustrated by Boris Artzybasheff.

SUMMARY: King Douda is vain and thinks himself very attractive. He summons his sailors and asks them if they know of any woman who is as good looking as himself that he may take as his bride. One sailor says he knows of a Princess Helena who is as attractive, but she would not be his bride because it would take twenty years to go to Boozan Island, where she lives, and back. The king went out to the countryside to cheer up after hearing this sad news, and there he met seven Simeons. They were simple people, all brothers, and each one had a talent. The first Simeon can build a tower; the second can see from the tower to anywhere in the world; the third can build ships; the fourth can sail ships; the fifth is a blacksmith who can make guns; and the sixth can recover whatever the guns shoot. The seventh Simeon claims his talent must remain hidden. The king takes six Simeons to work for him in the city; he locks the seventh Simeon away.

When the other six have done their work, the seventh Simeon is summoned and asked if he can steal the Princess, which he can do. After several adventures on the journey, which is much more quickly accomplished than normal with the Simeons' skills, Princess Helena arrives and marries the king. Instead of taking jobs as senators of the court, the simple Simeons prefer to return to their quiet peasant lives.

MEDIA: Pen and ink.

ANECDOTE: This story is an old Russian folktale. Artzybasheff was born in Ukraine and educated in St. Petersburg.

DISTINCTIONS: 1938 Caldecott Honor Book; 1938 Newbery Honor Book.

BIRTHDAY: Boris Artzybasheff: May 25, 1899.

SUBJECT: Folktales—Russian.

Shadow (Scribner, 1983). Translated and illustrated by Marcia Brown.

SUMMARY: The poetry is translated from French poet Blaise Cendrars (1887–1961), by Marcia Brown. To the shamans and storytellers of Africa, the shadow is more than the darkness and more than a reflection of ourselves that we see on the ground beside us when the sun is high in the sky. For them, the shadow comes forth when a storyteller speaks beside the fire and ash. It is a mystical trickster that lives in the forest. It is both prowler and dancer. It is always watching, but it is blind. It is not death, but it can be frightening. It spreads out at twilight and is heavy at night. It is always there in some form; it is the iris of our eye. The shadow is a spiritual belief and mystery of the past and present that we know and feel more than we understand.

MEDIA: Collage; paper, woodcuts, acrylics.

ANECDOTE: Marcia Brown's illustrations are inspired by her travels in Africa, but the idea for the book came from a book she read when she was a storyteller at the New York Public Library. She thought she might have difficulty finding a publisher for the book because she was a white woman writing about an African subject and also because the artwork would be difficult to duplicate. See more about Brown's artwork on this book in the Marcia Brown entry.

DISTINCTION: 1983 Caldecott Medal.

BIRTHDAY: Marcia Brown: July 13, 1918.

SUBJECTS: Shades and shadows—Poetry; Children's Poetry, French—Translations into English; Shadows—Poetry; French poetry; Africa—Poetry.

See Also: Brown, Marcia; *Cinderella, or The Little Glass Slipper*; *Puss in Boots*; *Skipper John's Cook*; *Stone Soup*.

Sing in Praise: A Collection of the Best Loved Hymns (Dutton, 1946). Selected by Opal Wheeler; illustrated by Marjorie Torrey.

SUMMARY: Stories, music, and lyrics are included for the following hymns: "Onward, Christian Soldiers"; "O God, Our Help in Ages Past"; "Faith of Our Fathers"; "A Mighty Fortress Is Our God"; "Rock of Ages"; "Jerusalem, the Golden"; "All Hail the Power of Jesus's Name"; "My Faith Looks Up to Thee"; "Now the Day Is Over"; "Abide with Me"; "Fairest Lord Jesus"; "Come, Thou Almighty King"; "Blest Be the Tie That Binds"; "Dear Lord and Father of Mankind"; "Christ the Lord Is Risen To-day";

"From Greenland's Icy Mountains"; "Nearer, My God, to Thee"; "Holy, Holy, Holy!" and "O Worship the King."

MEDIA: Undetermined.

ANECDOTE: The illustrations accompanying the stories are in black and white; the illustrations for the hymns are in color.

DISTINCTION: 1947 Caldecott Honor Book.

BIRTHDAY: Not available.

SUBJECTS: Hymns, English; Hymns, English—History and criticism.

Sing Mother Goose (Dutton, 1945). Music by Opal Wheeler; illustrated by Marjorie Torrey.

SUMMARY: The book contains music, lyrics, and illustrations for over fifty children's nursery rhymes, including "Little Bo Peep," "Little Boy Blue," "Three Wise Men of Gotham," "Hey, Diddle, Diddle," and "Pease Porridge Hot."

MEDIA: Undetermined.

ANECDOTE: The illustrations are both black-and-white and in color.

DISTINCTION: 1946 Caldecott Honor Book.

BIRTHDAY: Not available.

SUBJECT: Children's songs.

Skipper John's Cook (Scribner, 1951). Written and illustrated by Marcia Brown.

SUMMARY: One morning Si takes his dog George down to the wharf. The fishermen are friendly and throw Si a string of fish to cook for George. Si's best friend at the wharf is Skipper John, captain of the *Liberty Belle*. He cannot talk to Si today because he is busy trying to get his crew to board. The ship has no cook, and all the crew eats are beans morning, noon, and night. They refuse to go out to sea without a cook, so Skipper John nails up a sign with the announcement that a cook is wanted.

Si has cooked for George, so he decides to apply for the job. That afternoon, many cooks arrive with samples of their work to apply for the job as cook on the *Liberty Belle*. Mike, Davy, Eben, and Josh all bring beans—beans and hardtack, beans and salt pork, beans and bacon, and bean soup. When Si turns up in line, Skipper John sees how well fed George is, so he hires Si right then and there. Si goes home and cooks a favorite meal for George while his mother sews him a red shirt for the journey. Si packs his necessities in a sea bag, and off he goes in the morning.

He learns the ways of the ship quickly, then sets about working in the galley to prepare his first dinner for the men. George wanted fish, so Si fries him some with fried potatoes. The men on deck can smell it, and they are glad to have this same meal that evening after their hard day of work. In fact, this is the only food Si knows how to cook. Pretty soon, the men grow tired of it—every morning, noon, and night they eat fish. Just as he is about to cook his 259th fish, Si is approached by Skipper John, who asks him if he can cook anything else. Si replies that he can cook beans. So, every other meal became beans or fish.

When the *Liberty Belle* returns from sea, Si and Skipper John part their ways amicably. Skipper John tells Si that he is the best fish fryer he has ever seen. However, as soon as Si turns to go home, Skipper John is nailing up another sign for a new cook, one who can cook something besides fish and beans morning, noon, and night, and every time in between.

MEDIA: Undetermined.

ANECDOTE: Brown dedicated this book to her sister, Helen.

DISTINCTION: 1952 Caldecott Honor Book.

BIRTHDAY: Marcia Brown: July 13, 1918.

SUBJECTS: Cooking—Fiction; Fishing—Fiction.

See Also: Brown, Marcia; *Cinderella, or The Little Glass Slipper*; *Puss in Boots*; *Stone Soup*.

Small Rain: Verses from the Bible (Viking, 1943). Selected by Jessie Orton Jones; illustrated by Elizabeth Orton Jones.

SUMMARY: The book contains over two dozen short passages from the Bible illustrated for children. Examples include "Make a joyful noise"; "The Lord is my shepherd"; and "Blessed are the peacemakers." The book concludes with a listing of book, chapter, and verse citations so that readers may look them up in the Bible.

MEDIA: Undetermined.

ANECDOTE: Jessie and Elizabeth Jones were a mother–daughter team.

DISTINCTION: 1944 Caldecott Honor Book.

BIRTHDAY: Not available.

SUBJECT: Bible—Illustrations.

Smoky Night (Harcourt, 1994). Written by Eve Bunting; illustrated by David Diaz.

SUMMARY: Daniel and Mama (Gena) watch outside their apartment window as a riot takes place down on their street. Mama explains to Daniel what riots are and why people look both happy and angry at the same time when they steal things like shoes or other people's dry cleaning from smashed-out stores. In the night, smoke fills their building, and Daniel and Mama are rushed to a shelter behind Mr. Jackson and the Ramirez family, but Jasmine, David's cat, is nowhere to be found. Mrs. Kim of Kim Markets is with them, too. Mama tells Daniel she won't shop at Kim Markets because she believes it is better to stay with one's own people.

Later a firefighter brings in two cats to the shelter, a yellow one and a dirty carrot-colored cat that belongs to Mrs. Kim. He tells them that he found them hiding together. Daniel explains that the cats didn't get along before because they did not know each other, and Mama and Mrs. Kim get very quiet. Mama invites Mrs. Kim to bring her cat over

Cover of *Smoky Night*, written by Eve Bunting, illustrated by David Diaz. Bunting wrote this book as a response to the Los Angeles riots of 1992. Diaz's artwork received the Caldecott Medal in 1995, highlighting the fact that picture books for children sometimes deal with complex issues such as race. (Copyright © 1994 by David Diaz. Copyright © by Harcourt, Inc. All rights reserved.)

to their apartment when they can go back into their buildings, and Mrs. Kim accepts.

ANECDOTE: Diaz's wife, Cecelia, heard cheering and applause on their answering machine and thought perhaps they had won the Publisher's Clearing House Sweepstakes; instead, David had won the 1995 Caldecott Medal. Bunting wrote the book in response to the Los Angeles riots of 1992.

MEDIA: Acrylic paintings and photo-collages on watercolor paper.

DISTINCTION: 1995 Caldecott Medal.

SUBJECTS: Riots—California—Los Angeles—Fiction; Interpersonal relations—Fiction; Neighborliness—Fiction.

Snapshots from the Wedding (Putnam, 1997). Written by Gary Soto; illustrated by Stephanie Garcia.

SUMMARY: Maya, the flower girl for Isabel's and Rafael's wedding, narrates this "photo album." The photos are actually three-dimensional shadow boxes with figures of the wedding party, celebrants, and guests. Details that personalize the traditional wedding include the groom's broken arm in a cast from a softball injury and Tío Trino jump-starting someone's car to go to the reception. The reception includes a mariachi band as well as another band that plays oldies but goodies. Maya still has a bit of *mole* on her face when she goes to sleep that night; it has been a wedding that she will not forget.

MEDIA: Sculpty clay, acrylic paints, wood, fabric, and found objects.

ANECDOTE: The book begins with a glossary of twelve Spanish words that are used throughout Maya's narrative.

DISTINCTION: 1998 Pura Belpré Illustrator Award.

BIRTHDAY: Gary Soto: April 12, 1952.

SUBJECTS: Weddings—Fiction; Mexican Americans—Fiction.

Snow (Farrar, Straus and Giroux, 1998). Written and illustrated by Uri Shulevitz.

SUMMARY: Nobody believes boy with dog when he points to the snowflakes and suggests that a lot of snow may be coming. The grandfather with beard; man with hat; and woman with umbrella all think he's making too much of it. The radio and television do not agree either. Eventually, however, flakes accumulate until the entire town is covered with the fluffy white stuff.

MEDIA: Ink and watercolor washes.

ANECDOTE: Shulevitz's first picture book was *The Moon in My Room*.

DISTINCTIONS: 1999 Caldecott Honor Book; 1999 Charlotte Zolotow Award.

BIRTHDAY: Uri Shulevitz: February 27, 1935.

SUBJECTS: Snow—Fiction; City and town life—Fiction.

See Also: The Fool of the World and the Flying Ship.

Snow White and the Seven Dwarfs

(Coward, 1938). Retold and illustrated by Wanda Gág.

SUMMARY: The traditional story is retold (for plot summary, see *Snow-White*, translated by Randall Jarrell).

MEDIA: Possibly lithographs.

ANECDOTE: Gág released her book to coincide with Disney's film version of the tale, which she thought sentimentalized and trivialized the original.

DISTINCTION: 1939 Caldecott Honor Book.

BIRTHDAY: Wanda Gág: March 11, 1893.

SUBJECTS: Folklore—Germany; Fairy tales.

See Also: ABC Book; Gág, Wanda; *Millions of Cats.*

Snow-White and the Seven Dwarfs

(Farrar, Straus and Giroux, 1972). Translated by Randall Jarrell; illustrated by Nancy Ekholm Burkert.

SUMMARY: The story is the same as the traditional story. The Queen looks in the mirror and asks it who is the fairest of them all, and the mirror answers that Snow-White is the fairest. The jealous Queen sends a huntsman to the woods to kill the girl and bring back her liver and lungs as tokens. On seeing Snow-White's fear, the huntsman allows her to run away into the forest. There, she meets the dwarfs by resting in their cottage. The Queen disguises herself as an old woman and tricks Snow-White into biting a poison apple. Snow-White lies in a glass coffin in the woods. A prince convinces the dwarfs to let him have the coffin, and in the bouncing of his servants carrying it, the bit of poison apple pops out of her throat, and she wakens. The wicked old Queen dies from dancing in hot iron slippers after she goes to the palace and recognizes Snow-White, who has become the young new Queen.

Front cover of *Snow-White and the Seven Dwarfs*, translated by Randall Jarrell, illustrated by Nancy Ekholm Burkert. Burkert achieved what many consider to be her masterpiece picture book through her use of brush and colored inks. The book was awarded a Caldecott Honor in 1973. (Reprinted by permission of Farrar, Straus and Giroux, LLC: *Snow-White and the Seven Dwarfs: A Tale from the Brothers Grimm* translated by Randall Jarrell, pictures by Nancy Ekholm Burkert. Pictures copyright © 1972 by Nancy Ekholm Burkert. www.fsgkidsbooks.com.)

MEDIA: Brush and colored inks.

ANECDOTE: Many consider *Snow-White* to be Burkert's masterpiece artwork.

DISTINCTION: 1973 Caldecott Honor Book.

BIRTHDAYS: Nancy Ekholm Burkert: February 16, 1933; Randall Jarrell: May 6, 1914.

SUBJECTS: Folklore—Germany; Fairy tales.

Snowflake Bentley

(Houghton Mifflin, 1998). Written by Jacqueline Briggs Martin; illustrated by Mary Azarian.

SUMMARY: This is a biography of Wilson Bentley. Bentley is fascinated with snowflakes and devises a way to photograph them after they fall but before they melt. Sidebars to Bentley's biographical account add information such as the fact that, by 1926, he had spent $15,000 on equipment and had earned only $4,000 from the sale of his photographs. Bentley showed slide shows of his pictures on sheets hung over clotheslines and sold copies of his photos to colleges and universities where they were collected and used as a reference for scientists and artists. The book concludes with a photograph of Wilson Bentley at his camera and three samples of his amazing snowflake photographs.

MEDIA: Woodcuts, hand-tinted with watercolors.

ANECDOTE: Mary Azarian lived about an hour away from where Wilson Bentley lived and worked in Jericho, Vermont. A marker monument in the town commemorates his contribution to the world. She heard she won the Caldecott Medal just after helping a woman dig her car out of the snow. Bentley's book, *Snow Crystals*, with hundreds of his photographs of snowflakes, is still in print and used as a reference by those interested in the subject.

DISTINCTION: 1999 Caldecott Medal.

BIRTHDAYS: Mary Azarian: December 8, 1940; Jacqueline Briggs Martin: April 15, 1945.

SUBJECTS: Bentley, W.A. (Wilson Alwyn), 1865–1931; Snowflakes; Nature photography; Meteorologists—United States—Biography; Photographers—United States—Biography; Scientists; Snow.

The Snowy Day (Viking, 1962). Written and illustrated by Ezra Jack Keats.

SUMMARY: It has snowed in the night, and Peter puts on his red snowsuit and goes out and makes tracks, tracks with toes pointing out; tracks with his toes pointing in; straight line tracks. With a stick, he punches snow down from trees onto his head. He is not old enough yet to enter a snowball fight with the older boys. Instead, he makes a snow angel and a snowman and slides down a hill. He stuffs a snowball in his pocket and goes inside to warm up. He tells his mother about the fun he had; he thinks about it in the bathtub. When he checks his snowsuit pocket, he is sad to feel that the snowball is not there. He goes to bed and dreams that the snow has all melted overnight, but instead new snow has fallen and continues to come down, and the fun can begin again. This time, Peter asks his friend from across the hall to join him.

MEDIA: Collage; papers, paints, and gum-eraser stamps.

ANECDOTE: The book is one of the first picture books to feature an African American child as any other child in a universal situation. Keats had kept 1940 *Life* magazine photographs of a black boy whose face and look in his clothes he found intriguing enough to use as a model.

DISTINCTION: 1963 Caldecott Medal.

BIRTHDAY: Ezra Jack Keats: March 11, 1916.

SUBJECTS: Snow—Fiction; African Americans—Fiction.

So You Want to Be President? (Philomel, 2000). Written by Judith St. George; illustrated by David Small.

SUMMARY: The book traces common traits in several presidents, who are depicted in caricature—for example, how many presidents were born in a log cabin; how many served in the military; what sports they played; which ones played musical instruments; what jobs they had previously, and so forth. At the end of the book are lists of the presidents featured on which pages in the book; a listing of the forty-two presidents (through Clinton) with their years in office, birthplace, year of birth, and a comment about their administration. A short bibliography closes the volume.

MEDIA: Watercolor, ink, and pastel chalk.

ANECDOTE: The book was published in the year 2000, when one of the closest presidential elections in history, between George W. Bush and former Vice President Al Gore, ended in controversy.

DISTINCTION: 2001 Caldecott Medal.

BIRTHDAY: David Small: February 12, 1945.

SUBJECTS: Presidents—United States—Miscellanea; Presidents—Miscellanea.

Society of Children's Book Writers and Illustrators. Organization. The largest organization in the world devoted solely to the creators of literature for children, SCBWI was founded in 1971 by a group of children's writers in Los Angeles. In 2005, there were over 19,000 members in seventy regions worldwide. The organization provides a network for authors and illustrators, agents, editors and publishers, educators, librarians, booksellers and others to share their common efforts, concerns, and celebrations related to the production of children's literature.

Each year, the society sponsors two international conferences and several regional events. It has lobbied successfully for such issues as new copyright legislation, equitable treatment of authors and artists, and fair contract terms. Helping interested writers and artists along their journey to publication is one of the society's benefits, as well as providing consistent and meaningful support to published authors and artists. The organization publishes a bimonthly newsletter, the *SCBWI Bulletin*, which, among other articles and columns, contains current marketing information.

Each year since 1973 SCBWI awards its Golden Kite Award to members with outstanding work in picture book text, picture book illustration, fiction, and nonfiction categories. It is the only award given by the authors' and artists' peers. Winners of picture book text awards include authors such as Amy Timberlake, Sarah Wilson, J. Patrick Lewis, Jane Kurtz, and Deborah Hopkinson, among others. Golden Kite winners for illustration in picture books have included Loren Long, Marla Frazee, Beth Krommes, David Shannon, Amy Walrod, and Uri Shulevitz.

The society gives grants to works in progress to encourage the future of the profession and quality work in children's books. The Don Freeman Memorial Grant-in-Aid stipend, named in honor of the picture book artist of *Corduroy*, is awarded to a member artist working in picture books. Likewise, the Barbara Karlin Grant is an annual award given to encourage the efforts of aspiring picture book writers.

Contact: Society of Children's Book Writers and Illustrators, 8271 Beverly Boulevard, Los Angeles, CA, 90048; (323) 782-1010; Web site: http://www.scbwi.org; email: scbwi @scbwi.org.

Society of Illustrators and Society of Illustrators Museum. Organization and Museum. Founded on February 1, 1901, the society is the only national organization committed exclusively to the art of illustration. Its mission is to promote the appreciation of illustration in the past, present, and future and to stimulate interest in, and the creation of, quality art in illustration. The organization supports the profession both aesthetically and ethically by providing a network for the illustrator community, sponsoring exhibitions, lectures and educational events, and encouraging younger artists. Prominent former members include Howard Pyle, N. C. Wyeth, and Maxfield Parrish, among others. The society also plays a large role in maintaining the Museum of American Illustrators in New York; the organization and the facility are housed in the same location.

The Museum of American Illustration (also known as the Society of Illustrators Museum), provides permanent and changing exhibits for more than 200 years of American illustration in all formats, including books and periodicals for children and adults, posters, and other media. Exhibits highlight both historical and contemporary art. Each year an exhibit of the best illustration of the previous year is put on display for eight weeks. Scholars of illustration find resource material at the Norman Price Library, which houses books on illustration as well as biographical and other archival materials available for research.

Contact: Museum of American Illustration at the Society of Illustrators, 128 East 63rd Street, New York, NY 10021-7303; (212) 838-2560; Web site: http://www.societyillustrators.org; email: info@societyillustrators.org.

Song and Dance Man (Knopf, 1988). Written by Karen Ackerman; illustrated by Stephen Gammell.

SUMMARY: Grandpa is a song-and-dance man from the old vaudeville days. When his three grandkids visit, Grandma calls out that supper will be in one hour, and Grandpa takes the children upstairs to go through his old showtime things in the attic. Finding his tap shoes, striped vest, bowler hat, and cane, Grandpa tosses powder on the floor and does a little soft-shoe for the children. He tells them an old vaudeville joke about how to make an elephant float, plays the banjo and sings, and then he dons a silk top hat and gold-tipped cane to tap-dance a resounding finale. The grandkids love the show; it is better than anything on television. Grandpa holds the railing as they go back downstairs. When the grandkids get ready to go, they say they would have loved to have seen Grandpa dance on the vaudeville stage back when, but Grandpa tells them that he would not trade the olden days for any time he has spent with them. Still, the kids wonder about that as they see him glance back up the attic steps when he turns out the light.

MEDIA: Line drawings in colored pencil.

ANECDOTE: Gammell has said he would rather draw than write, though he has written some of his own books.

DISTINCTION: 1989 Caldecott Medal.

BIRTHDAY: Stephen Gammell: February 10, 1943.

SUBJECTS: Entertainers—Fiction; Grandfathers—Fiction.

See Also: The Relatives Came.

Song of Robin Hood (Houghton Mifflin, 1947). Edited by Anne Malcolmson; illustrated by Virginia Lee Burton; music arranged by Grace Castagnetta.

SUMMARY: This book contains music and lyrics for eighteen ballads of Robin Hood with more than 500 individual verses. The titles of the songs are "Robin Hood and Little John"; "Robin Hood and the Stranger"; "Robin Hood and the Tanner"; "Robin Hood and the Prince of Aragon"; "Robin Hood and the Curtal Friar"; "Robin Hood and Allen A. Dale"; "Robin Hood and Maid Marian"; "Robin Hood and the Bishop"; "Robin Hood and the Butcher"; "Robin Hood and the Bold Pedlar"; "Robin Hood and Guy of Gisborne"; "Robin Hood and the Golden Arrow"; "Robin Hood and the Ranger"; "Robin Hood Rescuing Will Stutly"; "Robin Hood and the Bishop of Hereford"; "Robin Hood's Golden Prize"; "Robin Hood Rescuing Three Squires"; and "Robin Hood's Death."

MEDIA: Scratchboard.

ANECDOTE: Malcolmson collected the original ballads of Robin Hood because she was dissatisfied with the way his story had been separated from the music over the years. Burton explains that the sheer number of verses made necessary the tiny print and small illustrations that characterize the book.

DISTINCTION: 1948 Caldecott Honor Book.

BIRTHDAY: Virginia Lee Burton: August 30, 1909.

SUBJECT: Robin Hood (Legendary character)—Songs and music.

See Also: The Little House.

Song of the Swallows (Scribner, 1949).
Written and illustrated by Leo Politi.

SUMMARY: On a day in spring, Juan runs to the Mission of Capistrano. Old Julian is the mission's bell-ringer, and he has told Juan the story of the origin of the mission many times. Juan likes the colors of the many flowers and how they look against the old stone walls of the mission. He especially likes the swallows, *las golondrinas*, that roost under the arches and on the beams of the roof. Their song and flapping wings make the mission particularly pleasant. They arrive on St. Joseph's Day in March and leave at the end of the summer. Juan keeps track of the swallows' activities while they are at the mission, such as building their nests and feeding their young. At the end of summer, he and Julian watch them fly away.

Juan asks Julian where they go each year, and Julian does not know, but he does know that they like fresh water and flowers. Juan has the idea to grow flowers near his old adobe home in hopes of attracting swallows the following spring. He plants his garden and often sings "La Golondrina," a song he learned in school. The next spring, on St. Joseph's Day, Juan and other children wait for the swallows. Sure enough, they come to the mission yet again. When Juan checks at home, two swallows have decided to make their nest near his new garden, and he is happy.

The book contains words and music for two songs about the swallows of Capistrano.

MEDIA: Tempera.

ANECDOTE: Politi enjoyed drawing children best of all and attempted to imbue his illustrations with the love and joy of family life.

DISTINCTION: 1950 Caldecott Medal.

BIRTHDAY: Leo Politi: November 21, 1908.

SUBJECTS: Swallows—Fiction; California—Fiction.

See Also: Juanita; Pedro, the Angel of Olvera Street.

Soul Looks Back in Wonder (Dial, 1993).
Written by Maya Angelou and others, illustrated by Tom Feelings.

SUMMARY: The book is an anthology of thirteen poems by black poets celebrating African creativity that binds black people together from their ancestors to the future, through their years of struggle, enabling them to endure. Poems and poets are "Mother of Brown-Ness" by Margaret Walker; "Look at Us" by Darryl Holmes; "Boyz n Search of Their Soular System" by Eugene B. Redmond; "To You" by Langston Hughes; "History of My People" by Walter Dean Myers; "window morning" by Mwatabu Okantah; "Destiny" by Haki R. Madhubuti; "I Love the Look of Words" by Maya Angelou; "Africa You Are Beautiful" by Rashidah Ismaili; "Rhythms, Harmones, Ancestors (A Spirit Rap)" by Askia M. Touré; "I am the creativity" by Alexis De Veaux; "Under the Rainbow" by Lucille Clifton; and "Who Can Be Born Black" by Mari Evans. An introduction describes Tom Feelings' intentions with the book. Brief contributors' biographies follow the poems, and the book ends with a quotation by Malcolm X about the value of education.

MEDIA: Colored pencils, stencil cut-outs, collage, and spray paint.

ANECDOTE: This was the first book Feelings illustrated in full color.

DISTINCTION: 1994 Coretta Scott King Award for Illustration.

BIRTHDAY: Tom Feelings: May 19, 1933.

SUBJECTS: American poetry—African

American authors; African Americans—poetry; Children's poetry—American.

The Spider and the Fly (Simon and Schuster, 2002). Written by Mary Howitt; illustrated by Tony DiTerlizzi.

SUMMARY: DiTerlizzi illustrates the famous verse by Mary Howitt. The original title of the 1829 verse was "The Spider and the Fly: An Apologue: A New Version of an Old Story." It first appeared in *The New Year's Gift* and then again five years later in Howitt's *Sketches of Natural History*. The book concludes with a cautionary note from Spider about the moral of the verse as well as biographies of Howitt and DiTerlizzi.

MEDIA: Lamp black and titanium white holbein Acryla gouache and Berol Prismacolor pencil on Strathmore 5-ply, plate Bristol board and reproduced in silver and black duotone, graphite, and Adobe Photoshop.

ANECDOTE: DiTerlizzi took the inspiration for his designs from 1920s and 1930s Hollywood horror movies.

DISTINCTION: 2003 Caldecott Honor Book.

BIRTHDAY: Not available.

SUBJECTS: Spiders—Poetry; Flies—Poetry; Children's poetry—English; Conduct of life—Poetry; English poetry.

Starry Messenger (Farrar, Straus and Giroux, 1996). Written and illustrated by Peter Sís.

SUMMARY: This is a biography of Galilei Galileo, the Italian astronomer, mathematician, scientist, philosopher, and physicist. The story goes from Copernicus' first theory that the earth revolved around the sun through Galileo's birth in Pisa, Italy, "with stars in his eyes," through his education, early work with telescopes (and publication of his findings in *The Starry Messenger*), his trial with the church, house imprisonment, eventual blindness, and death. The Church admitted it had been wrong about Galileo's findings and its

Cover of *Starry Messenger*, written and illustrated by Peter Sís. The 1997 Caldecott Honoree for this book about Galileo illustrated the Newbery Award–winning novel *The Whipping Boy* by Sid Fleischman ten years earlier. (Reprinted by permission of Farrar, Straus and Giroux, LLC: *Starry Messenger* by Peter Sís. Copyright © 1996 by Peter Sís. www.fsgkidsbooks.com.)

treatment of him 350 years later. Each page spread features maps and drawings in the sixteenth- and seventeenth-century Italian style with added information about the stars and heavens in small script type throughout.

MEDIA: Pen and brown ink and watercolor.

ANECDOTE: Peter Sís was born in Brno, Czechoslovakia, and once wrote Maurice Sendak a letter without expecting a reply. Sendak did not write back; he telephoned instead. Sís worked as a disc jockey while he attended art school. After immigrating to the United States to work on a film associated with the 1984 Olympics (and being left behind when the Czechs and other Soviet-bloc countries did not attend out of political protest), he became well known for his illustrations of Sid Fleischman's Newbery-Award-winning novel, *The Whipping Boy* (1986). The quotes from Galileo in the book are from *Discoveries and Opinions of Galileo*, translated by Stillman Drake.

DISTINCTION: 1997 Caldecott Honor Book.

BIRTHDAY: Peter Sís: May 11, 1949.

SUBJECTS: Galilei Galileo, 1564–1642; Galileo, 1564–1642; Astronomers—Italy—Biography; Scientists—Italy—Biography; Astronomers; Scientists.

The Steadfast Tin Soldier (Scribner, 1953). Translated by M. R. James; illustrated by Marcia Brown.

SUMMARY: The Tin Soldier has one leg because they ran out of tin when making a box of twenty-five tin soldiers; all the rest of the soldiers are alike. A boy receives the box for his birthday. There are many other toys in the room as well, including a paper castle with a dancing paper lady that wears a dress with a bright spangle on the sash. She stands *en point* with one leg in the air, so the Tin Soldier thinks she has one leg like he does and falls in love with her. A series of misadventures separates the Tin Soldier from the lady, including a fall out the third-story window (from the work of a troll and the wind). The Tin Soldier falls into a crack in the sidewalk. Other misadventures include sailing in a newspaper boat down a gutter; a brush with a rat; and being swallowed by a fish in the canal. Amazingly, the Tin Soldier reappears when a maid filets the fish, and he is back in the house where he started. The paper lady is still there dancing, steadfast on one foot. The Tin Soldier shoulders his arms and stands on one leg, steadfast as well. They just look at each other like before, neither toy saying a word.

Suddenly, a boy (perhaps inspired by the troll) throws the Tin Soldier into the fire. There the soldier's paint melts and he gets very hot from either the flames or from his love for the paper dancer, or both. When a door opens, the paper lady flies on the wind into the fire. The Tin Soldier melts down to a tin heart, and the blackened spangle on the dancer's dress is all that is left of her as both burn in the heat of the flames. The implication is that the spirits of the soldier and the lady are together forever, through a tragic end.

MEDIA: Undetermined.

ANECDOTE: The blue-violet and red colors of the drawings heighten the tragic aspect of the story.

DISTINCTION: 1954 Caldecott Honor Book.

BIRTHDAY: Marcia Brown: July, 13, 1918.

SUBJECT: Toys—Fiction.

See Also: Brown, Marcia; *Cinderella, or The Little Glass Slipper*; *Once a Mouse*; *Puss in Boots*; *Shadow*; *Skipper John's Cook*; *Stone Soup*.

Stellaluna (Harcourt, 1993). Written and illustrated by Janell Cannon.

SUMMARY: A new baby fruit bat named Stellaluna travels with her mother to find food. On the way one night, an owl attacks her mother and Stellaluna is knocked down. She grabs a twig and hangs there upside down for as long as she can. By daybreak, she slips off and falls into a bird's nest where there are three baby birds. Flap, Flitter, and Pip, the babies, accept Stellaluna, and their mother feeds her a grasshopper, which she eats only after she has grown very hungry. The baby bat adapts to the birds' ways except for sleeping—she still must hang by her feet at night to sleep. Once, Mama returns to the nest to see the bat and her three babies all hanging onto the outside edge of the nest by their tiny feet. She calls them back into the nest right away and tells Stellaluna that she will not be able to stay there if she continues to teach her babies bad habits. Stellaluna agrees.

Front cover of the popular picture book, *Stellaluna*, written and illustrated by Janell Cannon. Cannon achieved her unlikely images of friendly looking bats through the media of Liquitex acrylics and Prismacolor pencils on Bristol board. (Copyright © 1993 by Janell Cannon. Copyright © by Harcourt, Inc. All rights reserved.)

When the birds learn to fly, the bat flies with them. When they learn to land on a branch, the bat sort of learns to land on a branch. She is embarrassed by her clumsiness and decides to fly all day so that she does not land clumsily in front of the birds. When they fly home, she keeps on going. She sleeps by her thumbs because she has promised not to sleep anymore by her feet. As she is sleeping by herself, a bat comes by and asks her why she is sleeping upside down. Eventually, more bats arrive, and Stellaluna tells her story. Then, one bat comes forward, sniffs her fur, and recognizes her as her baby, Stellaluna.

Her mother teaches her to fly at night, and Stellaluna fills up at a mango tree. Excited, she goes to visit Flitter, Pip, and Flap, and share her new life with them. They come back with her and discover that they cannot see at night. Stellaluna rescues them. The birds marvel at her skill with night flying, and she admits not to be able to land on her feet. They all wonder how they can be so different yet also so much alike. Stellaluna declares that no matter the mystery, they are friends.

The book concludes with "Bat Notes" that give scientific information about bats such as the anatomy of their wings, kinds of bats, lifestyles, and details about fruit bats in particular.

MEDIA: Liquitex acrylics and Prismacolor pencils on Bristol board.

ANECDOTE: Cannon wanted to depict creatures that are not often considered cute and cuddly; this was her first children's book.

DISTINCTION: *New York Times* Best Book for Children.

BIRTHDAY: Janell Cannon: November 3, 1957.

SUBJECTS: Bats—Fiction; Birds—Fiction.

Stevie (Harper, 1969). Written and illustrated by John Steptoe.

SUMMARY: Robert's mother tells him that her friend Mrs. Mack has to work all week, and she is going to begin taking care of her little boy, Stevie. Robert is an only child, and he is not happy about younger Stevie staying with them. Stevie stays all week, plays with Robert's toys, tags along with him wherever he goes, and gets dirty footprints on his bed. When the Macks leave, and Stevie no longer comes to stay, Robert misses him and remembers all the times they used to play together and the things they used to do.

MEDIA: Possibly pastel.

ANECDOTE: Steptoe created *Stevie* when he was just seventeen years old, and it was published when he was nineteen. The entire book appeared in *Life* magazine and was praised there as "a new kind of book for black children." Steptoe was just thirty-eight years old when he died.

DISTINCTION: Of historical/scholarly interest. *Stevie* was the first mainstream American picture book for children with a universal theme created by an African American.

BIRTHDAY: John Steptoe: September 14, 1950.

SUBJECT: Friendship—Fiction.

See Also: Mother Crocodile; *Mufaro's Beautiful Daughters*; *The Story of Jumping Mouse*.

The Stinky Cheese Man and Other Fairly Stupid Tales (Viking, 1992). Written by Jon Scieszka; illustrated by Lane Smith.

SUMMARY: In a well-known example of the postmodern "fractured fairy tale," this book contains ten irreverent stories that bend, twist, and shake up the traditional fairy tales on which they are based. Titles are "Chicken Licken"; "The Princess and the Bowling Ball"; "The Really Ugly Duckling"; "The Other Frog Prince"; "Little Red Running Shorts"; "Jack's Bean Problem"; "Cinderumpelstiltskin, or The Girl Who Really Blew It"; "The Tortoise and the Hair"; "The Stinky Cheese Man"; and "The Boy Who Cried 'Cow Patty.'"

MEDIA: Oil and mixed media.

ANECDOTE: The book is a compilation of stories Scieszka read to young people during author visits. Both the author and artist cite *Mad* magazine, Monty Python, and comic books as influences. Smith decided to become an artist when he grew up when he received a D on a fourth-grade math paper. The book has more pages (fifty-six) than the traditional picture book (thirty-two) because both author and artist found it necessary for the pacing of the humor in the stories.

DISTINCTION: 1993 Caldecott Honor Book.

BIRTHDAYS: Jon Sciesczka: September 8, 1954; Lane Smith: August 25, 1959.

SUBJECTS: Fairy Tales—United States; Children's Stories—American; Fairy tales; Short stories.

Stone Soup (Scribner, 1947). Written and illustrated by Marcia Brown.

SUMMARY: Three hungry soldiers in red uniforms are working their way back home after the wars. They spy a village of peasants and wonder whether they might have a good dinner and beds to sleep in there. The peasants are afraid of strangers, and they hide all of their food under beds and in lofts and down wells. When the soldiers arrive, they ask Paul and Francoise for food and shelter. The couple tells them that it has been a poor harvest, and they have little to eat themselves. They hear the same at the homes of Albert and Louise and Vincent and Marie.

The soldiers suggest to the villagers that they make a pot of stone soup for them all. The villagers are intrigued and bring the soldiers the things they ask for. These include a pot, three stones, water, fire to boil it on, then also a carrot, cabbage, beef, potatoes, barley, and milk. Each of the villagers brings something from their hiding places to the large pot of soup cooking in the center of the village. Finally, the soldiers say the soup is like the last kind they had with the king, and the villagers are quite happy. All that is needed is bread, a roast, and cider. These are supplied, and there is a great feast in the town with drinking and dancing. Afterwards, when the three soldiers ask for beds to lay their heads, they are given the finest beds in town for teaching the people to make stone soup—one sleeps in the priest's bed; one in the baker's; and one at the mayor's. The next day, the peasants thank the soldiers as they leave for teaching them how to make stone soup, such a tasty meal from just three stones.

MEDIA: Possibly ink and watercolor.

ANECDOTE: This book was the first of several folktales and fairy tales that Brown illustrated in her career.

DISTINCTION: 1948 Caldecott Honor Book.

BIRTHDAY: Marcia Brown: July 13, 1918.

SUBJECT: Folklore—France.

See Also: Brown, Marcia; *Cinderella, or The Little Glass Slipper*; *Dick Whittington and His Cat*; *Once a Mouse*; *Skipper John's Cook*; *Shadow*.

The Storm Book (Harper, 1952). Written by Charlotte Zolotow; illustrated by Margaret Bloy Graham.

SUMMARY: A little boy is studying the sky and grass outside his home as the stillness and heat give way to a summer thunder and lightning storm. Zolotow's poetic text describes what a storm is like in the country, the city, and for a fisherman coming in to shore. The boy's mother is informative and reassuring about the lightning and thunder for the boy, and she curls her arm around him gently as the storm stops, and a rainbow appears in the sky.

MEDIA: Undetermined.

ANECDOTE: Charlotte Zolotow's first picture book was *The Park Book* (Harper, 1944) and was edited by Ursula Nordstrom.

DISTINCTION: 1953 Caldecott Honor Book.

BIRTHDAY: Charlotte Zolotow: June 26, 1915.

SUBJECT: Storms—Fiction.

A Story a Story (Atheneum, 1970). Adapted and illustrated by Gail E. Haley.

SUMMARY: This story is adapted from an African folktale. Nyame, the Sky God, owns all the stories of the world. He keeps them in a gold box by his throne. Ananse, the small Spider man, wants to buy stories from the Sky God. Nyame tells him that in order to buy his stories he must bring him three things—Osebo, a leopard with horrible teeth; Mmboro, a hornet with a sting like fire; and Mmoatia, a fairy no one ever sees. Through a series of cunning maneuvers, the Spider man presents all three to the Sky God. Sky God calls his court and announces that all of his stories now belong to Ananse and will now be called Spider stories. Over time, Spider stories have come to mean stories where small people or animals succeed over forces larger than themselves.

MEDIA: Woodcuts.

ANECDOTE: Haley researched the book for one year, learning about African cooking and dancing. It took her another year to write and illustrate the book. The book contains some words from Africa. Haley explains in the beginning that it is a custom of African languages to repeat words and phrases to emphasize their meaning. For example, "so small, so small" means very small.

DISTINCTION: 1971 Caldecott Medal.

BIRTHDAY: Gail E. Haley: November 4, 1939.

SUBJECT: Folklore—Africa.

The Story about Ping (Viking, 1933). Written and illustrated by Marjorie Flack and Kurt Wiese.

SUMMARY: Ping is a beautiful duck that lives with lots of relatives on a boat with two wise eyes on the Yangtze River in China. Every morning, the dozens of family members march down a plank off the boat to the river. At the end of the day, they march back up. The last duck in line returning to the boat receives a spanking with a switch. Ping always tries to avoid being last. One day, he is fishing wrong side up when it is time to climb the plank, and he misses the call. Rather than be the one to receive the spanking, Ping swims off and does not get on the boat. The next day, he swims up to a fishing boat and is caught by a boy. The boy's family says they will have duck for dinner and puts a basket over Ping. Later on, the boy releases Ping and puts him back in the water. Along the bank of the river, Ping spies his family and rejoins them. Though he is late again, he climbs the plank to their boat home, even though he does receive a spanking for being last.

MEDIA: Lithographs.

ANECDOTE: The book was one of the first picture book collaborations between a well-known author and an established illustrator.

DISTINCTION: *New York Times* Best Book for Children.

BIRTHDAYS: Marjorie Flack: October 23, 1897; Kurt Wiese: April 27, 1887.

SUBJECTS: Ducks—Fiction; Yangtze River (China)—Fiction; China—Fiction.

See Also: You Can Write Chinese.

The Story of Ferdinand (Viking, 1936).
Written by Munro Leaf; illustrated by Robert Lawson.

SUMMARY: Unlike the other bulls in the field, Ferdinand does not like to play by butting heads and snorting and trying to look strong and powerful. Instead, he prefers to sit beneath a cork tree and smell the flowers of the field. His mother, the cow, is concerned and asks him why he does not play and butt with the others, but she is understanding when he explains his preference. As the bull grows, young Ferdinand becomes very large and strong, but he still enjoys sitting in the shade smelling flowers and does not engage in the rivalries of the others.

One day, five men come to the field to choose a bull for the bullfights in Madrid. The other bulls compete for their attention, hoping one of them will be chosen. Ferdinand is not interested and goes to sit down beneath the cork tree. When he does, he sits on a bee, and the bee stings him. At the pinch, Ferdinand jumps and bucks his head and runs around in a way that draws the men's attention to his size and strength. They take him to Madrid. A large audience of people, including ladies with flowers in their hair, waits for a big fight. The banderilleros with their pins, picadores with their spears, and the matador with his sword all parade into the ring. Finally, the door is opened for Ferdinand to enter. The banderilleros, picadores, and the matador are all afraid of him because he is so large and strong. Instead of charging as everyone expects, however, Ferdinand goes out to the middle of the ring and sits down, smelling the flowers in the ladies' hair. There is nothing anyone can do but take him back home to the field, where he no doubt continues to this day to sit quietly, smelling the flowers.

MEDIA: Black-and-white etchings.

ANECDOTE: This book is often referred to as one of the first American children's picture books suspected of having a subversive intent. Published in the ominous years before World War II, detractors labeled it as promoting communism, fascism, and anarchism. The book was banned in civil war-torn Spain, and Hitler had it burned as propaganda. Others view it as a parable of pacifism. Leaf, who wrote the story on a legal pad for Lawson in less than an hour, simply explained that it was a book written to entertain children. The book has been translated into at least sixty languages and has remained in print for more than sixty years.

DISTINCTIONS: *New York Times* Best Book for Children; NYPL 100 Picture Books Everyone Should Know; *100 Best Books for Children*.

BIRTHDAYS: Munro Leaf: December 4, 1905; Robert Lawson: October 4, 1892.

SUBJECT: Bulls—Fiction.

See Also: Wee Gillis.

The Story of Jumping Mouse (Lothrop, 1984). Retold and illustrated by John Steptoe.

SUMMARY: A young mouse lives near a big river in some brush. There, he hears stories from the older mice. He enjoys all the stories, but his favorite story is one about a faraway place. The mouse wants to visit the far-off land very much. Even though the elders warn him that it is a long, difficult journey, one day the mouse starts off. When he comes to the river, he needs a way to cross. He meets Magic Frog, who names him Jumping Mouse and gives him powerful jumping legs. She helps him cross the river and tells him to keep up hope on his challenging way.

After more difficult traveling, Jumping Mouse meets an old mouse who asks him about his strange legs. Jumping Mouse explains his dream of seeing the faraway place just once in his life. The old mouse tries to talk Jumping Mouse out of going farther. He used to have the same kinds of dreams, but all he ever found was desert. Jumping Mouse stays with the old mouse under the berry bush for a while until he decides it is time to move on. A snake gets the old mouse and makes Jumping Mouse sad. Across the stream, Jumping Mouse meets a bison. The bison is groaning because it is dying. It cannot see the fresh grass to eat. Jumping Mouse names him Eyes-of-a-Mouse and lets him borrow his to see. Jumping Mouse can no longer see. The buffalo is happy that he has new sight. He leads him across the grassy place to the mountains where Jumping Mouse must cross.

Starting up the mountain, Jumping Mouse encounters a wolf. At first he is afraid, but the wolf is also dying because it has lost its sense of smell. Jumping Mouse names him Nose-of-a-Mouse and gives him his sense of smell. The fox helps him cross the mountains for being so kind. When Jumping Mouse leaves the fox, he realizes that it will be a difficult journey indeed now with no sight and no sense of smell. He begins to cry. Suddenly, he hears the rough voice of the Magic Frog. Magic Frog tells him that his generosity has brought him to the far-off place. She tells him to jump as high as he can. He follows her instructions and jumps higher and higher. As he does so, he begins to feel very powerful. Suddenly he can see the wonderful earth below and smell the freshness of the wind and all life. Magic Frog says she is giving him a new name—Eagle—and Jumping Mouse has transformed into a majestic bald eagle that will live in the far-off place forever.

MEDIA: Graphite pencil and india ink on paper.

ANECDOTE: Steptoe's first picture book, *Stevie*, was published by Harper when he was just seventeen years old. This story is retold from the way it appears in *Seven Arrows* by Hymeyohsts Storm.

DISTINCTION: 1985 Caldecott Honor Book.

BIRTHDAY: John Steptoe: September 14, 1950.

SUBJECTS: Indians of North America—Great Plains—Folklore; Mice—Folklore.

The Stray Dog (HarperCollins, 2001). Written and illustrated by Marc Simont.

SUMMARY: On a nice day, a family goes on a picnic outside the city. While they are there, a little dog comes to play with the children. They name him Willy. When it is time to go home, the children want to take Willy home with them, but the father says he must belong to somebody, so they need to leave him behind. On their way home, the little girl says that maybe Willy did not belong to anybody. All that week, each of the family members thinks about Willy. Finally, they go back to the park for a picnic that Saturday, where, happily they see Willy again. However, this time he is running fast away from a dogcatcher.

When they ask about it, the dogcatcher explains that the dog does not belong to anybody because he does not have a collar or leash. The boy takes off his belt and presents it as the dog's collar and the girl her ribbon as his leash. They say his name is Willy, and he belongs to them. Back at home, they clean up Willy and take him to the park where people walk their pedigree dogs. Willy meets these intriguing types of dogs, but most of all he fits right in with his new family.

MEDIA: Watercolor and gouache.

ANECDOTE: The story is a retelling of a true story by Reiko Sassa of adopting a stray dog.

DISTINCTION: 2002 Caldecott Honor Book.

BIRTHDAY: Marc Simont: November 23, 1915.

SUBJECT: Dogs—Fiction.

Strega Nona (Prentice-Hall, 1975). Written and illustrated by Tomie dePaola.

SUMMARY: An old lady called "Grandma Witch," Strega Nona, lives in the town of Calabria a long time ago. Strega Nona can cure ills such as headaches, warts, and other problems. She can help women who want husbands. However, since she is getting old, she is beginning to need help keeping up her house and garden, so she puts up a sign in the village. Big Anthony answers her request for help, but Big Anthony is a person who does not pay attention. Strega Nona gives him chores to do around her house such as sweeping and washing the dishes. For his work, she gives him three coins, plus room and board. One thing he must never do, however, is touch her pasta pot. The pot is very valuable, and Strega Nona never lets anyone touch it.

One day as Big Anthony is doing his duties, he hears Strega Nona singing. When he finds her, she is singing a rhyming song over her pasta pot. The pot makes pasta, and then it stops making it when Strega Nona sings for it to stop. Big Anthony knows the pot is magic; he does not see Strega Nona throw three kisses into it when she is done. Unfortunately, when Big Anthony goes to town to fetch water the next day, he tells everyone there about the pasta pot. Nobody believes him; they call him a liar. Big Anthony is determined to prove them wrong. When Strega Nona leaves one day to visit her friend, Strega Amelia, over the mountain, Big Anthony gets his chance.

He remembers the magic words and sings them over the pot. The pot begins making pasta. He runs to the town square to tell everyone, and they come to Strega Nona's, where there is plenty of pasta for all. Even the priests and nuns of the village have their fill, and still the pot is making pasta. When Big Anthony accepts the applause and compliments from the crowd, he does not notice that the pot keeps making pasta. He does not know about the three kisses. Soon, pasta is flowing from the pot and all through the house and on out the door. Pasta runs down

the road and into the village. The villagers try to keep the pasta from coming by blocking the roads with mattresses and tables, but it flows through their town's streets anyway.

The pasta is just about ready to cover the town, when Strega Nona happens to walk by on her way back from her friend's. She knows immediately what has happened. She sings the magic words, blows the three kisses, and the pot stops. "*Grazia*," say the grateful townspeople. Then they become angry with Big Anthony and want to string him up. Strega Nona stops them, saying that the punishment must fit the crime. She takes a fork and hands it to Big Anthony. She tells him that he is the one who wanted pasta, and she wants to sleep in her bed that night, so he had better start eating.

MEDIA: Watercolor and felt-tip pen over graphite.

ANECDOTE: In the original manuscript for the book, the Big Anthony character was a servant girl named Concetta. DePaola decided that there were enough daft servant girls in literature, so he changed the character to a boy who doesn't pay attention. Contrary to popular belief, Strega Nona is not a retelling of an Italian folktale. The character of Strega Nona is an original character created by dePaola, but the story is a reworking of the "Porridge Pot" folktale.

DISTINCTION: 1976 Caldecott Honor Book.

BIRTHDAY: Tomie dePaola: September 15, 1934.

SUBJECTS: Strega Nona (fictitious character)—Fiction; Folklore—Italy.

The Sun Is a Golden Earring (Henry Holt, 1962). Written by Natalia M. Belting; illustrated by Bernarda Bryson.

SUMMARY: People of the earth have always wondered about the sky. Before there was science, there were stories and sayings. This book tells of the various explanations of the sun, moon, stars, wind, and so forth in terms of very brief stories or sayings (two to eight lines each) from around the world. These include stories from India; Hungary; Solomon Islands; Hawaiian Islands; Siberia; Estonia; Society Islands; Lapland; the Marquis Islands; North American Utes; Malaya; Mongolia; North American Navajo; North American Chippewa; and Polynesia.

MEDIA: Pencil.

ANECDOTE: Bryson is well traveled in Europe, Asia, and New Zealand, and her work has also appeared in *Scientific American*.

DISTINCTION: 1963 Caldecott Honor Book.

BIRTHDAY: Not available.

SUBJECTS: Tales; Folklore; Universe—Fiction.

Swamp Angel (Dutton, 1994). Written by Anne Issacs; illustrated by Paul O. Zelinsky.

SUMMARY: This is an original tall tale of Angelica Longrider, "born" on August 1, 1815. She was given an ax to play with in her cradle, and she helped a wagon train of pioneers out of Dejection Swamp when she was twelve years old. From that day on, she became known as Swamp Angel. There are lots of stories about Swamp Angel, but the most daring is how she fights the huge bear, Thundering Tarnation, which has been wreaking havoc on the settlements for some time. After many days of tumbling in wide and big ways, including one bout where Angel throws Tarnation up into the sky, Angel snores so loud a huge pine tree falls on the bear, and he dies. Angel lays his pelt across the state of Montana to form what people today call the Shortgrass Prairie. Tarnation's bear form is still visible in the sky where the stars mark the place where Angel threw him.

MEDIA: Oil on cherry, maple, and birch veneers.

ANECDOTE: Zelinsky made his own swamp angel out of bent wire and tape while working on the book.

DISTINCTION: 1995 Caldecott Honor Book.

BIRTHDAYS: Anne Isaacs: March 2, 1949; Paul O. Zelinsky: February 14, 1953.

SUBJECTS: Tall tales; Frontier and pioneer life—Tennessee—Fiction; Tennessee—Fiction.

See Also: Rapunzel; Rumpelstiltskin.

Swimmy (Pantheon, 1963). Written and illustrated by Leo Lionni.

SUMMARY: Swimmy is a little black fish in a school of little red ones. He is the fastest swimmer. One day a large tuna fish swims through the school and eats up all of the red fish. Though he escapes, Swimmy is alone and frightened. As he swims through the ocean, however, he comes upon many wondrous sights that cheer him up. One is a medusa; another is a lobster. There are also seaweed and an eel and sea anemones. Before long, Swimmy finds another school of little red fish just like himself hiding behind rocks and plants. He asks them to come out and swim with him, but they answer that they are afraid the big fish will eat them. Swimmy says they must think of something, and he swims about thinking of an idea. He comes back and tells them that if they swim in formation, they can look like a big fish when they swim all together, and that this will protect them. He trains them all to do this and then takes his place as the large fish's eye. Their strategy works; the big fish do not bother them, and they can swim all they like.

MEDIA: Watercolor, rubber stamping, and pencil.

ANECDOTE: Leo Lionni published his autobiography, *Between Worlds*, in 1997.

DISTINCTION: 1964 Caldecott Honor Book.

BIRTHDAY: Leo Lionni: May 5, 1910.

SUBJECT: Fish—Fiction.

See Also: Alexander and the Wind-Up Mouse; Frederick; Inch by Inch.

Sylvester and the Magic Pebble (Windmill, 1969). Written and illustrated by William Steig.

SUMMARY: Donkey Sylvester Duncan likes to collect colored pebbles. He lives with his parents at Acord Road in Oatsdale. One day while on vacation, Sylvester comes upon a shiny red pebble. When he picks up the pebble, it is raining, and he wishes the rain would stop. Instantly, the rain stops. Sylvester is amazed to see that his wish is granted, so he tries out using the pebble to make it rain and stop again. He starts on his way to take the magic pebble home, thinking how wonderful it is that anyone can have anything he or she might wish for now that he has a magic pebble.

On his way, he meets a lion and becomes so afraid that his thoughts become jumbled. Intead of wishing he were home or some other way out of his situation, Sylvester wishes he were a rock. He becomes a rock, and the lion leaves, but there is just one problem now—the pebble sits beside the rock, and he must be holding the pebble for its magic to work. The only way for Sylvester to become a donkey again is the very unlikely chance that someone will see the magic pebble, pick it up, and wish that the rock would become a donkey.

In the meantime, Sylvester's parents are very worried when he does not come home. In the morning, they start out looking for him. All the neighbors and the police cannot find him. All of the dogs in the town of Oatsdale go looking. They sniff the rock on Strawberry Hill that was actually Sylvester, but it smells like a rock instead of a donkey. His parents search for a month straight when they figure something horrible has happened to him, and they will never see their son again. They go about their days completely lost without their son.

Fall comes, and Sylvester tries to sleep more often so that he does not have to deal with his sadness and hopelessness at being a rock with little to no chance of turning back into a donkey. During the winter, a wolf climbs on top of the rock and howls. In the spring, Mr. and Mrs. Duncan come out to Strawberry Hill. Mr. Duncan says they should try to cheer up. Sylvester wakes up when he feels the warmth of his mother sitting on him. Mr. Duncan sees the lively red pebble and picks it up. He places the pebble on the rock and tells his wife that Sylvester would have liked this pebble for his collection. Sylvester, as a rock, cannot speak.

Mrs. Duncan says that she wishes Sylvester were there with them to enjoy the day. Mr. Duncan agrees, and Sylvester thinks to himself that he wishes he were himself again. Suddenly, he becomes his donkey self, with the picnic things on his back. The family is overjoyed to be together again. Back at home, Mr. Duncan puts the magic pebble in a safe. They might wish for something in the future, but right now they had all they wanted.

MEDIA: Watercolor.

ANECDOTE: This book was the first of Steig's several Caldecott and Newbery recognitions. He was a frequent contributor of cartoons to *The New Yorker*.

DISTINCTION: 1970 Caldecott Medal.

BIRTHDAY: William Steig: November 14, 1907.

SUBJECTS: Donkeys—Fiction; Magic—Fiction; Missing children—Fiction.

See Also: The Amazing Bone; *Doctor De Soto*.

T

The Talking Eggs: A Folktale from the American South (Dial, 1989). Retold by Robert D. San Souci; illustrated by Jerry Pinkney.

SUMMARY: A widow lives in the country with her two daughters, Rose and Blanche. Rose is the widow's favorite daughter because she is most like herself—mean and pretentious. Blanche is a sweet girl who works hard while her mother and sister sit around just talking. One day the widow sends Blanche to the well for some water. While she is there, Blanche sees an old woman in a tattered black shawl who asks her for a drink. The girl brings her some cool, fresh water, and the woman thanks her, saying that God will bless her generous spirit. When Blanche returns home, the water she has brought her mother has turned warm, and her mother and sister are angry at her for taking so long. They dump out the water and strike Blanche. Blanche goes running and crying to the woods.

There she meets the old woman again, who takes her home with her to comfort the girl. Blanche, however, must promise not to laugh at what she will see there. The old woman's home is deep in the woods. There, Blanche sees a two-headed cow that brays like a mule and a yard full of chickens of every color. The

woman asks Blanche to light a fire and cook supper. While she does this, the woman takes off her head and sets it in her lap, then puts it back on again. The girl becomes frightened, but the woman is still kind to her, so she does not say anything that might upset her. Out of a beef bone and one grain of rice magically appear a stew and potful of rice. This magic happens because Blanche does not complain about the poor beginnings for the meal.

After supper, the woman takes the girl out back, where they watch dozens of rabbits dressed up in clothes dance to a banjo that one rabbit plays. After this, the little girl goes to bed and falls asleep. In the morning, the old woman has Blanche milk the two-headed cow. It has the sweetest milk she has ever tasted. Then the woman tells Blanche she must go home. She may go to the henhouse first and take any talking eggs she finds there that want to go with her. She must not take any that don't want to go. On her way home, she is to throw an egg over her left shoulder in the road, where it will break and give her a surprise. She must do this for all the eggs she takes with her, and life at home will be better.

As Blanche heads home, she does as the old woman instructed her. The eggs turn into jewels and gold, fancy clothes, and even a horse and carriage. When she arrives home, the widow cooks for her the first time in a long time so that she can find out where Blanche got all the nice things. After Blanche goes to sleep, the widow and Rose conspire to find the old woman and the eggs to get more riches for themselves; they then plan to take everything to the city and leave Blanche with nothing.

Rose finds the old woman and tells her that her sister told her about the house, and she would like to see it. The old woman tells her as long as she does not laugh at what she sees, she may come in. Once inside, however, Rose laughs and makes fun of the unusual sights. Rose repeats all of the same activities as Blanche, except that she complains when it is time to cook and makes general bad comments about everything. She goes to bed without the full meal that had appeared for Blanche. She makes fun of the cow in the morning and gets only a little bit of sour milk. When the woman removes her head to brush her hair, Rose catches hold of it and tells her she will not put it back until she receives all the presents her sister got.

The old woman tells her to take the eggs that want to go with her and throw them over her right shoulder on the way home. Instead, Rose grabs the more beautiful, jeweled eggs that did not want to go. She throws them over her right shoulder on her way home, and a wolf and snakes, frogs, and yellow-jacket bees and other creatures come after her all the way home. When she arrives home, Rose and the widow discover that Blanche has already gone to the city to live well with her riches. When they try to find the old woman's cabin again, they can never find it.

MEDIA: Pencil, colored-pencil, and watercolor.

ANECDOTE: The story is adapted from a Creole folktale among Louisiana stories collected by Alcee Fortier and published in the late nineteenth century. Its origins most likely are European, and the story may have come to America with French immigrants who settled in the Mississippi Delta of the South.

DISTINCTIONS: 1990 Caldecott Honor Book; 1990 Coretta Scott King Honor Book for Illustration.

BIRTHDAYS: Jerry Pinkney: December 22, 1939; Robert D. San Souci: October 10, 1946.

SUBJECT: Folklore—United States.

See Also: Minty: The Young Harriet Tubman; Mirandy and Brother Wind; The Ugly Duckling.

Tar Beach (Crown, 1991). Written and illustrated by Faith Ringgold.

SUMMARY: Eight-year-old third grader Cassie Louise Lightfoot is flying over the George Washington Bridge in New York City. She has told her brother, Be Be, to lie still on the mattress they are on the rooftop and not tell anyone she has flown. Tar Beach is the rooftop where she and her family have cookouts, play cards, and look up at the city lights and stars, and Cassie sleeps there, dreaming of flying. She is claiming the bridge for her father, who helped build it in 1931, the same year that she was born. Daddy worked the high steel in building the bridge but was not allowed to join the Union because he was nonwhite and a half-breed, half Native American and half African American, and because Grandpa did not join. Cassie dreams of claiming the bridge and the Union Building for Daddy by flying over them. Daddy, she says, will own the building because she has claimed it for him. Mommy will not be unhappy anymore because she cannot find work in the winter. Cassie wants her to be happy like their neighbors Mr. and Mrs. Honey next door and have ice cream every night. She flies over the ice cream factory to claim it just to make sure. When Be Be wants to know how Cassie flies, she tells him that it is easy; all you need is somewhere to go that you cannot get to by any other means. Soon enough, you find yourself flying among the stars.

MEDIA: Acrylic on canvas.

ANECDOTES: This book is adapted from a story quilt also created by Faith Ringgold. The quilt is part of the collection of the Solomon R. Guggenheim Museum in New York City. Ringgold grew up in Harlem, and the George Washington Bridge was part of the cityscape where she lived. Tar Beach is a rooftop that Ringgold sees from her apartment. The story is a blend of autobiography and fiction where Cassie emancipates her father by flying to freedom, echoing African American folktales where slaves fly to freedom.

DISTINCTION: 1992 Caldecott Honor Book.

BIRTHDAY: Faith Ringgold: October 8, 1930.

SUBJECTS: African Americans—Fiction; Flight—Fiction; Harlem (New York, N.Y.)—Fiction.

T-Bone, the Baby Sitter (Harper, 1950).
Written and illustrated by Clare Turlay Newberry.

SUMMARY: Mr. and Mrs. Pinny have a new baby, and T-Bone, their black-and-white cat, seems to like to babysit. Wherever the baby is, there is T-Bone lying right beside her. One day, T-Bone feels mischievous. While the baby is getting her bath, T-Bone gets into her clean clothes and scratches them out on the floor. He grabs one of Mrs. Pinny's nylon stockings and drags it under the couch. He gets into the hats in the closet and starts tearing one with a pink feather to bits. The baby watches this and thinks it is very funny.

Mrs. Pinny is so angry with T-Bone over the hat that she tells Aunt Mabel, who just then comes to visit. Aunt Mabel suggests she take the cat back with her to catch mice at her ranch. Mrs. Pinny lets him go. The next day, however, the baby cries when there is no T-Bone to keep her company. No matter what Mrs. Pinny does to soothe her, the baby goes back to crying as soon as she is done. When Walter Pinny gets home from work, Mrs. Pinny tells him about the day and that they must get T-Bone back.

T-Bone does not like it at Aunt Mabel's either. The other animals are too noisy, and Aunt Mabel gives him only a bowl of milk to eat. He is glad to see Mr. Pinny come for him, and he goes right home. The baby is the happiest of them all with the reunion, and she says her very first word right there and then as she's hugging T-Bone. She says, "Kitty!"

MEDIA: Possibly pen, ink, and charcoal.

ANECDOTE: Newberry used her own baby daughter and cat named T-Bone as models for this story.

DISTINCTION: 1951 Caldecott Honor Book.

BIRTHDAY: Clare Turlay Newberry: April 10, 1903.

SUBJECTS: Babysitters—Fiction; Cats—Fiction.

See Also: April's Kittens; Marshmallow.

Ten, Nine, Eight (Greenwillow, 1983).
Written and illustrated by Molly Bang.

SUMMARY: This counting book counts down from ten to one, starting with ten toes and moving to familiar objects in a little girl's room as she counts down to sleep time.

MEDIA: Gouache.

ANECDOTE: Bang's parents were both medical researchers. She illustrated health manuals for the United Nations International Children's Emergency Fund (UNICEF) and Johns Hopkins before turning her hand to children's books.

DISTINCTION: 1984 Caldecott Honor Book.

BIRTHDAY: Molly Bang: December 29, 1943.

SUBJECTS: Lullabies; Counting.

See Also: When Sophie Gets Angry—Really, Really Angry.

The Thanksgiving Story (Atheneum, 1954). Written by Alice Daligliesh; illustrated by Helen Sewell.

SUMMARY: The book is divided into five sections: "Two Ships and a Big Adventure"; "A Ship Sails Alone"; "The New Land"; "New Homes in a New Land"; and "A Time of Thanksgiving." The stories describe the journey of one family, the Hopkinses, from Southampton, England, to Plymouth to what would be called much later, Plymouth, Masachusetts. Giles, Constance, and Damaris Hopkins have a new brother born on the *Mayflower*. Since he was born on the ocean, he was named Oceanus. The pilgrims are visited by Samoset, Massasoit, and Squanto in their settlement of New Plymouth. Squanto shows them how to plant corn. Only fifty-one settlers survive the first winter. Another new baby, Peregrine, whose name means pilgrim or wanderer, is born on the *Mayflower* as it is anchored off Cape Cod. Finally, there is the great feast of the pilgrims and Native people that lasts three days, full of food and games.

MEDIA: Undetermined.

ANECDOTE: Daligliesh's novel *The Courage of Sarah Noble* won a Newbery Honor Award the same year as this book earned a Caldecott Honor.

DISTINCTION: 1955 Caldecott Honor Book.

BIRTHDAYS: Alice Daligliesh: October 7, 1893; Helen Sewell: June 27, 1896.

SUBJECTS: Pilgrims (New Plymouth Colony)—Fiction; Thanksgiving Day—Fiction.

There Was an Old Lady Who Swallowed a Fly (Viking, 1997). Written and illustrated by Simms Taback.

SUMMARY: This book depicts the rhyming folk poem about an accumulation of things the old lady swallows. Cut-outs in the pages reveal all the things the old lady has swallowed until the hole grows so big from her swallowing the fly, the spider, the bird, the cat, the dog, the cow, and finally the horse that she dies, of course. The pages also contain sidebars about the goings-on such as newspaper clippings with headlines about the events and observations from the animals and the artist. The page about the bird contains names and illustrations of different species of birds.

MEDIA: Mixed media and collage on kraft paper in color.

ANECDOTE: Versions of the folk rhyme from such places around the country as Georgia, Colorado, and Ohio are collected in *Hoosier Folklore* (December 1947).

DISTINCTION: 1998 Caldecott Honor Book.

BIRTHDAY: Simms Taback: February 13, 1932.

SUBJECTS: Folk songs—English—Texts; Toys and movable books—Specimens; Folk songs; Nonsense verses; Toys and movable books.

See Also: Joseph Had a Little Overcoat.

They Were Strong and Good (Viking, 1940). Written and illustrated by Robert Lawson.

SUMMARY: The book tells the story of six lives, the author's grandparents on both sides and his parents, and concludes when he is born. The theme is that none of the six people entered the history books or became famous, but they all contributed, as all ancestors do, to the country where they lived and the family who would be descended from them. Lawson's maternal grandfather was a Scottish sea captain; his maternal grandmother was a shy Dutch girl from a farm in New Jersey. His mother was a shy, intelligent girl who was educated in a convent and learned four languages, embroidery, and how to play the organ. His paternal grandfather was a preacher from England who lived in Alabama. His paternal grandmother enjoyed his voice when he was fighting Satan. At fourteen, his father took part in the Civil War as a guidon bearer for the Confederates and was hit by a Menie ball in the leg. When he sought his future in New York after the war, the author's mother met him there and felt sorry for his limp and enjoyed his Southern accent. All of these family members, according to Lawson, were strong and good and, like many readers' families, helped make America what it is today.

MEDIA: Brush and ink.

ANECDOTE: Lawson is the only person ever to receive both a Newbery Medal and a Caldecott Medal. This book depicts some of Lawson's ancestors owning slaves.

DISTINCTION: 1941 Caldecott Medal.

BIRTHDAY: Robert Lawson: October 4, 1892.

SUBJECT: Family.

See Also: Four and Twenty Blackbirds; Wee Gillis.

Thirteen Moons on a Turtle's Back: A Native American Year of Moons (Philomel, 1992). Retold by Joseph Bruchac and Jonathan London; illustrated by Thomas Locker.

SUMMARY: While they are looking at a turtle's back, Grandfather tells Sozap that there are always thirteen scales on the shell, and these correspond to the thirteen new moons of the year. He says that the Abenaki know that each moon has a name and its own stories. Other Native people also have names for the moons, while others do not. Grandfather embarks on telling the stories he learned from his grandfather. So begins this book of thirteen poems for thirteen moons, each with the name of a moon and a story from a group of Native people.

The First Moon is "Moon of Popping Trees" (Northern Cheyenne); Second Moon, "Baby Bear Moon" (Potawatomi); Third Moon, "Maple Sugar Moon" (Anishinabe); Fourth Moon, "Frog Moon" (Cree); Fifth Moon, "Budding Moon" (Huron); Sixth Moon, "Strawberry Moon" (Seneca); Seventh Moon, "Moon When Acorns Appear" (Pomo); Eighth Moon, "Moon of Wild Rice" (Menominee); Ninth Moon, "Moose-Calling Moon" (Micmac); Tenth Moon, "Moon of Falling Leaves" (Cherokee); Eleventh Moon, "Moon When Deer Drop Their Horns" (Winnebago); Twelfth Moon, "Moon When Wolves Run Together" (Lakota Sioux); and Thirteenth Moon, "Big Moon" (Abenaki).

MEDIA: Possibly oil paintings on canvas.

ANECDOTE: There are thirteen moon cycles (from one new moon to the next) throughout the seasons of one full year. The thirteen scales on a turtle's back are thought by some Native Americans to correspond with the moons, showing that we should strive to keep our lives and all of nature in balance.

DISTINCTION: Native American Indian-commended.

BIRTHDAYS: Joseph Bruchac: October 16, 1942; Jonathan London: March 11, 1947; Thomas Locker: 1937.

SUBJECTS: Indians of North America—Legends—Poetry; Children's poetry, American; Seasons—Poetry; Indians of North America—Legends; Indians of North America—Poetry; American poetry—Collections.

Three Jovial Huntsmen (Bradbury, 1973). Written and illustrated by Susan Jeffers.

SUMMARY: The rhyming text tells of three jovial huntsmen who go out hunting on St. David's day and never bring home any game. They think they see something, but then they're not sure. They see a sailboat in the woods, but maybe it's just a house with smoke coming out the chimney. One thinks he sees the moon, but another says it was cheese. One sees a hedgehog; the other a pincushion. They end up getting sprayed by skunks and go back home, leaving the woods and the creatures within it quite intact.

MEDIA: Pen-and-ink drawings with wash overlays painted in oils.

ANECDOTE: Jeffers lived near the woods in New York state. Her first attempt at this book did not sell to a publisher; her revision won the Caldecott Honor. Randolph Caldecott himself also illustrated this story in his time, along with another story that later received a Caldecott Medal when it was redone—*Frog Went A-Courtin'*.

DISTINCTION: 1974 Caldecott Honor Book.

BIRTHDAY: Susan Jeffers: October 7, 1942.

SUBJECT: Nursery rhymes.

The Three Pigs (Clarion, 2001). Retold and illustrated by David Wiesner.

SUMMARY: The text begins as the traditional three little pigs' story with the wolf, the three pigs, and the houses made of straw, sticks, and bricks, but soon something extraordinary happens. When the wolf blows down the house of sticks, the pig emerges from behind the frame of the illustration, safe and sound, and begins another amazing adventure through the picture book itself. The pigs fold up pages into a paper airplane and fly away for several pages until they crash. Soon they realize they have landed in another storybook altogether, a nursery rhyme book with softer colors and differently designed illustrations. They run out of that one and into a black-and-white-line-drawn book about dragons. They befriend the dragon in the story, and soon, they are in what appears to be a museum gallery of picture book illustrations with some of the characters from the other books. They find the panels of their own original book lying flat on the floor of the gallery-like space and pick them up on end again like windows or wall paintings. When they reenter the three pigs' story, how-

ever, now they have brought the dragon and other characters with them. The dragon scares away the wolf, and the pigs begin messing with the letters of the text over their heads until it reads that they live happily ever after.

MEDIA: Watercolor, gouache, colored inks, pencil, and colored pencil on Fabriano hot press paper.

ANECDOTE: Wiesner says that this book resulted from the pigs at the end of his book, *Tuesday*, suddenly taking to the air. He decided to give the pigs a book of their own. The book makes an excellent subject for the discussion of picture books as a genre.

DISTINCTION: 2002 Caldecott Medal.

BIRTHDAY: David Wiesner: February 5, 1956.

SUBJECTS: Pigs—Fiction; Characters in literature—Fiction.

See Also: Tuesday; Wiesner, David.

Thy Friend, Obadiah (Viking, 1969). Written and illustrated by Brinton Turkle.

SUMMARY: Obadiah Starbuck is befriended by a seagull that will not leave his side. At first Obadiah is annoyed by the gull. It follows him all around Nantucket town, where he lives. It follows him to the wharf, to the Meeting House with his family (which includes Father, Mother, Moses, Asa, Rebecca, and Rachel) on First Day (Sunday). One day, Mother sends Obadiah on an errand to the mill for flour. On the way home, the boy slips on the ice on Jacob Slade's hill and loses the penny Slade had given him and gets the flour wet. Other gulls are perched on the roofs of Orange Street, but the friendly seagull is not around. Later Obadiah sees the gull with a fishhook wrapped around its beak down at the wharf. He removes the hook from the bird's beak, and the gull flies away. Obadiah thinks the gull may be gone for good, until Mother sees it perched outside his window on the chimney when the boy is in bed. Obadiah agrees that by helping the gull, he is now also the gull's friend.

MEDIA: Undetermined.

ANECDOTE: This book is the second of four Obadiah books set in nineteenth-century Nantucket.

DISTINCTION: 1970 Caldecott Honor Book.

BIRTHDAY: Brinton Turkle: August 15, 1915.

SUBJECTS: Friendship; Seagulls—Fiction; Nantucket Island (Mass.)—Fiction; Quakers—Fiction.

Tibet Through the Red Box (Farrar, Straus and Giroux, 1998). Written and illustrated by Peter Sís.

SUMMARY: When the author was a child, his father, who was a filmmaker, was sent away on a film project to Tibet, many miles away from their home in Prague, Czechoslovakia. He was to document the building of a road to Tibet by the Chinese military and was to be gone a total of two months. He was told the road would bring medicine and other advantages of the twentieth century to isolated Tibet. The officials told him to stay with the camp and not stray because if they did, they would surely run into "brigands." The two months stretched to fourteen over a long and adventurous trial. To the young author, Christmases came and went without his beloved father. Peter was not well and fell, resulting in a long stay in a "white" bed, partly paralyzed. When he woke one particular day after a long recovery, his father was there, touching various parts of his body, and when he did, Peter was able to feel them again.

The book is a mystical journey through the red box that represents Tibet for Peter. The box belongs to his father and contains diaries, maps, and other treasures from his experience there. His father got lost away from his employers and spent time trying to locate Lhasa so that he could warn the Dalai Llama of the

Front cover of *Tibet Through the Red Box*, written and illustrated by Peter Sís. The mystical mysteries of the red box in this book for older readers are evoked through watercolor, pen and ink, and oil pastel. Sís received the Caldecott Honor for his work in 1999. (Reprinted by permission of Farrar, Straus and Giroux, LLC: *Tibet Through the Red Box* by Peter Sís. Copyright © 1998 by Peter Sís. www.fsgkids books.com.)

approaching road and what he had determined would be the resulting threats to the Tibetan way of life. All along the way, he encountered a gentle, happy, and generous people, no brigands of any sort. A mysterious "Jingle Boy," wearing red and bells and bringing him a letter from his family, blends and mingles in his memory, and in Peter's retelling from childhood, with the Dalai Llama Peter's father sees.

Throughout the book, Tibet is presented in all of its mystery, splendor, and wonder. Peter understands how impossible it is for his father to share everything he experienced while he was away and how he may never understand all of it himself. The book is a journey through two memories and a faraway and different land, and it is also a journey of a man back to his son and a son back to his father.

MEDIA: Watercolor, pen and ink, and oil pastel.

ANECDOTE:The back flap of the book shows a photograph of Peter with his father and his son.

DISTINCTION: 1999 Cadecott Honor Book.

BIRTHDAY: Peter Sís: May 11, 1949.

SUBJECT: Tibet (China)—Description and travel.

See Also: Starry Messenger.

Time Flies (Crown, 1994). Conceived and illustrated by Eric Rohmann.

SUMMARY: This is a wordless picture book. A bird flies into the window of a natural history museum where there are dinosaur skeletons on display. A flash of lightning outside the window marks a magic moment when the viewer's perception is altered to go back in time, and the dinosaurs appear to be living outside in their own time as the viewer follows close-ups of the bird's journey. It is unclear whether the bird is actually flying around the large dinosaurs in a diorama display or whether time itself has "flown." The bird flies around several different kinds of dinosaurs, around their large heads and legs, giving a sense of how really large they are compared to the tiny bird. Finally, the bird exits back out the museum window, which a dinosaur gargoyle guards.

MEDIA: Oil.

ANECDOTE:Rohmann has said that he creates the pictures for most of his books before he writes the words. This book has no words at all.

DISTINCTION: 1995 Caldecott Honor Book.

BIRTHDAY: Eric Rohmann: October 26, 1957.

SUBJECTS: Stories without words; Birds—Fiction; Dinosaurs—Fiction; Time travel—Fiction.

See Also: My Friend Rabbit.

Time of Wonder (Viking, 1957). Written and illustrated by Robert McCloskey.

SUMMARY: The book describes living on an island in Penobscot Bay off the coast of Maine for the summer. One can see rain approaching as the clouds dump showers on each island on their way to this one. Foggy mornings turn yellow as the sun burns it off and presents a clear day. Sailboats dot the water at the height of summer when visitors arrive for their vacations. Children play on large rocks that once were covered by glaciers. The end of summer brings hurricane season, and this is a challenge for all who live on the islands. Seagulls sit down, all facing the same direction. Boats gets anchored or hoisted up from the beach. The storm surge is visible in the distance as the hurricane shoves the water ahead of it. At the height of the storm, the cabin door can unlatch, spilling Parchesi games, lamps, whipping hair, and everything inside. People put dish towels underneath doors to try to keep out the spray of salt. They sing to try to keep calm. Finally the moon shines, and the storm starts to lose its strength. The wind slows to a lullaby.

Outside the next morning, trees have fallen, and people must clean them up. Seaweed washed up on the beach gets used to fertilize the garden. Children find shells and arrowheads in a hole where a tree has uprooted, and they realize that Native American children probably played on that same spot many years ago. Amazingly, the hummingbirds are still around, though they will leave soon. The sunflowers have sprung back up from where the storm flattened them and have turned their faces again toward the sun. Finally, it is time to leave for the summer and go back to school. Children take a last breath of salty air with some sadness about leaving and some eagerness to go back to school. It is a time of wonder about the new things discovered and the new questions one has, such as where do hummingbirds go during a hurricane.

MEDIA: Casein.

ANECDOTE: McCloskey was the first artist to ever receive two Caldecott Medals. He lived on an island off the coast of Maine with his family, which was the inspiration for this book.

DISTINCTION: 1958 Caldecott Medal.

BIRTHDAY: Robert McCloskey: September 15, 1914.

SUBJECTS: Islands—Fiction; Maine—Fiction.

See Also: Blueberries for Sal; Journey Cake, Ho!; Make Way for Ducklings; McCloskey, Robert; *One Morning in Maine.*

Timothy Turtle (Welch, 1946). Written by Al Graham; illustrated by Tony Palazzo.

SUMMARY: Timothy Turtle of Took-a-look Lake has a business with a duck called Turtle & Drake where he shuffles passengers across the lake on his back. He has everything a turtle could want except that he wants to be famous. The pine tree and Frothingham W. Frog both suggest that he become an adventurer and explore beyond Took-a-look Hill. Timothy goes home and packs a bag, ties it to the top of his shell, and heads out. As he begins the long climb up the hill, some rocks come tumbling down and tip him over. He cannot right himself again, but he tries to do so by rocking back and forth until finally he completes a somersault and manages to get back on his feet. This adventure is enough for Timothy, and he heads back home to Took-a-look Lake, where he is greeted by all the animals. Barnaby Bee, who was present on the hill to see Timothy's somersault, tells everyone about his feat, and Timothy becomes famous after all for managing to do what no other turtle before him has done.

MEDIA: Possibly pen and ink and watercolor.

ANECDOTE: Graham wrote for *The Saturday Evening Post* and *The New Yorker.* Palazzo's artwork appeared at the Museum of Modern Art and the Chicago Art Institute.

DISTINCTION: 1947 Caldecott Honor Book.

BIRTHDAYS: Al Graham: 1897; Tony Palazzo: 1902.

SUBJECTS: Turtles—Fiction; Stories in rhyme.

Tom Tit Tot (Scribner, 1965). Retold and illustrated by Evaline Ness.

SUMMARY: The story is an English version of Rumplestiltskin. A woman bakes five pies and tells her daughter to put them on the windowsill, where their crusts will soften, or "come again." Misunderstanding, the daughter eats the pies, since she thinks they will reappear. At supper, the woman asks the daughter for a pie, but they are all gone. The daughter admits to eating them, and the woman goes to her spinning wheel and sings about her daughter eating all the pies. The king goes by and hears the woman singing. When he inquires, the woman does not want to tell about her daughter eating five pies in one day, so she changes the words to her song to say that her daughter spun five skeins today.

The king says he will marry the woman's daughter under the following conditions—for eleven months out of the year, she could live well and be rich, but for the twelfth month, he expected her to spin five skeins every day. If she did not do this, he would kill her. The woman agrees, thinking they can figure out the skein business with plenty of time. The king and the woman's daughter are married. At the end of eleven months, the king locks her in a room, and she is expected to spin the skeins. She is at a loss. A small black thing comes into the room and offers to spin them for her. He says that if she can't guess its name by the end of the month, then she will be his. The queen guesses names such as Bill, Mark, Nicodemus, Sammie, and Methusalem, but none of these is correct.

Front cover of *Tops & Bottoms*, written and illustrated by Janet Stevens. This 1996 Caldecott Honor book opens vertically rather than horizontally. (Copyright © 1995 by Janet Stevens. Copyright © by Harcourt, Inc. All rights reserved.)

The king tells the queen that he was out hunting and saw a little black thing spinning and singing that its name was Tom Tit Tot. The woman knows what to do. The next day, she guesses a few more names with the black thing—Solomon, Zebedee—but then she guesses its correct name. The black thing gives out a shriek and disappears, never to be seen again.

MEDIA: Woodcuts.

ANECDOTE: The folktale is derived from the way the story appears in *English Folk and Fairy Tales*, edited by Joseph Jacobs.

DISTINCTION: 1966 Caldecott Honor Book.

BIRTHDAY: Evaline Ness: April 24, 1911.

SUBJECTS: Fairy Tales—England; Folklore—England.

See Also: Sam, Bangs & Moonshine.

Tops & Bottoms (Harcourt, 1995). Written and illustrated by Janet Stevens.

SUMMARY: This book opens vertically rather than horizontally. There is a lazy bear who is the son of a hardworking bear. Bear has lots of land and money, but no ambition. Hare and Mrs. Hare live nearby. Hare lost all his land when he lost a bet with a tortoise and had to sell his land to Bear to pay off the debt. Now, Hare's family is hungry, and he and Mrs. Hare comes up with a plan. They offer to go into business with Bear. They will work a field for Bear, while letting him sleep. They will split the profits in half. All Bear has to do is tell Hare which half of the crops he wants, the tops or the bottoms. Between yawns, Bear agrees to the plan and says that he will take the tops of the field's crops. When the rabbits plant and weed carrots, radishes, and beets and give Bear the leafy tops and take the vegetable bottoms for themselves, Bear makes them plant again. This time he wants the bottoms of the plants.

So, this time the Hare family plants lettuce,

broccoli, and celery. The family takes the leafy vegetable tops, and Bear gets nothing but roots. The next year Bear demands a crop where he receives both tops and bottoms. Again, he sleeps the entire time that the rabbit family plants and tends to the field. This time, they plant corn. At harvest time, they remove the roots and give them to Bear and the tassels on top of the cornstalks and give them to Bear, too. They keep the ears of corn from the middle of the stalks for themselves. Now, Bear is wide awake and not happy. He tells them he no longer wants to be in business with the Hare and his family. By now, Hare can feed his family and even opens a vegetable stand to earn money. With the money, he buys back his land. Bear never again sleeps through all seasons but now tends his own fields, and though they remain neighbors, Bear and the rabbits never go back into business together.

MEDIA: Watercolor, colored pencil, and gesso on paper made by hand by Ray Tomasso, Denver, Colorado.

ANECDOTE: At one time, Stevens designed fabrics for Hawaiian shirts.

DISTINCTION: 1996 Caldecott Honor Book.

BIRTHDAY: Janet Stevens: January 17, 1953.

SUBJECTS: African Americans—Folklore; Folklore—United States; Hares—Folklore; Bears—Folklore.

The Treasure (Farrar, Straus and Giroux, 1978). Written and illustrated by Uri Shulevitz.

SUMMARY: Isaac is a man who goes to bed hungry every night. One night he has a dream. He is told in the dream to go to the capital city and look for a treasure underneath the Royal Bridge. Isaac thinks this is only a dream, so he ignores it. When he has the dream a third time, he thinks maybe he should check it out.

Isaac walks most of the long journey to the

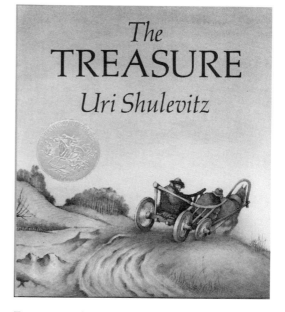

Front cover of *The Treasure*, written and illustrated by Uri Shulevitz. Before finally deciding on watercolors, Shulevitz tried several different media for illustrating what would later become a 1980 Caldecott Honor book. (Reprinted by permission of Farrar, Straus and Giroux, LLC: *The Treasure* by Uri Shulevitz. Copyright © 1978 by Uri Shulevitz. www.fsgkids books.com.)

capital city. When he gets to the Royal Bridge, he finds it is heavily guarded. He comes by every day and walks around the bridge from morning until night, though he does not dare search under it. Finally, a guard asks him why he keeps coming around. Isaac tells him about his dream. The guard says that if he listened to his dreams, he would go look for treasure in the city. The poor man comes from underneath the stove of a man named Isaac.

Isaac returns home, getting a ride here or there, but mostly walking back over the mountains and through the forests. He digs underneath his stove, and there he finds the treasure. He is never hungry again and sends a fine ruby to the guard for his kindness.

MEDIA: Watercolor with black line on acetate.

ANECDOTE: For this book, Shulevitz

tried out different media before deciding on watercolors. The other media included inks, oils, opaque watercolors, and tempera paints.

DISTINCTION: 1980 Caldecott Honor Book.

BIRTHDAY: Uri Shulevitz: February 27, 1935.

SUBJECT: Folklore—England.

A Tree Is Nice (Harper, 1956). Written by Janice Udry; illustrated by Marc Simont.

SUMMARY: The book describes all the niceties of trees for the very young. Trees make shade; they can be climbed; they provide safety for cats from dogs; they drop leaves in which children can play in the autumn; they drop sticks that children can draw with in the sand; and much more.

MEDIA: Gouache over watercolor.

ANECDOTE: Udry wrote the book after seeing a place where many trees were cut down and replaced with a housing development. Simont received so many questions about his biography after winning his Caldecott Medal for this book that the facts of his own life started sounding like someone else's life to him.

DISTINCTION: 1957 Caldecott Medal.

BIRTHDAYS: Marc Simont: November 23, 1915; Janice Udry: June 14, 1928.

SUBJECT: Trees.

Truck (Greenwillow, 1980). Written and illustrated by Donald Crews.

SUMMARY: In this wordless picture book, the viewer follows a truck full of new tricycles as it makes its delivery from one city, through a tunnel, down a hill, stopping at a truck stop, through the rain, onto the highway, through the fog and over a bridge, to its delivery station at the other end where the back is opened to reveal the many colorful tricycle boxes inside.

MEDIA: Four halftone separations with black line drawings.

ANECDOTE: Crews' first book for children was *We Read: A to Z*, published in 1967.

DISTINCTION: 1981 Caldecott Honor Book.

BIRTHDAY: Donald Crews: August 30, 1938.

SUBJECTS: Trucks—Fiction; Stories without words.

See Also: Freight Train.

Tuesday (Clarion, 1991). Conceived and illustrated by David Wiesner.

SUMMARY: At a lily pond somewhere in the United States around 8:00 P.M. on a Tuesday, something magical happens that is apparently recorded only by this book's illustrator. A turtle on a log watches as frogs take off into the air on lily pads. Thousands of flying frogs on lily pads flip and spin in the air, scaring away birds, flying over houses, and past windows where a man in a kitchen is eating a late-night sandwich. The frogs get caught in laundry on the line, fly in and out of houses, flick on the television from the remote in front of an asleep old woman, get chased by dogs, then chase dogs, then fall off their lily pads, getting caught in the branches of trees. They return to the pond in the wee hours of the next morning. The next day, detectives puzzle over the fallen lily pads and water droplets they see all over the road. The next Tuesday, at right about the same time, pigs begin to fly, and luckily the illustrator is on the scene again to catch their takeoff.

MEDIA: Watercolor.

ANECDOTE: The flying pigs at the end of this book resurface in Wiesner's *The Three Pigs.* The artist started working on his "frog book" while riding on an airplane. He chose the day Tuesday for the magical day of the week because of the "ooze" sound in the word. His first interest in frogs arose after illustrating a March 1989 cover for *Cricket* magazine. When Wiesner first showed his editor the dummy book for *Tuesday*, she laughed, and they both "sat around making pig and frog noises for awhile." The man eating the sandwich is Wiesner himself because he wanted to be in the middle of the story. One of the frogs flying by the window in that scene waves at the viewer. In order to make his frogs appear more real, Wiesner studied nature photographs and sculpted a clay model of a frog.

DISTINCTION: 1992 Caldecott Medal.

BIRTHDAY: David Wiesner: February 5, 1956.

SUBJECT: Frogs—Fiction.

See Also: Sector 7; The Three Pigs; Wiesner, David.

The Two Reds (Harcourt, 1951). Written by William Lipkind (pseud. Will); illustrated by Nicholas Mordivanoff (pseud. Nicolas).

SUMMARY: The two Reds are a boy named Joey with red hair and a red cat whose name is known only to cats but may be Mr. Furpatto Purrcatto. They both live on St. Mark's Place, where it is very noisy. The backyards are much quieter. Both Red the boy and Red the cat like fish; however, the cat likes the goldfish that Red the boy keeps in a bowl, so the two Reds are not friends. One morning, the day is fine, and the two Reds find themselves walking down the street at the same time. Red the cat is hungry from being out all night dancing. They see a horse, pigeon, and a gypsy's parrot. None of these serve what ei-ther Red wants in terms of entertainment or, in the case of Red the cat, food.

Suddenly, Red the boy smells fire, and Red the cat smells fish. The boy looks through a peek-hole in a fence. He sees a club called the Signal Senders dressed in feathered head-dresses and initiating a new member around a camp fire. He watches the show, but then he is seen and chased away as a spy. The cat finds a fish vendor on St. Mark's Place and steals away a small fish as he is chased by the fishman. Running down toward a street corner on one side is the boy with the Signal Senders behind him; down the other side is the cat with the fishman close to him. There is a big collision of boys and fishman and cat. The two Reds hurry away from the crowd and sit on a stoop, while the fishman chases the gang of boys away. The two Reds make an agreement that the cat will not harm the boy's goldfish or annoy his friends, and now they are together all the time.

MEDIA: Acetate separations using pen, ink, and brush.

ANECDOTE: The red of both "reds" stands out against the other artwork in the book.

DISTINCTION: 1951 Caldecott Honor Book.

BIRTHDAY: William Lipkind: December 17, 1904.

SUBJECTS: Cats—Fiction; Color—Fiction.

See Also: Finders Keepers.

U

The Ugly Duckling (Morrow, 1999). Story by Hans Christian Andersen, adapted and illustrated by Jerry Pinkney.

SUMMARY: The traditional ugly duckling story of the misfit duck that turns into a beautiful swan is retold in full text and lavishly depicted with Pinkney's watercolors.

MEDIA: Watercolor.

ANECDOTE: Pinkney was a nominee for the Hans Christian Andersen Award.

DISTINCTION: 2000 Caldecott Honor Book.

BIRTHDAYS: Hans Christian Andersen: April 2, 1805; Jerry Pinkney: December 22, 1939.

SUBJECTS: Fairy tales; Andersen, H.C. (Hans Christian), 1805–1875.

See Also: Half a Moon and One Whole Star; Mirandy and Brother Wind; The Patchwork Quilt.

Umbrella (Viking, 1958). Written and illustrated by Yaro Yashima.

SUMMARY: Momo, which means "peach" in Japanese, has turned three, and for her birthday she receives her first umbrella and some rain boots. She cannot wait until a rainy day arrives so that she may try them out; she even gets up one night at midnight, just to look at them. On one sunny day, she suggests she could use her umbrella to shield out the sun, but her mother tells her she must wait for rain to use her umbrella. On a windy day, she says maybe she can use her umbrella to block the wind, but her mother tells her the wind might damage the umbrella. Finally, a rainy day arrives, and Momo can use her umbrella and rain boots. She stands right up tall like a lady who is grown-up. She listens to the sound of the rain on the umbrella. She watches it outside her nursery school window; it rains all day. When her father comes to pick her up, she does not forget her umbrella as she has her scarf or mittens before. Now that Momo is a big girl she does not remember this first day of using an umbrella nor the fact that it was also the first day she walked without holding either of her parents' hands.

MEDIA: Watercolor; pencil and brush for direct separations.

ANECDOTE: The book is dedicated to Momo on her eighth birthday.

DISTINCTION: 1959 Caldecott Honor Book.

BIRTHDAY: Taro Yashima: September 21, 1908.

SUBJECTS: Umbrellas—Fiction; Rain and Rainfall—Fiction.

See Also: Crow Boy.

Uptown (Henry Holt, 2000). Written and illustrated by Bryan Collier.

SUMMARY: Uptown is many things, like the Metro-North train that goes over the Harlem River. The book shows the sights, smells, tastes, and sounds one encounters Uptown. These include chicken and waffles, jazz, the Apollo Theater, brownstones, 125th Street shopping, barbershops, Van Der Zee photographs, basketball at Ruckers, swing awnings on windows, sisters dressed in yellow, an orange sunset over the Hudson, and a song sung by the Boys Choir of Harlem. This uptown Harlem neighborhood is the boy narrator's home.

MEDIA: Watercolor and collage.

ANECDOTE: This book was Bryan Collier's picture book debut.

DISTINCTION: 2001 Coretta Scott King Award for Illustration.

BIRTHDAY: Not available.

SUBJECTS: African Americans—Fiction; Harlem (New York, N.Y.)—Fiction.

V

Van Allsburg, Chris (1949–). Artist and author. The famed author and illustrator of the late-twentieth-century Christmas classic *The Polar Express* was born in Grand Rapids, Michigan, on June 18, 1949. Van Allsburg's father ran a dairy that turned milk into ice cream. Though he was admired for his skill at art from an early age, Van Allsburg became involved in more social activities such as playing ball. After high school, he thought he might major in prelaw or forestry at the University of Michigan. On a lark, he enrolled in a figure drawing course and realized that art truly was his passion. After taking a sculpture class, he declared a major in fine arts.

At college, Chris met a woman named Lisa, and the couple was married. After he received his B.F.A., Chris decided to continue his studies for a M.F.A. in sculpture at the Rhode Island School of Design (RISD), and the two moved to Providence. There he worked with turning and laminating hardwood, molding latex, rubber, silicone, and plaster and learned how to cast metal through a variety of techniques. To relax between sculpting projects, he would often make large narrative drawings. His drawings led to his being invited to join the staff of RISD, which he did in 1977. Lisa took on a job as a teacher.

Lisa often brought home children's books from school and commented to Chris that he could do a book of equal or better quality. At the time, Chris was focusing more on his sculpture and was preparing for an exhibit in a New York gallery. Lisa was producing a local television show when she met children's book artist David Macauley and brought him home to dinner. When Macauley saw Van Allsburg's drawings, he joined Lisa in encouraging Chris to show his portfolio to Macauley's publisher, Houghton Mifflin. Van Allsburg didn't want to take the time just then to do so, so Lisa took on this role and actually acquired some manuscript assignments for Chris as an illustrator. When Chris read the stories written by others, he found that they did not interest him, and besides, he was hard at work on his sculpture. After the show in New York, he gave the manuscripts another look but decided that instead he would write a story of his own. That first book became *The Garden of Abdul Gasazi*, which, after Lisa again acted as agent and showed it to Walter Lorraine, was purchased and published by Houghton Mifflin in 1979. This first picture book received a Caldecott Honor Book Award in 1980. The bull terrier in that story that may or may not have turned into a duck has made cameo appearances in each of Van Allsburg's subsequent picture books.

Author-illustrator Chris Van Allsburg sits at his attic studio worktable in Providence, Rhode Island. The influence of Van Allsburg's early work as a sculptor at the Rhode Island School of Design is apparent in many of his picture books. (AP/Wide World Photos.)

Jumanji (Houghton Mifflin, 1981) came next. For one of his assignments to students, Van Allsburg asked them to find a believable way to put wild animals inside a house, including the details of the domestic interior. Chris did the assignment right alongside his students and realized that he had a picture book on his hands when he had completed the assignment. The book won the Caldecott Medal in 1982. Other picture books quickly followed every one to two years throughout the 1980s and 1990s: *Ben's Dream* (Houghton Mifflin, 1982); *The Wreck of the Zephyr* (Houghton Mifflin, 1983); *The Mysteries of Harris Burdick* (Houghton Mifflin, 1984); *The Polar Express* (Houghton Mifflin, 1985); *The Stranger* (Houghton Mifflin, 1986); *The Alphabet Theatre Proudly Presents the Z Was Zapped* (Houghton Mifflin, 1987); *Two Bad Ants* (Houghton Mifflin, 1988); *Just a Dream* (Houghton Mifflin, 1990); *The Wretched Stone* (Houghton Mifflin, 1991); *The Widow's Broom* (Houghton Mifflin, 1992); *The Sweetest Fig* (Houghton Mifflin, 1993); and *Bad*

Day at Riverbend (Houghton Mifflin, 1995). *Zathura: A Space Adventure* (Houghton Mifflin) was published in 2002. In addition to illustrating his own picture books, Van Allsburg also illustrated some books by Mark Halprin, including *Swan Lake* (Houghton Mifflin, 1989); *City in Winter* (Viking, 1996); and *The Veil of Snows* (Viking, 1997).

Van Allsburg's picture book art is characterized by its soft, surrealistic edges and play with light and shadow. The real and the fantastic blend one into the other effortlessly, often taking readers by surprise or putting them off balance. His stories are marked by mystery—he usually leaves some element of knowledge shrouded in the unknown before a story begins and as it ends. Readers are not often sure what might happen after the story ends, and they find themselves wondering. Van Allsburg purposely leaves the story open-ended enough at both beginning and ending so that the reader's imagination becomes engaged and an active participant in the story. This is an important technique in helping the reader suspend disbelief and enjoy the fantasies he creates. This device is often reflected in the artwork as well, when characters, animals, and scenes are literally cut off at the edge of a page, leaving the reader to imagine the portions that he or she does not see. Perhaps the strongest example of Van Allsburg inviting the reader in to his books is *The Mysteries of Harris Burdick*, which contains simply a series of fourteen pictures with captions beneath them that leave the reader full of curiosity and wonder and wanting to invent his or her own story to go with the picture. Many teachers have used the book as story starters for creative writing assignments with their students.

In addition to the Caldecott distinctions earned by his first two picture books, Van Allsburg won the 1986 Caldecott Medal for *The Polar Express*, arguably his most popular picture book. In its first five years it sold over a million copies and remained on the *New York Times* Bestseller List for weeks. Van Allsburg himself has admitted what millions of adults and children know about the story as well—that it is a book about the gift of faith, about the desire to believe in something. Van Allsburg discovered the theme organically as an artist should, after the story was already written and not as a theme he set out to write a story about. He simply followed the boy on the train in his imagination and went where it led. In 2004, the book was made into an animated film starring Tom Hanks as the voice of the conductor and several other characters. Van Allsburg added scenes about a mysterious hobo and other adventures on the train to expand the story for film. At the end of both the book and the film, however, the bell continues to ring for all those who continue to believe.

DISTINCTIONS: 1982, 1986 Caldecott Medal (one of only seven multiple gold medalists) for *Jumanji* and *The Polar Express*, respectively; 1980 Caldecott Honor Book Award for *The Garden of Abdul Gasazi*.

Further Reading: Allis, Sam. "Rhinoceros in the Living Room." *Time* (November 13, 1989): 108; Hubbard, Kim, and Dirk Mathison. "Chris Van Allsburg, A Rare Bird among Illustrators, Brings His Art to a Fresh Christmas Treasure." *People* 32, no. 24 (December 11, 1989): 142–144; Ford, Elizabeth A. "Resurrection Twins: Visual Implications in *Two Bad Ants*." *Children's Literature Association Quarterly* 15, no. 1 (1990 Spring): 8–10; Lessem, Don. "The Illustrator Man." *The Boston Globe Magazine* (November 6, 1988): 21–23+; Newmeyer, Peter. "How Picture Books Mean: The Case of Chris Van Allsburg." *Children's Literature Association Quarterly* 15, no. 1 (1990 Spring): 2–8; Stanton, Joseph. "The Dreaming Picture Books of Chris Van Allsburg." *Children's Literature: Annual of the Modern Language Association Division of Children's Literature and the Children's Literature Association* 24 (1996): 161–179.

See Also: The Garden of Abdul Gasazi; *Jumanji*; *The Polar Express*.

The Very Hungry Caterpillar (Philomel, 1969). Written and illustrated by Eric Carle.

SUMMARY: A very small caterpillar pops out of an egg on a leaf. He is very hungry and begins his journey through an apple on Monday; two pears on Tuesday; three plums on Wednesday; four strawberries on Thursday; five oranges on Friday; a mixture of ten sweet and spicy foods on Saturday (now he has a stomach ache); and a green leaf on Sunday, which makes him feel better. In the paper for each page are holes that signify the caterpillar chomping straight through the book. At the end of the book, the caterpillar has grown very large and builds himself a cocoon. Later, he becomes a beautiful butterfly.

MEDIA: Collage.

ANECDOTE: Carle refreshed the artwork for the book's twentieth-anniversary edition in 1989 using archival materials and slightly brighter and more textured colors.

The book has been translated into thirty languages and has sold 20 million copies worldwide.

DISTINCTIONS: *New York Times* Best Book for Children; NYPL 100 Picture Books Everyone Should Know; *100 Best Books for Children.*

BIRTHDAY: Eric Carle: June 25, 1929.

SUBJECTS: Toy and movable books—Specimens; Caterpillars—Fiction; Toy and movable book.

See Also: Brown Bear, Brown Bear, What Do You See?; Carle, Eric; Eric Carle Museum of Picture Book Art.

A Very Special House (Harper, 1953). Written by Ruth Krauss; illustrated by Maurice Sendak.

SUMMARY: Through this rhyming story, a small boy imagines a house where the doors, walls, and tables are very special. Beds are for jumping; tables are to rest one's feet upon; walls are for drawing; and so forth. Also, he can bring home animals (an old lion is able to eat the stuffing out of chairs); they can all play they are chickens, then sing opera and sprinkle cracker crumbs under all the cushions. A giant spills his drink, and a rabbit eats a chunk out of the door. He realizes by the end of the book that the house does not exist anywhere except in his own mind, but that is very well.

MEDIA: Possibly pen and ink.

ANECDOTE: Krauss incorporates a kind of child's stream-of-consciousness in the text that emphasizes her attention to the interior life.

DISTINCTION: 1954 Caldecott Honor Book.

BIRTHDAYS: Ruth Krauss: July 25, 1901; Maurice Sendak: June 10, 1928.

SUBJECTS: Imagination—Fiction; Houses—Fiction; Stories in rhyme.

See Also: In the Night Kitchen; Sendak, Maurice; *Where the Wild Things Are.*

The Village of Round and Square Houses (Little, Brown, 1986). Written and illustrated by Ann Grifalconi.

SUMMARY: A girl, Osa, tells of her village where men live in square houses and women in round ones. The village is Tos, at the base of the Naka Mountain in the Bameni Hills of West Africa. When their elders, Gran'pa Oma and Uncle Domo, visit the round house for dinner, the women and children bring out stools for their comfort and as a sign of respect. The elders, who are respected for being closer to the ancestors than the rest, ask to see the children and then ask them what they have learned that day. Mama and Gran'ma Tika cook the meal. After dinner, the men retire to their square houses to smoke and talk. Gran'ma smokes also, after everything has calmed down. She smokes a pipe outside, looking up at the evening sky.

She tells Osa a story about when Naka erupted, destroyed everything in its path, and covered the people with ash. When they returned to their village after enduring Naka's anger, they saw only one round and one square house were spared. Quickly, the chief gave orders to the people to rebuild their lives. He ordered the tall gray people to build more square houses; the round gray people to build round houses. Children were to pick stones out of the soil so the villagers might replant their crops.

Gran'ma explains that this is how the custom began and this is how the people grew to like it. The women liked being together to talk and laugh while they worked, and the men got used to being together relaxing in the evenings in the square houses together at the end of the day. The children still clear the land of small stones. Gran'ma says the custom will continue at least until Naka speaks to them again.

MEDIA: Possibly pastels.

ANECDOTE: Grifalconi learns this story from a woman she met in Tos, the real village of thatched-roof houses on the side of a volcano in the Cameroons of Central Africa that is described in the book.

DISTINCTION: 1987 Caldecott Honor Book.

BIRTHDAY: Ann Grifalconi: September 22, 1929.

SUBJECT: Folklore—Cameroon.

A Visit to William Blake's Inn: Poems for Innocent and Experienced Travelers

(Harcourt, 1981). Poems by Nancy Willard; illustrated by Alice and Martin Provensen.

SUMMARY: This book is an anthology of fifteen original poems related to Blake's work and an imaginary inn. The poems are "William Blake's Inn for Innocent and Experienced Travelers"; "Blake's Wonderful Car Delivers Us Wonderfully Well"; "A Rabbit Reveals My Room"; "The Sun and Moon Circus Soothes the Wakeful Guests"; "The Man in the Marmalade Hat Arrives"; "The King of Cats Orders an Early Breakfast"; "The Wise Cow Enjoys a Cloud"; "Two Sunflowers Move into the Yellow Room"; "The Wise Cow Makes Way, Room, and Believe"; "Blake Leads a Walk on the Milky Way"; "When We Come Home, Blakes Calls for Fire"; "The Marmalade Man Makes a Dance to Mend Us"; "The King of Cats Sends a Postcard to His Wife"; and "The Tiger Asks Blake for a Bedtime Story." There are also an Introduction, Epilogue, and "Blake's Advice to Travelers," which is a quote from "Proverbs of Hell" in *The Marriage of Heaven and Hell*.

MEDIA: Undetermined.

ANECDOTE: This book also won the 1982 Newbery Medal. The book is the only one to date to be honored by both Newbery

Front cover of *A Visit to William Blake's Inn: Poems for Innocent and Experienced Travelers*, written by Nancy Willard, illustrated by Alice and Martin Provensen. This collection of original poems inspired by William Blake's poetry received not only a 1982 Caldecott Honor but also the 1982 Newbery Medal. (Copyright © 1981 by Alice Provensen and Martin Provenson. Copyright © by Harcourt, Inc. All rights reserved.)

and Caldecott distinctions. Willard asked the Provensens if they would depict William Blake close to his actual appearance from available images.

DISTINCTIONS: 1982 Newbery Medal; 1982 Caldecott Honor Book.

BIRTHDAYS: Nancy Willard: June 26, 1936; Alice Provensen: August 14, 1918; Martin Provensen: July 10, 1916.

SUBJECTS: Blake, William, 1757–1827—Poetry; Children's Poetry—American; American poetry.

W

Wash. Artist's medium. Ink or watercolor paint is diluted significantly with water and spread thin over a surface, creating a thin, transparent covering of color.

The Wave (Houghton Mifflin, 1964). Written by Margaret Hodges; illustrated by Blair Lent.

SUMMARY: A grandson, Tada, lives on a mountainside in Japan with his grandfather, Ojiisan. Ojiisan, who is respected as a sage by the people of the village, warns of an impending earthquake. Just as he predicted, a small earthquake rocks the village. On another day, he looks out at the ocean drawing back from the shore an unusual distance. Though he has never seen the phenomenon before, he remembers what his father and ancestors told. There is not enough time to warn the people at the bottom of the mountain. Ojiisan tells Tada to light a pine torch. Ojiisan throws the torch into his rice field where the rice was ripe and ready for picking. The field ignites, creating a large signal. Tada does not understand why his grandfather would want to burn an entire year's work before it could be harvested, and he begins to cry.

The villagers near the shore see the massive fire on the mountainside and begin to race up the mountain to help. When the first of them arrive, Ojiisan tells them not to put it out, that he set it as a warning to all 400 villagers to try to get them away from the shore. When nothing happens, the men are angry with the old man. Even Tada calls him crazy. Suddenly, Ojiisan points to the shore, and there they all watch a huge tidal wave (tsunami) swell up and crash over the village. The spray from the wave is so vast that it goes halfway up the mountain. Soon, the entire village is covered by water, and when the wave retreats, everything is destroyed.

The man explains that this is why he set fire to his rice fields. There is room, he says, for them to stay at his homeland on the mountain until they rebuild. The villagers are eternally grateful to the old man for saving their lives. The men fall down out of respect before him, and they build a temple in his honor.

MEDIA: Ink and cardboard cutouts.

ANECDOTE: The story is adapted from Lafacadio Hearn's *Gleanings in Buddha-Fields*.

DISTINCTION: 1965 Caldecott Honor Book.

BIRTHDAY: Blair Lent: January 22, 1930.

SUBJECTS: Folklore—Japan; Tsunamis—Fiction.

The Way to Start a Day (Scribner, 1978). Written by Byrd Baylor; illustrated by Peter Parnall.

SUMMARY: The book encourages young people to greet the sun as it comes up and sing to it to celebrate the new day. Through poetic language, the text tells about cultures past and present that have sunrise traditions, such as the cave people; people in Peru; the Aztecs; people in the Congo and China; Egypt; Japan; India; and Native Americans in Arizona. Many brought gifts to the sun such as gold, flowers, sacred smoke, or a song or a new baby. Some believe that the sunrise heralds a life that will live only one day, so we should rejoice and greet that new life represented by the sun's colorful and brilliant appearance over the horizon.

MEDIA: Possibly pen and ink.

ANECDOTE: The author and artist collaborated on several books about the Southwest.

DISTINCTION: 1979 Caldecott Honor Book.

BIRTHDAYS: Byrd Baylor: March 28, 1924; Peter Parnall: May 23, 1936.

SUBJECTS: Sun (in religion, folklore, etc.); Sun worship.

See Also: The Desert Is Theirs; Hawk, I'm Your Brother; When Clay Sings.

Wee Gillis (Viking, 1938). Written by Munro Leaf; illustrated by Robert Lawson.

SUMMARY: A boy named Wee Gillis lives in Scotland. His actual name is Alastair Roderic Craigellachie Dalhousie Gowan Donny-bristle MacMac, but because that is a long name to say, people just call him Wee Gillis. Wee Gillis' mother's relatives are all Lowlanders. They live in the Lowlands and take care of long-haired cows. It takes a lot of breath to call the cows in at night to be milked. Wee Gillis' father's relatives are all Highlanders. They hunt for stags, and it takes a lot of lung power to hold one's breath long enough not to chase away a stag.

The Lowlanders and the Highlanders each think the other silly.

When he gets old enough, Wee Gillis spends one year in the Lowlands. There, he eats a big bowl of oatmeal every morning and goes out to take care of the long-haired cows. When he is late one day bringing them back from the fields so the Lowlanders can milk them, they teach him that he has to shout very loudly to the cows when the mist comes down so they will go where he wants them to go. When the year is up, Wee Gillis is able to shout very loudly, and his lungs are strong.

The next year, he lives and works with the Highlanders. Every morning he has a large bowl of oatmeal. When he stalks the stags, he waits and he waits, until finally, he sighs. His sigh chases away a stag. The Highlanders teach him that he must hold his breath so long that it will not chase away the deer. When the year is up, Wee Gillis' lungs are even stronger.

After a few years of going back and forth between the Highlanders and the Lowlanders, it comes time for Wee Gillis to choose with whom he would like to live forever. Uncle Angus from the Highlands and Uncle Andrew from the Lowlands take him to a spot in between and begin making their arguments in a polite manner about why he should choose their way of life. After a while, they lose their manners and begin shouting and jumping about. Suddenly, a very large man appears and sits on a rock. He is carrying a large set of bagpipes. He is sad because he has made the bagpipes too large and is not able to make them work.

The two uncles feel sorry for him, and each try to work the bagpipes. Neither one succeeds. No one thinks it worth letting young Wee Gillis try, but when he looks so much as if he wants to, the large man asks if he would like to do so. "Aye," is Wee Gillis' reply. First he takes a large breath just like when he was getting ready to call the cows in the Lowlands, then he holds his breath just like he did when he was stalking stags in the Highlands.

When he blows the pipes, Wee Gillis fills out the bag and makes them work just fine. The big man teaches him to play music, and from that day on, he visits both the Highlands and the Lowlands with the biggest bagpipes in Scotland and is welcome anywhere he goes.

MEDIA: Drawings in pen and tempera.

ANECDOTE: Leaf was educated at the University of Maryland and Harvard. His first book for children was *Grammar Can Be Fun*, which he wrote after overhearing a mother lecture her son about saying "ain't."

DISTINCTION: 1939 Caldecott Honor Book.

BIRTHDAYS: Munro Leaf: December 4, 1905; Robert Lawson: October 4, 1892.

SUBJECT: Scotland—Fiction.

See Also: The Story of Ferdinand.

What Do You Do With a Tail Like This?

(Houghton Mifflin, 2003). Written by Robin Page; illustrated by Steve Jenkins.

SUMMARY: Close-up illustrations of animal parts ask questions such as the one in the title. Turn the page, and the full picture of the animals shows them doing what their parts can do. Parts and their animals include noses: platypus, hyena, African elephant, and American alligator, and star-nosed mole; ears: yellow-winged bat, field cricket, antelope jackrabbit, hippotamus, and humpback whale; tails: striped skunk, giraffe, five-lined skink, scorpion, and spider monkey; eyes: chameleon, bald eagle, horned lizard, four-eyed fish, and bush baby; feet: chimpanzees, blue-footed booby, water strider, geckos, and mountain goat; mouths: brown pelican, mosquito, giant anteater, egg-eating snake, and archerfish. Pages in the back list all of the animals with paragraphs of further information about each.

MEDIA: Cut-paper collage.

ANECDOTE: The author and artist of this book are a couple with three children.

DISTINCTION: 2004 Caldecott Honor Book.

Front cover of *What Do You Do With a Tail Like This?* written by Robin Page, illustrated by Steve Jenkins. Jenkins used cut-paper collage in this 2004 Caldecott Honor book. (Copyright © 2003 by Robin Page; illustrations by Steve Jenkins. Copyright © by Houghton Mifflin Company. All rights reserved.)

BIRTHDAY: Steve Jenkins: 1952.

SUBJECTS: Sense organs; Animals—Physiology; Animals—Miscellanea; Animals—Questions and Answers.

What Do You Say, Dear? (Scott, 1958).

Written by Sesyle Joslin; illustrated by Maurice Sendak.

SUMMARY: In a question-and-response format, outlandish situations are presented to the reader to answer with the appropriate polite response. For example, if you are shopping downtown and walking backward because that is your preference and you bump into a crocodile, what should you say? "Excuse me," of course.

MEDIA: Pen and ink with watercolor wash separations.

ANECDOTE: The subtitle of this book is *A Book of Manners for All Occasions*. Inside, it is also described as "A Handbook of Etiquette for Young Ladies and Gentleman to Be Used as a Guide for Everyday Social Behavior."

The story arose out of a game Joslin used to play with her children.

DISTINCTION: 1959 Caldecott Honor Book.

BIRTHDAY: Maurice Sendak: June 10, 1928.

SUBJECTS: Etiquette; Etiquette for children and teenagers.

See Also: In the Night Kitchen; Sendak, Maurice; *Where the Wild Things Are.*

What James Likes Best (Atheneum, 2003). Written and illustrated by Amy Schwartz.

SUMMARY: In "The Twins," James, Mommy, and Daddy all take an express bus to visit new twin babies. While they are there, they see the twins' toys, and James receives a treat. The vignette ends with the narrator asking the reader what she or he thinks James liked best. In "Grandma's House," they take a taxi to Grandma's and Auntie's. James has cheese with little forks and plays with hats. His grandmother gives him a purple car. The narrator again asks the reader/listener which of these James may have liked best. In "The County Fair," the family gets in a yellow car in a parking garage and drives out to the fair. They enjoy the fair, and the narrator asks what James liked best. The scenario continues through walking to a playdate at Angela's in "Angela."

MEDIA: Gouache and pen and ink.

ANECDOTE: Amy Schwartz is married to the children's literature historian, Leonard Marcus. She dedicated the book to their son, Jacob.

DISTINCTION: 2004 Charlotte Zolotow Award.

BIRTHDAY: Amy Schwartz: April 2, 1954.

SUBJECTS: Transportation—Fiction; Family—Fiction.

Wheel on the Chimney (Lippincott, 1954). Written by Margaret Wise Brown; illustrated by Tibor Gergely.

SUMMARY: It is considered good luck in Hungary if a stork takes up residence on top of a house. Some farmers tie a wheel to the chimney to encourage storks to build their nest there. The book describes the stork's migration and other habits throughout the seasons of the year.

MEDIA: Possibly gouache.

ANECDOTE: A similar story about storks won the 1955 Newbery Award—*The Wheel on the School*, by Meindert De Jong, illustrated by Maurice Sendak. The story was about storks on roofs in Holland.

DISTINCTION: 1955 Caldecott Honor Book.

BIRTHDAY: Margaret Wise Brown: May 23, 1910.

SUBJECT: Storks—Fiction.

See Also: Brown, Margaret Wise; *Goodnight Moon*; *The Little Island.*

When Clay Sings (Scribner, 1972). Written by Byrd Baylor; illustrated by Tom Bahti.

SUMMARY: The Native people say that pottery remembers the hands that made it and that clay sings for many years. They teach children to respect broken pieces of pottery they find and use the pieces to teach about the ancestors and their way of life. Sometimes the children find enough pieces to put a design back together again like a jigsaw puzzle, a design such as a bird that suddenly looks at them with its eye. The prose poem of the text ruminates over what might have been the stories connected with the old pottery—a woman designing it while her husband was out hunting and her children playing nearby, a child sick and being given medicine from a bowl. The designs depicted come from areas in Utah, Colorado, Arizona, and New Mexico where the Mogollon, Anasazi, Hohokam, and Mimbres people live.

MEDIA: Undetermined.

ANECDOTE: Baylor is the illustrator of four Caldecott Honor books.

DISTINCTION: 1973 Caldecott Honor Book.

BIRTHDAY: Byrd Baylor: March 28, 1924.

SUBJECTS: Indian Pottery—Southwest, New; Indians of North America—Southwest, New.

See Also: The Desert Is Theirs; Hawk, I'm Your Brother; The Way to Start a Day.

When I Was Young in the Mountains

(Dutton, 1982). Written by Cynthia Rylant; illustrated by Diane Goode.

SUMMARY: The narrator tells of how life was when she was young living in the mountains of West Virginia. Grandfather came home covered in coal dust except for his lips with which he kissed the top of her head. Grandmother made dinner of okra and corn bread. If the narrator ate too much okra, Grandmother walked with her in the middle of the night to the johnny-house, and she promised not to eat too much of it again. When it was hot, she went to the swimming hole, where she jumped into the dark and muddy water whether she saw a snake in it or not. On her way home, she got butter at Mr. and Mrs. Crawford's store. Mr. and Mrs. Crawford looked alike and always smelled sweet. She pumped water from a well to fill a round tub for her bath. After their baths, she and her brother stood by the old black stove to warm up while Grandmother heated up cocoa.

They went to church on Sundays, and sometimes the congregation all went down to the swimming hole for baptisms. Grandmother cried when cousin Peter was laid back in the water, getting his shirt wet. At night, they could hear the sounds of frogs and other noises. If a black snake came into the yard, Grandmother tried to scare it off with a hoe. Once, a very long snake did not leave, and Grandmother used the hoe to kill it. The children draped the dead snake over their shoulders and took it to school to show everyone.

In the evenings, Grandfather sharpened the girl's pencils with his jackknife and Grandmother either shucked beans or braided her hair. They listened to the call of the bobwhite. The little girl narrator did not feel the need to see the seashore or the desert when she lived in the mountains. What she had there was pleasant enough.

MEDIA: Watercolor and fine-colored pencil.

ANECDOTE: The author grew up in a four-room house in Cool Ridge, West Virginia, in the mountains of Appalachia, where her grandparents and other relatives lived. This book was written as a tribute to her grandparents.

DISTINCTION: 1983 Caldecott Honor Book.

BIRTHDAYS: Cynthia Rylant: June 6, 1954; Diane Goode: September 14, 1949.

SUBJECTS: Mountain life—Fiction; United States—Social life and customs—twentieth century—Fiction.

See Also: The Relatives Came.

When Sophie Gets Angry—Really, Really Angry

(Blue Sky, 1999). Written and illustrated by Molly Bang.

SUMMARY: Sophie tugs on toy Gorilla to keep her sister from having him, but her mother says it is her sister's turn. When her sister grabs Gorilla away, Sophie trips and falls over a toy truck. Now Sophie is *really* angry! What does she do? She kicks and screams, but then she runs. She runs and runs, then slows down and cries. Finally, she is taking in the scents and sights of nature all around her that calm her down and make her feel better. When she goes back home, she is no longer angry, and things are all right again.

MEDIA: Gouache.

ANECDOTE: Bang is also the author and artist of *Picture This: How Picture Books Work* (SeaStar, 2000).

Front cover of *When Sophie Gets Angry—Really, Really Angry*, written and illustrated by Molly Bang. In 2000, Bang received a Charlotte Zolotow Book Award for her text for this book as well as a Caldecott Honor for the artwork. (From *When Sophie Gets Angry—Really, Really Angry . . .* by Molly Bang. Published by the Blue Sky Press/Scholastic Inc. Jacket illustration copyright © 1999 by Molly Bang. Reprinted by permission.)

DISTINCTIONS: 2000 Charlotte Zolotow Award; 2000 Caldecott Honor Book.

BIRTHDAY: Molly Bang: December 29, 1943.

SUBJECT: Anger—Fiction.

See Also: Ten, Nine, Eight.

When Will the World Be Mine?: The Story of a Snowshoe Rabbit (Scott, 1953).

Written by Miriam Schlein; illustrated by Jean Charlot.

SUMMARY: Little Snowshoe Rabbit is born in the spring and cannot see much above his bramble home. He can smell, though, and he smells sweet grass and asks his mother to bring him some. When she does, he asks whether he can go out into the field and see the grass for himself. She has him wait to be stronger and bigger, and then the sweet grass will be his. When he is in the field, he can hear a tinkling sound, but his mother says that his ears need to grow bigger before he can go find what is making that sound. When his ears grow bigger, he hops out and sees the stream that is causing the noise, and the stream is also his. The bunny is not quite sure how these things are "his," but his mother keeps instructing him as he sees snow, rain, bushes, his new white coat of fur that replaces his brown one, and so forth. His mother teaches him that he has now grown big enough to explore the world on his own and have his own family and adventures. The world as he needs it is his because he has knowledge of it and how to get along in it.

MEDIA: Lithographs.

ANECDOTE: Charlot illustrated the Newbery medalist books *And Now Miguel* and *Secret of the Andes*. He was of Mexican descent but did not make his first visit to Mexico until he was in his twenties.

DISTINCTION: 1954 Caldecott Honor Book.

BIRTHDAY: Jean Charlot: February 7, 1898.

SUBJECT: Rabbits—Fiction.

See Also: A Child's Good Night Book.

Where the Buffaloes Begin (Warne, 1981).

Written by Olaf Baker; illustrated by Stephen Gammell.

SUMMARY: Ten-year-old Little Wolf wants to locate the lake to the south where, according to the story told by the tribe's eldest member, Nawa, the buffaloes climb out from under the water onto the shore and begin running on the prairie. In the early morning, Little Wolf rides a wild pony to the lake, where he calls out and magically sees the bison emerge from the water covered by the mist. They begin their stampede onto the prairie. Meanwhile, the Assiniboin, the enemy of Little Wolf's people, are working their way toward the camp. The buffaloes run with Little Wolf until they encircle him and his pony as one of their own. They run with him until they outrun the Assinboin and save Little Wolf's people.

MEDIA: Possibly pencil drawings.

ANECDOTE: The book is dedicated to the author's friend, Red Eagle.

DISTINCTION: 1982 Caldecott Honor Book.

BIRTHDAY: Stephen Gammell: February 10, 1943.

SUBJECTS: Indians of North America—Fiction; Bison—Fiction.

See Also: Song and Dance Man.

Where the Wild Things Are (Harper, 1963). Written and illustrated by Maurice Sendak.

SUMMARY: Max wears his wolf suit and hammers a nail into the wall and chases the the dog with a fork. His mother calls him "wild thing." Max says he will eat her up, and she sends him to bed without supper. As Max is in his room, a forest grows and a sailboat with his name on it comes by on an ocean. Max gets in and sails for what seems like a long time to "where the wild things are." The wild things try to scare Max with their roars and teeth, eyes and claws, but Max tells them to be quiet with a magic trick, and they are still. The monsters agree that Max must be the wildest thing of all. They make him king. The king commences playtime, and he and the monsters roar at the moon, swing from trees, and parade through the forest. When Max tells them to stop, they do. He sends the monsters off to bed without their supper.

Max smells good food and decides to leave his post as king of wild things. The monsters ask him not to go, that they love him so much they will eat him up. Max gets in his private sailboat and sails back the long journey to his bedroom. There, he finds his hot supper waiting for him.

MEDIA: India ink line over full-color tempera.

ANECDOTE: Sendak himself has admitted that this popular book is about a little boy who "discharges his anger at his mother" through fantasy. Aesthetically, the book represents the imagination pictorially and "reality" through text. In this way, as the forest (or imagination) grows in Max's room, it takes up more and more of the page until finally the borders are all gone, and the full page is covered with illustration. This comes to a climax in the three wordless, double-page spreads depicting the "wild rumpus." As Max works his way back to reality, the text and borders pick back up until the last page, when Max realizes his mother's love for him through finding the supper that is still hot. That text appears on a page alone, with no pictures at all. Max's easing out of anger might also be said to be represented by his beginning to slip the wolf suit off his head at the end of the book.

Sendak drew a dummy book back in 1956 that was virtually the same story but called *Where the Horses Are.* Unhappy with the results, he put the book away until 1963 after he had written and/or illustrated more than twenty children's books. The new title occurred to him on May 10, 1963, when he decided that he just did not draw horses well. He made a new dummy for the story in miniature, trimming down the text significantly and changing the horses to monsters. This new small, handmade book was almost exactly the story as it appears in full picture book form today.

A few anecdotes about the illustrations have surfaced over the years as the status of the book as canonized children's literature cemented and Sendak's reputation grew as a true artistic genius by observers from inside and outside the children's literature community. For example, Sendak has said that Max's personality has appeared in other characters in his books—namely, as Kenny, Martin, and

Rosie—and Max is actually patterned after Sendak himself. Max's physical appearance as a young boy with dark hair repeats in several of Sendak's books as well. Sendak was influenced by *King Kong* films growing up, and while he said he had never seen the photograph, one day a woman showed him a still photo from a *King Kong* film side by side with his picture of one of the wild things emerging from a cave, and they were almost identical. Max's dog is similar to the dog in *Higgledy Diggledy Pop*, which is said to have been patterned after Sendak's own pet, Jennie.

The book was groundbreaking in American children's picture books and picture books around the world because it artfully opened up the possibility of depicting children's aggressive, complex, and perhaps less attractive sides, their inner turmoils of growing up. The book was the first of Sendak's trilogy of books exploring the interior and dream-state lives of children that included *In the Night Kitchen* and *Outside Over There*. The book was not universally commended at first—many adults, parents, and critics thought children might be frightened by the monsters and found the subject of children's anger in a picture book, especially one typically read at bedtime, perhaps a bit too unsettling. However, though some children did not favor the monsters, others did, and the book has gone on to be translated into at least fifteen languages and has sold more than 2 million copies worldwide. Both for its own intrinsic qualities and for its influence on books that came afterward, *Where the Wild Things Are* has become one of the true classics of the American picture book form. Sendak designed an operatic version of the story in 1979.

DISTINCTION: 1964 Caldecott Medal.

BIRTHDAY: Maurice Sendak: June 10, 1928.

SUBJECTS: Fantasy; Monsters—Fiction.

See Also: In the Night Kitchen; Sendak, Maurice.

White Snow, Bright Snow (Lothrop, 1947). Written by Alvin R. TressELT; illustrated by Roger Duvoisin.

SUMMARY: The postman, farmer, policeman, and the policeman's wife see and smell that snow is on its way. The policeman's wife feels it coming in her big toe. They each prepare in different ways. The postman puts on galoshes; the farmer goes to get a shovel out of his barn; the policeman fastens his coat; and the policeman's wife finds the cough medicine. As the snow falls, different things happen to the characters. The postman falls; the farmer shovels a path; the policeman falls ill from getting his feet wet; and his wife nurses him by his side. Meanwhile, the animals have gone into hibernation, and the children play or dream of playing in the snow. The snow deepens and covers everything with white caps—fenceposts; church steeples—and buries cars. Finally, the long winter season begins to warm and brighten. The postman enjoys the sunshine, delivering the mail more slowly; the farmer lets his cows out of the barn; the policeman goes for a walk in the park, swinging his club; and his wife tends to a lilac bush and crocuses. The children watch for the first robin, and it is clear that spring has come.

MEDIA: Acetate separations in India ink.

ANECDOTE: Roger Duvoisin was surprised to win the 1948 Caldecott Medal for this book, thinking that everyone would be tired of the recent long winter. He described doing the illustrations as easy because he was drawing snow on a white page.

DISTINCTION: 1948 Caldecott Medal.

BIRTHDAYS: Roger Duvoisin: August 28, 1904; Alvin Tressell: September 30, 1916.

SUBJECT: Snow—Fiction.

Why Mosquitoes Buzz in People's Ears (Dial, 1975). Retold by Verna Aardema; illustrated by Leo and Diane Dillon.

SUMMARY: Mosquito tells Iguana that he saw a farmer digging yams almost as big as he is. Iguana, tired of Mosquito's lies, put sticks in his ears. When the iguana passes by the python, he does not hear Python's hello, so he does not respond. Python decides Iguana must be plotting some trick against him, so he slithers into Rabbit's hole. Shocked to see the big snake, Rabbit hops out and away for dear life. Seeing this makes Crow caw the danger signal, and hearing this makes Monkey leap from tree to tree until he breaks a branch and accidentally kills one of Mother Owl's owlets. Mother Owl is so saddened by the death of one of her babies that she does not hoot for the morning sun to come up. It stays dark. Because of this, King Lion calls a meeting of all of the animals.

At the meeting, King Lion asks each animal who is to blame for Mother Owl's distress. Backward in turn, each animal—the monkey, the crow, the rabbit, and the snake—explain what happened. Iguana has not heard the call to come to the meeting because of the sticks in his ears, so King Lion sends the antelope to fetch him. All the animals laugh when they see the sticks in Iguana's ears. King Lion pulls the sticks out and asks him if he has been plotting something against the big snake. Iguana says that the snake is his friend, that he never saw or heard the snake when he passed by. He had put the sticks in his ears because he was tired of listening to the mosquito's lies. All the animals blame the mosquito for all the problems, and Mother Owl is satisfied and hoots for the sun to come up once again.

Mosquito has been listening to the council meeting from a nearby bush. He doesn't fly near but instead hides himself beneath a leaf and is never brought before the council. Mosquitoes from that time until now have whined in people's ears, asking if the animals are still angry with them. Each time they do so, people give them a swat that tells them the answer.

MEDIA: India ink; watercolor; pastels; vellum and frisket masks.

ANECDOTE: To get out of household chores when she was a child, Verna Aardema liked to go to a nearby swamp and think up stories. Although it is not written into the story, the Dillons drew a little red bird in each scene as an observer of what was happening. The Dillons are the only back-to-back Caldecott Medalists. After winning for this book, they won in 1977 for *Ashanti to Zulu*.

DISTINCTION: 1976 Caldecott Medal.

BIRTHDAYS: Verna Aardema: June 6, 1911; Diane Dillon: March 13, 1933; Leo Dillon: March 2, 1933.

SUBJECTS: Folklore—Africa, West; Animals—Folklore.

See Also: *Ashanti to Zulu: African Traditions*; Dillon, Diane and Leo.

Why the Sun and the Moon Live in the Sky (Houghton Mifflin, 1968). Written by Elhinstone Dayrell; illustrated by Blair Lent.

SUMMARY: The sun and the water were good friends who both live on the earth. The sun visits the water often, but the water never visits the sun. When the sun asks the water why this is so, the water explains that the sun does not have a big enough house for him and all of his people to visit. If he and his people come over, they drive the sun out. The water explains that he needs a very large house for him and his people to visit the sun. The sun promises to build such a house and goes back to his wife, the moon, who agrees.

After they had built the large house, the sun invites the water and his people to come over. The water visits, bringing more and more of his people. Each time that the water asks the sun if it is still all right for more of his people, fish, and all the water animals to enter the house, the sun and the moon say it is all right. However, they really have no idea how many people the water is bringing. The water becomes knee-deep; then it goes to the top of the sun's head. Soon the sun and the moon are on the rooftop of the house because there are so many water people inside. The water still asks if is all right that more water people come, and the sun says yes. However, now the sun and the moon have to go up to the sky. They have been there ever since.

MEDIA: Preseparated pen and ink in three colors.

ANECDOTE: William Sleator, reteller and author of *The Angry Moon*, a 1971 Caldecott Honor Book, wrote the musical version of this story.

DISTINCTION: 1969 Caldecott Honor Book.

BIRTHDAY: Blair Lent: January 22, 1930.

SUBJECT: Folklore—Africa.

See Also: The Angry Moon; *The Funny Little Woman*.

Wiesner, David (1956–). Artist and author. David Wiesner was born the fifth child and second son of George and Julia Wiesner on February 5, 1956, in Bridgewater, New Jersey. Several of Wiesner's siblings were interested in art, and they frequently passed down art supplies to him so that he would have materials to experiment with on a frequent basis. Many of the Wiesner children sat and watched the television art program that featured John Nagey giving art lessons. Aside from entertaining himself through art, Wiesner grew up playing outdoors where his siblings and neighborhood cohorts made up games and imaginative adventures. It was not unusual to turn a sidewalk into a brook or river in their imaginations or a cluster of trees into a deep forest.

Once his older brother and sisters began growing up and leaving home, Wiesner inherited a second-floor bedroom to himself. His father saw that he was taking art seriously as a potential career when he turned his bedroom into an art studio. Wiesner knew he had the support of his parents when his father brought home an old oak drafting table and took it upstairs and put it in Wiesner's room.

The table became one of his most cherished possessions.

Graduating from high school in 1974, Wiesner went to the Rhode Island School of Design. There he thrived on open-ended assignments where he could express his vivid imagination. One assignment in his sophomore year involved depicting "metamorphosis." In response, Wiesner created a ten-foot by forty-inch mural that portrayed orange slices turning into sailboats turning into fish. The project became the precursor of his later picture book *Free Fall* (Lothrop, 1988). Wiesner also studied oils about this time but returned to watercolors, which he preferred. He studied with Tom Sgouros, to whom he later dedicated *Tuesday* (Clarion, 1991). Another influence was the work of illustrator Lynd Ward, especially the wordless book *Mad Man's Drum*, made up of 130 woodcuts. Wiesner's friend, Michael Hays, suggested that he take a look at the book, and when Wiesner was in Philadelphia, he went to the Hunt Library at Carnegie Mellon University and examined the artwork firsthand. In his senior year, the artist created a forty-page wordless book based on a short story by Fritz Leiber called "Gonna Roll the Bones."

Wiesner graduated with a B.F.A. in 1978. After college, he moved to New York City, where he pursued work as an illustrator. He illustrated some works by other people, including *Honest Andrew* (1980) by Gloria Skurzynski, *The Ugly Princess* (1981) by Nancy Luenn, and *Kite Flyer* (1986) by Dennis Haseley. In March 1979, he was encouraged by Trina Schart Hyman, who helped his work appear on the cover of *Cricket* magazine. An apartment fire in 1983 destroyed all of his belongings, including his artwork as well as his beloved oak drawing table that his father had given him when he was young. Determined to keep creating, Wiesner came back from this loss and continued to use his imagination in unique and artful ways that began to extend his reputation.

By 1987, Wiesner had married Kim Kahng, a surgeon who also enjoys writing. Together, they retold *The Loathsome Dragon* (Putnam, 1987), which David illustrated. The next year, the first picture book Wiesner wrote and illustrated appeared, *Free Fall* (Lothrop, 1988). The book echoed back to the large mural he had made at college. In the book, figures "metamorphize"—the characters walk, float, fly, and ride through a dream sequence. The book also incorporated a dragon similar to one from the book he created with his wife. In a sign of good things to come, Wiesner's first picture book was awarded a Caldecott Honor Book Award in 1989.

In March 1989, Wiesner was again asked to illustrate the cover of *Cricket* magazine. He was given free reign over the subject matter other than having the information that the March issue of the magazine contained articles about St. Patrick and frogs. Since Wiesner particularly liked drawing frogs, he began playing around with that subject. From old sketchbooks and copies of *National Geographic*, he began to put together an idea of a frog on a lily pad looking as if it were sailing on a flying saucer. The cover he created showed several frogs doing just that, flying over a spring swamp scene on their lily pad flying saucers. One of the more fascinating aspects of Wiesner's work is the way his imagination on one project triggers further creative ideas for another, providing visual links from one work he produces to the next. He would return to these images of frogs in the not too distant future.

In the meantime, he created *Hurricane* (Clarion, 1990), which is an autobiographical book about David and his brother George enduring a hurricane together and then playing on a tree's fallen branches, imagining they are a jungle, a galleon, and a spaceship. Inserting realism even further into this book, Wiesner used actual wallpaper from his room as a child on page 13. It is not difficult to imagine a child with elephant heads, ships in bottles, rockets, books, medals, and magnifying glasses on the walls growing up with a creative sensibility.

Returning to the frog theme he had initiated for the *Cricket* cover, in 1991, his picture book *Tuesday* appeared. He chose the title because of the "ooze" sound in the word that reminded him most of frogs for the single day of the week that this odd occurrence was to take place. The nearly wordless book struck the Caldecott committee as so original that they awarded Wiesner a Caldecott Medal in 1992. Again picking up a thread from one book and leading it to another, Wiesner found himself wondering where the pigs at the end of *Tuesday* went and what they did when they got there. The result of his exploration led to *The Three Pigs*, an amazingly creative book that not only is a fractured fairy tale of the three little pigs but also tears apart at the borders and design of picture books in general and contains visual allusions to other children's stories and modes of illustration. This tour de force won for the artist a companion Caldecott Medal in 2002, ten years after *Tuesday*.

Between the two medalist books, Wiesner designed *Sector 7*, which he created after a visit to the top of the Empire State Building on a foggy day when he was all alone. This book was awarded a Caldecott Honor Book Award in 2000. His other books include *June 29, 1999* (Clarion, 1992), in which vegetables from Holly Evans' science project fly over Levittown, Anchorage, and Providence; and *Moo!* (Clarion, 1996). In all, David Wiesner has four Caldecott distinctions to date, putting him near the top of the list of awardees for illustration in American children's picture books several years before his fiftieth birthday. David and Kim have two sons, Kevin and Jaime. One can only imagine where the artist will next take the picture book art form in the future.

DISTINCTIONS: 1992, 2002 Caldecott Medals (one of only seven multiple gold medalists); 1989, 2000 Caldecott Honor Books.

Further Reading: Johnson, Nancy J. "Interview with the 2002 Caldecott Medal Winner, David Wiesner." *Reading Teacher* 56, no. 4 (December 2002–January 2003) 400–404; Nodelman, Perry. "Private Places on Public View: David Wiesner's Picture Books." *Mosaic: A Journal for the Interdisciplinary Study of Literature* 34, no. 2 (June 2001): 1–16; Wiesner, David. "Caldecott Acceptance Speech." *Horn Book Magazine* 68, no. 4 (July/August 1992): 416–422.

See Also: Free Fall; Sector 7; The Three Pigs; Tuesday.

The Wild Birthday Cake (Doubleday, 1949). Written by Lavinia R. Davis; illustrated by Hildegard Woodward.

SUMMARY: Johnny looks down Broomstick Hill on a beautiful spring morning in the countryside. He sees the adults gardening, but he is going to look for adventure. He is wearing his new hiking outfit and sneakers and carrying a backpack with food and provisions for his adventure. He begins walking—to where, he's not sure. When Miss Tibbetts asks him if he would like to help her dig up dandelions from her garden, Johnny says no. He says the same thing to Mr. and Mrs. Stout, who are transplanting roses. At the Professor's house, he sees that he has been transporting his turtles from his garden to the woods. Johnny wants to help him, but the Professor tells him he is finished already. He reminds Johnny, though, about coming down to his house that evening to have cake with him to help him celebrate his seventy-fifth birthday.

Johnny forgot about his best friend's birthday. He has gotten him neither a card nor a gift. What's worse, he has just emptied his prancing horse bank buying the backpack he is wearing. He keeps walking as he thinks about what might make a good present. He sees a columbine. He has learned about columbines from the Professor; so he picks it to give him as a gift, but it doesn't work out too well as something to put in his backpack. At Penton's Pasture, he sees some ducks flying overhead and forgets about the Professor's birthday from their beauty and wonder. He keeps walking until he gets into the Big Woodlot. There it becomes hot. He peels off some birch bark and thinks he might make a card out of it for the Professor when he gets home.

As he is in the woods, the ducks land on a pond. He marvels at them again; they fly away and leave one duck behind. The duck is hurt; Johnny feeds the duck some cake from his backpack and manages to catch her and take her home. His mother, however, won't allow the duck in the house and asks him to put her in the shed. Johnny's heart is heavy. When he visits the Professor, he sees three baby ducks with no mother in his garden pond and decides to make the difficult decision to give the Professor the duck for his birthday. It is clear that the female mallard and motherless mallard ducklings enjoy one another. Johnny helps the Professor name the duck, and they name her Birthday Cake because she was caught by cake and was a birthday present for the Professor. Johnny can visit Birthday Cake at the Professor's house any time that he likes.

MEDIA: Undetermined.

ANECDOTE: The year this book won a Caldecott Honor Book Award, there were five honor books.

DISTINCTION: 1950 Caldecott Honor Book.

BIRTHDAY: Unavailable.

SUBJECTS: Ducks—Fiction; Birthdays—Fiction.

Woodcut. Artist's medium. A design is cut into a block of plain-grain wood; then it is used in a relief process for printing.

Working Cotton (Harcourt, 1992). Written by Sherley Anne Williams; illustrated by Carole Byard.

Front cover of *Working Cotton*, written by Sherley Anne Williams, illustrated by Carole Byard. Byard used acrylics on Stonehendge white paper to depict this story of migrant workers. For her efforts, she received a Caldecott Honor in 1993. (Copyright © 1992 by Carole Byard. Copyright © by Harcourt, Inc. All rights reserved.)

SUMMARY: Shelan works cotton in the fields. She starts early in the morning, when the workers get their rides. Daddy picks in a row with Ruise and Jesmarie. Mamma cares for Leanne and the baby. Shelan is old enough to help Mamma with her sack but not to have a sack of her own. Daddy picks very fast. The cotton smells dusty in the heat and can make one sneeze. For lunch, the family eats corn bread and greens. Shelan's sisters want lots of water when they get thirsty. It is a long, hot day in the cotton fields. Other children are there, but they will be moved on the next day, and different children with their families will work near them tomorrow. Daddy sees a cotton flower that signals good luck. When it's almost dark, the bus comes to take the workers back. A day in the cotton fields is hard work that starts early and ends late, but the family is together.

MEDIA: Acrylic on Stonehendge white paper.

ANECDOTE: The book is based on Williams' *The Peacock Poems*, which was a National Book Award nominee.

DISTINCTION: 1993 Caldecott Honor Book.

BIRTHDAYS: Sherley Anne Williams: August 25, 1944; Carole Byard: July 22, 1941.

SUBJECTS: Migrant labor—Fiction; Cotton picking—Fiction; Family life—Fiction; African Americans—Fiction.

X, Y, Z

Yo! Yes? (Orchard, 1993). Written and illustrated by Chris Raschka.

SUMMARY: In a series of one- or two-word questions and answers, two boys, one black and one white, meet and agree to become friends.

MEDIA: Watercolor and charcoal pencil.

ANECDOTE: Chris Raschka says that he thought up the idea for this book on his way to the post office one morning in May.

DISTINCTION: 1994 Caldecott Honor Book.

BIRTHDAY: Not available.

SUBJECTS: Friendship—Fiction; Race relations—Fiction; African Americans—Fiction.

Yonie Wondernose (Doubleday, 1944). Written and illustrated by Marguerite de Angeli.

SUMMARY: Yonie is a seven-year-old Pennsylvania Dutch boy who lives with Mom, Pop, Malinda, Lydia, Nancy, and Granny in Pennsylvania's Lancaster County. He has an older brother, Ammon, who is grown-up and living away on his own. Yonie's real name is Jonathan, but he is called Yonie Wondernose because he is curious. He looks in pots and ovens to see what's cooking; he watches Nathan Straub plant bean seeds. Like his father, Yonie does not wear buttons on his coat but instead wears hooks and eyes to keep his jacket closed. Mom cuts his hair using a bowl as a guide.

One day, Yonie is left as the only "man" in the house with Granny and Nancy, as the others go visiting. Yonie has chores to do while they are away, and he is determined to not be a wondernose and forget his duties. When he goes to the pasture, he sees a knothole in a tree and has to look inside. When he fetches water, he stops to watch an airplane flying overhead. When he returns to the kitchen, Granny is not there. He looks inside the painted chest that Granny always said had things in it that were over 200 years old. The chest came to America from the old country. Granny is trapped in the chicken house, but Yonie doesn't find her from being curious. He finds her from hearing her calls.

That night, lightning strikes the barn. Yonie helps Granny release and guide the animals to safety. As the fire truck comes to put out the fire, Yonie forgets for a time what else he must do to help rescue animals and belongings. He remembers his father calling him Wondernose, however, and continues helping to save the day. When Pop arrives home, the Bishop informs him that everyone will come together to help him rebuild. The pig has had piglets, and Pop allows Yonie to have one as a reward.

MEDIA: Color separations done in pen, ink, pencil, and watercolor.

ANECDOTE: De Angeli lived with two families in Amish country, Lancaster, Pennsylvania, for a few days on different occasions. She often referred to Amish children as examples to her own children about good behavior and living without the latest conveniences.

DISTINCTION: 1945 Caldecott Honor Book.

BIRTHDAY: Marguerite de Angeli: March 14, 1889.

SUBJECTS: Family Life—Pennsylvania—Fiction; Amish—Fiction; Pennsylvania Dutch—Fiction; Pennsylvania—Fiction.

You Can Write Chinese (Viking, 1945). Written and illustrated by Kurt Wiese.

SUMMARY: The book shows Chinese characters with drawings shadowed behind them that suggest their meaning and origins. For example, two tree-shaped characters side by side create the word for forest. Words depicted include pool, mouth, the middle, tongue, axle, car, railroad, fish, bird, goat, horse, pig, family, language, to speak, bamboo, stone, eye, to see, gaze, ear, woman, mother, child, good, how are you, to eat, field, ox, rice, water, and mountain.

MEDIA: Ink and watercolor separations.

ANECDOTE: Wiese illustrated more than 300 books in a career that spanned four decades.

DISTINCTION: 1946 Caldecott Honor Book.

BIRTHDAY: Kurt Wiese: April 27, 1887.

SUBJECT: Chinese Language—Writing.

Zin! Zin! Zin! A Violin (Simon and Schuster, 1995). Written by Lloyd Moss; illustrated by Marjorie Priceman.

SUMMARY: One mournful trombone is soon joined by a swinging trumpet, and they become a duo. When a bright French horn joins in, they are now a trio. The mellow cello forms a quartet; the strings of a violin form a quintet, and so on. The rhymes introducing each instrument give characteristics of the instrument and its sound along with the word for counting the number of instruments proceeding all the way to a chamber group of ten.

MEDIA: Gouache.

ANECDOTE: The author is a disc jockey for New York City's only all-classical music radio station, WQXR.

DISTINCTION: 1996 Caldecott Honor Book.

BIRTHDAY: Marjorie Priceman: January 8, 1958.

SUBJECTS: Musical instruments—Fiction; Music—Fiction; Counting; Stories in rhyme.

Caldecott Medalists and Honor Books, by Year

1938

MEDALIST: *Animals of the Bible, a Picture Book*, illustrated by Dorothy P. Lathrop; text selected by Helen Dean Fish (Lippincott).

Honor Books

* *Four and Twenty Blackbirds*, illustrated by Robert Lawson; text compiled by Helen Dean Fish (Stokes).
* *Seven Simeons: A Russian Tale*, retold and illustrated by Boris Artzybasheff (Viking).

1939

MEDALIST: *Mei Li* by Thomas Handforth (Doubleday)

Honor Books

* *Andy and the Lion* by James Daugherty (Viking).
* *Barkis* by Clare Turlay Newberry (Harper).
* *The Forest Pool* by Laura Adams Armer (Longmans).
* *Snow White and the Seven Dwarfs* by Wanda Gág (Coward).
* *Wee Gillis*, illustrated by Robert Lawson; text by Munro Leaf (Viking).

1940

MEDALIST: *Abraham Lincoln* by Ingri and Edgar Parin d'Aulaire (Doubleday).

Honor Books

* *Cock-a-Doodle Doo* by Berta and Elmer Hader (Macmillan).
* *Madeline* by Ludwig Bemelmans (Viking).
* *The Ageless Story* by Lauren Ford (Dodd).

1941

MEDALIST: *They Were Strong and Good* by Robert Lawson (Viking).

Honor Book

* *April's Kittens* by Clare Turlay Newberry (Harper).

1942

MEDALIST: *Make Way for Ducklings* by Robert McCloskey (Viking).

Honor Books

* *An American ABC* by Maud and Miska Petersham (Macmillan).
* *In My Mother's House*, illustrated by Velino Herrera; text by Ann Nolan Clark (Viking).

- *Paddle-to-the-Sea* by Holling C. Holling (Houghton Mifflin).
- *Nothing at All* by Wanda Gág (Coward).

1943

MEDALIST: *The Little House* by Virginia Lee Burton (Houghton Mifflin).

Honor Books

- *Dash and Dart* by Mary and Conrad Buff (Viking).
- *Marshmallow* by Clare Turlay Newberry (Harper).

1944

MEDALIST: *Many Moons*, illustrated by Louis Slobodkin; text by James Thurber (Harcourt).

Honor Books

- *Small Rain: Verses from the Bible*, illustrated by Elizabeth Orton Jones; text selected by Jessie Orton Jones (Viking).
- *Pierre Pigeon*, illustrated by Arnold E. Bare; text by Lee Kingman (Houghton Mifflin).
- *The Mighty Hunter* by Berta and Elmer Hader (Macmillan).
- *A Child's Good Night Book*, illustrated by Jean Charlot; text by Margaret Wise Brown (W.R. Scott).
- *Good-Luck Horse*, illustrated by Plato Chan; text by Chih-Yi Chan (Whittlesey).

1945

MEDALIST: *Prayer for a Child*, illustrated by Elizabeth Orton Jones; text by Rachel Field. (Macmillan).

Honor Books

- *Mother Goose*, illustrated by Tasha Tudor (Oxford University Press).
- *In the Forest* by Marie Hall Ets (Viking).
- *Yonie Wondernose* by Marguerite de Angeli (Doubleday).

- *The Christmas Anna Angel*, illustrated by Kate Seredy; text by Ruth Sawyer (Viking).

1946

MEDALIST: *The Rooster Crows* by Maud and Miska Petersham (Macmillan).

Honor Books

- *Little Lost Lamb*, illustrated by Leonard Weisgard; text by Golden MacDonald, pseud. [Margaret Wise Brown] (Doubleday).
- *Sing Mother Goose*, illustrated by Marjorie Torrey; music by Opal Wheeler (Dutton).
- *My Mother Is the Most Beautiful Woman in the World*, illustrated by Ruth Gannett; text by Becky Reyher (Lothrop).
- *You Can Write Chinese* by Kurt Wiese (Viking).

1947

MEDALIST: *The Little Island*, illustrated by Leonard Weisgard; text by Golden MacDonald, pseud. [Margaret Wise Brown] (Doubleday).

Honor Books

- *Rain Drop Splash*, illustrated by Leonard Weisgard; text by Alvin Tresselt (Lothrop).
- *Boats on the River*, illustrated by Jay Hyde Barnum; text by Marjorie Flack (Viking).
- *Timothy Turtle*, illustrated by Tony Palazzo; text by Al Graham (Welch).
- *Pedro, the Angel of Olvera Street* by Leo Politi (Scribner).
- *Sing in Praise: A Collection of the Best Loved Hymns*, illustrated by Marjorie Torrey; text selected by Opal Wheeler (Dutton).

1948

MEDALIST: *White Snow, Bright Snow*, illustrated by Roger Duvoisin; text by Alvin Tresselt (Lothrop).

Honor Books

- *Stone Soup* by Marcia Brown (Scribner).
- *McElligott's Pool* by Dr. Seuss, pseud. [Theodor Seuss Geisel] (Random House).
- *Bambino the Clown* by Georges Schreiber (Viking).
- *Roger and the Fox*, illustrated by Hildegard Woodward; text by Lavinia R. Davis (Doubleday).
- *Song of Robin Hood*, illustrated by Virginia Lee Burton; text edited by Anne Malcolmson (Houghton Mifflin).

1949

MEDALIST: *The Big Snow* by Berta and Elmer Hader (Macmillan).

Honor Books

- *Blueberries for Sal* by Robert McCloskey (Viking).
- *All Around the Town*, illustrated by Helen Stone; text by Phyllis McGinley (Lippincott).
- *Juanita* by Leo Politi (Scribner).
- *Fish in the Air* by Kurt Wiese (Viking).

1950

MEDALIST: *Song of the Swallows* by Leo Politi (Scribner).

Honor Books

- *America's Ethan Allen*, illustrated by Lynd Ward; text by Stewart Holbrook (Houghton Mifflin).
- *The Wild Birthday Cake*, illustrated by Hildegard Woodward; text by Lavinia R. Davis (Doubleday).
- *The Happy Day*, illustrated by Marc Simont; text by Ruth Krauss (Harper).
- *Bartholomew and the Oobleck* by Dr. Seuss, pseud. [Theodor Seuss Geisel] (Random House).
- *Henry Fisherman* by Marcia Brown.

1951

MEDALIST: *The Egg Tree* by Katherine Milhous (Scribner).

Honor Books

- *Dick Whittington and His Cat* by Marcia Brown (Scribner).
- *The Two Reds*, illustrated by Nicolas, pseud. (Nicholas Mordvinoff); text by Will, pseud. [William Lipkind] (Harcourt).
- *If I Ran the Zoo* by Dr. Seuss, pseud. [Theodor Seuss Geisel] (Random House).
- *The Most Wonderful Doll in the World*, illustrated by Helen Stone; text by Phyllis McGinley (Lippincott).
- *T-Bone, the Baby Sitter* by Clare Turlay Newberry (Harper).

1952

MEDALIST: *Finders Keepers*, illustrated by Nicolas, pseud. (Nicholas Mordvinoff); text by Will, pseud. [William Lipkind] (Harcourt).

Honor Books

- *Mr. T. W. Anthony Woo* by Marie Hall Ets (Viking).
- *Skipper John's Cook* by Marcia Brown (Scribner).
- *All Falling Down*, illustrated by Margaret Bloy Graham; text by Gene Zion (Harper).
- *Bear Party* by William Pène Du Bois (Viking).
- *Feather Mountain* by Elizabeth Olds (Houghton Mifflin).

1953

MEDALIST: *The Biggest Bear* by Lynd Ward (Houghton Mifflin).

Honor Books

- *Puss in Boots*, illustrated by Marcia Brown; text translated from Charles Perrault by Marcia Brown (Scribner).

- *One Morning in Maine* by Robert McCloskey (Viking).
- *Ape in a Cape: An Alphabet of Odd Animals* by Fritz Eichenberg (Harcourt).
- *The Storm Book*, illustrated by Margaret Bloy Graham; text by Charlotte Zolotow (Harper).
- *Five Little Monkeys* by Juliet Kepes (Houghton Mifflin).

1954

MEDALIST: *Madeline's Rescue* by Ludwig Bemelmans (Viking).

Honor Books

- *Journey Cake, Ho!* illustrated by Robert McCloskey; text by Ruth Sawyer (Viking).
- *When Will the World Be Mine?* illustrated by Jean Charlot; text by Miriam Schlein (W. R. Scott).
- *The Steadfast Tin Soldier*, illustrated by Marcia Brown; text by Hans Christian Andersen, translated by M. R. James (Scribner).
- *A Very Special House*, illustrated by Maurice Sendak; text by Ruth Krauss (Harper).
- *Green Eyes* by A. Birnbaum (Capitol).

1955

MEDALIST: *Cinderella, or The Little Glass Slipper*, illustrated by Marcia Brown; text translated from Charles Perrault by Marcia Brown (Scribner).

Honor Books

- *Book of Nursery and Mother Goose Rhymes*, illustrated by Marguerite de Angeli (Doubleday).
- *Wheel on the Chimney*, illustrated by Tibor Gergely; text by Margaret Wise Brown (Lippincott).
- *The Thanksgiving Story*, illustrated by Helen Sewell; text by Alice Dalgliesh (Scribner).

1956

MEDALIST: *Frog Went A-Courtin'*, illustrated by Feodor Rojankovsky; text retold by John Langstaff (Harcourt).

Honor Books

- *Play with Me*, by Marie Hall Ets (Viking).
- *Crow Boy* by Taro Yashima (Viking).

1957

MEDALIST: *A Tree Is Nice*, illustrated by Marc Simont; text by Janice Udry (Harper).

Honor Books

- *Mister Penny's Race Horse* by Marie Hall Ets (Viking).
- *1 Is One* by Tasha Tudor (Walck).
- *Anatole*, illustrated by Paul Galdone; text by Eve Titus (McGraw-Hill).
- *Gillespie and the Guards*, illustrated by James Daugherty; text by Benjamin Elkin (Viking).
- *Lion* by William Pène du Bois (Viking).

1958

MEDALIST: *Time of Wonder* by Robert McCloskey (Viking).

Honor Books

- *Fly High, Fly Low* by Don Freeman (Viking).
- *Anatole and the Cat*, illustrated by Paul Galdone; text by Eve Titus (McGraw-Hill).

1959

MEDALIST: *Chanticleer and the Fox*, illustrated by Barbara Cooney; text adapted by Barbara Cooney from Chaucer's *Canterbury Tales* (Crowell).

Honor Books

- *The House That Jack Built: La Maison Que Jacques a Batie* by Antonio Frasconi (Harcourt).
- *What Do You Say, Dear?* illustrated by Maurice Sendak; text by Sesyle Joslin (W. R. Scott).
- *Umbrella* by Taro Yashima (Viking).

1960

MEDALIST: *Nine Days to Christmas*, illustrated by Marie Hall Ets; text by Marie Hall Ets and Aurora Labastida (Viking).

Honor Books

- *Houses from the Sea*, illustrated by Adrienne Adams; text by Alice E. Goudey (Scribner).
- *The Moon Jumpers*, illustrated by Maurice Sendak; text by Janice May Udry (Harper).

1961

MEDALIST: *Baboushka and the Three Kings*, illustrated by Nicolas Sidjakov; text by Ruth Robbins (Parnassus).

Honor Book

- *Inch by Inch*, by Leo Lionni (Obolensky).

1962

MEDALIST: *Once a Mouse . . . A Fable Cut in Wood*, retold and illustrated by Marcia Brown (Scribner).

Honor Books

- *Fox Went Out on a Chilly Night: An Old Song* by Peter Spier (Doubleday).
- *Little Bear's Visit*, illustrated by Maurice Sendak; text by Else H. Minarik (Harper).
- *The Day We Saw the Sun Come Up*, illustrated by Adrienne Adams; text by Alice E. Goudey (Scribner).

1963

MEDALIST: *The Snowy Day* by Ezra Jack Keats (Viking).

Honor Books

- *The Sun Is a Golden Earring*, illustrated by Bernarda Bryson; text by Natalia M. Belting (Henry Holt).
- *Mr. Rabbit and the Lovely Present*, illustrated by Maurice Sendak; text by Charlotte Zolotow (Harper).

1964

MEDALIST: *Where the Wild Things Are* by Maurice Sendak (Harper).

Honor Books

- *Swimmy* by Leo Lionni (Pantheon).
- *All in the Morning Early*, illustrated by Evaline Ness; text by Sorche Nic Leodhas, pseud. [Leclaire Alger] (Henry Holt).
- *Mother Goose and Nursery Rhymes*, illustrated by Philip Reed (Atheneum).

1965

MEDALIST: *May I Bring a Friend?* illustrated by Beni Montresor; text by Beatrice Schenk de Regniers (Atheneum).

Honor Books

- *Rain Makes Applesauce*, illustrated by Marvin Bileck; text by Julian Scheer (Holiday).
- *The Wave*, illustrated by Blair Lent; text by Margaret Hodges (Houghton Mifflin).
- *A Pocketful of Cricket*, illustrated by Evaline Ness; text by Rebecca Caudill (Henry Holt).

1966

MEDALIST: *Always Room for One More*, illustrated by Nonny Hogrogian; text by Sorche Nic Leodhas, pseud. [Leclair Alger] (Henry Holt).

Honor Books

- *Hide and Seek Fog*, illustrated by Roger Duvoisin; text by Alvin Tresselt (Lothrop).
- *Just Me* by Marie Hall Ets (Viking).
- *Tom Tit Tot*, retold and illustrated by Evaline Ness (Scribner).

1967

MEDALIST: *Sam, Bangs & Moonshine* by Evaline Ness (Henry Holt).

Honor Book

- *One Wide River to Cross*, illustrated by Ed Emberley; text adapted by Barbara Emberley (Prentice-Hall).

1968

MEDALIST: *Drummer Hoff*, illustrated by Ed Emberley; text adapted by Barbara Emberley (Prentice-Hall).

Honor Books

- *Frederick* by Leo Lionni (Pantheon).
- *Seashore Story* by Taro Yashima (Viking).
- *The Emperor and the Kite*, illustrated by Ed Young; text by Jane Yolen (World).

1969

MEDALIST: *The Fool of the World and the Flying Ship*, illustrated by Uri Shulevitz; text retold by Arthur Ransome (Farrar, Straus and Giroux).

Honor Books

- *Why the Sun and the Moon Live in the Sky*, illustrated by Blair Lent; text by Elphinstone Dayrell (Houghton Mifflin).

1970

MEDALIST: *Sylvester and the Magic Pebble* by William Steig (Windmill Books).

Honor Books

- *Goggles!* by Ezra Jack Keats (Macmillan).
- *Alexander and the Wind-Up Mouse* by Leo Lionni (Pantheon).
- *Pop Corn & Ma Goodness*, illustrated by Robert Andrew Parker; text by Edna Mitchell Preston (Viking).
- *Thy Friend, Obadiah* by Brinton Turkle (Viking).
- *The Judge: An Untrue Tale*, illustrated by Margot Zemach; text by Harve Zemach (Farrar).

1971

MEDALIST: *A Story a Story*, retold and illustrated by Gail E. Haley (Atheneum).

Honor Books

- *The Angry Moon*, illustrated by Blair Lent; text retold by William Sleator (Atlantic).
- *Frog and Toad Are Friends* by Arnold Lobel (Harper).
- *In the Night Kitchen* by Maurice Sendak (Harper).

1972

MEDALIST: *One Fine Day*, retold and illustrated by Nonny Hogrogian (Macmillan).

Honor Books

- *Hildilid's Night*, illustrated by Arnold Lobel; text by Cheli Durán Ryan (Macmillan).
- *If All the Seas Were One Sea* by Janina Domanska (Macmillan).
- *Moja Means One: Swahili Counting Book*, illustrated by Tom Feelings; text by Muriel Feelings (Dial).

1973

MEDALIST: *The Funny Little Woman*, illustrated by Blair Lent; text retold by Arlene Mosel (Dutton).

Honor Books

- *Anansi the Spider: A Tale from the Ashanti*, adapted and illustrated by Gerald McDermott (Henry Holt).
- *Hosie's Alphabet*, illustrated by Leonard Baskin; text by Hosea, Tobias, and Lisa Baskin (Viking).
- *Snow-White and the Seven Dwarfs*, illustrated by Nancy Ekholm Burkert; text translated by Randall Jarrell, retold from the Brothers Grimm (Farrar, Straus and Giroux).
- *When Clay Sings*, illustrated by Tom Bahti; text by Byrd Baylor (Scribner).

1974

MEDALIST: *Duffy and the Devil*, illustrated by Margot Zemach; retold by Harve Zemach (Farrar).

Honor Books

- *Three Jovial Huntsmen* by Susan Jeffers (Bradbury).
- *Cathedral* by David Macaulay (Houghton Mifflin).

1975

MEDALIST: *Arrow to the Sun* by Gerald McDermott (Viking).

Honor Book

- *Jambo Means Hello: Swahili Alphabet Book*, illustrated by Tom Feelings; text by Muriel Feelings (Dial).

1976

MEDALIST: *Why Mosquitoes Buzz in People's Ears*, illustrated by Leo and Diane Dillon; text retold by Verna Aardema (Dial).

Honor Books

- *The Desert Is Theirs*, illustrated by Peter Parnall; text by Byrd Baylor (Scribner).
- *Strega Nona* by Tomie dePaola (Prentice-Hall).

1977

MEDALIST: *Ashanti to Zulu: African Traditions*, illustrated by Leo and Diane Dillon; text by Margaret Musgrove (Dial).

Honor Books

- *The Amazing Bone* by William Steig (Farrar, Straus and Giroux).
- *The Contest*, retold and illustrated by Nonny Hogrogian (Greenwillow).
- *Fish for Supper* by M. B. Goffstein (Dial).
- *The Golem: A Jewish Legend* by Beverly Brodsky McDermott (Lippincott).
- *Hawk, I'm Your Brother*, illustrated by Peter Parnall; text by Byrd Baylor (Scribner).

1978

MEDALIST: *Noah's Ark* by Peter Spier (Doubleday).

Honor Books

- *Castle* by David Macaulay (Houghton Mifflin).
- *It Could Always Be Worse*, retold and illustrated by Margot Zemach (Farrar, Straus and Giroux).

1979

MEDALIST: *The Girl Who Loved Wild Horses* by Paul Goble (Bradbury).

Honor Books

- *Freight Train* by Donald Crews (Greenwillow).

- *The Way to Start a Day*, illustrated by Peter Parnall; text by Byrd Baylor (Scribner).

1980

MEDALIST: *Ox-Cart Man*, illustrated by Barbara Cooney; text by Donald Hall (Viking).

Honor Books

- *Ben's Trumpet* by Rachel Isadora (Greenwillow).
- *The Garden of Abdul Gasazi* by Chris Van Allsburg (Houghton Mifflin).
- *The Treasure* by Uri Shulevitz (Farrar, Straus and Giroux).

1981

MEDALIST: *Fables* by Arnold Lobel (Harper).

Honor Books

- *The Bremen-Town Musicians*, retold and illustrated by Ilse Plume (Doubleday).
- *The Grey Lady and the Strawberry Snatcher* by Molly Bang (Four Winds).
- *Mice Twice* by Joseph Low (McElderry/ Atheneum).
- *Truck* by Donald Crews (Greenwillow).

1982

MEDALIST: *Jumanji* by Chris Van Allsburg (Houghton Mifflin).

Honor Books

- *Where the Buffaloes Begin*, illustrated by Stephen Gammell; text by Olaf Baker (Warne).
- *On Market Street*, illustrated by Anita Lobel; text by Arnold Lobel (Greenwillow).
- *Outside Over There* by Maurice Sendak (Harper).

- *A Visit to William Blake's Inn: Poems for Innocent and Experienced Travelers*, illustrated by Alice and Martin Provensen; text by Nancy Willard (Harcourt).

1983

MEDALIST: *Shadow*, translated and illustrated by Marcia Brown; original text in French: Blaise Cendrars (Scribner).

Honor Books

- *A Chair for My Mother* by Vera B. Williams (Greenwillow).
- *When I Was Young in the Mountains*, illustrated by Diane Goode; text by Cynthia Rylant (Dutton).

1984

MEDALIST: *The Glorious Flight: Across the Channel with Louis Blériot* by Alice and Martin Provensen (Viking).

Honor Books

- *Little Red Riding Hood*, retold and illustrated by Trina Schart Hyman (Holiday).
- *Ten, Nine, Eight* by Molly Bang (Greenwillow).

1985

MEDALIST: *Saint George and the Dragon*, illustrated by Trina Schart Hyman; text retold by Margaret Hodges (Little, Brown).

Honor Books

- *Hansel and Gretel*, illustrated by Paul O. Zelinsky; text retold by Rika Lesser (Dodd).
- *Have You Seen My Duckling?* by Nancy Tafuri (Greenwillow).
- *The Story of Jumping Mouse: A Native American Legend*, retold and illustrated by John Steptoe (Lothrop).

1986

MEDALIST: *The Polar Express* by Chris Van Allsburg (Houghton Mifflin).

Honor Books

- *The Relatives Came*, illustrated by Stephen Gammell; text by Cynthia Rylant (Bradbury).
- *King Bidgood's in the Bathtub*, illustrated by Don Wood; text by Audrey Wood (Harcourt).

1987

MEDALIST: *Hey, Al*, illustrated by Richard Egielski; text by Arthur Yorinks (Farrar, Straus and Giroux).

Honor Books

- *The Village of Round and Square Houses* by Ann Grifalconi (Little, Brown).
- *Alphabatics* by Suse MacDonald (Bradbury).
- *Rumpelstiltskin* by Paul O. Zelinsky (Dutton).

1988

MEDALIST: *Owl Moon*, illustrated by John Schoenherr; text by Jane Yolen (Philomel).

Honor Book

- *Mufaro's Beautiful Daughters: An African Tale* by John Steptoe (Lothrop).

1989

MEDALIST: *Song and Dance Man*, illustrated by Stephen Gammell; text by Karen Ackerman (Knopf).

Honor Books

- *The Boy of the Three-Year Nap*, illustrated by Allen Say; text by Diane Snyder (Houghton Mifflin).
- *Free Fall* by David Wiesner (Lothrop).

- *Goldilocks and the Three Bears* by James Marshall (Dial).
- *Mirandy and Brother Wind*, illustrated by Jerry Pinkney; text by Patricia C. McKissack (Knopf).

1990

MEDALIST: *Lon Po Po: A Red-Riding Hood Story from China* by Ed Young (Philomel).

Honor Books

- *Bill Peet: An Autobiography* by Bill Peet (Houghton Mifflin).
- *Color Zoo* by Lois Ehlert (Lippincott).
- *The Talking Eggs: A Folktale from the American South*, illustrated by Jerry Pinkney; text by Robert D. San Souci (Dial).
- *Hershel and the Hanukkah Goblins*, illustrated by Trina Schart Hyman; text by Eric Kimmel (Holiday House).

1991

MEDALIST: *Black and White* by David Macaulay (Houghton Mifflin).

Honor Books

- *Puss in Boots*, illustrated by Fred Marcellino; text by Charles Perrault, translated by Malcolm Arthur (Di Capua/Farrar, Straus and Giroux).
- *"More More More," Said the Baby: Three Love Stories* by Vera B. Williams (Greenwillow).

1992

MEDALIST: *Tuesday* by David Wiesner (Clarion Books).

Honor Book

- *Tar Beach* by Faith Ringgold (Crown Publishers).

1993

MEDALIST: *Mirette on the High Wire* by Emily Arnold McCully (Putnam).

Honor Books

* *The Stinky Cheese Man and Other Fairly Stupid Tales*, illustrated by Lane Smith; text by Jon Scieszka (Viking).
* *Seven Blind Mice* by Ed Young (Philomel Books).
* *Working Cotton*, illustrated by Carole Byard; text by Sherley Anne Williams (Harcourt).

1994

MEDALIST: *Grandfather's Journey* by Allen Say; text edited by Walter Lorraine (Houghton Mifflin).

Honor Books

* *Peppe the Lamplighter*, illustrated by Ted Lewin; text by Elisa Bartone (Lothrop).
* *In the Small, Small Pond* by Denise Fleming (Henry Holt).
* *Raven: A Trickster Tale from the Pacific Northwest* by Gerald McDermott (Harcourt).
* *Owen* by Kevin Henkes (Greenwillow).
* *Yo! Yes?* illustrated by Chris Raschka; text edited by Richard Jackson (Orchard).

1995

MEDALIST: *Smoky Night*, illustrated by David Diaz; text by Eve Bunting (Harcourt).

Honor Books

* *John Henry*, illustrated by Jerry Pinkney; text by Julius Lester (Dial).
* *Swamp Angel*, illustrated by Paul O. Zelinsky; text by Anne Issacs (Dutton).
* *Time Flies* by Eric Rohmann (Crown).

1996

MEDALIST: *Officer Buckle and Gloria* by Peggy Rathmann (Putnam).

Honor Books

* *Alphabet City* by Stephen T. Johnson (Viking).
* *Zin! Zin! Zin! A Violin*, illustrated by Marjorie Priceman; text by Lloyd Moss (Simon and Schuster).
* *The Faithful Friend*, illustrated by Brian Pinkney; text by Robert D. San Souci (Simon and Schuster).
* *Tops & Bottoms*, adapted and illustrated by Janet Stevens (Harcourt).

1997

MEDALIST: *Golem* by David Wisniewski (Clarion).

Honor Books

* *Hush! A Thai Lullaby*, illustrated by Holly Meade; text by Minfong Ho (Melanie Kroupa/Orchard Books).
* *The Graphic Alphabet* by David Pelletier (Orchard Books).
* *The Paperboy* by Dav Pilkey (Richard Jackson/Orchard Books).
* *Starry Messenger* by Peter Sís (Frances Foster Books/Farrar, Straus and Giroux).

1998

MEDALIST: *Rapunzel* by Paul O. Zelinsky (Dutton).

Honor Books

* *The Gardener*, illustrated by David Small; text by Sarah Stewart (Farrar, Straus and Giroux).
* *Harlem*, illustrated by Christopher Myers; text by Walter Dean Myers (Scholastic).

- *There Was an Old Lady Who Swallowed a Fly* by Simms Taback (Viking).

1999

MEDALIST: *Snowflake Bentley*, Illustrated by Mary Azarian; text by Jacqueline Briggs Martin (Houghton Mifflin).

Honor Books

- *Duke Ellington: The Piano Prince and the Orchestra* illustrated by Brian Pinkney text by Andrea Davis Pinkney (Hyperion).
- *No, David!* by David Shannon (Scholastic).
- *Snow* by Uri Shulevitz (Farrar, Straus and Giroux).
- *Tibet Through the Red Box* by Peter Sis (Frances Foster).

2000

MEDALIST: *Joseph Had a Little Overcoat* by Simms Taback (Viking).

Honor Books

- *A Child's Calendar* illustrated by Trina Schart Hyman; text by John Updike (Holiday House).
- *Sector 7* by David Wiesner (Clarion Books).
- *When Sophie Gets Angry—Really, Really Angry* by Molly Bang (Scholastic).
- *The Ugly Duckling*, illustrated by Jerry Pinkney; text by Hans Christian Andersen; adapted by Jerry Pinkney (Morrow)

2001

MEDALIST: *So You Want to Be President?* Illustrated by David Small; written by Judith St. George (Philomel).

Honor Books

- *Casey at the Bat*, illustrated by Christopher Bing; written by Ernest Thayer (Handprint).
- *Click, Clack, Moo: Cows That Type*, illustrated by Betsy Lewin; written by Doreen Cronin (Simon and Schuster).
- *Olivia* by Ian Falconer (Atheneum).

2002

MEDALIST: *The Three Pigs* by David Wiesner (Clarion/Houghton Mifflin).

Honor Books

- *The Dinosaurs of Waterhouse Hawkins*, illustrated by Brian Selznick; written by Barbara Kerley (Scholastic)
- *Martin's Big Words: The Life of Dr. Martin Luther King, Jr.*, illustrated by Bryan Collier; written by Doreen Rappaport (Jump at the Sun/Hyperion).
- *The Stray Dog* by Marc Simont (HarperCollins).

2003

MEDALIST: *My Friend Rabbit* by Eric Rohmann (Roaring Brook Press/Millbrook Press).

Honor Books

- *The Spider and the Fly*, illustrated by Tony DiTerlizzi; written by Mary Howitt (Simon and Schuster Books for Young Readers).
- *Hondo & Fabian* by Peter McCarty (Henry Holt).
- *Noah's Ark* by Jerry Pinkney (SeaStar Books, a division of North-South Books). Inc.)

2004

MEDALIST: *The Man Who Walked between the Towers* by Mordicai Gerstein (Roaring Brook Press).

Honor Books

- *Ella Sarah Gets Dressed*, illustrated by Margaret Chodos-Irvine (Harcourt).
- *What Do You Do With a Tail Like This?* by Steve Jenkins and Robin Page (Houghton Mifflin).
- *Don't Let the Pigeon Drive the Bus* by Mo Willems (Hyperion).

2005

MEDALIST: *Kitten's First Full Moon* by Kevin Henkes (Greenwillow).

Honor Books

- *The Red Book* by Barbara Lehman (Houghton Mifflin).
- *Coming on Home Soon* illustrated by E. B. Lewis; written by Jacqueline Woodson (Putnam).
- *Knuffle Bunny: A Cautionary Tale* by Mo Willem; (Hyperion).

Caldecott Medalists and Honor Books, by Illustrator

Adams, Adrienne: *The Day We Saw the Sun Come Up*, text by Alice E. Goudey; 1962 Honor Book.

————. *Houses from the Sea*, text by Alice E. Goudey; 1960 Honor Book.

*Azarian, Mary: *Snowflake Bentley*, text by Jacqueline Briggs Martin; 1999 Medalist.

Bahti, Tom: *When Clay Sings*, text by Byrd Baylor; 1973 Honor Book.

Bang, Molly: *When Sophie Gets Angry—Really, Really Angry*; 2000 Honor Book.

————. *Ten, Nine, Eight*; 1984 Honor Book.

————. *The Grey Lady and the Strawberry Snatcher*; 1981 Honor Book.

Baskin, Leonard: *Hosie's Alphabet*; Hosea, Tobias, and Lisa Baskin; 1973 Honor Book.

*Bemelmans, Ludwig: *Madeline's Rescue*; 1954 Medalist.

Bileck, Marvin: *Rain Makes Applesauce*, text by Julian Scheer; 1965 Honor Book.

Bing, Christopher: *Casey at the Bat*, text by Ernest Thayer; 2001 Honor Book.

Birnbaum, A.: *Green Eyes*; 1954 Honor Book.

***Brown, Marcia: *Shadow*, trans. from the French by Marcia Brown; 1983. Medalist.

————. *Once a Mouse*; 1962 Medalist.

————. *Cinderella, or The Little Glass Slipper*; 1955 Medalist.

————. *The Steadfast Tin Soldier*, trans. from Hans Christian Andersen by M. R. James; 1954 Honor Book.

————. *Puss in Boots*; 1953 Honor Book.

Bryson, Bernarda: *The Sun Is a Golden Earring*, text by Natalia M. Belting; 1963 Honor Book.

Burkert, Nancy Ekholm: *Snow-White and the Seven Dwarfs*, text by Randall Jarrell; 1973 Honor Book.

Byard, Carole: *Working Cotton*, text by Sherley Anne Williams; 1993 Honor Book.

Charlot, Jean: *When Will the World be Mine?*, text by Miriam Schlein; 1954 Honor Book.

Collier, Brian: *Martin's Big Words: The Life of Dr. Martin Luther King, Jr.*, text by Doreen Rappaport; 2002 Honor Book.

**Cooney, Barbara: *Ox-Cart Man*, text by Donald Hall; 1980 Medalist.

————. *Chanticleer and the Fox*; 1959 Medalist.

Crews, Donald: *Truck*; 1981 Honor Book.

————. *Freight Train*; 1979 Honor Book.

Daugherty, James: *Gillespie and the Guards*, text by Benjamin Elkin; 1957 Honor Book.

de Angeli, Marguerite: *Book of Nursery and Mother Goose Rhymes*; 1955 Honor Book.

dePaola, Tomie: *Strega Nona*; 1976 Honor Book.

*Diaz, David: *Smoky Night*, text by Eve Bunting; 1995 Medalist.

*Indicates number of gold medals

**Dillon, Leo, and Diane: *Ashanti to Zulu: African Traditions*, text by Margaret Musgrove; 1977 Medalist.

———. *Why Mosquitoes Buzz in People's Ears*, text by Verna Aardema; 1976 Medalist.

DiTerlizzi, Tony: *Spider and the Fly*, text by Mary Howitt; 2003 Honor Book.

Domanska, Janina: *If All the Seas Were One Sea*; 1972 Honor Book.

du Bois, William Pène: *Lion*; 1957 Honor Book.

Duvoisin, Roger: *Hide and Seek Fog*, text by Alvin Tresselt; 1966 Honor Book.

*Egielski, Richard: *Hey, Al*, text by Arthur Yorinks; 1987 Medalist.

Ehlert, Louise: *Color Zoo*; 1990 Honor Book.

Eichenberg, Fritz: *Ape in a Cape: An Alphabet of Odd Animals*; 1953 Honor Book.

*Emberley, Ed: *Drummer Hoff*, text by Barbara Emberley; 1968 Medalist.

———. *One Wide River to Cross*, text by Barbara Emberley; 1967 Honor Book.

*Ets, Marie Hall: *Just Me*; 1966 Honor Book.

———. *Nine Days to Christmas*, text by Marie Hall Ets and Aurora Labastida; 1960 Medalist.

———. *Mister Penny's Race Horse*; 1957 Honor Book.

———. *Play with Me*; 1956 Honor Book.

Falconer, Ian: *Olivia*; 2001 Honor Book.

Feelings, Tom: *Jambo Means Hello: Swahili Alphabet Book*, text by Muriel Feelings; 1975 Honor Book.

———. *Moja Means One: Swahili Counting Book*, text by Muriel Feelings; 1972 Honor Book.

Fleming, Denise: *In the Small, Small Pond*; 1994 Honor Book.

Frasconi, Antonio: *The House That Jack Built—La Maison Que Jacques a Batie*; 1959 Honor Book.

Freeman, Don: *Fly High, Fly Low*; 1958 Honor Book.

Galdone, Paul: *Anatole and the Cat*, text by Eve Titus; 1958 Honor Book.

———. *Anatole*, text by Eve Titus; 1957 Honor Book.

*Gammell, Stephen: *Song and Dance Man*, text by Karen Ackerman; 1989 Medalist.

———. *The Relatives Came*, text by Cynthia Rylant; 1986 Honor Book.

———. *Where the Buffaloes Begin*, text by Olaf Baker; 1982 Honor Book.

Gergely, Tibor: *Wheel on the Chimney*, text by Margaret Wise Brown; 1955 Honor Book.

*Gerstein, Mordicai: *The Man Who Walked between the Towers*; 2004 Medalist.

*Goble, Paul: *The Girl Who Loved Wild Horses*; 1979 Medalist.

Goffstein, M. B.: *Fish for Supper*; 1977 Honor Book.

Goode, Diane: *When I Was Young in the Mountains*, text by Cynthia Rylant; 1983 Honor Book.

Graham, Margaret Bloy: *The Storm Book*, text by Charlotte Zolotow; 1953 Honor Book.

Grifalconi, Ann: *The Village of Round and Square Houses*; 1987 Honor Book.

*Haley, Gail E.: *A Story a Story*; 1971 Medalist.

*Henkes, Kevin: *Kitten's First Full Moon*; 2005 Medalist.

———. *Owen*; 1994 Honor Book.

**Hogrogian, Nonny: *The Contest*; 1977 Honor Book.

———. *One Fine Day*; 1972 Medalist.

———. *Always Room for One More*; text by Sorche Nic Leodhas [pseud. Leclair Alger]; 1966 Medalist.

*Hyman, Trina Schart: *A Child's Calendar*; text by John Updike; 2000 Honor Book.

———. *Hershel and the Hanukkah Goblins*; text by Eric Kimmel; 1990 Honor Book.

———. *Saint George and the Dragon*; text by Margaret Hodges; 1985 Medalist.

———. *Little Red Riding Hood*; 1984 Honor Book.

Isadora, Rachel: *Ben's Trumpet*; 1980 Honor Book.

Jeffers, Susan: *Three Jovial Huntsmen*; 1974 Honor Book.

Johnson, Stephen T.: *Alphabet City*; 1996 Honor Book.

*Keats, Ezra Jack: *Goggles!*; 1970 Honor Book.

———. *The Snowy Day*; 1963 Medalist.

Kepes, Juliet: *Five Little Monkeys*; 1953 Honor Book.

Lehman, Barbara: *The Red Book*; 2005 Honor Book.

*Lent, Blair: *The Funny Little Woman*; text by Arlene Mosel; 1973 Medalist.

———. *The Angry Moon*; text by William Sleator; 1971 Honor Book.

———. *Why the Sun and the Moon Live in the Sky*; text by Elphinstone Dayrell; 1969 Honor Book.

———. *The Wave*, text by Margaret Hodges; 1965 Honor Book.

Lewin, Betsy: *Click, Clack, Moo: Cows That Type*; text by Doreen Cronin; 2001 Honor Book.

Lewin, Ted: *Peppe the Lamplighter*; text by Elisa Bartone; 1994 Honor Book.

Lewis, E. B: *Coming on Home Soon*; text by Jacqueline Woodson; 2005 Honor Book.

Lionni, Leo: *Alexander and the Wind-Up Mouse*; 1970 Honor Book.

———. *Frederick*; 1968 Honor Book.

———. *Swimmy*; 1964 Honor Book.

———. *Inch by Inch*; 1961 Honor Book.

Lobel, Anita: *On Market Street*; text by Arnold Lobel; 1982 Honor Book.

*Lobel, Arnold: *Fables*; 1981 Medalist.

———. *Hildilid's Night*; text by Cheli Durán Ryan; 1972 Honor Book.

———. *Frog and Toad Are Friends*; 1971 Honor Book.

Low, Joseph: *Mice Twice*; 1981 Honor Book.

*Macaulay, David: *Black and White*; 1991 Medalist.

MacDonald, Suse: *Alphabatics*; 1987 Honor Book.

Marcellino, Fred: *Puss in Boots*, text by Charles Perrault, trans. by Malcolm Arthur; 1991 Honor Book.

———. *Castle*; 1978 Honor Book.

———. *Cathedral*; 1974 Honor Book.

Marshall, James: *Goldilocks and the Three Bears*; 1989 Honor Book.

McCarty, Peter: *Hondo & Fabian*; 2003 Honor Book.

**McCloskey, Robert: *Time of Wonder*; 1958 Medalist.

———. *Journey Cake, Ho!*, text by Ruth Sawyer; 1954 Honor Book.

———. *One Morning in Maine*; 1953 Honor Book.

———. *Blueberries for Sal*; 1949 Honor Book.

———. *Make Way for Ducklings*; 1941 Medalist.

*McCully, Emily Arnold: *Mirette on the High Wire*; 1993 Medalist.

McDermott, Beverly Brodsky: *The Golem: A Jewish Legend*; 1978 Honor Book.

*McDermott, Gerald: *Raven: A Trickster Tale from the Pacific Northwest*; 1994 Honor Book.

———. *Arrow to the Sun*; 1975 Medalist.

———. *Anansi the Spider: A Tale from the Ashanti*; 1973 Honor Book.

Meade, Holly: *Hush! A Thai Lullaby*, written by Minfong Ho; 1997 Honor Book.

*Montresor, Beni: *May I Bring a Friend?*, text by Beatrice Schenk de Regniers; 1965 Medalist.

Myers, Christopher: *Harlem*, written by Walter Dean Myers; 1998 Honor Book.

*Ness, Eveline: *Sam, Bangs & Moonshine*; 1967 Medalist.

———. *Tom Tit Tot*; 1966 Honor Book.

———. *A Pocketful of Cricket*, text by Rebecca Caudill; 1965 Honor Book.

———. *All in the Morning Early*, text by Sorche Nic Leodhas, pseud. [Leclaire Alger]; 1964 Honor Book.

Parker, Robert Andrew: *Pop Corn & Ma Goodness*; text by Edna Mitchell Preston; 1970 Honor Book.

Parnall, Peter: *The Way to Start a Day*; text by Byrd Baylor; 1979 Honor Book.

———. *Hawk, I'm Your Brother*; text by Byrd Baylor; 1977 Honor Book.

————. *The Desert Is Theirs*; text by Byrd Baylor; 1976 Honor Book.

Peet, Bill: *Bill Peet: An Autobiography*; 1990 Honor Book.

Pelletier, David: *The Graphic Alphabet*; 1997 Honor Book.

Pilkey, Dav: *The Paperboy*; 1997 Honor Book.

Pinkney, Brian: *Duke Ellington: The Piano Prince and the Orchestra*; text by Andrea Davis Pinkney; 1999 Honor Book.

————. *The Faithful Friend*; text by Robert D. San Souci; 1996 Honor Book.

Pinkney, Jerry: *Noah's Ark*; 2003 Honor Book.

————. *The Ugly Duckling*, by Hans Christian Andersen, adapted by Jerry Pinkney; 2000 Honor Book.

————. *John Henry*; text by Julius Lester; 1995 Honor Book.

————. *The Talking Eggs: A Folktale from the American South*; text by Robert D. San Souci; 1990 Honor Book.

————. *Mirandy and Brother Wind*; text by Patricia C. McKissack; 1989 Honor Book.

Plume, Ilse: *The Bremen-Town Musicians*; 1981 Honor Book.

Priceman, Marjorie: *Zin! Zin! Zin! A Violin*; text by Lloyd Moss; 1996 Honor Book.

*Provensen, Alice, and Martin: *The Glorious Flight: Across the Channel with Louis Bleriot*; 1984 Medalist.

————. *A Visit to William Blake's Inn: Poems for Innocent and Experienced Travelers*; text by Nancy Willard; 1982 Honor Book.

Raschka, Chris: *Yo! Yes?*, edited by Richard Jackson; 1994 Honor Book.

*Rathmann, Peggy: *Officer Buckle and Gloria*; 1996 Medalist.

Reed, Philip: *Mother Goose and Nursery Rhymes*; 1964 Honor Book.

Ringgold, Faith: *Tar Beach*; 1992 Honor Book.

*Rohmann, Eric: *My Friend Rabbit*, 2003 Medalist.

————. *Time Flies*; 1995 Honor Book.

*Rojankovsky, Feodor: *Frog Went A-Courtin'*, text by John Langstaff; 1956 Medalist.

*Say, Allen: *Grandfather's Journey*, edited by Walter Lorraine; 1994 Medalist.

————. *The Boy of the Three-Year Nap*; text by Diane Snyder; 1989 Honor Book.

*Schoenherr, John: *Owl Moon*; text by Jane Yolen; 1988 Medalist.

Selznick, Brian: *The Dinosaurs of Waterhouse Hawkins*, written by Barbara Kerley; 2002 Honor Book.

*Sendak, Maurice: *Outside Over There*; 1982 Honor Book.

————. *In the Night Kitchen*; 1971 Honor Book.

————. *Where the Wild Things Are*; 1964 Medalist.

————. *Mr. Rabbit and the Lovely Present*; text by Charlotte Zolotow; 1963 Honor Book.

————. *Little Bear's Visit*; text by Else H. Minarik; 1962 Honor Book.

————. *The Moon Jumpers*; text by Janice May Udry; 1960 Honor Book.

————. *What Do You Say, Dear?*; text by Sesyle Joslin (W. R. Scott); 1959 Honor Book.

————. *A Very Special House*; text by Ruth Krauss; 1954 Honor Book.

Sewell, Helen: *The Thanksgiving Story*, text by Alice Dalgliesh; 1955 Honor Book.

Shannon, David: *No, David!*; 1999 Honor Book.

*Shulevitz, Uri: *Snow*; 1999 Honor Book.

————. *The Treasure*; 1980 Honor Book.

————. *The Fool of the World and the Flying Ship*; text by Arthur Ransome; 1969 Medalist.

*Sidjakov, Nicolas: *Baboushka and the Three Kings*; text by Ruth Robbins; 1961 Medalist.

*Simont, Marc: *The Stray Dog*; 2002 Honor Book.

————. *A Tree Is Nice*; text by Janice Udry; 1957 Medalist.

Sís, Peter: *Tibet through the Red Box*; 1999 Honor Book.

————. *Starry Messenger*; 1997 Honor Book.

*Small, David: *So You Want to Be President?*,

written by Judith St. George; 2001 Medalist.

———. *The Gardener*, written by Sarah Stewart; 1998 Honor Book.

Smith, Lane: *The Stinky Cheeseman and Other Fairly Stupid Tales*, text by Jon Scieszka; 1993 Honor Book.

*Spier, Peter: *Noah's Ark*; 1978 Medalist.

———. *Fox Went Out on a Chilly Night*; 1962 Honor Book.

*Steig, William: *The Amazing Bone*; 1977 Honor Book.

———. *Sylvester and the Magic Pebble*; 1970 Medalist.

Steptoe, John: *Mufaro's Beautiful Daughters: An African Tale*; 1988 Honor Book.

———. *The Story of Jumping Mouse: A Native American Legend*; 1985 Honor Book.

Stevens, Janet: *Tops and Bottoms*; adapted by Janet Stevens; 1996 Honor Book.

*Tabeck, Simms: *Joseph Had a Little Overcoat*; 2000 Medalist.

———. *There Was an Old Lady Who Swallowed a Fly*; 1998 Honor Book.

Tafuri, Nancy: *Have You Seen My Duckling?*; 1985 Honor Book.

Tudor, Tasha: *1 is One*; 1957 Honor Book.

Turkle, Brinton: *Thy Friend, Obadiah*; 1970 Honor Book.

**Van Allsburg, Chris: *The Polar Express*; 1986 Medalist.

———. *Jumanji*; 1982 Medalist.

———. *The Garden of Abdul Gasazi*; 1980 Honor Book.

*Ward, Lynd: *The Biggest Bear*; 1953 Medalist.

**Wiesner, David: *The Three Pigs*; 2002 Medalist.

———. *Sector 7*; 2000 Honor Book.

———. *Tuesday*; 1992 Medalist.

———. *Free Fall*; 1989 Honor Book.

Willems, Mo: *Don't Let the Pigeon Drive the Bus*; 2004 Honor Book.

———. *Knuffle Bunny: A Cautionary Tale*; 2005 Honor Book.

Williams, Vera B.: *"More More More," Said the Baby: Three Love Stories*; 1991 Honor Book.

———. *A Chair for My Mother*; 1983 Honor Book.

*Wisniewski, David: *Golem*; 1997 Medalist.

Wood, Don: *King Bidgood's in the Bathroom*; text by Audrey Wood; 1986 Honor Book.

Yashima, Taro: *Seashore Story*; 1968 Honor Book.

———. *Umbrella*; 1959 Honor Book.

———. *Crow Boy*; 1956 Honor Book.

*Young, Ed: *Seven Blind Mice*; 1993 Honor Book.

———. *Lon Po Po: A Red-Riding Hood Story from China*; 1990 Medalist.

———. *The Emperor and the Kite*; text by Jane Yolen; 1968 Honor Book.

*Zelinsky, Paul O.: *Rapunzel*, retold by Paul O. Zelinsky; 1998 Medalist.

———. *Swamp Angel*, written by Anne Isaacs; 1995 Honor Book.

———. *Rumpelstiltskin*; 1987 Honor Book.

———. *Hansel and Gretel*; text by Rika Lesser; 1985 Honor Book.

*Zemach, Margot: *It Could Always Be Worse*; 1978 Honor Book.

———. *Duffy and the Devil*; text by Harve Zemach; 1974 Medalist.

———. *The Judge: An Untrue Tale*, text by Harve Zemach; 1970 Honor Book.

Caldecott Medalists and Honor Books, by Author

Aardema, Verna. Illus. Leo and Diane Dillon. *Why Mosquitoes Buzz in People's Ears.*

Ackerman, Karen. Illus. Stephen Gammell. *Song and Dance Man.*

Alger, Leclaire (pseud. Sorche Nic Leodhas). Illus. Evaline Ness. *All in the Morning Early.*

———. Illus. Nonny Hogrogrian. *Always Room for One More.*

Andersen, Hans Christian. Illus. Jerry Pinkney. *The Ugly Duckling.*

Armer, Laura Adams. *The Forest Pool.*

Artzybasheff, Boris. *Seven Simeons: A Russian Tale.*

d'Aulaire, Ingri, and Edgar Parin. *Abraham Lincoln.*

Baker, Olaf. Illus. Stephen Gammell. *Where Buffaloes Begin.*

Bang, Molly. *The Grey Lady and the Strawberry Snatcher.*

———. *Ten, Nine, Eight.*

———. *When Sophie Gets Angry—Really, Really, Angry.*

Bartone, Elisa. Illus. Ted Lewin. *Peppe the Lamplighter.*

Baskin, Hosea, Tobias, and Lisa. Illus. Leonard Baskin. *Hosie's Alphabet.*

Baylor, Bryd. Illus. Peter Parnall. *The Desert Is Theirs.*

———. *Hawk, I'm Your Brother.*

———. *The Way to Start a Day.*

———. Illus. Tom Bahti. *When Clay Sings.*

Belting, Natalia M. Illus. Bernarda Bryson. *The Sun Is a Golden Earring.*

Bemelmans, Ludwig. *Madeline.*

———. *Madeline's Rescue.*

Birnbaum, A. *Green Eyes.*

Du Bois, William Pène. *Bear Party.*

———. *Lion.*

Brown, Marcia. *Cinderella, or The Little Glass Slipper.*

———. *Dick Whittington and His Cat.*

———. *Henry Fisherman.*

———. *Puss in Boots.*

———. *Shadow.*

———. *Skipper John's Cook.*

———. *Stone Soup.*

Brown, Margaret Wise. Illus. Jean Charlot. *A Child's Good Night Book.*

———. Illus. Leonard Weisgard. *The Little Island.*

———. *Little Lost Lamb.*

———. Illus. Tibor Gergely. *Wheel on the Chimney.*

Buff, Mary, and Conrad. *Dash and Dart.*

Bunting, Eve. Illus. David Diaz. *Smoky Night.*

Burton, Virginia Lee. *The Little House.*

Carle, Eric. *The Very Hungry Caterpillar.*

Caudill, Rebecca. Illus. Evaline Ness. *A Pocketful of Cricket.*

Chodos-Irvine, Margaret. *Ella Sarah Gets Dressed.*

Clark, Ann Nolan. Illus. Velino Herrera. *In My Mother's House.*

Cooney, Barbara. *Chanticleer and the Fox.*

Crews, Donald. *Freight Train.*

———. *Truck.*

Cronin, Doreen. Illus. Betsy Lewin. *Click, Clack, Moo: Cows That Type.*

Daligliesh, Alice. Illus. Helen Sewell. *The Thanksgiving Story.*

Daugherty, James. *Andy and the Lion.*

Davis, Lavinia R. Illus. Hildegard Woodward. *Roger and the Fox.*

———. *The Wild Birthday Cake.*

Dayrell, Elhinstone. Illus. Blair Lent. *Why the Sun and the Moon Live in the Sky.*

de Angeli, Marguerite. *Book of the Nursery and Mother Goose Rhymes.*

———. *Yonie Wondernose.*

dePaola, Tomie. *Strega Nona.*

de Regniers, Beartrice Schenk. Illus. Beni Montresor. *May I Bring a Friend?*

Domanska, Janina. *If All the Seas Were One Sea.*

Ehlert, Lois. *Color Zoo.*

Eichenberg, Fritz. *Ape in a Cape: An Alphabet of Odd Animals.*

Elkin, Benjamin. Illus. James Daugherty; *Gillespie and the Guards.*

Emberley, Barbara. Illus. Ed Emberley; *Drummer Hoff.*

———. *One Wide River to Cross.*

Ets, Marie Hall. *In the Forest.*

———. *Just Me.*

———. *Mister Penny's Race Horse.*

———. *Mr. T. W. Anthony Woo.*

———. *Play with Me.*

———, and Aurora Labastida. Illus. Marie Hall Ets. *Nine Days to Christmas.*

Falconer, Ian. *Olivia.*

Feelings, Muriel. Illus. Tom Feelings. *Jambo Means Hello: Swahili Alphabet Book.*

———. *Moja Means One: Swahili Counting Book.*

Field, Rachel. Illus. Elizabeth Orton Jones. *Prayer for a Child.*

Fish, Helen Dean. Illus. Dorothy P. Lathrop; *Animals of the Bible, a Picture Book.*

———. Illus. Robert Lawson. *Four and Twenty Blackbirds.*

Flack, Marjorie. Illus. Jay Hyde Barnum. *Boats on the River.*

Fleming, Denise. *In the Small, Small Pond.*

Ford, Lauren. *The Ageless Story.*

Frasconi, Antonio. *The House That Jack Built—La Maison Que Jacques a Batie.*

Freeman, Don. *Fly High, Fly Low.*

Gág, Wanda. *Nothing at All.*

———. *Snow White and the Seven Dwarfs.*

Gerstein, Mordicai. *The Man Who Walked between the Towers.*

Goble, Paul. *The Girl Who Loved Wild Horses.*

Goffstein, M. B. *Fish for Supper.*

Goudey, Alice E. Illus. Adrienne Adams. *The Day We Saw the Sun Come Up.*

———. *Houses from the Sea.*

Graham, Al. Illus. Tony Palazzo. *Timothy Turtle.*

Grifalconi, Ann. *The Village of Round and Square Houses.*

Hader, Berta, and Elmer. *The Big Snow.*

———. *Cock-a-Doodle Doo.*

———. *The Mighty Hunter.*

———. *White Snow, Bright Snow.*

Haley, Gail E. *A Story a Story.*

Hall, Donald. Illus. Barbara Cooney. *Ox-Cart Man.*

Handforth, Thomas. *Mei Li.*

Henkes, Kevin. *Kittens First Full Moon.*

———. *Owen.*

Ho, Minfong. Illus. Holly Meade. *Hush! A Thai Lullaby.*

Hodges, Margaret. Illus. Blair Lent. *The Wave.*

Hogrogian, Nonny. *The Contest.*

———. *One Fine Day.*

Holbrook, Stewart. Illus. Lynd Ward. *America's Ethan Allen.*

Holling, Holling C. *Paddle-to-the-Sea.*

Howitt, Mary. Illus. Tony DiTerlizzi. *The Spider and the Fly.*

Hymen, Trina Schart. *Little Red Riding Hood.*

Isaacs, Anne. Illus. Paul O. Zelinsky. *Swamp Angel.*

Isadora, Rachel. *Ben's Trumpet.*

James, M. R. Illus. Marcia Brown. *The Steadfast Tin Soldier.*

Jarrell, Randall. Illus. Nancy Ekholm Burkert. *Snow-White and the Seven Dwarfs.*

Jeffers, Susan. *Three Jovial Huntsmen.*

Jenkins, Steve. Illus. Robin Page. *What Do You Do With a Tail Like This?*

Johnson, Stephen T. *Alphabet City.*

Jones, Jessie Orton. Illus. Elizabeth Orton Jones. *Small Rain: Verses from the Bible.*

Joslin, Sesyle. Illus. Maurice Sendak. *What Do You Say, Dear?*

Keats, Ezra Jack. *Goggles!*

———. *The Snowy Day.*

Kepes, Juliet. *Five Little Monkeys.*

Kerley, Barbara. Illus. Brian Selznick. *The Dinosaurs of Waterhouse Hawkins.*

Kimmel, Eric. Illus. Trina Schart Hymen. *Hershel and the Hannukkah Goblins.*

Kingman, Lee. Illus. Arnold E. Bare. *Pierre Pigeon.*

Krauss, Ruth. Illus. Marc Simont. *The Happy Day.*

———. Illus. Maurice Sendak. *A Very Special House.*

Langstaff, John. Illus. Feodor Rojankovsky. *Frog Went A-Courtin'.*

Lawson, Robert. *They Were Strong and Good.*

Leaf, Munro. Illus. Robert Lawson. *Wee Gillis.*

Lehman, Barbara. *The Red Book.*

Lesser, Rika. Illus. Paul O. Zelinsky. *Hansel and Gretel.*

Lester, Julius. Illus. Jerry Pinkney. *John Henry.*

Lobel, Arnold. *Fables.*

Lionni, Leo. *Alexander and the Wind-Up Mouse.*

———. *Frederick.*

———. *Inch by Inch.*

———. *Swimmy.*

Lipkind, William (pseud. Will). Illus. Nicholas Mordvinoff (pseud. Nicolas). *Finders Keepers.*

———. *The Two Reds.*

Lobel, Arnold. *Frog and Toad Are Friends.*

———. Illus. Anita Lobel. *On Market Street.*

Low, Joseph. *Mice Twice.*

Macauley, David. *Black and White.*

———. *Castle.*

———. *Cathedral.*

MacDonald, Suse. *Alphabetics.*

Malcolmson, Anne. Illus. Virginia Lee Burton. *Song of Robin Hood.*

Marshall, James. *Goldilocks and the Three Bears.*

Martin, Jacqueline Briggs. Illus. Mary Azarian. *Snowflake Bentley.*

McCarty, Peter. *Hondo & Fabian.*

McCloskey, Robert. *Blueberries for Sal.*

———. *Make Way for Ducklings.*

———. *One Morning in Maine.*

———. *Time of Wonder.*

McCully, Emily Arnold. *Mirette on the Highwire.*

McDermott, Beverly Brodsky. *The Golem: A Jewish Legend.*

McDermott, Gerald. *Anansi the Spider: A Tale from the Ashanti.*

———. *Arrow to the Sun.*

———. *Raven: A Trickster Tale from the Pacific Northwest.*

McGinley, Phyllis. Illus. Helen Stone. *All Around the Town.*

———. *The Most Wonderful Doll in the World.*

McKissack, Patricia. Illus. Jerry Pinkney. *Mirandy and Brother Wind.*

Milhous, Katherine. *The Egg Tree.*

Minarik, Else H. Illus. Maurice Sendak. *Little Bear's Visit.*

Mosel, Arlene. Illus. Blair Lent. *The Funny Little Woman.*

Moss, Lloyd. Illus. Marjorie Priceman. *Zin! Zin! Zin! A Violin.*

Mugrove, Margaret. Illus. Leo and Diane Dillon. *Ashanti to Zulu: African Traditions.*

Myers, Walter Dean. Illus. Christopher Myers. *Harlem: A Poem.*

Ness, Evaline. *Sam, Bangs & Moonshine.*

———. *Tom Tit Tot.*

Newberry, Clare Turlay. *April's Kittens.*

———. *Barkis.*

———. *Marshmallow.*

Olds, Elizabeth. *Feather Mountain.*

Peet, Bill. *Bill Peet: An Autobiography.*

Peletier, David. *The Graphic Alphabet.*

Perrault, Charles. Illus. Fred Marcellino. *Puss in Boots.*

Petersham, Maud, and Miska. *An American ABC.*

———. *The Rooster Crows.*

Pilkey, Dav. *The Paperboy.*

Pinkney, Andrea Davis. Illus. Brian Pinkney. *Duke Ellington: The Piano Prince and the Orchestra.*

Pinkney, Jerry. *Noah's Ark.*

Plume, Ilse. *The Bremen-Town Musicians.*

Politi, Leo. *Juanita.*

———. *Pedro, the Angel of Olvera Street.*

———. *Song of the Swallows.*

Preston, Edna Mitchell. Illus. Robert Andrew Parker. *Pop Corn & Ma Goodness.*

Prevensen, Alice, and Martin. *The Glorious Flight: Across the Channel with Louis Bleriot.*

Ransome, Arthur. Illus. Uri Shulevitz. *The Fool of the World and the Flying Ship.*

Rappaport, Doreen. Illus. Bryan Collier. *Martin's Big Words: The Life of Dr. Martin Luther King, Jr.*

Raschka, Chris. *Yo! Yes?*

Rathmann, Peggy. *Officer Buckle and Gloria.*

Reed, Philip. *Mother Goose and Nursery Rhymes.*

Reyher, Becky. Illus. Ruth Gannett. *My Mother Is the Most Beautiful Woman in the World.*

Ringgold, Faith. *Tar Beach.*

Robbins, Ruth. Illus. Nicolas Sidjakov. *Babouschka and the Three Kings.*

Rohmann, Eric. *My Friend, Rabbit.*

———. *Time Flies.*

Rylant, Cynthia. Illus. Stephen Gammell. *The Relatives Came.*

———. *When I Was Young in the Mountains.*

St. George, Judith. Illus. David Small. *So You Want to Be President?*

San Souci, Robert D. Illus. Brian Pinkney. *The Faithful Friend.*

———. Illus. Jerry Pinkney. *The Talking Eggs: A Folktale from the American South.*

Sawyer, Ruth. Illus. Kate Seredy. *The Christmas Anna Angel.*

———. Illus. Robert McCloskey. *Journey Cake, Ho!*

Say, Allen. *Grandfather's Journey.*

Scheer, Julian. Illus. Marvin Bileck. *Rain Makes Applesauce.*

Schlein, Miriam. Illus. Jean Charlot. *When Will the World Be Mine?*

Schreiber, Georges. *Bambino the Clown.*

Scieszka, Jon. Illus. Lane Smith. *The Stinky Cheese Man and Other Fairly Stupid Tales.*

Sendak, Maurice. *In the Night Kitchen.*

———. *Outside Over There.*

———. *Where the Wild Things Are.*

Seuss, Dr. (pseud. Theodor Seuss Geisel). *Bartholomew and the Oobleck.*

———. *If I Ran the Zoo.*

———. *McElligott's Pool.*

Shannon, David. *No, David!*

Shulevitz, Uri. *Fool of the World.*

———. *Snow.*

———. *The Treasure.*

Simont, Marc. *The Stray Dog.*

Sís, Peter. *Starry Messenger.*

———. *Tibet through the Red Box.*

Sleator, William. Illus. Blair Lent. *The Angry Moon.*

Snyder, Diane. Illus. Allen Say. *The Boy of the Three-Year Nap.*

Spier, Peter. *Fox Went out on a Chilly Night: An Old Song.*

———. *Noah's Ark.*

Steig, William. *The Amazing Bone.*

———. *Sylvester and the Magic Pebble.*

Steptoe, John. *Mufaro's Beautiful Daughters: An African Tale.*

———. *The Story of Jumping Mouse: A Native American Legend.*

Stevens, Janet. *Tops and Bottoms.*

Stewart, Sarah. Illus. David Small. *The Gardener.*

Tabeck, Simms. *Joseph Had a Little Overcoat.*

———. *There Was an Old Lady Who Swallowed a Fly.*

Tafuri, Nancy. *Have You Seen My Duckling?*

Thayer, Ernest Lawrence. Illus. Christopher Bing. *Casey at the Bat: A Ballad of the Republic Sung the Year 1888.*

Thurber, James. Illus. Louis Slobodkin. *Many Moons.*

Titus, Eve. Illus. Paul Galdone. *Anatole.*

———. *Anatole and the Cat.*

Tresselt, Alvin. Illus. Roger Duvoisin. *Hide and Seek Fog.*

———. Illus. Leonard Weisgard. *Rain Drop Splash.*

Tudor, Tasha. *Mother Goose.*

———. *1 Is One.*

Turkle, Brinton. *Thy Friend, Obadiah.*

Turlay, Clare. *T-Bone, the Baby Sitter.*

Udry, Janice May. Illus. Maurice Sendak. *The Moon Jumpers.*

———. Illus. Marc Simont. *A Tree Is Nice.*

Updike, John. Illus. Trina Schart Hyman. *A Child's Calendar.*

Van Allsburg, Chris. *The Garden of Abdul Gasazi.*

———. *Jumanji.*

———. *The Polar Express.*

Ward, Lynd. *The Biggest Bear.*

Wheeler, Opal. Illus. Marjorie Torrey. *Sing Mother Goose.*

———. *Sing in Praise: A Collection of the Best Loved Hymns.*

Wiese, Kurt. *Fish in the Air.*

———. *You Can Write Chinese.*

Wiesner, David. *Free Fall.*

———. *Sector 7.*

———. *The Three Pigs.*

———. *Tuesday.*

Willard, Nancy. Illus. Alice and Martin Provensen. *A Visit to William Blake's Inn: Poems for Innocent and Experienced Travelers.*

Willems, Mo. *Don't Let the Pigeon Drive the Bus.*

———. *Knuffle Bunny: A Cautionary Tale.*

Williams, Sherley Anne. Illus. Carole Byard. *Working Cotton.*

Williams, Vera B. *A Chair for My Mother.*

———. *"More More More," Said the Baby: Three Love Stories.*

Wisniewski, David. *Golem.*

Wood, Audrey. Illus. Don Wood. *King Bidgood's in the Bathtub.*

Woodson, Jacqueline. Illus. E. B. Lewis. *Coming on Home Soon.*

Yashima, Taro. *Crow Boy.*

———. *Seashore Story.*

———. *Umbrella.*

Yolen, Jane. Illus. Ed Young. *The Emperor and the Kite.*

———. Illus. John Schoenherr. *Owl Moon.*

Yorinks, Arthur. Illus. Richard Egielski. *Hey, Al.*

Young, Ed. *Lon Po Po: A Red-Riding Hood Story from China.*

———. *Seven Blind Mice.*

Zelinsky, Paul O. *Rapunzel.*

———. *Rumpelstiltskin.*

———. *The Swamp Angel.*

Zemach, Harve. Illus. Margot Zemach. *Duffy and the Devil.*

———. *The Judge: An Untrue Tale.*

Zemach, Margot. *It Could Always Be Worse.*

Zion, Gene. Illus. Margaret Bloy. *All Falling Down.*

Zolotow, Charlotte. Illus. Maurice Sendak. *Mr. Rabbit and the Lovely Present.*

———. Illus. Margaret Bloy Graham. *The Storm Book.*

Caldecott Medalists and Honor Books, by Title

Abraham Lincoln, by Ingri and Edgar Parin d'Aulaire.

The Ageless Story, by Lauren Ford.

Alexander and the Wind-Up Mouse, by Leo Lionni.

All Around the Town, by Phyllis McGinley; illus. Helen Stone.

All Falling Down, by Gene Zion; illus. Margaret Bloy.

All in the Morning Early, by Leclaire Alger (pseud. Sorche Nic Leodhas); illus. Evaline Ness.

Alphabet City, by Stephen T. Johnson.

Alphabetics, by Suse MacDonald.

Always Room for One More, by Leclair Alger (pseud. Sorche Nic Leodhas); illus. Nonny Hogrogian.

The Amazing Bone, by William Steig.

An American ABC, by Maud and Miska Petersham.

America's Ethan Allen, by Stewart Holbrook; illus. Lynd Ward.

Anansi the Spider: A Tale from the Ashanti, adapted and illus. by Gerald McDermott.

Anatole, by Eve Titus; illus. Paul Galdone.

Anatole and the Cat, by Eve Titus; illus. Paul Galdone.

Andy and the Lion, by James Daugherty.

The Angry Moon, retold by William Sleator; illus. Blair Lent.

Animals of the Bible, a Picture Book, selected by Helen Dean Fish; illus. Dorothy P. Lathrop.

Ape in a Cape: An Alphabet of Odd Animals, by Fritz Eichenberg.

April's Kittens, by Clare Turlay Newberry.

Arrow to the Sun, by Gerald McDermott.

Ashanti to Zulu: African Traditions, by Margaret Mugrove; illus. Leo and Diane Dillon.

Baboushka and the Three Kings, by Ruth Robbins; illus. Nicolas Sidjakov.

Bambino the Clown, by Georges Schreiber.

Barkis, by Clare Turlay Newberry.

Bartholomew and the Oobleck, by Theodor Seuss Geisel (pseud. Dr. Seuss).

Bear Party, by William Pène du Bois.

Ben's Trumpet, by Rachel Isadora.

The Big Snow, by Berta and Elmer Hader.

The Biggest Bear, by Lynd Ward.

Bill Peet: An Autobiography by Bill Peet.

Black and White, by David Macaulay.

Blueberries for Sal, by Robert McCloskey.

Boats on the River, by Marjorie Flack; illus. Jay Hyde Barnum.

Book of the Nursery and Mother Goose Rhymes, illus. Marguerite de Angeli.

The Boy of the Three-Year Nap, by Diane Snyder; illus. Allen Say.

The Bremen-Town Musicians, retold and illus. Ilse Plume.

Casey at the Bat: A Ballad of the Republic Sung

the Year 1888, by Ernest Lawrence Thayer; illus. Christopher Bing.

Castle, by David Macaulay.

Cathedral, by David Macaulay.

A Chair for My Mother, by Vera B. Williams.

Chanticleer and the Fox, adapted and illus. Barbara Cooney.

A Child's Calendar, John Updike; illus. Trina Schart Hyman.

A Child's Good Night Book, by Margaret Wise Brown; illus. Jean Charlot.

The Christmas Anna Angel, by Ruth Sawyer; illus. Kate Seredy.

Cinderella, or The Little Glass Slipper, trans. and illus. Marcia Brown.

Click, Clack, Moo: Cows That Type, by Doreen Cronin; illus. Betsy Lewin.

Cock-a-Doodle Doo, by Berta and Elmer Hader.

Color Zoo, by Lois Ehlert.

Coming On Home Soon, by Jacqueline Woodson; illus. by E. B. Lewis.

The Contest, retold and illus. Nonny Hogrogian.

Crow Boy, by Taro Yashima.

Dash and Dart, by Mary and Conrad Buff.

The Day We Saw the Sun Come Up, by Alice E. Goudey; illus. Adrienne Adams.

The Desert Is Theirs, by Bryd Baylor; illus. Peter Parnall.

Dick Whittington and His Cat, by Marcia Brown.

The Dinosaurs of Waterhouse Hawkins, by Barbara Kerley; illus. Brian Selznick.

Drummer Hoff, adapted by Barbara Emberley; illus. Ed Emberley.

Duffy and the Devil, retold by Harve Zemach; illus. Margot Zemach.

Duke Ellington: The Piano Prince and the Orchestra, by Andrea Davis Pinkney; illus. Brian Pinkney.

The Egg Tree, by Katherine Milhous.

The Emperor and the Kite, by Jane Yolen; illus. Ed Young.

Fables, by Arnold Lobel.

The Faithful Friend, by Robert D. San Souci; illus. Brian Pinkney.

Feather Mountain, by Elizabeth Olds.

Finders Keepers, by William Lipkind (pseud. Will); illus. Nicholas Mordvinoff (pseud. Nicolas).

Fish for Supper, by M. B. Goffstein.

Fish in the Air, by Kurt Wiese.

Five Little Monkeys, by Juliet Kepes.

Fly High, Fly Low, by Don Freeman.

The Fool of the World and the Flying Ship, retold by Arthur Ransome; illus. Uri Shulevitz.

The Forest Pool, by Laura Adams Armer.

Four and Twenty Blackbirds, by Helen Dean Fish; illus. Robert Lawson.

Fox Went out on a Chilly Night: An Old Song, by Peter Spier.

Frederick, by Leo Lionni.

Free Fall, by David Wiesner.

Freight Train, by Donald Crews.

Frog and Toad Are Friends, by Arnold Lobel.

Frog Went A-Courtin', retold by John Langstaff; illus. Feodor Rojankovsky.

The Funny Little Woman, retold by Arlene Mosel; illus. Blair Lent.

The Garden of Abdul Gasazi, by Chris Van Allsburg.

The Gardener, by Sarah Stewart; illus. David Small.

Gillespie and the Guards, by Benjamin Elkin; illus. James Daugherty.

The Girl Who Loved Wild Horses, by Paul Goble.

The Glorious Flight: Across the Channel with Louis Bleriot, by Alice and Martin Prevensen.

Goggles! by Ezra Jack Keats.

Goldilocks and the Three Bears, by James Marshall.

Golem, by David Wisniewski.

The Golem: A Jewish Legend, by Beverly Brodsky McDermott.

Grandfather's Journey, by Allen Say.

The Graphic Alphabet, by David Peletier.

Green Eyes, by A. Birnbaum.

The Grey Lady and the Strawberry Snatcher, by Molly Bang.

Hansel and Gretel, retold by Rika Lesser; illus. Paul O. Zelinsky.

The Happy Day, by Ruth Krauss; illus. Marc Simont.

Harlem, by Walter Dean Myers; illus. Christopher Myers.

Have You Seen My Duckling?, by Nancy Tafuri.

Hawk, I'm Your Brother, by Byrd Baylor; illus. Peter Panall.

Henry Fisherman, by Marcia Brown.

Hershel and the Hanukkah Goblins, by Eric Kimmel; illus. Trina Schart Hyman.

Hey, Al, by Arthur Yorinks; illus. Richard Egielski.

Hide and Seek Fog, by Alvin Tresselt; illus. Roger Duvoisin.

Hondo and Fabian, by Peter McCarty.

Hosie's Alphabet, by Hosea, Tobias, and Lisa Baskin; illus. Leonard Baskin.

The House That Jack Built—La Maison Que Jacques a Batie, by Antonio Frasconi.

Houses from the Sea, by Alice E. Goudey; illus. Adrienne Adams.

Hush! A Thai Lullaby, by Minfong Ho; illus. Holly Meade.

If All the Seas Were One Sea, by Janina Domanska.

If I Ran the Zoo, by Theodor Seuss Geisel (pseud. Dr. Seuss).

In the Forest, by Marie Hall Ets.

In My Mother's House, by Ann Nolan Clark; illus. Velino Herrera.

In the Night Kitchen, by Maurice Sendak.

In the Small, Small Pond, by Denise Fleming.

Inch by Inch, by Leo Lionni.

It Could Always Be Worse, retold and illus. Margot Zemach.

Jambo Means Hello: Swahili Alphabet Book, by Muriel Feelings; illus. Tom Feelings.

John Henry, by Julius Lester; illus. Jerry Pinkney.

Joseph Had a Little Overcoat, by Simms Taback.

Journey Cake, Ho!, by Ruth Sawyer; illus. Robert McCloskey.

Juanita, by Leo Politi.

The Judge: An Untrue Tale, by Harve Zemach; illus. Margot Zemach.

Jumanji, by Chris Van Allsburg.

Just Me, by Marie Hall Ets.

King Bidgood's in the Bathtub, by Audrey Wood; illus. Don Wood.

Kitten's First Full Moon, by Kevin Henkes.

Knuffle Bunny: A Cautionary Tale, by Mo Willems.

Lion, by William Pène du Bois.

Little Bear's Visit, by Else H. Minarik; illus. Maurice Sendak.

The Little House, by Virginia Lee Burton.

The Little Island, by Margaret Wise Brown (pseud. Golden MacDonald); illus. Leonard Weisgard.

Little Lost Lamb, by Margaret Wise Brown (pseud. Golden MacDonald); illus. Leonard Weisgard.

Little Red Riding Hood, retold and illus. Trina Schart Hyman.

Lon Po Po: A Red-Riding Hood Story from China, by Ed Young.

Madeline, by Ludwig Bemelmans.

Madeline's Rescue, by Ludwig Bemelmans.

Make Way for Ducklings, by Robert McCloskey.

Many Moons, by James Thurber; illus. Louis Slobodkin.

Marshmallow, by Clare Turlay Newberry.

Martin's Big Words: The Life of Dr. Martin Luther King, Jr., by Doreen Rappaport; illus. Bryan Collier.

May I Bring a Friend?, by Beatrice Schenk de Regniers; illus. Beni Montresor.

McElligott's Pool, by Theodor Seuss Geisel (pseud. Dr. Seuss).

Mei Li, by Thomas Handforth.

Mice Twice, by Joseph Low.

The Mighty Hunter, by Berta and Elmer Hader.

Mirandy and Brother Wind, by Patricia C. McKissack; illus. Jerry Pinkney.

Mirette on the High Wire, by Emily Arnold McCully.

Mister Penny's Race Horse, by Marie Hall Ets.

Moja Means One: Swahili Counting Book, by Muriel Feelings; illus. Tom Feelings.

The Moon Jumpers, by Janice May Udry; illus. Maurice Sendak.

"More More More," Said the Baby: Three Love Stories, by Vera B. Williams.

The Most Wonderful Doll in the World, by Phyllis McGinley; illus. Helen Stone.

Mother Goose, illus. Tasha Tudor.

Mother Goose and Nursery Rhymes, illus. Philip Reed.

Mr. Rabbit and the Lovely Present, by Charlotte Zolotow; illus. Maurice Sendak.

Mr. T. W. Anthony Woo, by Marie Hall Ets.

Mufaro's Beautiful Daughters: An African Tale, by John Steptoe.

My Friend, Rabbit, by Eric Rohmann.

My Mother Is the Most Beautiful Woman in the World, by Becky Reyher; illus. Ruth Gannett.

Nine Days to Christmas, by Marie Hall Ets and Aurora Labastida; illus. Marie Hall Ets.

No, David!, by David Shannon.

Noah's Ark, by Jerry Pinkney.

Noah's Ark, by Peter Spier.

Nothing at All, by Wanda Gág.

Officer Buckle and Gloria, by Peggy Rathmann.

Olivia, by Ian Falconer.

On Market Street, by Arnold Lobel; illus. Anita Lobel.

One Fine Day, retold and illus. Nonny Hogrogian.

1 Is One, by Tasha Tudor.

One Morning in Maine, by Robert McCloskey.

One Wide River to Cross, adapted by Barbara Emberley; illus. Ed Emberley.

Outside Over There, by Maurice Sendak.

Owen, by Kevin Henkes.

Owl Moon, by Jane Yolen; illus. John Schoenherr.

Ox-Cart Man, by Donald Hall; illus. Barbara Cooney.

Paddle-to-the-Sea, by Holling C. Holling.

The Paperboy, by Dav Pilkey.

Pedro, the Angel of Olvera Street, by Leo Politi.

Peppe the Lamplighter, by Elisa Bartone; illus. Ted Lewin.

Pierre Pigeon, by Lee Kingman; illus. Arnold E. Bare.

Play with Me, by Marie Hall Ets.

A Pocketful of Cricket, by Rebecca Caudill; illus. Evaline Ness.

The Polar Express, by Chris Van Allsburg.

Pop Corn & Ma Goodness, by Edna Mitchell Preston; illus. Robert Andrew Parker.

Prayer for a Child, by Rachel Field; illus. Elizabeth Orton Jones.

Puss in Boots, trans. and illus. by Marcia Brown.

Puss in Boots, by Charles Perrault; illus. Fred Marcellino.

Rain Drop Splash, by Alvin Tresselt; illus. Leonard Weisgard.

Rain Makes Applesauce, by Julian Scheer; illus. Marvin Bileck.

Rapunzel, by Paul O. Zelinsky.

Raven: A Trickster Tale from the Pacific Northwest, by Gerald McDermott.

The Red Book, by Barbara Lehman.

The Relatives Came, by Cynthia Rylant; illus. Stephen Gammell.

Roger and the Fox, by Lavinia R. Davis; illus. Hildegard Woodward.

The Rooster Crows, by Maud and Miska Petersham.

Rumpelstiltskin, by Paul O. Zelinsky.

Saint George and the Dragon, retold by Margaret Hodges; illus. Trina Schart Hyman.

Sam, Bangs & Moonshine, by Evaline Ness.

Seashore Story, by Taro Yashima.

Sector 7, by David Wiesner.

Seven Blind Mice, by Ed Young.

Seven Simeons: A Russian Tale, retold and illus. Boris Artzybasheff.

Shadow, trans. and illus. Marcia Brown.

Sing Mother Goose, music by Opal Wheeler; illus. Marjorie Torrey.

Sing in Praise: A Collection of the Best Loved Hymns, selected by Opal Wheeler; illus. Marjorie Torrey.

Skipper John's Cook, by Marcia Brown.

Small Rain: Verses from the Bible, selected by Jessie Orton Jones; illus. Elizabeth Orton Jones.

Smoky Night, by Eve Bunting; illus. David Diaz.

Snow, by Uri Shulevitz.

Snow-White and the Seven Dwarfs, trans. Randall Jarrell; illus. Nancy Ekholm Burkert.

Snow White and the Seven Dwarfs, by Wanda Gág.

Snowflake Bentley, by Jacqueline Briggs Martin; illus. Mary Azarian.

The Snowy Day, by Ezra Jack Keats.

Song of Robin Hood, edited by Anne Malcolmson; illus. Virginia Lee Burton.

So You Want to be President?, by Judith St. George; illus. David Small.

Song and Dance Man, by Karen Ackerman; illus. Stephen Gammell.

Song of the Swallows, by Leo Politi.

The Spider and the Fly, by Mary Howitt; illus. Tony DiTerlizzi.

Starry Messenger, by Peter Sís.

The Steadfast Tin Soldier, trans. M. R. James; illus. Marcia Brown.

The Stinky Cheese Man and Other Fairly Stupid Tales, by Jon Scieszka; illus. Lane Smith.

Stone Soup, by Marcia Brown.

The Storm Book, by Charlotte Zolotow; illus. Margaret Bloy Graham.

A Story a Story, by Gail E. Haley.

The Story of Jumping Mouse: A Native American Legend, by John Steptoe.

The Stray Dog, by Marc Simont.

Strega Nona, by Tomie dePaola.

The Sun Is a Golden Earring, by Natalia M. Belting; illus. Bernarda Bryson.

Swamp Angel, by Anne Issacs; illus. Paul O. Zelinsky.

Swimmy, by Leo Lionni.

Sylvester and the Magic Pebble, by William Steig.

The Talking Eggs: A Folktale from the American South, by Robert D. San Souci; illus. Jerry Pinkney.

Tar Beach, by Faith Ringgold.

T-Bone, the Baby Sitter, by Clare Turlay.

Ten, Nine, Eight, by Molly Bang.

The Thanksgiving Story, by Alice Dalgliesh; illus. Helen Sewell.

There Was an Old Lady Who Swallowed a Fly, by Simms Tabeck.

They Were Strong and Good, by Robert Lawson.

Three Jovial Huntsmen, by Susan Jeffers.

The Three Pigs, by David Wiesner.

Thy Friend, Obadiah, by Brinton Turkle.

Tibet through the Red Box, by Peter Sís.

Time Flies, by Eric Rohmann.

Time of Wonder, by Robert McCloskey.

Timothy Turtle, by Al Graham; illus. Tony Palazzo.

Tom Tit Tot, retold and illus. by Evaline Ness.

Tops and Bottoms, by Janet Stevens.

The Treasure, by Uri Shulevitz.

A Tree Is Nice, by Janice Udry; illus. Marc Simont.

Truck, by Donald Crews.

Tuesday, by David Wiesner.

The Two Reds, by William Lipkind (pseud. Will); illus. Nicholas Mordivanoff (pseud. Nicolas).

The Ugly Duckling, by Hans Christian Andersen; illus. Jerry Pinkney.

Umbrella, by Yaro Yashima.

The Very Hungry Caterpillar, by Eric Carle.

A Very Special House, by Ruth Krauss; illus. Maurice Sendak.

The Village of Round and Square Houses, by Ann Grifalconi.

A Visit to William Blake's Inn: Poems for Innocent and Experienced Travelers, by Nancy Willard; illus. Alice and Martin Provensen.

The Wave, by Margaret Hodges; illus. Blair Lent.

The Way to Start a Day, by Byrd Baylor; illus. Peter Parnall.

Wee Gillis, by Munro Leaf; illus. Robert Lawson.

What Do You Say, Dear?, by Sesyle Joslin; illus. Maurice Sendak.

Wheel on the Chimney, by Margaret Wise Brown; illus. Tibor Gergely.

When Clay Sings, by Byrd Baylor; illus. Tom Bahti.

When I Was Young in the Mountains, by Cynthia Rylant; illus. Diane Goode.

When Sophie Gets Angry—Really, Really, Angry, by Molly Bang.

When Will the World Be Mine?, by Miriam Schlein; illus. Jean Charlot.

Where the Buffaloes Begin, by Olaf Baker; illus. Stephen Gammell.

Where the Wild Things Are, by Maurice Sendak.

White Snow, Bright Snow, by Berta and Elmer Hader.

Why Mosquitoes Buzz in People's Ears, retold by Verna Aardema; illus. Leo and Diane Dillon.

Why the Sun and the Moon Live in the Sky, by Elhinstone Dayrell; illus. Blair Lent.

The Wild Birthday Cake, by Lavinia R. Davis; illus. Hildegard Woodward.

Working Cotton, by Sherley Anne Williams; illus. Carole Byard.

Yo! Yes?, by Chris Raschka.

Yonie Wondernose, by Marguerite de Angeli.

You Can Write Chinese, by Kurt Wiese.

Zin! Zin! Zin! A Violin, by Lloyd Moss; illus. Marjorie Priceman.

Charlotte Zolotow Book Awards for Best Picture Book Text

1998

Winner

- Williams, Vera B., *Lucky Song* (Greenwillow, 1997).

Honor Book

- Kasza, Keiko, *Don't Laugh, Joe!* (Putnam, 1997).

Highly Commended

- Bauer, Marion Dane. *If You Were Born a Kitten*. Illus. JoEllen McAllister Stammen (Simon, 1997).
- Cooper, Elisha. *Country Fair* (Greenwillow, 1997).
- Fleming, Denise. *Time to Sleep* (Henry Holt, 1997).
- McKissack, Patricia C. *Ma Dear's Aprons*. Illus. Floyd Cooper (Atheneum, 1997).
- Waber, Bernard. *Bearsie Bear and the Surprise Sleepover Party* (Houghton Mifflin, 1997).
- Wells, Rosemary. *Bunny Cakes* (Dial, 1997).

1999

Winner

- Shulevitz, Uri. *Snow* (Farrar, Straus and Giroux, 1998).

Honor Books

- Meade, Holly. *John Willy and Freddy McGee* (Cavendish, 1998).
- Steig, William. *Pete's a Pizza* (Harper, 1998).

Highly Commended

- Fleming, Denise. *Mama Cat Has Three Kittens* (Henry Holt, 1998).
- Henkes, Kevin. *Circle Dogs*. Illus. Dan Yaccarino (Greenwillow, 1998).
- Jones, Bill T., and Susan Kuklin. *Dance*. Photographs by Susan Kuklin (Hyperion, 1998).
- Reiser, Lynn. *Little Clam* (Greenwillow, 1998).
- Stuve-Bodeen, Stephanie. *Elizabeti's Doll*. Illus. Christy Hale (Lee, 1998).

2000

Winner

- Bang, Molly. *When Sophie Gets Angry—Really, Really, Angry* (Scholastic, 1999).

Honor Books

- Best, Cari. *Three Cheers for Catherine the Great!* Illus. Giselle Potter (DK, 1999).
- Feiffer, Jules. *Bark, George* (Harper, 1999).

Highly Commended

- Diakité, Baba Wagué. *The Hatseller and the Monkeys* (Scholastic, 1999).
- George, Kristine O'Connell. *Little Dog Poems*. Illus. June Otani (Clarion, 1999).
- Graham, Joan Bransfield. *Flicker Flash*. Illus. Nancy Davis (Houghton Mifflin, 1999).
- Howard, Elizabeth Fitzgerald. *When Will Sarah Come?* Illus. Nina Crews (Greenwillow, 1999).
- Schwartz, Amy. *How to Catch an Elephant* (DK, 1999).
- Thomas, Joyce Carol. *You Are My Perfect Baby*. Illus. Nneka Bennett (Harper, 1999).
- Zimmerman, Andrea, and David Clemesha. *Trashy Town* (Harper, 1999).

2001

Winner

- Banks, Kate. *The Night Worker*. Illus. Georg Hallensleben (Farrar, Straus and Giroux, 2000).

Honor Book

- Myers, Christopher. *Wings* (Scholastic, 2000).

Highly Commended

- Christian, Peggy. *If You Find a Rock*. Illus. Barbara Hirsch Lember (Harcourt, 2000).
- Cronin, Doreen. *Click, Clack, Moo: Cows That Type*. Illus. Betsy Lewin (Simon, 2000).
- Harjo, Joy. *The Good Luck Cat*. Illus. Paul Lee (Harcourt, 2000).
- Kajikawa, Kimiko. *Yoshi's Feet*. Illus. Yumi Heo (DK, 2000).
- Pinkney, Sandra L. *Shades of Black: A Celebration of Our Children*. Photographs by Myles C. Pinkney (Scholastic, 2000).

- Van Laan, Nancy. *When Winter Comes*. Illus. Susan Gaber (Atheneum, 2000).

2002

Winner

- Willey, Margaret. *Clever Beatrice*. Illus. Heather Solomon (Atheneum, 2001).

Honor Book

- Jenkins, Emily. *Five Creatures* (Farrar, Straus and Giroux, 2001).

Highly Commended

- Look, Lenore. *Henry's First Moon Birthday*. Illus. Yumi Heo (Atheneum, 2001).
- MacDonald, Margaret Read. *Mabela the Clever*. Illus. Tim Coffey (Whitman, 2001).
- Russo, Marisabina. *Come Back, Hannah* (Harper, 2001).
- Stock, Catherine. *Gugu's House* (Clarion, 2001).
- Wong, Janet S. *Grump*. Illus. John Wallace (McElderry, 2001).

2003

Winner

- Keller, Holly. *Farfallina & Marcel* (Greenwillow, 2002).

Honor Book

- Swanson, Susan Marie. *The First Thing My Mama Told Me*. Illus. Christine Davenier (Harcourt, 2002).

Highly Commended

- Andrews-Goebel, Nancy. *The Pot That Juan Built*. Illus. David Diaz (Lee, 2002).
- Banks, Kate. *Close Your Eyes*. Illus. Georg Hallensleben (Farrar, Straus and Giroux, 2002).
- Henkes, Kevin. *Owen's Marshmallow Chick* (Greenwillow, 2002).

- Herrera, Juan Felipe. *Grandma and Me at the Flea*. Illus. Anita de Lucio-Brock (Children's Book Press, 2002).
- McMullen, Kate, and Jim. *I Stink!* (Harper, 2002).
- Okimoto, Jean Davies, and Elaine M. Aoki. *The White Swan Express: A Story about Adoption*. Illus. Meilo So (Clarion, 2002).
- Schertle, Alice. *All You Need for a Snowman*. Illus. Barbara Lavallee (Harcourt, 2002).
- Shannon, David. *Duck on a Bike* (Scholastic, 2002).
- Wilson, Karma. *Bear Snores On*. Illus. Jane Chapman (McElderry, 2002).
- Wong, Janet S. *Apple Pie Fourth of July*. Illus. Margaret Chodos-Irvine (Harcourt, 2002).

2004

Winner

- Schawartz, Amy. *What James Likes Best* (Atheneum, 2003).

Honor Books

- Coy, John. *Two Old Potatoes and Me*. Illus. Carolyn Fisher (Knopf, 2003).
- O'Connell, Rebecca. *The Baby Goes Beep*. Illus. Ken Wilson-Max (Roaring, 2003).
- Paye, Won-Ldy, and Margaret H. Lippert. *Mrs. Chicken and the Hungry Crocodile*. Illus. Julie Paschkis (Henry Holt, 2003).
- Rumford, James. *Calabash Cat and His Amazing Journey* (Houghton Mifflin, 2003).
- Shannon, George. *Tippy-Toe Chick, Go!* Illus. Laura Dronzek (Greenwillow, 2003).

Highly Commended

- Banks, Kate. *Mama's Coming Home*. Illus. Tomek Bogacki (Farrar, Straus and Giroux, 2003).
- Chandra, Deborah, and Madeleine Comora. *George Washington's Teeth*. Illus.

Brock Cole (Farrar, Straus and Giroux, 2003).
- Fleming, Denise. *Buster* (Henry Holt, 2003).
- Frame, Jeron Ashford. *Yesterday I Had the Blues*. Illus. R. Gregory Christie (Tricycle, 2003).
- Jenkins, Steven, and Robin Page. *What Do You Do With a Tail Like This?* (Houghton Mifflin, 2003).
- Nye, Naomi Shihab. *Baby Radar*. Illus. Nancy Carlson (Greenwillow, 2003).
- Perkins, Lynne Rae. *Snow Music* (Greenwillow, 2003).
- U'Ren, Andrea. *Mary Smith* (Farrar, Straus and Giroux, 2003).
- Willems, Mo. *Don't Let the Pigeon Drive the Bus* (Hyperion, 2003).

2005

Winner

- Henkes, Kevin. *Kitten's First Full Moon* (HarperCollins, 2004).

Honor Books

- Thompson, Lauren. *Polar Bear Night*. Illus. Stephen Savage (Scholastic, 2004).
- Willems, Mo. *Knuffle Bunny: A Cautionary Tale* (Hyperion, 2004).
- Woodson, Jacqueline. *Coming On Home Soon*. Illus. E. B. Lewis (Putnam, 2004).

Highly Commended

- Beaumont, Karen. *Baby Danced the Polka*. Illus. Jennifer Plecas (Dial, 2004).
- Buehner, Caralyn. *Superdog: The Heart of a Hero*. Illus. Mark Buehner (HarperCollins, 2004).
- Dunrea, Olivier. *BooBoo* (Houghton Mifflin, 2004).
- Durant, Alan. *Always and Forever*. Illus. Debi Gliori (Harcourt, 2004).

- English, Karen. *Hot Day on Abbott Avenue.* Illus. Javaka Steptoe (Clarion, 2004).
- Hoberman, Mary Ann. *Whose Garden Is It?* Illus. Jane Dyer (Harcourt, 2004).
- Horowitz, Dave. *A Monkey Among Us* (HarperCollins, 2004).
- MacLachlan, Patricia, and Emily MacLachlan. *Bittle.* Illus. Dan Yaccarino (HarperCollins, 2004).
- Schaefer, Carole Lexa. *The Biggest Soap.* Illus. Stacey Dressen-McQueen (Farrar, Straus and Giroux, 2004).

Coretta Scott King Book Awards and Honor Books

Only *picture books* among the award and honor books are listed.

1970

No picture book winner.

1971

No picture book winner.

1972

No picture book winner.

1973

No picture book winner.

1974

Illustrator Award Winner

Ray Charles, illus. George Ford; by Sharon Bell Mathis.

1975

No picture book winner.

1976

No picture book winner.

1977

No picture book winner.

1978

Illustrator Award Winner

Africa Dream, illus. Carole Byard; by Eloise Greenfield.

Author Honor Books

Mary McCleod Bethune, by Eloise Greenfield.
Barbara Jordan, by James Haskins.

1979

Author Honor Book

I Have a Sister, My Sister Is Deaf, illus. Deborah Ray; by Jeanne W. Peterson.

1980

Illustrator Award Winner

Cornrows, illus. Carole Byard; by Camille Yarborough.

1981

Illustrator Honor Books

Grandmama's Joy, illus. Carole Byard; by Eloise Greenfield.
Count on Your Fingers African Style, illus. Jerry Pinkney; by Claudia Zaslavsky.

1982

Illustrator Honor Book

Daydreamers, illus. Tom Feelings; by Eloise Greenfield.

1983

Illustrator Honor Book

Just Us Women, illus. Pat Cummings; by Jeanette Caines.

1984

Illustrator Award Winner

My Mama Needs Me, illus. Pat Cummings; by Mildred Walter.

1985

No picture book winner.

1986

Illustrator Award Winner

The Patchwork Quilt, illus. Jerry Pinkney; by Valie Flournoy.

1987

Illustrator Award Winner

Half a Moon and One Whole Star, illus. Jerry Pinkney; by Crescent Dragonwagon.

Honor Book

C.L.O.U.D.S., by Pat Cummings.

1988

Illustrator Award Winner

Mufaro's Beautiful Daughters: An African Tale, illus. and written by John Steptoe.

Honor Book

What a Morning! The Christmas Story in Black Spirituals, illus. Ashley Bryan; selected by John Langstaff.

1989

Illustrator Award Winner

Mirandy and Brother Wind, illus. Jerry Pinkney; by Patricia McKissack.

Honor Book

Storm in the Night, illus. Pat Cummings; by Mary Stolz.

1990

Illustrator Award Winner

Nathaniel Talking, illus. Jan Spivey; by Eloise Greenfield.

Honor Book

The Talking Eggs, illus. Jerry Pinkney; by Robert San Souci.

1991

Author Honor Book

When I Am Old with You, illus. David Soman; by Angela Johnson.

1992

Illustrator Award Winner

Tar Beach, illus. and written by Faith Ringgold.

Honor Books

All Night, All Day: A Child's First Book of African American Spirituals, illus. and selected by Ashley Bryan.

Night on Neighborhood Street, illus. Jan Spivey Gilchrist; by Eloise Greenfield.

Author Honor Book

Night on Neighborhood Street, illus. Jan Spivey Gilchrist; by Eloise Greenfield.

1993

Illustrator Award Winner

The Origin of Life on Earth: An African Creation Myth, illus. Kathleen Atkins Wilson; retold by David Anderson.

Honor Books

Little Eight John, illus. Wil Clay; by Jan Wahl.
Sukey and the Mermaid, illus. Brian Pinkney; by Robert San Souci.
Working Cotton, illus. Carole Byard; by Sherley Anne Williams.

1994

Illustrator Award Winner

Soul Looks Back in Wonder, illus. Tom Feelings; by Phyllis Fogelman.

Honor Books

Brown Honey in Broom Wheat Tea, illus. Floyd Cooper; by Joyce Carol Thomas.
Uncle Jed's Barbarshop, illus. James Ransome; by King Mitchell.

1995

Illustrator Award Winner

The Creation, illus. James Ransome; by James Weld.

Honor Books

The Singing Man, illus. Terea Shaffer; by Angela Shelf Medearis.
Meet Danitra Brown, illus. Floyd Cooper; by Nikki Grimes.

1996

Illustrator Honor Book

The Faithful Friend, illus. Brian Pinkney; by Robert San Souci.

1997

Illustrator Award Winner

Minty: A Story of Young Harriet Tubman, illus. Jerry Pinkney; by Alan Schroeder.

Honor Books

The Palm of My Heart: Poetry by African American Children, illus. Gregorie Christie; edited by Davida Adedjouma.
Running the Road to ABC, illus. Reynold Ruffins; by Denize Lauture.
Neeny Coming, Neeny Going, illus. Synthia Saint James; by Karen English.

1998

Illustrator Award Winner

In Daddy's Arms I Am Tall: African Americans Celebrating Fathers, illus. Javaka Steptoe; by Alan Schroeder.

Honor Books

Ashley Bryan's ABC of African American Poetry, illus. and written by Ashley Bryan.
Harlem, illus. Christopher Myers; by Walter Dean Myers.
The Hunterman and the Crocodile, illus. and written by Baba Wagué Diakité.

1999

Illustrator Award Winner

i see the rhythm, illus. Michele Wood; by Toyomi Ig.

Honor Books

I Have Heard of a Land, illus. Floyd Cooper; by Joyce Carol Thomas.

The Bat Boy and His Violin, illus. E. B. Lewis; by Gavin Curtis.

Duke Ellington: The Piano Prince and His Orchestra, illus. Brian Pinkney; by Andrea Davis Pinkney.

2000

Illustrator Award Winner

In the Time of the Drums, illus. Brian Pinkney; by Kim L. Siegelson.

Honor Books

My Rows and Piles of Coins, illus. E. B. Lewis; by Tololwa M. Mollel.

Black Cat, by Christopher Myers.

2001

Illustrator Award Winner

Uptown, illus. and written by Bryan Collier.

Honor Books

Freedom River, by Bryan Collier.

Only Passing Through: The Story of Sojourner Truth, illus. R. Gregory Christie; by Anne Rockwell.

2002

Illustrator Award Winner

Goin' Someplace Special, illus. Jerry Pinkney; by Patricia McKissack.

Honor Book

Martin's Big Words, illus. Bryan Collier; by Doreen Rappoport.

2003

Honor Books

Rap a Tap Tap: Here's Bojangles—Think of That, illus. and written by Leo and Diane Dillon.

Visiting Langdon, illus. Bryan Collier; by Willie Perdomo.

2004

Illustrator Award Winner

Beautiful Blackbird, by Ashley Bryan.

Honor Books

Almost to Freedom, by Colin Bootman.

Thunder Rose, illus. Kadir Nelson; by Jerdine Nolan.

2005

Illustrator Award Winner

ellington was not a street, illus. Kadir Nelson; by Ntozake Shange.

Honor Books

God Bless the Child, illus. Jerry Pinkney; by Billie Holiday and Arthur Herzog Jr.

The People Could Fly: The Picture Book, illus. Leo and Diane Dillon; by Virginia Hamilton.

Pura Belpré Medalists and Honor Books

1996

Narrative Honor Book

- *The Bossy Gallito/El Gallo de Bodas: A Traditional Cuban Folktale*, by Lucía González; illus. Lulu Delacre.

Illustration Medal Winner

- *Chato's Kitchen*, illus. Susan Guevara; by Gary Soto.

Honor Books

- *Pablo Remembers: The Fiesta of the Day of the Dead*, illus. and written by George Ancona.
- *The Bossy Gallito/El Gallo de Bodas: A Traditional Cuban Folktale*, illus. Lulu Delacre; by Lucía González.

1998

Narrative Honor Book

- *Laughing Tomatoes and Other Spring Poems/ Jitomates risueños y otros poemas de primavera*, by Francisco Alarcón; illus. Maya Christina Gonzalez.

Illustration Medal Winner

- *Snapshots from the Wedding*, illus. Stephanie Garcia; by Gary Soto.

Honor Books

- *In My Family/En mi familia*, illus. Carmen Lomas Garza.
- *The Golden Flower: A Taino Myth from Puerto Rico*, illus. Enrique O. Sánchez; by Nina Jaffe.
- *Gathering the Sun: An Alphabet in Spanish and English*, illus. Simón Silva; by Alma Flor Ada; English translation by Rosa Zubizarreta.

2000

Narrative Honor Book

- *From the Bellybutton of the Moon and Other Summer Poems/Del Ombligo de la Luna y Otro Poemas de Verano*, by Francisco X. Alarcón; illus. Maya Christina Gonzalez.

Illustration Medal Winner

- *Magic Window*, illus. Carmen Lomas Garza.

Honor Books

- *Barrio: Jose's Neighborhood*, by George Ancona.
- *The Secret Stars*, illus. Felipe Dávalos; by Joseph Slate.

- *Mama & Papa Have a Store*, illus. and written by Amelia Lau Carling.

2002

Narrative Honor Book

- *Iguanas in the Snow*, by Francisco X. Alarcón; illus. Maya Christina Gonzalez.

Illustration Medal Winner

- *Chato and the Party Animals*, illus. Susan Guevara; by Gary Soto.

Honor Book

- *Juan Bobo Goes to Work*, illus. Joe Cepada; retold by Marisa Montes.

2004

Illustration Medal Winner

- *Just a Minute: A Trickster*, by Yuyi Morales.

Illustration Honor Books

- *First Day in Grapes*, illus. Robert Casilla; by L. King Pérez.
- *The Pot That Juan Built*, illus. David Diaz; by Nancy Andrews-Goebel.
- *Harvesting Hope: The Story of Cesar Chavez*, illus. Yuyi Morales; by Kathleen Krull.

Narrative Honor Book

- *My Diary from Here to There/Mi Diario de Aquí Hasta Allá*, by Amada Irma Pérez.

Reading Rainbow Books, by Title

This is the complete listing; most, but not all, are picture books.

Abiyoyo, by Pete Seeger; illus. Michael Hays.

Abuela, by Arthur Dorros, illus. Elisa Kleven.

The Adventures of Taxi Dog, by Debra and Sal Barracca, illus. Mark Buehner.

Albert the Running Bear's Exercise Book, by Barbara Isenberg and Marjorie Jaffe; illus. Diane de Groat.

Alejandro's Gift, by Richard E. Albert; illus. Sylvia Long.

Alexander and the Terrible, Horrible, No Good, Very Bad Day, by Judith Viorst; illus. Ray Cruz.

Allistair in Outer Space, by Marilyn Sadler; illus. Roger Bollen.

Allistair's Time Machine, by Marilyn Sadler, illus. Roger Bollen.

All about Whales, by Dorothy Hinshaw Patent.

All the Colors of the Race, by Arnold Adoff; illus. John Steptoe.

All Those Secrets of the World, by Jane Yolen; illus. Leslie Baker.

Alligator Shoes, by Arthur Dorros.

Aloha Dolores, by Barbara Samuels.

Alvin Ailey, by Andrea Davis Pinkney; illus. Brian Pinkney.

Always My Dad, by Sharon Dennis Wyeth, illus. Rául Colón.

The Always Prayer Shawl, by Sheldon Oberman; illus. Ted Lewin.

Amazing Bats, by Frank Greenaway; photos by Jerry Young and Frank Greenaway.

The Amazing Bone, by William Steig.

Amazing Grace, by Mary Hoffman; illus. Caroline Binch.

Amazon Diary: The Jungle Adventure of Alex Winters, by Hudson Talbott and Mark Greenberg.

Amelia's Fantastic Flight, by Rose Bursik.

Amy: The Story of a Deaf Child, by Lou Ann Walker; photos by Michael Abramson.

And Still the Turtle Watched, by Sheila MacFill-Callahan; pictures by Barry Moser.

Angel Child, Dragon Child, by Michelle Maria Surat; illus. Vo-Dinh Mai.

Animal Cafe, by John Stadler.

Anno's Journey, by Mitusmasa Anno.

Ant Cities, by Arthur Dorros.

Apt. 3, by Ezra Jack Keats.

Archibald Frisby, by Michael Chesworth.

The Art Lesson, by Tomie dePaola.

Arthur's Eyes, by Marc Brown.

Aunt Eater Loves a Mystery, by Doug Cushman.

Ayu and the Perfect Moon, by David Cox.

Baby Animals on the Farm, by Hans-Heinrich Isenbart; trans. Elizabeth D. Crawford; photos by Ruth Rau.

Backyard Insects, by Ronald Goor and Millicent E. Selsam; photos by Ronald Goor.

Badger's Parting Gifts, by Susan Varley.

The Banza, by Diane Wolkstein; illus. Marc Brown.

Barn Dance!, by Bill Martin Jr. and John Archambault; illus. Ted Rand.

Bea and Mr. Jones, by Amy Schwartz.

Begin at the Beginning, by Amy Schwartz.

Being Adopted, by Maxine B. Rosenberg; photos by George Ancona.

Belioz the Bear, by Jan Brett.

Ben's Trumpet, by Rachel Isadora.

Best Friends, by Steven Kellogg.

Better Homes and Gardens New Junior Cookbook, edited by Gerald Knox.

Better Homes and Gardens Step-by-Step Kid's Cookbook, edited by Gerald Knox.

The Bicycle Man, by Allen Say.

The Big Balloon Race, by Eleanor Coerr; illus. Carolyn Croll.

Big City Port, by Ellen DelVecchio and Betsy Maestro; illus. Giulio Maestro.

The Big Hello, by Janet Schulman; illus. Lillian Hoban.

Bill and Pete Go Down the Nile, by Tomie dePaola.

The Bionic Bunny Show, by Laurence Krasny Brown and Marc Brown.

Bird Watch, by Jane Yolen; illus. Ted Lewin.

Blackberry Ink, by Eve Merriam; pictures by Hans Wilhelm.

The Books of Pigericks, by Arnold Lobel.

Bored—Nothing to Do!, by Peter Spier.

Born in the Gravy, by Denys Gazet.

Borreguita and the Coyote, by Verna Aardema; illus. Petra Mathers Bossyboots by David Cox.

Boundless Grace, by Mary Hoffman; pictures by Caroline Binch.

The Brand New Kid, by Katie Couric; illus. Marjorie Priceman.

Bread Bread Bread, by Ann Morris; photos by Ken Heyman.

Bringing the Rain to Kapiti Plain, by Verna Aardema; illus. Beatriz Vidal.

Brush, by Pere Calders; illus. Carme Sole Vendrell.

The Bug Book and the Bug Bottle, by Dr. Hugh Danks; illus. Joe Weissman.

Bugs, by Nancy Winslow Parker and Joan Richards Wright; illus. Nancy Winslow Parker.

Busy, Busy Squirrels, by Colleen Stanley Bare.

A Cache of Jewels and Other Collective Nouns, by Ruth Heller.

Cactus, by Cynthia Overbeck; photos by Shabo Hani.

Caps for Sale, by Esphyr Slobodkina.

The Car Washing Street, by Denise Lewis Patrick; illus. John Ward.

The Carousel, by Liz Rosenberg; illus. Jim LaMarche.

Casey at the Bat, by Ernest Lawrence Thayer; illus. Ken Bachaus.

Cat & Canary, by Michael Foreman.

Caves, by Roma Gans; illus. Giulio Maestro.

Celebrate the Fifty States, by Loreen Leedy.

A Chair for My Mother, by Vera B. Williams.

Changes, by Marjorie N. Allen and Shelley Rotner; photos by Shelley Rotner.

Charlie Parker Played Be Bop, by Chris Raschka.

Check It Out! The Book about Libraries, by Gail Gibbons.

Chickens Aren't the Only Ones, by Ruth Heller.

The Chipmunk Song, by Joanne Ryder; illus. Lynne Cherry.

The Cloud Book, by Tomie dePaola.

Cloudy with a Chance of Meatballs, by Judi Barrett; illus. Ron Barrett.

Come a Tide, by George Ella Lyon; illus. Stephen Gammell.

Come Away from the Water, Shirley, by John Burningham.

Come Out, Muskrats, by Jim Arnosky.

Commander Toad series, by Jane Yolen; illus. Bruce Degen.

Conga Crocodile, by Nicole Rubel.

Cordelia, Dance!, by Sarah Stapler.

"Could Be Worse!," by James Stevenson.

Coyote Dreams, by Susan Nunes; illus. Ronald Himler.

Creatures of the Sea, by John Christopher Fine.

Crictor, by Tomi Ungerer.

Dabble Duck, by Anne Leo Ellis; illus. Sue Truesdell.

Daddy Is a Monster Sometimes, by John Steptoe.

Dakota Dugout, by Ann Turner; illus. Ronald Himler.

The Dancing Man, by Ruth Lercher; illus. Ruth Lercher.

Dancing with the Indians, by Angela Shelf Medearis; illus. Samuel Byrd.

Darcy and Gran Don't Like Babies, by Jane Cutler; illus. Susannah Ryan.

A Day in the Life of a Marine Biologist, by David Paige; photos by Roger Ruhlin.

A Day Underwater, by Deborah Kovacs.

The Day Jimmy's Boa Ate the Wash, by Trinka Hakes Noble; illus. Steven Kellogg.

A Day's Work, by Eve Bunting; illus. Ronald Himler.

Daydreamers, by Eloise Greenfield; illus. Tom Feelings.

Deer at the Brook, by Jim Arnosky.

Delphine, by Molly Bang.

The Desert Alphabet Book, by Jerry Pallotta; illus. Mark Astrella.

Desert Giant: The World of the Saguaro Cactus, by Barbara Bash.

Diego, by Jonah Winter; illus. Jeanette Winter.

Digging Up Dinosaurs, by Aliki.

Dinosaur Bob and His Adventures with the Family Lazardo, by William Joyce.

Dinosaur Time, by Peggy Parish; illus. Arnold Lobel.

Dinosaurs! A Drawing Book, by Michael Emberley.

Dive to the Coral Reefs, by Paul Erickson, Les Kaufman, and Elizabeth Tayntor.

Don't Laugh at Me, by Steve Seskin and Allen Shamblin; illus. Glin Dibley.

The Dream Eater, by Christian Garrison, illus. Diane Goode.

Duncan and Delores, by Barbara Samuels.

Earth Hounds, as Explained by Professor Xargle, by Jeanne Willis; illus. Tony Ross.

Easy Origami, by Dokuohtei Nakano; trans. Eric Kenneway.

Easy-to-Make Spaceships That Really Fly, by Mary and Dewey Blcksma; illus. Marisabina Russo.

Eats Poems, by Arnold Adoff; illus. Susan Russo.

Ed Emberley's Science Flip Books, by Ed Emberley.

The Edible Pyramid: Good Eating Every Day, by Loreen Leedy.

Egg to Chick, by Millicent E. Selsam; illus. Barbara Wolff.

Egg-Carton Zoo, by Hans Blohm and Rudi Haas.

Emma, by Wendy Kesselman; illus. Barbara Cooney.

Emma's Dragon Hunt, by Catherine Stock.

An Enchanted Hair Tale, by Alexis De Veaux; illus. Cheryl Hanna.

Enemy Pie, by Derek Munson; illus. Tara Calahan King.

Everett Anderson's Goodbye, by Lucille Clifton; illus. Ann Grifalconi.

Fathers, Mothers, Sisters, Brothers: A Collection of Family Poems, by Mary Ann Hoberman; illus. Marylin Hafner.

Feelings, by Aliki.

Fill It Up! All about Service Stations, by Gail Gibbons.

Find Waldo Now, by Martin Handford.

Fireflies!, by Julie Brinckloe.

The First Dog, by Jan Brett.

A Fish Hatches, by Joanna Cole and Jerome Wexler.

Flight, by Robert Burleigh; illus. Mike Wimmer.

Florence and Eric Take the Cake, by Jocelyn Wild.

Fly Away Home, by Eve Bunting; illus. Ronald Hilmer.

The Flyaway Pantaloons, by Joseph Sharples; illus. Sue Scullard.

Flying, from the Let's Discover library.

Follow the Drinking Gourd, by Jeanette Winter.

Fox on the Job, by James Marshall.

Free to Be . . . A Family: A Book about All Kinds of Belonging, by Marlo Thomas and Friends.

Frog and Toad Together, by Arnold Lobel.

Frogs, Toads, Lizards and Salamanders, by Nancy Winslow Parker and Joan Richards Wright; illus. Nancy Winslow Parker.

From Blossom to Honey, by Ali Mitgutsch.

The Furry News: How to Make a Newspaper, by Loreen Leedy.

Galimoto, by Karen Lynn Williams; illus. Catherine Stock.

The Garden of Abdul Gasazi, by Chris Van Allsburg.

George Shrinks, by William Joyce.

Georgia Music, by Helen V. Griffith; illus. James Stevenson.

Germs Make Me Sick!, by Melvin Berger; illus. Marylin Hafner.

A Gift for Abuelita: Celebrating the Day of the Dead, by Nancy Leunn; illus. Robert Chapman.

A Gift for Tía Rosa, by Karen T. Taha; illus. Dee DeRosa.

The Gift of the Sacred Dog, by Paul Goble.

Gila Monsters Meet You at the Airport, by Marjorie Weinman Sharmat; illus. Byron Barton.

Giving Thanks: A Native American Good Morning Message, by Chief Jake Swamp; illus. Erwin Printup Jr.

The Goat in the Rug, by Charles L. Blood and Martin Link; illus. Nancy Winslow Parker.

Going Buggy! Jokes about Insects, by Peter and Connie Roop; illus. Joan Hanson.

Gracias te damos: Uno-of Renda delos Naxiuos Americanos al amanecer de Cadia dia Spanish Version.

The Grandad Tree, by Trish Cooke; illus. Sharon Wilson.

Grandfather's Journey, by Allen Say.

Grandmama's Joy, by Eloise Greenfield; illus. Carole Byard.

The Great Kapok Tree: A Tale of the Amazon Rain Forest, by Lynne Cherry.

Great Newspaper Crafts, by F. Virginia Walter; illus. Teddy Cameron Long.

Great Women in the Struggle, by Toyomi Igus, Veronica Freeman Ellis, Diane Patrick, and Valerie Wilson Wesley.

Gregory, the Terrible Eater, by Mitchell Sharmat; illus. Jose Aruego and Ariane Dewey.

Growing Vegetable Soup, by Lois Ehlert.

Guess What?, by Beau Gardner.

Hail to Mail, by Samuel Marshak; trans. Richard Pevear; illus. Vladimir Radunsky.

Half a Moon and One Whole Star, by Crescent Dragonwagon; illus. Jerry Pinkney.

Halmoni and the Picnic, by Sook Nyul Choi; illus. Karen M. Dugan.

Hand Rhymes, collected and illus. Marc Brown.

The Handmade Alphabet, by Laura Rankin.

Harlequin and the Gift of Many Colors, by Remy Charlip and Burton Supree.

Harriet's Recital, by Nancy Carlson.

Harry and Lulu, by Arthur Yorinks; illus. Martin Matje.

Hector, the Accordion-Nosed Dog, by John Stadler.

Helping Out, by George Ancona.

Here Is the Coral Reef, by Madeleine Dunphy; illus. Tom Leonard.

Hey, Little Ant, by Phillip and Hannah Hoose; illus. Debbie Tilley.

Hide and Seek, by Jennifer Coldrey and Karen Goldie-Morrison.

Hill of Fire, by Thomas P. Lewis; illus. Joan Sandin.

Hip Cat, by Jonathan London; illus. Woodleigh Hubbard.

The Hippopotamus Song: A Muddy Love Story, by Michael Flanders and Donald Swann; illus. Nadine Bernard Westcott.

Home: A Collaboration of Thirty Distinguished Authors and Illustrators of Children's Books to Aid the Homeless, edited by Michael J. Rosen.

The Homeless Hibernating Bear, by Kids Livin' Life.

Honey, I Love and Other Love Poems, by Eloise Greenfield; illus. Diane and Leo Dillon.

Hooray for Snail!, by John Stadler.

Horace, by Holly Keller.

Hot-Air Henry, by Mary Calhoun; illus. Erick Ingraham.

Hotel Animal, by Keith DuQuette.

The House That Jack Built, illus. Jenny Stow.

How a Book Is Made, by Aliki.

How Many Stars in The Sky?, by Lenny Hort; paintings by James E. Ransome.

How Much Is a Million?, by David M. Schwartz; illus. Steven Kellogg.

How My Parents Learned to Eat, by Ina R. Friedman; illus. Allen Say.

How Tall, How Short, How Faraway, by David A. Adler; illus. Nancy Tobin.

How the Second Grade Got $8,205.50 to Visit the Statue of Liberty, by Nathan Zimelman; illus. Bill Slavin.

How to Dig a Hole to the Other Side of the World, by Faith McNulty; illus. Marc Simont.

How to Hide an Octopus & Other Sea Creatures, by Ruth Heller.

How to Make an Apple Pie and See the World, by Marjorie Priceman.

How You Were Born, by Joanna Cole; photos by Margaret Miller.

Humphrey the Lost Whale: A True Story, by Wendy Tokuda and Richard Hall; illus. Hanako Wakiyama.

I Am an Artist, by Pat Lowery Collins; illus. Robin Brickman.

I Can Be an Archeologist, by Robert E. Pickering.

I Can Be an Oceanographer, by Paul P. Spiera.

I Got Community, by Melrose Cooper; illus. Dale Gottlieb.

I Have a Friend, by Keiko Narahashi.

I Have a Sister, My Sister Is Deaf, by Jeanne Whitehouse Peterson; illus. Deborah Ray.

I Like the Music, by Leah Komaiko; illus. Barbara Westman.

I Made It Myself, by Sabine Lohf.

I Read Signs, by Tana Hoban.

I Want a Dog, by Dayal Kaur Khalsa.

I Wonder Why Soap Makes Bubbles: And Other Questions about Science, by Barbara Taylor.

If at First You Do Not See, by Ruth Brown.

If You Are a Hunter of Fossils, by Byrd Baylor; illus. Peter Parnall.

If You Give a Mouse a Cookie, by Laura Joffe Numberoff; illus. Felicia Bond.

If You Take a Pencil, by Fulvio Testa.

If a Bus Could Talk, by Faith Ringgold.

I'm Flying!, by Alan Wade; illus. Petra Mathers.

I'm Going to Be a: Firefighter, Police Officer, by Edith Kunhardt; illus. Ronald Himler.

I'm New Here, by Bud Howlett.

Imogene's Antlers, by David Small.

The Incredible Painting of Felix Clousseau, by Jon Agee.

Indians of the Americas, from the New True Book series.

Introduction to Musical Instruments Series: Brass/Percussion/Strings/Woodwind, by Dee Lillegard.

Ira Sleeps Over, by Bernard Waber.

Is There Life in Outer Space?, by Franklin M. Branley; illus. Don Madden.

Is This a Baby Dinosaur?, by Millicent E. Selsam.

Is This a House for Hermit Crab?, by Megan McDonald; illus. S. D. Schindler.

The Island of the Skog, by Steven Kellogg.

It Rained on the Desert Today, by Ken and Debby Buchanan; illus. Libba Tracy.

Jack, the Seal and the Sea, by Gerald Aschenbrenner.

Jafta Series, by Hugh Lewin; illus. Lisa Kopper.

Jamaica's Find, by Juanita Havill; illus. Anne Sibley O'Brien.

Jambo Means Hello: Swahili Alphabet Book, by Muriel Feelings; illus. Tom Feelings.

The Jolly Postman, by Janet and Allen Ahlberg.

Jumanji, by Chris Van Allsburg.

June 29, 1999, by David Wiesner.

Just Us Women, by Jeanette Caines; illus. Pat Cummings.

Kate Shelley and the Midnight Express, by Margaret K. Wetterer; illus. Karen Ritz.

Keep the Lights Burning, Abbie, by Peter and Connie Roop; illus. Peter E. Hanson.

The Kids around the World Cookbook, by Deri Robins; illus. Charlotte Stowell.

Koko's Kitten, by Dr. Francine Patterson; photos by Ronald H. Cohn.

Knots on a Counting Rope, by Bill Martin Jr. and John Archambault; illus. Ted Rand.

Kwanzaa, by Deborah Newton Chocolate; illus. Melodye Rosales.

La tortillería *Spanish Version*, by Gary Paulsen; paintings by Ruth Wright Paulsen.

The Lady and the Spider, by Faith McNulty; illus. Bob Marstall.

The Lady with the Ship on Her Head, by Deborah Nourse Lattimore.

Ladybug, by Harrie Watts.

The Legend of the Bluebonnet, by Tomie dePaola.

The Legend of the Indian Paintbrush, by Tomie dePaola.

Legend of the Milky Way, by Jeanne M. Lee.

Lemonade for Sale, by Stuart J. Murphy; illus. Tricia Tusa.

Lenses! Take a Closer Look, by Siegfried Aust; illus. Helge Nyncke.

Let's Go Swimming with Mr. Sillypants, by M. K. Brown.

The Letter Jesters, by Cathryn Falwell.

Liang and the Magic Paintbrush, by Demi.

The Life Cycle of the Honeybee, by Paula Z. Hogan; illus. Geri K. Strigenz.

The Life Cycle of the Whale, by Paula Z. Hogan; illus. Karen Halt.

Lights! Camera! Action!, by Gail Gibbons.

Lion Dancer: Ernie Wan's Chinese New Year, by Madeline Slovenz-Low and Kate Waters; photos by Martha Cooper.

The Little Engine That Could, by Watty Piper; illus. George and Doris Hauman.

Little Nino's Pizzeria, by Karen Barbour.

The Little Painter of Sabana Grande, by Patricia Maloney Markun; illus. Robert Casilla.

The Little Pigs' Puppet Book, by N. Cameron Watson.

The Little Red Lighthouse and the Great Gray Bridge, by Hildegarde H. Swift and Lynd Ward.

A Living Desert, by Guy J. Spencer; photos by Tim Fuller.

The Long Silk Strand: A Grandmother's Legacy to Her Granddaughter, by Laura E. Williams; illus. Grayce Bochak.

The Long Way to a New Land, by Joan Sandin.

Look at This, by Harlow Rockwell.

The Lotus Seed, by Sherry Garland; illus. Tatsuro Kiuchi.

Loudmouth George and the Sixth-Grade Bully, by Nancy Carlson.

Louis the Fish, by Arthur Yorinks; illus. Richard Egielski.

Ludlow Laughs, by Jon Agee.

Lulu's Lemonade, by Barbara deRubertis; illus. Paige Billin-Frye.

Maebelle's Suitcase, by Tricia Tusa.

The Maestro Plays, by Bill Martin Jr.; illus. Vladimir Radunsky.

The Magic School Bus Inside the Earth, by Joanna Cole; illus. Bruce Degen.

The Magic Wings: A Tale from China, by Diane Wolkstein; illus. Robert Andrew Parker.

The Make Me Laugh! Joke Books, by Joan Hanson.

Make Way for Ducklings, by Robert McCloskey.

Making Musical Things, by Ann Wiseman.

Making the Team, by Nancy Carlson.

Mama Bear, by Chyng Feng Sun; illus. Lolly Robinson.

Mama Don't Allow, by Thacher Hurd.

Mama Provi and the Pot of Rice, by Sylvia Rosa-Cassanova; illus. Robert Roth.

Manatees, by Emilie U. Lepthien.

The Many Lives of Benjamin Franklin, by Aliki.

Mapping Penny's World, author/illustrator Loreen Leedy.

Maps and Globes, by Jack Knowlton; illus. Harriett Barton.

Martha Speaks, by Susan Meddaugh.

Marvelous Math: A Book of Poems, selected by Lee Bennett Hopkins; illus. Karen Barbour.

Math Curse (aka Math Cure), by Jon Scieszka; illus. Lane Smith.

Max, by Bob Graham.

Max, by Rachel Isadora.

Max Found Two Sticks, by Brian Pinkney.

Me and Neesie, by Eloise Greenfield; illus. Moneta Barnett.

Me on the Map, by Joan Sweeney; illus. Annette Cable.

Meanwhile Back at the Ranch, by Trinka Hakes Noble; illus. Tony Ross.

A Medieval Feast, by Aliki.

Meet the Orchestra, by Ann Hayes; illus. Karmen Thompson.

Messages in the Mailbox: How to Write a Letter, by Loreen Leedy.

The Microscope, by Maxine Kumin; illus. Arnold Lobel.

The Milk Makers, by Gail Gibbons.

Miranda, by Tricia Tusa.

Mirette on the High Wire, by Emily Arnold McCully.

Miss Nelson Has a Field Day, by Harry Allard and James Marshall.

Miss Nelson Is Back, by Harry Allard and James Marshall; illus. James Marshall.

Mitchell Is Moving, by Marjorie Weinman Sharmat; illus. Jose Aruego and Ariane Dewey.

The Mitten Tree, by Candace Christiansen; illus. Elaine Greenstein.

Mole Music, by David McPhail.

Molly's Pilgrim, by Barbara Cohen; illus. Michael J. Deraney.

Moog-Moog, Space Barber, by Mark Teague.

The Moon, by Robert Louis Stevenson; illus. Denise Saldutti.

Moon Tiger, by Phyllis Root; illus. Ed Young.

Moondogs, by Daniel Kirk.

Moonsong Lullaby, by Jamake Highwater; photos by Marcia Keegan.

Mouse Views: What the Class Pet Saw, by Bruce McMillan.

Mouthsounds, by Frederick R. Newman.

Mr. Tall and Mr. Small, by Barbara Brenner; illus. Mike Shenon.

Mrs. Huggins and Her Hen Hannah, by Lydia Dabcovich.

Mrs. Katz and Tush, by Patricia Polacco.

Mrs. Pig's Bulk Buy, by Mary Rayner.

The Mud Pony, by Caron Lee Cohen; illus. Shonto Begay.

Mufaro's Beautiful Daughters, by John Steptoe.

Mummies Made in Egypt, by Aliki.

Mundos a Explorar, by Girl Scouts of the U.S.A.

Music, Music for Everyone, by Vera B. Williams.

My America: A Poetry Atlas of the United States, selected by Lee Bennett Hopkins; illus. Stephen Alcorn.

My First Activity Book, by Angela Wilkes.

My First Cook Book, by Angela Wilkes.

My First Green Book: A Life-Size Guide to Caring for Our Environment, by Angela K. Wilkes.

My First Nature Book, by Angela K. Wilkes.

My Grandson Lew, by Charlotte Zolotow; illus. William Pene du Bois.

My Life with the Wave, by Octavio Paz; illus. Mark Buehner.

My Little Island, by Frane Lessac.

My Mama Had a Dancing Heart, by Libba Moore Gray; illus. Raul Colon.

My Mama Needs Me, by Mildred Pitts Walter; illus. Pat Cummings.

My Puppy Is Born, by Joanna Cole; photos by Margaret Miller.

My Shadow, by Robert Louis Stevenson; illus. Ted Rand.

Mystery on the Docks, by Thacher Hurd.

Nate the Great Mystery, Series by Marjorie Weinman Sharmat; illus. Marc Simont.

Nature All Year Long, by Clare Walker Leslie.

Neale S. Godfrey's Ultimate Kids' Money Book, by Neale S. Godfrey; illus. Randy Verougstraete.

Newspapers, by David Petersen.

Nicholas Bentley Stoningpot III, by Ann McGovern; illus. Tomie dePaola.

The Night I Followed the Dog, by Nina Laden.

Night Markets: Bringing Food to a City, by Joshua Horwitz.

Night on Neighborhood Street, by Eloise Greenfield; illus. Jan Spivey Gilchrist.

Nosey Mrs. Rat, by Jeffrey Allen; illus. James Marshall.

Oink, by Arthur Geisert.

The Old Banjo, by Dennis Haseley; illus. Stephen Gammell.

The Old Man Who Loved to Sing, by John Winch; illus. John Winch.

Old Turtle's Baseball Stories, by Leonard Kessler.

On Grandma's Roof, by Erica Silverman; illus. Deborah Kogan Ray.

On That Day, by Andrea Patel.

On the Day You Were Born, by Debra Frasier.

Once There Was a Tree, by Natalie Romanova; illus. Gennady Spirin.

One Hundred Hungry Ants, by Elinor J. Pinczes; illus. Bonnie Mackain.

One Monday Morning, by Uri Schulevitz.

One Round Moon and a Star For Me, by Ingrid Mennen; illus. Niki.

Only One, by Marc Harshman; illus. Barbara Garrison.

Opt: An Illusionary Tale, by Arline and Joseph Baum.

Our Big Home: An Earth Poem, by Linda Glase; illus. Elisa Kleven.

Our Teacher's in a Wheelchair, by Mary Ellen Powers.

Our Wet World, by Sneed B. Collard III; illus. James M. Needham.

Over the River and through the Wood, by Lydia Maria Child; illus. Iris Van Rynbach.

Owen, by Kevin Henkes.

Owl Moon, by Jane Yolen; illus. John Schoenherr.

Ox-Cart Man, by Donald Hall; illus. Barbara Cooney.

Pablo Picasso, by Ibi Lepscky; illus. Paolo Cardoni; trans. Howard Rodger MacLean.

The Paper Crane, by Molly Bang.

"Paper" through the Ages, by Shaaron Cosner; illus. Priscilla Kiedrowski.

The Patchwork Quilt, by Valerie Flournoy; illus. Jerry Pinkney.

Paul Bunyan, by Steven Kellogg.

People in the Rain Forest, by Saviour Pirotta.

A Peddler's Dream, by Janice Shefelman, illus. Tom Shefelman.

Perfect Crane, by Anne Laurin; illus. Charles Mikolaycak.

The Perfect Spot, by Robert J. Blake.

Perfect the Pig, by Susan Jeschke.

Pet Show!, by Ezra Jack Keats.

Pet Stories: You Don't Have to Walk, story collection by SeaStar Books, a division of North-South Books.

Peter and the Wolf, by Sergei Prokofiev; illus. Erna Voigt.

Peter's Chair, by Ezra Jack Keats.

Peter Spier's Rain, by Peter Spier.

The Philharmonic Gets Dressed, by Karla Kuskin; illus. Marc Simont.

A Picture Book of Harriet Tubman, by David A. Adler; illus. Samuel Byrd.

The Piggy in the Puddle, by Charlotte Pomerantz; illus. James Marshall.

Pig Pig Gets a Job, by David McPhail.

Pigs on a Blanket: Fun with Math and Time, by Amy Axelrod; illus. Sharon McGinley-Nally.

Pig William, by Arlene Dubanevich.

Pipsqueaks! Maze School, by Patrick Merrell.

The Pirate Cook Book, by Mary Ling; designed by Karen Lieberman.

Plane Song, by Diane Siebert; illus. Vincent Nasta.

Poem Stew, by William Cole; illus. Karen Ann Weinhaus.

Pointsettia and Her Family, by Felicia Bond.

The Polar Express, by Chris Van Allsburg.

The Popcorn Book, by Tomie dePaola.

The Puppy Who Wanted a Boy, by Jane Thayer; illus. Lisa McCue.

The Purple Coat, by Amy Hest; illus. Amy Schwartz.

Puss in Boots, by Charles Perrault; retold and illus. by Lorinda Bryan Cauley.

Raccoons and Ripe Corn, by Jim Arnosky.

Rainbow Crow, by Nancy Van Laan; illus. Beatriz Vidal.

Ramona: Behind the Scenes of a Television Show, by Elaine Scott; photos by Margaret Miller.

The Reason for a Flower, by Ruth Heller.

Rechinka's Eggs, by Patricia Polacco.

Red Leaf, Yellow Leaf, by Lois Ehlert.

Redbird, by Patrick Fort.

Regards to the Man in the Moon, by Ezra Jack Keats.

Regina's Big Mistake, by Marissa Moss.

A River Ran Wild, by Lynne Cherry.

The Robbery at the Diamond Dog Diner, by Eileen Christelow.

Rock Collecting, by Roma Gans; illus. Holly Keller.

Rodeo, by Cheryl Walsh Bellville.

Roly Goes Exploring, by Phillip Newth.

Ronald Morgan Goes to Bat, by Patricia Reilly Giff; illus. Susanna Natti.

Roses Sing on New Snow: A Delicious Tale, by Paul Yee; illus. Harvey Chan.

Round Trip, by Ann Jonas.

Rumpelstiltskin, by Paul O. Zelinsky.

The Runaway Duck, by David Lyon.

Ruth Law Thrills a Nation, by Don Brown.

Sailing with the Wind, by Thomas Locker.

The Salamander Room, by Anne Mazer; illus. Steve Johnson.

Sam Johnson and the Blue Ribbon Quilt, by Lisa Campbell Ernst.

Sam the Sea Cow, by Francine Jacobs; illus. Laura Kelley.

Saturday Sancocho, by Leyla Torres; illus. Leyla Torres.

The Science Book of Sound, by Neil Ardley; illus. Dorling Kindersley, London.

Science Magic Series with Sound/Light/Air/Water/Magnets/Forces, by Chris Oxlade.

The Scrambled States of America, by Laurie Keller.

The Seashore Book, by Charlotte Zolotow; illus. Wendell Minor.

Seashore Surprises, by Rose Wyler; illus. Steven James Petruccio.

The Secret Shortcut, by Mark Teague.

Shadowgraphs Anyone Can Make, by Phila H. Webb and Jane Corby.

Shadows and Reflections, by Tana Hoban.

Shake It to the One That You Love Best: Play Songs and Lullabies from Black Musical Traditions, collected and adapted by Cheryl Warren Mattox; illus. from the works of Varnette P. Honeywood and Brenda Joysmith.

Shake My Sillies Out, a Raffi song to read; illus. David Allender.

The Shaman's Apprentice: A Tale of the Amazon Rain Forest, by Lynne Cherry and Mark J. Plotkin.

Shoes, by Elizabeth Winthrop; illus. William Joyce.

A Show of Hands, by Linda Bourke and Mary Beth Sullivan.

The Sign Painter's Dream, by Roger Roth.

The Signmaker's Assistant, by Tedd Arnold.

Silent Lotus, by Jeanne M. Lee.

Simon's Book, by Henrik Drescher.

Sleep Is for Everyone, by Paul Showers; illus. Wendy Watson.

The Sleeping Beauty, by Mercer Mayer.

Smart Dog, by Ralph Leemis; illus. Chris L. Demarest.

Snakes Are Hunters, by Patricia Lauber; illus. Holly Keller.

The Snowy Day, by Ezra Jack Keats.

Snowy Day: Stories and Poems, edited by Caroline Feller Bauer; illus. Margot Tomes.

Soccer Sam, by Jean Marzollo; illus. Blanche Sims.

Someplace Else, by Carol P. Saul; illus. Barry Root.

Somewhere in the World Right Now, by Stacey Schuett.

Sophie and Lou, by Petra Mathers.

Sosu's Call, by Meshack Asare.

Space Case, by Edward Marshall; illus. James Marshall.

Spider's Web, by Christine Back and Barrie Watts.

Sports, by Tim Hammond; photos by Dave King.

Sports Pages, by Arnold Adoff; illus. Steve Kuzma.

The Star Spangled Banner, by Peter Spier.

Stay Away from the Junkyard!, by Tricia Tusa.

Stefan and Olga, by Betsy Day.

Stellaluna, by Janell Cannon.

Step into the Night, by Joanne Ryder; illus. Dennis Nolan.

Sterling: The Rescue of a Baby Harbor Seal, by Michael Filisky and Sandra Verrill White.

Stopping by Woods on a Snowy Evening, by Robert Frost; illus. Susan Jeffers.

Storms, by Seymour Simon.

The Story about Ping, by Marjorie Flack and Kurt Wiese.

A Story a Story, by Gail E. Haley.

The Story of a Castle, by John S. Goodall.

The Story of Ferdinand, by Munro Leaf; illus. Robert Lawson.

The Story of Mrs. Lovewright and Purrless Her Cat, by Lore Segal; illus. Paul O. Zelinsky.

Stringbean's Trip to the Shining Sea, by Vera B. Williams and Jennifer Williams.

Suho and the White Horse, by Yuzo Otsuka; illus. Suekichi Akaba.

Summer, by Ron Hirschi; photos by Thomas D. Mangelsen.

Sunken Treasure, by Gail Gibbons.

Sweet Clara and the Freedom Quilt, by Deborah Hopkinson; illus. James Ransome.

Take Action!: A Guide to Active Citizenship, by Marc and Craig Kielburger.

The Talking Eggs, by Robert D. San Souci; illus. Jerry Pinkney.

The Tamarindo Puppy and Other Poems, by Charlotte Pomerantz; illus. Byron Barton.

Tar Beach, by Faith Ringgold.

Taxi! Taxi!, by Cari Best; illus. Dale Gottlieb.

Taxi: A Book of City Words, by Betsy and Giulio Maestro.

Te presento a la orquesta Spanish Version, by Ann Hayes; illus. Karmen Thompson.

Teddy Bears Cure a Cold, by Susanna Gretz; illus. Alison Sage.

A Teeny Tiny Baby, by Amy Schwartz.

The Tenth Good Thing about Barney, by Judith Viorst; illus. Erik Blegvard.

The Terrible Thing That Happened at Our House, by Marge Blaine; illus. John Wallner.

There's a Nightmare in My Closet, by Mercer Mayer.

10 Things I Know Books, by Della Rowland and Wendy Wax; illus. Thomas Payne.

Thirteen Moons on a Turtle's Back, by Joseph Bruchac and Jonathan London; illus. Thomas Locker.

The 13th Clue, by Ann Jonas.

This House Is Made of Mud, by Ken Buchanan; illus. Libba Tracy.

This Is the Key to the Kingdom, by Diane Worfolk Allison.

The Three Bears, by Paul Galdone.

Three by the Sea, by Edward Marshall; illus. James Marshall.

Three Days on a River in a Red Canoe, by Vera B. Williams.

A Three Hat Day, by Laura Geringer; illus. Arnold Lobel.

The Three Little Javelinas, by Susan Lowell; illus. Jim Harris.

Through Grandpa's Eyes, by Patricia MacLachlan; illus. Deborah Ray.

Through Moon and Stars and Night Skies, by Ann Turner; illus. James Graham Hale.

Tiger, by Judy Allen; illus. Tudor Humphries.

Tight Times, by Barbara Shook Hazen; illus. Trina Schart Hyman.

Tillie and the Wall, by Leo Lionni.

Time Train, by Paul Fleischman; illus. Claire Ewart.

The Tin Forest, by Helen War; illus. Wayne Anderson.

Tin Lizzie and Little Nell, by David Cox.

The Titanic: Lost . . . and Found, by Judy Donnelly; illus. Keith Kohler.

To Sleep, by James Sage; illus. Warwick Hutton.

Today We Are Brother and Sister, by Arnold Adoff; illus. Glo Coalson.

Tooth-Gnasher Superflash, by Daniel Pinkwater.

Tornado Alert, by Franklyn M. Branley; illus. Guilio Maestro.

The Tortilla Factory, by Gary Paulsen; paintings by Ruth Wright Paulsen.

The Tortoise and the Hare, by Janet Stevens.

Town Mouse, Country Mouse, by Carol Jones.

The Train to Lulu's, by Elizabeth Fitzgerald Howard; illus. Robert Casilla.

The Tree in the Wood, adapted by Christopher Manson.

Tree Trunk Traffic, by Bianca Lavies.

Tulip Sees America, by Cynthia Rylant; illus. Lisa Desimini.

Trees, by Harry Behn; illus. James Endicott.

The Trek, by Ann Jonas.

The Tremendous Tree Book, by Barbara Brenner and May Garelick; illus. Fred Brenner.

Truck Song, by Diane Siebert; illus. Byron Barton.

The Turn About, Think About, Look About Book, by Beau Gardner.

Turtle and Tortoise, by Vincent Serventy.

Turtle in July, by Marily Singer; illus. Jerry Pinkney.

Twelve Snails to One Lizard, by Susan Hightower; illus. Matt Novak.

The Two of Them, by Aliki.

Tyrannosaurus Wrecks: A Book of Dinosaur Riddles, by Noelle Sterne; illus. Victoria Chess.

Ty's One-Man Band, by Mildred Pitts Walter; illus. Margot Tomes.

The Ugly Duckling, by Lorinda Cauley.

Uncle Jed's Barber Shop, by Margaree King Mitchell; illus. James Ransome.

Uncle Nacho's Hat, by Harriet Rohmer; illus. Veg Reisberg.

Uncle Willie and the Soup Kitchen, by DyAnne DiSalvo-Ryan.

Up and Down on the Merry-Go-Round, by Bill Martin Jr. and John Archambault; illus. Ted Rand.

The Upside Down Riddle Book, edited by Louis Phillips; graphics by Beau Gardner Urban.

Roosts, by Barbara Bash.

The Velveteen Rabbit, by Margery Williams; illus. William Nicholson.

Very Last First Time, by Jan Andrews; illus. Ian Wallace.

The Viking Children's World Atlas, by Michael Day and Jacqueline Tivers.

Visiting the Art Museum, by Laurence Krasny Brown and Marc Brown.

Wagon Wheels, by Barbara Brenner; illus. Don Bolognese.

The Wall, by Eve Bunting; illus. Ronald Himler.

Walter the Baker, by Eric Carle.

Watch the Stars Come Out, by Riki Levinson; illus. Diane Goode.

Water Dance, by Thomas Locker; illus. Thomas Locker.

Water, Water Everywhere, by Mark J. Rauzon and Cynthia Overbeck Bix.

Water: What It Is, What It Does, by Judith S. Seixas; illus. Tom Huffman.

Weather, by Rena K. Kirkpatrick; illus. Janetta Lewin.

Welcome to the Green House, by Jane Yolen; illus. Laura Regan.

Whale in the Sky, by Anne Siberell.

Whales and Other Sea Mammals, by Elsa Posell.

Whalewatch!, by June Behrens; photos by John Olguin.

What Does It Do? Inventions Then and Now, by Daniel Jacobs.

What Food Is This?, by Rosmarie Hausherr.

What Happens to a Hamburger, by Paul Showers; illus. Edward Miller.

What It's Like to Be a . . . Newspaper Reporter, by Janet Craig; illus. Richard Max Kolding.

What Makes Popcorn Pop?: And Other Questions about the World around Us, answered by Jack Myers.

What the Mailman Brought, by Carolyn Craven; illus. Tomie dePaola.

What's in the Deep? An Underwater Adventure for Children, by Alese and Morton Pechter.

What's Inside? Shells, by Angela Royston; photos by Andreas Von Einsiedel.

What's under My Bed?, by James Stevenson.

When Aunt Lena Did the Rumba, by Eileen Kurtis-Kleinman; illus. Diane Greenseid.

When I Was Young in the Mountains, by Cynthia Rylant; illus. Diane Goode.

When Panda Came to Our House, by Helen Zane Jensen.

Where the Wild Things Are, by Maurice Sendak.

The White Bicycle, by Rob Lewis.

Whoever You Are, by Mem Fox; illus. Leslie Staub.

Who's in Rabbit's House, by Verna Aardema; illus. Leo and Diane Dillion.

Why Mosquitoes Buzz in People's Ears, by Verna Aardema; illus. Leo and Diane Dillion.

Wilfrid Gordon McDonald Partridge, by Mem Fox; illus. Julie Vivas.

Will We Miss Them? Endangered Species, by Alexandra Wright; illus. Marshall Peck III.

Willie Jerome, by Alice Faye Duncan; illus. Tyrone Geter.

Winter, by Ron Hirschi; photos by Thomas D. Mangelsen.

A Winter Place, by Ruth Radin Yaffe; illus. Mattie Lou O'Kelley.

The Wonderful Happens, by Cynthia Rylant; illus. Coco Dowley.

The Wonderful Towers of Watts, by Patricia Zelver; illus. Frane Lessac.

Work, by Ann Morris.

Worksong, by Gary Paulsen; illus. Ruth Wright Paulsen.

Worlds to Explore: Handbook for Brownie and Junior Girl Scouts, by Girl Scouts of the U.S.A.

The Wreck of the Zephyr, by Chris Van Allsburg.

Yagua Days, by Cruz Martel; illus. Jerry Pinkney.

Zin! Zin! Zin! A Violin, by Lloyd Moss; illus. Marjorie Priceman.

Zoom, by Istvan Banyai.

Zora Hurston and the Chinaberry Tree, by William Miller; illus. Cornelius Van Wright and Ying-Hwa Hu.

APPENDIX I

Selected Review Periodicals

American picture books for children are regularly reviewed in the following publications, among others:

The Boston Globe
P.O. Box 2378
Boston, MA 02107-2378
http://www.boston.com

The Bulletin of the Center for Children's Books
501 E. Daniel St., MC-493
Champaign, IL 61820
http://www.lis.uiuc.edu/puboff/bccb/

The Horn Book Guide
The Horn Book, Inc.
56 Roland Street, Suite 200
Boston, MA 02129
http://www.hbook.com/guide.shtml

Horn Book Magazine
The Horn Book, Inc.
56 Roland Street, Suite 200
Boston, MA 02129
http://www.hbook.com

Kirkus Reviews
VNU US Literary Group

770 Broadway
New York, NY 10003
http://www.kirkusreviews.com

Library Journal
360 Park Avenue South
New York, NY 10010
http://www.libraryjournal.com

The New York Times Book Review
The New York Times Company
229 West 43rd Street
New York, NY 10036
http://www.NYTimes.com

Publishers Weekly
360 Park Avenue South
New York, NY 10010
http://www.publishersweekly.com

School Library Journal
360 Park Avenue South
New York, NY 10010
http://www.schoollibraryjournal.com

Collections of Books and Materials on Picture Books and Their Creators

Alice M. Jordon Collection
Boston Public Library
700 Boylston Street
Boston, MA 02116
http://www.bpl.org

Babbidge Library, Special Collections Department
University of Connecticut, Storrs
369 Fairfield Road
Storrs, CT 06269
http://www.lib.uconn.edu

Beincke Rare Book and Manuscript Library
Yale University
121 Wall Street
New Haven, CT 06520-2840
http://www.library.yale.edu/beinecke/

Carolyn Sherwin Bailey Historical Collection of Children's Books
Buley Library
Southern CT Sate College
501 Crescent Street
New Haven, CT 06515

Children's Literature Historical Collection
The State University of New York at Albany
1400 Washington Avenue
Albany, NY 12222
http://library.albany.edu/

Darton Collection
Milbank Memorial Library
Teachers College
Columbia University
525 West 120th Street
New York, NY 10027
http://lweb.tc.columbia.edu/cs/sc/childrens/darton.htm

The de Grummond Children's Literature Collection
University of Southern Mississippi
Box 5148
Hattiesburg, MS 39406
http://www.lib.usm.edu~degrum/

Central Children's Room
Donnell Library Center, 2nd Floor
New York Public Library
20 West 53rd Street
New York, NY 10019-6185
http://www.nypl.org/branch/collections/dch.html

The Dr. Seuss Collection
Mandeville Special Collections Library
University of California at San Diego
9500 Gilman Drive
La Jolla, CA 92093-0175

http://orpheus.ucsd.edu/speccoll/seusscoll.
html

Elizabeth Nesbitt Room
Information Sciences Library
University of Pittsburgh
135 N. Bellefield Avenue
Pittsburgh, PA 15260
http://www.library.pitt.edu/libraries/is/enroo
m/

The Five Owls Collection
Bush Library
Hamline University
1536 Hewitt Avenue
Saint Paul, MN 55104-1284
http://www.hamline.edu/bushlibrary/

**Gail E. Haley Collection of the Culture
of Childhood**
Appalachian State University Libraries
Appalachian State University
P.O. Box 32026
Boone, NC 28608-32026
http://www.library.appstate.edu/newlibrary/

Kerlan Collection
University of Minnesota
113 Elmer L Andersen Library
222 21st Street Avenue South
Minneapolis, MN 55455
http://special.lib.umn.edu/clrc/kerlan.html

**Library of Congress Children's Litera-
ture Center**
101 Independence Avenue SE
Thomas Jefferson Building, LJ 100
Washington, DC 20540-4620
http://www.loc.gov/rr/child/

**Mary Faulk Markiewicz Collection of
Early American Children's Books**
University of Rochester
River Campus Libraries

Rochester, NY 14627
http://www.library.rochester.edu/index.cfm?p
age=1440&fund=The Mary Faulk
Markiewicz Collection and Endowed
Fund&fundid=68

May Massee Collection
Emporia State University
1200 Commercial Street Box 4051
Emporia, KS 66801
http://www.emporia.edu/libsv/menu1/special
collections/maymassee.html

**Mazza Museum of International Art
from Picture Books**
The University of Findlay
1000 North Main Street
Findlay, OH 45840-3695
http://www.mazzamuseum.org/

The Pierpont Morgan Library
29 East 56th Street
New York, NY 10016
http://www.morganlibrary.org/index.html

Rosenbach Museum and Library
2008-2010 De Lancey Place
Philadelphia, PA 19103
http://www.rosenbach.org

**U.C.L.A. Library Department of Special
Collections**
A1713 Charles E. Young Research Library
Box 951575
Los Angeles, CA 90095-1575
http://www.library.ucla.edu/libraries/special/
scweb/

University of Oregon Special Collections
Knight Library, Second Floor North
15th and Kincaid Street
Eugene, OR 97403
http://libweb.uoregon.edu/speccoll/

Birthdays of Picture Book *Companion* Authors/Artists, Alphabetically

Adrienne Adams   February 8, 1906
Harry Allard   January 27, 1928
Hans Christian Andersen   April 2, 1805
Laura Adams Armer   January 12, 1874
Boris Artzybasheff   May 25, 1899
José Aruego   August 9, 1932
Frank Asch   August 6, 1946
Edgar d'Aulaire   September 30, 1898
Ingri d'Aulaire   December 27, 1904
Mary Azarian   December 8, 1940
Molly Bang   December 29, 1943
Arnold Edwin Bare   June 20, 1920
Leonard Baskin   August 15, 1922
Byrd Baylor   March 28, 1924
Ludwig Bemelmans   April 27, 1898
Barbara Helen Berger   March 1, 1945
Marcia Brown   July 13, 1918
Margaret Wise Brown   May 23, 1910
Joseph Bruchac   October 16, 1942
Ashley Bryan   July 13, 1923
Conrad Buff   January 15, 1886
Mary Marsh Buff   April 10, 1890
Virginia Lee Burton   August 30, 1909
Carole Byard   July 22, 1941
Janell Cannon   November 3, 1957
Eric Carle   June 25, 1929
Barbara Cooney   August 6, 1917
Donald Crews   August 30, 1938
Pat Cummings   November 9, 1950
Alice Dalgliesh   October 7, 1893
James Daugherty   June 1, 1889
Marguerite de Angeli   March 14, 1889

Diane Dillon   March 13, 1933
Leo Dillon   March 2, 1933
Crescent Dragonwagon   November 25, 1952
William Pène du Bois   May 9, 1916
Richard Egielski   July 16, 1952
Lois Ehlert   November 9, 1934
Benjamin Elkin   August 10, 1911
Barbara Emberley   December 12, 1932
Ed Emberley   October 19, 1931
Marie Hall Ets   December 16, 1893
Tom Feelings   May 19, 1933
Rachel Field   September 19, 1894
Helen Dean Fish   February 7, 1889
Marjorie Flack   October 23, 1897
Denise Fleming   January 31, 1950
Don Freeman   August 11, 1908
Wanda Gág   March 11, 1893
Stephen Gammell   February 10, 1943
Ruth Stiles Gannett   August 12, 1923
Mordicai Gerstein   November 25, 1935
Paul Goble   September 27, 1933
M. B. Goffstein   December 20, 1940
Margaret Bloy Graham   November 2, 1920
Eloise Greenfield   May 17, 1929
Ann Grifalconi   September 22, 1929
Susan Guevara   January 27, 1956
Berta Hader   February 6, 1891
Elmer Hader   September 7, 1889
Gail E. Haley   November 4, 1939
Donald Hall   September 20, 1928
Kevin Henkes   November 27, 1960
Mary Ann Hoberman   August 12, 1930

Nonny Hogrogian   May 7, 1932
Holling C. Holling   August 2, 1900
Clement Hurd   January 12, 1908
Pat Hutchins (British)   June 18, 1942
Trina Schart Hyman   April 8, 1939
Anne Isaacs   March 2, 1949
Susan Jeffers   October 7, 1942
Crockett Johnson   October 20, 1906
Stephen T. Johnston   May 29, 1964
Elizabeth Orton Jones   June 25, 1910
Ezra Jack Keats   March 11, 1916
Eric Kimmel   October 30, 1946
Robert Kraus   June 21, 1925
Ruth Krauss   July 25, 1901
John Langstaff   December 24, 1920
Dorothy Lathrop   April 16, 1891
Robert Lawson   October 4, 1892
Munro Leaf   December 4, 1905
Dom Lee   May 4, 1959
Lois Lenski   October 14, 1893
Blair Lent   January 22, 1930
Sorche Nic Leodhas   January 8, 1898
Julius Lester   January 27, 1939
Bétsy Lewin   May 12, 1937
E. B. Lewis   December 16, 1956
Leo Lionni   May 5, 1910
William Lipkind   December 17, 1904
Arnold Lobel   May 22, 1933
Jonathan London   March 11, 1947
Joseph Low   August 11, 1911
David Macaulay   December 2, 1946
Jacqueline Briggs Martin   April 15, 1945
Clare Newberry   April 10, 1903
Ted Lewin   May 6, 1935
Suse MacDonald   March 3, 1940
Fred Marcellino   October 25, 1939
James Marshall   October 10, 1942
Bill Martin Jr.   March 20, 1916
Robert McCloskey   September 15, 1914
Gerald McDermott   January 31, 1941
Phyllis McGinley   March 21, 1905
Patricia McKissack   August 9, 1944
Else Holmelund Minarik   September 13, 1920
Ken Mochizuki   May 18, 1954
Beni Montresor   March 31, 1926
Arlene Mosel   August 27, 1921
Walter Dean Myers   August 12, 1937
Evaline Ness   April 24, 1911
Clare Turlay Newberry   April 10, 1903
Peter Parnall   May 23, 1936

Bill Peet   January 29, 1915
Maud Petersham   August 5, 1889
Miska Petersham   September 20, 1888
Brian Pinkney   August 28, 1961
Jerry Pinkney   December 22, 1939
Leo Politi   November 21, 1908
Marjorie Priceman   January 8, 1958
Alice Provensen   August 14, 1918
Martin Provensen   July 10, 1916
Arthur Ransome   January 18, 1884
James E. Ransome   September 25, 1961
Doreen Rappaport   October 31, 1939
Ellen Raskin   March 13, 1928
Peggy Rathmann   March 4, 1953
H. A. Rey   September 16, 1898
Faith Ringgold   October 8, 1930
Eric Rohmann   October 26, 1957
Feodor Rojankovsky   December 24, 1891
Cynthia Rylant   June 6, 1954
Ruth Sawyer   August 5, 1880
Allen Say   August 28, 1937
John Schoenherr   July 5, 1935
Georges Schreiber   April 25, 1904
Jon Sciesczka   September 8, 1954
Uri Shulevitz   February 27, 1935
Maurice Sendak   June 10, 1928
Kate Seredy   November 10, 1899
Dr. Seuss (Theodor Geisel)   March 2, 1904
Helen Sewell   June 27, 1896
Uri Shulevitz   February 27, 1935
Nicolas Sidjakov   December 16, 1924
Marc Simont   November 23, 1915
Peter Sís   May 11, 1949
Louis Slobodkin   February 19, 1903
Esphyr Slobodkina   September 22, 1908
David Small   February 12, 1945
Lane Smith   August 25, 1959
Gary Soto   April 12, 1952
Peter Spier   June 6, 1927
William Steig   November 14, 1907
Javaka Steptoe   April 19, 1971
John Steptoe   September 14, 1950
William Steig   November 14, 1907
Janet Stevens   January 17, 1953
Sarah Stewart   August 27, 1939
Simms Taback   February 13, 1932
Gustaf Tenggren   November 3, 1896
Ernest Lawrence Thayer   August 14, 1863
James Thurber   December 8, 1894
Eve Titus   July 16, 1922

Alvin Tresselt   September 30, 1916
Tasha Tudor   August 28, 1915
Brinton Turkle   August 15, 1915
John Updike   March 18, 1932
Chris Van Allsburg   June 18, 1949
Judith Viorst   February 2, 1931
Lynd Ward   June 26, 1905
Leonard Weisgard   December 13, 1916
Kurt Wiese   April 27, 1887
David Wiesner   February 5, 1956
Nancy Willard   June 26, 1936
Margaret Willey   November 5, 1950

Sherley Anne Williams   August 25, 1944
Vera B. Williams   January 28, 1927
David Wisniewski   March 21, 1953
Taro Yashima   September 21, 1908
Jane Yolen   February 11, 1939
Arthur Yorinks   August 21, 1953
Ed Young   November 28, 1931
Paul O. Zelinsky   February 14, 1953
Harve Zemach   December 5, 1933
Margo Zemach   November 30, 1931
Gene Zion   October 5, 1913
Charlotte Zolotow   June 26, 1915

Birthdays of Picture Book *Companion* Authors/Artists, Daily

January

Sorche Nic Leodhas   January 8, 1898
Marjorie Priceman   January 8, 1958
Laura Adams Armer   January 12, 1874
Clement Hurd   January 12, 1908
Conrad Buff   January 15, 1886
Janet Stevens   January 17, 1953
Arthur Ransome   January 18, 1884
Blair Lent   January 22, 1930
Harry Allard   January 27, 1928
Julius Lester   January 27, 1939
Susan Guevara   January 27, 1956
Vera B. Williams   January 28, 1927
Bill Peet   January 29, 1915
Gerald McDermott   January 31, 1941
Denise Fleming   January 31, 1950

February

Judith Viorst   February 2, 1931
David Wiesner   February 5, 1956
Berta Hader   February 6, 1891
Helen Dean Fish   February 7, 1889
Adrienne Adams   February 8, 1906
Stephen Gammell   February 10, 1943
Jane Yolen   February 11, 1939
David Small   February 12, 1945
Simms Taback   February 13, 1932
Paul O. Zelinsky   February 14, 1953
Louis Slobodkin   February 19, 1903
Uri Shulevitz   February 27, 1935

March

Barbara Helen Berger   March 1, 1945
Dr. Seuss (Theodor Geisel)   March 2, 1904
Leo Dillon   March 2, 1933
Anne Isaacs   March 2, 1949
Suse MacDonald   March 3, 1940
Wanda Gág   March 11, 1893
Ezra Jack Keats   March 11, 1916
Jonathan London   March 11, 1947
Diane Dillon   March 13, 1933
Marguerite de Angeli   March 14, 1889
John Updike   March 18, 1932
Bill Martin Jr.   March 20, 1916
Phyllis McGinley   March 21, 1905
David Wisniewski   March 21, 1953
Byrd Baylor   March 28, 1924
Beni Montresor   March 31, 1926

April

Trina Schart Hyman   April 8, 1939
Mary Marsh Buff   April 10, 1890
Clare Turlay Newberry   April 10, 1903
Gary Soto   April 12, 1952
Jacqueline Briggs Martin   April 15, 1945
Dorothy Lathrop   April 16, 1891
Evaline Ness   April 24, 1911
Georges Schreiber   April 25, 1904
Kurt Wiese   April 27, 1887
Ludwig Bemelmans   April 27, 1898

May

Dom Lee   May 4, 1959
Leo Lionni   May 5, 1910
Ted Lewin   May 6, 1935
Nonny Hogrogian   May 7, 1932
William Pène du Bois   May 9, 1916
Peter Sís   May 11, 1949
Betsy Lewin   May 12, 1937
Eloise Greenfield   May 17, 1929
Ken Mochizuki   May 18, 1954
Arnold Lobel   May 22, 1933
Margaret Wise Brown   May 23, 1910
Peter Parnall   May 23, 1936
Boris Artzybasheff   May 25, 1899
Stephen T. Johnston   May 29, 1964

June

James Daugherty   June 1, 1889
Peter Spier   June 6, 1927
Cynthia Rylant   June 6, 1954
Maurice Sendak   June 10, 1928
Pat Hutchins (British)   June 18, 1942
Chris Van Allsburg   June 18, 1949
Arnold Edwin Bare   June 20, 1920
Robert Kraus   June 21, 1925
Elizabeth Orton Jones   June 25, 1910
Eric Carle   June 25, 1929
Lynd Ward   June 26, 1905
Charlotte Zolotow   June 26, 1915
Nancy Willard   June 26, 1936
Helen Sewell   June 27, 1896

July

John Schoenherr   July 5, 1935
Martin Provensen   July 10, 1916
Marcia Brown   July, 13, 1918
Ashley Bryan   July 13, 1923
Eve Titus   July 16, 1922
Richard Egielski   July 16, 1952
Carole Byard   July 22, 1941
Ruth Krauss   July 25, 1901

August

Holling C. Holling   August 2, 1900
Ruth Sawyer   August 5, 1880
Maud Petersham   August 5, 1889
Barbara Cooney   August 6, 1917
Frank Asch   August 6, 1946

José Aruego   August 9, 1932
Patricia McKissack   August 9, 1944
Benjamin Elkin   August 10, 1911
Don Freeman   August 11, 1908
Joseph Low   August 11, 1911
Ruth Stiles Gannett   August 12, 1923
Mary Ann Hoberman   August 12, 1930
Walter Dean Myers   August 12, 1937
Ernest Lawrence Thayer   August 14, 1863
Alice Provensen   August 14, 1918
Brinton Turkle   August 15, 1915
Leonard Baskin   August 15, 1922
Arthur Yorinks   August 21, 1953
Sherley Anne Williams   August 25, 1944
Lane Smith   August 25, 1959
Arlene Mosel   August 27, 1921
Sarah Stewart   August 27, 1939
Tasha Tudor   August 28, 1915
Allen Say   August 28, 1937
Brian Pinkney   August 28, 1961
Virginia Lee Burton   August 30, 1909

September

Elmer Hader   September 7, 1889
Jon Sciesczka   September 8, 1954
Else Holmelund Minarik   September 13, 1920
Robert McCloskey   September 15, 1914
H. A. Rey   September 16, 1898
Miska Petersham   September 20, 1888
Donald Hall   September 20, 1928
Taro Yashima   September 21, 1908
Esphyr Slobodkina   September 22, 1908
Ann Grifalconi   September 22, 1929
James E. Ransome   September 25, 1961
Paul Goble   September 27, 1933
Edgar d'Aulaire   September 30, 1898
Alvin Tresselt   September 30, 1916

October

Robert Lawson   October 4, 1892
Gene Zion   October 5, 1913
Alice Daligliesh   October 7, 1893
Susan Jeffers   October 7, 1942
Faith Ringgold   October 8, 1930
James Marshall   October 10, 1942
Lois Lenski   October 14, 1893
Joseph Bruchac   October 16, 1942
Ed Emberley   October 19, 1931
Crockett Johnson   October 20, 1906

Marjorie Flack   October 23, 1897
Fred Marcellino   October 25, 1939
Eric Rohmann   October 26, 1957
Eric Kimmel   October 30, 1946

November

Margaret Bloy Graham   November 2, 1920
Gustaf Tenggren   November 3, 1896
Janell Cannon   November 3, 1957
Gail E. Haley   November 4, 1939
Margaret Willey   November 5, 1950
Pat Cummings   November 9, 1950
Kate Seredy   November 10, 1899
William Steig   November 14, 1907
Leo Politi   November 21, 1908
Marc Simont   November 23, 1915
Mordicai Gerstein   November 25, 1935
Crescent Dragonwagon   November 25, 1952
Kevin Henkes   November 27, 1960
Ed Young   November 28, 1931
Margo Zemach   November 30, 1931

December

David Macaulay   December 2, 1946
Munro Leaf   December 4, 1905
Harve Zemach   December 5, 1933
James Thurber   December 8, 1894
Mary Azarian   December 8, 1940
Barbara Emberley   December 12, 1932
Leonard Weisgard   December 13, 1916
Marie Hall Ets   December 16, 1893
E. B. Lewis   December 16, 1956
Nicolas Sidjakov   December 16, 1924
William Lipkind   December 17, 1904
M. B. Goffstein   December 20, 1940
Jerry Pinkney   December 22, 1939
Feodor Rojankovsky   December 24, 1891
John Langstaff   December 24, 1920
Ingri d'Aulaire   December 27, 1904
Molly Bang   December 29, 1943

Subjects Listing of Picture Book *Companion* Titles

Subjects are per the Library of Congress catalog or close estimates when LOC subjects are not available.

AERIALISTS

The Man Who Walked between the Towers

AERIALISTS—FRANCE

The Man Who Walked between the Towers

AFRICA, EAST—SOCIAL LIFE AND CUSTOMS

Moja Means One: Swahili Counting Book

AFRICA—FICTION

Africa Dream
Mufaro's Beautiful Daughters: An African Tale

AFRICA—POETRY

Shadow

AFRICA—SOCIAL LIFE AND CUSTOMS

Ashanti to Zulu: African Traditions

AFRICAN AMERICANS—BIOGRAPHY

Duke Ellington: The Piano Prince and the Orchestra
Martin's Big Words: The Life of Dr. Martin Luther King, Jr.
Minty: A Story of Young Harriet Tubman

AFRICAN AMERICANS—CIVIL RIGHTS—HISTORY—TWENTIETH CENTURY

Martin's Big Words: The Life of Dr. Martin Luther King, Jr.

AFRICAN AMERICANS—CIVIL RIGHTS WORKERS—POETRY

ellington was not a street

AFRICAN AMERICANS—FICTION

Africa Dream
Coming On Home Soon
Cornrows
Goggles!
Goin' Someplace Special
In the Time of the Drums
Mirandy and Brother Wind
The Patchwork Quilt
The Snowy Day
Tar Beach
Uptown
Working Cotton
Yo! Yes!

AFRICAN AMERICANS—FOLKLORE

Tops & Bottoms

AFRICAN AMERICANS—MUSIC— HISTORY AND CRITICISM

i see the rhythm

AFRICAN AMERICANS—POETRY

ellington was not a street
Harlem: A Poem
Nathaniel Talking
Soul Looks Back in Wonder

AFRO-AMERICAN ARTISTS— POETRY

ellington was not a street

AFRO-AMERICAN GIRLS—POETRY

ellington was not a street

AIR PILOTS

The Glorious Flight: Across the Channel with Louis Blériot, July 25, 1909

AIRPLANES—DESIGN AND CONSTRUCTION

The Glorious Flight: Across the Channel with Louis Blériot, July 25, 1909

ALLEN, ETHAN, 1738–1789

America's Ethan Allen

ALPHABET

ABC Book
ABC Bunny
All Around the Town
Alphabet City
Alphabetics
An American ABC
Ape in a Cape: An Alphabet of Odd Animals
Ashanti to Zulu: African Traditions
Chicka Chicka Boom Boom
Hosie's Alphabet
On Market Street

ALPHABET RHYMES

All Around the Town
Alligators All Around (from *The Nutshell Library*)

AMERICAN POETRY

A Child's Calendar
ellington was not a street
Harlem: A Poem
In My Mother's House
Nathaniel Talking
The Rooster Crows: A Book of American Rhymes and Jingles
A Visit to William Blake's Inn: Poems for Innocent and Experienced Travelers

AMERICAN POETRY—AFRICAN AMERICAN AUTHORS

Soul Looks Back in Wonder

AMERICAN POETRY— COLLECTIONS

Thirteen Moons on a Turtle's Back

AMISH—FICTION

Yonie Wondernose

ANANSI (LEGENDARY CHARACTER)

Anansi the Spider: A Tale from the Ashanti

ANDERSEN, H. C. (HANS CHRISTIAN), 1805–1875

The Ugly Duckling

ANIMALS—FICTION

Bear Party
The Big Snow
Brown Bear, Brown Bear, What Do You See?
Chanticleer and the Fox
Fables
In the Forest
May I Bring a Friend?
Mice Twice
My Friend, Rabbit

Mr. T. W. Anthony Woo: The Story of a Cat and a Dog and a Mouse
Play with Me

ANIMALS—INFANCY—FICTION

Green Eyes
Kitten's First Full Moon

ANIMALS, LEGENDS AND STORIES OF

Cock-a-Doodle Doo: The Story of a Little Red Rooster

ANIMALS—MISCELLANEA

What Do You Do With a Tail Like This?

ANIMALS—PHYSIOLOGY

What Do You Do With a Tail Like This?

ANIMALS—PICTORIAL WORKS

Ape in a Cape: An Alphabet of Odd Animals

ANIMALS—QUESTIONS AND ANSWERS

What Do You Do With a Tail like This?

ANIMATORS—UNITED STATES—BIOGRAPHY

Bill Peet: An Autobiography

ANTISLAVERY MOVEMENTS—UNITED STATES

Minty: A Story of Young Harriet Tubman

APARTMENT HOUSES—FICTION

April's Kittens

ARCHITECTURE—GOTHIC

Cathedral: The Story of Its Construction

ASHANTI (AFRICAN PEOPLE)—FOLKLORE

Anansi the Spider: A Tale from the Ashanti

ASTRONOMERS

Starry Messenger

ASTRONOMERS—ITALY—BIOGRAPHY

Starry Messenger

AUTHORS, AMERICAN

Bill Peet: An Autobiography

AUTHORS, AMERICAN—TWENTIETH CENTURY—BIOGRAPHY

Bill Peet: An Autobiography

BABIES—ACTIVITIES

Pat the Bunny

BABIES—FICTION

"More More More," Said the Baby: Three Love Stories
My Mama Needs Me

BABYSITTERS—FICTION

T-Bone, the Baby Sitter

BAPTISTS—UNITED STATES—CLERGY—BIOGRAPHY

Martin's Big Words: The Life of Dr. Martin Luther King, Jr.

BASEBALL—POETRY

Casey at the Bat: A Ballad of the Republic Sung the Year 1888

BASEBALL PLAYERS—POETRY

Casey at the Bat: A Ballad of the Republic Sung the Year 1888

BATS—FICTION

Stellaluna

BEARS—FICTION

Bear Party (marsupial koalas)
The Biggest Bear
Blueberries for Sal
The Happy Day

Happy Birthday, Moon
Little Bear's Visit

BEARS—FOLKLORE

Goldilocks and the Three Bears
Tops & Bottoms

BEDTIME—FICTION

A Child's Goodnight Book
Goodnight Moon

BEDTIME PRAYERS

Prayer for a Child

BEHAVIOR—FICTION

Bear Party
Miss Nelson Is Missing!
No, David!
Olivia

BENTLEY, W.A. (WILSON ALWYN), 1865–1931

Snowflake Bentley

BIBLE—ILLUSTRATIONS

Small Rain: Verses from the Bible

BIBLE—NATURAL HISTORY

Animals of the Bible—A Picture Book

BIRDS—FICTION

Feather Mountain
Fly High, Fly Low
Hey, Al
Stellaluna
Time Flies

BIRTHDAYS—FICTION

Chato and the Party Animals
Happy Birthday, Moon
The Wild Birthday Cake

BISON—FICTION

Where the Buffaloes Begin

BLAKE, WILLIAM, 1757–1827—POETRY

A Visit to William Blake's Inn: Poems for Innocent and Experienced Travelers

BLANKETS—FICTION

Owen

BLÉRIOT, LOUIS (1872–1936)

The Glorious Flight: Across the Channel with Louis Blériot, July 25, 1909

BLUEBERRIES—FICTION

Blueberries for Sal

BOATS—FICTION

The Boats on the River
Pierre Pidgeon

BOOKS—FICTION

The Red Book

BOSTON (MASS.)—FICTION

Make Way for Ducklings

BROTHERS AND SISTERS—FICTION

Barkis
Peppe the Lamplighter

BULLIES—FICTION

Goggles!

BUS DRIVERS—FICTION

Don't Let the Pigeon Drive the Bus

CALIFORNIA—FICTION

Song of the Swallows

CARMEN LOMAS GARZA—FAMILY

Magic Windows

CASEY, BRIAN KAVANAGH (1859–1946)—POETRY

Casey at the Bat: A Ballad of the Republic Sung the Year 1888

CASTLES—FICTION

Castle

CATERPILLARS—FICTION

Farfallina & Marcel
The Very Hungry Caterpillar

CATHEDRALS

Cathedral: The Story of Its Construction

CATS—FICTION

Anatole and the Cat
April's Kittens
Chato and the Party Animals
Chato's Kitchen
Green Eyes
Hondo & Fabian
Kitten's First Full Moon
Marshmallow
Millions of Cats
T-Bone, the Baby Sitter
The Two Reds

CHAIRS—FICTION

A Chair for My Mother

CHARACTERS IN LITERATURE—FICTION

The Three Pigs

CHEESE—FICTION

Anatole

CHICKENS—FICTION

Rosie's Walk

CHILDREN—PRAYER BOOKS AND DEVOTIONS—ENGLISH

Prayer for a Child

CHILDREN'S POETRY

Book of Nursery and Mother Goose Rhymes
If All the Seas Were One Sea
The Rooster Crows: A Book of American Rhymes and Jingles

CHILDREN'S POETRY—AMERICAN

A Child's Calendar
All Around the Town
ellington was not a street
Harlem: A Poem
In My Mother's House
Nathaniel Talking
The Rooster Crows: A Book of American Rhymes and Jingles
Soul Looks Back in Wonder
Thirteen Moons on a Turtle's Back
A Visit to William Blake's Inn: Poems for Innocent and Experienced Travelers

CHILDREN'S POETRY—ENGLISH

Spider and the Fly
The House That Jack Built—La Maison Que Jacques a Batie

CHILDREN'S POETRY—FRENCH

The House That Jack Built—La Maison Que Jacques a Batie

CHILDREN'S POETRY, FRENCH—TRANSLATED INTO ENGLISH

Shadow

CHILDREN'S SONGS

Sing Mother Goose

CHILDREN'S STORIES, AMERICAN

Fables
The Stinky Cheese Man and Other Fairly Stupid Tales

CHILDREN'S STORIES—AUTHORSHIP

Bill Peet: An Autobiography

CHINA—FICTION

Fish in the Air
Mei Li
The Story about Ping

CHINESE LANGUAGE—WRITING

You Can Write Chinese

CHRISTMAS—FICTION

Baboushka and the Three Kings
The Christmas Anna Angel
The Polar Express

CITY AND TOWN LIFE

Alphabet City
Snow

CITY AND TOWN LIFE—FICTION

Goggles!

CITY AND TOWN LIFE—FOLKLORE

One Monday Morning

CITY AND TOWN LIFE—POETRY

All Around the Town

CIVIL RIGHTS WORKERS

Martin's Big Words: The Life of Dr. Martin Luther King, Jr.

CIVIL RIGHTS WORKERS—UNITED STATES—BIOGRAPHY

Martin's Big Words: The Life of Dr. Martin Luther King, Jr.

CLERGY

Martin's Big Words: The Life of Dr. Martin Luther King, Jr.

CLOTHING AND DRESS—FICTION

Ella Sarah Gets Dressed

CLOUDS—FICTION

Sector 7

CLOWNS—FICTION

Bambino the Clown

COLOR

Color Zoo
Freight Train

COLOR—FICTION

Brown Bear, Brown Bear, What Do You See?
The Red Book
The Two Reds

COLOR—STUDY AND TEACHING (ELEMENTARY)

Color Zoo

CONDUCT OF LIFE—POETRY

Spider and the Fly

CONSTRUCTION WORKERS—FICTION

The Night Worker

CONTESTS

Gillespie and the Guards

COOKING—FICTION

Skipper John's Cook

COTTON PICKING—FICTION

Working Cotton

COUNTING

All in the Morning Early
Just a Minute: A Trickster Tale and Counting Book
Moja Means One: Swahili Counting Book
1 Is One
Ten, Nine, Eight

COUNTING RHYMES

One Was Johnny (from *The Nutshell Library*)
1 Is One

COUNTRY LIFE—FICTION

All in the Morning Early

COWS—FICTION

Click, Clack, Moo: Cows That Type

CREATION—FOLKLORE

The Origin of Life on Earth: An African Creation Myth

CRICKETS—FICTION

A Pocketful of Cricket

CROCODILES—FICTION

Mother Crocodile

DANCE—FICTION

Mirandy and Brother Wind

DAY—FICTION

Lucky Song

DEER—FICTION

Dash and Dart

DESERT ECOLOGY

The Desert Is Theirs

DESERTS

The Desert Is Theirs

DINOSAURS—FICTION

Time Flies

DOGS—FICTION

Barkis
Finders Keepers
Harry the Dirty Dog
Hey, Al
Hondo & Fabian
Madeline's Rescue
Nothing-at-All
Officer Buckle and Gloria
The Poky Little Puppy
The Stray Dog

DOMESTIC ANIMALS—FICTION

Click, Clack, Moo: Cows That Type

DONKEYS—FICTION

Sylvester and the Magic Pebble

DRAGONS—FOLKLORE

Saint George and the Dragon

DREAMS—FICTION

Free Fall

DUCKS—FICTION

Make Way for Ducklings
The Story about Ping
The Wild Birthday Cake

DWELLINGS—FICTION

A House Is a House for Me

ECOLOGY

The Desert Is Theirs

ELEPHANTS—FOLKLORE

Seven Blind Mice

ELLINGTON, DUKE (1899–1974)

Duke Ellington: The Piano Prince and the Orchestra

EMILY DICKINSON (1830–1886)—FICTION

Emily

EMPIRE STATE BUILDING (NEW YORK, N.Y.)—FICTION

Sector 7

ENGLISH LANGUAGE—ALPHABET

Alphabatics

ENGLISH POETRY

Spider and the Fly

ENTERTAINERS—FICTION

Song and Dance Man

ETHNOLOGY—AFRICA

Ashanti to Zulu: African Traditions

ETIQUETTE

What Do You Say, Dear?

ETIQUETTE—FICTION

Mice Twice

ETIQUETTE FOR CHILDREN AND TEENAGERS

What Do You Say, Dear?

FABLES

Andy and the Lion
Chanticleer and the Fox
Fables
Once a Mouse
Seven Blind Mice

FABLES—AMERICAN

Fables

FAIRY TALES

The Bremen-Town Musicians
Cinderella, or The Little Glass Slipper
The Girl Who Loved Wild Horses
Hansel and Gretel
Little Red Riding Hood
Mufaro's Beautiful Daughters: An African Tale
Puss in Boots (Brown)
Puss in Boots (Marcellino)
Rumpelstiltskin
The Stinky Cheese Man and Other Fairly Stupid Tales
The Ugly Duckling

FAIRY TALES—AMERICAN

The Stinky Cheese Man and Other Fairly Stupid Tales

FAIRY TALES—ENGLAND

Tom Tit Tot

FAMILY

They Were Strong and Good

FAMILY—FICTION

What James Likes Best

FAMILY LIFE—FICTION

A Chair for My Mother
One Morning in Maine
The Patchwork Quilt
The Relatives Came
Working Cotton

FAMILY LIFE—PENNSYLVANIA—FICTION

Yonie Wondernose

FANTASY

Bartholomew and the Oobleck
Corduroy
Harold and the Purple Crayon
If I Ran the Zoo
In the Night Kitchen
Nothing Ever Happens on My Block
Outside Over There
Rain Makes Applesauce
Where the Wild Things Are

FATHERS AND DAUGHTERS—FICTION

Knuffle Bunny
Owl Moon

FATHERS AND DAUGHTERS—FOLKLORE

The Emperor and the Kite

FATHERS AND SONS—FICTION

The Night Worker
Peppe the Lamplighter

FISHING—FICTION

Fish for Supper
Henry—Fisherman

McElligott's Pool
Skipper John's Cook

FLIES—POETRY

Spider and the Fly

FLIGHT—FICTION

Hawk, I'm Your Brother
Tar Beach

FOLK SONGS

There Was an Old Lady Who Swallowed a Fly

FOLK SONGS—ENGLISH—TEXTS

There Was an Old Lady Who Swallowed a Fly

FOLK SONGS—FRANCE

One Monday Morning

FOLK SONGS, SCOTS

Always Room for One More

FOLK SONGS, SCOTS—SCOTLAND—TEXTS

Always Room for One More

FOLK SONGS—UNITED STATES

Frog Went A-Courtin'

FOLKLORE

Beautiful Blackbird
Between Earth and Sky: Legends of Native American Sacred Places
The Funny Little Woman
Goldilocks and the Three Bears
Golem
The Golem: A Jewish Legend
The Sun Is a Golden Earring

FOLKLORE—AFRICA

Anansi the Spider: A Tale from the Ashanti
The Origin of Life on Earth: An African Creation Myth

FOLKLORE—ARMENIA

The Contest: An Armenian Folktale

FOLKLORE—CAMEROON

The Village of Round and Square Houses

FOLKLORE—CARIBBEAN AREA

The Faithful Friend

FOLKLORE—CHINA

The Emperor and the Kite
Lon Po Po: A Red Riding Hood Story from China

FOLKLORE—ENGLAND

Saint George and the Dragon
Tom Tit Tot
The Treasure

FOLKLORE—FRANCE

Cinderella, or The Little Glass Slipper
Puss in Boots (Brown)
Puss in Boots (Marcellino)
Stone Soup

FOLKLORE—GERMANY

The Bremen-Town Musicians
Hansel and Gretel
Little Red Riding Hood
Rumpelstiltskin

FOLKLORE—INDIA

Once a Mouse
Seven Blind Mice

FOLKLORE—ITALY

Strega Nona

FOLKLORE—JAPAN

The Boy of the Three-Year Nap
Crow Boy
The Wave

FOLKLORE—MARTINIQUE

The Faithful Friend

FOLKLORE—MICHIGAN

Clever Beatrice

FOLKLORE—NORTH AMERICA

Between Earth & Sky: Legends of Native American Sacred Places

FOLKLORE—RUSSIA

Baboushka and the Three Kings
The Fool of the World and the Flying Ship: A Russian Tale

FOLKLORE—SENEGAL

Mother Crocodile

FOLKLORE—UNITED STATES

Journey Cake, Ho!
The Talking Eggs: A Folktale from the American South
Tops & Bottoms

FOLKLORE—ZAMBIA

Beautiful Blackbird

FOLKTALES—RUSSIAN

My Mother Is the Most Beautiful Woman in the World
Seven Simeons: A Russian Tale

FORTIFICATION—FICTION

Castle

FOXES—FICTION

One Fine Day
Roger and the Fox

FRANCE—FICTION

Madeline
Madeline's Rescue

FRENCH LANGUAGE—READERS

The House That Jack Built—La Maison Que Jacques a Batie

FRENCH POETRY

Shadow

FRIENDSHIP—FICTION

Farfallina & Marcel
George and Martha
Marshmallow
My Friend, Rabbit
Stevie
Thy Friend, Obadiah
Yo! Yes?

FROGS—FICTION

Frog and Toad Are Friends
Tuesday

FRONTIER AND PIONEER LIFE—TENNESSEE-FICTION

Swamp Angel

GALILEI, GALILEO, 1564–1642

Starry Messenger

GALILEO, 1564–1642

Starry Messenger

GAMES—FICTION

Jumanji

GARDENING—FICTION

The Carrot Seed
The Gardener

GEESE—FICTION

Farfallina & Marcel

GEORGE, SAINT, d. 303

Saint George and the Dragon

GEORGE, SAINT, d. 303—LEGENDS

Saint George and the Dragon

GOBLINS—FICTION

Hershel and the Hanukkah Goblins

GOLEM

Golem
The Golem

GRANDFATHERS—FICTION

Song and Dance Man

GRANDMOTHERS—FICTION

Coming on Home Soon
Fish for Supper
In the Time of the Drums
The Patchwork Quilt

GREAT-AUNTS—FICTION

Miss Rumphius

GREAT LAKES—FICTION

Paddle-to-the-Sea

GUARDS—FICTION

Gillespie and the Guards

HAIR—FICTION

Cornrows

HANDICRAFT

Magic Windows

HANUKKAH—FICTION

Hershel and the Hanukkah Goblins

HARES—FOLKLORE

Tops & Bottoms

HARLEM (NEW YORK, N.Y.)—FICTION

Tar Beach
Uptown

HARLEM (NEW YORK, N.Y.)—POETRY

Harlem: A Poem

HATS—FICTION

Caps for Sale

HAWKS—FICTION

Hawk, I'm Your Brother

HORSES—FICTION

The Girl Who Loved Wild Horses
Good-Luck Horse
Mister Penny's Race Horse

HOUSES—FICTION

A Very Special House

HUMAN ECOLOGY

Giving Thanks: A Native American Good Morn-ing Message

HUMMINGBIRDS—FICTION

The Forest Pool

HUMOROUS STORIES

Alexander and the Terrible, Horrible, No Good, Very Bad Day

HUNTING—FICTION

The Mighty Hunter

HYMNS, ENGLISH

Sing in Praise: A Collection of the Best Loved Hymns

HYMNS, ENGLISH—HISTORY AND CRITICISM

Sing in Praise: A Collection of the Best Loved Hymns

KINGS, QUEENS, RULERS, ETC.—FOLKLORE

One Monday Morning

IGBO (AFRICAN PEOPLE)—FICTION

In the Time of the Drums

IGUANAS—FICTION

The Forest Pool

ILA (AFRICAN PEOPLE)—FOLKLORE

Beautiful Blackbird

ILLUSTRATORS

Bill Peet: An Autobiography

ILLUSTRATORS—UNITED STATES—BIOGRAPHY

Bill Peet: An Autobiography

IMAGINATION—FICTION

And to Think I Saw It on Mulberry Street
Frederick
Sam, Bangs & Moonshine
A Very Special House

INDIAN POTTERY—SOUTHWEST, NEW

When Clay Sings

INDIANS OF NORTH AMERICA—FICTION

Did You Hear Wind Sing Your Name? An Oneida Song of Spring
The Girl Who Loved Wild Horses
Where the Buffaloes Begin

INDIANS OF NORTH AMERICA—FOLKLORE

The Angry Moon
Between Earth & Sky: Legends of Native American Sacred Places

INDIANS OF NORTH AMERICA—LEGENDS

Thirteen Moons on a Turtle's Back

INDIANS OF NORTH AMERICA—LEGENDS—POETRY

Thirteen Moons on a Turtle's Back

INDIANS OF NORTH AMERICA—NORTHWEST, PACIFIC—FOLKLORE

Raven: A Trickster Tale from the Pacific Northwest

INDIANS OF NORTH AMERICA—POETRY

In My Mother's House
Thirteen Moons on a Turtle's Back

INDIANS OF NORTH AMERICA—SOUTHWEST, NEW

When Clay Sings

INDIVIDUALITY—FICTION

Ella Sarah Gets Dressed

INSECTS—FICTION

Inch by Inch

INTERPERSONAL RELATIONS—FICTION

Smoky Night

INTERPLANETARY VOYAGES—FICTION

Nova's Ark

ISLANDS—FICTION

Time of Wonder

ITALIAN AMERICANS—FICTION

Peppe the Lamplighter

JAPAN—FICTION

Seashore Story

JAPANESE AMERICANS—EVACUATION AND RELOCATION, 1942–1945—FICTION

Baseball Saved Us

JAZZ MUSICIANS—UNITED STATES—BIOGRAPHY

Duke Ellington: The Piano Prince and the Orchestra

JEWS—FOLKLORE

Golem
The Golem

JUDAH LÖW BEN BEZALEEL, CA. 1525–1609

The Golem

KING, MARTIN LUTHER, JR., 1929–1968

Martin's Big Words: The Life of Dr. Martin Luther King, Jr.

KING, MARTIN LUTHER, JR., 1929–1968—QUOTATIONS

Martin's Big Words: The Life of Dr. Martin Luther King, Jr.

KITES—FICTION

Fish in the Air
Lucky Song

KITES—FOLKLORE

The Emperor and the Kite

KNIGHTS AND KNIGHTHOOD—FOLKLORE

Saint George and the Dragon

KOALAS—FICTION

Bear Party

LAMBS—FICTION

Little Lost Lamb

LAZINESS—FOLKLORE

The Boy of the Three-Year Nap

LETTERS—FICTION

The Gardener

LINCOLN, ABRAHAM (1809–1865)

Abraham Lincoln

LIONS—FICTION

Pierre (from *The Nutshell Library*)

LITERARY RECREATIONS

Black and White

LITTLE RED RIDING HOOD—ENGLISH

Little Red Riding Hood

LOS ANGELES (CALIF.)—FICTION

Chato and the Party Animals
Chato's Kitchen

LOST AND FOUND POSSESSIONS—FICTION

Knuffle Bunny

LULLABIES

Ten, Nine, Eight

MACHINERY—FICTION

The Little Machinery

MAGIC—FICTION

Sylvester and the Magic Pebble

MAINE—FICTION

One Morning in Maine
Time of Wonder

METEOROLOGISTS—UNITED STATES—BIOGRAPHY

Snowflake Bentley

MEXICAN AMERICAN FAMILIES

Magic Windows

MEXICAN AMERICANS—FICTION

Chato's Kitchen
Juanita
Pedro, the Angel of Olvera Street
Snapshots from the Wedding

MEXICAN AMERICANS—SOCIAL LIFE AND CUSTOMS

Magic Windows

MEXICO

Just a Minute: A Trickster Tale and Counting Book

MEXICO—FICTION

The Forest Pool

MEXICO—SOCIAL LIFE AND CUSTOMS

Magic Windows

MICE—FICTION

Anatole
Anatole and the Cat
Chato's Kitchen
Frederick
If You Give a Mouse a Cookie
Lilly's Purple Plastic Purse
My Friend Rabbit
Owen

MIGRANT LABOR—FICTION

Working Cotton

MISSING CHILDREN—FICTION

Sylvester and the Magic Pebble

MOHAWK INDIANS

Giving Thanks: A Native American Good Morning Message

MONKEYS—FICTION

Caps for Sale
Curious George
Five Little Monkeys

MONSTERS—FICTION

Where the Wild Things Are

MONTHS—POETRY

A Child's Calendar

MONTHS RHYMES

Chicken Soup with Rice (from *The Nutshell Library*)

MOON—FICTION

Grandfather Twilight
Happy Birthday, Moon
Kitten's First Full Moon
Many Moons

MORNING—FICTION

The Paperboy

MOTHER AND CHILD—FICTION

Blueberries for Sal
Coming on Home Soon
My Mama Needs Me

MOTHERS—FICTION

My Mother Is the Most Beautiful Woman in the World

MUSICIANS

Duke Ellington: The Piano Prince and the Orchestra

MUSICIANS—FICTION

Ben's Trumpet

NANTUCKET ISLAND (MASS.)—FICTION

Thy Friend, Obadiah

NASHVILLE (TENN.)—FICTION

Goin' Someplace Special

NATIVE AMERICANS—FICTION

The Mighty Hunter

NATURE—FICTION

Did You Hear Wind Sing Your Name? An Oneida Song of Spring

NATURE—RELIGIOUS ASPECTS

Giving Thanks: A Native American Good Morning Message

NATURE PHOTOGRAPHY

Snowflake Bentley

NEIGHBORHOODS—FICTION

Nothing Ever Happens on My Block

NEIGHBORLINESS—FICTION

Emily
Smoky Night

NEW ENGLAND—FICTION

Ox-Cart Man

NEW YORK CITY

The Man Who Walked between the Towers

NEW YORK (N.Y.)—FICTION

Peppe the Lamplighter

NEWSPAPER CARRIERS—FICTION

The Paperboy

NIGHT—FICTION

Grandfather Twilight
Half a Moon and One Whole Star
Hildilid's Night
The Moon Jumpers
The Night Worker

NONSENSE VERSES

There Was an Old Lady Who Swallowed a Fly

NORTH POLE—FICTION

The Polar Express

NURSERY RHYMES

Book of Nursery and Mother Goose Rhymes
Four and Twenty Blackbirds
If All the Seas Were One Sea
The House That Jack Built—La Maison Que Jacques a Batie
Mother Goose (Tudor)
Mother Goose and Nursery Rhymes (Reed)
The Rooster Crows: A Book of American Rhymes and Jingles
Three Jovial Huntsmen

NURSERY RHYMES—AMERICAN

The Rooster Crows: A Book of American Rhymes and Jingles

NURSERY RHYMES—ENGLISH

The House That Jack Built—La Maison Que Jacques a Batie

NURSERY RHYMES—FRENCH

The House That Jack Built—La Maison Que Jacques a Batie

ONEIDA INDIANS—FICTION

Did You Hear Wind Sing Your Name? An Oneida Song of Spring

OWLS—FICTION

Owl Moon

PAPER WORK

Magic Windows

PARENT AND CHILD—FICTION

"More More More," Said the Baby: Three Love Stories
Owen

PARIS (FRANCE)—FICTION

Madeline's Rescue

PARROTS—FICTION

The Forest Pool

PARTIES—FICTION

Chato and the Party Animals

PEDDLERS AND PEDDLING—FICTION

Caps for Sale

PEET, BILL

Bill Peet: An Autobiography

PEET, BILL—AUTOBIOGRAPHY

Bill Peet: An Autobiography

PENNSYLVANIA—FICTION

Yonie Wondernose

PENNSYLVANIA DUTCH—FICTION

Yonie Wondernose

PETIT, PHILIPPE, 1949–

The Man Who Walked between the Towers

PETS—FICTION

Hondo & Fabian

PHOTOGRAPHERS—UNITED STATES—BIOGRAPHY

Snowflake Bentley

PIGEONS—FICTION

Don't Let the Pigeon Drive the Bus

PIGS—FICTION

The Amazing Bone
Olivia
The Three Pigs

PILGRIMS (NEW PLYMOUTH COLONY)—FICTION

The Thanksgiving Story

PLAY—FICTION

Jumanji

POETRY—FICTION

Frederick

POETS—FICTION

Frederick

POLICE—FICTION

Officer Buckle and Gloria

POLICE DOGS—FICTION

Officer Buckle and Gloria

PRAYERS

Prayer for a Child

PREJUDICES—FICTION

Baseball Saved Us

PRESIDENTS—MISCELLANEA

So, You Want to Be President?

PRESIDENTS—UNITED STATES—BIOGRAPHY

Abraham Lincoln

PRESIDENTS—UNITED STATES—MISCELLANEA

So, You Want to Be President?

PRINCESSES—FICTION

Many Moons

PUEBLO INDIANS—FOLKLORE

Arrow to the Sun: A Pueblo Indian Tale

QUAKERS—FICTION

Thy Friend, Obadiah

QUILTING—FICTION

The Patchwork Quilt

RABBITS—FICTION

ABC Bunny
Goodnight Moon
Marshmallow
Mr. Rabbit and the Lovely Present
My Friend Rabbit
When Will the World Be Mine?

RACE RELATIONS—FICTION

Yo! Yes?

RAIN AND RAINFALL—FICTION

Umbrella

REVOLUTIONARIES—UNITED STATES—BIOGRAPHY

America's Ethan Allen

RIOTS—CALIFORNIA—LOS ANGELES—FICTION

Smoky Night

ROBIN HOOD (LEGENDARY CHARACTER)—SONGS AND MUSIC

Song of Robin Hood

ROBOTS—FICTION

Nova's Ark

ROTKÄPPCHEN

Little Red Riding Hood

SAFETY—FICTION

Officer Buckle and Gloria

SANTA CLAUS—FICTION

The Polar Express

SAVING AND INVESTMENT— FICTION

A Chair for My Mother

SCHOOLS—FICTION

Lilly's Purple Plastic Purse
Miss Nelson Is Missing!
Officer Buckle and Gloria

SCIENCE FICTION

Nova's Ark

SCIENTISTS

Snowflake Bentley
Starry Messenger

SCIENTISTS—ITALY—BIOGRAPHY

Starry Messenger

SCOTLAND—FICTION

All in the Morning Early

SEA LIONS—FICTION

Bambino the Clown

SEAGULLS—FICTION

Thy Friend, Obadiah

SEALS (ANIMALS)—FICTION

Bambino the Clown

SEASONS—FICTION

All Falling Down
Frederick
Green Eyes

SEASONS—POETRY

Thirteen Moons on a Turtle's Back

SEGREGATION—FICTION

Goin' Someplace Special

SELF-SERVICE LAUNDRIES— FICTION

Knuffle Bunny

SENSE ORGANS

What Do You Do With a Tail Like This?

SEPARATION (PSYCHOLOGY)— FICTION

Coming on Home Soon

SHADES AND SHADOWS—POETRY

Shadow

SHADOWS—POETRY

Shadow

SHAPE

Color Zoo

SHEEP—FICTION

Little Lost Lamb

SHELLS

House from the Sea

SHEPHERDS—FICTION

Little Lost Lamb

SHOPPING—FICTION

On Market Street

SHORT STORIES

The Stinky Cheese Man and Other Fairly Stupid Tales

SHOW-AND-TELL PRESENTATIONS—FICTION

A Pocketful of Cricket

SICK—FICTION

Madeline

SIGNS AND SIGNBOARDS

I Read Signs

SINGING—FICTION

Lucky Song

SISTERS—FICTION

Outside Over There

SKYSCRAPERS

The Man Who Walked between the Towers

SLAVE INSURRECTIONS—FICTION

In the Time of the Drums

SLAVE INSURRECTIONS—UNITED STATES—FICTION

In the Time of the Drums

SLAVES

Minty: A Story of Young Harriet Tubman

SLAVES—UNITED STATES—BIOGRAPHY

Minty: A Story of Young Harriet Tubman

SLEEP—FICTION

Half a Moon and One Whole Star

SNOW

Snowflake Bentley

SNOW—FICTION

Snow
The Snowy Day

SNOWFLAKES

Snowflake Bentley

SOLDIERS—UNITED STATES—BIOGRAPHY

America's Ethan Allen

SPANISH LANGUAGE MATERIALS—BILINGUAL

Magic Windows

SPEECHES, ADDRESSES, ETC., MOHAWK

Giving Thanks: A Native American Good Morning Message

SPIDERS—POETRY

Spider and the Fly

SPRING—FICTION

Did You Hear Wind Sing Your Name? An Oneida Song of Spring

STEAM SHOVELS—FICTION

Mike Mulligan and His Steam Shovel

STORIES IN RHYME

And to Think I Saw It on Mulberry Street
Brown Bear, Brown Bear, What Do You See?
Chicka Chicka Boom Boom

The Grey Lady and the Strawberry Snatcher
Half a Moon and One Whole Star
A House Is a House for Me
If I Ran the Zoo
The Judge: An Untrue Tale
Madeline
Madeline's Rescue
May I Bring a Friend?
McElligott's Pool
On Market Street
One Fish Two Fish Red Fish Blue Fish
1 Is One
Pop Corn & Ma Goodness
Seven Blind Mice
Timothy Turtle
A Very Special House

STORIES WITHOUT WORDS

Free Fall
Sector 7
Time Flies
Truck

STORKS—FICTION

Wheel on the Chimney

STORMS—FICTION

The Storm Book

STRAWBERRIES—FICTION

The Grey Lady and the Strawberry Snatcher

STREET SIGNS

I Read Signs

STREGA NONA (FICTITIOUS CHARACTER)—FICTION

Strega Nona

SUN (IN RELIGION, FOLKLORE, ETC.)

The Way to Start a Day

SUN—FICTION

The Day We Saw the Sun Come Up

SUN WORSHIP

The Way to Start a Day

SWALLOWS—FICTION

Song of the Swallows

TALES

The Sun Is a Golden Earring

TALL TALES

Clever Beatrice
Swamp Angel

TEACHERS—FICTION

Lilly's Purple Plastic Purse

TENNESSEE—FICTION

Swamp Angel

TEWA INDIANS—POETRY

In My Mother's House

THANKSGIVING DAY—FICTION

The Thanksgiving Story

THREE BEARS

Goldilocks and the Three Bears

TIBET (CHINA)—DESCRIPTION AND TRAVEL

Tibet Through the Red Box

TIGERS—FICTION

Leo the Late Bloomer

TIGHTROPE WALKING

The Man Who Walked between the Towers
Mirette on the High Wire

TIME TRAVEL—FICTION

Time Flies

TLINGIT INDIANS—FOLKLORE

The Angry Moon

TOADS—FICTION

Frog and Toad Are Friends

TOYS—FICTION

Corduroy
Knuffle Bunny
The Most Wonderful Doll in the World
The Steadfast Tin Soldier

TOYS AND MOVABLE BOOKS

The Very Hungry Caterpillar
There Was an Old Lady Who Swallowed a Fly

**TOYS AND MOVABLE BOOKS—
SPECIMENS**

The Very Hungry Caterpillar
There Was an Old Lady Who Swallowed a Fly

TRAFFIC SIGNS AND SIGNALS

I Read Signs

TRAINS—FICTION

The Little Engine That Could

TRANSPORTATION—FICTION

The Little Engine That Could
What James Likes Best

TREES

A Tree Is Nice

TRUCKS—FICTION

Truck

TSUNAMIS—FICTION

The Wave

**TUBMAN, HARRIET, 1820(?)–1913—
CHILDHOOD AND YOUTH**

Minty: A Story of Young Harriet Tubman

TURTLES—FICTION

Timothy Turtle

TYPEWRITERS—FICTION

Click, Clack, Moo: Cows That Type

TWILIGHT—FICTION

Grandfather Twilight

UMBRELLAS—FICTION

Umbrella

UNCLES—FICTION

The Gardener

UNDERGROUND RAILROAD

Minty: A Story of Young Harriet Tubman

UNITED STATES—HISTORY

An American ABC

**UNITED STATES—HISTORY—
REVOLUTION, 1775–1783**

America's Ethan Allen

**UNITED STATES—HISTORY—
REVOLUTION, 1775–1783—
BIOGRAPHY**

America's Ethan Allen

UNIVERSE—FICTION

The Sun Is a Golden Earring

**VERMONT—HISTORY—
REVOLUTION, 1775–1783**

America's Ethan Allen

VIRGIN ISLANDS—FICTION

Henry—Fisherman

**VISUAL PERCEPTION—STUDY AND
TEACHING (ELEMENTARY)**

Color Zoo

WAGONS—FICTION

Gillespie and the Guards

WALT DISNEY PRODUCTIONS

Bill Peet: An Autobiography

WEDDINGS—FICTION

Snapshots from the Wedding

WINDS—FICTION

Mirandy and Brother Wind

WINTER—FICTION

The Big Snow
Frederick
The Happy Day

WORK—FICTION

Frederick
The Night Worker

WORLD TRADE CENTER (NEW YORK, N.Y.)

The Man Who Walked between the Towers

WORLD WAR, 1941–1945—UNITED STATES—FICTION

Baseball Saved Us
Coming on Home Soon

YANGTZE RIVER (CHINA)—FICTION

The Story about Ping

YORUBA (AFRICAN PEOPLE)—FOLKLORE

The Origin of Life on Earth: An African Creation Myth

Award-Winning Picture Books, 2006–2010

2006

2006 Caldecott Awards

2006 Charlotte Zolotow Book Awards

2006 Coretta Scott King Book Awards

2006 Other Awards

2007

2007 Caldecott Awards

2007 Charlotte Zolotow Book Awards

2007 Coretta Scott King Book Awards

2007 Other Awards

2008

2008 Caldecott Awards

2008 Charlotte Zolotow Book Awards

2008 Coretta Scott King Book Awards

2008 Other Awards

2009

2009 Caldecott Awards

2009 Charlotte Zolotow Book Awards

2009 Coretta Scott King Book Awards

2009 Other Awards

2010

2010 Caldecott Awards

2010 Charlotte Zolotow Book Awards

2010 Coretta Scott King Book Awards

2010 Other Awards

Bibliography

PICTURE BOOKS (CITED IN THIS VOLUME)

Aardema, Verna. Illus. by Leo and Diane Dillon. *Why Mosquitoes Buzz in People's Ears: A West African Tale*. New York: Dial Press, 1975.

Ackerman, Karen. Illus. by Stephen Gammell. *Song and Dance Man*. New York: Knopf, 1988.

Alger, Leclaire (pseud. Sorche Nic Leodhas). Illus. by Evaline Ness. *All in the Morning Early*. New York: Holt, Rinehart, and Winston, 1963.

———. Illus. by Nonny Hogrogrian. *Always Room for One More*. New York: Holt, Rinehart and Winston, 1965.

Allard, Harry. Illus. by James Marshall. *Miss Nelson Is Missing!* Boston: Houghton Mifflin, 1977.

Andersen, Hans Christian. Illus. by Jerry Pinkney. *The Ugly Duckling*. New York: Morrow Junior Books, 1999.

Anderson, David A. Illus. by Kathleen Atkins Wilson. *The Origin of Life on Earth: An African Creation Myth*. Mt. Airy, MD: Sights Productions, ca. 1991.

———. *Yonie Wondernose*. Garden City, NY: Doubleday, 1944.

Angelou, Maya, et al. Illus. by Tom Feelings. *Soul Looks Back in Wonder*. New York: Dial, ca. 1993.

Armer, Laura Adams. *The Forest Pool*. New York: Longmans, Green, 1938.

Artzybasheff, Boris. *Seven Simeons: A Russian Tale*. New York: Viking Press, 1937.

d'Aulaire, Ingri, and Edgar Parin. *Abraham Lincoln*. New York: Doubleday, 1939.

Baker, Olaf. Illus. by Stephen Gammell. *Where the Buffaloes Begin*. New York: F. Warne, 1981.

Bang, Molly. *The Grey Lady and the Strawberry Snatcher*. New York: Four Winds Press, 1980.

———. *Ten, Nine, Eight*. New York: Greenwillow, 1983.

———. *When Sophie Gets Angry—Really, Really, Angry*. New York: Blue Sky Press, 1999.

Bartone, Elisa. Illus. by Ted Lewin. *Peppe the Lamplighter*. New York: Lothrop, Lee and Shepard, 1993.

Baskin, Hosea, Tobias, and Lisa. Illus. by Leonard Baskin. *Hosie's Alphabet*. New York: Viking Press, 1972.

Baylor, Bryd. Illus. by Peter Parnall. *The Desert Is Theirs*. New York: Scribner, 1975.

———. *Hawk, I'm Your Brother*. New York: Scribner, 1976.

———. *The Way to Start a Day*. New York: Scribner, 1978.

————. Illus. by Tom Bahti. *When Clay Sings*. New York: Scribner, 1972.

Bedard, Michael. Illus. by Barbara Cooney. *Emily*. New York: Doubleday, 1992.

Belting, Natalia M. Illus. by Bernarda Bryson. *The Sun Is a Golden Earring*. New York: Holt, Rinehart, and Winston, 1962.

Bemelmans, Ludwig. *Madeline*. New York: Simon and Schuster, 1939.

————. *Madeline's Rescue*. New York: Viking Press, 1953.

Berger, Barbara. *Grandfather Twilight*. New York: Philomel, ca. 1984.

Birnbaum, A. *Green Eyes*. Irvington, NY: Capitol, 1953.

duBois, William Pène. *Bear Party*. New York: Viking Press, 1951.

————. *Lion*. New York: Viking Press, 1956.

Brown, Marica. *Cinderella, or The Little Glass Slipper*. New York: Scribner, 1954.

————. *Dick Whittington and His Cat*. New York: Scribner, 1950.

————. *Henry Fisherman*. New York: Scribner, 1949.

————. *Once a Mouse*. New York: Scribner, 1961.

————. *Puss in Boots*. New York: Scribner, 1952.

————. *Shadow*. New York: Scribner, 1952.

————. *Skipper John's Cook*. New York: Scribner, 1951.

————. *Stone Soup*. New York: Scribner, 1947.

Brown, Margaret Wise. Illus. by Clement Hurd. *Goodnight Moon*. New York: Harper, 1947.

Brown, Margaret Wise. Illus. by Jean Charlot. *A Child's Good Night Book*. New York: W. R. Scott, 1943.

———— [pseud. Golden MacDonald]. Illus. by Leonard Weisgard. *The Little Island*. Garden City, NY: Doubleday, 1946.

———— [pseud. Golden MacDonald]. *Little Lost Lamb*. Garden City, NY: Doubleday, Doran, 1945.

————. Illus. by Tibor Gergely. *Wheel on the Chimney*. Philadelphia: Lippincott, 1954.

Bruchac, Joseph. Illus. by Thomas Locker. *Between Earth & Sky: Legends of Native American Sacred Places*. San Diego: Harcourt, Brace, 1996.

Bruchac, Joseph, and Jonathan London. Illus. by Thomas Locker. *Thirteen Moons on a Turtle's Back*. New York: Philomel, 1992.

Bryan, Ashley. *Beautiful Blackbird*. New York: Atheneum, 2003.

Buff, Mary, and Conrad. *Dash and Dart*. New York: Viking Press, 1942.

Bunting, Eve. Illus. by David Diaz. *Smoky Night*. San Diego: Harcourt, Brace, 1994.

Burton, Virginia Lee. *The Little House*. Boston: Houghton Mifflin, 1942.

————. *Mike Mulligan and His Steam Shovel*. Boston: Houghton Mifflin, 1939.

Cannon, Jane. *Stellaluna*. San Diego: Harcourt Brace Jovanovich, ca. 1993.

Carle, Eric. *The Very Hungry Caterpillar*. New York: Philomel, 1979.

Caudill, Rebecca. Illus. by Evaline Ness. *A Pocketful of Cricket*. New York: Holt, Rinehart, and Winston, 1964.

Chan, Chih-Yi. Illus. by Plato Chan. *Good-Luck Horse*. New York: McGraw-Hill, 1943.

Chodos-Irvine, Margaret. *Ella Sarah Gets Dressed*. San Diego: Harcourt, 2003.

Clark, Ann Nolan. Illus. by Velino Herrera. *In My Mother's House*. New York: Viking Press, 1941.

Collier, Bryan. *Uptown*. New York: Henry Holt, 2000.

Cooney, Barbara. *Chanticleer and the Fox*. New York: Crowell, 1958.

Crews, Donald. *Freight Train*. New York: Greenwillow Books, 1978.

————. *Truck*. New York: Puffin Books, 1980.

Cronin, Doreen. Illus. by Betsy Lewin. *Click, Clack, Moo: Cows That Type*. New York: Simon and Schuster Books for Young Readers, ca. 2000.

Daligliesh, Alice. Illus. by Helen Sewell. *The Thanksgiving Story*. New York: Atheneum, ca. 1954.

Daugherty, James. *Andy and the Lion*. New York: Viking Press, 1938.

Davis, Lavinia R. Illus. by Hildegard Woodward. *Roger and the Fox*. Garden City, NY: Doubleday, ca. 1947.

———. *The Wild Birthday Cake*. Garden City, NY: Doubleday, ca. 1949.

Dayrell, Elphinstone. Illus. by Blair Lent. *Why the Sun and the Moon Live in the Sky*. Boston: Houghton Mifflin, 1968.

de Angeli, Marguerite. *Book of the Nursery and Mother Goose Rhymes*. Garden City, NY: Doubleday, 1954.

De Coteau Orie, Sandra. Illus. by Christopher Canyon. *Did You Hear Wind Sing Your Name? An Oneida Song of Spring*. New York: Walker, 1995.

dePaola, Tomie. *Strega Nona*. Englewood Cliffs, NJ: Prentice-Hall, 1975.

de Regniers, Beatrice Schenk. Illus. by Beni Montresor. *May I Bring a Friend?* New York: Atheneum, 1964.

Domanska, Janina. *If All the Seas Were One Sea*. New York: Macmillan, 1971.

Dragonwagon, Crescent. Illus. by Jerry Pinkney. *Half a Moon and One Whole Star*. New York: Macmillan, 1986.

Du Bois, William Pène. *Bear Party*. New York: Viking Press, 1951.

Ehlert, Lois. *Color Zoo*. New York: Lippincott, 1989.

Eichenberg, Fritz. *Ape in a Cape: An Alphabet of Odd Animals*. San Diego: Harcourt Brace Jovanovitch, ca. 1952.

Elkin, Benjamin. Illus. by James Daugherty. *Gillespie and the Guards*. New York: Viking Press, 1956.

Emberley, Barbara. Illus. by Ed Emberley. *Drummer Hoff*. Englewood Cliffs, NJ: Prentice-Hall, 1967.

———. *One Wide River to Cross*. Englewood Cliffs, NJ: Prentice-Hall, 1966.

Ets, Marie Hall. *In the Forest*. New York: Viking Press, 1944.

———. *Just Me*. New York: Viking Press, 1965.

———. *Mr. Penny's Race Horse*. New York: Viking Press, 1956.

———. *Mr. T. W. Anthony Woo: The Story of a Cat and a Dog and a Mouse*. New York: Viking Press, 1951.

———. *Play with Me*. New York: Viking Press, 1955.

Ets, Marie Hall, and Aurora Labastida. Illus. by Marie Hall Ets. *Nine Days to Christmas*. New York: Viking Press, 1959.

Falconer, Ian. *Olivia*. New York: Atheneum, 2000.

Falls, C. B. *ABC Book*. New York: Doubleday, 1923.

Feelings, Muriel. Illus. by Tom Feelings. *Jambo Means Hello: Swahili Alphabet Book*. New York: Dial Press, 1974.

———. *Moja Means One: Swahili Counting Book*. New York: Dial Press, 1971.

Field, Rachel. Illus. by Elizabeth Orton Jones. *Prayer for a Child*. New York: Macmillan, 1944.

Fish, Helen Dean, ed. Illus. by Dorothy P. Lathrop. *Animals of the Bible, a Picture Book*. New York: Frederick A. Stokes, 1937.

———. Illus. by Robert Lawson. *Four and Twenty Blackbirds*. New York: J. B. Lippincott, 1937.

Flack, Marjorie. Illus. by Jay Hyde Barnum. *The Boats on the River*. New York: Viking Press, 1946.

———. Illus. by Kurt Wiese. *The Story about Ping*. New York: Viking Press, 1933.

Fleming, Denise. *In the Small, Small Pond*. New York: Henry Holt, 1993.

Flournoy, Valerie. Illus. by Jerry Pinkney. *The Patchwork Quilt*. New York: Dial Press, 1985.

Ford, Lauren. *The Ageless Story. The Ageless Story, with Its Antiphons*. New York: Dodd, Mead, 1939.

Frasconi, Antonio. *The House That Jack Built: La Maison Que Jacques a Batie*. New York: Harcourt, Brace, 1958.

Freeman, Don. *Corduroy*. New York: Viking Press, 1968.

———. *Fly High, Fly Low*. New York: Viking Press, 1957.

Gág, Wanda. *Millions of Cats*. New York: Coward McCann, 1928.

———. *Nothing at All*. New York: Coward McCann, 1941.

———. *Snow White and the Seven Dwarfs*. New York: Coward McCann, 1938.

Garza, Carmen Lomas. *Magic Windows*. San Francisco: Children's Book Press, 1999.

Goble, Paul. *The Girl Who Loved Wild Horses*. New York: Dutton, 1978.

Goffstein, M. B. *Fish for Supper*. New York: Dial Press, 1976.

Goldstein, Mordicai. *The Man Who Walked between the Towers*. Brookfield, CT: Roaring Brook Press, 2003.

Goudey, Alice E. Illus. by Adrienne Adams. *The Day We Saw the Sun Come Up*. New York: Scribner, 1961.

———. *Houses from the Sea*. New York: Scribner, 1959.

Graham, Al. Illus. by Tony Palazzo. *Timothy Turtle*. Cambridge, MA: Robert Welch, 1946.

Greenfield, Eloise. Illus. by Carole Byard. *Africa Dreaming*. New York: HarperCollins, 1977.

———. Illus. by Jan Spivey Gilchrist. *Nathaniel Talking*. New York: Black Butterfly Children's Books, 1988.

Grifalconi, Ann. *The Village of Round and Square Houses*. Boston: Little, Brown, 1986.

Hader, Berta, and Elmer. *The Big Snow*. New York: Macmillan, 1948.

———. *Cock-a-Doodle Doo*. New York: Macmillan, 1939.

———. *The Mighty Hunter*. New York: Macmillan, 1943.

Haley, Gail E. *A Story a Story: An African Tale*. New York: Atheneum, 1970.

Hall, Donald. Illus. by Barbara Cooney. *Ox-Cart Man*. New York: Viking Press, 1979.

Handforth, Thomas. *Mei Li*. Garden City, NY: Doubleday, 1938.

Henkes, Kevin. *Lilly's Purple Plastic Purse*. New York: Greenwillow Books, 1996.

———. *Kitten's First Full Moon*. New York: Greenwillow Books, 2004.

———. *Owen*. New York: Greenwillow Books, 1993.

Herron, Carolivia. Illus. by Joe Cepada. *Nappy Hair*. New York: Alfred A. Knopf, 1997.

Hill, Eric. *Where's Spot?* New York: Putnam, 1980.

Ho, Minfong. Illus. by Holly Meade. *Hush! A Thai Lullaby*. New York: Orchard, 1996.

Hoban, Tana. *I Read Signs*. New York: Greenwillow, 1983.

Hodges, Margaret. Illus. by Blair Lent. *The Wave*. Boston: Houghton Mifflin, 1964.

———. Illus. by Trina Schart Hyman. *Saint George and the Dragon*. New York: Little, Brown, 1984.

Hogrogian, Nonny. *The Contest*. New York: Greenwillow, 1976.

———. *One Fine Day*. New York: Macmillan, 1971.

Holbrook, Stewart. Illus. by Lynd Ward. *America's Ethan Allen*. Boston: Houghton Mifflin, 1949.

Holling, Holling C. *Paddle-to-the-Sea*. Boston: Houghton Mifflin, 1941.

Howitt, Mary. Illus. by Tony DiTerlizzi. *The Spider and the Fly*. New York: Simon and Schuster, 2002.

Hutchins, Pat. *Rosie's Walk*. New York: Macmillan, 1967.

Hymen, Trina Schart. *Little Red Riding Hood*. New York: Holiday House, 1983.

Igus, Toyomi. Illus. by Michele Wood. *i see the rhythm*. San Francisco: Children's Book Press, 1998.

Isaacs, Anne. Illus. by Paul O. Zelinsky. *Swamp Angel*. New York: Dutton Children's Books, 1994.

Isadora, Rachel. *Ben's Trumpet*. New York: Greenwillow, 1979.

James, M. R. Illus. by Marcia Brown. *The Steadfast Tin Soldier*. New York: Scribner, 1953.

Jarrell, Randall. Illus. by Nancy Ekholm Burkert. *Snow-White and the Seven Dwarfs*. New York: Farrar, Straus and Giroux, 1972.

Jeffers, Susan. *Three Jovial Huntsmen*. Scarsdale, NY: Bradbury Press, 1973.

Johnson, Crockett. *Harold and the Purple Crayon*. New York: Harper and Row, 1955.

Johnson, Stephen T. *Alphabet City*. New York: Viking Press, 1995.

Jones, Jessie Orton. Illus. by Elizabeth Orton Jones. *Small Rain: Verses from the Bible*. New York: Viking Press, 1943.

Joslin, Sesyle. Illus. by Maurice Sendak. *What Do You Say, Dear?* New York: Young Scott Books, 1958.

Keats, Ezra Jack. *Goggles!*. New York: Macmillan, 1969.

———. *The Snowy Day*. New York: Viking Press, 1962.

Keller, Holly. *Farfallina & Marcel*. New York: Greenwillow, 2002.

Kepes, Juliet. *Five Little Monkeys*. Boston: Houghton Mifflin, 1952.

Kerley, Barbara. Illus. by Brian Selznick. *The Dinosaurs of Waterhouse Hawkins*. New York: Scholastic, 2001.

Kimmel, Eric. Illus. by Trina Schart Hymen. *Hershel and the Hannukkah Goblins*. New York: Holiday House, 1989.

Kingman, Lee. Illus. by Arnold E. Bare. *Pierre Pidgeon*. Boston: Houghton Mifflin, 1943.

Kirk, David. *Nova's Ark*. New York: Scholastic, 1999.

Kraus, Robert. Illus. by José Aruego. *Leo the Late Bloomer*. New York: Harper, 1971.

Krauss, Ruth. Illus. by Crockett Johnson. *The Carrot Seed*. New York: Harper, ca. 1945.

———. Illus. by Marc Simont. *The Happy Day*. New York: Harper, 1949.

———. Illus. by Maurice Sendak. *A Very Special House*. New York: Harper, 1953.

Kunhardt, Dorothy. *Pat the Bunny*. New York: Simon and Schuster, 1940.

Langstaff, John. Illus. by Feodor Rojankovsky. *Frog Went A-Courtin'*. San Diego: Harcourt Brace Jovanovitch, 1955.

Lawson, Robert. *They Were Strong and Good*. New York: Viking Press, 1940.

Leaf, Munro. Illus. by Robert Lawson. *The Story about Ferdinand*. New York: Viking Press, 1936.

———. *Wee Gillis*. New York: Viking Press, 1938.

Lehman, Barbara. *The Red Book*. Boston: Houghton Mifflin, 2004.

Lesser, Rika. Illus. by Paul O. Zelinsky. *Hansel and Gretel*. New York: Dodd, Mead, 1984.

Lester, Julius. Illus. by Jerry Pinkney. *John Henry*. New York: Dial Press, 1994.

Lionni, Leo. *Alexander and the Wind-Up Mouse*. New York: Pantheon, 1969.

———. *Frederick*. New York: Random House, 1967.

———. *Inch by Inch*. New York: I. Obolensky, 1960.

———. *Swimmy*. New York: Pantheon, 1963.

Lipkind, William (pseud. Will). Illus. by Nicholas Mordvinoff (pseud. Nicolas). *Finders Keepers*. New York: Harcourt, 1951.

———. *The Two Reds*. New York: Harcourt, 1950.

Lobel, Arnold. *Fables*. New York: Harper, 1980.

———. *Frog and Toad Are Friends*. New York: Harper and Row, 1970.

———. Illus. by Anita Lobel. *On Market Street*. New York: Greenwillow Books, 1981.

Low, Joseph. *Mice Twice*. New York: Atheneum, 1980.

Lowrey, Janette Sebring. Illus. by Gustaf Tenggren. *The Poky Little Puppy*. New York: Simon and Schuster, 1942.

Macauley, David. *Black and White*. Boston: Houghton Mifflin, 1990.

———. *Castle*. Boston: Houghton Mifflin, 1977.

———. *Cathedral*. Boston: Houghton Mifflin, 1973.

MacDonald, Suse. *Alphabetics*. New York: Aladdin Books, 1992.

Malcolmson, Anne. Illus. by Virginia Lee Burton. *Song of Robin Hood*. Boston: Houghton Mifflin, [2000], 1947.

Marshall, James. *George and Martha*. Boston: Houghton Mifflin, 1972.

———. *Goldilocks and the Three Bears*. New York: Dial, 1988.

Martin, Bill, Jr. Illus. by Eric Carle. *Brown Bear, Brown Bear, What Do You See?* New York: Holt, Rinehart, and Winston, 1967.

Martin, Bill, Jr., and John Archambault. Illus. by Lois Ehlert. *Chicka Chicka Boom Boom*. New York: Simon and Schuster, 1989.

Martin, Jacqueline Briggs. Illus. by Mary Azarian. *Snowflake Bentley*. Boston: Houghton Mifflin, 1998.

McCarty, Peter. *Hondo and Fabian*. New York: Henry Holt, 2002.

McCloskey, Robert. *Blueberries for Sal*. New York: Viking Press, 1948.

———. *Make Way for Ducklings*. New York: Viking Press, 1941.

———. *One Morning in Maine*. New York: Viking Press, 1952.

———. *Time of Wonder*. New York: Viking Press, 1957.

McCully, Emily Arnold. *Mirette on the High Wire*. New York: G. P. Putnam's Sons, 1992.

McDermott, Beverly Brodsky. *The Golem: A Jewish Legend*. Philadelphia: Lippincott, 1976.

McDermott, Gerald. *Anansi the Spider: A Tale from the Ashanti*. New York: Holt, Rinehart, and Winston, 1972.

———. *Arrow to the Sun*. New York: Viking Press, 1974.

———. *Raven: A Trickster Tale from the Pacific Northwest*. San Diego: Harcourt Brace Jovanovich, 1993.

McGinley, Phyllis. Illus. by Helen Stone. *All Around the Town*. Philadelphia: Lippincott, 1948.

———. *The Most Wonderful Doll in the World*. Philadelphia: Lippincott, 1950.

McKissack, Patricia. Illus. by Jerry Pinkney. *Goin' Someplace Special*. New York: Atheneum, 2001.

———. *Mirandy and Brother Wind*. New York: Knopf, 1988.

Milhous, Katherine. *The Egg Tree*. New York: Scribner, 1950.

Minarik, Else H. Illus. by Maurice Sendak. *Little Bear's Visit*. HarperCollins, 1961.

Mochizuki, Ken. Illus. by Dom Lee. *Baseball Saved Us*. New York: Lee and Low, 1993.

Mosel, Arlene. Illus. by Blair Lent. *The Funny Little Woman*. New York: Dutton, 1972.

Moss, Lloyd. Illus. by Marjorie Priceman. *Zin! Zin! Zin! A Violin*. New York: Simon and Schuster, 1995.

Mugrove, Margaret. Illus. by Leo and Diane Dillon. *Ashanti to Zulu: African Traditions*. New York: Dial Press, 1976.

Myers, Walter Dean. Illus. by Christopher Myers. *Harlem: A Poem*. New York: Scholastic, 1997.

Ness, Evaline. *Sam, Bangs & Moonshine*. New York: Holt, Rinehart, and Winston, 1966.

———. *Tom Tit Tot: An English Folktale*. New York: Scribner, 1965.

Newberry, Clare Turlay. *April's Kittens*. New York: Harper and Brothers, 1940.

———. *Barkis*. New York: Harper, 1938.

———. *Marshmallow*. New York: Harper and Brothers, 1942.

Numeroff, Laura Joffe. Illus. by Felicia Bond. *If You Give a Mouse a Cookie*. New York: Harper and Row, 1985.

Olds, Elizabeth. *Feather Mountain*. Boston: Houghton Mifflin, 1951.

Page, Robin. Illus. by Steve Jenkins. *What Would You Do With a Tail Like This?* Boston: Houghton Mifflin, 2003.

Peet, Bill. *Bill Peet: An Autobiography*. Boston: Houghton Mifflin, 1989.

Peletier, David. *The Graphic Alphabet*. New York: Orchard, 1996.

Perrault, Charles. Illus. by Fred Marcellino. *Puss in Boots*. New York: Farrar, Straus, and Giroux, 1990.

Petersham, Maud, and Miska. *An American ABC*. New York: Macmillan, 1941.

———. *The Rooster Crows: A Book of American Rhymes and Jingles*. New York: Macmillan, 1945.

Pilkey, Dav. *The Paperboy*. New York: Orchard Books, ca. 1996.

Pinkney, Andrea Davis. Illus. by Brian Pinkney. *Duke Ellington: The Piano Prince and the Orchestra*. New York: Hyperion, 1998.

Pinkney, Jerry. *Noah's Ark*. New York: SeaStar/North-South Books, 2002.

Piper, Watty. Illus. by Lois Lenski. *The Little Engine That Could*. New York: Platt and Munk, 1930.

Plume, Ilse. *The Bremen-Town Musicians*. Garden City, NY: Doubleday, 1980.

Politi, Leo. *Juanita*. New York: Scribner, 1948.

———. *Pedro, the Angel of Olvera Street*. New York: Scribner, 1946.

———. *Song of the Swallows*. New York: Scribner, 1949.

Preston, Edna Mitchell. Illus. by Robert Andrew Parker. *Pop Corn & Ma Goodness*. New York: Viking Press, 1969.

Prevensen, Alice, and Martin. *The Glorious Flight: Across the Channel with Louis Blériot*. New York: Viking Press, ca. 1983.

Ransome, Arthur. Illus. by Uri Shulevitz. *The Fool of the World and the Flying Ship*. New York: Farrar, Straus and Giroux, 1968.

Rappaport, Doreen. Illus. by Bryan Collier. *Martin's Big Words: The Life of Dr. Martin Luther King, Jr.* New York: Hyperion Books for Children, 2001.

Raschka, Chris. *Yo! Yes?* New York: Orchard Books, 1993.

Raskin, Ellen. *Nothing Ever Happens on My Block*. New York: Atheneum, 1966.

Rathmann, Peggy. *Officer Buckle and Gloria*. New York: Putnam, 1995.

Reed, Philip. *Mother Goose and Nursery Rhymes*. New York: Atheneum, 1963.

Rey, H. A. *Curious George*. Boston: Houghton Mifflin, 1941.

Reyher, Becky. Illus. by Ruth Gannett. *My Mother Is the Most Beautiful Woman in the World*. New York: Howell, Soskin, 1945.

Ringgold, Faith. *Tar Beach*. New York: Crown, 1991.

Robbins, Ruth. Illus. by Nicolas Sidjakov. *Baboushka and the Three Kings*. Boston: Houghton Mifflin, 1960.

Rohmann, Eric. *My Friend, Rabbit*. Brookfield, CT: Roaring Brook Press, 2002.

———. *Time Flies*. New York: Crown, 1994.

Ryan, Cheli Durán. Illus. by Arnold Lobel. *Hildilid's Night*. New York: Macmillan, 1971.

Rylant, Cynthia. Illus. by Stephen Gammell. *The Relatives Came*. New York: Bradbury Press, 1985.

———. *When I Was Young in the Mountains*. New York: Dutton, 1982.

St. George, Judith. Illus. by David Small. *So You Want to Be President?* New York: Philomel Books, 2000.

San Souci, Robert D. Illus. by Brian Pinkney. *The Faithful Friend*. New York: Simon and Schuster, 1995.

———. Illus. by Jerry Pinkney. *The Talking Eggs: A Folktale from the American South*. New York: Dial Press, 1989.

Sawyer, Ruth. Illus. by Kate Seredy. *The Christmas Anna Angel*. New York: Viking Press, 1944.

———. Illus. by Robert McCloskey. *Journey Cake, Ho!* New York: Viking Press, 1953.

Say, Allen. *Grandfather's Journey*. Boston: Houghton Mifflin, 1993.

Scheer, Julian. Illus. by Marvin Bileck. *Rain Makes Applesauce*. New York: Holiday House, 1964.

Schlein, Miriam. Illus. by Jean Charlot. *When Will the World Be Mine?: The Story of a Snowshoe Rabbit*. New York: W. R. Scott, 1953.

Schreiber, Georges. *Bambino the Clown*. New York: Viking Press, 1947.

Scieszka, Jon. Illus. by Lane Smith. *The Stinky Cheese Man and Other Fairly Stupid Tales*. New York: Viking Press, 1992.

Sendak, Maurice. *In the Night Kitchen*. New York: Harper and Row, 1970.

———. *Nutshell Library*. New York: Harper and Row, 1962.

———. *Outside Over There*. Calligraphy by Jeanyee Wong. New York: Harper and Row, 1981.

———. *Where the Wild Things Are*. New York: Harper and Row, 1963.

Seuss, Dr. (pseud. Theodor Seuss Geisel). *And to Think I Saw It on Mulberry Street*. New York: Vanguard Press, 1937.

———. *Bartholomew and the Oobleck*. New York: Random House, 1949.

———. *If I Ran the Zoo*. New York: Random House, 1950.

———. *McElligott's Pool*. New York: Random House, 1947.

Shange, Ntozake. Illus. by Kadir Nelson. *ellington was not a street*. New York: Simon and Schuster, 2004.

Shannon, David. *No, David!* New York: Blue Sky Press, 1998.

Shulevitz, Uri. *One Monday Morning*. New York: Scribner, 1967.

———. *Snow*. New York: Farrar, Straus and Giroux, ca. 1998.

———. *The Treasure*. New York: Farrar, Straus and Giroux, 1978.

Siegelson, Kim L. Illus. by Brian Pinkney. *In the Time of the Drums*. New York: Hyperion, 1999.

Simont, Marc. *The Stray Dog*. New York: HarperCollins, 2001.

Sís, Peter. *Starry Messenger*. New York: Frances Foster, 1996.

———. *Tibet Through the Red Box*. New York: Farrar, Straus and Giroux, 1998.

Sleator, William. Illus. by Blair Lent. *The Angry Moon*. Boston: Little, Brown, 1970.

Slobodkina, Esphyr. *Caps for Sale*. New York: Scott, 1940.

Snyder, Diane. Illus. by Allen Say. *The Boy of the Three-Year Nap*. Boston: Houghton Mifflin, 1988.

Soto, Gary. Illus. by Susan Guevara. *Chato and the Party Animals*. New York: Putnam, 2000.

———. *Chato's Kitchen*. New York: Putnam, 1995.

Spier, Peter. *Fox Went out on a Chilly Night: An Old Song*. New York: Doubleday, 1961 [1989].

———. *Noah's Ark*. Garden City, NY: Doubleday, 1977.

Steig, William. *The Amazing Bone*. New York: Farrar, Straus and Giroux, 1976.

———. *Doctor De Soto*. New York: Farrar, Straus and Giroux, 1982.

———. *Sylvester and the Magic Pebble*. New York: Windmill Books, 1969.

Steptoe, Javaka, ed. and illus. *In Daddy's Arms I Am Tall*. New York: Lee and Low, 1997.

Steptoe, John. *Mufaro's Beautiful Daughters: An African Tale*. New York: Lothrop, Lee and Shepard Books, 1987.

———. *Stevie*. New York: HarperCollins, 1969.

———. *The Story of Jumping Mouse: A Native American Legend*. New York: Lothrop, Lee, and Shepard Books, 1984.

Stevens, Janet. *Tops and Bottoms*. San Diego: Harcourt Brace Jovanovich, 1995.

Stewart, Sarah. Illus. by David Small. *The Gardener*. New York: Farrar, Straus and Giroux, 1997.

Swamp, Jake Chief. Illus. by Erwin Printup Jr. *Giving Thanks: A Native American Good Morning Message*. New York: Lee and Low, 1995.

Tabeck, Simms. *Joseph Had a Little Overcoat*. New York: Random House, 1977.

———. *There Was an Old Lady Who Swallowed a Fly*. New York: Viking Press, 1997.

Tafuri, Nancy. *Have You Seen My Duckling?* New York: Greenwillow, 1984.

Thayer, Ernest Lawrence. Illus. by Christopher Bing. *Casey at the Bat: A Ballad of the Republic Sung the Year 1888*. Brooklyn, NY: Handprint Books, 2000.

Thurber, James. Illus. by Louis Slobodkin. *Many Moons*. New York: Harcourt, Brace, 1943.

Titus, Eve. Illus. by Paul Galdone. *Anatole*. New York: Whittlesey House, 1956.

———. *Anatole and the Cat*. New York: Whittlesey House, 1957.

Tresselt, Alvin. Illus. by Roger Duvoisin. *Hide and Seek Fog*. New York: Lothrop, Lee and Shepard, 1965.

———. *White Snow Bright Snow*. New York: Lothrop, Lee and Shepard, 1947.

———. Illus. by Leonard Weisgard. *Rain Drop Splash*. New York: Lothrop, Lee and Shepard Co., 1946.

Tudor, Tasha. *Mother Goose*. New York: Random House, 1944.

———. *1 is One*. New York: Oxford University Press, 1956.

Turkle, Brinton. *Thy Friend, Obadiah*. New York: Viking Press, 1969.

Turlay, Clare. *T-Bone, the Baby Sitter*. New York: Harper, 1950.

Udry, Janice May. Illus. by Maurice Sendak. *The Moon Jumpers*. New York: Harper, 1959.

———. Illus. by Marc Simont. *A Tree Is Nice*. New York: Harper, 1956.

Updike, John. Illus. by Trina Schart Hyman. *A Child's Calendar*. New York: Holiday House, 1999.

Van Allsburg, Chris. *The Garden of Abdul Gasazi*. Boston: Houghton Mifflin, 1979.

———. *Jumanji*. Boston: Houghton Mifflin, 1981.

———. *The Polar Express*. Boston: Houghton Mifflin, 1985.

Walter, Mildred Pitts. Illus. by Pat Cummings. *My Mama Needs Me*. New York: Lothrop, Lee and Shepard, 1983.

Ward, Lynd. *The Biggest Bear*. Boston: Houghton Mifflin, 1952.

Wheeler, Opal. Illus. by Marjorie Torrey. *Sing Mother Goose*. New York: E. P. Dutton, 1945.

———. *Sing in Praise: A Collection of the Best Loved Hymns*. New York: E. P. Dutton, 1946.

Wiese, Kurt. *Fish in the Air*. New York: Viking Press, 1948.

———. *You Can Write Chinese*. New York: Viking Press, 1945.

Wiesner, David. *Free Fall*. New York: Lothrop, Lee and Shepard, 1988.

———. *Sector 7*. New York: Clarion Books, 1999.

———. *The Three Pigs*. New York: Clarion Books, 2001.

———. *Tuesday*. New York: Clarion Books, 1991.

Willard, Nancy. Illus. by Alice and Martin Provensen. *A Visit to William Blake's Inn: Poems for Innocent and Experienced Travelers*. New York: Harcourt Brace Jovanovich, 1981.

Willems, Mo. *Don't Let the Pigeon Drive the Bus*. New York: Hyperion, 2003.

———. *Knuffle Bunny: A Cautionary Tale*. New York: Hyperion, 2004.

Willey, Margaret. Illus. by Heather Solomon. *Clever Beatrice*. New York: Atheneum, 2001.

Williams, Sherley Anne. Illus. by Carole Byard. *Working Cotton*. San Diego: Harcourt Brace Jovanovitch, 1992.

Williams, Vera B. *A Chair for My Mother*. New York: Greenwillow Books, 1982.

———. *"More More More," Said the Baby: Three Love Stories*. New York: Greenwillow Books, 1990.

Wisniewski, David. *Golem*. New York: Clarion Books, 1996.

Wood, Audrey. Illus. by Don Wood. *King Bidgood's in the Bathtub*. San Diego: Harcourt Brace Jovanovich, 1985.

Woodson, Jacqueline. Illus. by E. B. Lewis. *Coming on Home Soon*. New York: Penguin, 2004.

Yarbrough, Camille. Illus. by Carole Byard. *Cornrows*. [New York: Coward, McCann, and Geoghegan, 1979]. New York: Putnam, 1996.

Yashima, Taro. *Crow Boy*. New York: Viking Press, 1955.

———. *Seashore Story*. New York: Viking Press, 1967.

———. *Umbrella*. New York: Viking Press, 1958.

Yolen, Jane. Illus. by Ed Young; *The Emperor and the Kite*. New York: Putnam, 1967.

———. Illus. by John Schoenherr. *Owl Moon*. New York: Philomel Books, 1987.

Yorinks, Arthur. Illus. by Richard Egielski. *Hey, Al*. New York: Farrar, Straus and Giroux, 1986.

Young, Ed. *Lon Po Po: A Red-Riding Hood Story from China*. New York: Philomel Books, 1989.

———. *Seven Blind Mice*. New York: Philomel Books, 1992.

Zelinsky, Paul O. *Rapunzel*. New York: Dutton, 1997.

———. *Rumpelstiltskin*. New York: Dutton, 1986.

Zemach, Harve. Illus. by Margot Zemach. *Duffy and the Devil*. New York: Farrar, Straus and Giroux, 1973.

———. *The Judge: An Untrue Tale*. New York: Farrar, Straus and Giroux, 1969.

Zemach, Margot. *It Could Always Be Worse*. New York: Farrar, Straus and Giroux, 1976.

Zion, Gene. Illus. by Margaret Bloy Graham. *All Falling Down*. New York: Harper, 1951.

———. *Harry the Dirty Dog*. New York: Harper, 1956.

Zolotow, Charlotte. Illus. by Maurice Sendak. *Mr. Rabbit and the Lovely Present*. New York: Harper and Row, 1962.

———. Illus. by Margaret Bloy Graham. *The Storm Book*. New York: HarperCollins, 1952.

ANTHOLOGIES

HarperCollins Treasury of Picture Book Classics: A Child's First Collection. New York: HarperCollins, 2002.

Schulman, Janet, and Simon Boughton, eds. *The 20th Century Children's Book Treasury: Picture Books and Stories to Read Aloud*. New York: Knopf, 1998.

ABOUT AUTHORS AND ARTISTS

Aardema, Verna. *A Bookworm Who Hatched*. Illus. by Dede Smith. Katonah, NY: R. C. Owens, 1992.

Adams, Adrienne. "The Artist at Work: Color Separation." *Horn Book* 41 (April 1965): 153–155.

Alderson, Brian. *Ezra Jack Keats: Artist and Picture-Book Maker*. Greta, LA: Pelican, 1994.

Allen, Terry J. "Mary Azarian." *Horn Book* (July/August 1999): 430–433.

Averill, Esther. "Feodor Rojankovsky, Illustrator." *Horn Book* 19 (May 1943): 151–157.

———. "Unfinished Portrait of an Artist, Feodor Rojankovsky." *Horn Book* 32 (August 1956): 246–253.

Azarian, Mary. "Caldecott Medal Acceptance." *Horn Book* (July/August 1999): 423–429.

Bader, Barbara. *American Picturebooks: From Noah's Ark to The Beast Within*. New York: Macmillan, 1976.

Bechtel, Louise Seaman. "Alice Dalgliesh and Her Books." *Horn Book* 23 (March 1947): 126–134.

Bodmer, George. "Donald Crews: The Signs and Times of an American Childhood—Essay and Interview." *African American Review* 32, no. 1 (Spring 1998): 107–117.

Boekhoff, P. M., and Kallen, Stuart. *Dr. Seuss*. Farmington Hills, MI: Greenhaven Press, 2002.

Brooks, Donna. "Paul O. Zelinsky: Geishas on Tractors." *Horn Book* (July/August 1998): 442–449.

Brown, Marcia. "1992 Laura Ingalls Wilder Award Acceptance Speech." *Journal of Youth Services in Libraries* 5, no. 4 (Summer 1992): 363.

———. "Organized Wonders: Laura Ingalls Wilder Acceptance Speech." *Horn Book* 68, no. 4 (July 1, 1992): 429.

Brown, Margaret Wise. "Creative Writing for Very Young Children." *Book of Knowledge Annual*, 1951, 81.

Bunting, Eve. *Once Upon a Time*. Katonah, NY: R. C. Owen, 1995

Burton, Virginia Lee. "Making Picture Books." *Horn Book* 19 (July/August 1943): 228–229.

———. "Symphony in Comics." *Horn Book* 17 (July/August 1941): 307–311.

Carle, Eric, Flora, and Tiger. *19 Very Short Stories from My Life*. New York: Philomel, 1997.

———. *The Art of Eric Carle*. New York: Philomel, 1996.

Cech, John. *Angels and Wild Things: The Archetypal Poetics of Maurice Sendak*. University Park: University of Pennsylvania Press, 1995.

Commire, Anne. *Something about the Author*, series. Detroit: Gale, 1971–1998.

Cooney, Barbara. "The Artist at Work: Scratchboard Illustration." *Horn Book* 40 (April 1964): 163–164.

Cummings, Pat, ed. *Talking with Artists: Conversations with Victoria Chess* [et al.], vol. 1. New York: Simon and Schuster, 1992.

———. *Talking with Artists: Conversations with Thomas B. Allen* [et al.], vol. 2. New York: Simon and Schuster, 1995.

———. *Talking with Artists: Conversations with Peter Catalanotto* [et al.], vol. 3. New York: Simon and Schuster, 1999.

Davis, Mary Gould. "Helen Dean Fish, 1889–1953." *Horn Book* (April 1953): 89.

———. *Randolph Caldecott, 1846–1886*. Philadelphia: Lippincott, 1946.

dePaola, Tomie. *On My Way*. New York: Putnam. 2001.

———. *Here We All Are*. New York: Putnam, 2000.

———. *26 Fairmont Avenue*. New York: Puffin, 1999.

Diaz, Cecelia. "David Diaz." *Horn Book* (July/August 1995): 434–435.

Egielski, Richard. "Caldecott Medal Acceptance." *Horn Book* (July/August 1987): 433–435.

Eichenberg, Fritz. "Feodor Rojankovsky, Friend of Children." *American Artist* 21 (January 1957): 28–35.

Elleman, Barbara. *Tomie dePaola: His Art and His Stories*. New York: Putnam, 1999.

———. *Virginia Lee Burton: A Life in Art*. New York: Houghton Mifflin, 2002.

Engen, Rodney. *Randolph Caldecott: Lord of the Nursery*. London: Oresko Books, 1976.

Evans, Dilys. "David Wisniewski." *Horn Book* (July/August 1997): 424–426.

Evans, Ernestine. "Wanda Gág as Writer." *Horn Book* 11 (November 1935): 184.

Gág, Wanda. *Growing Pains*. New York: Coward McCann, 1940.

———. "A Hotbed of Feminists." *Nation* 124 (June 22, 1927): 691.

Gauch, Patricia Lee. "Ed Young." *Horn Book* (July/August 1990): 430–435.

———. "John Schoenherr." *Horn Book* (July/August 1988): 460–463.

Hare, W. John, et al. *Tasha Tudor: The Direction of Her Dreams*. New Castle, DE: Oak Knoll, 1998.

Hearn, Michael Patrick. "Maurice Sendak." *Riverbank Review* (Summer 1999): 10–13.

———. "Wanda Gág: American Picture Book Illustrator." *American Book Collector* 4, no. 5 (1983 September–October): 25–43.

Hepperman, Christine. "Meindert DeJong." *Riverbank Review* (Winter 1998/1999): 18–20.

Higgins, James E. "Kate Seredy: Storyteller." *Horn Book* (April 1968): 162–168.

"The Humor of Ludwig Bemelmans." *Publishers Weekly* 134 (October 22, 1938).

Hutchins, Michael, ed. *Yours Pictorially: Illustrated Letters of Randolph Caldecott*. London: Warne, 1976.

Hyman, Trina Schart. *Self Portrait: Trina Schart Hyman*. Reading, MA: Addison Wesley, 1981.

Joyce, William, et al. *The World of William Joyce Scrapbook*. New York: HarperCollins, 1998.

Kassen, Aileen. "Kate Seredy: A Person Worth

Knowing." *Elementary English* (March 1968): 303–315.

Keats, Ezra Jack. "Dear Mr. Keats." *Horn Book* (June 1972): 306–310.

Kingman, Lee. "Virginia Lee Burton's Dynamic Sense of Design." *Horn Book* 46 (October–December 1970): 449–460.

Koch, John. "An Interview with Jane Yolen." *The Writer* 110, no. 3 (March 1, 1997): 20.

"Kurt Wiese, Busiest Illustrator, Has 14 Juveniles on Fall Lists." *Publishers Weekly* 158 (October 28, 1950): 1924–1925.

Lanes, Selma G. *The Art of Maurice Sendak.* New York: Abradale Press, 1984.

Lent, Blair. "The Artist at Work: Cardboard Cuts." *Horn Book* 41 (August 1965): 408–409, 411–412.

———. "On Illustrating *Tikki Tikki Tembo.*" *Owlet among the Colophons III* (November 1968): 1, 3.

Lester, Julius. "John Henry." *Horn Book* (January/February 1996): 28–31.

Levine, Arthur A. "Emily Arnold McCully." *Horn Book* (July/August 1993): 430–432.

Lionni, Leo. *Between Worlds: The Autobiography of Leo Lionni.* New York: Knopf, 1997.

Livsey, Rosemary. "Leo Politi, Friend of All." *Horn Book* (March/April 1949): 97–108.

Macaulay, David. "Caldecott Medal Acceptance." *Horn Book* (July/August 1991): 410–421.

———. "Chris Van Allsburg." *Horn Book* (July/August 1986): 425–429.

———. "David Wiesner." *Horn Book* (July/August 1992): 423–428.

Marantz, Sylvia, and Kenneth Marantz. "Interview with Ashley Bryan." *Horn Book* (March/April 1988): 173–179.

Marcus, Leonard S. *Author Talk: Conversations with Judy Blume* [et al.], New York: Simon and Schuster, 2000.

———. *A Caldecott Celebration: Six Artists and Their Paths to the Caldecott Medal.* New York: Walker, 1998.

———. *Margaret Wise Brown: Awakened by the Moon.* Boston: Beacon Press, 1992.

———. "Rearrangement of Memory: An Interview with Allen Say." *Horn Book* (May/June 1991): 295–303.

———. *Side by Side: Five Favorite Picture-Book Teams Go to Work.* New York: Walker, 2001.

———. *Ways of Telling: Conversations on the Art of the Picture Book.* New York: Dutton, 2002.

Massee, May. "Ingri and Edgar d'Aulaire." *Horn Book* 11 (September 1935): 265–270.

———. "The Petershams." *Publishers Weekly* 126 (October 20, 1934): 1467–1470.

McCulley, Emily Arnold. "Caldecott Medal Acceptance." *Horn Book* (July/August 1993): 424–429.

McElmeel, Sharron L. *100 Most Popular Picture Book Authors and Illustrators: Biographical Sketches and Bibliographies.* Englewood, CO: Libraries Unlimited, 2000.

McKissack, Frederick, and Patricia McKissack. "How to Write a Children's Book." *Highlights Foundation 1988 Report*, pp. 25–26.

Mordinoff, Nicolas. "Artist's Choice: *Crow Boy.*" *Horn Book* 32 (December 1956): 429–430.

Petersham, Maud. "Illustrating Books for Children." *Elementary English Review* 2 (March 1925): 85–89.

Pitz, Henry. "Ludwig Bemelmans." *American Artist* 15 (May 1951): 1508–1510.

Preiss, Byron, ed. *The Art of Leo and Diane Dillon.* New York: Ballantine Books, 1981.

Rathmann, Peggy. "Caldecott Medal Acceptance." *Horn Book* (July/August 1996): 424–427.

Raymond, Allen. "Artist, Writer and Teacher: Ashley Bryan." *Teacher K-8* (May 1995): 36–39.

Sadler, Glenn Edward. "Maurice Sendak and Dr. Seuss: A Conversation." *Horn Book* (September/October 1989): 582–588.

Say, Allen. "Caldecott Medal Acceptance." *Horn Book* (July/August 1994): 427–431.

———. "Grandfather's Journey." *Horn Book* (January/February 1995): 30–32.

Say, Yuriko. "My Father." *Horn Book* (July/August 1994): 432–435.

Schoenherr, John. "Caldecott Medal Acceptance." *Horn Book* (July/August 1988): 457–459.

Schwartz, Anne. "Stephen Gammell." *Horn Book* (July/August 1989): 456–459.

Scott, Alma. *Wanda Gág: The Story of an Artist.* Minneapolis: University of Minnesota Press, 1940.

Seaman, Louise H. " 'Berta and Elmer' [Hader] and Their Picture Books." *Horn Book* 4 (August 1928): 52–57.

Silvey, Anita. *100 Best Books for Children.* New York: Houghton Mifflin, 2004.

———, ed. *Children's Books and Their Creators.* Boston: Houghton Mifflin, 1995.

———, ed. *The Essential Guide to Children's Books and Their Creators.* Boston: Houghton Mifflin, 2002.

———. "An Interview with Cynthia Rylant." *Horn Book* (November/December 1987): 695–702.

Snyder, Dianne. "The Boy of the Three-Year Nap." *Horn Book* (March/April 1989): 176–178.

Sparrow, C. G. "Ingri and Edgar Parin d'Aulaire." *American Scandinavian Review* 30 (May 1942): 49–53.

Steele, Vincent. "Tom Feelings: A Black Arts Movement." *African American Review* 32, no. 1 (1998 Spring): 119–124.

Tudor, Tasha, and Richard Brown. *Drawn from New England: Tasha Tudor.* Cleveland, OH: William Collins, 1979.

———. *The Private World of Tasha Tudor.* Boston: Little, Brown, 1992.

Van Allsburg, Chris. "Caldecott Medal Acceptance." *Horn Book* (July/August 1986): 420–424.

———. "David Macaulay: The Early Years." *Horn Book* (July/August 1991): 422–425.

Ward, Diane. "Cynthia Rylant." *Horn Book* (July/August 1993): 420–423.

Wiesner, David. "Caldecott Medal Acceptance." *Horn Book* (July/August 1992): 416–422.

Wisniewski, David. "Caldecott Medal Acceptance." *Horn Book* (July/August 1997): 418–423.

Yep, Laurence. *In My Own Words: The Lost Garden.* Englewood Cliffs, NJ: Julian Messner, 1991.

Yolen, Jane. *A Letter from Phoenix Farm.* Photos by Jason Stemple. Katonah, NY: Owen, 1992.

Young, Ed. "Caldecott Medal Acceptance." *Horn Book* (July/August 1990): 425–429.

Zelinsky, Paul O. "Caldecott Medal Acceptance." *Horn Book* (July/August 1998): 433–441.

Zemach, Margot. *Self-Portrait: Margot Zemach.* Illus. by Margot Zemach. New York: Harper, 1985.

ABOUT PICTURE BOOKS

Allen, Marjorie N. *100 Years of Children's Books in America, Decade by Decade.* New York: Facts on File, 1996.

Apseloff, Marilyn. "Children's Literature: Picture Books, Poetry, and Fiction." In Glenn Edward Sadler; ed. Intro. by U. C. Knoepflmacher. *Teaching Children's Literature: Issues, Pedagogy, Resources.* New York: Modern Language Association, 1992, pp. 170–171.

Association for Library Service to Children. *The Newbery and Caldecott Awards: A Guide to the Medal and Honor Books,* 2004 ed. Chicago: American Library Association, 2004.

Bader, Barbara. *American Picturebooks: From Noah's Ark to The Beast Within.* New York: Macmillan, 1976.

———. *The World in 32 Pages: One Hundred Years of American Picturebooks.* New York: Winslow, 2001.

Baird, Shirley. "The Popularization of Folk Songs through Children's Picture Books." *Children's Literature Association Quarterly* 11, no. 3 (1986 Fall): 142–144.

Bang, Molly. *Picture This: Perception and Composition.* Boston: Little, Brown, 1992.

Bodmer, George R. "The Post-Modern Alphabet: Extending the Limits of the Contemporary Alphabet Book, from Seuss to Gorey." *Children's Literature Association Quarterly* 14, no. 3 (1989 Fall): 115–117.

Carpenter, Humphrey, and Mari Pritchard. *The Oxford Companion to Children's Literature.* Oxford: Oxford University Press, 1974.

Doonan, Jane. "The Object Lesson: The Picture Books of Anthony Browne." *Word & Image: A Journal of Verbal/Visual Enquiry* 2, no. 2 (April–June 1986): 159–172.

Dubow, Rhona. "Picture Books as Literature." *CRUX: A Journal on the Teaching of English* 20, no. 4 (October 1986): 12–16.

Edmonds, Leslie. "The Treatment of Race in Picture Books for Young Children." *Book Research Quarterly* 2, no. 3 (Fall 1986): 30–41.

Gilson, Nancy. "Words on Pictures: Critics Lament Lack of Children's Picture Books with Illustrations That Whisper." *The Columbus Dispatch,* February 10, 2002.

Hegel, Claudette. *Newbery and Caldecott Trivia and More for Every Day of the Year.* Westport, CT: Libraries Unlimited, 2000.

Higonnet, Margaret R. "The Playground of the Peritext." *Children's Literature Association Quarterly* 15, no. 2 (1990 Summer): 47–49.

Johnston, Margaret. "Surprised by Joy: The World of Picture-Books." in Sheila A. Egoff, *One Ocean Touching: Papers from the First Pacific Rim Conference on Literature.* Metuchen, NJ: Scarecrow Press, 1979, pp. 147–154.

Kiefer, Barbara Z. *The Potential of Picturebooks: From Visual Literacy to Aesthetic Understanding.* Englewood Cliffs, NJ: Prentice-Hall, 1995.

Kummerling-Meibauer, Bettina. "Metalinguistic Awareness and the Child's Developing Concept of Irony: The Relationships between Pictures and Texts in Ironic Picture Books." *Lion and the Unicorn* 23, no. 2 (April 1999): 157–183.

Landis, Sonia. "Picture Books as Literature." *Children's Literature Association Quarterly* 10, no. 2 (1985 Summer): 51–54.

Liddell, Mary. "*Little Machinery* Reviews." *Horn Book* 10 (January 1934): 25.

Lipson, Eden Ross. *The New York Times Parent's Guide to the Best Books for Children,* 3rd ed. New York: Three Rivers Press, 2000.

Lobel, Arnold. "A Good Picture Book Should . . ." In Betsy Hearne, and Marilyn Kaye, eds. *Celebrating Children's Books: Essays on Children's Literature in Honor of Zena Sutherland.* New York: Lothrop, Lee and Shepard, 1981, pp. 73–80.

MacCann, Donnarae, and Gloria Woodard, eds. *The Black American in Books for Children: Readings in Racism.* Metuchen, NJ: Scarecrow Press, 1985.

Manna, Anthony L. "Reading Jerry Pinkney Reading." *Children's Literature Association Quarterly* 16, no. 4 (Winter 1991–1992): 269–275.

Marantz, Kenneth A., and Sylvia S. Marantz. *Creating Picturebooks: Interviews with Editors, Art Directors, Reviewers, Booksellers, Professors, Librarians, and Showcasers.* Jefferson, NC: McFarland, 1997.

Marantz, Sylvia S. *Picture Books for Looking and Learning: Awakening Visual Perceptions through the Art of Children's Books.* Phoenix, AZ: Oryx Press, 1992.

Marantz, Sylvia S., and Kenneth A. Marantz. *The Art of Children's Picture Books: A Selective Reference Guide,* 2nd ed. New York: Garland, 1995.

———. *Artists of the Page: Interviews with Children's Book Illustrators.* Jefferson, NC: McFarland, 1992.

———. *Multicultural Picture Books: Art for Illuminating Our World,* 2nd ed. Lanham, MD: Scarecrow Press, 2005.

———. *Multicultural Picture Books: Art for Understanding Others,* 2 vols. Worthington, OH: Linworth, 1994–1997.

Marcus, Leonard S. *Goodnight Moon, with a 50th Anniversary Retrospective.* New York: HarperCollins, 1997.

Martin, Michelle H. *Brown Gold: Milestones of African American Children's Picture Books, 1845–2002.* New York: Routledge, 2004.

Matthias, Margaret and Graciela Italiano. "Louder Than a Thousand Words." In Robert Bator ed., *Signposts to Criticism of Children's Literature.* Chicago: American Library Association, 1983, pp. 161–165.

Meyer, Susan E. *A Treasury of the Great Children's Book Illustrators.* New York: Harry N. Abrams, 1997.

Moebius, William. "Introduction to Picturebook Codes." *Word & Image: A Journal of Verbal/Visual Enquiry* 2, no. 2 (April–June 1986): 141–158.

Moerk, Ernst L. "Picture-Book Reading by Mothers and Young Children and Its Impact upon Language Development." *Journal of Pragmatics: An Interdisciplinary Monthly of Language Studies* 9, no. 4 (August 1985): 547–566.

Nikola-Lisa, W. "The Image of the Child in the Picture Books of Ezra Jack Keats." In Sylvia Patterson Iskander, ed., *The Image of the Child.* Battle Creek, MI: Children's Literature Association, 1991.

———. "John Henry: Then and Now." *African American Review*, 32, no. 1 (1998 Spring): 51–56.

———. "Letters, Twigs, Hats, and Peter's Chair: Object Play in the Picture Books of Ezra Jack Keats." *Children's Literature Association Quarterly* 16, no. 4 (Winter 1991–1992): 255–258.

Nikolajeva, Maria, and Carole Scott. *How Picturebooks Work.* New York: Garland, 2001.

Nist, Joan. "The Image of the Child in Picture Books: Adult-Child Perspectives." In Sylvia Patterson Iskander, ed., *The Image of the Child.* Battle Creek, MI: Children's Literature Association, 1991, pp. 223–230.

Nodelman, Perry, ed. and introd. "Art Theory and Children's Picture Books." *Children's Literature Association Quarterly* 9, no. 1 (Spring 1984): 15–33.

———, ed. *Touchstones: Reflections on the Best in Children's Literature, Volume 3: Picture Books.* West Layfayette, IN: Children's Literature Association, 1989.

———. *Words about Pictures: The Narrative Art of Children's Picture Books.* Athens and London: University of Georgia Press, 1988.

Paley, Nicholas. "Experiments in Picture Book Design: Modern Artists Who Made Books for Children 1900–1985." *Children's Literature Association Quarterly* 16, no. 4 (Winter 1991–1992): 264–269.

Pavonetti, Linda M., ed. *Children's Literature Remembered: Issues, Trends, and Favorite Books.* Westport, CT: Libraries Unlimited, 2004.

Perrot, Jean. "Deconstructing Maurice Sendak's Postmodern Palimpsest." *Children's Literature Association Quarterly* 16, no. 4 (Winter 1991–1992): 259–263.

Pflieger, Pat. "Fables into Picture Books." *Children's Literature Association Quarterly* 9, no. 2 (Summer 1984): 73–75, 80.

Potter, Joyce. "Manger and Star: The Christmas Story in Modern Picture Books." *Children's Literature Association Quarterly* 13, no. 4 (Winter 1988): 185–191.

Reinstein, P. Gila. "Sex Roles in Recent Picture Books." *Journal of Popular Culture* 17, no. 4 (Spring 1984): 116–123.

Roethler, Jacque. "Reading in Color: Children's Book Illustrations and Identity Formation for Black Children in the United States." *African American Review* 32, no. 1 (1998 Spring): 95–105.

Schmidt, Nancy J. "Children's Books about Africa in Series: Picture Books." *Africana Journal: A Bibliographic and Review Quarterly* 3, no. 1 (1972): 3–5.

Segal, Elizabeth. "Picture Books and Princesses: The Feminist Contribution." In Priscilla A. Ord, ed., *Proceedings of the Eighth Annual Con-*

ference of the Children's Literature Association, University of Minnesota, March 1981. New Rochelle: Department of English, Iona College, 1982, pp. 77–83.

Selden, Rebecca; and Sarah Smedman. "The Art of the Contemporary Picture Book." In Priscilla A. Ord, ed. *Proceedings of the Seventh Annual Conference of the Children's Literature Association*, Baylor University, March 1980. New Rochelle: Department of English, Iona College, 1982.

Silvey, Anita. *100 Best Books for Children*. New York: Houghton Mifflin, 2004.

———, ed. *Children's Books and Their Creators*. Boston: Houghton Mifflin, 1995.

———. *The Essential Guide to Children's Books and Their Creators*. Boston: Houghton Mifflin, 2002.

Stephens, John. "Language, Discourse, and Picture Books." *Children's Literature Association Quarterly* 14, no. 3 (1989 Fall): 106–110.

Taylor, Mary-Agnes. "Notes from a Dark Side of the Nursery: Negative Images in Alphabet Books," In Sylvia Patterson Iskander, ed. *The Image of the Child*. Battle Creek, MI: Children's Literature Association, 1991, pp. 287–292.

Torsney, Cheryl B. "The Politics of Low and High Culture: Representations of Music in Some Recent Children's Picture Books." *The Lion and the Unicorn: A Critical Journal of Children's Literature* 16, no. 2 (December 1992): 176–183.

Whitehurst, G. J., F. L. Falco, C. J. Lonigan, J. E. Fischel, B. D. DeBaryshe, M. C. Valdez-Menchaca, and M. Caulfield. "Accelerating Language Development through Picture Book Reading." *Developmental Psychology* 24, no. 4 (July 1988): 552–559.

Winslow, David. "Children's Picture Books and the Popularization of Folklore." *Keystone Folklore* 14 (1969): 142–157.

Wong, Hertha D. "Pictographs as Autobiography: Plains Indians Sketchbooks of the Late Nineteenth and Early Twentieth Centuries." *American Literary History* 1, no. 2 (Summer 1989): 295–316.

Woolman, Bertha, and Patricia Litsey. *The Caldecott Award*. Minneapolis: T. S. Denison, 1998.

Zelditch, Bernice. "For Fresh-New Sea-Farers: Social and Political Values in Children's Picture Books." in Stella Lees, ed., *A Track to Unknown Water*. Metuchen, NJ: Scarecrow Press, 1987, pp. 55–65.

DISSERTATIONS AND THESES

Flannery-Quinn, Suzanne Marie. *The Portrayals of Male Parents in Caldecott Award-winning American Picture Books (1938–2002): Examining the Culture of Fatherhood Presented to Young People*. Ph.D. diss., Syracuse University, 2003.

Karel, Amanda Irene. *"Did My First Mother Love Me?": Adoption as Portrayed in Children's Picture Books*. M.A. thesis, Eastern Michigan University, 2002.

McConnell, Melissa Ann. *The Presence of Stereotypes about Librarians: A Content Analysis of Children's Picture Books*. M.L.S. thesis, Central Missouri State University, 1998.

Mitchell, Deirdre Ruth. *Reading Character in the Caldecotts: Adult and Child Perceptions of Character Traits in Children's Picture Books*. Ph.D. diss., Ohio University, 1999.

Yau, Rittchell Ann. *The Portrayal of Immigration in a Selection of Picture Books Published Since 1970*. Ed.D. diss., University of San Francisco, 2003.

RELATED WORKS

Bossert, Jill. *Children's Book Illustration: Step by Step Techniques—A Unique Guide from the Masters*. New York: Watson-Guptill, 1998.

Hurlimann, Bettina. *Picture-Book World*. New York: Oxford University Press, 1968.

Johnson, Paul. *Pictures and Words Together: Children Illustrating and Writing Their Own Books*. Portsmouth, NH: Heinemann, 1997.

Marcus, Leonard. Illus. by Maurice Sendak. *Dear Genius: The Letters of Ursula Nordstrom*. New York: HarperCollins, 2000.

Marcus, Leonard, and the Children's Book Council. *75 Years of Children's Book Week Posters*. New York: Knopf, 1994.

Shulevitz, Uri. *Writing with Pictures: How to Write and Illustrate Picture Books*. New York: Watson-Guptill, 1985.

Slade, Catharine. *The Encyclopedia of Illustration Techniques*. Philadelphia: Running Press Book, 1997.

REFERENCES

Lima, Carolyn W., and John A. Lima. *A to Zoo: Subject Access to Children's Picture Books*. 6th ed. Westport, CT: Greenwood Press, 2001.

Quinnam, Barbara, comp. *Fables, from Incunabula to Modern Picture Books: A Selective Bibliography*. Washington, DC: Library of Congress, 1966.

VISUAL

Getting to Know: Gerald McDermott. Color, 21 minutes. Produced by Soundworks. Distributed by Harcourt, Brace, 1996.

Getting to Know: William Steig. Color, 20 minutes. Weston Woods, 1995.

Good Conversation! A Talk with the McKissacks. Color, 20 minutes. Tim Podell Productions, 1997.

Maurice Sendak. Color, 15 minutes. Weston Woods, 1986.

Meet Ashley Bryan: Storyteller, Artist, Writer. Color, 23 minutes. American School, 1992.

Meet Leo Lionni. Color, 19 minutes. American School, 1992.

Meet the Caldecott Illustrator: Jerry Pinkney. Color, 21 minutes. American School, 1991.

Meet the Picture Book Author: Cynthia Rylant.

Color, 10 minutes. Produced by Miller-Brody, 1990

Trumpet Video Visits Donald Crews. Color, 19 minutes. Trumpet Club, 1992.

A Visit with Eve Bunting. Color, 19 minutes. Houghton Mifflin/Clarion, 1990.

A Visit with Barbara Cooney. Color, 25 minutes. Viking/Puffin, 1995.

A Visit with Jerry Pinkney. Color, 25 minutes. Dial/Puffin, 1995.

A Visit with Paul O. Zelinsky. Color, 25 minutes. Dutton/Puffin, 1995.

WEB SITES

"Caldecott Medal Homepage." *American Library Service to Children Division of the American Library Association*. http://scils.rutgers.edu/~kvander/Culture/illustration.html, accessed February 1, 2004.

"Children's Picture Book Database at Miami University." *Miami University*. http://www.lib.muohio.edu/pictbks/, accessed June 3, 2003.

"Early Illustrators of Children's Books from the 19th and 20th Centuries." Kay E. Vandergrift, Rutgers University. http://scils.rutgers.edu/~kvander/HistoryofChildLit/illus.html, accessed February 1, 2004.

"Illustration and the Art of the Picture Book." Kay E. Vandergrift. Rutgers University. http://scils.rutgers.edu/~kvander/Culture/illustration.html, accessed: February 1, 2004.

"100 Picture Books that Everyone Should Know." *New York Public Library*. http://kids.nypl.org/reading/recommended2.cfm?ListID=61, accessed May 20, 2005.

"Picturing Books." Denise I. Matulka. http://picturingbooks.imaginarylands.org/, accessed February 1, 2004.

Index

Location of main entries is indicated by bold page numbers.

About the Author

CONNIE ANN KIRK is Adjunct Professor of Languages and Literature at Mansfield University and School Librarian at All Saints Academy. Her previous books include *J. K. Rowling: A Biography* (2003), *Emily Dickinson: A Biography* (2004), *Mark Twain: A Biography* (2004), and *Sylvia Plath: A Biography* (2004), all available from Greenwood Press.

DATE DUE

JUL 1 6 2009			